THE Sober Kitchen

THE *Sober*
Kitchen

Recipes and Advice for a
Lifetime of Sobriety

Liz Scott

The Harvard Common Press
Boston, Massachusetts

THE HARVARD COMMON PRESS
535 Albany Street
Boston, Massachusetts 02118
www.harvardcommonpress.com

Printed in the United States of America
Printed on acid-free paper

Library of Congress Cataloging-in-Publication Data

Scott, Liz.
    The sober kitchen : recipes and advice for a lifetime of sobriety / Liz Scott.
        p.   cm.
    Includes bibliographical references and index.
    ISBN 1-55832-220-5 (hc : alk. paper)—ISBN 1-55832-221-3 (pbk : alk. paper)
    1. Cookery.   2. Alcoholism—Diet therapy.   I. Title.
TX714.S3925   2003
641.5'631—dc21

                                                                                2003007557

Special bulk-order discounts are available on this and other Harvard Common Press books.
Companies and organizations may purchase books for premiums or resale, or may arrange a
custom edition, by contacting the Marketing Director at the address above.

10 9 8 7 6 5 4 3 2 1

Cover design by Night & Day Design
Cover photograph by Amos Chan
Interior design by Ralph Fowler

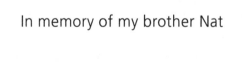

In memory of my brother Nat

"Affliction comes to us, not to make us sad, but sober,
not to make us sorry, but wise."

—Henry Ward Beecher

Contents

Phase One

Saving Your Life and Staying Sober   1

During this early stage of recovery, getting and staying sober is the prime objective, while repairing your body from the damage of addiction by developing healthy eating and drinking habits will help you to cope with common cravings that require attention. Simple, nourishing recipes to quench, calm, and satisfy, without taxing your energy and time, are presented during this phase.

Phase Two

Getting Comfortable and Feeding Your Inner Child   155

As the difficult period of early recovery begins to wane, it is time to rediscover what comfort means to you. Homestyle meals that warm your heart and bring you closer to family and friends help to create an atmosphere of love and support, while providing a positive sense of who you are.

Phase Three

Enhancing Your Health and Becoming a Sober Gourmet   313

Extend the life you saved by making positive changes to your diet that will affect your overall health, while discovering the functionality of food. Come full circle by renovating classic dishes with a sober outlook and celebrating your sobriety.

Foreword

Sobriety is much more than not using alcohol and illegal drugs. Stopping alcohol and drug use is the easy part of sobriety. Every alcoholic and drug addict has stopped, as Mark Twain said about cigarette smoking, hundreds of times. The hard part of being sober is creating a whole new life that does not revolve around getting high on alcohol and other drugs.

Sobriety is also not what people who have never had an alcohol or a drug problem do. As a practicing psychiatrist, I have been permitted into the inner lives of thousands of patients over the years. One of my patients, a woman physician who suffered from Obsessive-Compulsive Disorder (OCD), lost her husband of 25 years to a rapidly developing colon cancer when she was 55, just when she was looking forward to her golden years with her soul mate. This woman had never been addicted to alcohol or drugs. In her darkest hour, she did not turn to me or to another therapist for help. She turned for help to her friends in recovery from addiction. Later I asked her why she did that. Here is what she told me: "People who have confronted addiction and built sober lives in recovery are not like other people. They have fallen to the depths of human suffering and pulled themselves out. To do that, they have had to understand life and their limitations, as well as their abilities, in whole new ways. They have a well-tempered wisdom that people not in recovery seldom achieve. I was sure that I could find in my friends in recovery the experience, strength, and hope that I needed to go on after my devastating loss." Unless you understand this woman's logic, you don't get what it means to be "sober."

Liz Scott not only gets it at a deep level, but she has also brought her passion for food—cooking it and eating it—into the lifelong process of recovery. She understands that one of the central elements of a sober life is a healthy relationship with food. This is especially to be treasured after the disordered relationships with food that characterize almost everyone addicted to alcohol and other drugs. In the misery of addiction, healthy eating is an early casualty.

The great discovery of Bill Wilson, the founder of Alcoholics Anonymous, was that the only way he could stay sober was to help suffering alcoholics. That is the twelfth of the twelve steps. Bill Wilson should have gotten a Nobel Prize for that discovery. He didn't. Instead, his prize was helping millions of alcoholics get well—a far bigger reward than the one given in Stockholm each year. Liz Scott understands this principle of recovery. Honoring it, she is passing on in her book what she has found useful about food to help people in recovery build and sustain healthy, happy, sober lives.

In this wise and loving book there is a road map for a sober relationship with food and with one's own body. Liz Scott writes with an unmistakable sense of the joy that comes from escaping that dark and lonely trap of addiction. The experience of addiction makes the discovery of healthy eating all the more precious to her and her readers.

Many people in the grip of addiction cannot imagine a sober life. They see nothing but losses as they contemplate giving up their abusive lovers—the alcohol and other drugs that have decimated their lives for years. This book is a powerful antidote to that hopeless attitude. It radiates the love of the sober life. This book celebrates the little miracles that are all around us every day, surprising and beautiful miracles that cannot be seen through the dense fog of active addiction. Liz Scott's book is one of those little miracles.

—*Robert L. DuPont, M.D.*

Author of *The Selfish Brain: Learning from Addiction*; founding director of the National Institute on Drug Abuse (NIDA); president of the Institute for Behavior and Health, Inc.; vice-president of Bensinger DuPont and Associates; and clinical professor of psychiatry at Georgetown Medical School

Preface

As a professional chef in recovery I was faced with a daunting prospect: Did I have to abandon the career I loved to protect my sobriety? Early in treatment, I was warned of the danger of being around alcohol. "People, places, and things" associated with drinking and drug use had to be avoided at all costs; cravings could be triggered and recovery could be at risk. When my counselor looked me straight in the eye and said, "You may have to find a new career," I realized what I was up against.

Cooking was my life. After working on the periphery of the food business for years, I had finally become a professional chef and I loved my job. My livelihood had become my lifeline and I honestly felt, after many career twists and turns, that I had finally found my calling. Give it up? There had to be another way.

It is true that the culinary world is not conducive to sobriety, especially the restaurant scene. In addition to being around alcohol nearly all the time and using it as a staple cooking ingredient, the lifestyle of a chef practically screams relapse. Long, tiring hours, poor eating habits, constant adrenaline rushes, and late-night socializing all come with the territory. Although I hardly ever drank when I worked, I always made up for it when the night came to a close. It was my "reward" for all the hard work and frenzied activity of the day.

Fortunately for me, I had already begun to trade in the hectic pace of traditional chef work for the more civilized life of a "personal chef" and was slowly building up a solid clientele in my vicinity. I liked being my own boss, working reasonably normal hours, and catering parties and events. I had eliminated a lot of the "slipperiness" of my environment. But cooking without alcohol? I wasn't sure if I could. Everything I knew from my culinary training and first-hand experience told me it was necessary as a "flavor enhancer" and besides, it evaporated in the heating process, right?

Despite what just about every professional chef and gourmet food writer has said, I discovered that alcohol does not "burn off" when cooked. In fact, as much as 85 percent of the original alcohol content can find its way to your plate, depending upon the type of alcohol used and the cooking method employed. And there was more. Recent addiction studies indicated that not only can traces of ingested alcohol activate brain activity in the addicted, but visual stimuli or cues (such as simply *looking* at a wine bottle), as well as the mere aroma of alcohol itself could induce craving, the primary mechanism researchers believe is behind the unfortunately too-common relapse and a return to a life of alcohol and drugs. It was too much of a risk to take. Abstinence had to be total. It was clear that alcohol had to go.

I began to experiment with sober substitutes in dishes that called for everything from wine to sambuca. To simply leave it out didn't seem to go along with the essence of good cooking. In the past, I had successfully replaced alcohol in recipes when clients had requested me to do so. Couldn't I use my training, palate, and a little creativity to develop new recipes and redesign old ones that would be sober safe and maybe even healthier and tastier than the original? I decided to make it my quest and that is essentially how this book was born. But there's a lot more to it.

As I began to educate myself on the disease of addiction and familiarize myself with all the current research, I discovered a disturbing fact. There was virtually no attention given to basic diet and nutrition in the field of treatment. True, there were several books that referred to vitamin deficiency, mostly in late-stage alcoholism, and a few that suggested drastic changes in diet or intense nutritional therapy that mainly revolved around sugar avoidance and hypoglycemia, but none of these publications proved to be practical guides for the vast majority of us in recovery. In addition, the treatment field as a whole appeared to dismiss their recommendations. But I learned it was not for lack of interest or need that diet was ignored. As I spoke with numerous people who worked in the substance dependence field, many told me they often felt their efforts were frustrated by the obvious absence of practical diet and nutrition information that they could pass on to their patients. Much is said about the

inability of formal treatment to help addicts and alcoholics stay clean and sober, but in many ways the effectiveness of treatment can only be determined by the research information and tools currently available. Without any helpful guidelines to impart, treatment professionals are left with little dietary advice except to say "don't drink." Surely, this is not sufficient. When a Type II diabetic is diagnosed, extensive and informative consultations and publications on diet and nutrition are offered to the patient. They are not told just to avoid sugar (a fallacy in itself) and sent on their way. Bookstores are filled with cookbooks and nutritionally informative guides that address everything from arthritis to diabetes to PMS, acknowledging that eating has an enormous impact on every disease. Why was addiction recovery so far behind?

Although today addiction is accepted as a brain disease by the medical community and the majority of the population as a whole, it was not long ago that moral integrity and pure weakness of intent were considered to be the only obstacles to long-term sobriety. When my brother Nat began battling his heroin addiction in the 1960s, with many periods of successful abstinence unfortunately followed by a return to opiates and alcohol, it was assumed that his inability to stay clean and sober was entirely due to a lack of desire and willpower to change. Although scientific research was beginning to reveal many underlying causes for substance dependence, few accepted the disease premise and, as a result, treatment was primarily based on attempts to control behavior. This, along with the enormous stigma attached to alcoholism and drug addiction, slowed down the pace of advancement in research and treatment. Despite strides made in psychiatry, neurobiology, and physiology, the connection between thought, emotion, and the physical body was not yet considered to be particularly important, if it existed at all. Consequently, Western medicine was slow to embrace what other cultures have known for centuries—mind, body, and spirit are intricately connected and each aspect is an important one in the quest for total healing. We know now that willpower alone cannot resolve diseases of the brain just because they tend to manifest themselves in behavior and personality changes. Lifestyle issues, such as stress management and exercise, pharmacology, and, of course, diet and nutrition, are important factors to consider as well. As we begin to attend to the whole person, especially in addiction, we may find that treatment can be far more successful than previously thought.

We are now lucky to live at a time when it is possible to explore the human body and mind in vast technological detail, particularly with advanced tools that allow us to witness neurochemical activity as it happens. When my brother was alive, the concept of brain cells communicating with each other was laughable. Today we know better, while the mapping of the human genome will provide more information than we ever believed possible. As studies continue and results are analyzed, the connection between brain chemistry, addiction, genetics, and behavior will thankfully be much better understood, paving the way for better treatment and ultimate prevention.

On a similar note, we also live at a time when healthy eating is more than a popular trend; for many, it has become an important way of life. And with a return to family values and the knowledge that food has the ability to comfort and heal, quality cooking and eating has become something from which everyone can benefit—physically, emotionally, and spiritually. I've always respected the power of food to enhance our lives and, as a result, the recipes and information in this book reflect my direct experience with, and intense interest in, the many wonderful ways that cooking and eating good food can contribute to our lives. There is as much information on ingredients, food history, and cook-

ing techniques in this book as there is on addiction and recovery. However, as an alcoholic who knows only too well the symptoms of post-acute withdrawal and the inability, especially at the beginning of recovery, to focus and concentrate, I have tried to make this book as easy to read and utilize as possible. I often recall with a smile one person's response on learning I was writing this book, "A cookbook for alcoholics! What a great idea, as long as we don't have to follow directions!"

I also know that developing healthy eating habits and attempting a new lifestyle are goals that need to be attained through small and significant steps if they are to have any long-term impact. Changes in diet cannot and should not be thrust upon us, particularly as some magical solution to our addiction. We all know there is no quick-fix dietary answer to getting and staying sober and enjoying the recipes from this book will not guarantee your sobriety. What I am hoping is that you will discover how including good food in the recovery process may play a significant and often overlooked part in its success and, at the very least, help to make the ups and downs of the journey a bit easier to understand and accept. In addition, spending our energy and time concentrating on preparing meals, learning about nutrition and how it relates to our disease, as well as sharing food with others and reacquainting ourselves with the pleasures of the table may even help to prevent some of the typical preoccupations with negative and unproductive thinking we all experience. The more we participate in our own recovery and the better educated we become, the more our chances of achieving success and quality in our sobriety can increase.

We are often told that being proud of our recovery is an important aspect of our progress, but being proud implies that we shouldn't feel ashamed of our disease. Too many of us are compelled to make up socially acceptable reasons why we no longer drink rather than admit to the reality of our illness. Maybe having a cookbook and eating guide that addresses the specific issues we face will convince us, as well as the rest of the world, that we have nothing to be ashamed of. Although the continued stigma attached to addiction is slowly beginning to wane, it's been said that real change will only come through the advocacy of those of us who are in recovery—that we need to show our faces, tell our stories, and demonstrate that there is hope, that recovery is real. I have written this book in that spirit and in the spirit of service to those who still suffer from this insidious disease. Shirley Chisholm once said, "Service is the rent you pay for room on this earth." To those who do not yet have the means to pay, know that there will be plenty of healing room to share until you do.

Acknowledgments

We often hear that once we begin our recovery journey, helpful and influential people, golden opportunities, and even a bit of serendipity suddenly appear as if thoughtfully placed in our path to assist us, encourage us, and validate our new life's passage. My journey has been no exception. From the moment I met my literary agent, now dear friend and most exuberant of cheerleaders, Larry Chilnick, I knew I was headed in the right direction. Without his persistence and immense enthusiasm, I believe *The Sober Kitchen* would never have seen the light of day. Larry, I will never be able to thank you enough for everything you have done and continue to do—you have single-handedly changed my life and I will be forever grateful.

I could not have been graced with finer representation than Michael Carlisle and I must thank everyone at Carlisle & Company for their exquisite attention to details from the proposal to the final product. A big thank you to the multitalented Susanna Chilnick for her beautiful food photography, which superbly enhanced the proposal.

To my extended family at The Harvard Common Press—thank you for welcoming me into your fold with open arms and giving my book the most personalized and loving attention any author could hope for. To Bruce Shaw, HCP publisher, for his flattering confidence in my work and abilities and the many people in Boston whose splendid efforts and enthusiasm for *The Sober Kitchen* will be long remembered: Valerie Cimino, Jodi Marchowsky, Christine Alaimo, Sunshine Erickson, Abbey Phalen, Dana Garczewski, Virginia Downes, Skye Stewart, Beatrice Wikander, Michele Caterina, and Ralph Fowler for his fantabulous book design. Most of all, from the bottom of my heart, I want to express my greatest gratitude to Pam Hoenig, surely the most amazing and talented editor to ever grace the publishing world! Your passion, direction, and golden touch made *The Sober Kitchen* the absolute best it could be, dare I say, far above and beyond anyone's expectations—you insisted on nothing less. You will never know how much it has meant to have you at the helm and I thank you so very, very much.

Long before I could only dream of a project such as this, however, I had to take that final scary step out of the cloud of addiction into a sun-filled life of recovery, and there are many people who helped to pave the pathway and shine their light so I could see more clearly. I must thank Marilyn Roll for helping me see the direction my life might have taken if not for that important phone call. To everyone at High Focus for an excellent treatment program, and especially to Carl Ryder for being the first to make me realize that with sobriety, anything is possible. To every fellow alcoholic and addict who participated in those early challenging days as we took the leap together and faced our demons. Most especially to Jim Plunkett and his lovely family for their continued friendship and support. To my long-lost friend Margot—wherever you may be—I still think of you often and thank you for your all-too-short friendship. I would also like to thank everyone connected to the Rutgers School and Institute of Alcohol and Drug Studies, where I gleaned invaluable research and education on the subject of addiction. In particular, the instruction of Dr. Carlton Erickson, Dr. Larissa Pohorecky, and the inimitable Patricia Burke, all of whom, including the many participants of the summer program, assisted not only in the development and direction of my ideas, but in my own personal journey of recovery. A thank you also to Ray Dreitlein for his encouragement and valuable comments. To Dr. Jesse Rosenthal—many thanks for reviewing my writing on psychiatric matters and offering wonderful encouragement. And a special thank you to my gang of recovery friends on the Internet, in particular those at Recovery_also, whose warmth, enthusiasm, and humor helped me get through many a difficult time.

Just as there are new faces that appear to us as we make this recovery journey, so there are those that have been there loyally all along. To my dear friend Jennifer Pruden—if it is true that what you put out into the universe will come back to you tenfold, then you most certainly have every joy and advantage to look forward to.

Your friendship has been a priceless asset in my life. Thanks also to Anna Stenstrom for her kindness and thoughtfulness, and Sherri Skok for her immense patience and loyalty. To Jimmy Youngman for being the knight in shining armor on more than one occasion, while providing inspiration and advice on the joys of sobriety. Thanks also to Marion Wright, Gerry Buckley, Hilary Belsky, Billy Callahan, and everyone else whose words of encouragement and genuine interest in the book were so very much appreciated. Appreciation is also due for my loyal clients who exhibited the utmost patience and understanding with my erratic schedule and publishing deadlines. A big thank you to the Hopkins family—Janet, Beau, Robert, Peter, and, of course, Savo—for letting me become an integral part of your wonderful clan. To Ellen Waksman and her family, Evelyn Dvorin, and Bev and Ed Goldschmidt for welcoming me into your kitchens and displaying great enthusiasm and understanding for the importance of this project.

When those of us in recovery need to find words to express to our families the gratitude, love, and compassion they deserve, it is sometimes difficult to know how and where to begin. In many ways, the writing of this book has been my way of expressing these sentiments, as well as serving as an important catharsis for me and the closest members of my family. Having already lost one child to the horrific disease of addiction, my mother lived in fear for too many years that it would happen again. I can never begin to express to her my sadness and regret over that chapter of our lives, but I am hoping that in some small way this book will help us to heal. Mom, your love and support during good times and bad, tragedy and elation, and everything in between has meant more to me than you will ever realize. Without you by my side, I doubt very much that I would have come this far. Here's to the rest of the journey together—may it be softly warming to the heart, easy on the mind, and serenely satisfying to the soul. To my brother Rich—your words, deeds, and pride in your "little sister" meant so much to me through the years and still do. I wish you and my wonderful sister-in-law Nancy the best that life can offer in the years ahead. Thank you both for all your support. Thanks as well to my most incredible nephew Dustin, the M.D., whose deft uncovering of important journal articles, as well as abundant enthusiasm, was indispensable. To Mandy, my beautiful niece, for her thoughtfulness and encouragement. And to the newest members of the family, Helen and Bret, for their kindness and interest. Thanks to my real-life (but still magically fairy-like) godmother Connie for years and years of undying affection and optimism. And to "little Liz," I hope that this book helps to validate your journey as well.

Know that you are much loved by all of us and cherished especially by me.

Last, but certainly not least, big hugs, kisses, peacock feathers, and tuna treats to my feline best friend "Baby," whose companionship got me through many late nights on the computer and who instinctively knew when it was time to close up shop and head for bed. Prompting me with a soft, loving nudge of the paw and a dainty meow, I have perhaps learned my greatest and most poignant lesson from you and the 13 years we have shared together on this earth—although today is all we have, tomorrow is always another today, and with it, just as sure as the dawn will break, comes the precious gift of living, and the promise and comfortable reassurance of a most heavenly and unconditional love, if we only look around us with the clarity of a sober mind and an open, loving heart.

Introduction

Addiction, Recovery, and the Role of Food

Maintaining a clean and sober lifestyle can be a formidable task for the millions of people who suffer from addiction to alcohol and drugs. It is estimated that 14 percent of the population struggles with alcohol dependence and abuse alone, while a recent government report concluded that many more Americans may still be in denial. These numbers, as alarming as they are, don't come close to including the number of people whose lives have been devastated by the addiction of a family member, loved one, or friend. Remarkably, it is believed that one in four children under the age of 18 lives in a home where alcoholism or alcohol abuse is a fact of daily life.

Currently, only one in five alcoholics will receive any treatment for their addiction, while the disease concept unbelievably continues to be questioned by some. At the same time, however, although many people find the prospect of a sober life difficult to achieve, there are numerous others who have found recovery and are living normal and productive lives. If we knew all the answers as to why some make it and others don't, the disturbing statistics above would no doubt be greatly diminished. We do know that quality treatment, support groups, and therapy appear to contribute positively, while pharmacology holds much future promise. Likewise, attention to food and diet, an aspect often overlooked, also appears to have a positive impact.

Food can make a difference in the recovery from many illnesses and diseases, and good food can often promote good results on many different levels. Recovery from addiction can be no different. Poor eating habits, giving in to constant cravings, and denying chemically abused bodies of needed nutrition can only be detrimental to the process. We can help ourselves and increase our chances of success if we pay attention to what we eat. And cooking and preparing meals for ourselves, as well as others, utilizing the power of food as a healer of body, mind, and spirit, can only contribute to the quality of our recovery and the lives of those affected by our addiction. This is not only true in the early weeks and months of recovery. Concentrating on diet and nutrition may help us through the entire winding course that we must travel towards a lifetime of sobriety.

Feeding the Phases of Recovery

Research and experience have shown that recovery from alcohol and drug dependence follows three phases, with each one lasting about a year, although many people move through these phases at a slower or more rapid pace, depending upon individual factors. These phases are also referred to as stages, or early, middle, and late recovery. There are no definite moments in time when we move from one phase to another, but in general, we can tell from the experience of others as well as through therapy and support groups when we are ready to address issues that are part of the next phase.

Phase One, or early recovery, usually revolves around one task—remaining sober while we grapple with physical changes, emotional roller coasters, and intense cravings. In some ways, it is the hardest stage to go through, and often the light at the end of the tunnel is barely visible, but it does get better and we begin the healing process. During this time, food can play an important role by replenishing lost nutrition, soothing tired minds and bodies, and calming cravings that could steer us in the wrong direction.

By Phase Two, or middle recovery, we begin to feel more comfortable with sobriety and start the process of reacquainting ourselves with who we are. For some, this stage is a welcome respite, while for others, it is sometimes a period of nongrowth that can jeopardize our sobriety and the progress we have made. During this time, food can play an important role as a motivator of change and a tool for rediscovery, not only of ourselves, but also those around us. Through cooking and eating, we may glean better insight into who we are and witness how good food can help in rebuilding our relationships and the place we call home.

Phase Three, or late recovery, is characterized by making further positive lifestyle changes that can prolong our lives and assist us in enjoying the best of health in body, mind, and spirit. Continued growth within ourselves, our families, and society is an ongoing, lifelong task that this period will set into motion. In many ways, food has its most important role to play in this stage, by opening us up to new and healthy ways of eating and living and offering potential protection from future illness and disease, while expanding our horizons and helping us to celebrate our sobriety.

How to Use This Book

You don't have to be an alcoholic in recovery to benefit from the information and recipes in this book. Obviously, drug dependency is a parallel disease and we know that if you have struggled with an addiction to drugs, like all alcoholics, you will need to avoid mind-altering substances and go through an identical healing process. Although my own problem was with alcohol and I often refer to the reader as an alcoholic, this book is meant to address all substance dependencies. For the purposes of food and recovery, they are one and the same; we are fraternal twins of the same disease.

Similarly, if someone you care about—a family member or friend—is battling an addiction, this book will offer insight and encouragement, helping you to better understand not only the nature of the disease, but also the process of recovery. You are the ones that have suffered the most in many ways and you deserve to be included at every stage to heal your own wounds as well as those of the person you love.

If you are new to recovery, then you will no doubt find the recipes and information in Phase One extremely applicable to your current experiences. While proving to be valuable tools to help us move forward, viewing our recovery in terms of the phases will, if nothing else, make us aware of the improvement and strides we have already made. But since this book is not at all meant to be a recovery diet plan or rigid program, skipping ahead to future chapters and topics is fine and even encouraged. I've used the phase guidelines to organize the recipes and information because of the practical relevancy of particular eating habits and health goals to the physical, emotional, and psychological symptoms that characterize each stage. This is also reflected in the choice of recipe categories for each phase, as well as the topics that are discussed in headings and sidebars. For example, you will find that the Phase One recipes tend to require less effort and time, since this is often a hectic and energy-sapped period for most of us. On the other hand, some people find that the phases overlap, in which some early issues from Phase One tend to persist, while other later issues, normally addressed in Phase Three, are already well under control. Feel free to read as much as you can and enjoy as many recipes as possible from all of the sections at a rate that feels comfortable. Similarly, for those who have already achieved sobriety and may even have a good number of healthy years under their belts, the recipes and current research contained in the book may prove helpful in keeping you well informed as you continue your journey and offer assistance and support to others.

Saving Your Life and Staying Sober

During this early stage of re-covery, which lasts anywhere from six months to a year and a half, there is only one real objective and that is to not drink. For most of us, staying sober is an overwhelming prospect. We have spent years, maybe even a lifetime, relying on substances to get us through the day (and night). Whether we are recuperating in a rehabilitation facility, outpatient program, or within another support system, we all share a common dilemma: How do we cope with the compulsion to "pick up" and attempt to put our sober selves back in charge?

Behavioral Treatment Offers Helpful Guidelines

The assistance of twelve-step programs and other support groups, as well as behavioral therapy and the support of loved ones can help get us through this difficult time by offering advice and guidelines that teach us to cope with challenges and set realistic goals. For example, during Phase One we can't expect to fix every terrible problem that our addiction created. Putting a temporary bandage on these issues and simply holding things together for future evaluation and resolution is often the best tactic to employ. Taking on too much too soon can exacerbate the symptoms of post-acute withdrawal and propel us into a downward spiral of stress and anxiety, which may lead to compulsive behavior, physical cravings, and ultimate relapse. Applying these guidelines to diet and nutrition is the logical and most conducive way to view your eating habits and your relationship with food during this time.

The stress management acronym of Alcoholics Anonymous—*H A L T*—is a good thing to remember during Phase One. Try to avoid becoming *H*ungry, *A*ngry, *L*onely, or *T*ired. It's simple but sound advice. And there is a reason that hunger plays a prominent role in managing our stress. Often, people in recovery confuse hunger for food with hunger for drugs or alcohol. Many of the symptoms of chemical craving mimic those of hunger, such as dizziness, nausea, headache, and irritability. Recognizing this similarity will help us to see things in their proper perspective, while devising and sticking to an eating plan will go a long way in lessening the frequency of these symptoms. In addition, many of us suffer from post-acute withdrawal, a period lasting weeks, months, and sometimes even years and characterized by difficulty in concentration, memory, and sleeping. Eating well can help to move us through this period at a somewhat quicker pace.

An Opportunity to Begin a New Relationship with Food

In Phase One of recovery, we probably have yet to establish a healthy eating pattern; years of

Simple Goals for Phase One

EAT BREAKFAST EVERY MORNING. If you are not used to eating breakfast on a regular basis, now is the time to start. Once you set the routine in motion, your body will wake up in the morning anticipating nourishment. Even a simple bowl of cereal will start you off on the right track for the rest of the day. Keep a good supply of some favorite cold and hot cereals on hand—even the sugary sweet versions that may appeal to you at this time can serve as stepping stones toward healthier varieties later on. Eventually start adding some sliced fruit or berries or prepare a quick scrambled egg with toast. If time and energy allow, skip ahead to "Weekend Breakfasts and Brunches: Welcoming Starts to Leisurely Days" (page 159) for some old favorites and more substantial nourishment.

KEEP SNACKS AND BEVERAGES READILY AVAILABLE. When hunger hits, be prepared with a good supply of healthy snacks and beverages to keep you going until your next meal. Take time out to replenish your energy and de-stress from the demands of the day. Keep your cupboards and fridge stocked with a variety of snacks, such as nuts and yogurt, that you can grab at a moment's notice, and if you spend a good amount of time in your car, consider carrying a small tote bag with ice packs for cool beverages and perishable nibbles.

PLAN YOUR MEALS FOR THE DAY. If you are on a hectic schedule, by far the best solution is to bring your lunch or dinner with you. Soups, sandwiches, and reheatable leftovers (especially if you have access to a microwave) are ideal for those on the go. Remember that dinnertime is when we can be particularly vulnerable to "happy hour" temptations. If you have a plan, whether it be to have a quick dinner at home with your family, join a friend for a hamburger, or zap last night's leftover spaghetti in the microwave, you'll be less likely to go astray.

DON'T EAT ANYTHING PREPARED WITH ALCOHOL AND AVOID FOODS WITH "TRIGGER EFFECTS." Eating out in Phase One can sometimes be precarious, especially if you don't know exactly what's on your plate. Ask how things are prepared if you are not sure and refrain from ordering dishes that remind you of your drinking days, which could set off some unwanted triggers and cause you to let your guard down.

nutritional neglect and possible extremes of overeating the wrong foods or not eating at all have become a poor habit. Now is the time to break that cycle. Eating well and eating often is incredibly important right now and starting a new, healthy relationship with food will increase your chances of success during this tough time. Particular vitamins and minerals tend to be in short supply during active drinking and drugging and need replenishing (see page 7). Concentrating on those nutrients during your Phase One eating can only make early recovery easier and healthier. Similarly, rehydrating your body with lots of healthy fluids is a good idea. Refreshing beverages and nutritionally packed soups will help you to regain your strength and stamina. But, again, try not to do everything at once, even if you are feeling infinitely better. Apply realistic goals and don't get ahead of yourself by trying to become a health guru overnight. There will be plenty of time in Phases Two and Three to clean up your act. Do you want that chocolate chip cookie (or two or three)? Go ahead. Hungry for a large order of fries? Indulge. Despite what you've heard, there's no such thing as "death by chocolate," and the occasional large order of French fries won't kill you. Choosing a drink instead, however, just might. Go easy on yourself. What you are attempting to accomplish right now is the hardest thing you will ever do in your life. Each day congratulate yourself on staying sober. Worry about saturated fat later.

Planning Ahead and Taking the Time to Eat

Now more than ever, you will probably be pressed for time. Chances are you are attending numerous meetings and/or participating in outpatient group or individual therapy. In addition, you must keep up with your daily routine of work and family responsibilities. There doesn't seem to be enough time in the day to accomplish everything and sometimes taking the time to eat becomes a low priority. Working a full program of recovery is essential to our success; we know this from the advice we receive in treatment and support groups and from those who have successfully achieved sobriety before us. Making time to eat and nourish yourself is part of any successful program and should become an integral part of your newly sober life.

So, how do you eat well and often when your day seems to consist of dashboard dining and stale cups of coffee? Here is where a little planning can go a long way. To help you out, the recipes in Phase One are designed to address the symptoms and needs of this early period of recovery. They are easily prepared, travel well, and offer good sustenance throughout the day. "Beverages: A Whole New World of Refreshment" provides a wealth of refreshing and rejuvenating beverages for the newly sober you, while "When the Craving Hits: Snacks, Sugar, and Feeding the Chocolate Monster" is packed full of delicious solutions to soothe and satisfy the sudden and powerful cravings we all experience. You'll find the nourishment and sustenance we all need in "The Serenity of Soup: Remedies That Nourish the Body, Mind, and Spirit," while "Keeping It Simple: Satisfying Suppertime Solutions" provides quick and easy answers to the question, "What's for dinner?" without stressing our tired bodies and minds. Before you know it, you'll be feeling healthier, livelier, and full of hopeful promise as the healing process of Phase One progresses and your sober self gets back in charge.

1 *Beverages*

A Whole New World of Refreshment

One of the first questions we alcoholics ask ourselves is, "What do I drink now?" It is as if we have suddenly been cut off from the world of beverages and feel like our future will be nothing but Shirley Temples and Virgin Marys. This couldn't be further from the truth.

When we were drinking, it is unlikely that any other form of liquid apart from alcohol passed our lips, except for water, of course, when we were ferociously thirsty and dehydrated. The world of smoothies, protein drinks, herbal teas, and fruit blends was probably a foreign place to us. Even those fancy mixed tropical drinks (which at least had a few vitamins) were no doubt unappealing to us. After all, you had to drink so many of them before you *knew* you were drinking.

Well, welcome to a whole new world of refreshing, quenching, and even soothing beverages! The choices are overwhelming. So where do we begin? The best place to start is by listening to your body. In the early days and weeks of recovery, it is probably screaming out for hydration. I have always found it odd that people refer to quitting drinking as "drying out" when, in actuality, it's really the other way around. Alcohol makes you lose most of the water you take into your body. It dehydrates cells and removes fluid from the blood. Even once you stop drinking, your body continues to eliminate alcohol, its by-products, and other toxins for several weeks. Drinking plenty of fluids during this time will help this process along. But which fluids and beverages?

Obviously, water is great. It's a good idea to carry around bottled water with you wherever you go. Keep some in the car, next to your bed, on your desk at work. If the quality of your tap water is questionable, drink spring water or purified water or get one of those water filter jugs or a faucet filter. Water, water everywhere . . . drink up and drink often.

Fruit juices are a good choice, too. You'll get lots of nutrients and can satisfy some of your sweet cravings in the process. Vegetable juices are also winners. There are all kinds of interesting combinations out there these days, loaded with vitamins and minerals that your body most likely is in great need of. Explore the beverage section of your grocery store (while avoiding the beer aisle!) and try a few different blends, or make your own. Mix some grapefruit juice with orange-flavored seltzer or have some iced tea with a splash of lemonade. Just be sure to stay away from anything that may be a trigger for you during this time. If your drink of choice was a screwdriver, then maybe orange juice should take a back seat to tomato juice. Or if white wine was your poison, steer clear of white grape juice for a while. Remember, your addiction is so clever, it just may persuade you to take that extra step and add the vodka or uncork the bottle. Don't tease the tiger, as they say. It has a way of sneaking up on you.

What about sugary drinks like sodas? People seem to crave them all the time. It is, of course, the sugar and sometimes the caffeine they are after. Drinking these all day is probably not a good idea, but having them with snacks and meals tends to lessen their direct effect on blood glucose and will help to avoid unwanted spikes and dips in energy and mood. The same goes for coffee and tea. I know there are folks out there who will say caffeine is an evil drug that coffeehouses are pushing on us unconscionably, but moderate caffeine consumption, especially with meals, is not unhealthy unless your doctor has restricted your caffeine intake due to a heart condition or another medical problem. Ask your physician if you are not sure.

Teas are a whole other world to explore. Green tea is one of the healthiest things you can drink; it contains loads of antioxidants and has less caffeine than coffee. Herbal teas, generally caffeine free, can actually soothe and relax us. Chamomile is good for digestion, while dandelion root tea can be cleansing to the liver. Go into a health food store some time and look at the variety of teas and tea blends available. Try some different ones in the evening with honey or lemon. Most of them make delicious iced tea as well. The only questionable herb that has recently been used in teas, tonics, and capsules is valerian root. It is supposed to induce sleep and is considered by some to be a mood-altering substance. I personally would leave it off my list of herbal remedies and explore the other possibilities.

Milk is a great source of protein, is packed with vitamin A and riboflavin, and can be a refreshing drink with a meal or snack, as can yogurt-based smoothies. Some people find that dairy products upset their stomachs; this may be an indication that you are lactose intolerant. However, before deciding whether or not this is the case for you, give your body the chance to recuperate from your addiction before blaming indigestion on other things. Until you're back

Alcohol Takes Its Toll

Recovering Vitamins and Minerals

Active drinking can destroy our bodies. In addition to simply eating poorly, with alcohol often supplying as much as 50 percent of our sustenance, chronic drinking can reduce the body's ability to absorb, process, use, and store nutrients. Since alcohol has a direct, toxic effect on the gastrointestinal tract, most of the vitamins and minerals that are extracted from the small amount of food we do eat cannot be absorbed through the intestinal wall and make their way into the bloodstream. In addition, alcohol consumption is toxic to the liver, the organ that processes nutrients, so our ability to use the vitamins and minerals that may already be present in our bodies is severely compromised. Many water-soluble vitamins, such as B_1 (thiamine), B_6, and folate, cannot be processed, while fat-soluble vitamins, such as A, D, and E, cannot be absorbed properly. The liver is also responsible for manufacturing the transport system that escorts minerals throughout the body. If it is unable to do this, minerals cannot get out and may build up to toxic levels.

Alcohol has been found to be extremely detrimental to the body's antioxidant levels, the important nutrients that protect against free radicals (unstable molecules that steal electrons from healthy molecules, subsequently promoting disease and aging). A study in France of 102 recovering alcoholics found that blood levels of antioxidants (vitamins C and E, beta-carotene, and selenium) were particularly low, while concentrations of free radicals were particularly high, leading researchers to believe that much of alcohol's damage occurs because of the lack of antioxidants in the blood to deal with these scavenger molecules.

It is clear that increasing our intake of vitamins and minerals that were depleted during our active drinking and drugging may go a long way towards improving our health. In most cases, once we are on a regular balanced diet, a lot of the nutritional damage caused by alcohol becomes reversible, so it appears that boosting our nutrients through food may actually be the best remedy for us at this time. Here is a list of vitamins and minerals to make a point of including in your diet:

VITAMIN A: This vitally important antioxidant is necessary for cell reproduction, infection fighting, and healthy vision. Dark green, leafy vegetables and orange and yellow fruits and veggies are the best food sources.

VITAMIN B_1 (THIAMINE): Extremely important for brain function, thiamine deficiency on some level is common in 30 to 80 percent of alcoholics. Although dramatic deficiencies can result in the rare syndrome called Wernicke-Korsakoff, in which irreversible confusion, amnesia, and muscular incoordination occur, most of us could use some extra thiamine, especially during Phase One. Good sources include whole grains, nuts, legumes, potatoes, and most meats, particularly pork.

VITAMIN B_2 (RIBOFLAVIN): Like thiamine, riboflavin is needed to digest and use proteins and carbohydrates and is also beneficial to the moist tissue of the body, such as the eyes, mouth, nose, and throat. Sources are primarily foods of animal origin, such as meat, fish, eggs, and yogurt, although dark green vegetables including broccoli and spinach are also good providers.

VITAMIN B_3 (NIACIN): Deficiency of this important nutrient, which allows oxygen to flow into body tissues, is often common in chronic alcoholics. Including more niacin-rich foods at this time can promote a healthy appetite and help to metabolize sugars and fats. Most breads and cereals are enriched with niacin, but it is also available from meat and dairy products.

VITAMIN B_6 (PYRIDOXINE): Alcohol destroys this important vitamin and over 50 percent of active alcoholics are deficient. Vitamin B_6 is important for transmitting nerve impulses and essential for getting energy and other nutrients from the food we eat. Good sources include beans, nuts, seeds, chicken, eggs, prunes, and potatoes.

FOLIC ACID: Also called folate, this essential nutrient takes part in protein metabolism and the production of new body cells and tissues. Beans, dark green leafy vegetables, and most fruits are good dietary sources.

VITAMIN C: A powerful antioxidant, vitamin C protects the immune system, participates in healing, and is important for vascular function. Citrus fruits are the most common sources, but green peppers, broccoli, tomatoes, strawberries, and many other fresh fruits and vegetables also provide a good supply.

VITAMIN E: This is another important antioxidant required to maintain a healthy reproductive system, muscles, and nerves. It may also have heart-health advantages as well. Vegetables, nuts, oils, and seeds are the best sources.

VITAMIN K: A lesser-known nutrient, but one vital for making specialized proteins found in blood plasma as well as kidney tissue, vitamin K is often depleted by excessive alcohol intake. Although the friendly bacteria in your intestines produce vitamin K (see "Making

Friends with Bacteria," page 347), many leafy greens including cabbage, lettuce, and spinach also provide a healthy amount, as does cheese and most fruits and cereals.

CALCIUM: Not just for strong bones, this mineral contributes to healthy cardiac and muscle function and is often unable to be properly absorbed by active alcoholics. Although dairy products are touted as the best source of calcium, meat, whole grains, beans, and many fruits and vegetables may actually be better sources for our bodies to utilize. Calcium-enriched fruit juices are excellent Phase One beverage choices.

MAGNESIUM: Tissue magnesium, as opposed to that present in the blood, is often reduced in chronic drinkers, causing muscle weakness and degeneration. This important mineral can be obtained from bananas and dark green fruits and vegetables (magnesium is present in chlorophyll, the green pigment of plants), as well as seeds, nuts, beans, and grains.

POTASSIUM: An important nutrient known as a principal electrolyte, potassium is necessary for maintaining proper fluid balance in the body and contributes to nerve transmission and muscle activity. Electrolyte depletion is often a post-intoxication concern and is normally addressed in the hospital during detoxification. Bananas, prunes, raisins, and milk are the best dietary sources.

SELENIUM: A trace mineral with powerful antioxidant capability, selenium apparently works with vitamin E to protect the heart muscle. It may also be protective against certain types of cancer. Fruits and vegetables grown in selenium-rich soil provide a good source, as do seafood, meat, eggs, dairy products, and Brazil nuts.

ZINC: This mineral tends to be excreted in large amounts in chronic drinkers and is important for enzyme and insulin formation, as well as for growth and healing. Zinc in plants is unfortunately difficult to absorb, which is why vegetarians also tend to be short in supply. Better dietary sources include shellfish, beef, and eggs.

A Note About Supplements: Although it has now been established that all adults can benefit from taking a daily multivitamin, speak with a health professional before beginning any supplement regimen that exceeds the Recommended Daily Allowance (RDA) and see the "Resources" section for a reading list to learn more about specific vitamins and minerals.

on a healthy track, it will be hard to know exactly what your body is really allergic to or finding difficult to digest. Again, a physician can guide you in this regard.

Here are some ideas for refreshing beverages, both hot and cold, to quench your thirst, feed your body, and get you started in Phase One. Here's to you and your healthy recovery!

Old-Fashioned Lemon Barley Water

MAKES 4 SERVINGS Lemon barley water has been a traditional restorative for children and people with low constitutions since the nineteenth century. This is no surprise, as lemons contain an enormous amount of citric acid and bioflavonoids, both purported to cleanse the system of toxins and regulate body temperature, while barley is one of the heartiest, most nutritious grains around. Look for barley in the dried-bean-and-grain section of your local supermarket and keep it on hand for this, as well as for some splendid soups and pilafs.

Lemon barley water is not unlike a drink I have often heard recommended by old-timers in recovery to calm cravings and thirst, which consists of corn syrup and lemon juice over ice. Not surprisingly, both are grain-based beverages that also take advantage of the healing power of lemons and the satisfyingly sweet taste of sugar that we crave at this time. If you've never tried sipping a glass of lemon barley water, give this old-fashioned recipe a try and see what you think. I dare say it would give even Gatorade a run for its money in the thirst-quenching department and may provide welcome relief for sudden cravings.

½ cup dried barley
4 cups water
Juice of 1 lemon
3 tablespoons sugar

1. In a medium-size saucepan, combine the barley and water and bring to a boil. Reduce the heat to medium-low and let simmer for 3 to 4 minutes.

2. Pour the barley water through a fine mesh strainer into a 1-quart heat-proof container and add the lemon juice and sugar. Stir to combine.

3. Allow the mixture to cool somewhat, then transfer to the refrigerator and chill well. Serve over ice.

Barley Water

The Original Kitchen Quencher

Famed nineteenth-century French chef George Auguste Escoffier was well aware of the potential danger of his kitchen staff playing the "one for the sauce, one for me" game with the restaurant's alcohol supply. A stickler for order and discipline, Escoffier strictly forbade drinking on the job. To remedy the problem, he asked a doctor friend of his to concoct a nonalcoholic drink that would quench the thirst and relieve the stress of his kitchen workers. The result was a healthy and pleasant barley drink available in huge vats in every hotel kitchen Escoffier oversaw.

Homestyle Lemonade

MAKES 4 SERVINGS Both tart and sweet, lemonade is an excellent thirst-quencher. After juicing the lemons and discarding the seeds, keep any resulting lemon pulp and add it to your drink for a truly homestyle appearance and enhanced flavor.

1 cup fresh lemon juice
3 tablespoons sugar, or more to taste
3 cups cold water

In a pitcher, combine the lemon juice and sugar and stir until the sugar has dissolved. Add the cold water, stir well, and serve over ice.

Fizzy Lemony Ade: Substitute lemon-flavored sparkling water or seltzer for the plain water. Garnish with a lemon slice.

Pink Lemonade: Add 2 teaspoons nonalcoholic grenadine or cherry juice with the water and stir well.

Strawberry Lemonade: In a food processor or blender, puree 1½ cups hulled and halved strawberries. Using a wooden spoon, force the puree through a fine mesh strainer to remove the seeds and add the liquid to the lemon juice-and-sugar mixture, whisking well to combine, before adding the water. Taste for sugar.

Ginger-Honey Lemonade

MAKES 4 SERVINGS The wonderfully medicinal and highly fragrant gingerroot adds a refreshing twist to traditional lemonade. If you have yet to encounter the intensity of fresh ginger, you are in for a pleasant surprise! Easily found in your local grocer's produce section, gingerroot adds the perfect zest to stir fries, baking, and beverage making. Here, the subtle sweetness of honey teams up with lemon and ginger for a delicious, thirst-quenching experience. Use a sharp paring knife or vegetable peeler to remove the gingerroot's bumpy skin.

3 cups water
½ cup honey
¼ cup sugar
¼ cup peeled and chopped fresh ginger
    (about one 4-inch piece)
1 cup fresh lemon juice

(continued on page 12)

Ginger
An Ancient Cure-All Makes a Comeback

The medicinal properties of ginger have been known for centuries. Chinese cooks have added ginger to dishes not only for its intense flavor, but to counter the effects of potential toxins in animal protein and stimulate digestion, while the ancient Greeks utilized ginger's ability to counteract vertigo and motion sickness. During the Middle Ages, ginger was thought to remedy the plague and, in the form of gingerbread, provide muster for knights going into battle. Today, the healing nature of ginger is being recognized in the West for its anti-inflammatory properties in the treatment of arthritis and bursitis, as a remedy for nausea and menstrual cramps, and as a possible aid in cardiovascular health through the reduction of platelet aggregation.

We all remember being given a glass of ginger ale to calm an upset stomach and, indeed, the medicinal properties of ginger can serve us well at this time if problems with indigestion, nausea, or aches and pains due to inflammation occur. If you're feeling a bit like a knight coming *out* of battle during the frequent difficult days of Phase One recovery, let ginger work its magic by incorporating it into your diet. Ginger teas are available on the market and are quite delicious with a squirt of honey and lemon. Munching on crystallized candied ginger is an excellent remedy for nausea and something to keep in mind as a replacement for motion sickness medications such as Dramamine, which contain sedatives that are best avoided in recovery. Keep a piece of fresh gingerroot in your refrigerator bin for quick additions to rice dishes, stir-fries, soups, and baking. And keep some good old ginger ale around for refreshment. Let the healing properties of ginger work for you while enjoying its zesty and delicious flavor.

(continued from page 11)

1. In a medium-size saucepan, bring the water, honey, sugar, and ginger to a boil, stirring until the sugar has dissolved. Reduce the heat to low and simmer for 5 minutes. Allow to cool, then strain through a fine-mesh strainer into a pitcher.

2. Add the lemon juice and stir well to combine. Serve over ice.

Lemons and Limes

Worth More Than a Twist

If your experience with lemons and limes is limited to a tiny twist in a mixed drink, you're in for a real treat. Homemade lemon and lime drinks, from Old-Fashioned Lemon Barley Water to Refreshing Limeade, are easy to make and unbeatable in the thirst-quenching department.

In addition to being a great source of vitamin C, lemons provide modest amounts of calcium and magnesium. They are also one of the top sources of potassium, which works with sodium to regulate the body's water balance and keep us properly hydrated. Limes, also an excellent provider of vitamin C, are historically associated with the prevention of scurvy, a severe vitamin C deficiency suffered by British sailors at sea until they were fed copious amounts of limes (hence, the nickname "limey").

When purchasing lemons, look for firmness and lack of blemishes. Thin-skinned lemons will yield more juice, while thicker rinds are easier for grating. Limes should be bright green and feel heavy for their size.

For fresh juice, 4 to 6 medium-size lemons and 7 to 10 medium-size limes will yield about one cup. To maximize juice yield, gently press and roll the fruit before cutting in half. In addition, a few seconds in the microwave will encourage juice yield. Whole lemons and limes will keep fresh under refrigeration for 10 days to two weeks.

Refreshing Limeade

MAKES 4 SERVINGS Limes, although full flavored, contain a bit more acid than lemons and may require a touch more sugar. The highly aromatic, specialty Key limes from Florida, made famous in Key lime pie, can also be used but will result in a more yellow-colored drink, like lemonade, while tasting distinctly more acidic.

1 cup fresh lime juice
¼ cup sugar
3 cups cold water

In a pitcher, combine the lime juice and sugar and stir until the sugar has dissolved. Add the water, stir well, and serve over ice.

Lemon-Lime Sparkler: Substitute ½ cup of the lime juice with lemon juice and use lemon-lime sparkling water or seltzer instead of plain water. Garnish with a lime wedge.

Raspberry-Lime Cooler: Add 1 tablespoon raspberry syrup to the lime juice-and-sugar mixture and substitute raspberry-flavored seltzer for the water.

"Limey" Ginger Ale: Reduce the sugar to 2 tablespoons and substitute ginger ale for the water.

Citrus Fruit Cooler

MAKES 4 SERVINGS Lemon and lime juices wake up ordinary orange juice, while grapefruit adds a delicious tang in this not-too-sweet fruit blend. You can use orange and grapefruit juice from the carton or squeeze your own, if feeling ambitious. Serve with a slice of fresh orange and a sprig of mint for a summertime treat.

¼ cup fresh lemon juice

2 tablespoons fresh lime juice

¼ cup sugar, or more to taste

1 cup orange juice

1 cup grapefruit juice

1 cup cold water

4 slices fresh orange (optional)

4 fresh mint sprigs (optional)

In a pitcher, combine the lemon and lime juices with the sugar and stir until the sugar has dissolved. Add the orange and grapefruit juices and water, stir well, and serve over ice, garnished with an orange slice and mint sprig, if desired.

Grapefruit Is Not Always a Good Mixer

If you enjoy grapefruit or grapefruit juice on a regular basis and are on medication, be sure to check with your doctor to ensure it is not a bad "mix." Some medicines, particularly those prescribed for blood pressure and cholesterol, may interact with certain enzymes present in grapefruit and cause a dangerous reaction by neutralizing enzymes in the digestive tract that would otherwise slow down the absorption of the drug. This could indirectly and dramatically alter your dosage. If this is the case for you, substitute orange, pineapple, or any other citrus fruit juice, all of which are safe alternatives.

Quick Quenchers

Keep a good supply of juices, sodas, and seltzers on hand to help you create instant refreshment without fuss and to relieve the boredom of plain club soda or fruit juice. Mix and match your own combinations depending on your taste and thirst quotient. Just be sure to refrain from using any mixers that may pose a personal trigger for you, especially during Phase One. For instance, opt for club soda if tonic water reminds you of gin or vodka.

Here are a few ideas to get you started:

- ORANGEADE: 2 parts orange juice, 1 part seltzer or club soda

- GRAPEFRUIT COOLER: 3 parts grapefruit juice, 1 part seltzer or club soda

- PINEAPPLE PUNCH: 1 part pineapple juice, 1 part orange juice, 1 part ginger ale

- CRANAPPLE PLEASER: 2 parts cranberry juice, 1 part apple juice, splash of orange juice

- LIME TONIC: 2 parts tonic water, 1 part lemon-lime soda, splash of Rose's lime juice

- WHITE GRAPE QUENCHER: 2 parts white grape juice, 1 part seltzer or club soda, squeeze of lemon

Homemade Iced Tea

MAKES 2 QUARTS Bottled iced teas have become so popular these days that many folks have foregone making homemade iced tea in favor of convenience. But too often these purchased teas taste less like real tea and more like sugary flavored drinks. If you prefer decaffeinated and/or diet iced teas, your choices become limited. And when thirst is an issue, these pricey bottled teas begin to soak up your wallet! Why not make your own iced tea to have on hand for immediate refreshment? You can choose from caffeinated, decaf, herbal, and a multitude of delicious flavors, add your own sugar or sweetener according to taste, and save quite a few pennies in the process.

    4 cups boiling water
    8 regular teabags or 10 herbal teabags
    4 cups cold water

In a large saucepan or heat-proof pitcher, pour the boiling water over the teabags and allow to steep for 5 to 8 minutes. Remove the teabags, add the cold water, and serve over ice or refrigerate.

Lemon Iced Tea: Add ½ cup fresh lemon juice with the cold water. Garnish with a lemon wedge.

Ginger Iced Tea: Add a 2-inch piece peeled fresh ginger, cut into ¼-inch-thick rounds, to

Not All Drink Enhancers Are Created Equal

Although many common drink enhancers or flavorings traditionally found behind the bar or in the beer or beverage aisle of your grocer *do* contain alcohol, some do not and can be added to an otherwise plain club soda or seltzer for added flavor and refreshment. Here are a few to look for as well as those to avoid:

ROSE'S SWEETENED LIME JUICE: The traditional enhancer of the British "lager and lime," this sweet and tart concoction adds a welcome zest to any plain soda water or even cola without a drop of alcohol.

GRENADINE: Made from pomegranates, which accounts for the intense red color and flavor, this fruit juice concentrate can enhance any citrus drink, such as lemonade or orange juice. Rarely does grenadine contain alcohol, but be sure to check the label before purchasing.

CHERRY JUICE: Maraschino cherries, the common garnish for many drinks, come bottled in this sweet, red juice that can be added to beverages for color and flavor. The popular cherry-flavored cola is just one of its many combination possibilities. However, read the label to ensure that your cherries have not been soaked in any form of alcohol. Vodka, rum, and brandy are common culprits.

ANGOSTURA BITTERS: This potent liquid made from the distillation of aromatic herbs and plants contains a high level of alcohol and is sometimes mistakenly added to "nonalcoholic" drinks by those who are unaware. Steer clear of this dangerous enhancer.

TRIPLE SEC: Technically a liqueur, this strong, orange-flavored enhancer is often used in small amounts (as in margaritas) and consequently is assumed to be alcohol-free. Not so! Keep it out of your cupboard and substitute with orange juice concentrate instead.

the water when steeping and remove with the teabags. Sweeten with honey, if desired, while still warm.

Minted Iced Tea: Add a handful of fresh mint sprigs when steeping and remove with the teabags. Garnish with a mint sprig.

Orange Iced Tea: Add four 2-inch-long strips orange rind (removed with a vegetable peeler) to the water when steeping and discard with the teabags. Garnish with an orange slice.

Fennel-Scented Iced Tea

MAKES 4 SERVINGS Fennel is an excellent aid to digestion and here the seeds impart a refreshing aroma to iced tea. You can make this with any herbal tea you like, although an orange- or lemon-flavored one would be particularly delicious.

4 cups water
1 tablespoon fennel seeds
½ cup honey
4 herbal teabags
Lemon wedges for garnish

1. Combine the water, fennel seeds, and honey in a medium-size saucepan and bring to a boil. Remove from the heat, add the teabags, and allow to steep for 5 minutes.
2. Strain through a fine mesh strainer into a 1-quart heat-proof container and chill.
3. Serve over ice with a lemon wedge.

Black Currant Iced Tea with Exotic Spice

MAKES 4 SERVINGS One of my favorite teas is Twinings Blackcurrant, a blend of black oriental tea and

An Ode to Fennel

Long considered a medicinal plant, the fragrant and feathery fennel is reputed to cleanse the body of toxins from alcohol and dietary excesses, while easing digestion and flatulence. The bulb itself, which bears tall, celery-like stalks with bright green, delicate foliage, is a delicious addition to salads and savory dishes, while the seeds can impart a mild licorice flavor to beverages, both hot and cold. Popular since ancient Roman times, fennel has been honored in art and literature as a symbol of courage and strength. Longfellow paid tribute to this tradition in this poem:

Above the lowly plants it towers
The fennel, with its yellow flowers,
And in an earlier age than ours,
Was gifted with the wondrous powers,
Lost vision to restore.
It gave new strength, and fearless mood;
And gladiators, fierce and rude,
Mingled it in their daily food;
And he who battled and subdued,
A wreath of fennel wore.

—from "The Goblet of Life"
 Henry Wadsworth Longfellow (1807–1842)

the fruity flavor of black currants. Currants (both black and red) are far more popular in Europe than in America, where they are used to make juice, syrups, and delicious jams and jellies. They are high in vitamin C and protective phytochemicals called polyphenols that fight free radicals and encourage cardiovascular health. Polyphenols are also found in red grapes, hence the touting of red wine as a beneficial beverage. (See "The Abstinent Approach: Wine-Free Ways to Increase Your Polyphenols," page 411).

The addition of cinnamon and ginger to this iced tea adds a fragrant and exotic twist. Try it hot sometime as a soothing drink on a chilly night.

4 cups water
4 black currant teabags
2 cinnamon sticks
2 teaspoons peeled and chopped fresh ginger
4 teaspoons sugar

1. In a medium-size saucepan, bring the water to a boil and add the teabags, cinnamon sticks, and ginger. Remove from the heat, cover, and allow to steep for 8 to 10 minutes.

2. Strain the tea through a fine-mesh strainer into a heat-proof container. Add the sugar and stir to dissolve. Chill and serve over ice.

Green Tea Punch

MAKES 4 SERVINGS The aroma and flavor of green tea lends itself beautifully to this refreshing, not-too-sweet punch while providing important antioxidants. Use a strong green tea such as gunpowder or tencha and allow it to steep for at least 15 minutes to obtain maximum flavor.

Simple syrup is a staple in restaurant kitchens and is used as a base for sorbets as well as sweet drinks. It is easy to make and will keep indefinitely in the refrigerator. Simply bring to a boil equal parts of water and sugar (one cup water, one cup sugar), stirring until the sugar dissolves. Allow it to cool and pour into an airtight container. For this recipe you will only need a small amount of simple syrup, but it is worth making at least a cup at a time and storing the rest. It can also be added to lemonades and other tart beverages as a light sweetener instead of sugar or honey.

¼ cup simple syrup, or more to taste (see headnote)
½ cup fresh lemon juice

The Benefits of Becoming a *Tea*totaler

Did you know that drinking just two cups of tea a day could increase your antioxidant levels? Studies have shown that powerful compounds known as polyphenols protect against cancer by preventing free radicals from harming cells and may even protect against heart disease by inhibiting blood platelets from clumping together and clearing artery walls of harmful cholesterol. Green tea, oolong tea, and black tea are all protective, whether decaffeinated or not, but green tea, due to its unique processing, appears to hold the greatest benefits.

Another type of tea made from the young branches of the same plant may even help curb sweet cravings. Kukicha twig tea (available in health food stores) is particularly bitter and is believed by Chinese philosophers to balance the body's desire for sugary substances. Since Western diets tend to be deficient in bitter tastes, preferring instead the sensations of salt, sour, sweet, and pungent, increasing this taste sensation in your diet might lessen your desire for sugar. In addition to bitter-tasting teas, quinine—a bitter alkaloid found in tonic water—may also balance a craving for sweet. Provided it is not a trigger for you, drinking plain tonic water may help lessen sugar cravings. Other dietary sources of bitter include salad greens such as endive and escarole and green leafy vegetables, including broccoli rabe, chard, and dandelion greens.

1 cup strong brewed green tea
2 cups white grape juice
2 cups seltzer or club soda

Combine all the ingredients in a pitcher and stir well. Chill in the refrigerator and serve over ice.

Hot Chamomile Cranberry Tea

MAKES 4 SERVINGS This unlikely combination is a favorite of many of my clients and friends in recovery, no doubt because of the sweet-and-tart tang of the cranberry juice coupled with the delicacy of the chamomile tea. It is a great after-dinner quaff, as cranberry juice cleanses the palate while chamomile settles the stomach. Make a one-cup serving for yourself (with one teacup of chamomile and ¼ cup cranberry juice) or a full teapot to share with family and friends. This after-dinner "drink" will surely become a habit in your house!

4 chamomile teabags
4 cups boiling water
1 cup cranberry juice cocktail,
    at room temperature
Sugar to taste

Steep the teabags in the boiling water in a teapot for 8 minutes. Discard the teabags and add the cranberry juice. Stir and serve immediately in teacups. Add sugar to taste.

Spiced Citrus Hot Tea

MAKES 4 SERVINGS This is a particularly warming drink on a cold evening and can be made with any type of tea, including an herbal variety. Use ordinary orange juice without extra pulp and don't forget to remove the whole spices before serving!

4 cups water
½ cup sugar
4 teabags
2 cinnamon sticks
8 cloves
8 black peppercorns
1 cup orange juice

1. Combine the water and sugar in a medium-size saucepan and bring to a boil. Remove from the heat and add the teabags, cinnamon sticks, cloves, and peppercorns. Cover and allow to steep for 10 minutes.

2. Discard the teabags and remove the whole spices using a slotted spoon. Stir in the orange juice and serve immediately.

Herbal Remeteas

Herbal teas are not only popular because of their fragrant aroma, pleasant taste, and naturally caffeine-free composition, they may provide medicinal benefits as well. For centuries, people have infused leaves, blossoms, seeds, and roots of flowers, fruits, and spices to make soothing beverages that help to heal body, mind, and soul.

- Feel a cold coming on? Have a cup of rose-hip tea, familiarly known as Red Zinger, for a boost of vitamin C.

- Tummy upset from too many chocolate chip cookies? Peppermint tea may calm your digestion.

- Need to unwind from a busy day? Chamomile tea will soothe your nerves and rest your mind.

- Stamina a bit sluggish? Echinacea tea can help stimulate your immune system.

Whether by the bag or in bulk, herbal teas are a great addition to your beverage repertoire. Beware, however, that many herbal remedies in the form of tinctures, or liquid solutions, can contain a good amount of alcohol. Herbs in capsule form do not, by nature, pose this threat. But, as with all types of medication, be sure to consult your doctor before embarking on any self-prescribed herbal regimen.

Sweet Ginger Tea

MAKES 1 SERVING This soothing warm drink is really not a tea at all, but an infusion of medicinal ginger-root, fennel seeds, and cinnamon stick. Sip this when you are feeling a bit delicate in the stomach but still crave something sweet.

1 cup water
One 1-inch piece fresh ginger, peeled and
    cut into 4 slices
1 teaspoon fennel seeds
1 cinnamon stick
1 heaping tablespoon light brown sugar

1. Combine all the ingredients in a small saucepan and bring to a boil, stirring occasionally. Allow to simmer for 1 minute and remove from the heat. Let the ingredients infuse for 5 minutes.

2. Strain through a fine mesh strainer into a drinking mug and serve.

Chai for Two

MAKES 2 SERVINGS Chai is actually the word for tea in many parts of the Eastern world. Recently, it has become a popular alternative to café au lait, a close Western cousin. Essentially a spiced milk tea, it consists of black tea, milk, a combination of spices, and a sweetener. You can buy powdered chai, to which you add hot water or milk, but homemade chai is really easy to prepare yourself and much more aromatic than instant versions.

Ordinary teabags will do just fine, but strong specialty black teas will be more intense in flavor. Feel free to substitute decaf tea if you prefer. You can use low-fat milk if you like, but some chai aficionados swear by half-and-half. As a compromise, I use regular whole milk in this recipe, though I have also had success with soymilk. Sugar actually helps to bring out the full robustness of the spices, so add as much as you like. Honey can be substituted as well.

Cardamom, a popular pungent spice used in East Indian and Scandinavian cooking, comes in seed-filled pods or ground. The pods are worth finding, as they contribute much more flavor. If your supermarket does not carry them, try a specialty grocer or health food store. In a pinch, you can substitute ground cardamom.

The next time you feel like taking a tea break, invite a friend over and have "chai for two." Serve with Cinnamon Crunchies (page 66) and enjoy!

1½ cups water
⅔ cup whole milk
1 cinnamon stick
8 cardamom pods, lightly crushed,
    or ½ teaspoon ground cardamom
4 cloves
One ½-inch piece fresh ginger, peeled and
    roughly chopped
6 black peppercorns
4 teaspoons sugar, or more to taste
2 teabags, black or Darjeeling

1. In a medium-size saucepan, combine all the ingredients, except the teabags. Stir and bring to a boil. Reduce the heat to low and allow to simmer for 10 minutes.

2. Remove from the heat and add the teabags. Cover and allow to steep for 5 minutes.

3. To serve, pour through a tea strainer into two cups. Add more sugar, if desired.

Chocolate Chai for Two: Use chocolate-flavored milk or soymilk instead of regular and proceed as directed above. Reduce the sugar to taste.

Iced Chai: Let cool after straining and pour over ice for a refreshing alternative to iced tea or coffee.

Easy Café au Lait

MAKES 4 SERVINGS If you enjoy coffee, as many of us do, especially in early recovery, but realize you need to cut down on your caffeine intake, café au lait is a great way to wean yourself away from heavy-duty java. At first you may want to add only a touch of warm milk, but eventually you will find that equal parts coffee and milk are just as satisfying as that cup of Joe you used to down with abandon. Of course, if you are already decaffeinated, café au lait is equally delicious prepared with decaf coffee. Try making this with some of the flavored coffees available on the market or experiment with the variations on pages 20 and 21.

Scalding means a liquid has been heated to just below the boiling point. When little bubbles begin

Nonalcoholic Wine and Beer
Traces of Alcohol and Cue Reactivity

Consuming so-called alcohol-free beer and wine, although perhaps incapable of making us drunk, may actually pose serious triggers to craving and relapse. By definition, a beverage can be labeled "nonalcoholic" if its alcohol content is less than 0.05 percent. Researchers believe, however, that not only can trace amounts of alcohol cause cravings, but other subtle cues may jeopardize our sobriety.

Cue reactivity is an important aspect of addiction research that looks at the possible environmental and internal triggers that activate brain activity in alcoholics and addicts. For example, it has been found that merely looking at a glass of beer or a piece of familiar drug paraphernalia can activate the pleasure pathway of the addicted brain as seen in Positron Emission Tomography (PET) scans, technologically advanced equipment that pictorially reveals how the brain is actually functioning. And ingesting small amounts of alcohol before the stimuli are administered will heighten the response to these visual cues.

Since our brains have tremendous recall ability, smelling, viewing, and certainly tasting anything that reminds us of our addiction can be a potential problem, most especially in the early stage of recovery. Cue reactivity accounts for the often-reported feeling of craving that addicts get when they drive by locations where they used to buy drugs, or the ability of ice tinkling in a glass to remind alcoholics of their last glass of scotch. The anticipation alone of a drink or drug may raise levels of the brain chemical dopamine, an important neurotransmitter involved in feelings of elation and pleasure. For this reason, addiction specialists advise staying away from *anything* that may spark addictive recognition when trying to remain clean and sober—scientific evidence of the "people, places, and things" concept and yet another reason to keep alcohol out of the kitchen.

to sizzle around the edges of the pan, your milk is ready.

2 cups hot coffee
2 cups milk, whole, 2 percent, or 1 percent, scalded
Sugar to taste (optional)

Pour equal amounts of hot coffee and milk into a mug, stir, and serve. Add sugar if desired.

Cinnamon Café au Lait   Add 2 cinnamon sticks to the milk before scalding it. Let steep for 5 minutes before combining with the coffee. Remove the sticks before serving.

Vanilla Café au Lait: Scrape the seeds from one-half of a vanilla bean and whisk into the milk before scalding. Steep for 5 minutes and stir well before combining with the coffee.

Is Caffeine Addictive?

Ask anyone who has tried to give up his or her morning coffee and you will hear an emphatic "yes!" Caffeine is classified as a psychoactive drug because it alters behavior and feelings. Symptoms of caffeine intoxication include nervousness, diuresis (excess urination), rapid heartbeat, insomnia, and muscle twitching. Physical withdrawal includes throbbing headache, lethargy, and gastrointestinal distress. Yet, we are told that moderate consumption of caffeine may actually boost athletic performance, ease congestion due to colds and flu, and enhance the pain-relieving effects of aspirin. And, when in the form of a foamy cappuccino or an afternoon cup of tea, caffeine can be a pleasant respite for many of us. So where does caffeine fit into a recovery plan, especially in Phase One?

The greatest drawback of caffeine consumption mentioned by fellow recovering alcoholics is often the least talked about: caffeine can kill our appetite for food. Since eating often and regularly is an important aspect of early recovery, excess caffeine may prevent us from sticking to a healthy and balanced eating schedule. Additionally, the anxiety and nervousness that can occur from too many cups of java may actually set us up for susceptibility to triggers and cravings. If caffeine is drastically reducing your appetite for food, consider cutting down or switching to tea, which contains somewhat less of this powerful drug. Or try brewing a pot of half regular and half decaffeinated coffee (there are actually some of these mixes available in the supermarket) to cut back and help lessen any withdrawal. Similarly, many soft drinks contain high levels of caffeine, so beware of how much you may be consuming and consider substituting them with seltzers or decaffeinated versions of popular sodas.

Incidentally, although mild tolerance and withdrawal are two characteristics of heavy caffeine consumption that coincide with chemical addiction, surprisingly it is not generally considered to be addicting, according to the *Diagnostic and Statistical Manual of Mental Disorders-IV* (DSM-IV), because it does not, by definition, produce true dependence and loss of control.

Mocha au Lait: Whisk in 2 tablespoons unsweetened cocoa powder to the milk before scalding. Continue as directed above.

Decaf Mochaccino

MAKES 4 SERVINGS This rich coffee-and-chocolate blend is a popular coffee bar offering. Use a good quality semisweet chocolate and be sure to whisk in the hot coffee to help create volume for maximum results.

½ cup heavy or whipping cream
4 ounces semisweet chocolate,
    broken into pieces
4 cups freshly brewed decaffeinated coffee
Whipped cream
Ground cinnamon

1. In a large saucepan, bring the cream to a simmer. Reduce the heat to low, add the chocolate, and stir until completely melted and smooth.

2. Gradually whisk in the coffee and carefully ladle the mochaccino into cups. Garnish each with a dollop of whipped cream and a sprinkle of cinnamon and serve immediately.

Creamy Hot Chocolate

MAKES 2 SERVINGS If your experience with hot chocolate is to simply tear open a packet and add hot water, you are in for a real chocolate treat. The quality of the chocolate that you use will determine the success of your outcome and, depending on how sweet you like your hot chocolate, you can use milk chocolate, semisweet, or even bittersweet. You may also use low-fat milk if you prefer less richness. Hot chocolate, unlike hot cocoa, is generally made with solid chocolate, while the latter makes use of unsweetened cocoa powder. Some chocolate lovers will use both for added flavor. This recipe is by far the easiest and creamiest one I know.

2 cups whole milk
3 ounces chocolate of your choice,
    broken into pieces
Miniature marshmallows

1. In a medium-size saucepan, bring the milk to a simmer over medium heat. Add the chocolate, reduce the heat to low, and whisk until melted and smooth, about 1 minute.

2. Increase the heat to medium and continue to whisk until the mixture returns to a simmer, about 2 minutes. Immediately pour into mugs, garnish with the marshmallows, and serve.

White Hot Chocolate: Use 4 ounces white chocolate, broken into pieces, for the chocolate of your choice and continue as directed above.

Orange Milk Chocolate: Add ½ teaspoon grated orange rind to the milk when simmering and use milk chocolate.

Double Dutch Hot Chocolate: Add 2 tablespoons unsweetened cocoa powder and 2 tablespoons sugar to the milk when simmering, whisking well to blend. Use semisweet as the chocolate of choice and continue as directed above, for a doubly delicious result.

Hot Spiced Cocoa with Cinnamon Whipped Cream

MAKES 3 TO 4 SERVINGS Using unsweetened cocoa powder allows you to make your hot cocoa as sweet as you like. Dutch-processed cocoa powder, which is dark and rich, has been treated with an alkali to neutralize its acidity. It is the preferred choice of serious hot cocoa makers and is widely used in baking as well.

I use low-fat milk in this instance to lighten the consistency and encourage second helpings. Serve in a warmed pitcher or coffee pot with the whipped cream on the side. It's a great alternative to a pot of after-dinner coffee.

CINNAMON WHIPPED CREAM
1 cup heavy or whipping cream
2 heaping tablespoons confectioners' sugar
¼ teaspoon ground cinnamon

HOT COCOA
½ cup unsweetened cocoa powder
½ cup granulated sugar, or more to taste
1 teaspoon ground cinnamon
¼ teaspoon ground nutmeg
1 quart low-fat milk (2 percent or 1 percent)
Cinnamon sticks for garnish

1. To make the whipped cream, in a medium-size mixing bowl whip the heavy cream, confectioners' sugar, and cinnamon together with an electric mixer until stiff peaks form. Transfer to a serving bowl and chill until ready to serve.

2. To make the hot cocoa, in a medium-size saucepan combine the cocoa powder, granulated sugar, cinnamon, and nutmeg and whisk together. Add 1 cup of the milk, combine well, and cook over medium heat until the mixture just comes to a boil, whisking often. While still whisking, add the remainder of the milk in a steady stream. Bring to a simmer and heat through. Do not allow the milk to boil again and be sure to whisk often.

3. Remove from the heat and pour into a warmed pitcher or coffee pot. Provide cups or mugs with a cinnamon stick for each guest and serve the whipped cream on the side.

Fruit Smoothies

Blenders all over the country have enjoyed a comeback, thanks to the popularity of smoothies. Variations abound, from nonfat to protein packed to carb boosting. For those of us in recovery, most of our experiences with these types of drinks are probably in the form of piña coladas or frozen margaritas. In fact, if the idea of a blended drink is a trigger for you at this stage, don't even bother and simply pour yourself a glass of orange juice instead—it's best not to conjure up any dangerous associations at this time. But if sweet, fruity drinks appeal to you now as a refreshing beverage to calm your thirst and cravings, they are a great way to deliver a glassful of nutrients, especially those valuable antioxidants.

Smoothies essentially consist of three components: fresh or frozen fruit, an added flavoring or sweetener, and a liquid of choice, generally milk, fruit juice, or yogurt. The number of combinations is endless, but there are a few that are especially tasty and offer a good dose of some much-needed vitamins and minerals such as vitamin C, potassium, and calcium.

There are a few tips to making good smoothies that are easy to remember. Freezing your fruit (or using frozen bagged fruit) will eliminate the need for adding ice cubes, which tend to clunk around in the blender, giving everyone within 20 yards of the kitchen a splitting headache. It may even spark a memory or two of the familiar sound of crushing ice, which might pose a trigger for you. Using frozen fruit ensures a cold and smooth consistency without the use of ice and is the best way I have found to utilize a plethora of fresh fruit that might otherwise go bad sitting on the counter. Just wash them, cut them into large chunks, and freeze in resealable plastic bags for use anytime. Bananas (peeled), strawberries, peaches, even melon chunks and blueberries are suitable. Fruit that you buy already frozen, such as raspberries, may have some added sugar or sweet syrup, so be mindful of adding more sweetener until you have tasted the result. Of course, if you like your smoothies just cool and not ice cold, you needn't use frozen fruit at all. Merely chilled fruit and liquids will result in a more "drinkable" smoothie and may even be preferable to you early on.

Using flavored yogurts is a great way to create different flavor combinations. If blueberries are scarce, use blueberry yogurt. If peaches are not in season, peach yogurt will substitute nicely. One of the best-flavored yogurts around is a banana-vanilla combination, sometimes called "banilla." If you are a fan of banana milkshakes and smoothies, try using "banilla" yogurt in place of fresh bananas sometime. Obviously, the more fresh fruit you use, the better the nutrient and fiber content, but in a pinch, flavored yogurts can really enhance your smoothies and provide the taste you are after.

Finally, one of the best things about smoothies is that if you are not completely satisfied with the outcome, you can always pour it back into the blender and add something else! What other recipes give you that kind of leeway? Too thick? Add some milk or juice. Too thin? Add more fruit. Too tart? Add some honey or sugar. Too sweet? Add a squeeze of lemon juice. One of my favorite combinations is strawberry-grapefruit with a little honey. One day I whipped up the smoothie as usual, but the taste was so tart, probably due to the particularly unsweet strawberries I had on hand, that I couldn't drink it without pouring half the honey jar into it. I put it back in the blender with a scoop of low-fat vanilla ice cream instead and *voila*! A delicious new concoction! Don't be afraid to play with your food when making smoothies. Be creative and have fun.

Additives in Smoothies?

Try adding one tablespoon of any of the following to your smoothies for extra nutritional benefits:

- Wheat germ for vitamin E and folic acid
- Protein powder for vegetarians who need a protein boost
- Brewer's yeast for iron, selenium, and chromium to aid glucose tolerance
- Peanut butter for added protein and niacin
- Psyllium husk powder for extra dietary fiber

Strawberry-Banana Smoothie

MAKES TWO SERVINGS The powerful amount of potassium and vitamin C in this version is perfect for early recovery. If you like, you can substitute vanilla soymilk for the regular milk for added protein and flavor.

> 1 cup fresh or frozen strawberries,
>   hulled and halved
> 1 ripe banana, peeled and cut into 1-inch pieces
> 1 tablespoon sugar
> 1 cup milk

Place all the ingredients in a blender and process until smooth. Serve immediately.

Pineapple-Mango Smoothie

MAKES 1 SERVING This tropical combination is sure to quench any thirst, while also providing the essential vitamins A, C, and D. Bags of frozen mango pieces will allow you to whip this up in no time. If buying fresh mangoes, look for those that are at least half tinged with red, yellow, or orange. When ripe, they are slightly soft to the touch, but not bruised or mushy. For smoothie purposes, removing the skin first with a vegetable peeler or paring knife is probably the best way to get at the flesh. Once peeled, you must carefully cut around the flat, stone-like pit in the center. You can scrape away some of the flesh when you get closer to the seed. Try not to include any of the white, stringy pith. If you can't find mango nectar, substitute apricot nectar, which is similarly thick, or orange juice, if necessary. Feel free to add a scoop of vanilla ice cream or frozen yogurt for added creaminess and calcium.

1 ripe mango, peeled, pitted, diced, and then frozen (or use 1 cup frozen mango pieces)
½ cup pineapple juice
½ cup mango nectar
Honey to taste

Combine all the ingredients in a blender and process until smooth. Serve immediately.

Blueberry Passion Yogurt Smoothie

MAKES 1 SERVING If you like blueberries, you will love this blueberry triple whammy! Touted as one of the best brain foods around, blueberries contain a high concentration of antioxidants and have been shown to improve short-term memory. They may even be able to reverse deficits in motor coordination that generally appear in middle age. Researchers are currently testing the power of blueberries in the laboratory to reverse Alzheimer-like brain damage.

This smoothie provides an intense concentra-tion of flavor thanks to the blueberry juice, available in most health food stores. If you can't find blueberry juice, you can substitute half blueberry syrup and half water. In a pinch, red grape juice will do nicely. Try making this with strawberries or raspberries, too. Even a mixed-berry combination would be delicious.

½ cup fresh or frozen blueberries, picked over for stems
½ cup blueberry yogurt (half of an 8-ounce container)
½ cup blueberry juice, well chilled

Combine all the ingredients in a blender and process until smooth. Serve immediately.

Orange Creamsicle Smoothie

MAKES 1 SERVING If you fondly remember the flavor of orange creamsicles, this smoothie will send you to the comfort zone in no time. Vitamin C never tasted so good! You can substitute frozen orange juice concentrate for the sherbet or sorbet.

1 scoop orange sherbet or sorbet
One 8-ounce container vanilla yogurt
1 tablespoon honey
¼ cup milk

Combine all the ingredients in a blender and process until smooth. Serve immediately.

Fudgsicle Smoothie: If fudgsicles are your passion, try substituting chocolate sorbet or frozen yogurt for the orange sherbet.

Savory Lassi

MAKES 1 SERVING Popular in India and Pakistan, and often seen on Middle Eastern restaurant menus, lassi are chilled yogurt-based drinks, not unlike smoothies, but much lighter and generally unsweetened. They are particularly refreshing with a meal that has some "heat" to it, as the yogurt tends to soothe the taste buds. This recipe is for a savory version and is an excellent accompaniment to any curry dish or refreshing on its own.

½ cup plain yogurt
½ cup water
⅛ teaspoon celery salt
¼ teaspoon cumin seeds

Combine all ingredients in a blender and process until smooth. Pour over ice and serve.

Sweet Rose Lassi

MAKES 1 SERVING Rosewater has been around for centuries as a fragrant addition to Eastern cooking. It is also one of the few "extracts" that does not contain alcohol as a preservative. Orange blossom water is similar, although a little less floral in its fragrance. You could substitute it for the rosewater, if you like, for a slightly different taste. Both waters are available in specialty food stores and are used in many exotic desserts such as Greek baklava and Indian rice pudding called *kheer*. Enjoy this light and fragrant drink on its own or with something sweet.

½ cup plain yogurt
½ cup water
2 teaspoons sugar
½ teaspoon rosewater

Combine all the ingredients in a blender and process thoroughly. Pour over ice and serve.

Cranberry Lassi

MAKES 1 SERVING Cranberries have long been considered an aid in urinary tract health. More recently, they have been determined to be rich in flavonoids, the same antioxidants contained in red wine, and are just as good at absorbing potentially dangerous free radicals in the body. In addition, cranberries can promote the healthy dilation of blood vessels and contribute to healthy gums. Surely, the humble cranberry deserves to be consumed more often than at Thanksgiving time!

Try this thirst-quenching lassi as an alternative to plain cranberry juice.

¼ cup plain yogurt
¾ cup cranberry juice
Juice of ½ lemon
2 teaspoons sugar
Lemon wedge for garnish

Combine all the ingredients in a blender and process. Serve over ice with a lemon wedge.

Careful of Kefir

When browsing the yogurt section of your supermarket or health food store, you may come across kefir, a slightly sour drink reminiscent of liquid yogurt in both taste and texture. Strawberry and vanilla are the most common flavors and, upon first glance, you might be tempted to grab a bottle and add it to your newfound beverage repertoire. But read the label carefully. Kefir is actually fermented milk and can contain about 2½ percent alcohol. Originally made from mare or camel's milk by the medieval Moghuls, kefir is now produced from cow's milk, but the fermentation result is the same. Kumiss, a similar concoction, also contains alcohol and is often sold as a digestive aid.

The Perfect Milkshake

MAKES 2 SERVINGS Milkshakes really belong somewhere between beverages and dessert. Although many of us like to slurp our shakes with burgers and fries, they may just be the perfect choice for something sweet *after* dinner, especially since there are so many "dessert-like" possibilities. From Rocky Road to Strawberry Cheesecake, you are only limited by the variety of ice cream or frozen yogurt in your grocer's freezer. Even then, you can add just about anything you like, from peanut butter to Oreo cookies. The basic proportions for two 8-ounce servings are as follows, but you can add more or less milk, depending on how cold or soft your ice cream is and how thick or thin you like your milkshakes.

1 pint ice cream or frozen yogurt, softened
1 cup milk

Put the ice cream and milk in a blender and process until smooth. Serve immediately with a straw (the straw is key for slurping!).

Chocolate Peanut Butter Milkshake: Use chocolate ice cream, chocolate milk, and 2 tablespoons smooth peanut butter.

Butterscotch Pecan Milkshake: Use butter pecan ice cream, milk, and ¼ cup butterscotch topping swirled in.

***Dulce de Leche* Milkshake:** Use *dulce de leche* ice cream and milk and sprinkle with toffee bits.

Mocha Latte Milkshake: Use coffee ice cream and chocolate milk and top with whipped cream and a dash of ground cinnamon.

Strawberry Fudge Swirl Milkshake: Use strawberry ice cream, milk, and fudge or chocolate sauce swirled in. Top with a chocolate-dipped strawberry.

Banana Milkshake: Substitute 1 medium-size, very ripe banana, peeled and sliced, for half the ice cream. Add ½ cup banana yogurt for a boost of flavor.

Classic Black-and-White Milkshake: Pour 2 tablespoons chocolate syrup in the bottom of the glass and pour a vanilla milkshake over. Swirl with your straw.

Caramel Apple Milkshake

MAKES 2 SERVINGS Here is one of my very favorite combinations that is always a real treat. Use chunky applesauce to retain little pieces of apple in the blending process and add more cinnamon if you are a fan of its taste. Cinnamon ice cream, if available, really intensifies the flavor and takes this shake to delicious heights!

½ pint vanilla bean ice cream, softened
½ cup milk
½ cup cinnamon applesauce
¼ cup prepared caramel sauce
Dash of ground cinnamon (optional)
Apple wedges dipped in caramel sauce for garnish

1. Combine all the ingredients in a blender, except for the apple wedges, and process until smooth.
2. Garnish each serving with the caramel-dipped apples.

2 When the Craving Hits

Snacks, Sugar, and Feeding the Chocolate Monster

If you are craving snack food, sugar, and chocolate, you probably know you are not alone. These voracious cravings are a normal part of recovery and everyone has experienced them at one time or another, particularly during Phase One. You know the feeling. The snack attack hits and you're itching to indulge. Maybe it's late at night or between meals. Since many of us confuse our hunger for food to mean a hunger for alcohol or drugs, we may think we're experiencing a craving to drink or use. That can be dangerous. Our anxiety levels increase while irritability and irrational thinking set in and, before we know it, we are off and running in the wrong direction. Here's just one person's memorable story:

"I distinctly recall one evening when a ravenous snack urge struck me full force. Driving home after my meeting, I made a high-speed, tire-screeching turn into the nearest convenience store to find what I believed was the only thing that could satisfy my uncontrollable craving—a bag of Ruffles potato chips and a container of onion dip! No, another brand of ridged chip would not suffice in my crazed state. 'Where's the Ruffles?!' I screamed.

Getting the Basics Straight
Understanding Macronutrients and the Glycemic Index

Vitamins and minerals are called micronutrients, smaller components of the larger macronutrients known as protein, fat, and carbohydrates. Although much disagreement exists as to the appropriate proportion of macronutrients in the ideal diet, particularly with the sensationalized high-protein diet programs that exist, in essence a good balance is to consume about 20 to 30 percent of our daily calories from protein, up to 30 percent from fat, and about 40 to 60 percent from carbohydrates. Within these percentages, it is the quality of each macronutrient that is particularly important. For example, protein derived from fish and vegetables (like soy) is often a better bet than those from animal sources that may contain a large amount of saturated fat. In the fat category, monounsaturated and polyunsaturated fats are better for us than saturated fats. And in the carbohydrate world, the traditional complex versus refined carbohydrate discussion still holds true, but we also have a new tool and method of categorization, which helps differentiate "healthy" carbohydrates from "not-so-healthy" ones, called the Glycemic Index.

The Glycemic Index (GI) tells us how much our blood sugar rises after eating a particular carbohydrate. On a scale of 0 to 100, with pure glucose set at the top, carbohydrates are classified as low (55 or less), moderate (56 to 70), and high (greater than 70). Those carbohydrates that

'Don't you have Ruffles?!! I have to have Ruffles with my dip!' Finally, eyeing the desired blue bag, I grabbed the goods, stood in line to pay (which seemed like forever!), and raced back to the car. As I turned the key and felt my heart pumping at double speed, I suddenly discovered a moment of sober clarity. What am I, nuts? Why am I so hungry, not to mention obsessed with this blue bag sitting next to me on the car seat? I started to think back on my day. I hadn't eaten dinner yet . . . it was nearly 10:00 P.M. As a matter of fact, I didn't recall eating much for lunch either . . . there wasn't time. Breakfast was a few cups of coffee and, oh yes, I did manage to wolf down a yogurt or something. Or was that yesterday? Well, at least I'm not drinking!

Although a cold beer would go down nicely just about now."

Eating throughout the day is an important habit to begin in Phase One. Even small amounts of nutritious snacks can keep our glucose levels stable and our moods from fluctuating haphazardly, avoiding vulnerable moments when triggers can be acted upon and relapse becomes a real possibility. As part of a complete recovery program, what we eat and when we eat it can contribute to our success and well being.

It's a good idea to keep a supply of healthy snacks with us "on the road" and to take the time to eat and refresh ourselves. Most people, regardless of whether they are battling with the disease of addiction or not, neglect to do this are rapidly digested and cause quick spikes in blood glucose are not particularly good for us because they can put stress on the pancreas, which must produce a flood of insulin in order to bring glucose levels down to normal. For diabetics, in particular, who need to monitor their blood sugar levels, high glycemic-rated foods can be particularly disruptive. And, for all of us, quick rises and falls in blood sugar can negatively affect our moods and our appetite.

In general, highly processed foods that are easy to digest often have higher GI values, while those that are in a more natural state tend to be lower on the GI scale. Fiber and fat content, as well as acidity, all affect the rate at which carbohydrates are metabolized and, ultimately, predict their GI rating. Since we normally eat foods in combination with one another, we can lower the effects of a high glycemic-rated food by consuming it with lower glycemic-rated carbohydrates, protein, fat, or fiber. This means that basically no food is really off limits—it is the combination in which we eat these foods and the overall balance of high and low GI-rated foods that will determine whether or not the final effects on our blood sugar and ultimately our moods and appetite are detrimental or acceptable.

Hundreds of foods have been tested for a Glycemic Index rating, and there are numerous publications and online sources where you can view a complete or partial list (see the "Resources" section). Throughout the book we'll be looking at the advantages of using the Glycemic Index in our diet planning. Adding this valuable tool to our recovery cooking will provide a better understanding of basic nutrition and help to keep us well fed and nourished through the phases of recovery.

and end up devouring junk food in record time as they drive from place to place. Don't start this bad habit now. We have the tremendous opportunity to begin a new eating plan, and since we probably never had an eating plan to begin with, the slate is pretty clean and ready to be filled with all kinds of good habits!

Most nutritious snacks require little or no cooking at all. Having a well-stocked pantry and refrigerator of select ingredients that can be thrown together in a flash is more than half the battle. Just a little preparation and planning will go a long way in helping us deal with sudden urges and cravings, instead of endlessly reaching into that bag of potato chips while staring into the fridge trying to decide what to devour next.

Think of your snacks as mini-meals, with all the components of a regular meal, only smaller in portion size. When at home, take the time to sit down, set a place for yourself at the table, include a beverage, and savor your snack slowly and deliberately. When out and about, try as best you can to find a quiet and comfortable place to take your break and relish your food. Even just a few minutes will help to relax and refresh your body, mind, and spirit.

In this chapter we'll come up with some quick ideas for quelling those munchies and dig into some healthy dips and appetizers. We'll find that sugar, in and of itself, is not necessarily the enemy and create some delicious solutions to soothe a sweet tooth in what I fondly call "The

Doughnut Alternative." Finally, we'll meet face to face with the chocolate monster and discover that he may not be such a bad guy after all, provided that we put him in his place.

So, before you reach for that blue bag, let's start cooking up some satisfying snacks for when the craving hits!

Dips and Appetizers: Dipping into Nutrition

How often do we reach into a bag of chips to satisfy a sudden urge to munch? Potato, corn, tortilla chips . . . all empty calories with no long-lasting satisfaction. Cravings for carbohydrates such as these are not uncommon, even though they do not (generally) contain sugar. Why? Refined carbohydrates convert into sugar more rapidly than other foods and appear to "satisfy" us quickly, although that satisfaction is always short-lived. Even popular rice cakes, which are advertised as healthy, break down almost immediately in our system and quickly raise glucose levels. When eaten alone, rice cakes have one of the highest ratings on the Glycemic Index. But when combined with another, lower-rated food, such as peanut butter, they have longer-lasting effects of satiety and can contribute to steady energy levels. The same is true for those chips. Dipping into a bowl of something nutritious before devouring them can lessen their tumultuous effect. Although nothing will lessen the amount of saturated fat they contain, there are several reduced-fat versions you could try. My favorite is Cape Cod brand reduced-fat potato chips, made only with potatoes, canola oil, and salt. They are made without the addition of unhealthy partially hydrogenated oils and trans fatty acids and are satisfyingly crisp and flavorful. You might also take a peek at your local health food store for some interesting and healthful tortilla chip varieties, many of which are made with whole grains. Sweet potato chips, as well as plantain chips, are a good alternative to the usual potato chip. And tasty root vegetable chips, which include taro, batata, parsnip, and yuca, are now found under the Terra Chip brand in most supermarkets. But for now, when the craving hits for those crispy crunchies, try dipping them into these delicious bowls of energy and nutrition.

Are We Carbohydrate Addicts?

You may have heard this popular term and wonder, in light of your current cravings for carbs and sweets, if you may indeed be addicted to carbohydrates. Addiction science researchers caution us to use the term "addiction" with care and for good reason. We sometimes hear it applied to everything from cookies to television: "I'm addicted to Chips Ahoy" or "She's a soap opera addict." Although these may sometimes feel like addictions, they do not fit the medical definition of substance dependence and are not at all comparable.

But recently, carbohydrate addiction has become a hot topic in weight-loss circles and diet books, and advocates of the theory have even suggested that carbohydrate addiction fits the standard definition set by the American Psychiatric Association for psychoactive substance dependence, because the "addict" attempts to control or cut down use (dieting), increases his or her tolerance (eats greater and greater quantities), and even experiences withdrawal symptoms (the "crash" after the "rush").

Here's the basic idea: Carb addicts possess a compelling hunger or craving for carbohydrate-rich foods, including what they call "carbohydrate act-alikes," such as alcohol and sugar substitutes. In an attempt to feel better, these "addicts" will overindulge on foods such as cake, bread, pasta, potatoes, and lots of junk food in order to release the powerful neurochemical serotonin, which regulates our moods and emotions. However, in carb-addicted folks, it is suggested, something goes wrong with the wiring and serotonin does not rise appropriately, which interferes with the "stop eating" message from the brain and encourages the addict to keep on munching. This results in overeating, insulin resistance, and blood sugar fluctuations, ultimately leading to obesity and diseases, such as Type II diabetes. According to Dr. Andrew Weil, author of *Eating Well for Optimum Health*, the idea that eating refined starch and sugar *causes* insulin resistance is "simply false." He reminds us that insulin resistance is primarily determined by genetics, weight, and physical fitness. Overeating refined carbohydrates can exacerbate insulin resistance if you already have it (as is the case in some diabetics), but it will not *make* you insulin resistant. Even so-called carbohydrate-sensitive people can do quite well by simply avoiding high glycemic-rated carbohydrates.

As far as serotonin is concerned, we know that certain foods can stimulate an increase in neurochemical activity or there would be no such thing as comfort food. But in reality, many of our neurochemicals, not just serotonin, are affected by what we eat and drink, as well as what we do every day, and it is this complex interaction that is the basis of much research still to be done. We do know that the choice of carbohydrate plays an important role in how we immediately react to what we've eaten and that highly refined and processed foods tend to leave us wanting more, offering little satiation and, consequently, making us appear to be "addicted" because we simply keep eating out of hunger. Complex carbohydrates, or those with a lower Glycemic Index rating, on the other hand, contribute to a feeling of satisfaction (satiety) because they are metabolized more slowly, avoiding the often-reported sugar "high" followed by a "crash" of sorts, when high-glycemic foods are consumed.

As a remedy, carbohydrate addiction gurus suggest, among other things, decreasing the frequency of carbo-rich meals and saving them for special "reward" meals. The rest of the time, they encourage higher protein consumption. However, by reducing the amount of carbohydrates we eat throughout the day, we are depriving our bodies of their preferred energy source, particularly the brain, that fabulous organ we have already exposed to terrible abuse from addiction. In fact, by drastically reducing the amount of carbohydrates they eat during early recovery, some people report an increase in alcohol craving. I have heard this over and over from recovering alcoholics who, in an attempt to fix everything at once, diet early on and experiment with extremely low-carbohydrate eating plans. After all, alcohol is metabolized as a carbohydrate, and when the brain needs energy, it's not picky about what form it takes. What a convenient opening for our addiction to slither its way back into our lives and convince us that an ice cold beer is a really good "reward."

And finally, is it possible to become addicted to carbohydrates? We know that when we become addicted to drugs and alcohol, our brain chemistry is changed in lasting ways. Chronic exposure can alter both the number of neurochemical receptors and their sensitivity. This is called neuroadaptation and helps to explain the phenomena of tolerance and withdrawal, two important aspects of addiction as a brain disease. I am not convinced that potato chips have the same power. Moreover, substance dependence in the form of alcoholism and drug addiction is a chronic, progressive, and fatal disease. If we do not stop, we will die.

So, if you are choosing to eat more carbohydrates at this time, for whatever reason, you can rest assured it is far better than reaching for the bottle. And don't be too hard on yourself if your snacking is occasionally "out of control." It's still better to drive with a bag of Ruffles next to you instead of a six-pack.

Grateful for Guacamole

MAKES 4 SERVINGS Can something so smooth, creamy, and satisfying to our "fat tooth" really be good for us? You bet. The type of fat contained in the avocado is the healthy monounsaturated variety. It is also loaded with much-needed vitamins and minerals, including vitamin C and potassium.

Choose avocados called Hass or Calavo, which are smaller, have bumpy skin, and are dark green, sometimes almost black in color, as opposed to the Fuerte variety (larger, lighter green, and with a smooth skin), which generally lack flavor. If you can't find ripe avocados, keep them in a brown paper bag at room temperature for a couple of days until they are soft (but not mushy) and yielding to the touch. Cut-up avocado reacts when exposed to air, turning brown. To keep this from happening to your guacamole, squeeze the half of lime not used in the recipe to moisten a paper towel. Place this directly on the surface of any uneaten (hardly!) guacamole before covering with

plastic wrap and your dip will remain fresh and green in the fridge for next time. This is also a handy tip if you make your guacamole ahead of time or plan to take it with you for a snack at work. The acidic qualities of sour cream will also help to keep your guacamole from discoloring, but you can omit it if you like.

Use this as a dip with tortilla chips and raw vegetables. Guacamole is also a great addition to burritos and wraps as well as a topping for burgers or grilled chicken. So, dig in and be grateful (I know I am!).

2 ripe Hass avocados
1 lime
½ small onion, chopped
1 small, ripe tomato, seeded and chopped
1 tablespoon sour cream
Dash of Tabasco sauce
Pinch of salt and pepper

(continued on page 34)

The Avocado Advantage

Once upon a time, avocados were considered taboo for dieters, diabetics, and heart patients, due to their high fat content. But recent studies have shown that the type of fat avocados contain, the monounsaturated variety, may actually lead to improved HDL cholesterol (high-density lipoprotein, the good kind of cholesterol), lower triglycerides, and better diabetic glucose control. And there's more good news. A 2000 study in Honolulu discovered that avocados contain potent chemicals that may reduce liver damage and may be particularly promising for the treatment of viral hepatitis. In addition, this delicious fruit (often mistakenly referred to as a vegetable) contains phytochemicals that can aid in preventing cancer and is an excellent source of soluble fiber, folate, B_6, and potassium, as well as the antioxidant vitamins C and E.

Although guacamole may be your only acquaintance with this nutritional powerhouse, avocados also make great additions to salads and sandwiches and are a main ingredient in the familiar sushi bar offering called the California roll. So, get to know your avocado and enjoy the tremendous advantages it has to offer.

THE COLORADO AVOCADO SANDWICH

I was first introduced to this combination in Boulder, Colorado, and have loved it ever since. A good quality, nutty, whole-grain bread is the key, along with a perfectly ripe avocado. Give it a try and see what you think. It's perfect for a snack or light vegetarian lunch.

2 heaping teaspoons mayonnaise

2 slices whole-grain bread, preferably with seeds and nuts

2 slices Swiss or Jarlsberg cheese

½ ripe avocado, pitted, peeled, and thinly sliced

2 medium-size white mushrooms, wiped clean, stems trimmed, and thinly sliced

Salt and pepper to taste

Spread a heaping teaspoon of mayonnaise on each bread slice. Layer the cheese, avocado, and mushrooms on one bread slice and season with salt and pepper. Top with the other bread slice, and press down firmly before cutting into two to serve.

Chef's Note: If making ahead of time, sprinkle a little lemon or lime juice on the avocado and mushrooms before adding to your sandwich to prevent browning.

(continued from page 32)

1. With a sharp knife, slice the avocado in half lengthwise and twist apart. Discard the seed and scoop the flesh out of the peel into a medium-size mixing bowl.

2. Squeeze the juice from half the lime over the avocados and mash together with a fork or back of a wooden spoon. Add the onion, tomato, sour cream, and Tabasco, season with salt and pepper, and combine well. Transfer to a dipping bowl and serve.

Chef's Note: Use your hand-held immersion blender for a creamy and smooth result in no time at all! You can substitute 3 to 4 table-spoons of your favorite salsa for the onion and tomato. Hold back on the salt, however, and taste for "heat" before adding the Tabasco.

Easy Homemade Hummus

MAKES 4 SERVINGS Chickpeas, like other members of the bean family, are a rich source of protein, calcium, and iron. They double as complex carbohydrates and are a healthy addition to any diet. Tahini is a paste made from ground sesame seeds, an excellent source of calcium in itself, and the ingredient that gives hummus its characteristic flavor. You can find it in health food stores and specialty grocers. In addition, many supermarkets now carry tahini in the condiment aisle.

If you would like to start with dried chickpeas, you will need to soak them in water to cover overnight and cook them in fresh water until they are soft enough to process. Canned chickpeas should be drained and rinsed under cold running water before using.

There are lots of varieties of hummus these days, which has become a popular dip for pita bread and raw vegetables. If you want to experiment, try some of the variations below. Hummus also makes a terrific spread for bagels and a satisfy-

ing filling for sandwiches or wraps. It will keep, refrigerated, for up to one week.

Two 15-ounce cans chickpeas, drained and rinsed (about 3 cups)
Juice of 1 lemon
4 garlic cloves, peeled and minced
½ cup tahini
Salt and pepper to taste
1 teaspoon extra virgin olive oil

1. In a food processor or blender, process the chickpeas and lemon juice together until smooth. Add a touch of water if necessary to improve the consistency. Add the garlic, tahini, and a good pinch of salt and pepper and process for another minute.

2. Transfer to a serving bowl, taste for seasoning, drizzle the olive oil over the top, and serve chilled or at room temperature.

Horseradish Dill Hummus: Add 1 tablespoon chopped fresh dill and 2 teaspoons prepared horseradish when blending.

Pesto Hummus: Add 2 tablespoons prepared pesto sauce when blending.

Sun-dried Tomato Hummus: Add 2 tablespoons chopped oil-packed sun-dried tomatoes when blending.

Soybean Hummus with Roasted Peppers: Substitute canned soybeans for the chickpeas and add ¼ cup chopped roasted peppers when blending.

Black Bean and Corn Salsa

MAKES 4 SERVINGS This is a wonderful dip for tortilla chips and makes an excellent accompaniment to a Mexican-style dinner as well. Healthy black beans combine with the sweet crispness of corn and just the right amount of seasoning to wake up the flavors and keep you dipping for more.

This salsa will keep, refrigerated, for up to one week.

One 15-ounce can black beans,
   drained and rinsed
One 3-ounce can corn kernels, drained
1 medium-size, ripe tomato, seeded and diced
2 scallions, ends trimmed and cut ¼ inch thick
1 jalapeño (optional), seeded and minced
Juice of ½ lime
1 teaspoon red wine vinegar
1 tablespoon extra virgin olive oil
½ teaspoon ground cumin
1 tablespoon chopped fresh cilantro leaves
Salt and pepper to taste

Combine all the ingredients in a medium-size mixing bowl and blend together with a rubber spatula. Taste for "heat" and seasonings, cover with plastic wrap, and chill before serving.

Warm Jalapeño Bean Dip

MAKES 4 SERVINGS Spicy and scintillating, this dip served warm from the oven is sure to satisfy any craving for "heat" you can dish out. I prefer using pinto beans, but other varieties such as black or kidney beans will work equally well. Tortilla chips are the appropriate dippers here, although crisp pieces of green or red bell peppers will add a refreshing taste sensation and help to cool down the fire!

1 tablespoon canola oil
½ medium-size onion, peeled and diced
Salt
2 jalapeños, seeded and minced
Two 15-ounce cans pinto beans,
   drained and rinsed
1 tablespoon fresh lime juice

¼ cup water
1 teaspoon ground cumin
1 teaspoon pure maple syrup
Pepper to taste
½ cup shredded sharp cheddar cheese

1. Preheat the oven to 400 degrees.
2. Heat the oil in a large nonstick skillet over medium heat, add the onion and a pinch of salt and cook, stirring, until slightly softened, 3 to 4 minutes. Add the jalapeños and cook another minute. Add the beans and stir well, cooking for 1 to 2 minutes. Add the remaining ingredients, except the cheese, stir to combine, and cook 2 to 3 minutes, stirring a few times to prevent sticking. Remove from the heat.

(continued on page 36)

Craving Spicy Foods?

If you are experiencing an insatiable urge to eat spicy food, there may be a neurochemical explanation. According to the University of Washington Nutritional Sciences program, hot foods such as jalapeños, Tabasco sauce, and cayenne pepper are believed to secrete a neuropeptide called substance P, which is similar to endorphins, one of the natural opioid brain chemicals that make us feel good. This craving for "fire" is common among recovering alcoholics, especially during Phase One.

Since alcohol is known to increase the release of opioid peptides, including endorphins and enkephalines, which ultimately result in a rewarding experience, it may be that we are drawn to spicy food because of this neurochemical similarity. Coincidentally, Naltrexone, the FDA-approved treatment for reducing alcohol craving in early recovery, works by blocking the same reward system, and some alcoholics who have used this drug have reported a decreased ability to taste spice.

(continued from page 35)

3. Using a potato masher or the back of a wooden spoon, coarsely mash the bean mixture until it appears smooth, yet somewhat lumpy. Transfer to an ungreased 8-inch round casserole dish and top evenly with the cheese. Bake until the cheese is melted and the dip is heated throughout, 10 to 12 minutes. Serve immediately.

Chef's Note: *For ready-made, plan-ahead, individual portions, divide the mashed bean mixture between four 1-cup serving-size microwaveable custard cups or ramekins before topping each with cheese. Cover with plastic wrap and refrigerate. When ready to eat, microwave one portion at a time until heated through, 1 to 2 minutes.*

Cutting Crudités

Tips on Preparing Vegetables for Dipping

Having cut crudités, or raw vegetables, ready for dipping, will encourage you to snack on these healthy alternatives to chips. Here are some tips on preparing them for your favorite dip:

CARROTS: Choose medium-size, firm carrots. Trim the ends and peel, then cut in half or thirds, and again into quarters to make sticks. For even quicker snacking, a bag of washed and peeled baby carrots on hand will provide no excuse not to nibble on these vitamin-rich vegetables.

CELERY: Purchase celery hearts, which require less tedious scrubbing and virtually no peeling of the stringy outside fibers. Wash and cut into two- or three-inch pieces and then into thin sticks, if you prefer. The inside stalks are particularly sweet, tender, and tasty.

BELL PEPPERS: Green, red, orange, or yellow raw peppers make for perfect dipping, while providing oodles of antioxidants. Wash, cut them in half, and remove the core, seeds, and membrane. Slice into ½-inch-wide strips. These vegetables are particularly perishable, however, and should be eaten within a day or two.

CUCUMBERS: Kirbys and English seedless varieties are ideal for dipping and require very little preparation. Simply wash, trim off the ends, and cut into strips. No peeling is necessary, as they do not have waxy, tough exteriors like the common cucumber.

SQUASH: Raw zucchini and yellow summer squash are less likely to be found on the usual crudité plate, but are terrific for creamy dips, particularly ranch flavored or blue cheese. The outside skins should be scrubbed well to remove grit, then trimmed and cut as you would a cucumber. Peeling and seeding is unnecessary. Some grocers now carry baby zucchini and mini squash varieties, such as pattypan, which are tender and delicious as dippers. Just wash well and trim the tiny ends.

FENNEL: Another less likely candidate for crudité is the sweet and crunchy anise-flavored fennel, also excellent for digestion. Fennel is typically included on the vegetable platter offered with the Italian dip called *bagna cauda*, or "hot bath," made of anchovies and olive oil and served in some Italian restaurants. Cut off the fronds, or feathery leaves, trim the ends, peel the harder outside pieces, and cut into wedges or thin strips. Save the trimmings to make Southern Italian Pasta with Sardines and Fennel (page 391).

BROCCOLI AND CAULIFLOWER FLORETS: These can be found bagged and ready to go for those who prefer not to fuss with the whole head, although it is far more economical to cut your own florets and use the remaining stalks for soup making (page 87). Some find raw broccoli hard to digest, so a quick submerging in boiling salted water, then an ice bath, will help in this regard. Raw cauliflower is a particularly delicious dipper and a good source of fiber.

SUGAR SNAPS AND SNOW PEAS: Again, a quick dip in boiling water (also known as "blanching") will turn these pea family members into delicious dippers. I have recently found that the stringless sugar snaps don't even need blanching because they are super sweet and tender straight from the bag.

Although some prepared supermarket crudité platters may include cherry tomatoes, radishes, raw mushrooms, and even raw asparagus spears, I generally do not include them in my array of vegetables for dipping. They are either too difficult to hold onto (as in the case of cherry tomatoes, radishes, and mushrooms) or rather unappealing (as in the case of raw asparagus). However, in the early spring when thin asparagus spears appear, they can be quickly blanched in boiling salted water and become quite good as an interesting addition to the platter. This is also true of thin green beans, and the French *haricot verts*, which are particularly tender and sweet early in the season.

Cut raw vegetables will keep for many days if stored properly. Try to separate them into zipper-locked bags, with a folded paper towel to absorb excess moisture. This way the vegetables that are more likely to perish (bell peppers and cucumbers for instance) will not affect the hardier ones. A great way to keep crudités on hand is to purchase one of the popular plastic Tupperware containers with sections. Some are even designed for dips, with an indentation in the middle and six or so sections around for the vegetables. When a crunchy craving hits, just whip out the prepared container from the fridge and start munching!

Taking Your Kitchen's Inventory
Trashing Triggers and Adding Useful Equipment

As you begin your recovery cooking, it's a good idea to take a quick inventory of your pantry, refrigerator, cupboards, and drawers to dispose of any unwanted "paraphernalia" that might be lurking about, which could create a dangerous spark in your brain-cell activity. All products containing alcohol need to go, including extracts, marinades, drink enhancers, and condiments spiked with booze. If possible, let someone else pour them down the sink so you needn't take a whiff of the fumes.

Getting rid of other tools of the trade is also a good idea if they are personal triggers for you. I used to keep a corkscrew in the drawer next to my stove for opening corked vinegars and other nonalcoholic bottles of ingredients (I had already disposed of my favorite corkscrew for wine), but every time I opened the drawer, my eyes would instantly focus on the corkscrew, even though there were no doubt 50 other items in the drawer. Finally, I just threw it in the trash—out of sight, out of mind, as they say. Depending on your drink or drug of choice, any number of things may set you off, so think about which items you are better off without for now, whether they be bottle openers, spoons, or your favorite glass for drinking vodka, and put them out of your sight.

At the same time, it's a good idea to take a quick look at what sort of kitchen equipment you have for cooking and add to your inventory if possible. The basics are generally fine, such as sharp knives; a cutting board; mixing bowls; a variety of pots, pans, and skillets; as well as an electric mixer and blender (if not a memory jogger of mixed drinks and crushed ice). A food processor will be handy too, but it is not entirely necessary. Consider purchasing a hand-held immersion blender with a chopping attachment to make preparation easier and to save valuable time. Check for baking dishes and roasting pans, as well as cookie sheets and muffin tins, if you enjoy baking, to make sure they are in good condition. An instant-read thermometer is also a worthwhile investment.

Keeping a pepper grinder and a small bowl of kosher salt next to the stove will help you quickly season your cooking. It's also a good idea to keep a pitcher or ceramic holder full of wooden spoons, rubber spatulas, whisks, and other mixing and stirring utensils near the burners to make it easier to reach for the next necessary cooking tool.

Caramelized Onion and Bacon Dip

MAKES 4 SERVINGS If you like classic onion dip, you will love this delicious version that combines the sweetness of caramelized onions with the savory crunch of bacon and smooth sour cream. No powdered or artificial ingredients here! Whether served with veggies, crackers, or old reliable potato chips, this is a sure winner.

Just a little bacon adds the right amount of flavor and a nice addition of protein and thiamine. Reduced-fat sour cream helps to cut down on the saturated fat, while a dab of horseradish really wakes up all the flavors.

4 strips lean bacon or turkey bacon
1 medium-size onion, peeled and thinly sliced
1 cup reduced-fat sour cream
¼ cup mayonnaise
1 teaspoon prepared horseradish,
    or more to taste
Salt and pepper to taste

1. Fry the bacon in a medium-size skillet until crisp and golden. Drain on paper towels and set aside.

2. Pour out all but 1 tablespoon of the drippings. Add the sliced onion to the skillet and cook over medium-low heat, stirring, until golden and caramelized, about 5 minutes. Set aside to cool.

3. Chop the cooked bacon and onion into small pieces. You can also chop them briefly in a food processor. Add the remaining ingredients and blend thoroughly in the processor or by hand. Chill well before serving.

Fresh Fruit Salsa with Cinnamon Chips

MAKES 4 SERVINGS Feel like dipping but want a hint of sweetness? This refreshing salsa with cinnamon-sugared tortilla chips is a delicious alternative to plain fruit and a satisfying choice for an in-between meal sweet craving. Try creating your own combination from seasonal fruit offerings such as peaches, nectarines, apricots, pineapple, pears, papaya, raspberries, and/or blueberries. Add some chopped fresh mint and cilantro for an interesting flavor combination. Even a chopped jalapeño pepper will work nicely in this salsa and certainly spice up the result! I like using the flour tortillas, because they are lighter and interfere less with the fruit flavors, but corn tortillas could easily be substituted. You may also lightly spray the tortillas with cooking oil instead of brushing them with butter for a reduced-fat and lower-calorie result.

FRUIT SALSA
1 kiwi fruit, peeled and diced
1 ripe mango, peeled, seeded, and diced
1 cup fresh strawberries, hulled and diced
1 Golden Delicious apple, left unpeeled,
    cored, and diced
¼ medium-size cantaloupe or honeydew
    melon, seeded, flesh cut from the
    rind, and diced
3 tablespoons red or green jalapeño jelly
1 tablespoon fresh lemon juice
1 tablespoon honey

CINNAMON CHIPS
Ten 8-inch flour tortillas (fajita size)
¼ cup (½ stick) unsalted butter, melted
1 cup cinnamon sugar (¾ cup sugar mixed with
    ¼ cup ground cinnamon)

1. To make the fruit salsa, combine the diced fruit in a large mixing bowl and fold together gently. In a small mixing bowl, combine the jalapeño jelly, lemon juice, and honey and whisk together to combine. Pour this over the diced fruit and fold in to coat evenly. Cover with plastic wrap and chill for 20 minutes.

2. Preheat the oven to 350 degrees.

3. To make the cinnamon chips, brush the tortillas on both sides with the melted butter, stacking them on top of each other as you go along. Cut through the buttered tortillas to make 4 piles of wedges. Place the wedges in a single layer on 2 baking sheets that have been brushed lightly with the remaining melted butter. Bake, turning once, until crisp, 18 to 20 minutes.

4. Have ready the cinnamon sugar in a brown paper lunch bag and, working in batches, drop the hot tortilla chips into the bag and shake well to coat. Remove the chips and place on a wire rack to cool. (You can save the remaining cinnamon sugar in a dry, cool place for next time.)

5. Serve the cinnamon chips with the fruit salsa and enjoy!

Chef's Note: If you cannot find jalapeño jelly, substitute another fruit jelly such as raspberry or red currant.

Appetizers Bar-None

It's ironic that many of the snacks we might be craving at this time are hallmark dishes usually associated with bars and restaurants where alcohol reigns supreme. Before, we probably didn't blink an eye when the table next to us ordered up the Nachos Supreme or the Loaded Potato Skins. We were too busy downing our third round of tequila slammers to notice. But now, as strange as it seems, those goodies are awfully tempting. Could it be our addiction trying to cleverly slither its way back into our thoughts? What's a harmless visit to the old haunt to "pick up" a pizza going to do to us anyway? As the smell of alcohol wafts through the air and the glasses tinkle with ice, we may not notice our resolve waning. But suddenly, a friendly face offers us a quick libation while we wait for our order. Before we know it, the pizza is forgotten and we're off and running in a dangerous direction—just one of many possible scenarios—all because we had to have that pizza.

Does this mean we should avoid "bar food," such as chicken wings and pizza? Of course not. It just means we need to start creating some new and positive associations, while losing the old and unhealthy ones. Spicy chicken wings are just as delicious when shared with some sober buddies around the kitchen table as they are in a dimly lit corner of your local bar/restaurant. Cravings for pizza, potato skins, and other quintessential "bar food" are real—they are satisfying and comforting dishes that quell a carbohydrate urge and are not just your addiction's way of getting you to step into the danger zone. So, here are some delicious, at-home solutions to help you feed your hunger without jeopardizing your hard-earned recovery!

The Five-Minute Pizza

MAKES 1 TO 2 SERVINGS   When hunger hits with a fury, we need something substantial and we want it right away! Does the idea of pizza put a little piz-zazz in your step? But how healthy is it? Researchers have found that cooked tomatoes (found in pizza sauce) accompanied with a little fat (found in cheese) may actually be beneficial in the antioxidant department and that a slice of pizza can provide just what the doctor ordered. Okay, but where do we turn? A trip to Rusty's Tavern is definitely out of the question. Those 30-minute delivery services can be a tasty option, but even they're not quick enough! And frozen pizzas require preheated ovens and just as long a wait. How about whipping up a mini pizza snack in less than five minutes? Here's how to do it.

1 bagel, sliced in half
2 heaping tablespoons prepared marinara or
    pizza sauce
A drizzle of olive oil
A dash of dried oregano
½ cup shredded mozzarella cheese

1. Toast the bagel halves in a toaster or toaster oven until lightly golden. Transfer, toasted side up, to a flameproof dish or baking sheet. Spread the sauce evenly on top of the bagel halves, drizzle the olive oil, sprinkle the oregano, and top with the cheese.

2. Place under a broiler set to high until the cheese has melted, about 1 minute. Transfer to a plate and serve.

Variations: If you like toppings on your pizza, you're in luck. Even though this quick-broiling method prohibits adding toppings under the broiler (they would burn before the cheese melts!), there's an easy solution. Simply add your toppings *after* broiling and quickly zap in the microwave for about 20 seconds to heat through. *Voila!* Instant, personalized pizza. Here are a few topping ideas:

- Thin slices of pepperoni, salami, or spicy sausages, such as chorizo or andouille
- Diced ham, onion, and green pepper
- Sliced mushrooms and black olives
- Strips of marinated roasted peppers or sun-dried tomatoes
- Tiny broccoli florets and a sprinkle of Parmesan cheese
- Sliced cherry tomatoes and chopped fresh basil leaves

Pesto Pizza: Replace the marinara sauce with basil or sun-dried tomato pesto. Omit the olive oil and oregano and use shredded Parmesan, asiago, or mozzarella cheese.

Mexican Pizza: Replace the marinara sauce with prepared salsa and top with shredded cheddar cheese. Add sliced jalapeño peppers for a spicy finish.

Pita Bread Pizza: Although too big for your toaster, a quick minute or so under the broiler before adding the sauce and cheese will seal the surface of the pita and prevent a soggy result. Continue with any of the preparations suggested above and slice wedges with a pizza cutter or sharp knife before serving.

Chef's Note: To be sure you always have bagels on hand, buy a bag and keep them in the freezer. You can even preslice them or use mini bagels for smaller portions. When the craving hits, defrost for 1 minute in the microwave before toasting.

Recovery Note: Read marinara sauce labels before purchasing, as some products may contain alcohol in the form of wine, vodka, or other alcoholic beverages.

Microwave Nachos

MAKES 1 TO 2 SERVINGS This recipe is "supremely" easy to prepare when all the ingredients are at hand. Pile up your nachos with as many toppings as you like and utilize any leftover chili, cooked chicken, or beans you may have available for additional protein. Serve with a dollop of guacamole or sour cream in the middle for dipping and enjoy!

12 tortilla chips
⅔ cup shredded cheddar, Monterey Jack, or
    another quick-melting cheese
½ small onion, peeled and diced
2 tablespoons prepared jalapeño slices
2 tablespoons pitted and sliced black olives
1 plum tomato, seeded and diced
Dollop of guacamole (page 32) or sour cream
    (optional)

1. Arrange the tortilla chips on a microwave-proof plate, overlapping as necessary. Sprinkle the cheese and arrange the jalapeños, olives, and tomato evenly on top.

2. Microwave on high until the cheese has melted and the toppings are heated through, 2 to 3 minutes. Serve immediately.

Chef's Note: To make the nachos in the oven, preheat the oven to 400 degrees, arrange the nachos on a baking sheet, and bake until the cheese melts, 12 to 15 minutes. Transfer to a plate and serve.

Quick American Quesadillas with Ham and Cheese

MAKES 1 TO 2 SERVINGS A popular restaurant appetizer, these delicious wedges are fast and simple to whip up at home. Here, basic ham and cheese makes for a quick and satisfying filling, but you could also add some chopped scallions, tomatoes, or avocados for additional flavor and texture. In fact, quesadillas are a great way to use up leftover morsels of cooked chicken, steak, or even vegetables and canned beans. You can also substitute a whole wheat tortilla or try one of the flavored varieties for added interest, as well as using any number of quick-melting cheeses.

Keep opened bags of flour tortillas in the fridge, tightly sealed with plastic wrap. Packaged this way, they will stay fresh for several weeks and always be on hand for a quick snack.

Two 10-inch flour tortillas (burrito size)
2 thin slices ham (about 1 ounce)
½ cup shredded cheddar or Monterey Jack cheese
Canola oil

1. Place 1 tortilla on your work surface and evenly drape the ham slices over it. Sprinkle the cheese on the ham and place the other tortilla on top, pressing down firmly.

2. Heat a heavy medium-size skillet over medium-high heat. Brush lightly with oil. Add the quesadilla and cook until the cheese has melted and the tortilla begins to crisp and brown, 3 to 4 minutes per side, occasionally pressing down with a metal spatula.

3. Transfer to a cutting board, slice into 6 or 8 wedges, and serve.

The Greek Quesadilla: Substitute ⅓ cup crumbled feta cheese for the cheddar and add 1 tablespoon pitted and chopped Kalamata olives.

The Italian Quesadilla: Substitute ½ cup shredded mozzarella for the cheddar, prosciutto for the ham, and add 1 tablespoon chopped, oil-packed sun-dried tomatoes and 6 fresh basil leaves.

The French Quesadilla: Substitute ⅓ cup diced brie or camembert cheese for the cheddar and add 4 to 6 thin spears roasted asparagus (page 348).

The Vegetarian Quesadilla: Mix together ½ cup drained and rinsed canned kidney beans with 2 tablespoons prepared salsa and substitute for the ham.

The Quick Fix
Healthy Snack Ideas for Instant Gratification

Learning to control our need for immediate pleasure and relief is one of the toughest things we must attempt in Phase One on more than one level. But, when it comes to snacking, a little leeway is surely allowed. Here is my A to Z list of quick healthy fixes when any amount of time or fuss is not an option.

A: An apple a day may keep the doctor away, but a handful of *almond*s can keep us going. Nuts and seeds are an excellent choice for sustained energy, while providing a nutritional powerhouse of vitamins and minerals. For a savory craving, try hickory-smoked almonds and, to feed a sweet tooth, seek out candy-coated Jordan almonds or chocolate-covered almonds, often found in bridge mixes or sometimes on their own.

B: *Bing cherries* are deliciously sweet, ranging in color from deep red to nearly black. They are also one of the lowest glycemic-rated fruits at a modest 22, good for slow conversion to glucose and low in calories to boot. Buy cherries with stems (they will keep longer) and store in a plastic bag in the fridge.

C: A quick toasting, a little bit of butter, and a good sprinkling of cinnamon sugar turns regular sliced bread into *cinnamon toast*, a satisfying childhood snack destined to be a Phase One favorite. There is something about the aroma of cinnamon that soothes the savage breast and, since medieval times, it has been touted as a healing, medicinal spice. Try making it with a hearty, whole-grain bread for added nutrition.

D: A slice of *date nut bread* with a smear of whipped cream cheese can satisfy a sweet craving, while providing our bodies with protein and fiber. Commercially packaged date nut breads are sometimes presliced from mini loaves and are perfect for making snack-size cream cheese sandwiches to take on the road. Try using reduced-fat cream cheese, also called Neufchâtel.

E: Dieters know that hard-boiled *eggs* can fill you up in no time. Have some cooked and ready to peel when you feel like something salty. Simply dip your egg in a bit of kosher salt and accompany with a few whole-grain crackers. Hard-boiled eggs will keep unshelled for up to two weeks in the fridge.

F: *Fruit rolls or fruit leather* are simply pureed fruit that is spread very thin and then dried. Often a little sugar or honey is added. Choose products that are 100 percent fruit or fruit juice-concentrate (a healthier choice) over those with large amounts of high fructose corn syrup.

G: Whether white or red, seedless or not, *grapes* are one of the healthiest out-of-hand snacks you can eat. Cut clusters by snipping the stems with kitchen scissors and keep these presized portions in a bowl in the fridge for instant snacking. Table grapes, as they are called, are much sweeter and less acidic than their wine-making counterparts, so shouldn't pose a trigger for even the biggest former wine guzzler (I should know!).

H: If you've never tried *halvah*, you're in for a real treat. Made from ground sesame seeds and honey, it is available in most supermarkets and delis in wrapped bars and comes plain (vanilla-flavored), chocolate, or marbled. There is even a chocolate-covered variety that is quite tasty, but bear in mind, a little goes a long way. A few bites will satisfy a sweet tooth in no time and provide a generous amount of calcium in the process.

I: *Ice cream* is definitely one of the top 10 cravings in recovery, especially during Phase One. So how do we turn it into a reasonably healthy snack? Low-fat ice cream is a good choice, as is frozen yogurt. And, believe it or not, all those varieties that have lots of added nuts and bits of fruit and chocolate are better choices glucose-wise than just plain old vanilla, as they help to fill us up and lessen the immediate effects on the blood stream of sucrose and lactose. Portion size is really the key here. You may find that the Italian version, called gelato, and now available in supermarkets, may provide more satisfaction from smaller servings, as it is denser and usually more intensely flavored. Whichever you choose, try to stick to sensible, small portions and be sure to read labels for added rum, rum flavoring, and other alcohol-related additions.

J: Fruit *jams and jellies* can be a good choice for a sweet craving when spread on something healthy such as whole-wheat toast, English muffins, or crackers. Look for varieties that contain pieces of fruit, as found in preserves, and lower amounts of sugar and high fructose corn syrup. Many brands claim to be "pure fruit," but a quick label read will tell you if this is true. Gourmet jams in specialty shops will sometimes spike the jar with booze, such as amaretto or Grand Marnier, so be on the lookout when purchasing.

K: Also known as the Chinese gooseberry, *kiwi fruit* from New Zealand is gaining popularity. Both sweet and tart in taste, kiwi can be enjoyed on its own, or as an addition to fruit salads and desserts. To eat out-of-hand, simply chill, cut in half, and scoop out the attractive green flesh with a teaspoon. The tiny black seeds are completely edible and add to the excellent fiber content. One kiwi fruit contains 120 percent of the recommended daily allowance of vitamin C.

L: Real *licorice candies* are made from dark molasses and licorice root extract (without alcohol). Loaded with iron and calcium, they may also aid digestion and relieve a grumpy stomach. Unfortunately, the red pseudo-licorice candy we generally find in the candy aisle bears no connection to the real thing. Allsorts, a type of English licorice candy with colorful fruit and coconut pastels, may be a good choice if you find straight licorice a bit strongly flavored.

M: *McIntosh apples*, although not generally recommended for cooking, are terrific eating apples. Crisp and not too sweet, they pair up nicely with a small wedge of cheddar cheese and a couple of crackers for a nutritious and satisfying snack. Red Delicious apples are a good substitute and are generally found year round, as opposed to McIntosh, which are only in season from September through March.

N: *Navel oranges* from California and Florida are a natural take-along snack and can be incredibly refreshing when chilled and peeled or cut into wedges. Sweet and juicy, these oranges can fill a room with their lovely fragrance. Take a few on the road to quell thirst and sweet cravings.

O: Cookies can be a healthy snack when they are made from *oatmeal*, especially with the addition of raisins and nuts. Look for varieties with lots of oats for fiber and low-fat ingredients, or make the Oatmeal Spice Cookies on page 62. They may not be Oreos, but they still go great with a glass of milk!

P: I actually have two favorites here. *Peanut butter* is my first choice, as well as some of the other nut butters, such as almond, cashew, and soybean, now available in many supermarkets and always available in health food stores. When spread on graham crackers or oozing on a warm piece of toast, peanut butter is a favorite snack and offers a good dose of protein. Believe it or not, peanut butter was developed as a health food for the 1904 St. Louis World's Fair, but today's varieties can sometimes contain too much added sugar and hydrogenated oil, which take the healthiness down a notch. Natural peanut butter uses only peanuts and peanut oil and is the "natural" choice for a healthy snack. Number two choice for "p" is *popcorn*, available salted, buttered, cheese flavored, and caramel coated for that insatiable sweet tooth. Microwave bags give you freshly popped servings in an instant. Keep these handy bags in your desk drawer at work and zap up an afternoon snack to share with your coworkers.

Q: Who says you can't enjoy breakfast cereal for a snack? *Quick-cooking cereals* such as oat-meal, cream of wheat, and multigrain varieties can cook up in the microwave in no time. Drizzle a little maple syrup on top or add a spoonful of strawberry preserves to satisfy your sweet tooth and benefit from the sustained energy that these grains can provide.

R: *Raisins* are not just found in little red boxes anymore. These days you can buy them yogurt- or chocolate-covered, orange- or cherry-scented, or sprinkled with cinnamon. A handful of these sweet morsels provide a variety of vitamins and minerals and are especially rich in iron. Store opened bags of raisins tightly sealed at room temperature and they'll stay moist and fresh.

S: Before you reach for that blue bag of Ruffles, head a little farther on down the aisle and grab a bag of *sweet potato chips*. A tremendous source of vitamin A and fiber, these nutri-tious alternatives to the old tater chip are often lightly spiced and always satisfyingly crunchy. When the munchies hit, these guys fill in nicely and also make for a good sturdy dipping chip.

T: Those little cans of *tuna fish* with the flip tops were designed for quick access and easy travel. Take one along with a packet of crackers for a truly nutritious mini-meal on the go. The next time you're at the deli, ask for some extra mayo packets and plastic utensils and you'll always be prepared for instant tuna salad. Drain the oil or water and mix your salad right in the can.

U: The thick Japanese noodles called *udon* can be found in the refrigerated or Asian section of your grocery already cooked and in stay-fresh packs, usually accompanied by a flavorful broth-making packet. This means instant noodles that are not only healthy, but soothing and delicious as well. Half a package will do nicely for a modest snack, while a whole package, dressed up with some cooked chicken and veggies, can become a hearty meal at dinnertime.

V: As boring as they may sound, raw cut-up *vegetables*, such as celery, carrots, cucumbers, cauliflower, and broccoli can calm hunger pangs and keep our jaws busily munching. Keep a platter of these crudités, as they are called, in the fridge ready to go when the urge hits. And add some not-so-common veggies, such as sliced zucchini, fennel, and red cabbage for vari-ety. See Dipping into Nutrition (page 30) for some excellent alternatives to the usual com-mercial dips.

W: *Watermelon*, unlike its muskmelon cousins the cantaloupe and honeydew, is indeed pri-marily composed of H_2O. But who can think of a more thirst-quenching snack, especially when the temperature begins to rise? Keep slices ready for grabbing in the fridge or remove the rind and cut into squares for a less dribbly experience. I like to combine watermelon balls with blueberries and raspberries for an attractive fruit cup and to lessen, somewhat, the higher glycemic effect that watermelon has on blood sugar.

x: Okay, this isn't exactly a snack, but it is food related. Eating excessive amounts of carotene-containing foods can result in a yellow or orange-yellow coloring of the skin, called *Xanthosis cutis*, but don't let that keep you from consuming this powerful antioxidant found in orange-colored fruits and vegetables and their juices, such as carrots and apricots. If straight carrot juice doesn't appeal to you, try one of the blends on the market that also contains citrus juices. Apricot juice is hearty, sweet, and loaded with carotene and is usually sold in small cans for taking on the go.

y: *Yogurt* comes in all flavors, from vanilla to cappuccino, as well as nonfat, low-fat, and varieties made from whole milk or soy milk. Some have the fruit on the bottom, others are blended, and some even have a spoon attached for your convenience. Consequently, there is no excuse not to add yogurt to your arsenal of snack foods, as there is surely a flavor and version to suit everyone. Yogurt contains healthy, friendly bacteria that keep our intestinal systems running smoothly and is a good source of calcium, protein, and the B vitamins. Whether eaten alone, or in combination with fresh fruit or granola, yogurt is an excellent energy source and in-between meal snack.

z: German *zwieback* is not just for babies. Named because it is "twice-baked" (the same procedure used to make Italian biscotti), these slightly sweet, crispy crackers are easily digested and are a good choice for a sensitive stomach. European rusks, mini toast-like crackers found in the international food section of your grocery, are close cousins and come plain, whole wheat, and sometimes flavored. They make excellent bases for spreads and toppings, which lower somewhat their higher Glycemic Index rating, while satisfying that urge to crunch.

Oven Crisp Potato Skins

MAKES 1 TO 2 SERVINGS Probably the most popular bar food going, potato skins usually come deep fried and "loaded" with all kinds of saturated fat. This healthier version is just as satisfying and will surprise you at how easy it is to whip up with just a little planning. The next time you are baking a potato for a dinner side dish, throw a few more in the oven for when the potato skin craving hits. You'll be glad you did!

2 medium-size Idaho potatoes, baked in a preheated 400 degree oven until fork tender, about 1 hour
Nonstick cooking spray
Salt and pepper to taste
½ cup shredded cheddar cheese
2 teaspoons bacon bits or salad topping (such as McCormick Salad Toppins)
Sour cream (optional)

1. Preheat the oven to 475 degrees.

(continued on page 48)

Getting Misty from Cooking Sprays?

One of the most convenient cooking inventions of our time has been the handy can of cooking oil spray. A quick mist of vegetable oil, olive oil, or even garlic- or butter-flavored oils reduces the amount of fat in preparations such as baking and roasting and can add just enough of a light coating of oil to prevent sticking and contribute flavor. But how healthy is it and is there any danger of its use in recovery cooking?

Originally, chloroflurocarbons were used as aerosol propellants until we became aware of the danger they posed to public health and the environment. Thankfully, in 1978, they were banned from use, making cooking sprays quite safe for the average kitchen. However, some brands, Pam in particular, use grain alcohol for "clarity" purposes, which can pose a problem in the sober kitchen. This is an unnecessary added ingredient and the many brands that don't contain it do not suffer from any inferiority of performance. As little as the amount may be, I'd rather not spray alcohol haphazardly around the kitchen and breathe in the fumes, especially when other products are readily available. Reading labels, as always, is an important practice when shopping for products like these.

A relatively new and healthy alternative to spray cans is the oil mister or pump. Available in metal or plastic, you can fill the container with your choice of oil (without all the added propellant chemicals) and use the built-in pumping mechanism to create a propellant effect, allowing you to lightly mist anything from cookie sheets to potatoes for roasting. I keep one on hand for canola oil and another for olive oil and have found them to be extremely helpful in the kitchen. Oil misters can be purchased at kitchen supply and department stores or ordered online.

(continued from page 47)

2. Slice the potatoes lengthwise with a sharp knife and scoop out all but about ¼ inch of the potato next to the skin. Lightly spray each half on both sides with cooking oil and season with salt and pepper. Place cut side down on a baking sheet and bake until golden and crispy, 20 to 25 minutes.

3. Turn the potato skins cut side up and distribute the cheese over each one. Sprinkle with the bacon bits or salad topping and return to the oven until the cheese begins to melt, about 5 minutes. Serve immediately with sour cream, if desired.

Make Ahead Buffalo Chicken Wings with Blue Cheese Ranch Dip

MAKES 2 TO 4 SERVINGS Spicy buffalo wings may be just the thing for a snack craving, especially if "heat" is our desire. But, apart from strolling into that bar room, how do we satisfy the urge? Here's an easy solution and one that's easily adapted for quick, snack-size portions (see Chef's Note on next page).

This baked method results in much lower fat, so enjoy as many as you like! With some crisp celery sticks on the side and the luscious blue cheese ranch dip below, you'll be in buffalo wing utopia! Depending on your heat threshold, choose a hot sauce that is mild, medium, or three alarm.

BUFFALO WINGS
12 chicken wings, tips removed and cut in
    half at the joint
¼ cup (½ stick) unsalted butter
½ cup hot sauce of your choice

BLUE CHEESE RANCH DIP
½ cup prepared ranch dressing
⅓ cup crumbled blue cheese
Celery sticks (optional)

1. Preheat the oven to 400 degrees.

2. To make the wings, line a baking sheet with aluminum foil and arrange the chicken wing pieces evenly on it in a single layer. Bake until crispy and golden, 30 to 35 minutes, pouring off the accumulated fat halfway through the cooking time.

3. To make the dip, combine the ranch dressing and blue cheese in a small mixing bowl while the wings are baking. Chill until ready to use.

4. Prepare the coating for the wings by melting together the butter and hot sauce in a saucepan large enough to hold the cooked wings. Stir well to combine and remove from heat.

5. Transfer the baked wings with tongs to the saucepan, cover with a lid, and shake vigorously from side to side and up and down to coat the wings.

6. Serve immediately with the dip and celery sticks.

Chef's Note: To always have buffalo wings at the ready for when the craving hits, keep baked wing pieces (Step 2) in a food storage container in the fridge, then broil a snack portion (6 pieces) until crisp and heated through, 2 to 3 minutes per side. Melt 1 tablespoon of the butter with 2 tablespoons of the hot sauce in a small saucepan, add the broiled wings, cover and shake until coated, and you have buffalo wings in 5 minutes flat. Be sure to keep some Blue Cheese Ranch Dip on hand!

Recovery Note: Read hot sauce labels for the possible addition of whiskey, bourbon, or tequila.

The Road to Recovery Trail Mix

Trail mixes have become a popular addition to the candy aisle and are a great choice for quick snacking. Based on the backpacker's staple called GORP (Good Old Raisins and Peanuts), these mixes can contain anything from nuts and candy to granola and dried fruit.

When I first began recovery, I had the idea to create a Recovery Trail Mix, with all kinds of ingredients that would satisfy the nutritional needs and cravings we all experience, especially during Phase One. After a bit of experimentation, I settled on this one when it was passed around the room and devoured even before the counselor arrived one evening in an outpatient group. "Great stuff," proclaimed Jim, who was our resident two-fisted doughnut eater. I noticed at break time there were fewer trips to the Dunkin' Donuts across the street and everybody seemed a little more relaxed in their sharing.

Loaded with protein, fiber, magnesium, potassium, and vitamin E, The Road to Recovery Trail Mix is great to keep on hand as a nutritious and satisfying in-between meal snack. Use roasted, raw, salted, or unsalted nuts and seeds. You can substitute other nuts if you like, even chocolate-covered varieties, but try to keep the proportion of soybeans the same to preserve the protein content. Simply combine all the ingredients in a canister or zipper-lock bag and toss well. Store any bags of unused nuts and seeds in the fridge or freezer to retain freshness.

2 cups roasted soybeans
1 cup shelled pumpkin seeds
1 cup shelled sunflower seeds
1 cup dried banana chips
½ cup honey-roasted peanuts
½ cup mini semisweet chocolate chips

MAKES TWELVE ½-CUP SERVINGS

The Doughnut Alternative: Muffins, Scones, Quick Breads, and Cookies

A cup of coffee and a doughnut for dunking is as classically American as mom and apple pie. A dozen doughnuts can turn up at any gathering, from PTA meetings to twelve-step groups, and all of us, not just those in recovery, need to drastically rethink this unhealthy social snack habit. These fried and highly refined carbohydrates, which come raised (from yeast) or cake-like (with baking powder) are part of the "fast food" trend that has contributed to upping the obesity level and heart disease rate among Americans today. And "fast" is definitely the effect foods such as these have on our systems; quickly converted to glucose, we get a rush of pseudo-energy, particularly when accompanied by a jolt of caffeine from coffee. By the time our doughnut meeting is over, however, we're ready to fall asleep, as a surge of insulin floods our bloodstreams to cope with the fast rise of glucose. Add to that the enormous amount of saturated fat that a doughnut habit will add to our diet, and we are setting ourselves up for a permanently sluggish metabolism and inevitable weight gain.

Doughnuts are not, of course, the only culprits. How many times have we been tempted by the display case at the local diner full of mile-high cream pies, layer cakes, and three-tiered displays of gooey danishes and sticky buns? Sometimes if you look closely enough, you might find a low-fat corn muffin lurking behind that pile of glazed doughnuts but, more often than not, the choices for a healthy, yet sweet-tooth-satisfying snack to enjoy with our coffee or tea are terribly limited. If more elegant coffee bars are your hangout, you might find an almond biscotti or two, but only if you peek beyond the tray of tempting gourmet cheesecake and crème brûlée. If visual triggers are indeed hard to ignore, then how do we survive in a world of sweet temptation without over-indulging a voracious sweet tooth, especially during Phase One? Is there a satisfying alternative to quell this seemingly insatiable craving?

Consider the difference between an oatmeal cookie and a sugar cookie. Although the oatmeal cookie may have more calories and perhaps even a tad more fat, the sugar cookie has virtually no nutrition, especially if made completely with refined white flour, and lacks complex carbohydrates, which the oatmeal cookie possesses in the form of oats and perhaps raisins. Glycemically speaking, the oatmeal cookie is, of course, the smarter and healthier choice. And it is also the best choice for weight watchers, who will derive much more satiety from its ingredients in the long run. Working with our knowledge of things like fiber, complex carbohydrates, and the Glycemic Index, we can easily recognize baking recipes that will go a long way towards improving overall health, while satisfying the urge for something sweet. This isn't, of course, to suggest that the fat issue should be ignored. In general, "good" fats should be chosen over "bad" ones and, in particular, hydrogenated oils and trans fatty acids (found in stick and tub margarines as well as solid vegetable shortening like Crisco) should be avoided. But butter, eggs, sugar, and flour, the basic ingredients of baking, are not, in and of themselves, unhealthy. If we are careful about the amounts we eat, the actual fat and caloric content becomes less significant.

Self-discipline and moderation in satisfying immediate wants and needs are something those of us in recovery struggle with every day in nearly every aspect of our lives. When it comes to feeding our sugar cravings, we can help ourselves by making thoughtful, wiser, and more sensible choices. The recipes in this section will include more whole grains and whole wheat products, fruits of all varieties (even some vegetables!), nuts and seeds, and healthier oils, but be assured that in the flavor department there is no lack of excitement. Enjoy these goodies and share them with your family and friends. They'll be deliciously amazed and grateful you did.

Honey Nut and Wheat Muffins

MAKES 6 MUFFINS These hearty wheat muffins are truly healthy, especially with the addition of chopped walnuts, sunflower seeds, and honey. In addition, canola oil fills in for the usual butter, drastically reducing the amount of saturated fat. Raisins or other types of dried fruit would also make a nice addition and add a further hint of sweetness. Perfect as a snack, they are delicious served warm with a dab of light cream cheese, butter and a drizzle of honey, or a teaspoon of orange marmalade.

1 cup all-purpose flour
½ cup whole wheat flour
2 teaspoons baking powder
¼ teaspoon salt

½ cup honey
½ cup milk
¼ cup canola oil
1 large egg
½ teaspoon grated orange rind
¼ cup shelled sunflower seeds
¼ cup chopped walnuts
¼ cup raisins (optional)

1. Preheat the oven to 400 degrees. Lightly oil or butter a standard 12-cup muffin tin.

2. In a medium-size mixing bowl, whisk together the flours, baking powder, and salt. In another medium-size mixing bowl, whisk together the honey, milk, oil, egg, and orange rind to combine well. Add the flour mixture to the wet ingredients and stir to moisten and combine (a few lumps are okay). Stir in the sunflower seeds, chopped walnuts, and raisins, if using.

3. Pour the batter evenly among 6 of the muffin cups and bake until a toothpick inserted in the center comes out clean and the tops are lightly golden, 15 to 20 minutes. Allow to cool for 5 minutes before removing from the pan. Serve warm.

Chef's Note: If you are using salted sunflower seeds, be sure to reduce the amount of salt in the recipe to a pinch. Try using glazed walnuts if you can find them for a little added sweetness and crunch.

Sucrose on Trial

The Scoop on Sugar

Public enemy number one. Sweet poison. The scourge of modern society. The root of every problem that ever was and ever shall be. Yikes! If I were a sugar cube, I'd be shaking in my sugar bowl right now. Why is sugar so popularly singled out as the evil culprit of modern day dietary problems (even displacing fat from its throne) and is there any real evidence to

convict? And what about so many folks in recovery who claim they are "sugar addicts"? Is this a real possibility? Let's examine the facts before we invite the jury to pronounce its final verdict and delve a little deeper into the sugar canister to get the real scoop.

Facts first. Sugar is a carbohydrate and, as far as our bodies are concerned, it is metabolized just like any other starch, except that instead of being broken down into glucose only, it yields equal parts glucose and the low glycemic-rated fructose (which is actually a good thing in moderate amounts). As a result, sucrose, or common table sugar, has a moderate effect on blood sugar levels; it is neither high nor low on the Glycemic Index, but a modest 65 on a scale of 0 to 100. What tends to make sugar consumption so unhealthy is that it is usually eaten in ridiculously huge quantities in conjunction with highly refined flour and saturated fat, which is, of course, what also makes it taste so good. We're talking about America's enormous proclivity for store-bought cakes, cookies, and candies; all are highly processed, mass-produced, and not without some other undesirable substances like chemical additives and preservatives. So you can see that sugar, in and of itself, although lacking any nutritive value, is not the sole evil ingredient you may have thought it to be. It is, unfortunately, the company it keeps that, for the most part, has given sugar a bad rap. When sugar hangs out with healthier carbohydrates and even a few proteins, it can certainly be part of a healthy diet.

Now let's call a few witnesses to enlighten us as to why sugar is so appealing and why so many people, despite its bad reputation, crave its sweetness. Researchers believe that early man was genetically selected for sugar consumption, because those who ate it, probably available back then only in the form of ripened fruit and, perhaps, honey, had more immediate energy than those who consumed only protein and were, consequently, more likely to outwit, outrun, and outlast their sluggish counterparts. A taste for sugar is, in fact, the only instinctual taste modern man is born with, while the other "tastes" of sour, salt, bitter, and pungent are learned. The problem now seems to be that there is simply too much sugar available to us and when we overeat it, along with other carbohydrates, we end up storing glucose in the form of fat, awaiting the hunt that never takes place. So you see, it is *we* who are at fault here, not the sugar! Perhaps if we had to chase a bison or two on a daily basis, we would not be the obese society we have become.

Still, why do some people seem to be sugar "addicted"? And specifically, why do abstinent alcoholics tend to crave it more than most people? Our expert witnesses can shed some light in this direction.

A recent twin study at the University of North Carolina at Chapel Hill revealed that a craving for sweets and the urge to drink may actually stem from the same gene. Despite their different life experiences, researchers found that separated twin brothers tended to share a preference for sweets and alcohol. Those who reported "drinking more alcohol on occasion and having more alcohol-related problems" also reported cravings for sweets, particularly when depressed or nervous. Chances are their urges to eat sugar took place when they were not consuming alcohol. As many of us can attest, eating sweets is usually of no interest to the active alcoholic. It is only when we quit that we seem to "need" these foods to feel better. Additionally, the researchers have suggested that a child's early sweet tooth may be a predictor of alcoholism in later life. Obviously, since everyone is born with a craving for sugar and not everyone becomes alcoholic, there must be other factors involved. If brain chemistry is faulty from the start, then it seems likely that a person would try to alleviate the symptoms of an imbalance by utilizing whatever means are available to him or her. Since environment, as well as genetics, play key roles in the development of addictions, some sugar cravers may never reach for the bottle but might continue to satiate themselves with food. Others may find, after an exposure to drugs and alcohol, that chemical substances provide a more powerful remedy. When the alcohol is removed and abstinence is attempted, however, brain chemistry still remains disturbed and is even exacerbated by the effects of chronic and prolonged chemical dependence. Maybe sweet cravings step up in their intensity, in an attempt to correct the effects of this imbalance, by trying somehow to compensate for the lack of alcohol consumption. Unfortunately, sugar is not as powerful and incessant sweet urges and subsequent binges are usually short-lived in their ability to rectify the problem. One may continue to crave and eat sweets, as a type of "self-medication" as it were, particularly if they have not satisfied their body's glucose needs with a more balanced and regular eating plan.

Although we know that chronic drug and alcohol use can forever change our brain chemistry, the intensity of sugar craving, something we still have yet to fully understand, seems to wane somewhat after an initial settling-in period. Many alcoholics report that their sweet cravings tend to lessen as time passes, sometimes after only a few months, while others require a couple of years. Also, the more recent and escalating prescribing of antidepressants seems to have helped in reducing sugar and carbohydrate cravings by dealing directly with the chemical imbalance in abstinent alcoholics. These drugs have the ability to correct neurochemistry with long-lasting effects and have become useful tools in addiction treatment.

The verdict? Although sugar cravings appear unyielding at first, they may, in the end, help us to stay sober and get through a most difficult and trying time, as we develop better eating habits and incorporate healthy alternatives. In the meantime, until we progress in our recovery journey and learn to make smarter nutritional choices, eating a few extra cookies won't hurt. Therefore, the jury finds sugar "not guilty" and concludes that hands caught in the cookie jar are not, at this time, subject to any offense. Canister closed.

Whipping Up Flavored Cream Cheese

Instead of butter and jam on your muffin, scone, or quick bread, consider whipping up a deliciously flavored cream cheese spread to add a bit of protein and healthy carbs to your snack. Although savory flavored cream cheeses, such as salmon, vegetable, and chive, are readily available for purchase and appropriate for bagels and breads, sweet versions are a bit harder to come by, but certainly are easy to make.

Start out with an eight-ounce package of plain cream cheese, preferably a light version like Neufchâtel, and allow to soften at room temperature. Then simply add your choice of sweet enhancements to create any number of unusual, delicious spreads. A food processor or an electric mixer fitted with a paddle with make this preparation a snap, but hand mixing with a wooden spoon will certainly do the trick. When adding dried fruit, it's a good idea to soak it in a little warm water for 20 minutes to plump up the texture and flavor before using.

Here are a few of my favorite cream cheese combinations:

HONEY WALNUT CREAM CHEESE: Add ⅓ cup chopped walnuts and 2 tablespoons honey.

FRESH STRAWBERRY CREAM CHEESE: Add ½ cup hulled and chopped ripe strawberries and 2 tablespoons sugar.

CHERRY VANILLA CREAM CHEESE: Add ⅓ cup chopped dried cherries and 2 tablespoons vanilla sugar (page 168) or 2 tablespoons sugar and 1 teaspoon nonalcohol vanilla extract.

ORANGE PECAN CREAM CHEESE: Add 2 tablespoons orange marmalade and ⅓ cup chopped pecans.

LEMONY COCONUT CREAM CHEESE: Add 1 tablespoon grated lemon rind, 3 tablespoons sweetened flaked coconut, and 1 tablespoon sugar.

MAPLE CRANBERRY CREAM CHEESE: Add 3 tablespoons pure maple syrup and ¼ cup chopped dried cranberries.

CINNAMON RAISIN CREAM CHEESE: Add 2 tablespoons cinnamon sugar and ⅓ cup chopped seedless raisins.

BROWN SUGAR CARAMEL CREAM CHEESE: Add 2 tablespoons light brown sugar and combine well. Gently fold in ¼ cup prepared caramel topping, allowing streaks to remain.

To store your flavored cream cheese, scoop into plastic storage containers, smooth down the surface, and top with a piece of round, fitted wax or parchment paper before replacing the lid. Kept in this way, flavored cream cheeses will last up to three weeks in the refrigerator, although those with fresh fruit additions should be consumed within three to four days.

Blueberry Lemon Buttermilk Muffins

MAKES 12 STANDARD OR 24 MINI MUFFINS The nutritionally packed blueberry stars in this moist and delicious muffin that is especially satisfying as a mid-morning or afternoon snack. I like to use a lot more blueberries than are usually called for in most recipes, especially when they are at their height of sweetness. You can substitute canned or frozen blueberries when necessary, provided they do not contain heavy syrup and have been well drained.

Taking the time to cream together the butter and sugar into a nearly white marshmallow-type fluff before adding any further ingredients will ensure a perfect batch of muffins each time. Alternating your dry and wet ingredients and not over-beating will also produce excellent results. Remember these tips when making other types of muffins that call for creaming butter and sugar together and you will never be disappointed!

½ cup (1 stick) unsalted butter, softened

1 cup sugar

2 large eggs

¾ cup buttermilk

2 cups all-purpose flour

1 teaspoon baking powder

½ teaspoon baking soda

½ teaspoon salt

2 teaspoons grated lemon rind

1½ cups fresh blueberries, picked
  over for stems

1 tablespoon sugar for sprinkling on top (optional)

1. Preheat the oven to 375 degrees. Lightly oil or butter a standard 12-cup muffin tin or 2 mini muffin tins.

2. Beat together the butter and sugar in a large mixing bowl with an electric mixer until light and fluffy, about 5 minutes. In a small mixing bowl, lightly beat together the eggs and buttermilk. In a medium-size mixing bowl, combine the flour, baking powder, baking soda, and salt with a whisk.

3. Alternating between the wet and dry ingredients, add to the butter-and-sugar mixture, beating briefly on medium speed to combine after each addition. Do not overbeat. Stir in the lemon rind and blueberries. Spoon the batter into the prepared muffin tin and sprinkle with a little of the sugar, if desired.

4. Bake until lightly golden and a toothpick inserted in the middle comes out clean, about 25 minutes for standard size muffins and 20 minutes for mini muffins. Let cool for 5 minutes before removing from the pan.

Apple Cinnamon Pecan Muffins

MAKES 12 STANDARD OR 6 LARGE MUFFINS Grated apples make for a deliciously moist muffin and natural sweetness, while chopped pecans and wheat germ add to a delightfully crunchy topping. A great alternative to classic fruit Danish, these muffins travel well and will stay moist for days, so consider making a batch early in the week for mid-morning munchies with tea or coffee all week long.

Be sure to cream the butter and sugar to a fluffy white consistency, as in the Blueberry Lemon Buttermilk Muffins (left), to ensure a perfect result. These do very well in large-size muffin tins for heartier appetites, as well as the standard size.

MUFFINS

½ cup (1 stick) unsalted butter, softened

½ cup granulated sugar

1 large egg

½ cup milk

1½ cups all-purpose flour

2 teaspoons baking powder

½ teaspoon ground cinnamon

½ teaspoon salt

1 cup peeled, cored, and grated apple

TOPPING

⅓ cup firmly packed dark brown sugar

½ cup chopped pecans

2 tablespoons toasted wheat germ

½ teaspoon ground cinnamon

1. Preheat the oven to 400 degrees. Lightly grease or butter a 12-cup standard muffin tin or 6-cup large muffin tin.

2. To make the muffins, beat together the butter and granulated sugar in a large mixing bowl with an electric mixer until light and fluffy, about 5 minutes. In a small mixing bowl, lightly beat the egg with the milk. In a medium-size mixing bowl, combine the flour, baking powder, cinnamon, and salt with a whisk.

3. Alternating between the wet and dry ingredients, add to the butter-and-sugar mixture, beating briefly on medium speed to combine after each addition. Do not overbeat. Stir in the grated apples and spoon the batter into the prepared muffin tins.

4. To make the topping, mix together all the ingredients in a small bowl. Spoon the topping over each muffin evenly before baking. Bake until the tops are browned and a toothpick inserted in the middle comes out clean, 25 to 30 minutes. Allow to cool for 5 minutes before removing from the pan.

Easy English Scones

MAKES ABOUT 10 SCONES I first tasted the quintessential English scone baked by my roommate in London many years ago and have never forgotten the simplicity of its creation. Warm from the oven and topped with Devonshire clotted cream and jam, nothing is better with a cup of strong British tea. Today, we see many varieties of scones in supermarkets and bakeries, from oddly shaped drop scones to triangular wedges flavored with anything from raisins and blueberries to poppy seeds and almonds. But the plain English scone, not at all dissimilar in taste and texture to our American buttermilk biscuit, is truly a pleasure to bake and enjoy. Starting with this basic recipe, you can then add numerous flavors and enhancements and even vary the shape, if you like.

Baking in the British Isles utilizes self-rising flour far more often than in America. We see this also in many traditional Irish recipes, such as Barm Brack (page 60), so adding a bag to your pantry is not a bad idea, especially if you plan on expanding your baking skills. Be aware, however, that self-rising flour is not the same as self-rising cake flour, which is much finer in texture and better suited to delicate cake making.

Clotted cream, basically thickened, unpasteurized cream, is a true luxury, calorie and fat-wise, but if you are lucky enough to come across it in your supermarket or specialty food store, definitely give it a try at least once. It is the essence of what is called a "cream tea" in Britain. Otherwise, a nice alternative would be Neufchâtel (light) cream cheese. Try making some of the whipped-up versions of cream cheese on page 54 to add a flavor boost to your plain scones.

Although best when warm from the oven, scones will keep for two to three days and freeze quite well for up to a month when wrapped tightly in plastic.

1½ cups self-rising flour

1½ tablespoons sugar

Pinch of salt

3 tablespoons unsalted butter, softened and
    cut into pieces

⅔ cup milk

Flour for dusting

1. Preheat the oven to 425 degrees.

2. In a medium-size mixing bowl, stir together the flour, sugar, and salt. Add the butter pieces and, using a pastry blender or fork, work the butter lightly into the dry ingredients until the mixture has a sand-like consistency. Mix in the milk a little at a time to form a soft dough.

3. Turn the mixture out onto a lightly floured work surface and roll the dough into a circle about ¾ inch thick. If necessary, add a little more flour to prevent sticking. Using a biscuit cutter or the open end of a 2-inch-wide drinking glass dipped in flour, carefully cut out the scones. Gather the scraps together, reroll it, and cut out more scones.

4. Transfer to a lightly greased baking sheet and dust the tops with a little flour. Bake until golden brown on top, 12 to 15 minutes. Let cool on a wire rack and serve slightly warm.

Studded Scones: Stir in ½ cup dried currants, cranberries, blueberries, or diced crystallized ginger before rolling out.

Lemon Scones: Add 1 teaspoon *each* grated lemon rind and lemon juice to the mixture.

Orange Poppy Seed Scones: Add 2 teaspoons grated orange rind and 1 tablespoon poppy seeds to the mixture.

Chocolate Chip Walnut Scones: Add ½ cup mini semisweet chocolate chips and ¼ cup chopped walnuts to the mixture.

Whole Wheat Brown Sugar Scones

MAKES 7 TO 8 SCONES The nutritious addition of somewhat heavier whole wheat flour in this recipe requires some added oomph for rising, so I've included baking powder and an egg to that end. Deliciously satisfying, these hearty scones are particularly good served warm with a dab of butter and a sprinkle of cinnamon sugar.

½ cup whole wheat flour, plus more for dusting
½ cup self-rising flour

2 tablespoons firmly packed light brown sugar
1 teaspoon baking powder
½ teaspoon ground cinnamon
1½ tablespoons unsalted butter, softened
1 large egg
2 to 3 tablespoons milk, plus more for brushing

1. Preheat the oven to 450 degrees.

2. In a medium-size mixing bowl, combine the flours, brown sugar, baking powder, and cinnamon. Add the butter and, using a pastry blender or fork, work it into the dry ingredients until it forms a sand-like consistency. In a small mixing bowl, beat together the egg and 2 tablespoons of the milk, then add it a little bit at a time to the dry ingredients, stirring to just moisten. Add more milk, if necessary, to hold the dough together.

3. Turn the mixture out onto a lightly floured work surface and roll it out into a circle about ¾ inch thick. Using a biscuit cutter or the open end of a 2-inch-wide glass dipped in flour, carefully cut out the scones. Gather together the scraps, reroll them, and cut out more scones.

4. Transfer to a lightly greased baking sheet, brush the tops with milk and dust with whole wheat flour. Bake until nicely browned on top and a toothpick inserted in the center comes out clean, 15 to 20 minutes. Let cool on a wire rack or serve warm.

Nutty Whole Wheat Scones: Add 2 tablespoons *each* shelled sunflower seeds and chopped almonds, pecans, or hazelnuts to the mixture.

Fruity Whole Wheat Scones: Add ¼ cup diced assorted dried fruit to the mixture.

Oatmeal Brown Sugar Scones: Substitute quick-cooking rolled oats for the whole wheat flour and process briefly in a food processor before adding to the other dry ingredients. One-quarter cup chopped dried apricots would make a nice addition.

Best Banana Quick Bread

MAKES 1 LOAF Probably one of the most popular types of quick bread, soft, ripe bananas are the key to making successful banana breads. Don't hesitate to use darkened or bruised ones either, as the outcome will not reflect these imperfections, but instead, add to the flavor and moistness. Make this when you have a glut of overripe bananas and freeze the extra loaves. This recipe will also work well as a muffin, if you prefer.

It's important not to overwork this batter, as it may become "gummy," so beat the ingredients by hand instead of using an electric mixer. You can stir in ½ cup of chopped nuts if you like—walnuts are always a nice complement to bananas, although pecans and macadamias are also delicious choices. Below you will find a variation with chocolate chips, another great partner for bananas. Feel free to add both if you enjoy the combination.

½ cup canola oil

¾ cup sugar

2 large eggs, slightly beaten

2 teaspoons nonalcohol vanilla, or substitute vanilla sugar (page 168) for ¼ cup of the sugar above

2 medium-size ripe, soft bananas, peeled and mashed with a fork (about 1½ cups)

1½ cups all-purpose flour

1 teaspoon ground cinnamon

1 teaspoon baking powder

½ teaspoon baking soda

¼ teaspoon salt

Dash of ground nutmeg

½ cup chopped nuts (optional)

1. Preheat the oven to 350 degrees. Grease well and flour a 9 x 5-inch loaf pan, knocking out any excess.

2. In a large mixing bowl, beat together the oil and sugar with a wooden spoon. Add the eggs and vanilla and stir well to combine. Add the bananas and fold into the mixture. In a medium-size mixing bowl, whisk together the dry ingredients and add to the wet mixture in 3 batches, stirring well to combine each time. Do not overbeat. Stir in the nuts, if desired.

3. Pour the batter into the prepared loaf pan and bake until the top is golden and a toothpick inserted in the middle comes out clean, about 50 minutes. Let cool in the pan for 10 minutes before turning loaf out of the pan and transfer to a wire rack to cool completely before slicing.

Chocolate Chip Banana Quick Bread: Reduce the ground cinnamon to ½ teaspoon and add ¾ cup mini semisweet chocolate chips to the batter.

Pumpkin Quick Bread with Pepitas and Sunflower Seeds: Increase the sugar to 1½ cups and substitute canned unsweetened pumpkin puree for the mashed bananas. Add ¼ teaspoon *each* ground cloves and ground coriander. Stir in ¼ cup *each* pepitas (hulled pumpkin seeds) and hulled sunflower seeds.

Zucchini Loaf with Black Walnuts

MAKES 1 LOAF An unlikely vegetable takes center stage in this delicious cross between a cake and a bread. I remember when zucchini first appeared in a "bread" guise and wondered if it was someone's crazy idea of dealing with the plethora of zucchini that is grown in the summertime. However, I was won over by the taste and you will be too.

I like using black walnuts in this recipe—the walnut variety that boasts excellent omega-3 fatty acid content and is one of the few non-fish sources

(continued on page 60)

Using Nonalcohol-Based Vanilla

How Important Is It?

Vanilla extract, the most popular flavor enhancer in baking, is usually bottled in a solution that is at least 35 percent alcohol by volume. Ice creams, prepared baked goods, and numerous home recipes include it as an essential ingredient. But, for those of us in recovery, how important is it to avoid? Obviously, its prevalence is hard to ignore and, in reality, consuming cookies, cakes, and other dessert items that have been store prepared or baked by others using alcohol-based vanilla extract is of little consequence, since the amount, once distributed in the cooking process, is nearly infinitesimal.

However, if *we* are the ones doing the cooking or baking, holding an open bottle of vanilla extract could be as dangerous as holding a hand grenade. We know that the mere aroma of alcohol can send signals to our brain cells in record time. Especially during Phase One, these kinds of triggers may pose potential problems to our abstinence. For that reason, an alcohol-free kitchen necessarily means eliminating alcohol-based extracts.

Fortunately, numerous alternatives have recently been introduced to the cooking market that rival both the fragrance and taste of traditional extracts. Glycerin-based, alcohol-free vanilla can now be purchased at gourmet and cake decorating supply shops and online. Many other flavored extracts, from almond to mint to walnut, are also available. (See the "Resources" section for ordering information.)

Another alternative to traditional vanilla extract is vanilla powder, which is essentially the whole, dried vanilla bean, finely ground. It has the advantage of maintaining its flavor throughout the cooking process, even at high temperatures, unlike liquid extracts, which tend to dissipate somewhat. Vanilla powder can be substituted one for one when vanilla extract is required.

Of course, the best alternative is the highly prized, deliciously fragrant vanilla bean, from which all pure extracts, alcohol-based or not, derive their flavor. When the bean is slit open lengthwise and the thousands of tiny seeds are scraped directly into food preparations, the amazing aroma and taste it imparts are undeniably wonderful. Infusing sugar with vanilla beans will create super fragrant vanilla sugar (see page 168 for instructions) and is an excellent baking alternative—one that I utilize often.

Incidentally, Bourbon-Madagascar vanilla beans, the most popular in the world (Mexican and Tahitian are the others), do not contain bourbon or any other form of alcohol. They refer, instead, to the Bourbon Islands, to which Madagascar belongs.

(continued from page 58)
of it—but, if they are hard to come by, use regular walnuts or try chopped pecans or hazelnuts. This bread is particularly good toasted with a smear of butter or delicious as is for a take-along snack for afternoon coffee or tea. Be sure to let the loaf cool almost completely and use a serrated knife when slicing to prevent any "gummy" crumbs.

2 large eggs
¾ cup sugar
½ cup canola oil
1 cup freshly shredded zucchini, including skin
    (about 1 medium-size zucchini)
1 teaspoon nonalcohol vanilla, or substitute
    vanilla sugar (page 168) for ¼ cup of the
    sugar above
1 cup all-purpose flour
½ cup whole wheat flour
½ teaspoon salt
½ teaspoon baking soda
¼ teaspoon baking powder
1 teaspoon ground cinnamon
¼ teaspoon ground nutmeg
⅔ cup chopped black walnuts

1. Preheat the oven to 350 degrees. Grease a 9 x 5-inch loaf pan.

2. In a medium-size mixing bowl, beat together the eggs, oil, and sugar with a wooden spoon until well blended. Add the zucchini and vanilla and beat another minute.

3. In another medium-size mixing bowl, whisk together the remaining ingredients except for the nuts. Add the flour mixture in 2 batches to the oil mixture, beating well each time to combine. Stir in the walnuts.

4. Pour the batter into the prepared loaf pan. Bake until a toothpick inserted in the middle of the loaf comes out clean, 50 to 60 minutes. Allow to cool in the pan for 10 minutes, then loosen the edges with a sharp knife and turn out. Let cool completely on a wire rack before slicing.

Irish Tea Bread (Barm Brack)

MAKES 1 LOAF I first discovered this classic Irish tea bread when I was asked to cater a traditional St. Patrick's Day party with truly authentic menu choices and not just the usual corned beef and cabbage. Along with soda bread, barm brack is a typical Irish treat to accompany tea, its name deriving from a corruption of the Gaelic words *aran breac* or speckled bread.

Some recipes call for yeast, but this easy version calls for self-rising flour and requires very little preparation time, apart from macerating, or soaking, the fruit and nuts for several hours or overnight (see "Maceration: Infusing Flavor Without Alcohol," page 61). It is an excellent example of how liquids other than alcohol, in this case tea, can be used to infuse flavor and to soften dried fruit and nuts.

Below is the recipe I created for the party, studded with green pistachios and citron for a festive St. Patrick's Day presentation; however, any color or type of dried fruit and nut can be substituted, as shown in the variations below. The tea that I use to macerate the fruit in this recipe is a wonderfully aromatic honey vanilla chamomile, but other flavored herbal teas will do equally well. Lastly, I generally bake this in a long, thin loaf pan, usually used for pâtés, because of its "tea bread" size and attractive appearance. A standard loaf pan holds the same volume, however, and can be easily substituted but will require an additional 10 to 15 minutes of baking time.

1½ cups golden raisins
½ cup diced green citron
½ cup raw shelled pistachios
1 cup firmly packed light brown sugar
1 cup hot, strongly steeped honey vanilla
    chamomile tea
1 large egg
2¼ cups self-rising flour

1. In a medium-size mixing bowl, combine the raisins, citron, pistachios, and brown sugar. Add the hot tea, stir well, cover, and allow to macerate (soak) for several hours or overnight at room temperature.

2. Preheat the oven to 350 degrees. Grease and flour a 12 x 4½ x 2½-inch or standard 9 x 5 x 3-inch loaf pan, knocking out any excess flour.

3. Beat the egg into the macerated mixture. Add the flour in about ½-cup batches, beating well after each addition.

4. Pour the batter into the prepared loaf pan. Bake until a toothpick inserted in the middle comes out clean, about 1 hour. Let cool in the pan for 10 minutes before turning out and transferring to a wire rack to cool completely. Serve sliced thin, plain or toasted, with butter.

Cranberry Orange Pecan Barm Brack: Substitute dried cranberries for the raisins, diced candied orange peel for the citron, and chopped pecans for the pistachios. Macerate in orange-flavored herbal tea.

Black Tea Barm Brack: Substitute dried currants for the citron and chopped black walnuts for the pistachios. Macerate in black Irish or English breakfast tea.

Green Tea and Ginger Barm Brack: Substitute diced crystallized ginger for the citron and chopped almonds for the pistachios. Macerate in green tea.

Fennel Seed and Pine Nut Barm Brack: Add 1 tablespoon fennel seeds to the fruit mixture and substitute pine nuts for the pistachios.

Chocolate Chip Cherry Barm Brack: Substitute 1 cup dried cherries for the golden raisins and chopped hazelnuts for the pistachios. Omit the citron and macerate in a combination of ¾ cup plain tea and ¼ cup cherry juice. Stir in 1 cup mini semisweet chocolate chips before baking.

Maceration

Infusing Flavor Without Alcohol

Soaking food in a liquid in order to infuse it with flavor is called maceration and many fruit desserts are often prepared in this way. Usually alcohol in the form of wine, brandy, or rum is the liquid of choice, but it is by no means the only option. Tea, just as in the Barm Brack recipe (page 60), will often make an excellent starting point when substituting for macerating liquor because of its acidic quality in the form of tannins, the same substances found in red wine. By adding sugar in the form of molasses, corn syrup, or even simple syrup (page 16), along with other flavorful ingredients, we can replicate both the taste and consistency of many types of liqueurs. Of course, and rightly so, it will never be an exact replica, which could just as easily fool our taste buds and trigger a craving, but for the purposes of the recipe, it will fill in perfectly and fulfill the role of the original alcohol.

It's interesting to note that Auguste Escoffier, in his classic nineteenth-century cookbook, suggested using strong tea as a replacement for rum in several dessert recipes, including ice cream. For dark rum substitutions, I would even suggest adding a splash of molasses or dark corn syrup to the tea to enhance the flavor and color since molasses is, after all, the base ingredient of rum distillation. For a lighter color, simple syrup or light corn syrup could be used.

Flavored teas with a boost of fruit juice or syrup can also be excellent macerating liquids. For example, Earl Gray tea makes an ideal base for replicating orange-flavored liqueurs, as it contains the essence of bergamot, the oil from the peel of a small variety of orange. Adding a spoonful of orange juice concentrate to this would create a good macerating liquid that fills in nicely for a cordial like Curaçao or Cointreau.

Oatmeal Spice Cookies with Golden Raisins

MAKES ABOUT 3 DOZEN Cookies for a healthy snack? When they're oatmeal cookies, the answer is yes. Store-bought varieties tend to contain more sugar than anything else, but here the emphasis is on the oats and the result is moist, chewy, and delicious. Oats and oatmeal products are some of our best choices at this time because they metabolize at a slow rate, providing sustained energy while controlling hunger. Even when combined with sugar and refined carbohydrates, their power is not diminished. Something sweet that contains oats is a perfect solution to those ferocious sweet crav-ings. Take a few of these "for the road" to enjoy when the craving hits!

1 cup (2 sticks) unsalted butter, softened
¾ cup firmly packed light brown sugar
¼ cup granulated sugar
2 large eggs
1 teaspoon nonalcohol vanilla extract, or substitute vanilla sugar (page 168) for the granulated sugar above
1 cup all-purpose flour
½ teaspoon baking soda
½ teaspoon baking powder
½ teaspoon salt
½ teaspoon ground cinnamon
½ teaspoon ground allspice

More on Sugar

Common Cousins, Impersonators, and Imposters

White sugar is, of course, not the only sugar out there. But for the most part, there is little difference between ordinary table sugar and its close cousins. For instance, brown sugar is simply white sugar that has had molasses added to it in varying degrees (light or dark brown), while castor sugar (also called superfine) and confectioners' sugar are merely granulated white sugars that have been crushed to a finer texture or powder. Raw sugar, although it sounds as if it must be better for us in some way, is just the residue that is left after both molasses and white sugar have been extracted from the sugarcane. Demerara, Barbados, and Turbinado are all names of sugar in the raw and can come from any number of geographical locations, Guyana and Hawaii being the most popular.

Nutritionally, sugar has little to offer no matter what form it takes, although blackstrap molasses contains a modest amount of magnesium and iron. Honey, maple sugar, sorghum, and evaporated cane juice are all converted by the body to glucose, so there is little advantage in choosing one over another, except for flavor considerations in cooking and baking. Similarly, so-called natural or organic sugar holds no real advantage and is purely a matter of preference.

Sugar impersonators have been the subject of much controversy over the years, beginning

2 cups quick-cooking rolled oats

1 cup golden raisins

1. Preheat the oven to 350 degrees. Lightly grease a cookie sheet.

2. In a large mixing bowl, using an electric mixer beat together the butter, brown sugar, and granulated sugar until smooth and fluffy. Add the eggs and vanilla and beat to combine well.

3. In a medium-size mixing bowl, combine the remaining ingredients, except the raisins, and whisk together. On low speed, add the dry ingredients to the butter-and-egg mixture a little at a time until well blended. Stir in the raisins.

4. Drop the cookie dough by heaping tablespoons onto the prepared cookie sheet about

2 inches apart and bake until lightly golden on the edges, 10 to 12 minutes. Do not overbake.

5. Let the cookies cool on the cookie sheet for 1 to 2 minutes, then transfer to a cooling rack or brown paper bag to cool completely.

Ginger Cashew Granola Bar Cookies

MAKES 12 GRANOLA BARS Granola bars have been popular for a long time and many ready-made varieties are available, but they often contain a high concentration of partially hydrogenated oils and high-fructose corn syrup. Making your own is really

with saccharin, which research has shown may increase the chances of some types of cancer. Aspartame, better known as NutraSweet, is by far the most prevalent artificial sweetener, found in everything from diet sodas to sugar-free candy. Many people dislike the taste and find that they get headaches from its consumption, while others prefer it over sugary sodas and as a sugar substitute in coffee and tea. Too much of anything, of course, is probably not a good idea, so you might want to limit your intake of aspartame until we know more about its potential long-term side effects. A new kid on the block, sucralose, sold as Splenda, is derived from actual sugar and, so far, appears to be safe. Many diet sodas are beginning to replace aspartame with this alternative. Although some diet cookbook authors encourage baking with these types of sweeteners, I have never found them to be particularly tasteful when used in the kitchen and prefer to opt for the real thing.

Finally, you may see the term "sugar alcohols" on many diet food ingredient labels, particularly diabetic products, and wonder if this is something to avoid. Natural substances such as sorbitol, mannitol, and xylitol fall into this category and are used because they tend not to raise blood sugar levels, while containing half the calories of real sugar. Rest assured, however, that there is no form of alcohol present in these sweeteners and they are certainly safe to use in the sober kitchen. Large consumption of these substances can, however, wreak havoc with your digestion and it should be eaten in small amounts. Stevia, the new darling of these types of sugar imposters, is so intensely sweet that it must be diluted in water. Some people enjoy its mild licorice taste, while others find it to be too strongly flavored and difficult to use.

quite simple and allows you to adjust the amount of sweetness to your liking. More like a cookie than a snack bar, these delicious goodies make a great accompaniment to afternoon tea or coffee.

Oats are a great grain for sustaining energy levels and ginger is a wonderfully healing and delicious ingredient. I like cashews in this recipe, because they are a softer, sweeter nut than most, but you can substitute almonds or any other nut just as easily. When choosing a granola to use, one without lots of added nuts and fruits is best, especially when adding your own. However, the many interesting varieties of granola that are now available may indeed make for a delicious-flavored treat, without the necessity of too many additional ingredients. In fact, this recipe was inspired by a ginger-flavored granola I happen to adore. Feel free to experiment with different granolas (or even use the recipe on page 178) to create your own favorite combination.

Make a batch of these for a week's worth of snacking, provided the rest of the family doesn't devour them first!

1 cup granola

1 cup quick-cooking rolled oats

½ cup unsalted raw or dry-roasted cashews

¼ cup diced crystallized ginger

½ cup all-purpose flour

1 large egg, beaten

⅓ cup honey

⅓ cup canola oil

¼ cup firmly packed light brown sugar

¼ teaspoon ground ginger

¼ teaspoon ground cinnamon

1. Preheat oven to 325 degrees. Butter a 9-inch square baking pan. Line the bottom with a piece of parchment paper or wax paper cut to fit.

2. In a medium-size mixing bowl, combine the granola, oats, cashews, crystallized ginger, and flour and stir well to combine. In a small mixing bowl, combine the remaining ingredients and whisk well. Pour that into the granola mixture and stir well with a wooden spoon.

3. Transfer to the prepared pan and smooth evenly, pressing down with a spatula or your fingers. Bake until just lightly browned on the edges, 25 to 30 minutes.

4. Let cool completely and flip over onto a cutting board. Remove the paper and cut into 12 bars. Keep in an airtight container or wrap individually in plastic wrap or aluminum foil.

Cranberry Pecan Granola Bar Cookies: Substitute dried cranberries for the crystallized ginger and chopped pecans for the cashews. Omit the ground ginger.

Chocolate Chip Walnut Granola Bar Cookies: Substitute ½ cup mini semisweet chocolate chips for the crystallized ginger and chopped walnuts for the cashews. Omit the ground ginger and cinnamon.

Peanut Butter Crunch Granola Bar Cookies: Replace the cashews with unsalted peanuts and omit the crystallized ginger. Replace the canola oil with peanut butter (smooth or chunky).

Chunky Peanut Butter Cookies

MAKES ABOUT 3 DOZEN COOKIES Half of America's peanut crop is used to make peanut butter, and there is no doubt that this delicious spread is a popular choice for both kids and adults. Possessing a good amount of iron, niacin, and protein, peanut butter, particularly natural and organic varieties, is a great, glycemically healthy snack. However, this recipe is one instance in which natural is not necessarily better. Because natural peanut butter uses only peanuts and oil, without any additives, it tends towards separation and is distinctly remiss of sugar. I recommend using the standard supermarket version (you can substitute smooth if you prefer) in this recipe for the best results.

Chunky and chewy, these cookies will satisfy any urge for a sweet respite and are particularly tasty when warm and straight from the oven.

½ cup chunky peanut butter
½ cup (1 stick) unsalted butter, softened
½ cup granulated sugar
½ cup firmly packed light brown sugar
1 large egg
1 cup all-purpose flour
¼ cup whole wheat flour
¾ teaspoon baking soda
½ teaspoon baking powder
¼ teaspoon salt
1 cup unsalted raw or dry-roasted peanuts

1. Preheat the oven to 375 degrees.
2. In a large mixing bowl, beat together the peanut butter, butter, and both sugars until light and fluffy. Add the egg and beat to combine well.
3. In a medium-size mixing bowl, combine the remaining ingredients, except the peanuts, and whisk together. Add the dry ingredients to the butter mixture in 2 batches, beating until well combined. Stir in the peanuts. Form the dough into 1-inch-size balls and place 2 inches apart on an ungreased cookie sheet. Flatten in a criss-cross fashion with the back of a fork dipped in flour to prevent sticking, and bake until set and lightly golden around the edges, 10 to 12 minutes. Transfer to a wire rack or brown paper bag to cool.

Chunky Nut Butter Cookies: Substitute almond, cashew, or soybean butter for the peanut butter and increase the granulated sugar to ⅔ cup. Stir in coarsely chopped unsalted almonds, cashews, or whole roasted, unsalted soybeans.

Chocolate Chunk Peanut Butter Cookies: Reduce the peanuts to ½ cup and stir in 1 cup semisweet chocolate chunks.

Chewy Double Ginger Molasses Cookies

MAKES ABOUT 2½ DOZEN COOKIES Everyone just loves these soft-centered, chewy cookies, which go great with a cup of Hot Spiced Cocoa (page 21). The inclusion of crystallized ginger adds a real zip as well as offering therapeutic value, helping to ease digestion and even protecting DNA against dangerous carcinogens. In addition, blackstrap molasses is a good source of magnesium and iron. And you thought they just tasted great!

¾ cup canola oil
1 cup sugar, plus a bit more for rolling
1 large egg
⅓ cup blackstrap molasses
1¾ cups all-purpose flour
⅔ cup whole wheat flour
2 teaspoons baking soda
1 teaspoon ground ginger
1 teaspoon ground cinnamon
½ teaspoon salt
½ cup finely diced crystallized ginger

1. Preheat the oven to 350 degrees.
2. In a large mixing bowl, beat together the oil and sugar until well combined. Add the egg and molasses and beat for another 2 to 3 minutes.
3. In a medium-size mixing bowl, combine the remaining ingredients, except for the crystallized ginger, and whisk together. Add the dry ingredients to the oil mixture a little at a time, combining well after each addition. Stir in the crystallized ginger.
4. Form the cookie dough into balls about the size of small whole walnuts and roll in sugar to coat evenly. Place, without flattening, on an ungreased cookie sheet and bake until the cookies have spread out and the tops appear crackled, 8 to 10 minutes. Remove from the oven (the cookies will still be very soft) and let stand on the baking sheet

for 2 minutes before transferring to a wire rack or brown paper bag to cool.

Chef's Note: *You can buy "baker's cut" crystallized ginger at specialty food stores. If not available, chop crystallized ginger slices or chunks into a rough ¼-inch dice. To prevent sticking while chopping, add 1 teaspoon flour to your chopping board.*

Cinnamon Crunchies

MAKES EIGHTEEN 3 x 1½-INCH BARS   If you like cinnamon, you are in for a real treat with these crunchy cookie bars, which can satisfy a sweet craving from the delicious aroma alone. I have enjoyed these since I was a child and they always bring back fond memories of cooking with my mother in our small kitchen in the house where I grew up. I remember mixing everything by hand, which made the final product that much more satisfying, but feel free to utilize your electric mixer and food processor (for nut chopping) when whipping up these crunchy delights.

COOKIES
⅓ cup unsalted butter, softened
½ cup sugar
1 large egg yolk
2 tablespoons milk
1 cup all-purpose flour
½ teaspoon ground cinnamon
¼ teaspoon salt

CRUNCHY TOPPING
¼ cup sugar
½ teaspoon ground cinnamon
½ cup chopped pecans or walnuts
1 large egg white, slightly beaten

1. Preheat the oven to 350 degrees.
2. To make the cookies, beat together the butter and sugar in a medium-size mixing bowl until light and fluffy. Add the egg yolk and milk and beat well to combine.
3. In a small mixing bowl, combine the flour, cinnamon, and salt and whisk together. Add to the butter mixture and beat until smooth. Spread evenly in a 9-inch square ungreased baking pan and set aside.
4. To make the topping, combine the sugar, cinnamon, and nuts in a small mixing bowl and stir well. Using a pastry brush, coat the top of the cookie mixture in the pan with the egg white and be sure to cover the area completely. Sprinkle the topping mixture evenly over the egg white and bake until set and lightly golden, about 30 minutes.
5. Allow to cool for 10 minutes before using a sharp knife to cut into bars. Remove from the pan and let cool completely on a wire rack or brown paper bag.

The Ultimate Chocolate Chip Cookie

MAKES ABOUT 3 DOZEN COOKIES No section on cookie baking would be complete without a recipe for chocolate chip cookies, and since we are just about ready to face the chocolate monster, I thought this recipe might be the appropriate segue to our next section.

There are more recipes for chocolate chip cookies out there than you can shake a wooden spoon at and everyone I know has their favorite version, from Mrs. Fields to the classic Toll House. Here is a happy medium sure to please any chocolate chip cookie fan: crisp on the outside edges, but moist and chewy on the inside. This ultimate cookie snack, a favorite indulgence for just about everyone, should be savored, not devoured! Keep them in an airtight container to retain their soft, chewy centers.

1 cup (2 sticks) unsalted butter, softened

1½ cups firmly packed light brown sugar

½ cup granulated sugar

2 large eggs

1 tablespoon nonalcohol vanilla extract, or
   substitute vanilla sugar (page 168) for the
   granulated sugar above

2½ cups all-purpose flour

1 teaspoon baking powder

1 teaspoon baking soda

½ teaspoon salt

One 12-ounce bag semisweet chocolate chips or
   chunks

1 cup chopped walnuts

1. Preheat the oven to 350 degrees.

2. In a large mixing bowl, beat together the butter and both sugars until smooth and fluffy. Add the eggs and vanilla and beat to combine well.

3. In a medium-size mixing bowl, combine the remaining ingredients, except the chocolate chips and walnuts, and whisk together. Add the dry ingredients to the butter-and-sugar mixture a little at a time until well blended. Stir in the chocolate chips and walnuts.

4. Drop the cookie dough by heaping tablespoons onto an ungreased cookie sheet about 2 inches apart and bake until set and slightly golden on the edges, 9 to 11 minutes. For crispier cookies, bake 11 to 13 minutes. Do not overbake. Remove from the oven and allow to rest on the cookie sheet for 2 to 3 minutes before transferring to a wire rack or brown paper to cool.

Feeding the Chocolate Monster: Friend or Fiend?

When a snack attack hits and chocolate is your desire, where do you turn to satisfy the urge? I don't know anyone in early recovery who has not experienced this compulsion and raced to the candy aisle to feed the chocolate monster. Bill W., in the classic Big Book, *Alcoholics Anonymous*, even advised keeping chocolate bars in the car to quell any alcohol cravings. And although some have suggested that feeding a sweet tooth, particularly with chocolate, is merely a substitute for alcohol that will inevitably lead us back to the bottle, the logistics of our cravings are far more complex than that. To tell us not to give in to these natural urges is, for most, an unrealistic restriction and perhaps even poor judgment, considering the unwanted alternative. Obviously, munching on chocolate bars all day is not a great idea. But if we are attempting to eat properly with nutritiously planned meals, chocolate is certainly a treat that we have a right to enjoy.

So how do we feed this chocolate monster when it rears its demanding, fiendish head? For one thing, we know we can lessen the effect of certain refined carbohydrates by combining them with healthier complex carbohydrates and that even a certain amount of added protein and fat will slow down the quick metabolism of these types of foods. All chocolate treats are already and necessarily a combination of fat, protein, and carbohydrates (pure cocoa powder would be quite inedible!), which is what makes them so appealing to our taste buds. However, within these combinations, we can make better choices for chocolate snacks by selecting those that contain healthier fats, proteins, and carbs. For instance, a dark chocolate bar studded with whole almonds would be a better choice than a milk chocolate bar with crispy rice. Why? Because dark chocolate contains less sugar and more potent phytochemicals (see "Chocolate: The 21st Century Health Food?" page 70), while almonds contain healthy monounsaturated fat, in addition to numerous vitamins, minerals, and fiber, which will help to sustain energy levels. Crispy rice, identical to that found in rice cakes, is "poofed" and processed to high glycemic extremes and is virtually without any nutritional value, while milk chocolate will often contain more sugar and added unhealthy fats.

Another way to appease an overactive chocolate craving is to experience a "Lucy and Ethel" moment. Everyone is surely familiar with the classic "I Love Lucy" episode in which the girls wind up working in a chocolate factory, devouring pounds of chocolate candies in an attempt to fool their supervisor about their slow work performance. Afterwards, when they get home, Ricky and Fred present them each with a five-pound box of chocolates to make up for their male insensitivity, unaware of what has just transpired. If these TV episodes had been filmed in color, Lucy and Ethel would surely have been sickly green in the face when they saw their gifts. The idea of more chocolate was enough to have them racing to the medicine cabinet for some good old bicarbonate of soda! Interestingly, a recent study conducted by the Northwestern Cognitive Brain Mapping Group entitled "Changes in Brain Activity Related to Eating Chocolate: From Pleasure to Aversion" indicated that once participants began to eat chocolate beyond their satiation level, brain blood flow decreased in the part of the cortex associated with pleasure and increased in the region related to negative/unpleasant stimuli. This suggests that there is a limit to our chocolate craving, beyond which the enjoyment distinctly wanes. On a personal note, I can tell you that

after attending a chocolate truffle-making seminar (we're talking six straight hours of chocolate, chocolate everywhere!), I was convinced that I could not even enter the restaurant pastry kitchen (which always smells of chocolate), much less face a candy bar ever again! In general, if you are eating a balanced diet spread throughout the day, chocolate probably will not have the power you think it has. But, if you are sure you are eating a reasonably healthy diet and still classify yourself as a "chocoholic," try taking a tour of a chocolate factory one day, such as Hershey's or Ghirardelli's, or take a part-time job behind the counter of a Godiva chocolate store. Better yet, enroll in a cooking class on chocolate candy making or baking, and I guarantee you will be able to put your chocolate craving in perspective in no time flat and remove much of its mystique. Remember how a particularly overindulgent evening of drink used to swear us off alcohol forever (or at least a day or two)? Well, this is the same principle without the toxic repercussions and I promise your resolve will last a lot longer. Remember, too, that advertising has worked to convince most Americans that chocolate is a maniacal obsession, especially for women, and that we "need" it somehow when we are feeling unloved or depressed. Don't fall into the trap of believing that the chocolate monster controls *you*. It doesn't.

Similarly and finally, getting to know your own personal chocolate monster is certainly a worthwhile endeavor, as you may find, more often than not, that a little bit of chocolate will calm him down and put him in his place quite readily. Consider reaching for a slice of Chocolate Chip Banana Quick Bread (page 58) or a handful of chocolate-covered raisins. Maybe a mug of hot cocoa or a glass of chocolate soymilk will do the trick. Like many alcohol and drug cravings, chocolate cravings tend to pass more swiftly than we realize. If we can ride them out by using one of the many helpful psychological

Instant Chocolate-Dipped Strawberries

Hand-dipped chocolate-coated strawberries can be seen gracing many an elegant party dessert table and bakery window display. Chocolatiers pay close attention to the details, ensuring that the melted chocolate is at the ideal temperature for dipping (called tempering) before submerging oversized long-stem berries. A flourish of white or milk chocolate squiggles will often finish the presentation and the price will reflect this intensity of labor.

For the rest of us, however, dipping strawberries in melted chocolate may actually not be a bad choice when looking for a quick way to satisfy the chocolate monster, provided we don't go overboard on our dipping. Any size berries will do just fine. Simply wash and carefully dry the strawberries, leaving the leaves and hull to hold on to, and break your favorite plain chocolate bar into pieces (about two ounces of good quality milk, semisweet or bittersweet) into a small glass or ceramic bowl or ramekin. Microwave for 30 seconds, stir gently, and continue to heat in 10-second intervals until the chocolate is completely melted (usually less than a minute). *Voila!* In a flash, you have instant chocolate-dipped strawberries to enjoy warm like a fondue straight from the dipping bowl or chilled after 20 minutes in the fridge on wax or parchment paper. Chocolate-dipped strawberries make excellent garnishes for ice creams, puddings, and milkshakes and as part of a dessert tray with coffee and cookies. Beware of booze, however, when buying them. Fancy bakeshops will sometimes inject their berries with a dose of brandy or flavored liqueur before dipping. Ask if this is the case when offered these treats at formal buffets and parties.

tools we have in recovery, like thinking through our cravings and turning our attention to healthy distractions, we will find that the urge is practically over before it begins. If, however, you discover that, despite your best efforts, your friendly chocolate monster has a tendency to show up unannounced too often, demanding to be fed, be prepared by making some of the recipes in this section ahead of time so you will always be ready to soothe its restless appetite with some smart and delicious choices.

Fudge Brownies with Peanut Butter Cream Cheese Swirl

MAKES 16 BROWNIES Moist, chocolatey, gooey brownies are always at the top of any chocolate treat list. Here the addition of a peanut butter-and-cream-cheese swirl adds some protein as well as a delicious smooth texture. I had been making this brownie recipe, without the peanut butter swirl, for years when one of my clients requested a chocolate and peanut butter dessert for a party she was giving. This recipe was born and has been a hit ever since.

BROWNIES
⅓ cup unsalted butter
2 ounces unsweetened chocolate
1 cup granulated sugar
2 large eggs
¾ cup all-purpose flour
½ teaspoon baking powder
½ teaspoon salt

PEANUT BUTTER CREAM CHEESE
¼ cup (½ stick) unsalted butter, softened
1 cup chunky peanut butter
½ cup firmly packed light brown sugar
1 large egg
One 8-ounce package cream cheese, softened

1. Preheat the oven to 350 degrees. Grease an 8-inch square baking pan.

2. To make the brownies, melt the butter in a small saucepan over low heat, then add the chocolate squares and stir until completely melted. Transfer to a large mixing bowl and beat in the granulated sugar and eggs. Add the flour, baking powder, and salt and beat well to combine. Pour into the prepared pan and spread evenly.

3. To make the peanut butter cream cheese mixture, beat together the softened butter and peanut butter in a medium-size mixing bowl. Add the brown sugar and beat for 1 minute. Add the egg and softened cream cheese and continue to beat until smooth.

4. Using a tablespoon, drop dollops of the peanut butter mixture on top of the chocolate mixture. Using a knife, swirl the peanut butter dollops into the chocolate, distributing evenly. Bake until the edges begin to pull away from the baking pan and a tester inserted towards the edge comes out clean, 35 to 45 minutes.

5. Let cool completely in the pan before cutting into squares.

Chocolate

The 21st Century Health Food?

Able to lower cholesterol? High in antioxidants? Equivalent to the medicinal consumption of olive oil, red wine, and green tea? Surely we can't be talking about chocolate?! Yet recent research has indicated that those who are passionate about chocolate might actually be doing themselves a favor, reaping the many health benefits chocolate and cocoa powder seem to offer.

First used by Aztecs in the preparation of hot, stimulating, and restorative beverages, chocolate, made from the seeds of the tropical cacao tree called *theobroma* after the Greek word meaning "food of the gods," has since been considered a pleasurable treat verging on the erotic. (Casanova drank chocolate before bedding his conquests.) Yet only recently have researchers discovered that chocolate, when eaten in reasonable quantities and from high quality sources, may actually be an excellent health food. This is because chocolate contains high polyphenol levels, which are known to fight free radicals. In addition, cocoa butter, the fat that is present in chocolate, is processed as healthy monounsaturated fat, similar to olive oil, and could aid in lowering blood cholesterol levels. Dark chocolate, which contains more actual cocoa, is the preferred medicinal choice over those varieties that contain a lot of added trans fats and sugar.

We also hear much about the psychoactive effects of chocolate and how "chocoholics" claim it is their antidepressant of choice. In addition to containing some caffeine, chocolate boasts

Chocolate-Dipped Caramel Apples

MAKES 6 CARAMEL APPLES Some old treats never die and these delicious dipped apples are one of them. Fancy sweet shops and department stores sell these double-dipped apples at exorbitant gourmet prices, but you can easily make them at home, just like everybody did years ago. I have found that green Granny Smith apples are the best for dipping—they are crisp and less sweet than many other apples, which helps to balance the ultra-sweet coating—but there are so many varieties of apples on the market these days, feel free to try any one you like. Rather than picking the largest apples you can find, I think a smaller apple is far more manageable to dip, as well as to eat.

Making your own caramel from scratch requires a candy thermometer and a little bit of nerve if you are not used to working with cooked sugar. Instead, I have suggested taking a shortcut, using prepared caramel candies, which work very well and make this recipe a snap. Directions are given for stove-top as well as microwave melting.

another stimulant called theobromine, which, along with phenylethylamine, the so-called love chemical, may be responsible for the euphoric benefits that some people report. In reality, however, enormous quantities would need to be consumed to produce any noticeable effects, although some people, particularly women, find that eating chocolate can alleviate their anxiety and depression, particularly during premenstrual times. Another substance, called anandamide, appears to be found in both chocolate and marijuana, but in the case of chocolate, it is broken down by stomach acids before entering the bloodstream, ultimately having little effect on brain chemistry, if any. Similarly, although chocolate also contains modest amounts of magnesium and it has been suggested that chocolate cravings may be an indication of a deficiency of this mineral, many other foods boast good magnesium content, such as spinach and lima beans. But I don't recall anyone racing through the supermarket in search of the Birds Eye section, do you?

Of particular interest is a Spanish study revealing that the same alkaloid compounds found in alcohol are also present in chocolate, offering an explanation as to why many recovering alcoholics crave chocolate, especially in early sobriety. They admit, however, that a myriad of chemicals are involved in both alcohol and alleged chocolate "addiction" and that until we discover their details, it is hard to make a judgment on the correlation. Again, dark chocolate appears to hold the most similarity because it has a high percentage of cocoa, yet many chocolate cravings during recovery are reported to be of the less-intense milk chocolate variety, always in combination with ingredients that are highly refined and loaded with fat. This suggests that, once again, it is more likely to be the pleasurable, "feel good" brain chemical-enhancing effects of eating carbohydrates and sugar that we are ultimately seeking.

6 small to medium-size crisp apples

6 popsicle sticks

One 12-ounce bag caramels, unwrapped

2 tablespoons water

12 ounces good quality milk or semisweet
chocolate

1 cup chopped nuts (optional), such as almonds,
pecans, or peanuts

Chef's Note: *To take these apples totally over the top, you can drizzle some melted white chocolate or dark bittersweet chocolate over the finished apples, then let them set for another 30 minutes. You can also decorate with more chopped nuts, sprinkles, or coconut if you like. Chocolate-dipped caramel apples will keep in the refrigerator for 2 to 3 days.*

1. Wash and dry the apples. Insert the sticks into the stem part of the apple and set aside. Cover a baking sheet with lightly buttered parchment paper or aluminum foil.

2. In a small but deep bowl, microwave the unwrapped caramels and water together on high, stirring until smooth and all the pieces are melted, 2 to 3 minutes. (Alternatively, you can melt the caramels in the top of a double boiler over gently simmering water.) Let the mixture set a minute or two until the sauce is no longer steaming.

3. Carefully dip the apples into the hot caramel sauce and turn to coat well. Scrape the excess against the side of the bowl and place on the prepared baking sheet. Refrigerate for at least 1 hour.

4. Chop the chocolate into small pieces and melt in the top of a double boiler or in the microwave. Stir well until smooth. (For microwave melting, break the chocolate into small pieces and place in a glass or ceramic bowl. Start on high for 1 minute, stir well, then continue to microwave in 10-second intervals until the chocolate is completely smooth.) Transfer the melted chocolate to a small but deep bowl and set aside for 5 minutes. Meanwhile, prepare the caramel apples for dipping. Lift them off the paper or foil and mold any uneven bits of caramel back onto the surface of the apples. Now, dip the apples into the melted chocolate, using a spoon if necessary to coat evenly. Let the excess drip off and dip the bottom of the apple only into a bowl of the chopped nuts, if using.

5. Place on the baking sheet again and refrigerate until set, at least 30 minutes. Before eating, let stand at room temperature for 5 to 10 minutes.

Dark Chocolate Pudding

MAKES 4 SERVINGS Most of us probably think of pudding as coming from a box. We add some milk, bring it to a boil (or sometimes in the case of instant, merely whisk it together), and we've got pudding. Today, most kids no doubt assume it comes straight from the tub in the dairy section of the supermarket. Actually, homemade pudding was a staple for generations, before processed foods arrived on the scene. Traditional "cornstarch" puddings were popular and easy ways to serve up a quick dessert only a couple of generations ago. My grandmother used to make an Italian version she called *crema*, a vanilla pudding studded with citron and chocolate chips. Given the fact that homemade pudding doesn't take that much longer to make than the box variety, it's surprising more people don't cook their own. There is surely nothing to match the warm and creamy consistency of a homemade chocolate pudding. With very few ingredients, it is a snap to make and, once tasted, you will be wondering how you were ever able to eat the tub variety. For all you chocolate fans out there, I have included some extra good quality chocolate at the end for added richness and a gourmet touch. Serve warm or chilled with a dollop of whipped cream and savor the lusciousness that homemade pudding has to offer.

1½ cups sugar

½ cup unsweetened cocoa powder

⅓ cup cornstarch

¼ teaspoon salt

2 cups milk

2 cups light cream

8 ounces good quality semisweet or bittersweet chocolate, chopped

1. In a large saucepan, whisk together the sugar, cocoa powder, cornstarch, and salt. Add the milk and whisk to combine well. Over medium heat, whisk in the light cream and continue to whisk constantly until the mixture comes to a boil and thickens. Switch to a wooden spoon and, stirring constantly, allow to boil for 1 minute, taking care not to scorch the bottom of the saucepan. Reduce the heat if necessary. After 1 minute, remove from the heat and add the chopped chocolate. Stir with the wooden spoon until all the chocolate is melted and the pudding is thick and smooth.

2. Transfer to a large dessert dish or individual dishes (four 1-cup size or eight ½-cup size) and either cover with plastic wrap (to prevent a skin from forming) or let cool uncovered (for skin formation), depending on your preference. Serve warm or chilled.

Shortcut Chocolate Mousse with Fresh Raspberries

MAKES 4 SERVINGS Chocolate mousse equals total chocolate indulgence to most, but this simplified version, devoid of egg yolks and combined with the wondrously healthy raspberry will satisfy a desire for decadence without too much guilt.

Choose an excellent quality plain chocolate, preferably dark and high in cocoa content. Because this recipe contains raw egg whites, read up on using them in recipes, if it is a concern to you (see page 172). Consider making serving-size portions in one-cup plastic containers with lids to take on

the road, but be sure to have a refrigerator available for chilling until ready to eat.

4 ounces bittersweet or semisweet chocolate, broken into pieces, setting aside a small piece for garnish

½ cup heavy or whipping cream

2 large egg whites

1 cup fresh raspberries

1. In the top of a double boiler over simmering water (or in the microwave), melt the chocolate. Transfer to a medium-size mixing bowl and allow to cool for 10 to 15 minutes, stirring occasionally.

2. In another medium-size mixing bowl using an electric mixer, whip the cream to soft peaks. Wash the beaters thoroughly and dry well. In a third medium-size mixing bowl, beat the egg whites until stiff.

3. All at once, add the egg whites and whipped cream to the melted chocolate and vigorously whisk until completely blended, about 1 minute.

4. In a 1-quart serving dish or individual serving dishes, layer the mousse with the raspberries. Begin with a little of the mousse, sprinkle with a few raspberries, top with more mousse, then more raspberries, finishing with a smooth topping of mousse. Grate the reserved chocolate piece on the medium-sized side of a cheese grater onto the top for a decorative garnish. Cover with plastic wrap and chill at least 2 hours before serving.

Recovery Note: Restaurants will sometimes add brandy or a fruited liqueur to their chocolate mousse. Check with the waiter before ordering.

White Chocolate Bump Bark

Chocolate bark comes in many shapes and varieties. Popular at holiday times, it can be studded

(continued on page 75)

Your Life in a Box of Chocolates

If life is indeed like a box of chocolates, then it pays to read the labels to know what you might be getting. Chocolates laced with liqueurs and other types of alcohol are not uncommon, although, in general, many of the alcohol additions, especially to your average drugstore chocolate box, are in the form of extracts or flavorings. Still, containing 35 percent alcohol by volume and being reminiscent in taste of rum, brandy, or whiskey, these sweets can readily pose triggers by sparking off brain-cell recognition. Cherry cordials and bottle-shaped chocolates filled with booze are more obvious about being laden with alcohol. However, other subtler flavors may go unnoticed at first, surprising us with a quick reaction by our olfactory and taste senses as they perk up to this familiar substance. Again, reading labels is the only way to do your detective work and, after a while, you'll be able to recognize potential culprits quite readily. For example, Irish coffee- or crème-flavored chocolates will pretty much guarantee a dose of whiskey or a facsimile, while piña colada just might contain some rum flavoring. Expensive gourmet chocolate shops are more likely to lace their goodies with real booze, especially chocolate truffles, and usually it will be apparent by the name, such as dark chocolate rum truffle. Recently, some manufacturers have added chardonnay or merlot to their chocolates, reflecting the popularity of fine wine tasting. I suppose that microbrewed beers in chocolate vessels are not far behind!

Since we can't always be as vigilant as we may want, and if it's true that "you never know what you're gonna get," a quick remedy for a mistaken bite of alcohol-laced chocolate is the old discreet napkin trick, followed by replacing the taste in your mouth with something else that is strong flavored—a gulp of coffee or soda or a bite of some other dessert offering—to help drown out the taste. Reading those diagram inserts that come in most chocolate boxes that we tend to toss in the trash just might save you from an experience like this.

By the way, many chocolate products list something called "chocolate liquor" as an ingredient. This is a complete misnomer and has nothing to do with alcohol. Rather, it is the term used for the pure essence of chocolate derived from the cocoa bean before it is processed and refined into its final chocolate product.

(continued from page 73)

with nuts, dried fruit, and even cookie pieces. This recipe calls for white chocolate, which is not really chocolate at all, as it contains no chocolate liquor (a misnomer that means essence of chocolate), only cocoa butter, but provides a wonderful venue for the dark chocolate-covered nuts and raisins, which "bump" the surface. If you can find a good quality bridge mix, use that for the chocolate-covered nuts. I like to use almonds, rather than peanuts, although they can certainly be included if you prefer. I have even seen chocolate-covered soy nuts and walnuts, which would work nicely. Be sure to let this harden well in the fridge before breaking it into "bark" pieces. For those who prefer real chocolate rather than white, you can use the same amount of dark or milk chocolate for the bark.

> 1 pound good quality white chocolate,
>   chopped
> 1½ cups chocolate-covered nuts, such as
>   almonds, filberts, cashews, or pecans
> ½ cup chocolate-covered raisins or cranberries

1. Melt the chopped white chocolate in the top of a double boiler over gently simmering water, stirring occasionally until completely smooth, 4 to 5 minutes. Line a rimmed baking sheet with a piece of parchment paper or wax paper cut to fit. When the chocolate is melted, remove it from the heat and allow it to sit for a few minutes.

2. When the chocolate is still warm to the touch but not hot, add the chocolate-covered nuts and raisins and fold into the chocolate with a rubber spatula. Pour the entire mixture onto the prepared baking sheet and spread evenly with the spatula. "Bumps" of the larger nuts will appear and should be distributed evenly throughout. Place another piece of parchment or wax paper over the spread mixture and lightly press down.

3. Refrigerate the baking sheet for at least 1 hour, preferably overnight. Remove the paper and cut or break into bark pieces. Store in an airtight container in the refrigerator for up to 2 weeks.

Chef's Note: *For an attractive marbleized effect, melt a small milk or dark chocolate bar and drizzle over the white chocolate bump layer while it is still warm. Use the tip of a sharp knife to create swirled designs before refrigerating as above.*

The Chocolate Monster Trail Mix

MAKES ABOUT 5 SERVINGS Chocolate cravings that strike us on the road, particularly when we are unprepared, can often lead us to make poor snack choices. The all-too-convenient convenience store may end up being our downfall when we pop in to purchase something else and are faced with display after display of candy bars. Mindless grabbing and munching of these unhealthy goodies will not only add empty calories and weight to our diets, they may even prevent us from eating a proper meal later on because we have allowed ourselves to overindulge and fill up on the wrong thing. If your chocolate monster requires periodic feeding, especially during the early weeks and months of Phase One, it's a good idea to be prepared. This trail mix will surely do the trick and is a great take-along snack for those ravenous urges. Measure out one-cup servings into zipper-locked bags and carry one along with you to pick from during the day when the craving hits. If you have trouble finding chocolate-covered roasted soybeans (also called soynuts), substitute unsalted roasted soybeans or another type of chocolate-covered nut or dried fruit.

> 1 cup dark chocolate-covered almonds
> 1 cup chocolate-covered roasted soybeans
> 1 cup chocolate-covered raisins or
>   dried cherries
> 1 cup peanut M&Ms
> One 4-ounce bar bittersweet chocolate,
>   broken into bite-size pieces

In a canister or large zipper-locked bag, combine all the ingredients and toss well. Store in a dry, cool place.

Warm Chocolate Cup

MAKES 1 SERVING Rich and decadently delicious, this treat, although technically a beverage, should be reserved for feeding the chocolate monster when his appetite demands pure luxury. Based on an Italian-style favorite, the experience of this warm chocolate cup has been described as like sipping on a melted chocolate bar. I will never forget the first time I tasted a *cioccolata calda*, or hot chocolate, in Italy, at the Caffé Rivoire in Florence, where these delicacies are served. As a student, it was a luxury to sit at this expensive outdoor café,

and no doubt the thrill of that alone added to the memory, but I have never tasted any hot chocolate again to match its creaminess and richness.

A little goes a long way here, so save this for a special treat when nothing else but chocolate will do. *"Con panna?"* (with whipped cream?), the waiter at Rivoire's used to ask. A dollop of whipped cream will surely take this over the top. Enjoy!

**2 ounces highest quality milk or semisweet
   chocolate, broken into pieces**
½ cup light cream
Whipped cream for garnish (optional)

1. In a small heavy saucepan over low heat, melt the chocolate pieces in the cream, whisking to a smooth consistency and heating through.

2. Pour into a small teacup, top with whipped cream, if desired, and serve immediately.

3 | *The Serenity of Soup*

Remedies That Nourish the Body, Mind, and Spirit

Everyone knows that soup is a comforting and soothing remedy when we're feeling under the weather. A bowl of grandma's chicken soup can be the cure for all ills, while a piping hot mug of tomato soup on a cold winter's day can warm and coddle your insides like nothing else. Sometimes when the flu hits, the only food we can realistically swallow is a cup of hot broth to nourish our tender tummies.

It is no surprise, then, that soup is the number one choice for the unwell, including those of us in the early stages of addiction recovery. Not only is its warmth consoling to our ailing bodies, the fluid it provides is of utmost importance in flushing out toxins that can plague our organs, making us feel weak and listless. Soup can also deliver a powerful concentration of important nutrients, especially when vegetables are cooked down and pureed into a smooth, drinkable tonic.

During the early weeks and months of recovery, a delicate stomach affects many people and dehydration can be a real issue. Turning to soups for nourishment and comfort is an obvious way to provide your body with the vitamins and minerals it needs without overstressing your digestive system. A steaming bowl of delicious soup can breathe life into our being and offer a moment of quiet serenity during this difficult time.

Phase One is an excellent time to begin mastering the basic techniques of good soup making. Contrary to popular belief, making soup is one of the easiest cooking skills to learn. Once you know the simple rules, you will be whipping up varieties to rival even Campbell's! And once tasted, a return to the canned version will be nearly impossible. So, follow me into the soup kitchen as we embark on our quest for creating the best medicine around.

Chicken Soup for Body, Mind, and Soul

Chicken soup has the ability to feed every aspect of our being. It provides vitamins and minerals and liquid replenishment for our bodies. It eases our troubled minds with warm memories and nourishes our soul with calmness and serenity. Scientists have finally confirmed what grandma knew all along—chicken soup *is* medicine! Once you have mastered the simple art of making chicken broth, you will be off and running toward creating a multitude of soup variations, from Chicken Noodle to Farmhouse Chicken with Wild Rice. However, it should be noted that although homemade broth is, of course, far superior to canned versions and bouillon cubes, it is by no means a necessary step in creating any of the chicken soup recipes that follow. Sometimes convenience and ease of preparation will take priority, especially when we lack energy and resolve. Using prepared ingredients like canned broth and stock cubes is a great way to save time and effort, so feel free to take advantage of these items when necessary.

Chicken Soup
An Essential Drug?

Two Israeli physicians have nominated chicken soup to the World Health Organization's "List of Essential Drugs," suggesting that, when made in the traditional fashion (not with synthetic, powdered mixes), this ancient elixir meets all four criteria of the list of what constitutes a medicine: it must be "evidence-based, efficient, flexible, and forward looking." Although no major controlled trials have been performed, they cite anecdotal evidence accumulated over the centuries and maintain that chicken soup "is here to stay as part . . . of traditional effective remedies."

Meanwhile, vegetarians needn't despair, as Dr. James Duke of the USDA has proclaimed that "an old-fashioned vegetable soup . . . is a more powerful anticarcinogen (cancer fighter) than any known medicine." All the more reason to grab your soup spoon and take your medicine.

Basic Broth for Chicken Soup

MAKES 2 TO 3 QUARTS This recipe for basic broth will provide you with the groundwork for all the chicken soups that follow, in addition to making a flavorful stock for use in other types of soups and recipes. Here are a few helpful hints to get you started:

- Be sure to remove the giblets from the cavity of the chicken, as well as any solid fat pieces that often appear near the neck and cavity.

- Rinse the chicken well, inside and out, with cold water.

- It is not necessary to skin your chicken. As the broth cooks, you may skim some of the puddles of fat from the top if you like. Otherwise, wait until your broth is done, strain it, refrigerate it for several hours or overnight, and simply remove the solid layer of fat that has formed on the top.

- Consider adding one or two chicken backs (often sold in the frozen meat section of your grocer) to boost the flavor of your broth.

One 3- to 4-pound chicken or the equivalent
     amount of bone-in chicken pieces
1 large onion, peeled and cut into quarters
2 medium-size carrots, peeled and cut into halves
1 large celery stalk, ends trimmed and cut in half
1 bay leaf
1 handful fresh parsley, including stems
Kosher salt and pepper to taste

1. Place the chicken, vegetables, and herbs in a large soup pot (8- to 12-quart size) and add enough cold water to cover. Slowly bring to a boil, reduce the heat to low, and allow to gently simmer, uncovered, for 30 minutes. During this time, use a ladle or large spoon to skim the surface of any scum that rises to the top. You may also remove any fat puddles that appear.

2. When the surface seems clear, add a generous pinch of kosher salt and a grinding of black pepper, partially cover the pot with a lid, and continue to simmer for at least 1½ hours and up to 3 hours. The longer it simmers, the more flavorful the broth will become.

3. When the vegetables are quite tender and the chicken is falling off the bone, remove them from the pot with a slotted spoon and set them aside in a large bowl. Strain the broth through a colander into a clean pot. You now have a delicious homemade chicken broth that can be sipped on its own for warmth and nourishment or made more substantial by adding back the cooked chicken and vegetables. Simply debone your chicken, pull it into bite-size pieces, and return it to the soup pot along with the carrots and celery, which have been cut into smaller pieces. Taste to see if your soup needs additional salt, if you desire, before serving.

Too Much Fat Got You Down?

Doctors acknowledge that delicate stomachs and excess fat are not agreeable partners. If you are finding it hard to "stomach" anything but a clear, fat-free broth, try these easy tips:

- Use skinned chicken pieces to make your broth. Simply pull the skin away from the flesh with the aid of a small sharp knife to cut any stubborn connective tissue or ask your butcher to do it for you.
- When straining your broth, place a paper towel or piece of cheesecloth that has been moistened with cold water over the inside of the colander surface before pouring.
- For the leanest of broths, start with equal parts fat-free canned chicken stock and water in your recipe and cook boneless, skinless chicken breasts instead of those on the bone. This will also reduce your simmering time by half.

If you prefer to save the broth at this time, pour it into storage containers and refrigerate or freeze for later use. Homemade chicken broth will keep in the fridge for several days or in the freezer for up to 3 months. Similarly, if you are not planning to use the cooked chicken immediately, debone and save for a delicious chicken salad (page 335) or quick dinner reheat. Save the cooked carrots too for a ready-made vegetable side dish.

Congratulations! You have just passed Chicken Soup 101 with flying colors. Now let's explore some delicious and easy variations.

Shortcut for Basic Broth for Chicken Soup: If you begin with a flavorful canned or cubed chicken broth, you will only need to simmer the pot until your chicken pieces and vegetables are cooked. To yield about 2 quarts of broth, combine 1 quart prepared broth and 1 quart water. Add your chicken pieces (boneless is fine here), carrots, and celery only, bring to a simmer, and cook until the chicken and vegetables are tender, 20 to 30 minutes. Strain and continue as directed above.

Chicken Noodle Soup: This is by far one of the easiest and quickest ways to use your Basic Broth for Chicken Soup. Simply cook 6 to 8 ounces egg noodles (thin, medium, or wide) according to the package directions, drain, and add to your hot broth along with the cut-up chicken and vegetables. Add 1 heaping tablespoon finely chopped fresh parsley leaves and, *voila*, you have the best chicken noodle soup on the planet! Are you fond of the look of that "red label" chicken noodle soup from childhood? Add the same quantity of cooked spaghetti or linguine instead and slurp your way to the comfort zone.

Chicken and Rice Soup: Here's another easy variation on your Basic Broth recipe. Add some substance with 1 to 2 cups cooked long-grain rice, such as Carolina or Uncle Ben's. Even simpler, save that leftover white or brown rice from yesterday's Chinese take-out and add it to your broth along with the cut-up chicken and vegetables. A heaping tablespoon of finely chopped fresh parsley or basil leaves would make a fine addition as well.

Farmhouse Chicken Soup with Wild Rice: Once you have made your Basic Broth, you can add nearly any type of cooked vegetable, as well as rice, beans, or pasta. This hearty version is another meal in itself and is perfect for those who are on the mend with big appetites. Serve with warm corn bread (page 255) slathered in butter and listen to your insides hum with con-

tentment. To 1 recipe Basic Broth for Chicken Soup, including the cut-up chicken and vegetables, add 1 large russet or Idaho potato, peeled and diced; 1/2 cup frozen or fresh green peas; 1 cup frozen or fresh green beans cut into 1-inch pieces; 1 medium-size zucchini, ends trimmed and diced; and 1/2 cup frozen, fresh, or canned corn kernels. Cook at a gentle simmer until all vegetables are tender. Add 1/2 cup wild rice, cooked according to package directions, and season with salt and pepper to taste.
Serve piping hot with big spoons!

Chef's Note: I particularly like carrots in this soup so you may want to add another one to two to your broth when cooking the vegetables. You could also substitute the wild rice with brown rice or, in a pinch, any leftover cooked white rice you may have on hand. Feel free to add any other cooked vegetables you might enjoy, such as turnips, okra, cabbage, or mushrooms. The more, the better!

Basic Chicken Broth Italian Style: At the earliest sign of illness in the family, Italian mothers and grandmothers across the globe launch head first into serious chicken soup making. Below are three popular versions that would make even Tony Soprano purr. But first we need to make a slight adjustment to the Basic Broth for Chicken Soup by adding 2 crushed garlic cloves, an additional bay leaf, and 2 sprigs fresh thyme to the other ingredients. For the truly traditional at heart, make sure the parsley you use is the Italian flat-leaf variety. What you will have is a broth with just the right amount of Italian flair to create the following soups.

***Stracciatella* (Chicken Broth with Eggs and Parmesan):** For simple tastes and delicate stomachs, this soup is the perfect solution. Protein is provided in the form of egg drops or "little rags" as *stracciatelle* translates from the Italian; this soup is a relative of the Chinese egg drop soup and the Greek version called *avgolemono*, which also adds a squeeze of fresh lemon juice. Make the Basic Chicken Broth Italian Style. Reserve your cooked chicken and vegetables for another use. Beat together 3 large eggs, 3 tablespoons finely grated Parmesan cheese, 2 tablespoons finely chopped fresh parsley leaves, and a pinch of nutmeg. Bring the strained broth to a bubbling simmer and slowly whisk in the egg mixture. After about a minute of whisking, the egg will be cooked and look thread-like. Season with salt and pepper to taste and serve with more Parmesan cheese to sprinkle on top.

***Tortellini in Brodo* (Stuffed Pasta in Broth):** This is another easy Italian version that is a bit more substantial than *stracciatella*. Simply cook 9 ounces dried, fresh, or frozen tortellini in Basic Chicken Broth Italian Style for the time specified on the package, but do not add any more salt at this time. You can choose from any number of flavored tortellini with delicious fillings, such as cheese, meat, chicken, spinach, or even a gourmet variety like porcini mushroom or sun-dried tomato. I recently came across lemon and black pepper tortellini with chicken, which worked exceedingly well. You could also use the larger tortelloni, if you prefer. An optional tasty and authentic addition would be 1 cup fresh or frozen peas, cooked in the broth along with the tortellini. When the peas and tortellini are cooked, season with salt and pepper to taste, add 1 heaping tablespoon finely chopped fresh parsley leaves, and don't forget to pass the freshly grated Parmesan cheese for sprinkling on top. Again, reserve your cooked chicken and vegetables for another use or add them to your finished soup, following the instructions of page 79, for a heartier version.

***Zuppa alla Nonna* (Grandma's Soup):** This "meal in itself" soup is the version that was most commonly served in my house when my grandmother tied on her apron and the one I associate most closely with "comfort in a bowl." Every element was carefully prepared and kept in its own separate pot on the stove so we could dish out our own combination. First, make 1 recipe Basic Chicken Broth Italian Style, including the deboned chicken and cut-up vegetables. Keep it in a saucepan on the stove at a very gentle simmer. Cook 1 cup small pasta, such as *tubettini*, *acini di pepe*, or *ditalini*, in a pot of boiling salted water according to the package directions. Drain, rinse under cold water, return to the pot, and moisten with a ladle or two of the broth. Keep over very low heat. In another large pot, heat 1 tablespoon extra virgin olive oil over medium heat and quickly cook 3 garlic cloves, peeled and minced, without browning, about 1 minute, stirring. Add 1 head escarole, leaves washed and sliced into ½-inch-wide strips, to the pot and quickly stir. Be careful, as some of the hot oil may splatter from the addition of the wet escarole. Season with a pinch of salt and a grinding of pepper, reduce the heat to low, cover, and cook about 20 minutes, stirring occasionally. The escarole is done when most of the liquid has evaporated and the tough stems are fork tender. Moisten with a ladle of broth and keep over very low heat. Invite your diners to assemble the soup combination that

Pastina Primer for Soup

In Italy, there is a shape and size of pasta to fit all culinary occasions, from *zuppa* (soup) to *dolce* (dessert). *Pastina* ("little pasta") is ideal for soups, especially delicate chicken and vegetable broths. Try using any of the following *pastina* to add a touch of variety to your homemade soups, or add them to any number of prepared soups that could use a little more substance:

- *ACINI DI PEPE* (PEPPERCORNS): This tiny *pastina* that resembles little peppercorns is an excellent addition to chicken soup, especially Italian versions (see *Zuppa alla Nonna*, page 81).

- *ALFABETI* (ALPHABET PASTA): These little letters and numbers will take you back to childhood in no time. Cooked alphabets can add substance and texture to a simple canned tomato soup when time is limited.

- *CONCHIGLIETTE* (LITTLE SEA SHELLS): Baby sister of the more popular medium and large shells, these go great in a thick lentil soup for a hearty one-dish meal.

- *ORZI* (BARLEY): Not to be confused with *risi*, the rice-shaped *pastina*, these barley-sized bits are often seen in salads and used as side dishes. Soups, however, are their natural venue, especially light broths and particularly as an addition to *stracciatella* (page 81).

- *STELLINE* (LITTLE STARS): These petite sparklers are most often used for the simple nursery meal of *pastina* with butter and hot milk (page 116), but also have their place in soups like Chicken with Stars and Brodo with Pastina.

- *FARFALLINE* (LITTLE BUTTERFLIES): Farfalle, the larger butterfly pasta, is often a popular shape for salads and main course pasta dishes, but these little cousins tend to be underutilized. They make a nice addition to just about any type of soup and are delicious on their own with a little butter and Parmesan cheese.

- *TUBETTINI* (LITTLE TUBES): An excellent choice for Italian chicken soup, this shape also does well as an addition to split pea or navy bean soup. The slightly larger *tubetti* is used in classic minestrone, while the slightly larger still *ditalini* is the hands down choice for *pasta e fagioli*, also known as pasta fazool (page 363).

works for them in large bowls, taking what they want from each of the pots on the stove. And, oh yes, make sure there is plenty of freshly grated Parmesan cheese for sprinkling on top and loaves of fresh crusty Italian bread. *Abbondanza!*

Chef's Note: Instead of an "assembly line" presentation, you can, of course, serve this soup in one very large pot with everything in it, if you prefer.

Italian Wedding Soup: You can use the *Zuppa alla Nonna* recipe to create the classic Italian wedding soup by adding little meatballs. Mix together 1 pound ground pork (or use a combination of beef, veal, and pork) with 1 large egg, beaten, and ⅔ cup dry Italian-seasoned bread crumbs. Form 1-inch-size meatballs and drop them into the simmering pot of broth before serving. When they rise to the top (10 to 12 minutes), they are done and you're ready to serve!

Jewish Chicken Soup with Matzo Balls: Italian cooks don't hold a monopoly on nourishing chicken soup. In fact, many would argue that nothing beats an authentic Jewish chicken soup with matzo balls. Although there are as many different versions and recipes as there are Jewish grandmothers, the following additions to Basic Broth for Chicken Soup, to make a Basic Broth for Jewish Chicken Soup, are pretty well agreed upon: 1 medium-size parsnip, peeled and cut in half, 1 medium-size turnip, peeled and cut in half, and 1 medium-size bunch fresh dill, including stems, all added along with the other ingredients. The parsnip and turnip are usually added for flavor only and do not end up in the soup bowl. However, if you happen to like them, as I do, you can cut them into bite-size pieces and include them along with the carrots and celery. The fresh dill gives this soup a wonderful aroma and really makes this broth

To Italians, Escarole Means "Food"

Escarole is actually a type of endive and the word derives from the Latin *esca*, meaning "food." It is also the root of the word *edere*, from which we get the words "edible" and "eat." Escarole can also be used as a slightly bitter salad green or cooked as a side dish vegetable. The dark green outer leaves are rich in calcium, iron, and vitamins A and C.

Where's the Schmaltz?

Before all you matzo ball lovers out there start calling me a *schmo* for leaving out the *schmaltz* (chicken fat), let me apologize for using vegetable oil instead but also remind you that many of us may need to keep our fat consumption to a minimum during this time. Although it's true that our systems tend to fluctuate in early recovery from digestive delicacy to ravenous hunger for sweets and fat, it's probably best to keep animal fat intake to a low roar, especially when a queasy stomach can plague us in the early days and weeks of Phase One. If, however, your digestion is up to it and you simply cannot imagine Jewish Chicken Soup without it, feel free to *schmear* your matzo balls with some *schmaltz* and enjoy! I understand from die-hard matzo ball soup fans that the addition of a little seltzer water in the matzo ball mix helps to lighten the load.

stand out from the other versions. Don't replace it with dillweed, because it won't come close to replicating the flavor. If you cannot find fresh dill, simply leave it out and add more fresh parsley. Once you have prepared your broth, make the matzo balls: Blend together ¼ cup vegetable oil, 4 large eggs, beaten, and

1 cup matzo meal in a medium-size mixing bowl. Add ¼ cup of the chicken broth or water to moisten and season with salt and pepper. Combine well, cover with plastic wrap, and refrigerate for 20 minutes. Bring 2 to 3 quarts salted water to a boil, then reduce the heat to a simmer. Wetting your hands with cold water to prevent sticking, shape the chilled matzo meal mixture in your palms into 1-inch balls (makes about 16) and drop them carefully, one by one, into the simmering water. Cover the pot and cook until the matzo balls have doubled in size and are well puffed, 30 to 40 minutes. Remove with a slotted spoon and transfer to a large pot that contains a few ladles of the hot chicken broth. To serve, spoon 2 to 3 matzo balls into individual soup bowls and ladle the hot chicken broth over them. Add some of the cut-up chicken and vegetables. Garnish with a sprig of dill and serve.

Asian Chicken Broth with Tender Greens: This broth, delicately scented with ginger, is a welcome medicinal choice for digestive systems under stress. Adjust the recipe for Basic Broth for Chicken Soup by eliminating the bay leaf

Making the Most of Canned Soup and Mixes

Too exhausted to tackle a recipe from scratch, but longing for the comfort of home-cooked flavor? Many canned soup varieties, as well as dry mixes, lend themselves to a little doctoring, resulting in greater nutritional content and better taste. Here are just a few ideas of how to embellish those ready-made, pantry staples:

- **CANNED CHICKEN, BEEF, OR VEGETABLE BROTH: We've already seen how utilizing canned chicken broth can make for a short-cut version of homemade chicken soup. Taken one step further, prepared broth can become instant homemade soup with the addition of cooked chicken, vegetables, rice, pasta, or even diced tofu. Use the lower sodium varieties to compensate for any seasoned ingredients you may be adding. And any of these flavored broths can be used to create noodle and vegetable soups in no time. Simply cook thin egg noodles or broken pieces of vermicelli in the broth, but be sure to add about ½ cup water, as the pasta will absorb a lot of the liquid and may result in an overly salty soup. Also consider adding a cup of frozen "soup mix vegetables" (containing onion, celery, carrot, potato, green beans, peas, and sometimes okra) available in your vegetable freezer section. Keep a bag of these handy and use them when you're too tired to chop and peel. They add nutritional substance to any simple canned broth or dry mix without the work.**

- **DRY CHICKEN NOODLE SOUP MIX: This was a favorite staple of my grandmother, who often cooked broccoli florets in the pot as the soup simmered. All the valuable nutrients are retained, while adding a delicious flavor and texture to the result. Cauliflower florets are** and parsley and adding one 3-inch piece fresh ginger, peeled and roughly chopped. Refrain from salting the broth and instead add a few dashes of soy sauce at the beginning. Later, you can add more soy sauce to taste if necessary. When the broth is done and strained, reserve the chicken and vegetables for another use, add a large handful of tender greens such as baby spinach or watercress (only the delicate leafy tips) to the pot, and simmer until they are barely wilted, about 2 minutes. A splash of toasted sesame oil added at the end will tie together the flavors beautifully.

Consider adding any of the following to your finished Asian Broth: 1 small bunch scallions, thinly sliced; 1 cup firm tofu cut into small dice; 1 cup reserved cooked chicken breast, thinly sliced; 8 ounces cooked Chinese or Japanese noodles; or a handful of shiitake mushrooms, stems removed and caps thinly sliced.

Recovery Note: Read soy sauce labels carefully, especially those called tamari, as alcohol, often in the form of rice wine, is sometimes added as a preservative.

similarly well suited to this soup, as is diced zucchini or a handful of fresh spinach leaves. You can also create instant *stracciatella* (see page 81) and boost your protein, by whisking in an egg beaten with 1 tablespoon Parmesan cheese. If you will be adding ingredients to any type of prepared dry soup and need to simmer it for a little longer than instructed on the box, it's a good idea to add about ½ cup extra water to compensate for the evaporation.

- CONDENSED TOMATO SOUP: This classic familiar can holds a multitude of possibilities. First, instead of adding water, try milk or soymilk for additional calcium and protein. And for a heartier version, add leftover cooked rice, *pastina*, noodles, or barley. Drain a can of diced or stewed tomatoes and add this to the pot for a chunky style soup. Cooked beans such as cannellini are also a great addition, as are chopped fresh herbs such as basil, oregano, or parsley.

- CONDENSED CREAMED SOUPS: Although never quite as good as homemade, these soups can fill in nicely when you are in the mood for something smooth and creamy. They are also ideal for using leftover chicken and vegetables. Consider adding chunks of roasted chicken and cooked wild rice to a reconstituted can of cream of chicken soup. Or embellish your canned cream of asparagus soup with leftover oven-roasted asparagus cut into pieces. Any ingredients you choose should be precooked and added at the end to simply warm them through. And, as with condensed tomato soup, you could add milk when water is called for, or soymilk in place of regular milk, for additional nutrition and richness.

- BOUILLON CUBES: A little hot water is all you need for instant broth. Available in beef, chicken, fish, and vegetable flavored, use these in place of canned versions for a quick soup base.

Vegetable Soups for Vitality

The creaminess of a pureed vegetable soup can be luxuriously soothing and a great way to provide essential nutrients for our often-neglected bodies. The technique is so simple you will be quite amazed. All you will need is one of the following pieces of equipment: a standard blender, a hand-held immersion blender, or a food processor. If you happen to have a food mill hiding in the cupboard feeling neglected, you can use that as well. My first choice for the smoothest soups would be the standard-type blender. Also handy is the hand-held immersion blender, which I often use when only pureeing some of the soup for a chunkier texture. Food processors will not ultimately "blend" your soups, but they can be useful in breaking down larger pieces of vegetables.

Many people mistakenly assume that "creamed" soups contain, of all things, cream. This is not necessarily the case, as many vegetables provide enough starch of their own to make a creamy blended consistency quite possible. I cannot deny that a bit of cream added at the end will make just about any soup that much richer and smoother, but it is by no means essential in most cases. The cream adds a certain amount of fat, which makes the soup appealing to the palate. This can also be duplicated somewhat if butter is used in the beginning to soften or "sweat" the vegetables. If you are having some trouble digesting fatty foods in the early stages of recovery, by all means, eliminate the butter and cream and work up to it as you feel better.

Creamed Vegetable Soup

MAKES 4 SERVINGS The purest and most delicate of soups I have made in this fashion was, sadly, for a client of mine whose alcoholism prohibited just about all forms of nourishment in the late stages. Creamed Vegetable Soup, packed with nutrients and absent of fat, was the only soup she was able to digest with any regularity. If you are feeling a bit delicate and are tired of clear broth, this is a good choice.

2 large carrots, peeled and roughly chopped
1 large russet potato, peeled and diced
2 celery stalks, ends trimmed, any strings removed, and chopped
2 leeks (white part only), ends trimmed, washed well, and chopped
2 medium-size zucchini, ends trimmed and diced
1 small butternut squash, peeled, seeded, and cubed
2 handfuls baby spinach, washed well
Salt to taste

1. Put all the vegetables in a large soup pot, add enough water to cover, season with a pinch of salt, and bring to a simmer over medium heat. Cook until all vegetables are fork tender, about 20 minutes.

2. Carefully ladle the hot soup into a blender, filling the container no more than halfway, and process until completely smooth. Transfer to a clean pot and continue in batches until all of the soup is blended. If too thick, add a little more water to get the desired consistency. Taste for salt and add if necessary. Serve merely warm, not piping hot.

Chef's Note: You can vary this recipe depending on the vegetables you have on hand, but avoid the cruciferous types, such as cabbage, cauliflower, and broccoli, if digestion is a problem, as their high insoluble fiber content can cause gas and bowel distress.

Quick and Flavorful Vegetable Stock

MAKES 2 QUARTS For those who prefer a vegetarian base for their soups, homemade vegetable stock is actually quick and simple to make. I have never been pleased with any of the canned or cubed vegetable broths I have come across, as they tend to be too intensely carrot or tomato flavored, and usually contain way too much sodium. This recipe results in a delicate broth and is a basic guideline for vegetable stock. However, you can add any number of vegetable trimmings to intensify the flavor. If you think that you will be making this stock on a regular basis, begin saving mushroom stems, onion ends, celery tops, parsley stems, tomato cores, and other typical throwaways in the refrigerator. When you have a good variety of ingredients collected, simply throw them in a pot, cover with water and simmer for 30 to 40 minutes. Strain and refrigerate as you would chicken broth, or freeze for up to 6 months.

2 medium-size carrots, peeled and sliced

1 large celery stalk, ends trimmed and sliced

1 large onion, peeled and quartered

1 large leek (white and green parts), trimmed, washed well, and sliced

2 large garlic cloves, peeled and roughly chopped

1 bunch fresh parsley, with stems, washed well

4 sprigs fresh thyme or 1 teaspoon dried thyme

1 bay leaf

1 teaspoon black peppercorns

1 cup mushroom stems (optional)

½ cup tomato trimmings (optional)

Pinch of kosher salt

1. Combine all the ingredients in a 4-quart pot and add just enough cold water to cover. Bring to a boil, reduce the heat to low, and allow to gently simmer for 30 to 40 minutes.

2. Strain the stock through a colander into a clean pot or storage container.

Classic Potato and Leek Soup

MAKES 4 TO 6 SERVINGS One of the most famous "creamed" soups is the French classic, potato and leek, also called vichyssoise when served cold and ultra creamy and smooth. It is the perfect version to learn the basic technique of blended soup making. After that, you will be able to substitute nearly any type of vegetable for the potatoes, to create every variation from cream of asparagus to cream of zucchini.

Using leeks as opposed to onions in creamed soups is really a matter of tradition and choice. Since the flavor is more subtle, most chefs prefer to use leeks in many creamed soup varieties to allow the "starring" vegetable to dominate, but onions can certainly be substituted if you like. In fact, when the sweet types of onions are in season, such as Vidalias, you may find them even more preferable to leeks.

Let's start with the basic technique and follow it up with some common variations as well as a few interesting and delicious vegetable combinations.

2 tablespoons unsalted butter

2 medium-size leeks (white part only), ends trimmed, washed well, and chopped

Small pinch of salt

8 cups low-sodium chicken or vegetable broth, canned or homemade (page 78 or left)

6 medium-size Idaho or russet potatoes, peeled and diced

½ cup heavy or light cream

Pepper to taste

2 tablespoons chopped fresh chives (optional)

1. In a heavy-bottomed soup pot, melt the butter over medium heat, then add the leeks, sprinkle with the salt (this will help to keep them from browning and enhance their flavor), and cook, stirring, until the leeks are soft and translucent, about 10 minutes. Do not brown.

2. Add the broth and potatoes, bring to a simmer, and allow to cook, uncovered, until the potatoes are fork tender, 25 to 30 minutes. Add the cream, stir to combine, and remove from the heat.

3. Carefully transfer the hot soup in batches to a blender and process until smooth. Transfer to a clean pot or soup tureen. If using an immersion blender, carefully puree in the soup pot to the desired smoothness. You can certainly leave pieces of potato and leek if you prefer a chunkier soup. If the consistency is too thick, add a little more broth, cream, milk, or water. Taste for salt and pepper and adjust as necessary. If using, add the chives, stir, and serve.

Chef's Note: For queasy stomachs, this soup can be made without butter and cream. Merely skip step 1, add the leeks with the potatoes to the liquid in step 2, and continue as directed, omitting the cream addition at the end. If you are up to it, consider adding a touch of milk or soymilk before blending for smoothness and a bit of calcium and protein. You can follow this advice for all of the creamed soups that follow.

Common Variations for Soothing Blended Soups There are many variations of creamy blended soups, limited only by the variety of vegetables in your market. Try making some of the versions below, following the steps in the Potato and Leek Soup recipe and substituting the named vegetable for the potatoes. If you are feeling creative and have the time to spare, try reserving some small pieces of the vegetable, such as broccoli florets, for a garnish and to add substance to your pureed soup. Cook the reserved vegetable pieces in boiling salted water until tender and add to the pureed soup at the very end. If you are only partially blending your soup with an immersion blender or food processor, you won't need to do this, as you will already have a more rustic consistency.

Quick Tip for Flavoring Blended Soups

Blended vegetable soups are well suited to this time-saving tip. Instead of using canned or homemade broth, simply add water, throw in a large bouillon cube, and wait to add any additional seasoning until later on.

Cream of Asparagus Soup: Use 1½ pounds fresh asparagus, woody, thick ends removed and stalks roughly chopped. Reserve ⅔ cup asparagus tips for your garnish, prepared as described above, if desired.

Cream of Broccoli Soup: Use 1 large head broccoli, stems trimmed and peeled, and cut into florets, reserving 1 cup bite-size florets for garnish, prepared as described above, if desired. Finish with a squeeze of lemon juice to enhance the broccoli flavor.

Cream of Carrot with Ginger: Use 1½ pounds carrots (7 to 8 medium-size carrots), peeled and sliced. Add a 2-inch piece fresh ginger, peeled and chopped, 2 teaspoons sugar, and a dash of ground cinnamon and nutmeg. One cup cooked brown or wild rice, added after blending, would make an excellent addition.

Cream of Cauliflower Soup: Use 1 large head cauliflower, leaves removed, stem trimmed and peeled, and cut into florets, reserving 1 cup small florets for garnish, prepared as described above, if using. For a tasty variation, use roasted cauliflower instead (see page 348 for instructions), reducing the quantity of liquid in the soup to 6 cups and simmer only a brief 10 minutes before blending. Reserve several of the lacy roasted cauliflower slices to top each serving bowl. Serve with plenty of fresh ground pepper. A tablespoon of shredded cheddar cheese on top would also make a fine addition before serving.

Cream of Celery Soup: Trim and roughly chop 1 bunch celery, reserving 2 stalks to dice and cook as garnish, if desired. Sometimes the outer stalks are particularly large and coarse, so you may need to peel the outside using a vegetable peeler. This is particularly recommended if you are only partially blending your soup. You can also reserve some of the feathery celery hearts to serve and munch on as a soup accompaniment. As a variation, replace half of the bunch of celery with 2 medium-size celery root (also called celery knob or celeriac), peeled and diced. The wonderful celery flavor and aroma that it adds is well worth the somewhat tedious peeling required. Use a sharp knife to cut away the bumpy exterior before dicing.

Old-Fashioned Cream of Tomato Soup: There are numerous methods for creating this classic comforting soup, from using only fresh, vine-ripened tomatoes to slow roasting plum tomatoes and processing them laboriously through a food mill. This version is by far the simplest, but is still enormously satisfying. Drain two 28-ounce cans plum tomatoes. Squeeze the seeds from each tomato, then chop and add to the soup pot with the broth. Increase the amount of cream at the end to $3/4$ cup and, when blended, serve piping hot in a large mug. For Classic Tomato and Rice Soup, add 1 cup cooked white or brown rice before serving. Some chopped fresh basil leaves would also be a nice addition.

Cream of Tomato and Fennel Soup: Try making a creamed soup using this unique licorice-scented vegetable, which is a natural partner for tomatoes. Fennel (also known as anise) has long been acknowledged as an effective aid to digestion, a welcome characteristic in ingredients used for early recovery cooking. Roughly chop 1 fennel bulb, reserving some of the feathery tips for garnish, and cook, stirring, in the butter along with the leeks to release its powerful fragrance and flavor. If the outside stalks of the bulb seem a bit stringy, you may want to peel them a little as you would celery, especially if you are only partially blending your soup.

Creamy Autumn Blend Soup: Replace the potatoes with 1 large butternut squash, peeled, seeded, and diced, and one 15-ounce can unsweetened pumpkin puree. Add $1/2$ teaspoon ground ginger and $1/4$ teaspoon ground nutmeg to the pot while cooking. Garnish with purchased croutons or try making Toasted Rye Croutons (below) for an excellent accompaniment. This is a warming and sweet creamed soup, particularly welcome on a cool fall day, but delicious any time of year.

Toasted Rye Croutons

Unlike many traditional croutons, which are baked with oil or butter, these are merely toasted and well suited to soaking up your delicious and creamy soup without the added grease.

Cut one unsliced rye bread loaf (seeded or unseeded) into one-inch cubes and bake in a preheated 400 degree oven on an ungreased baking sheet until lightly golden and dry, 10 to 15 minutes. Shake the sheet occasionally to evenly brown. Let them cool completely before storing. They will keep for several days in an airtight container and make nice additions to salads as well.

Quick and Easy Country Style Vegetable Soup

MAKES 4 TO 6 SERVINGS If you enjoy the type of vegetable soup that demands a fork, then this one's for you! Large chunks of vegetables with minimal liquid are the key to its heartiness and satisfaction. Feel free to create your own rendition with your favorite vegetables once you have mastered this easy technique.

> 1 tablespoon unsalted butter
> 1 tablespoon olive oil
> 1 medium-size onion, peeled and diced
> 1 celery stalk, ends trimmed and sliced
> 2 medium-size carrots, peeled and sliced
> ½ small head (about 1 pound) white or Savoy cabbage, tough core removed and roughly chopped
> 8 cups low-sodium chicken or vegetable broth, canned or homemade (page 78 or 87), or water
> One 8-ounce can chopped or diced tomatoes
> 1 large Idaho or russet potato, peeled and cubed
> 1 medium-size zucchini, ends trimmed and cut into ½-inch-thick rounds
> 1 small can cream-style corn
> ½ cup frozen peas
> ½ cup frozen lima beans
> Salt and pepper to taste

1. In a heavy-bottomed soup pot, melt the butter with the olive oil over medium heat. Add the onion and cook, stirring, until soft, about 5 minutes. Add the celery and carrots and continue to cook, stirring, for another 2 to 3 minutes. Add the cabbage, stir well, and cook another 2 minutes. Add the broth and tomatoes, increase the heat to high, and bring to a simmer. Add the remaining vegetables and allow to simmer until all the vegetables are fork tender, 15 to 20 minutes.

2. Using a hand-held immersion blender, briefly pulse 3 or 4 times, just to tie together all the ingredients and add a bit of thickness. You can also achieve this consistency by taking 1 cup of your cooked soup, vegetables and all, blending it briefly in a food processor or blender, and returning the puree to the soup pot. Taste for seasoning and serve in large soup bowls with some crusty French or sourdough bread as an accompaniment.

Easy Minestrone: With a few minor changes, this soup can become an excellent minestrone. Use Italian-style canned diced tomatoes, or add 1 teaspoon dried oregano to the regular tomatoes. Replace the corn with ½ cup dry *ditalini* pasta to cook with the vegetables, stirring often and adding a touch of water if the soup becomes too thick. Replace the peas and lima beans with 1 cup drained and rinsed canned kidney beans, chickpeas, cannellini beans, or a combination of these, and add them during the last 10 minutes of cooking. Finish with 1 heaping tablespoon grated Parmesan or Romano cheese, stir well and serve.

Chunky Vegetable Beef or Hearty Turkey with Vegetable Soup: Simply add leftover diced cooked beef (a tender cut) or turkey to your finished soup to create an almost stew-like consistency. For added beef flavor, substitute canned low-sodium beef broth for the chicken broth. Although requiring a bit more time and effort, you can also make a deliciously flavorful vegetable beef soup by browning 1 pound cubed stewing beef in the butter and oil before adding the onion and proceeding as directed, allowing additional cooking time (1 to 1½ hours) for the beef to become tender and release its flavor before adding the rest of the vegetables. This version may require the addition of a little more liquid while cooking.

Vidalia Onion Soup with Whole-Grain Fontina Toasts

MAKES 4 SERVINGS French onion soup is a classic favorite. Although it does not always call for alcohol, traditional versions will often include at least ½ cup sweet white wine, port wine, or even hard cider. This subtle combination of sweet and sour is a trademark of the soup. In this recipe, by using Vidalia onions, which are wonderfully sweet by themselves (especially when caramelized), the need for added sugar (in the form of alcohol) is eliminated, while a splash of cider vinegar will balance out the flavors.

The melting properties and flavor of Fontina cheese are perfect for this dish, but mozzarella could also be used, as well as the classic Gruyère or

Tips on Storing and Freezing Your Homemade Soups

Soups are one of the best remedies for you at this time, and you'll be grateful that you have a good supply on hand for those days when you are not feeling up to par and don't relish the idea of cooking. Here are some important tips on storing and freezing:

- **THE COOL DOWN:** It is never a good idea to put hot soup in the fridge or freezer, as it can drastically alter the storage temperature and possibly spoil other food products. Instead, use this quick cool down method. Place your soup pot in the sink, surrounded by ice water. Stir occasionally and transfer to storage containers when the soup is lukewarm or cool.

- **THE COLD STORAGE:** Meat- and chicken-based soups will keep, refrigerated and tightly covered, for three to four days without any danger of spoilage. Vegetable-based soups, without dairy, may be kept up to one week. Any soup that has cheese, milk, or cream should be consumed within three days.

- **THE FREEZE OUT:** Soups freeze best and retain their flavor in small to medium-size, airtight containers. In general, three to four months would be my limit for all but dairy-based soups, which should be consumed within one month. Some argue that creamed soups should never be frozen as the consistency is spoiled. However, I have found that a slow defrost and reheat will greatly alleviate this problem, as will whisking while reheating. Similarly, soups that contain a large proportion of pasta, rice, or potatoes are usually not recommended for freezing; however, a soup like minestrone, with a small amount of pasta, for example, would be fine.

- **THE WARM UP:** Broth-based soups are easily reheated or defrosted in the microwave, but soups that contain dairy, such as creamed soups, will do better with a stove-top reheat over a low flame to avoid breakdown. If the consistency is too thick, add a touch of milk or water and whisk in while simmering.

Swiss. Cheese provides the protein here, so the soup, served with a crisp green salad, can be a complete meal in itself. I like to serve the toasts on the side for dipping into the flavorful broth.

2 tablespoons unsalted butter

2 tablespoons light olive oil

4 medium-size to large Vidalia onions (or another sweet onion variety), peeled and thinly sliced

Salt and pepper to taste

2 garlic cloves, peeled and minced

1 teaspoon dried thyme

Splash of cider vinegar

4 cups canned low-sodium beef broth

8 slices whole-grain baguette (½ inch thick)

1 cup shredded Fontina cheese

1. In a large skillet (preferably not nonstick, as this will delay the caramelizing somewhat), heat the butter and olive oil over medium heat together until the butter melts. Add the onions and sprinkle with salt and pepper. Stir well to coat, then cook over medium to high heat, stirring quite often. The onions will begin to soften and brown (naturally caramelize) as they cook. This may take up to 30 minutes or more. Stir more often as the browning process begins to prevent sticking. Once the onions are brown, add the garlic and thyme, stir, and cook another 2 to 3 minutes.

2. Sprinkle the vinegar over the onion mixture and, with a wooden spoon, scrape the bottom of the pan to get up all the accumulated caramelized bits. Transfer the contents of the skillet to a soup pot and add the beef broth. Over medium heat, bring to a low boil and simmer for 10 to 15 minutes. Give a generous grinding of pepper and taste for salt. Set aside.

3. Lightly toast both sides of the baguette slices on a baking sheet under a preheated broiler. Sprinkle equal amounts of the shredded cheese over each and return to the broiler until the cheese begins to melt, 1 to 2 minutes. Immediately serve the toasts with the ladled soup.

Cooking with Alcohol and Playing with Fire

The Proof Is in the Pudding

We hear it every day. Chefs on cooking shows and epicurean television hosts repeat it consistently: *"The alcohol will burn off."* This simple assumption has led many a good-intentioned cook, recovering alcoholic, addict, and their family members to unknowingly "play with fire" because, in reality, the original amount of alcohol contained in a recipe that could end up on your plate may be as much as 85 percent.

In 1992, a group of food and nutrition scientists published an article in the *Journal of the American Dietetic Association* that was the result of a study contracted by the United States Department of Agriculture (USDA) in order to determine alcohol retention in food preparation for the National Nutrient Data Bank. Their goal was to calculate the amount of alcohol that remained—if any—after several types of cooking methods were employed so that dietitians would know exactly how many energy units (calories) the alcohol contributed to the final calorie count of a prepared meal.

For example, if we wanted to know how many calories there are in a serving of, say, chicken marsala, we would simply add together the calories contained in the marsala, the chicken, and the other few ingredients, *after* cooking. This is an important distinction because cooking and heating very often change the final energy count of food. Although dietitians already knew the calorie content of thousands of cooked food ingredients, as well as the number of calories in alcoholic beverages poured straight from the bottle, they did not really know how cooking affected the final energy value of alcohol. The hypothesis that alcohol evaporated during cooking had never been validated by actual experimentation. Ironically, the purpose of their research had absolutely nothing to do with the study of alcoholism, addiction, or recovery. In fact, in the words of our friendly food scientists, this study was prompted by ". . . an increased interest in the use of wines, liqueurs, and distilled spirits. . . . to fulfill the needs of 'nouvelle' and 'light' cuisines. . . ."

The researchers selected six different recipes that called for various types of alcoholic beverages and studied the extent of alcohol loss in each one. The preparation methods they used included adding alcohol to a hot sauce, flaming, oven baking, simmering for a short time, and simmering for a long time. They also tested the effects of overnight refrigeration, without any heat application at all.

They began by preparing a sauce using Grand Marnier, an orange-flavored liqueur. The alcohol was added to a boiling hot liquid and no further cooking took place. This is a very common method of flavoring sauces and is similar to the way that many brandy, port, and madeira sauces are made. Chefs know that if these beverages are added too early, their flavors will dissipate. Consequently, they are always included at the very final stage of a sauce's preparation. The results of the Grand Marnier sauce, when tested for alcohol retention, indicated that between 83 percent and 85 percent of the original alcohol remained. Depending on how heavy-handed a chef might be with the bottle, we could be talking about a whole lot of alcohol here—not too different from grabbing the bottle yourself and taking a quick swig. The other tests were no less surprising.

When alcohol spends hours cooking away in a dish like pot roast, the study showed that even 2½ hours of simmering retained between four and six percent of the alcohol used, in this case, a Burgundy wine. Likewise, an orange chicken Burgundy recipe, which simmered for a briefer 10 minutes, retained up to 60 percent of its original alcohol. And a baked dish of scalloped oysters made with dry sherry retained between 41 percent and 49 percent.

Surprisingly, in the brandy Alexander pie, which was loaded with liqueur and never actually cooked, the alcohol content ended up being *less* potent than the Grand Marnier sauce, which was subjected to heat. By being exposed to the air and kept under refrigeration overnight, some of its alcohol managed to evaporate, but it still tallied in with a whopping 70 percent to 77 percent. The scientists determined that eating one piece of their pie was the equivalent of drinking about a third of a glass of wine!

Of particular interest was the result of the cherries jubilee recipe, which entailed the setting alight of the brandy. You know the technique—that fancy flaming thing that chefs love to do in front of an audience. The theatrics of flaming alcohol, or flambéing, is no doubt the main reason that the myth of alcohol evaporation has persisted. When we see such a rigorously burning, "flamboyant" spectacle, it's hard to believe that *anything* could be left in the aftermath, never mind the booze you just poured in the pan. But, in fact, flambéing, which is merely the result of alcohol vapor combustion, retains nearly 78 percent of a dish's original alcohol content, a formidable amount.

The researchers concluded, "The assumption that all alcohol is evaporated when heat is applied during cooking is not valid." Their results were submitted to the USDA, which contracted the study in the first place, and the facts and figures found their way to the USDA Table of Nutrient Retention Factors, Release 4, in 1998. It was added to their online data sometime in 1999 and now anyone can access this information on the Internet at the USDA web site. The nutrient table also lists the retention factors for 18 important vitamins and minerals in hundreds of foods and tells us the different percentages that remain of each after various methods of cooking, just as in the alcohol study. Printing out the table is easy to do and you may find it helpful as a reference in your kitchen when trying to determine the advantages of certain cooking methods over others. It will also be handy to wave around when skeptics question the results of the alcohol study.

Incidentally, at the inaugural luncheon honoring George W. Bush, tasters were on hand in the kitchen, not only to ensure that the new president was not being poisoned, but also to make sure that the mushrooms that accompanied the tenderloin of beef were not cooked in wine for the teetotalling Texan. Apparently, they had read the study.

Bowls of Sustenance: Bean- and Grain- Based Soups

Some of the most satisfying and heartiest soups around are those made from the inexpensive, humble, and versatile bean. A member of the plant family called legumes, which also include lentils, peas, and soybeans, these little guys pack a punch in the nutrition department and are an irreplaceable staple in the vegetarian diet. However, research has shown that beans and all legumes are a healthy addition to any diet and may help manage blood cholesterol as well as glucose levels. They are high in protein, fiber, and the B vitamins and can contribute to a steady release of energy in the body due to their slow metabolizing rate.

Grains, which are also great providers of sustenance, can be found in the familiar mushroom barley soup and are often added, in the form of rice and corn, to chicken-based broths. The less familiar wheat berry makes a hearty European-style soup and is delicious when added to broths where barley or rice is called for.

Taking advantage of these nutritious ingredients will be beneficial to our health and well-being at this early time in our recovery, not to mention making our soup choices even more tempting and delicious!

Hearty Split Pea Soup with Ham

MAKES 4 TO 6 SERVINGS One of everybody's favorite soups is split pea with (or without) ham and surprisingly it is one of the easiest soups to make. Split peas do not require presoaking, as some legumes and beans do, so the preparation time is very brief. The addition of a ham bone, if you happen to have one, is an excellent enhancement, but not necessary. You could also use a smoked ham hock instead, if you like its intensity of flavor. Whatever you choose, consider adding the diced pieces of ham at the final stage, as they are a rich source of thiamine (vitamin B_1), one of several important nutrients that alcohol can deplete.

1 tablespoon unsalted butter
1 tablespoon olive oil
1 medium-size onion, peeled and diced
1 medium-size carrot, peeled and diced
1 celery stalk, ends trimmed and diced
8 cups low-sodium chicken or vegetable broth, canned or homemade (page 78 or 87)
One 16-ounce bag dried green split peas, picked over and rinsed
1 ham bone, trimmed of fat, or smoked ham hock
One ¼-pound piece deli ham or ham steak, diced
Salt and pepper to taste

1. Melt the butter with the olive oil in a soup pot over medium heat, then cook the onion, carrot, and celery, stirring until softened, 8 to 10 minutes. Add the broth, split peas, and ham bone, stir well, and bring to a simmer. Allow to cook until the split peas are tender to the bite, 45 to 50 minutes.

2. Turn off the heat, remove the ham bone, add the diced pieces of ham, and let sit for 5 minutes. Taste for the addition of salt and pepper. (Since ham contains a lot of sodium, it is wise to wait until the flavors marry before adding any salt.) You may also pulse the soup briefly with a hand-held immersion blender (or puree a cup or two of the finished soup in a blender, returning this to the pot) for a creamier consistency. Serve with croutons or crackers, if desired.

Recovery Note: *Watch for the addition of sherry in many gourmet versions of split pea soup.*

Beans and Grains

The Perfect Low GI Foods

When various beans and grains were tested for a glycemic response and ultimate Glycemic Index rating, they fared extraordinarily well. On a scale of 0 to 100, with pure glucose equaling 100, these common soup ingredients were all 55 or less, which means they are slowly absorbed by the body, have a prolonged metabolic release, and affect blood sugar minimally.

Soy beans	18
Barley	25
Kidney beans	27
Lentils	30
Black beans	30
Split peas	32
Chick peas	33
Navy beans	38
Hominy	40
Wheat berries	41
Sweet corn	55
Brown rice	55

Lentil Soup with Swiss Chard

MAKES 4 TO 6 SERVINGS Lentils are another healthy legume that contributes to steady energy release in the body and is a good source of calcium and iron. Swiss chard (with stalks of green, red, or sometimes yellow or orange) is also a great provider of these nutrients, as well as magnesium, a mineral that is vital for effective nerve and muscle functioning and one in which alcoholics are usually deficient. Consequently, this soup delivers a powerful punch of good nutrition with every spoonful. If you would like to substitute or add other greens, such as spinach, collards, or kale, feel free to create your own nutritious combination.

Be sure to rinse and pick over your dried lentils before adding them to the pot. They are notorious for keeping company with tiny little pebbles that must be discarded. I find the brown common lentil is best for soup making, although there are other varieties you may discover, such as the Egyptian red or orange lentil, which I use in curry dishes, and the tiny French *de puy* lentils, the crème de la crème of pulses (dried legumes), which I reserve for a starring role and often use to make lentil salad or pilaf.

2 tablespoons olive oil
1 medium-size onion, peeled and diced
1 celery stalk, ends trimmed and diced
1 garlic clove, peeled and minced
1 bunch Swiss chard, stems removed, leaves washed, and roughly chopped
1 cup drained canned chopped tomatoes
2 cups dried brown lentils, picked over and rinsed
8 cups low-sodium chicken or vegetable broth, canned or homemade (page 78 or 87), or canned beef broth (see page 104)
1 bay leaf
1 teaspoon ground cumin
Salt and pepper to taste

1. In a heavy-bottomed soup pot, heat the olive oil over medium heat. Add the onion and celery and cook, stirring, until softened, about 5 minutes. Add the garlic and cook, stirring, another minute. Add the Swiss chard and stir well to coat. Add the remaining ingredients, bring to a simmer, and cook until the lentils are soft but not mushy, about 25 minutes.

2. A few quick pulses of a hand-held immersion blender will tie this soup together or puree a small amount in a blender or food processor and return to the pot. Thin out with additional broth or water if necessary and taste for seasoning before serving.

Variation: You can turn this soup into a hearty meal by simply adding 3 cooked and sliced Italian sausages, sweet or hot, according to your preference, and 1 cup small pasta (shells or *ditalini* are excellent choices) that have been cooked in salted boiling water following the package directions. Serve with a drizzle of extra virgin olive oil.

The Painful Truth About Lentils

Sadly, if you are suffering from gout or gouty arthritis, painful joint conditions often associated with heavy alcohol consumption, you may want to pass on the lentil soup. A certain group of proteins called purines, to which lentils belong, and which also includes organ meats, sardines, anchovies, and some shellfish, is conducive to raising levels of uric acid in the blood, sometimes bringing on acute attacks or exacerbating an already existing problem. Drinking plenty of water can help in preventing crystal deposits from forming, while eliminating caffeine may ultimately reduce uric acid levels. Check with your doctor about temporarily eating a low-purine diet if you experience a bout of this common and painful illness.

Spicy Black Bean Soup with Cilantro Sour Cream

MAKES 4 TO 6 SERVINGS   Black beans are one type of dried beans that benefits from an overnight soak. Simply place them in a pot of cold water and let them soften. Drain and rinse before cooking. If you are pressed for time, bring the pot of beans and water to a boil, turn off the heat, and allow to sit for an hour. This will also soften them and reduce an otherwise long cooking time. Drain and rinse before using.

This soup is a favorite request of many of my clients in recovery. There is something about the

spiciness that seems, ironically, to relieve anxiety and stress. In addition to affecting our neurochemicals (see Craving Spicy Foods?, page 35), I would suspect that, as we begin to repair our bodies, we reawaken our dormant taste buds and suddenly crave foods that stimulate our palates. It is a good sign that we are on our way to better health.

If you are not sure of the heat intensity of your jalapeño peppers, be sure to taste a small piece before deciding how much to add. Remember that much of the heat resides in the seeds, so if you would prefer a slightly less "potent" soup, by all means remove them. Also take care when chopping hot peppers in general, as the juice is easily transferred from your hands to whatever you may touch next, possibly irritating your eyes. Always wash your hands, knife, and cutting board well after chopping hot peppers.

2 tablespoons olive oil

1 medium-size onion, peeled and diced

1 celery stalk, ends trimmed and diced

1 medium-size green bell pepper, seeded and diced

2 garlic cloves, peeled and minced

1 jalapeño, or more to taste, finely chopped (see headnote)

2 cups dried black beans (also called turtle beans), picked over and rinsed

8 cups low-sodium chicken or vegetable broth, canned or homemade (page 78 or 87)

1 smoked ham hock

1 bay leaf

1 tablespoon ground cumin

2 teaspoons chili powder

1 teaspoon ground coriander

1 cup sour cream

2 tablespoons chopped fresh cilantro leaves

Juice of ½ lime

Dash of Tabasco sauce (optional)

Salt and pepper to taste

1. Heat the olive oil over medium heat in a large soup pot. Add the onion, celery, and bell pepper

and cook, stirring, until softened, about 10 minutes. Add the garlic and jalapeño and cook, stirring, another 2 minutes. Add the broth, beans, ham hock, bay leaf, cumin, chili powder, and coriander and bring to a low simmer. Reduce the heat to medium-low and allow the beans to cook until tender, when they are soft on the inside and beginning to fall apart. Add water if necessary and stir to prevent sticking. This may take anywhere from 1 to 2 hours.

2. While the beans are cooking, mix the sour cream and cilantro together in a small bowl. Set aside in the refrigerator, covered with plastic wrap.

3. When the beans are cooked, remove the pot from the heat. Discard the ham hock and bay leaf and, with a hand-held immersion blender, pulse 4 or 5 times to cream some of the soup. Alternatively, you can remove 2 cups of the beans, puree them in a blender or food processor, and return them to the soup pot. Stir well to combine.

4. Just before serving, add the lime juice and Tabasco, if using, and season with salt and pepper. Serve with a dollop of the cilantro sour cream on top.

Chef's Note: For those who crave a really spicy soup with a little more substance, consider adding a diced chorizo (spicy Spanish sausage) when sautéing your onion, celery, and bell pepper. Cajun andouille sausage could also be used or even the more common Italian pepperoni will serve to spice up your soup!

Recovery Note: Many chefs will add sherry to black bean soup, although I must admit I have never found it to be particularly appealing, even before recovery. The smoked ham hock adds flavor enough, while the fresh lime juice and Tabasco sauce added just before serving will provide adequate "bite."

White Bean Soup with Canadian Bacon and Sage

MAKES 4 TO 6 SERVINGS White beans can take the name of cannellini, navy, Small California, and Great Northern. It doesn't matter which one you choose, but it would be helpful to allow an overnight soak as with the Spicy Black Bean Soup (page 97) to cut down on cooking time.

Bacon is a traditional flavoring accompaniment to beans. By using Canadian bacon, we cut down on unnecessary fat that may be upsetting to the digestive system without compromising flavor. Once you begin to feel better, substitute regular strip bacon or even Italian pancetta, which has a lovely yet intense flavor. However, bear in mind that you will want to use a low-sodium version of the broth of your choosing, if not just plain water, because bacon, and especially pancetta, contains a large amount of sodium. The addition of fresh sage also adds a great taste and aroma. If fresh is not available, use dried leaves but refrain from using powdered sage, as it tends to lack any real flavor.

2 tablespoons olive oil
1 medium-size onion, peeled and chopped
¼ pound Canadian bacon, strip bacon, or pancetta, diced
2 medium-size carrots, peeled and coarsely chopped
1 celery stalk, ends trimmed and diced
2 cups dried white beans, picked over and rinsed
8 cups low-sodium chicken or vegetable broth, canned or homemade (page 78 or 87)
1 sprig fresh parsley
1 sprig fresh thyme
1 bay leaf
Leaves from 1 small bunch fresh sage or 2 tablespoons rubbed dried sage
Salt and pepper to taste

1. In a heavy-bottomed pot, heat the olive oil over medium heat, then add the onion and bacon and cook, stirring, until the onion is soft and, in the case of strip bacon or pancetta, most of the fat has been rendered, about 5 minutes. Add the carrots and celery and cook, stirring, for another 5 minutes. Add the remaining ingredients, except the salt, bring to a simmer, and cook until the beans are tender to the bite, anywhere from 45 minutes to 1½ hours. Stir occasionally to prevent sticking and add water if the mixture is too thick.

2. As with most bean soups, a few pulses of a hand-held immersion blender will improve the final consistency (alternatively you can remove 2 cups of the beans, puree them in a blender or food processor, and return them to the soup pot). Check for the addition of salt, adjust if necessary, and serve.

Fermented Foods, Yeast Breads, and Vinegars

Don't They Contain Alcohol?

When we hear that something is fermented, we immediately assume that it must contain alcohol and, therefore, is a product we should avoid. This is not necessarily the case and requires just a bit of easy food chemistry to understand why.

Fermentation is a process by which a living cell obtains energy in the absence of oxygen. These cells, or microorganisms, are typically yeasts and bacteria. By breaking down and converting sugars and amino acids contained in products such as grape juice or milk, where they have either accidentally or intentionally been added, they are able to obtain their desired energy and, in the process, give off certain by-products. For example, when yeast breaks down sugar or glucose, the end result is ethyl alcohol and carbon dioxide; this is the process that is used to make alcoholic beverages. When bacteria breaks down lactose, a sugar found in milk, the result is lactic acid. This is the fermentation process that is used to make yogurt, buttermilk, and cheese. Similarly, microorganisms are added to things like crushed soybeans and grains to encourage fermentation and the production of healthy live organisms, such as is found in Japanese miso and tempeh. Soy sauce is also made through fermentation and, surprisingly, this same chemical process is also responsible for common food products like pickled cucumbers, olives, and sauerkraut. None of these contain alcohol, of course, as they do not undergo alcohol-specific fermentation. A word of caution, however. Some fermented products, such as miso, tamari soy sauce, and other Asian ingredients, will contain *added* alcohol, as a preservative. This usually indicates that the product is of inferior quality because its aging process has been rushed and, therefore, is not something you would want to buy anyway. Always read your labels to be sure.

What about bread? Doesn't it involve the fermentation of yeast? Bread is indeed made through a simple fermentation of sugar and starch by yeast. However, in the presence of plenty of oxygen, the reaction results in primarily carbon dioxide and water. If the bread dough has a limited oxygen supply, a small amount of alcoholic fermentation may occur. While the carbon dioxide that is produced causes the dough to rise, any alcohol that may result is rapidly evaporated in the baking process. But, alcohol doesn't really totally evaporate, does it? In this case, with higher temperatures and very miniscule amounts of fermentation by-product, the answer is actually yes, at least enough for us not to be needlessly concerned. A scoop of commercial French vanilla ice cream probably has more alcohol from a teaspoon of vanilla extract added at the factory than a loaf of yeast bread. In either case, the amount is infinitesimal.

What about vinegars made from red and white wines? As long as we are on the subject of fermentation, it bears mentioning that vinegar, derived from the French words *vin aigre*, meaning "sour wine," often carries a question mark to those in recovery when discussing the avoidance of alcohol-containing food ingredients. After all, vinegars are made from any number of alcoholic beverages, including red wine, white wine, cider, sherry, and even champagne. However, when bacteria is added to a diluted alcohol solution, such as red or white wine, the process of fermentation is carried a step further; alcohol is now converted to acetic acid (the familiar sour flavor of vinegar) and the resulting liquid becomes vinegar, with no trace of alcohol. But what about the taste? Isn't that a potential trigger? Generally, through clarification, pasteurization, and sometimes distillation, most of the initial flavoring dissipates. Consequently, when you see pricey wine vinegars made from Cabernet or Chardonnay, they will not taste much different from your average red or white wine vinegars, and are definitely not worth the added investment, especially if you are a former wine drinker and the mere name can set off a mental trigger. Balsamic vinegar, on the other hand, differentiated by its fermentation in various wood barrels which impart a unique, earthy flavor, is definitely a vinegar worth investing in. Its pungent and fragrant flavor will wake up many a dish and greatly enhance your cooking. Other flavored vinegars, like raspberry, are actually infused after the fermentation with fruit, berries, and sometimes flowers. These can make for excellent components of alcohol substitutions in cooking and we'll be looking at some of their uses further along.

Finally, I was once asked a question about fermentation that at first seemed silly, but on reflection was a valid and interesting thought. Can we, as humans, cause fermentation to occur in our bodies by ingesting certain bacteria or enzymes that break down glucose and amino acids? Here's what I discovered: Fermentation that produces lactic acid is actually a common human function. Characterized by the all too familiar muscle stiffness when inactive people suddenly start to exercise, lactic acid fermentation occurs when the oxygen in muscles is depleted. Normally, with plenty of oxygen to spare, we metabolize glucose into water and carbon dioxide. But when we overdo it in the exercise department and our muscles use up oxygen faster than our blood can supply it, a localized anaerobic (lacking oxygen) condition occurs. Lactic acid is produced and aches and pains are the result. Eventually, after a few days of rest, an oxygen-plentiful atmosphere returns and lactic acid moves on to be converted to other chemicals.

As for alcohol fermentation, fortunately, we are not capable of becoming human breweries or distilleries. We cannot, by nature, produce alcohol in our own bodies, regardless of what we consume, through fermentation or otherwise. In essence, it is impossible because we simply lack the genetic information necessary to do so. However, depending on physiological conditions, varying degrees of endogenous alcohol may be present in our bodies and it is this notion, also called the "auto-brewery syndrome" that has been used (unsuccessfully) as a drunk driving defense when questioning the validity of blood alcohol tests. Since documented concentrations have been negligible, endogenous alcohol ultimately has no forensic and little medical significance.

Hot-and-Sour Soup with Pork and Tofu

MAKES 2 TO 4 SERVINGS Many people enjoy the "heat" of a hot-and-sour soup when they are struck with a nasal cold, as it rapidly opens up those stuffy sinuses. Similarly, people in recovery who enjoy spicy food when they are on the mend will also get a boost from this powerful soup. Personally, until my eyes begin to tear while eating, I keep adding pepper! You can, of course, adjust the amount of pepper according to your own "heat" threshold. It is ground white pepper that gives hot-and-sour soup its potency and, although I am not a huge fan of cooking with white pepper, it is irreplaceable in this recipe.

Pork has been added, instead of chicken, to include a little thiamine (vitamin B_1), a basic nutrient we tend to be short on in early recovery, but you can easily substitute any thinly sliced poultry or beef you may have on hand. Additional protein appears here in the form of tofu (soybean curd), which is available in most any supermarket. It is made from curdled soymilk, which is extracted from ground cooked soybeans. The curds are drained and pressed into blocks or cakes. Tofu is available silken, soft, firm, and extra-firm in its consistency, depending on how much whey has been removed. In general, firm and extra-firm tofu is perfect for soups and stir-fries, while the softer varieties are often mashed and used in recipes to replace high-fat cheeses and creams. The wonderful thing about tofu is that it acts like a sponge, absorbing any flavors you may care to impart, making it particularly good when marinated. Some commercial varieties come pre-flavored and also baked, resulting in a firmer and denser cake. These could be substituted here if you like. If you wish to make your hot-and-sour soup completely vegetarian, omit the pork, double the amount of diced tofu, and use a vegetable broth. I have, on occasion, used a purchased organic mushroom stock, with excellent results.

This soup is incredibly easy to prepare, so it's not all that necessary to make a large batch at once in order to save time later. In fact, the "hot" and "sour" characteristics tend to dissipate over time.

Your local Chinese take-out may find its soup sales diminishing once you start whipping up this wonderfully therapeutic soup on a regular basis!

4 cups low-sodium chicken or vegetable broth,
   canned or homemade (page 78 or 87)
One 1-inch piece fresh ginger, left unpeeled and
   thickly sliced
1 garlic clove, peeled and smashed
2 small thin boneless loin pork chops (4 ounces),
   trimmed of fat and thinly sliced
2 tablespoons soy sauce
1 teaspoon sugar
1 bunch scallions, ends trimmed and thinly sliced
8 shiitake mushrooms, stems removed and caps
   thinly sliced
½ cup canned bamboo shoots, drained
½ cup canned sliced water chestnuts, drained
½ teaspoon white pepper, or more to taste
3 tablespoons rice vinegar or white wine vinegar
Salt to taste
Half of a 15-ounce block firm or extra firm tofu,
   drained and cut into ½-inch dice
2 tablespoons cornstarch mixed with
   3 tablespoons cold water
1 large egg, lightly beaten
2 teaspoons toasted sesame oil

1. Bring the broth to a simmer in a large pot. Add the ginger and garlic and allow to simmer very slowly for about 15 minutes.

2. Marinate the thinly sliced pork in a medium-size mixing bowl with the soy sauce and sugar.

3. Using a slotted spoon, remove the ginger pieces and garlic from the broth and discard. Add to the pot the scallions, mushrooms, pork and its marinade, bamboo shoots, water chestnuts, white pepper, and vinegar and cook over low heat for 10 minutes. At this point, you can taste for "heat" and add more white pepper, if desired. You can also taste for salt at this time.

4. Add the tofu and cornstarch mixture, increase the heat to medium, and stir a minute or two, until the soup begins to thicken. Add the beaten egg slowly while continuing to stir until the egg strands set, about a minute. Lastly, add the sesame oil, stir to distribute, and serve immediately for the best flavor.

Miso Soup

MAKES 4 SERVINGS A cup of miso soup to the Japanese is like a mug of morning coffee to most of us—something we can't imagine beginning our day without! You may be familiar with this delicious and healthy broth if you frequent sushi restaurants, or may have come across dry packet versions in your supermarket, now more easily found as the nutritional benefits of miso are acknowledged in the West.

Miso is a fermented soy food that is made by adding *koji*, or microorganisms grown on rice, barley, and soybeans, to crushed cooked soybeans, salt, and water, which triggers fermentation. It has a pungent and distinct flavor and can be used in marinades, dressings, main dishes, and soup. Similar in appearance and consistency to peanut butter, miso is generally found in the refrigerator section of health food stores or Asian markets. Depending on the amount of salt and the addition of rice or barley, miso can vary from light gold in color to deep brown. The lighter, sweet white miso, called *shiro*, is generally the one called for in miso soup.

Dashi is the traditional Japanese stock used in this soup, but you can substitute a light broth or water in its place. If you are using water, you may need to add about ⅛ teaspoon salt to the pot. Wakame, a type of sea vegetable, is also a traditional ingredient and comes dried, in flakes or strips, and sometimes in instant form. Check the label for reconstituting instructions and chop the strips if necessary. If you are browsing your health food store or Asian market for miso, you will probably also come across these ingredients as well. If not, use the recommended substitutions as follows.

Although miso is one of the soy products we will be exploring in detail in Phase Three, it is worth making this incredibly nutritious and comforting soup now when we may most appreciate its medicinal value. Miso is high in protein, phytochemicals, and beneficial enzymes and bacteria, which can help to get our systems back on track and make our insides hum and purr.

½ cup dried wakame

6 cups dashi (recipe follows), vegetable broth, canned or homemade (page 87), or water

¼ cup shiro miso (white soybean paste)

Half of a 15-ounce block soft or firm tofu, drained and cut into ½-inch dice

3 scallions, thinly sliced

1. Soak the wakame in warm water to cover until softened, about 15 minutes. Drain through a sieve.

2. Heat the dashi in a medium-size saucepan over high heat until it simmers. Ladle about ½ cup of hot stock into a measuring cup, add the miso, and stir with a fork to combine well. Pour the mixture back into the saucepan, add the wakame, tofu, and scallions, stir well, and simmer for 1 minute. Serve immediately.

Dashi in a Dash

MAKES 6 CUPS Fish stock called dashi is the base liquid for miso soup and other traditional Japanese dishes. Although it is possible to buy it ready made, making your own is really an easy and quick process. A jaunt through an Asian market or health food store will turn up the two essential ingredients–kombu, dried kelp, and *katsuo bushi*, dried bonito (fish) flakes.

6 cups cold water

One 12-inch piece *kombu*

¾ cup bonito flakes

1. Bring water and *kombu* to a boil in a medium-size saucepan. Remove from the heat, discard the *kombu*, and add the bonito flakes.

2. Let stand for 5 minutes, then pour through a fine sieve lined with cheesecloth or a coffee filter into a clean saucepan. You are now ready to make the miso soup! If you prefer, you can cool down the dashi and refrigerate it in an airtight container for 3 to 4 days until ready to use.

Portobello Mushroom and Barley Soup

One of the healthiest grains around is barley. It is excellent for glycemic control because it is metabolized by the body at a very slow rate. This translates into sustained energy and fewer mood fluctuations.

Mushroom barley soup is a classic combination and is often prepared with chunks of stewing beef for added flavor. Here, portobello mushrooms provide a boost of flavor, while fresh dill adds a fragrant and medicinal touch.

1 tablespoon unsalted butter

1 tablespoon olive oil

1 medium-size onion, peeled and diced

1 medium-size carrot, peeled and diced

1 celery stalk, ends trimmed and diced

Salt and pepper to taste

6 ounces portobello mushrooms, stems discarded and caps sliced

1 cup pearl barley

8 cups low-sodium beef, chicken, or vegetable broth, canned or homemade (page 78 or 87)

Handful fresh dill sprigs

1 large sprig fresh parsley

1 bay leaf

1. Melt the butter with the olive oil in a soup pot over medium heat, then add the onion, carrot,

and celery, season lightly with salt and pepper, and cook, stirring, for 10 minutes, without browning. Add the mushrooms and cook, stirring, for another 5 minutes. Add the pearl barley and stir well. Add the broth and herbs, bring to a simmer, and cook until the barley is tender, about 40 minutes.

2. Before serving, remove the bay leaf and stems of the dill and parsley. Taste for the addition of salt and pepper and adjust if required.

Chef's Note: There are numerous varieties of fresh mushrooms available these days. Feel free to substitute any of these for the portobellos. You can also use dried mushrooms (about 1 ounce) that have been soaked in warm water to rehydrate them. Save the soaking liquid (straining it first to remove any grit) and add it to your soup for a boost of flavor.

"Where's the Beef" Broth Recipe?

Homemade beef broth can contribute to a delicious array of dishes from soups to stews, but frankly, it's a lot of work to make. Roasting beef bones for hours and adding them to simmering pots of aromatic vegetables is a luxurious, time-consuming endeavor that really only large restaurants can accommodate. However, if you would like to experiment with making a homemade beef broth, recipes are easy to find. Just beware that many cookbooks will tell you to "deglaze" your roasting pan with wine. For stock making, this is completely unnecessary and water can be used instead. For our purposes, a far less bothersome alternative is to use canned beef broth, preferably low-sodium. There are many on the market, as well as beef-flavored bouillion cubes, that you can make use of whenever beef broth is called for.

Hearty Barley and Vegetable Soup

Although barley is the featured ingredient here, the addition of lentils and split peas makes this soup truly hearty and satisfying. Simple to make and surprisingly quick to cook, you'll enjoy the variety of flavors and textures as you eat your way to good health.

Canned vegetable broth, generally too intensely flavored with carrot or tomato to be used in most soups, finds a perfect home with these ingredients, although homemade vegetable broth is certainly welcome. And the addition of fresh marjoram unites the flavors beautifully. As with many soups of this type, a few quick pulses with a hand-held immersion blender will create just the right amount of thickness and tie everything together.

2 tablespoons olive oil

1 medium-size onion, peeled and diced

1 large celery stalk, trimmed and diced

3 medium-size carrots, peeled and diced

Salt and pepper to taste

1 garlic clove, peeled and minced

4 cups vegetable broth, canned or homemade (page 87)

4 cups water

One 15-ounce can plum tomatoes with juices, roughly chopped

½ cup pearl barley

¼ cup dried brown lentils, picked over and rinsed

¼ cup dried green or yellow split peas, picked over and rinsed

1 bay leaf

2 sprigs fresh marjoram or 1 teaspoon dried marjoram

1 cup canned chickpeas, drained and rinsed

1. Heat the olive oil in a soup pot over medium heat, then add the onion, celery, and carrots, season lightly with salt and pepper, and, stirring a few times, cook until slightly softened, about 5 minutes. Add the garlic and cook, stirring, 1 minute more.

2. Add all the remaining ingredients except the chickpeas, stir well, bring to a simmer, and allow to cook, covered, until the barley, lentils, and split peas are tender, about 45 minutes. Stir occasionally to prevent sticking. Add the chickpeas and simmer 5 minutes more.

3. Remove the marjoram sprigs and bay leaf. Using a hand-held immersion blender, pulse 3 or 4 times for a creamier consistency (or puree a cup or two of the finished soup in a blender, returning this to the pot). Taste for seasoning, adjust if necessary, and serve.

Hearty Barley and Vegetable Soup with Chicken: Substitute chicken broth for the vegetable broth and 1 cup diced cooked chicken for the chickpeas.

Wheat Berry Soup with Smoked Turkey

MAKES 4 TO 6 SERVINGS I am always looking for ways to utilize the healthy and delicious qualities of wheat berries and this soup is surely one of the best I have found. Based on the traditional French Provençal *soupe d'epeautre*, which uses a variety of wheat kernels similar to wheat berries, this soup is definitely a meal in itself.

Wheat berries can sometimes be found in the supermarket, especially near Easter, when traditional Italian wheat pies are made. You can also look for them in Italian delis and groceries, or in specialty food stores, either locally or online.

A smoked turkey wing adds a delicious rustic aroma (a smoked ham hock could be substituted)

and the addition of diced lean smoked turkey provides all the protein that's needed for this hearty dish.

1 tablespoon unsalted butter
1 tablespoon olive oil
1 medium-size onion, peeled and chopped
1 medium-size celery stalk, ends trimmed and chopped
1 large carrot, peeled and diced
1 medium-size turnip, peeled and diced
Salt and pepper to taste
4 cups low-sodium chicken or vegetable broth, canned or homemade (page 78 or 87)
4 cups water
1 smoked turkey wing
1 cup wheat berries
1 bay leaf
2 sprigs fresh thyme or ½ teaspoon dried thyme
1 teaspoon dried sage
3 fresh parsley sprigs
One 15-ounce can white beans, drained and rinsed
One ¼-pound piece lean smoked turkey, diced
Croutons for serving (optional)

1. Melt the butter with the olive oil in a soup pot, then cook the onion, celery, carrot, and turnip, lightly seasoned with salt and pepper, until slightly softened, about 5 minutes. Add the remaining ingredients, except the white beans, diced turkey, and croutons, stir well, bring to a simmer, and cook, covered, until the wheat berries are tender, about 1 hour.

2. Remove the bay leaf, herb sprigs, and turkey wing. Add the white beans and diced turkey and cook for 5 minutes to heat through. Taste for seasoning and add salt and pepper if necessary. Serve piping hot with croutons.

Hominy and Edamame Chowder

East meets West in this hearty and nutritious soup containing both bean and grain. Don't be put off by the ingredients, which are not always easy to find, but well worth the trek to a specialty store or two.

Hominy (also called *pozole*) has been eaten by American Indians for centuries and, when in a dry state, is ground and turned into the more familiar "grits" of the South. White hominy can be bought cooked and canned in most grocery stores and has a wonderful flavor not unlike that of popcorn.

Edamame beans (fresh soybeans) have been a staple of Asian countries for even longer and are now quite often seen in American grocery freezer sections, either shelled or unshelled. They cook up quickly and also make a great nutritious snack. They are an excellent addition to a vegetarian diet as a source of protein (see page 358). The closest substitution I have found for edamame are fava beans (also not always easy to find) or the more common lima beans, which you could use here instead.

Although not a chowder in the true sense of the word, the addition of potatoes makes this soup chunky and thick and very much like traditional chowders in consistency and taste. Here the use of milk instead of broth makes for a soothing creaminess while, at the same time, providing a good dose of much needed calcium.

¼ cup (½ stick) unsalted butter
1 large onion, peeled and chopped
½ medium-size red bell pepper, seeded and
    diced
½ medium-size green bell pepper, seeded
    and diced
Salt and pepper to taste
¼ cup all-purpose flour
2 quarts milk (whole or 2 percent fat)
Two 14.5-ounce cans hominy, drained

2 large russet potatoes, peeled and cut into ½-inch
    dice
1 cup frozen edamame beans, shelled, or lima
    beans, thawed
1 teaspoon ground cumin
½ teaspoon paprika

1. Melt the butter in a heavy-bottomed large pot over medium heat. Add the onion and bell peppers, sprinkle with salt and pepper to taste, and cook, stirring, until softened, 8 to 10 minutes. Do not allow the butter to brown; reduce the heat if necessary to keep this from happening.

2. Add the flour and stir to coat the vegetables, cooking another 2 minutes. Using a wire whisk, add the milk and continue to slowly whisk over medium heat until the milk begins to bubble around the edge of the pot. Add the hominy, potatoes, edamame beans, cumin, paprika, and a good pinch of salt and stir to combine with a wooden spoon. Keep at a low simmer and cook until the potatoes are fork tender, 15 to 20 minutes. Stir often to prevent sticking and reduce the heat if necessary.

3. Add a touch more milk if the soup becomes too thick too soon. Taste for the addition of salt, which will probably be necessary, as only milk has been used as a liquid.

4. Serve piping hot with oyster soup crackers or croutons.

Fish and Seafood Chowders and Soups

Soups based on fish and seafood can be wonderfully satisfying and comforting. Chowders, gumbos, and stew-like varieties are practically meals in themselves and provide an excellent source of protein with little saturated fat. In addition, fish cooks almost immediately in hot liquid, making for a super easy preparation, while at the same time imparting a distinctive and delicious flavor of the sea to your soup or chowder. Consider keeping bags of frozen shrimp, scallops, and other shellfish or fish fillets on hand to add to your soups, when a trip to the fresh fish department of your grocer is not possible. Many varieties of fish, especially shrimp, are flash frozen at sea, and there is virtually no difference between you or your fishmonger defrosting the product. Often, you will save money, especially when buying in quantity. Some varieties of fish, such as the salmon fillets called for in the Salmon and Corn Chowder with Dill, should be purchased fresh for maximum flavor, but if you live a distance from the shore, frozen fillets may be your only option. They are certainly fine to use in a pinch, especially in soup making.

If you find removing the skin from your fish fillets too tedious a prospect, your friendly fishmonger will happily do it for you. He or she can also suggest specific choices for your mixed fish soups based on knowledge and experience with different varieties, textures, and tastes, as well as other customers' preferences and comments. Make friends with your fish department and you'll always be well advised and catered to!

Salmon and Corn Chowder with Dill

MAKES 4 SERVINGS Fresh salmon, with its excellent omega-3 fatty acids, is a popular fish for soups and chowders. Easy to make and wonderfully soothing, this soup is really a substantial meal when rounded out with a tossed salad.

Corn, one of the lower glycemic grains, is perfect here, although I will sometimes substitute a can of yellow hominy, drained, when available. Roughly cube instead of dicing your potatoes, as the larger cut definitely contributes to the heartiness of this chowder. Dill is, of course, a natural partner for salmon, but chopped fennel fronds (the leafy tops) would also be a nice and somewhat different touch.

Once added, the salmon will be done in a mere 5 minutes. If overcooked, the bite-size fillet pieces will fall apart, so be sure that all the vegetables are tender before proceeding to this step. The addition of heavy cream is a delicious component, however, light cream or milk can be substituted with a somewhat less rich and creamy result. Serve in deep bowls with big spoons and pass oyster crackers or saltines to break up and sprinkle on top.

2 tablespoons unsalted butter
2 medium-size leeks (white part only), ends
    trimmed, washed well, and sliced
Salt and pepper to taste
2 large russet or Idaho potatoes, peeled and cut
    into 1-inch cubes
1 cup frozen corn kernels, thawed
5 cups low-sodium chicken or vegetable broth,
    canned or homemade (page 78 or 87)
2 tablespoons chopped fresh dill
1 cup heavy cream
One 1-pound skinless salmon fillet, any remaining
    pinbones removed and cut into 1-inch pieces
2 tablespoons cornstarch mixed with 3 tablespoons
    cold water

1. Melt the butter in a soup pot over medium heat, add the leeks, season lightly with salt and pepper, and cook, stirring a few times, until softened but not browned, about 5 minutes. Add the potatoes and corn and stir for 1 minute. Add the broth and dill, bring to a simmer, and cook until the potatoes are fork tender, about 15 minutes.

2. When the potatoes are done, add the cream to the soup pot and stir well to incorporate.

3. While keeping the soup at a low simmer, add the salmon pieces and carefully stir to distribute. Cook until the fish is opaque in the center, about 5 minutes. Stir in the cornstarch mixture and stir constantly while bringing to a low boil, 2 to 3 minutes. Taste for the addition of salt and pepper and serve immediately.

Dill

An Herbal Lullaby?

The word "dill" comes from an old Norse word meaning "lull" and, in fact, mothers used to put dill sprigs in their babies' cradles to help them fall asleep. Dill has also been touted as an aid to digestion and can stimulate a poor appetite, all welcome characteristics for Phase One recovery.

Easy Chunky Cioppino

MAKES 4 TO 6 SERVINGS Its creation credited to Italian immigrants in San Francisco, cioppino is a soupy stew of fish and tomatoes, not unlike French bouillabaisse, a classic fish dish of Provence. The choice of seafood is generally not as important as its freshness and local availability. Consequently, Dungeness crab became an integral part of San Francisco cioppino. Here, however, a quick visit to the seafood department of your supermarket will provide you with all you need to whip up this tasty,

satisfying dish, no matter where you live.

One of the usual ingredients found in cioppino or bouillabaisse is wine. An easy substitution with vinegar and fruit juice will provide the necessary tang and enhancement to an already flavorful soup. French or sourdough bread is an excellent accompaniment for dipping into this delicious broth.

¼ cup olive oil
2 medium-size onions, peeled and chopped
2 medium-size celery stalks, ends trimmed and sliced
Salt and pepper to taste
4 garlic cloves, peeled and minced
1 teaspoon dried thyme
1 teaspoon dried oregano
1 teaspoon dried rosemary
1 bay leaf
¾ cup unsweetened red grape juice
¼ cup red wine vinegar
4 cups low-sodium chicken or vegetable broth, canned or homemade (page 78 or 87)
1 cup water
One 28-ounce can diced tomatoes, drained
¼ teaspoon crushed red pepper
One 6½-ounce can chopped clams with their juice
One 1-pound cod or scrod fillet, any remaining pinbones removed and cut into 1-inch pieces
One ½-pound sea bass or red snapper fillet, skinned and cut into 1-inch pieces
½ pound large shrimp, peeled and deveined
½ cup fresh basil leaves, roughly chopped

1. Heat the olive oil in a soup pot over medium heat and add the onions and celery. Season lightly with salt and pepper and cook until softened, 6 to 8 minutes, stirring occasionally. Add the garlic, thyme, oregano, rosemary, and bay leaf and stir for 1 minute. Add the grape juice and vinegar, bring to a boil, and allow to boil until reduced by half, about 5 minutes. Add the broth, water, tomatoes, red pepper, and clams with juice, stir, and bring to a

simmer. Cook at a low simmer over medium-low heat for 15 minutes, stirring occasionally.

2. Add the fish and simmer just until cooked through, about 5 minutes. Taste for the addition of salt and pepper and season if necessary.

3. Just before serving, stir in the basil, then ladle into large serving bowls.

Recovery Note: Almost undoubtedly, restaurant versions of cioppino will contain wine, so be sure to ask before ordering. Similarly, I have seen prepared jars of cioppino simmering sauce, all of which have contained red or white wine, so read labels carefully if you are purchasing these products.

Bay Scallop and Haddock Gumbo

MAKES 5 TO 6 SERVINGS The most important aspect of Creole gumbo is the making of a roux and, until I discovered this microwave method, I rarely took the time to prepare gumbos for my clients, as I couldn't spare the 20 to 30 minutes of constant stirring while other dishes needed attention. Thanks to Gwen McKee, author of *The Little Gumbo Book*, I now readily make gumbo soup for everyone! Gwen's quick roux is a wonderful trick, allowing me to chop the vegetables while the roux is cooking, and I thank her for letting me adapt her recipe here.

Gumbo, a derivation of the African word for okra, usually contains this unusual fuzzy vegetable, which can be found fresh or frozen, either of which is perfectly fine for this recipe. Indeed a package of frozen sliced okra will save a lot of preparation time and not detract from the final outcome. Other ingredients often included are tomatoes, one or several types of meat or shellfish, and the aromatic filé powder, made from the ground dried leaves of the sassafras tree, always added at the very end for maximum flavor. Along with the okra,

filé powder helps to thicken the gumbo, in addition to imparting a distinct flavor. It is readily available in the spice section of most supermarkets, not far from the Creole seasoning blends, which you will also be using in this dish.

Traditionally served over a scoop of white rice, gumbo also tastes great over brown basmati rice, a delicious, not to mention healthier, choice. Bear in mind that gumbo freezes exceedingly well and even may even intensify in flavor, so don't be afraid to make a large batch. Similarly, Gwen has a great idea for freezing the accompanying rice—simply place in a zippered-top bag and, when needed, break off a piece for your bowl of gumbo.

MICROWAVE ROUX
½ cup canola oil
½ cup all-purpose flour

GUMBO
1 large onion, peeled and diced
1 large celery stalk, ends trimmed and diced
1 large green bell pepper, seeded and diced
3 garlic cloves, peeled and minced
One 10-ounce package frozen cut okra, thawed, or 1 pound fresh okra, trimmed and sliced
One 28-ounce can chopped tomatoes
4 cups low-sodium chicken or vegetable broth, canned or homemade (page 78 or 87)
2 cups water
2 teaspoons Creole seasoning, or more to taste
2 bay leaves
1 pound bay scallops
One ½-pound skinless haddock fillet, cut into 1-inch pieces
Filé powder to taste
Salt and pepper to taste
3 cups cooked brown basmati rice
1 bunch scallions, ends trimmed and thinly sliced

1. Whisk together the canola oil and flour in a large microwaveable bowl. Microwave, uncovered,

on high for 5 minutes. Whisk and continue to microwave in 1-minute intervals until the roux is the color of mahogany and the aroma is evident (reminiscent of fried chicken!).

2. Because both the bowl and the roux will be incredibly hot, take care to use oven mitts to remove it from the microwave. Carefully transfer the cooked roux to a large soup pot and add the onion, celery, green pepper, and garlic. Over medium heat, cook and stir occasionally until the vegetables have softened somewhat, about 3 minutes. Add the okra, stir well to combine and allow to cook for 10 to 15 minutes over medium-low heat, stirring occasionally. The okra will appear stringy and even "slimy" as it cooks down. Add the tomatoes, broth, water, Creole seasoning, and bay leaves, bring to a simmer, and cook for 45 minutes, uncovered, stirring occasionally.

3. Add the bay scallops and haddock and cook at a low simmer until opaque and slightly firm, 10 to 12 minutes. Taste for the addition of salt and pepper and add if necessary. Remove from the heat, remove the bay leaves, stir in the filé powder, and serve over a scoop of rice, garnishing with some sliced scallions.

Shrimp Gumbo: Substitute 1½ pounds shelled and deveined medium-size shrimp for the scallops and haddock.

Mixed Gourmet Gumbo: Replace the scallops and haddock with 1 pound shelled and deveined medium-size shrimp; ½ pound diced boneless, skinless chicken breast; and ¼ pound cubed ham. Right before serving, stir in 4 ounces lump crabmeat, picked over for shells and cartilage.

Coconut Curry Soup with Shrimp and Butternut Squash

MAKES 4 SERVINGS Thai and Indian soups that combine coconut milk, shrimp and hot chilés are popular items on restaurant menus and in gourmet food stores. The smooth and refreshing taste of coconut pairs nicely with the intensity of hot spices. However, in this version, I've cut down on the "heat" somewhat in favor of a more complex blend of flavors. Curry powder provides just the right amount of spice, while butternut squash adds a sweetly satisfying dimension. Many supermarkets carry peeled and cut-up butternut squash at a slightly higher price. This will cut down on preparation time if you would like to utilize the convenience.

Baby salad-size shrimp are perfect for this dish. They generally come precooked and defrost in no time. They are a handy addition to your freezer staples, as they can be added to anything from quick pasta dishes to soups and salads. This soup is not a good candidate for freezing, but you will probably find there is very little left after serving!

2 tablespoons unsalted butter
1 medium-size onion, peeled and chopped
2 tablespoons peeled and chopped fresh ginger
2 teaspoons mild curry powder
2 cups butternut squash (about one 1-pound squash), peeled, seeded, and cut into ½-inch cubes
1 medium-size red potato, peeled and cut into ½-inch cubes
5 cups low-sodium chicken or vegetable broth, canned or homemade (page 78 or 87)
1 pound frozen cooked baby salad shrimp, defrosted
½ cup frozen small peas, thawed
½ cup canned unsweetened coconut milk
Salt and pepper to taste
1 tablespoon chopped fresh cilantro leaves

1. Melt the butter in a soup pot over medium-low heat, add the onion and ginger, and cook, stirring a few times, until the onion is softened and the ginger fragrant, about 5 minutes, without browning. Add the curry powder, stir to coat, and cook for 1 minute. Add the squash and potato and stir well. Add the broth, bring to a simmer, and cook, covered, over low heat until the potato and squash are fork tender, about 15 minutes.

2. Add the shrimp, peas, and coconut milk and stir well to combine. Allow to simmer gently over medium-low heat for 3 to 4 minutes. Taste for salt and pepper and adjust if necessary.

3. Just before serving, stir in the chopped cilantro, then ladle into soup bowls.

Cold Soups

When it's simply too warm outside to even think of eating hot soup, a refreshing cold soup may be just the answer. Gazpacho and vichyssoise (cold potato and leek soup) are probably the best known varieties, but many creamed vegetable soups lend themselves to a cold presentation; cream of celery, asparagus, or zucchini are just a few that you might enjoy.

Fruit-based soups are also a wonderful alternative. Somewhere between a fruit punch and a smoothie in consistency, they are usually served with the added attraction of a nutritious garnish of succulent, choice pieces of cut-up fruit and will often make for a delicious and light dessert. Whenever you choose to enjoy these cooling concoctions, they are a great addition to your soup repertoire and another way to quench a thirst while increasing your nutritional intake.

Quickie Gazpacho

MAKES 4 SERVINGS A really good gazpacho outcome generally requires an intense amount of chopping and preparation, but not so here. This simple version, with fewer ingredients, is equally refreshing on a hot day and a snap to put together. Be sure to use your blender and not your food processor; a few quick pulses in the blender will adequately chop without a foamy result. If you prefer a little more "heat," add extra Tabasco sauce or, better yet, garnish with a chopped hot cherry pepper!

> 3 Kirby cucumbers or 1 English cucumber, ends trimmed and roughly chopped
> 1 quart tomato juice
> 1 teaspoon garlic salt
> 1 teaspoon ground cumin
> Juice of ½ lemon
> Dash of Tabasco sauce
> Pepper to taste
> Salt to taste

GARNISHES (OPTIONAL):
> 1 small cucumber, peeled, seeded, and thinly sliced
> 6 medium-size radishes, ends trimmed and thinly sliced
> 1 medium-size ripe avocado, peeled, pitted, and diced

1. Allow the chopped cucumbers to soak in the tomato juice in a large mixing bowl for 1 hour at room temperature.

2. Transfer the cucumbers and tomato juice to a blender, add the garlic salt, cumin, lemon juice, and Tabasco, season with pepper, and blend on high for a few seconds. Transfer to a bowl, cover with plastic wrap, and chill in the refrigerator for at least 2 hours.

3. Before serving, taste and add salt if desired. Ladle into soup bowls and garnish with thin slices

of cucumber, radishes, or diced avocado, if desired. This soup will keep in the fridge for 2 to 3 days, but do not attempt to freeze.

Gazpacho with Shrimp: Add 4 to 6 cooked and chilled cocktail shrimp to the serving bowl before pouring for a heartier version.

Chef's Note: If you are unable to find Kirby or English cucumbers, you can use 2 medium-size waxy-coated cucumbers, but you will need to peel and seed them before chopping.

Recovery Note: Watch for "spiked" restaurant versions of gazpacho that may contain tequila, vodka, or angostura bitters.

Watercress Vichyssoise

MAKES 4 TO 6 SERVINGS The mystique of vichyssoise is quickly dispelled when we realize it is simply a cold version of the humble potato and leek soup with some minor alterations. Smooth, rich, and creamy, it is a wonderful cold soup that can be quickly embellished with any number of nutritious leafy greens. Here I've chosen traditional watercress, an excellent source of calcium, potassium, and vitamin C, but spinach, arugula, or Swiss chard could easily be substituted.

You will definitely need to use a standard blender for this version, which will allow us to dispense with tedious straining. Since we're not cooking for the Cordon Bleu judges (hardly!), a few stray pieces of potato are perfectly fine. Substitute light cream or milk if you prefer less fat, but be sure your soup is thick enough to incorporate it.

When chilling the soup, be sure to place the plastic wrap directly on the surface to keep a skin from forming. And before serving, give the soup a quick stir with a wire whisk to smooth out the consistency.

1 recipe Classic Potato and Leek Soup (page 87)
¾ cup heavy cream
2 bunches watercress
Salt to taste

1. Prepare the potato and leek soup according to the directions, except add the extra heavy cream before blending. Use a standard blender instead of an immersion blender for as smooth a consistency as possible. Transfer to a bowl or storage container and cover the surface with plastic wrap. Chill well.

2. Remove the leaves from the watercress and discard the stems, saving a few sprigs for garnish. Cook the leaves in boiling salted water for 2 minutes, drain, and run under cold running water until cool. Put the cooked leaves in the blender and add a little cold water (no more than ½ cup) as needed to help blend the leaves into a fine puree. Transfer the mixture to the chilled vichyssoise and whisk well to combine. Taste now for the addition of salt, adjust if necessary, and serve in chilled soup bowls with a sprig of watercress to garnish.

Strawberry Soup with Honeyed Fruit

MAKES 4 SERVINGS Chilled fruit soups are a fun and refreshing way to get those essential vitamins and minerals, which so many popular fruits provide. Strawberries are particularly well suited for this type of dish and offer a nice base for a dollop of honeyed fruit salad.

You can use fresh or frozen strawberries (packed without syrup) and any number of seasonal ripe fruits your grocer has to offer. The ingredients for the honeyed fruit below are only a suggestion—be creative and select a variety of your favorites. A dollop of sour cream, crème fraîche, or plain yogurt provides the perfect finishing touch.

STRAWBERRY SOUP

2 pints fresh strawberries, washed and hulled, or one 16-ounce package frozen strawberries (without syrup), thawed

½ cup sugar

½ cup water

Juice of ½ lemon

HONEYED FRUIT

2 cups mixed fresh fruit, such as blueberries, raspberries, or blackberries (left whole); honeydew melon or cantaloupe (shaped with a melon baller); and kiwi, mango, or papaya (peeled and diced)

2 tablespoons honey

¼ cup sour cream, crème fraîche, or plain yogurt

Fresh mint sprigs

1. In a food processor, combine the strawberries, sugar, and water and process until smooth. Strain the puree through a medium-mesh sieve to remove most, but not all, of the seeds. (If you do not mind the seeds, you needn't strain the mixture at all.) Transfer to a medium-size mixing bowl and stir in the lemon juice. If the soup is too thick, add a little more water. Cover with plastic wrap and chill for at least 1 hour.

2. Place the prepared fruit in a medium-size mixing bowl. Fold in the honey, cover with plastic wrap, and chill until ready to serve.

3. To present the soup, place ½ cup per serving of the fruit mixture in the center of a soup bowl. Ladle the strawberry soup around it and garnish with a dollop of the sour cream and a mint sprig.

4 | *Keeping It Simple*

Satisfying Suppertime Solutions

Wen time is limited and stamina is low, the idea of creating a lavishly orchestrated dinner with all the fixings is unrealistic and exhausting. Indeed, at the beginning of our recovery we may not even be terribly interested in food or, at best, our appetites tend to be sporadic and extreme. One day we may wish for nothing heavier than a bowl of tomato soup, while the next day finds us ravenous for a double cheeseburger with all the fixings. Bouncing back and forth from one appetite extreme to the other is common in early recovery. Eating small meals throughout the day, whether we are hungry or not, can help to temper these ups and downs. But, still the challenge remains—how do we keep from overextending ourselves in the kitchen, especially at dinnertime, while providing our bodies with much needed nutrition and sustenance?

Simple dinners that are fast and easy to prepare can mean the difference between eating something healthy and not eating at all. In this chapter, we'll come up with some excellent quick preparations that will turn dinner making into a snap. With the help of a well-stocked pantry and some ready-made products, dinner will be on the table in no time and good nutrition is only a bite away.

Pasta dishes are an obvious solution for satisfying, quick meals and the recipes that follow can be prepared while the water is boiling. Stir-fries and rice can produce dinner in minutes, while sautéing, broiling, and pan-frying are more quick methods that will not tax our time or energy. Making use of the microwave is another time saver, especially for vegetables. We'll be exploring all of these options in this chapter, with hints on adding quick flavor, as well as ways to supplement your main dishes with healthy, prepared side dishes. Of course, if you are up to it, feel free to skip ahead to Supportive Sides, Vegetables, and Complements (page 225) for some excellent accompaniments. But for now, don't feel obligated to make everything from scratch. There will be plenty of time in Phases Two and Three to explore dinner making in greater depth. Keeping it simple is the name of the game in Phase One and, like much of what we face during this early stage of recovery, small steps are the best way to reach our larger goals. In addition, by learning to set aside the time, albeit limited, for sitting down and eating dinner, whether alone or with family and friends, we are creating good habits. By adding some much needed structure and discipline to our lives, we contribute positively to *every* aspect of our blossoming recovery and not just our stomachs!

Pasta: Fast Food, Pronto!

When dinnertime suddenly descends upon us, and cooking options are limited, a quick pasta preparation may be just the answer. In the time it takes for the water to boil, everything we need to create a satisfying meal can be easily whipped up without much effort.

Pasta, contrary to what some diet gurus may tell us, is a healthy carbohydrate, particularly when made from hard durum wheat, which contains more protein, offering a better balance of macronutrients. Similarly, those pastas that contain eggs offer even more protein and satiety. And cooking our pasta to the perfect *al dente* degree (still a bit chewy, but not at all underdone) can contribute to its sustained metabolic release by lowering its Glycemic Index rating below that of other starches such as bread and even some potatoes.

There are now a myriad of pasta choices on the market, ranging from organic whole wheat to interesting flavored varieties, all of which are worth trying out. Whether dry, fresh, or frozen, it is a good idea to keep a supply on hand for spontaneous preparations. Similarly, keep your pantry stocked with prepared sauces and canned goods that can be added to your pasta creations. All of this will make for easy and quick cooking that will satisfy hunger pangs without delay. A bowl of salad greens (straight from the bagged salad section of your supermarket) with your favorite dressing will round out the meal perfectly with much-needed nutrients and fiber.

Some of the recipes in this section contain more than a little fat in the form of butter and cream. Obviously, if you are feeling that you can't stomach rich food, try a lighter preparation with a simple tomato-based sauce. Many of us, however, will be craving the comfort that only a creamy sauce can provide, so happily enjoy these recipes during Phase One, when we are less concerned with saturated fat and more interested in simply obtaining nourishment. A bowl of fettuccine Alfredo is still a better choice than four Snickers bars. Later on, these rich dishes will become occasional treats as part of a healthy diet.

So, put that water on to boil and let's get cooking!

Pastina with Milk and Butter

MAKES 2 LARGE SERVINGS Pamper yourself with *pastina*, one of the quickest prepared and most comforting pasta dishes around. Usually reserved for babies and children, because it is gentle on the stomach and easy to eat, "babies" of all ages who need a little pampering after a rough day can certainly benefit from a bowl of this nutritious "little pasta." Sometimes cooked in broth and sprinkled with parsley and Parmesan cheese, *pastina* is also traditionally made with hot milk and a little butter, definitely my preferred version and one you will no doubt enjoy for its creaminess and simplicity of flavor.

One serving of *pastina* contains 12 grams of protein and is a good way to include this macronutrient in your diet when digestion is a problem. Half a box will make two generous adult servings, which you could share with someone else who needs a little TLC, or save to reheat for another quick meal.

1⅓ cups (½ a box) *pastina*
⅓ cup milk
2 tablespoons unsalted butter
Salt to taste

1. Bring a medium-size pot of salted water to a boil.

2. Cook the *pastina* according to the package directions, then drain well. Combine the milk, butter, and cooked *pastina* in the hot pot and stir until the butter has melted. Season with salt and serve immediately.

Pasta with Fresh Herbs, Butter, and Parmesan

MAKES 2 TO 3 SERVINGS This is an easy preparation idea for a summertime dinner when fresh herbs are plentiful in the garden, although any time of year will suit this delicious dish. You can create any combination of herbs you like or simply use chopped Italian parsley for a singularly flavorful version. Finishing it with Parmigiano-Reggiano, the best of the Parmesan cheeses, will make all the difference.

Any size or shape pasta will do. I usually use a spaghetti or linguine for this recipe, in particular, one that is egg based, for added protein. Fresh or dried fettuccine, the classic Italian egg noodle, would also be a good choice.

8 ounces spaghetti, linguine, or fettuccine
¼ cup (½ stick) unsalted butter
1 tablespoon *each* chopped fresh parsley and
    basil leaves
1 teaspoon *each* chopped fresh thyme and
    marjoram leaves
Salt and pepper to taste
Freshly grated Parmesan cheese

1. Bring a large pot of water to a boil, add a good pinch of salt, and cook the pasta according to the package directions.

2. In a small saucepan, melt the butter over medium heat and stir in the herbs. Remove from the heat and set aside.

3. When the pasta is cooked, drain well, reserving about ½ cup of the cooking water, and return to the hot pot. Add the herb butter and reserved cooking water and season with salt and pepper, tossing well to coat. Transfer to a warm platter or individual bowls to serve and pass the Parmesan cheese for sprinkling.

Pasta with Fresh Herbs and Tomatoes: Add one 15-ounce can plum tomatoes (or 4 to 5 medium-size vine-ripened plum tomatoes), drained, seeded, and roughly chopped, along with the herb butter, tossing and seasoning well. During the summer, when fresh, succulent tomatoes are available, use any variety, even cherry tomatoes cut in half, and toss briefly to coat, not to cook. Drizzle a little extra virgin olive oil over all before sprinkling with the cheese.

Chef's Note: Although dried herbs are fine in many dishes, I wouldn't recommend substituting them here, as not only the fragrance but the texture of fresh herbs is what we are after. However, in a pinch, you could increase the amount of the more commonly found fresh parsley and basil, while reducing the thyme and marjoram to a pinch of the dried alternative without much loss of flavor.

Linguine with Garlic and Olive Oil

MAKES 2 TO 3 SERVINGS If you love garlic and hot red pepper, you will adore this classic quick pasta dish, traditionally known as *aglio e olio*. My grandmother used to whip this up for a late-night supper and was never stingy with the garlic. An excellent quality extra-virgin olive oil will provide enormous flavor for this simple dish, which also makes an excellent side for any type of broiled or grilled meat.

8 ounces linguine
¼ cup extra virgin olive oil
4 large garlic cloves, peeled and thinly sliced
Pinch of salt
¼ teaspoon red pepper flakes

1. Bring a large pot of water to a boil, add a generous pinch of salt, and cook the linguine ac-

Stuffed Pastas for Fast Flavor

Try any of these deliciously flavored store-bought stuffed pastas for one serving (four ounces) of a super quick supper:

- Chicken-stuffed tortellini tossed with 1 tablespoon unsalted butter and 1 teaspoon chopped fresh sage leaves.

- Pumpkin ravioli tossed with 1 tablespoon *each* unsalted butter and finely minced crystallized ginger.

- Tricolor cheese tortellini tossed with a drizzle of extra virgin olive oil, a dash of red pepper flakes, and a sprinkle of Parmesan cheese.

- Meat-stuffed ravioli tossed with ½ cup warm tomato sauce, 1 tablespoon light cream, and 1 tablespoon roughly chopped fresh basil leaves.

- Lobster ravioli tossed with 1 tablespoon *each* unsalted butter and light cream and 1 teaspoon chopped fresh tarragon leaves.

cording to the package directions. Drain well and set aside.

2. Add the olive oil to the hot pot and over medium heat, cook the garlic, stirring, until fragrant but not browned, about 1 minute. Add the salt, pepper flakes, and the cooked linguine and toss well to coat. Drizzle with a little more olive oil, if desired, and serve immediately.

Variation: This dish welcomes a number of additions. Consider adding any of the following: 1 cup cooked broccoli or cauliflower florets, asparagus tips, sliced zucchini, or strips of roasted peppers. In addition, ¼ cup toasted pine nuts or ½ cup pitted and chopped Sicilian green or black olives would add a nice texture and taste. Finish with a freshly grated strong-flavored cheese like Pecorino Romano.

Easy Fettuccine Alfredo

MAKES 2 TO 3 SERVINGS This dish is essentially the adult version of macaroni and cheese, made famous by restaurateur Alfredo de Lello in the 1920s. It is a deliciously creamy concoction that will make you hum with pleasure, even if it is a bit extravagant in the fat department. Enjoy it on occasion, when you are in the mood for something rich and creamy.

Although many people enjoy fettuccine Alfredo as a main course, it also makes an excellent side dish for simply prepared steak or fish. Serve with a crisp green salad to complement the richness of the sauce.

8 ounces fettuccine
½ cup light or heavy cream
Salt and pepper to taste
Dash of ground nutmeg
2 tablespoons unsalted butter
½ cup freshly grated Parmesan cheese

Put a Lid on It!

Helpful Hints for Cooking Pasta

If it's true that a watched pot never boils, then dinnertime may seem like eons away when pasta is on the menu. Here are some tips to help speed up the process:

- Choose a pot or saucepan for the water that is big enough to do the job, but not too large to require ages of waiting for the water to boil. Yes, the instructions on the box usually recommend cooking the pasta in a lot of water, but, in general, about half the amount is okay, if you keep an eye on the pasta as it cooks to prevent sticking. Spaghetti, linguine, and other "tall" pastas will benefit from a deeper pot, but can also be coaxed into fitting a shallower one as they soften, about a minute after submersion. Remember that less water means less time.

- Put a lid on your pot of water to help it boil more quickly. The build-up of hot steam under the cover will raise the temperature of the water so it can achieve its boiling point (212 degrees) faster than if the steam escaped into the air. And don't salt the water until *after* it comes to a boil. Salt raises the boiling temperature and will force you to wait longer before you can add the pasta.

- Keep your pot at a "full rolling boil," one that is not disturbed even when stirred, for ideal pasta cooking. A high flame will help to circulate the water around the pasta better and keep

1. Bring a large pot of water to a boil, add a generous pinch of salt, and cook the fettuccine according to the package directions.

2. In a small saucepan, heat the cream with the salt, a grinding of fresh pepper, and the nutmeg over medium-low heat. Do not allow to boil.

3. When the fettuccine is cooked, drain well and return to the hot pot. Add the butter and toss to melt and coat. Add the heated cream and Parmesan and toss well. Taste for seasoning and serve on a warmed platter with an additional sprinkle of grated Parmesan.

Fettucine Tomato Alfredo: Add 1 tablespoon tomato paste to the warm light cream.

Roasted Garlic Fettuccine Alfredo: Add 1 to 2 tablespoons roasted garlic puree (see page 120) to the warm light cream.

Chef's Note: Leftover diced cooked chicken, turkey, and ham can be easily added to this dish for a heartier and more protein-packed dinner. Warm the meat briefly in the microwave before adding or heat directly in the pot. Cooked shrimp would also make a nice addition.

Recovery Note: White wine is sometimes lurking in embellished restaurant Alfredo sauces. Read the menu or ask your waiter.

it from sticking. And don't waste good olive oil by pouring it into your pot to supposedly prevent sticking. Oil and water don't mix and the hot oil that rises to the top may create some dangerous spattering. A rolling boil and frequent stirring are all that is required.

- Stir occasionally, especially if you are using a smaller than recommended pot size. And test the pasta at least a minute or two *before* the suggested cooking time. Drain the pasta when it is *al dente*, or firm to the bite, not mushy and falling apart. Pasta was meant to be eaten this way—ask any Italian. Besides, it will improve its glycemic value by metabolizing at a slower rate, providing sustained energy.

- Don't run cold water over the pasta unless you are preparing it way ahead of time and need to stop the cooking or if you're going to use it in cold dishes like salad or in a lasagne. If you rinse cooked pasta, you are rinsing off an outside coating of starch that will help your sauce cling to it. For dishes that will be served immediately, drained hot pasta, when added to sauce that is cool or at room temperature, will quickly transfer its heat. You can return the pasta and add sauce to the still plenty hot saucepan you used for boiling. Stir together and serve. In most cases, no further heat will be necessary.

- Don't be afraid to cook more pasta than you plan to eat. Kept in a plastic container or covered bowl in the fridge, leftover pasta (drizzled with a little olive oil to prevent sticking if not dressed in sauce) will provide a fast and easy reheat for particularly busy or energy-sapped evenings.

Slow Roasting for Instant Flavor

Roasted Garlic and Peppers

Roasted garlic can add a delicious flavor to many pasta dishes, entrees, and even mashed pota-toes. Also popular as a low-fat spread for bread and toast, it has become a staple ingredient for the home cook and restaurant chef alike. Although it is possible to purchase prepared versions in jars or at deli counters, certainly a convenience when time is limited, there is nothing to com-pare to an aromatic head of garlic roasted at home.

Similarly, charring and roasting your own peppers will save considerable expense and offer yet another fast way to add intense flavor to a simply prepared dish. So, consider setting aside some time to make these wonderful ingredients at home to have on hand in the kitchen. Actu-ally, the amount of work time is minimal, compared to the slow roasting time that is necessary to develop flavor. Plop them in the oven and forget about them, until the enticing aroma wafts from the kitchen. You'll be glad you did!

To make one head of roasted garlic, preheat the oven to 300 degrees. (If you have a terra-cotta roaster, follow the directions included in the packaging.) With a sharp paring knife, cut about ¼ inch off the top of the head of garlic, slightly exposing the cloves. Drizzle with olive oil, sprinkle with salt and pepper, and wrap loosely in aluminum foil. Place on a baking sheet and roast for 30 minutes. Open up the foil and continue to roast until the head is golden and the cloves are soft, another 45 minutes to 1 hour. Allow to cool, then gently squeeze the cloves from their casings into a small bowl. Leave whole or puree with a fork or in a food processor to make a paste. Roasted garlic will keep in the refrigerator for 1 week. One large head of garlic will yield about ⅓ cup of puree.

To roast bell peppers, char the lightly oiled skin of the whole pepper to black by rotating it over an open flame, such as that from a gas-top stove, outdoor grill, or under the broiler. When completely blackened, place the peppers in a brown paper bag and allow the steam to help loosen the charred skin and continue to cook the pulp. When cool enough to handle, scrape off the blackened bits with the back of a knife. Do not run them under water to clean, because much of the essential oil and ultimate flavor will be lost. Cut them open, remove the stem and seeds, cut the pepper into strips, and store in an airtight container in the refrigerator, drizzled with a little olive oil, for up to one week. You can also make a paste from roasted peppers by pureeing them in a food processor. Add a little olive oil, salt, and pepper to enhance their flavor. Roasted pepper puree makes a delicious dip as well as a light sauce for pasta. One medium-size pepper will yield about ⅔ cup of puree.

Penne with Pesto Cream Sauce

MAKES 2 TO 3 SERVINGS Making use of prepared ingredients can be a real time saver in the Phase One kitchen. Pesto sauce is available in jars or in the refrigerated section of your grocer and is handy for adding intense flavor to anything from pasta to chicken. Sun-dried tomato pesto has also become quite popular and is readily available in most supermarkets. When there is no time or energy to make these classic sauces from scratch, good quality store-bought versions can pinch-hit beautifully.

This creamy pesto sauce is deliciously indulgent and will definitely stick to your ribs. Sauce clings nicely to penne, but any other shape pasta will fill in just as well.

> 8 ounces penne pasta
> ⅔ cup light or heavy cream
> ⅓ cup prepared pesto sauce
> Salt and pepper to taste
> Freshly grated Parmesan cheese

1. Bring a large pot of water to a boil, add a generous pinch of salt, and cook the penne according to the package directions.

2. In a medium-size saucepan, simmer the cream over medium heat, stirring occasionally with a whisk, until it has reduced by a third. Remove from the heat and stir in the pesto sauce.

3. When the penne is cooked, drain well, reserving about ¼ cup of the cooking water, and return it to the hot pot. Add the reserved cooking water and pesto cream, season with salt and pepper, and toss to coat the pasta well with the sauce. Serve immediately, sprinkled with the cheese.

Bowties with Creamy Carbonara Sauce

MAKES 2 TO 3 SERVINGS This is another quick sauce preparation that could easily be called "bowties with bacon and eggs." True carbonara aficionados will insist on using pancetta—a flavorful Italian bacon that has been cured but not smoked—instead of the bacon and refrain from adding cream, but I have found that the version below is more appealing to most American palates. In addition, some recipes call for white wine, which is completely unnecessary, while others add garlic and olive oil. If you have been lucky enough to come across pancetta in your soup-making endeavors, by all means use it here. Otherwise bacon, even turkey bacon, will work well.

I once had this served to me in a French restaurant with a raw egg yolk in the middle of the pasta dish, with the intention, I suppose, that I do the final tossing myself. (I was tempted to enter the kitchen and ask why the chef wanted me to do his job for him!) My dinner companion was appalled and quickly lost his appetite. In this recipe, however, the egg will be cooked in the cream, so there is no chance of offending, nor any need to worry about the dangers of salmonella from raw eggs (see page 172 for a detailed discussion of eggs).

Bowties, also called *farfalle* (butterflies), are my pasta of choice for this dish, although the more traditionally used spaghetti or another type of pasta would be fine too.

> 8 ounces bowtie pasta
> ¼ pound bacon or pancetta, diced
> 1 cup light or heavy cream
> 2 tablespoons unsalted butter
> 2 large egg yolks, slightly beaten
> Salt and pepper to taste
> ½ cup freshly grated Parmesan or Pecorino
>   Romano cheese
> 1 tablespoon finely chopped fresh parsley leaves

1. Bring a large pot of water to a boil, add a generous pinch of salt, and cook the bowties according to the package directions.

2. In a medium-size nonstick skillet, fry the bacon until brown and crisp and most of the fat has been rendered. Remove the bacon to drain and reserve 1 tablespoon of the rendered fat.

3. In a medium-size saucepan, heat the cream with the butter and simmer over medium heat, whisking occasionally, until slightly thickened, about 12 minutes. Remove from the heat and allow to cool for 10 minutes, then stir in the egg yolks using a wire whisk.

4. When the bowties are cooked, drain well and return to the hot pot. Add the bacon, the reserved fat, the cream mixture, and plenty of freshly ground pepper. Toss well to coat. Add the grated cheese and taste for salt, adding if necessary. Serve immediately, sprinkled with the parsley.

Chef's Note: Reheating this dish can be a bit tricky because of the eggs and cream, as excessive heat may cause the sauce to curdle. If using a microwave, set it to half power and stir often. If reheating on a stove-top, add a touch of milk and heat, covered, over low heat.

Presto Pasta Puttanesca

MAKES 2 TO 3 SERVINGS Named after the "ladies of the night," puttanesca sauce is renowned for its spiciness and ease of preparation. Usually served with spaghetti, I think this sauce is delicious over any type of pasta, especially those that have nooks and crannies to hold the bits of olives and capers that stud the red sauce. Assertive olives like Kalamata or Gaeta are ideal here and can sometimes be bought pitted to save time. Small capers are preferable to the large ones and should be well drained.

If you think you dislike anchovies, try them in this recipe, where they virtually melt away, leaving a subtle yet delicious flavor in their wake. Since many of the ingredients in puttanesca are quite well salted, it's best to taste the final result before adding any more.

8 ounces rotini, gemelli, or radiatore pasta
2 tablespoons olive oil
2 large garlic cloves, peeled and minced
1 ounce (½ can) anchovy fillets, chopped
One 15.5-ounce can crushed tomatoes
2 tablespoons small capers, drained
½ cup cured black olives, such as Kalamata or
   Gaeta, pitted and roughly chopped
¼ teaspoon red pepper flakes
Pinch of sugar
Salt to taste
2 tablespoons roughly chopped fresh
   parsley leaves

1. Bring a large pot of water to a boil, add a generous pinch of salt, and cook the pasta according to the package directions.

2. Heat the olive oil in a heavy skillet over medium heat, add the garlic and anchovies, and cook for 1 minute, stirring constantly. Do not brown the garlic. Stir in the tomatoes and bring to a simmer. Add the remaining ingredients and cook over low heat until nicely thickened, 15 to 20 minutes, stirring occasionally to prevent sticking.

3. When the pasta is cooked, drain well, and return to the hot pot. Add the cooked sauce and toss well to coat. Taste for the addition of salt, adjust if necessary, and serve immediately, sprinkled with the parsley.

Quick Spaghetti and Meatballs

MAKES 2 TO 3 SERVINGS A jar of prepared marinara sauce is the key to this easy recipe that is sure to please a hearty appetite. Consider doubling the quantity of meatballs and sauce for another, even quicker, meal—you'll only need to cook some pasta. Extra meatballs can be stored right in the sauce in an airtight container in the refrigerator or freezer.

I will sometimes add a few crushed garlic cloves to the meat mixture when time allows. You could also add a little finely chopped onion, if you like.

½ **pound lean ground beef or a combination of beef, veal, and pork**
1 large egg
½ **cup dry Italian-seasoned bread crumbs**
One 26-ounce jar good quality marinara or other spaghetti sauce
8 ounces spaghetti or other pasta
Freshly grated Parmesan cheese for serving

1. In a medium-size mixing bowl, combine the ground meat with the egg and bread crumbs and mix well.

2. Pour the marinara sauce, plus a little water, into a large saucepan and bring to a simmer.

3. Put a large pot of water on to boil.

4. Shape the meat mixture with your hands into 1½-inch balls, about the size of a golf ball (½ pound of meat will make 6 or 7 meatballs of this size). Drop them gently into the simmering sauce and stir ever so slightly to submerge them. Reduce the heat to low, cover the pot, and allow to cook for 20 to 30 minutes, occasionally stirring gently to prevent sticking.

5. Salt the boiling water and add the pasta. Cook according to the package instructions, then drain.

6. Serve the meatballs and the sauce over the cooked spaghetti and sprinkle with grated Parmesan.

Turkey Meatballs: Substitute ground turkey for the meat, but do not use ground turkey breast, as it is far too lean for this recipe. Buy a combination of dark and white meat, often referred to simply as "lean ground turkey."

Chef's Note: You can use plain bread crumbs but you will need to add salt and pepper to

taste. You may also want to add ½ teaspoon garlic powder and ½ teaspoon each dried oregano and parsley to replicate the flavor of seasoned crumbs.

Recovery Note: Remember to read labels when purchasing prepared ingredients such as spaghetti sauce, which can sometimes contain wine, vodka, and other alcoholic beverages.

Planning Ahead for Dinner on the Go

Sometimes, out of pure necessity, we must grab our dinner on the run as we go about our business of attending recovery meetings or fulfilling family and work obligations. The dinner hour can be a dangerous time for us, as many will attest, for that, more often than not, is the time when we headed for the bar after work, not to be seen again for quite some time.

With a little conscious planning, we can avoid problems before they arise. If you know you have a busy schedule ahead of you, take a moment to think about where and how you will fit dinner into the agenda. Will you be near a favorite diner or fast food stop where you can grab a bite to eat? Is it possible to make a quick trip back home for a light supper before heading out for the evening? Put to use that amazing power you had to seek out alcohol and drugs by directing it instead toward strategizing your dinner plans.

Bring containers of leftovers to reheat if you will have access to a microwave. Load up on a supply of healthy snacks to tide you over until you get home. Or prepare yourself with the classic take-along meal: the sandwich. Whatever you do, don't leave yourself open to trouble. Tiredness and hunger can be a lethal combination and one that is best to avoid at all costs.

Linguine with Pink Clam Sauce

MAKES 2 TO 3 SERVINGS Classic linguine with clam sauce, either white or red, is usually quite easy to make, but often the recipe will call for white or red wine as one of its ingredients. Instead of using an alcohol substitute in this dish, I've eliminated the need for it altogether by creating a "pink" clam sauce of tomatoes and cream. Laced instead with some fragrant chopped fresh basil, this dish will become a favorite on quick pasta nights.

Fresh clams require a bit of scrubbing and time, so canned clams will fill in nicely here. However, for a little extra in the presentation department, you can purchase a dozen or so littleneck clams and cook them in the sauce before adding the cream.

3 tablespoons olive oil

3 large garlic cloves, peeled and chopped

One 15.5-ounce can diced tomatoes, drained

1 tablespoon tomato paste

Dash of paprika

Two 6.5-ounce cans chopped clams, drained, juice reserved

8 ounces linguine

1/3 cup light cream

2 tablespoons chopped fresh basil leaves

Salt and pepper to taste

1. Bring a large pot of water to a boil.

2. Heat the olive oil in a large skillet over medium heat and cook the garlic, stirring, until fragrant but not browned, about 1 minute. Add the tomatoes, tomato paste, paprika, and a little of the reserved clam juice, stir to combine, cover, and cook over low heat for 10 to 12 minutes, stirring occasionally. Add more clam juice if the sauce becomes too thick.

3. Salt the boiling water and cook the linguine according to the package directions, then drain.

4. Add the clams to the skillet and cook, covered, over low heat for about 5 minutes. Remove the lid from the skillet, add the cream and the basil, season with salt and pepper, and stir to combine. Bring to a simmer and cook over low heat an additional 2 to 3 minutes, stirring often. Add the drained cooked linguine, toss well to coat, and serve immediately.

Variation: This preparation can be easily adapted for other types of shellfish. Try using

---

Breakfast for Dinner?

A Quick Scramble for Fast Nutrition

Who said you can't eat breakfast for dinner? Not just a great advertising ploy, chowing down on breakfast fare at dinnertime is not a bad idea for Phase One fast food eating. Whipping up a couple of scrambled eggs and toasting some bread may be just the answer for a light, nourishing supper for folks in a hurry or those with no energy to spare. Check out some delicious variations for old reliable scrambled eggs (page 169) or consider frying up one or two eggs to top off your toast. Eggs provide every essential vitamin we require and are a good protein source at this time.

How about a plate of quickly prepared French toast? Skip ahead to "Weekend Breakfasts and Brunches" (page 159) for some delicious ideas on how to make a morning meal your evening delight. Something sweet and nourishing may be just what you are after. For those who lack even an ounce of energy, fixing a bowl of cereal, hot or cold, topped with some sliced fruit and enhanced with protein-rich milk or soymilk will provide some excellent sustenance. Yogurt and granola are good choices as well. A cup of soothing herbal tea to wash it all down, and you'll be ready for a good night's sleep with plenty of stored energy to face the next day.

shelled and deveined shrimp, baby scallops, mussels, or a combination. Frozen bags of cleaned shellfish, sometimes packaged as an assortment, make this version even easier.

Recovery Note: Beware that a pink sauce in restaurants will often indicate a vodka sauce. Similarly, clam sauces that contain wine will generally say so on the menu, but to be sure, ask before ordering.

Angel Hair Pasta with Shrimp, Artichokes, and Feta Cheese

MAKES 2 TO 3 SERVINGS This elegant dish is deceivingly easy to make with the assistance of prepared ingredients, while angel hair pasta, cooked in a matter of seconds, will have you enjoying this meal in no time flat.

I like using fresh angel hair, also called *cappellini*, in this recipe, but the dried form is also fine. Buy shelled and cleaned shrimp and crumbled feta to save time. Some feta cheese comes flavored with herbs, olives, or sun-dried tomatoes, which would add a boost of flavor.

> 2 tablespoons olive oil
> 12 to 15 large or jumbo shrimp, shelled and
>   deveined
> Salt and pepper to taste
> One 6-ounce jar marinated artichoke hearts,
>   drained
> One 10-ounce jar marinara or other
>   spaghetti sauce
> ¼ cup water
> 8 ounces angel hair pasta
> ½ cup crumbled feta cheese

1. Bring a large pot of water to a boil.

2. Heat the olive oil in a medium-size skillet over medium heat. Add the shrimp, sprinkle with salt and pepper, and cook until no longer pink, about 1 minute per side. Add the artichoke hearts, marinara sauce, and water, stir to combine, reduce the heat to low, and cook, covered, for 4 to 5 minutes.

3. Salt the boiling water, cook the angel hair according to the package directions, and drain well. To serve, spoon the sauce over the pasta and sprinkle with the feta cheese.

Rigatoni with Chickpeas and Roasted Peppers

MAKES 2 TO 3 SERVINGS Nutritionally potent chickpeas pair up nicely with roasted red peppers in this satisfying dish. Homemade roasted peppers (see page 120)—or those purchased either from the deli department of your supermarket or marinated in olive oil from a jar—add a unique and delicious flavor.

Hearty rigatoni is the ideal pasta here, although other shapes of pasta, such as wagon wheels or rotini, would work well too. Leftovers make a delicious cold pasta salad for lunch or a light supper, so doubling this recipe is certainly encouraged.

> 3 tablespoons olive oil
> ½ cup diced red onion
> Salt and pepper to taste
> 3 garlic cloves, peeled and roughly chopped
> 2 teaspoons finely chopped fresh rosemary leaves
>   or 1 teaspoon dried rosemary
> 1 cup canned chickpeas, drained and rinsed
> ⅔ cup thinly sliced roasted red peppers
> ¼ cup balsamic vinegar
> ½ cup low-sodium chicken or vegetable broth
> 8 ounces rigatoni pasta
> Extra virgin olive oil for drizzling

1. Bring a large pot of water to a boil. Add a generous pinch of salt, cook the rigatoni according to the package directions, and drain well.

2. Heat the olive oil in a large skillet over medium heat. Add the onion, sprinkle with salt and pepper, and cook, stirring, until slightly softened, about 3 minutes. Add the garlic and cook another minute. Add the rosemary, chickpeas, peppers, vinegar, and broth and cook at a low simmer until the liquid is slightly reduced, 3 to 4 minutes. Add the drained rigatoni and toss well to combine. Taste for seasoning, drizzle a little extra virgin olive oil over all, and serve immediately.

Stir-Fries for Fast Nourishment

Stir-frying is most certainly a healthy and quick way to prepare a nourishing Phase One dinner. However, many recipes for classic Asian stir-fried dishes contain a good number of ingredients that need to be properly peeled, sliced, chopped, or diced in some fashion before the cooking can even begin. Although the actual stir-fry may take as little as 5 to 10 minutes, the precooking time could run into hours, especially if you are not a whiz with your chef's knife.

Do not despair! These days we are happily aided by supermarket packets of washed, peeled, and chopped fresh and frozen vegetables that will lighten our load considerably. We can even purchase presliced chicken, pork, or beef, ready to go for a quick stir-fry dinner, not to mention bottled sauces and condiments to finish the dish. Still, I would encourage utilizing the nutri-

tional advantages that only truly unprocessed, fresh ingredients can provide, while not taxing our time or energy too greatly. To that end, these recipes are limited to two or three main ingredients at most. Enhanced with flavor from the wonderfully healing garlic and ginger and the satisfying taste of soy sauce and sesame oil, we can't do much better for our bodies at this time, while we attempt to nourish ourselves back to health.

Easily prepared, quick-cooking basmati rice is the ideal accompaniment to stir-fried dishes, while jasmine and Japanese varieties are also good choices. Whether steamed in a rice cooker or prepared according to the package directions, your rice will be ready within 15 minutes from the onset of cooking. Carolina long-grain rice and the many brown varieties are, of course, excellent selections in terms of health and, if you can spare the time (usually at least 25 minutes of cooking time), consider those as well. Although I am not fond of "minute" cooking rices, as they tend to lack any nutritional value as well as flavor, feel free to use them as quick time savers on particularly busy nights. In any case, making extra rice is always a good idea. Topped with leftovers or a quickly microwaved frozen vegetable, it may be just what the doctor ordered before we plop into bed after a long, rough day. Precooked rice is also the basis for the delicious one-dish rice dinners that follow the stir-fries, so save that extra rice whenever possible.

The Basic Stir-Fry

MAKES 2 SERVINGS Simple stir-fries require high heat, a minimal amount of oil, and a flavorful liquid. Ingredients that are ready to go are also key. In fact, it is not even necessary to use a wok, although if you have one, by all means use it. Instead, a sauté or fry pan (the same we will be using for sautéing fillets later on in this chapter) will certainly work fine. Large wooden spoons and spatulas are great for quickly moving the food around in the pan.

Your choice of oil for stir-frying should not interfere with the Asian flavors of the dish, which may be the case with olive oil. Canola or peanut oil would be a better neutral choice in terms of taste. These oils also possess a slightly higher smoking point (the temperature at which the oil will start to break down and smoke), a desirable characteristic for high-temperature stir-frying. Grapeseed oil, now becoming more available, may be the best choice of all, as it never interferes with flavor and has the highest of all oil smoking points. Toasted sesame oil is never used for frying, but rather at the end of the cooking preparation, when it can be drizzled over a stir-fry for a delicious finish.

Keep in mind that the smaller the cut of food, the faster it will cook. If some of the packaged broccoli florets you purchase appear a bit large, do not hesitate to cut them in half to a uniform size. Similarly, you may want to opt for a bag of shredded rather than sliced carrots, as these will cook in no time. Crisp tender is the consistency we are after, but if left too long in the pan, vibrant vegetables will become mushy and discolored. They will also lose many of their nutrients, so be sure not to overdo it. Stir-frying, by definition, means brief cooking over very high heat with constant and brisk movement of the ingredients; keeping this in mind will always provide perfect results.

For chopping fresh ginger and garlic, a small food processor is indispensable. You could also use the same hand-held immersion blender recommended for soups, which often comes with a handy chopping attachment. These tools will save you a lot of frustration and grief if you do not have the patience for knife work. They are also great for chopping fresh herbs in large quantities. As an even greater time saver, you can purchase jars of chopped garlic and ginger in your supermarket and spoon out what you need, although fresh is surely the way to go if you can manage it.

Finally, your choice of liquid should complement the main ingredients. Water and a bit of soy sauce would be just fine, but you can also add a little more flavor by using a chicken, beef, or vegetable broth. Chinese cooks are fond of adding a little sherry to stir-fries for its sweetness (sometimes a tablespoon or two). If you run across a recipe like this, you can easily substitute straight apple juice. For larger amounts of sherry substitution, I would combine a little sherry vinegar with the apple juice to replicate the proper acidity.

This recipe uses beef as an example, but another type of meat or poultry could be substituted. We are also using broccoli here as the main vegetable; a powerhouse of nutrition, it should become a staple in everyone's diet (see page 416 on the amazing health benefits of eating broccoli).

2 tablespoons soy sauce
1 tablespoon cornstarch
½ teaspoon sugar
6 ounces top sirloin, trimmed of any fat and
    cut into ¼-inch-thick strips
1½ tablespoons canola or peanut oil
One ½-inch piece fresh ginger, peeled and
    minced (about 1 tablespoon)
1 to 2 large garlic cloves, to your taste, peeled
    and minced
2 cups broccoli florets
½ cup low-sodium beef, chicken, or
    vegetable broth
Toasted sesame oil for drizzling
Salt and pepper to taste
2 cups hot cooked rice

1. In a medium-size mixing bowl, whisk together the soy sauce, cornstarch, and sugar. Add the beef, stir to coat, and set aside.

2. Heat the canola oil in a wok or large skillet over high heat. Add the beef mixture and stir-fry until no longer pink, about 2 minutes. Remove the beef from the pan.

3. Add the ginger and garlic (you may add a

touch more oil, if necessary, to prevent sticking) to the pan and cook for 30 seconds, without browning. Add the broccoli and stir-fry until it is heated and coated with oil, about 1 minute. Pour in the broth, stir to combine, and cook, covered, over medium heat until crisp tender, about 3 minutes.

4. Return the beef to the pan and stir-fry to reheat and coat with the sauce, about 1 minute. Taste for the addition of salt and pepper, drizzle with a little sesame oil, and serve immediately over rice.

Stir-Fried Beef with Peppers and Onions: Replace the broccoli with 1 cup bell pepper strips (green or red, or a combination) and 1 cup onion cut into ½-inch pieces. Add 1 tablespoon hoisin sauce (see page 131) to the broth and season the dish liberally with freshly ground black pepper.

Sweet Chili Stir-Fried Pork: Replace the beef with strips of boneless pork from thin-cut loin chops. Substitute 1 cup thinly sliced carrots for half the broccoli and ¼ cup pineapple juice for half the broth. Add 1 tablespoon prepared chili sauce to the broth mixture and omit the sesame oil at the end.

Gingered Chicken with Water Chestnuts and Cashews: Replace the beef with thinly sliced boneless, skinless chicken breasts and increase the ginger to 2 tablespoons. Substitute 1 bunch scallions, ends trimmed and cut into 1-inch pieces, and one 3½-ounce can sliced water chestnuts, drained, for the broccoli. Add ½ cup unsalted raw or roasted cashews with the broth.

Stir-Fried Shrimp with Snow Peas: Replace the beef with raw large shrimp, peeled and deveined. Substitute 1 bunch scallions, ends trimmed and cut into 1-inch pieces, and 1 cup snow peas, strings pulled, for the broccoli. Reduce the covered cooking time to 1 minute.

Sesame Tofu with Broccoli and Bean Sprouts: Replace the beef with one 15-ounce block extra-firm tofu, cut into 1-inch dice and patted dry with paper towels, and add 1 tablespoon sesame seeds to the soy mixture. Decrease the broccoli to 1 cup and add 2 cups fresh bean sprouts and ½ cup shredded carrots towards the end of the cooking time. Drizzle generously with more soy sauce and sesame oil.

Recovery Note: Bottled Asian sauces can add a great boost of flavor, but read labels for common additions of wine, sherry, and other alcoholic beverages. Lesser quality soy sauces of the tamari kind may contain alcohol as a preservative and should be avoided.

Stirring Up the Salad Bar

Your local deli or supermarket salad bar may be just the place to find what you need for a delicious stir-fry dinner. With a little planning, you can save yourself an enormous amount of chopping and slicing. If visiting the salad bar for lunch, grab an extra container and pick out some fresh raw veggies for a later stir-fest. Look for sliced onions (red or yellow) and bell peppers, broccoli florets, shredded carrots, snow peas, and any other fresh, attractive-looking ingredients. Create your own medley—about two cups total will do—and stir up a delicious dinner in no time.

When Rice Takes Center Stage

Rice has been cultivated for thousands of years, and for nearly half of the world's population, it is the number one diet staple today. Like the pasta dishes we saw earlier, main course rice dishes can be wonderfully satisfying and easy to prepare, making them an excellent choice for Phase One dinners that require little effort. The key will be to have your rice already cooked, so save that extra white or brown rice from yesterday's Chinese take-out or make a large pot when time allows and stick it in the fridge for later. Brown rice, because it is less processed, is, of course, far better in terms of nutrition, but precooked basmati, jasmine, and long-grain varieties will provide good sustenance when combined with other nutritious ingredients. In general, one cup of raw uncooked rice will yield four cups cooked, enough for two to three hearty appetites, when used as the main ingredient. Cooked rice will keep in the fridge for up to one week or consider freezing portions in plastic zippered-top bags and microwaving or submerging them in boiling water to revive when needed.

Again, having a well-stocked pantry will make these dishes even easier to whip up, as will a varied spice rack for bursts of flavor. Accompanied by a side salad, these main course rice dishes will serve us well on hungry Phase One nights. They also make excellent side dishes for simply prepared meats, chicken, or fish, so any leftovers can be happily served again!

Ginger Fried Rice

MAKES 1 TO 2 SERVINGS Classic Chinese fried rice is essentially a dish made up of leftovers and is generally named after the ingredient that predominates, such as chicken fried rice or shrimp fried rice. Here, the wonderfully healing fresh gingerroot is the dominating flavor, but you can add any number of leftover pieces of meat or cooked vegetables if you like.

My clients often request this dish when they are feeling a bit under the weather, as it is easily digested and calming to the stomach. For a boost of protein, I like to add some cooked edamame beans, but you can substitute lima beans or peas if you prefer, or leave them out entirely.

2 cups cooked white or brown rice, chilled
¼ cup low-sodium chicken or vegetable broth
1 tablespoon soy sauce
1 teaspoon toasted sesame oil
1½ tablespoons canola or peanut oil
1 bunch scallions, ends trimmed and finely chopped
2 tablespoons peeled and finely chopped fresh ginger
Salt and pepper to taste
½ cup edamame beans (optional), cooked in water to cover until tender and drained

1. Place the rice in a large mixing bowl and separate the grains using a fork or your fingertips. Set aside.

2. In a small mixing bowl, stir together the broth, soy sauce, and sesame oil and set aside.

3. Heat the canola oil in a large nonstick skillet or wok over high heat, add the scallions and ginger, season with a little salt and pepper, and stir-fry for about 30 seconds. Add the rice and edamame beans, if using, and stir-fry quickly to heat through, 2 to 3 minutes. Add the broth mixture and toss to coat evenly. Taste for additional seasoning and serve immediately.

Egg-Ginger Fried Rice: Lightly beat 1 large egg and scramble it in the skillet or wok before cooking the scallions and ginger. Remove, break into small pieces, and add later with the broth mixture. Additional oil may be needed when stir-frying.

Recovery Note: *The addition of Chinese rice wine or sake is sometimes called for in fried rice recipes. Substitute rice vinegar or sushi vinegar for small amounts (1 to 2 tablespoons) and see "Demystifying Deglazing" (page 134) for suggestions on substituting for larger measurements (¼ to ½ cup).*

Indonesian Nasi Goreng

MAKES 2 SERVINGS This classic rice dish from Indonesia has gained popularity with those who enjoy a bit of "heat" on their dinner plate. *Nasi goreng* is basically fried rice with the addition of some unique spices and diced ham or other types of meat, chicken, or shrimp. You can make this as hot as you like by adding additional jalapeño peppers or serving it with chili sauce or Tabasco sauce on the side. An accompaniment of plain yogurt or raita (page 261) and pita bread will help cool down your palate!

3 cups cooked white long-grain rice, chilled
1 tablespoon canola or peanut oil
1 small onion, peeled and chopped
1 large garlic clove, peeled and minced
1 jalapeño, seeded and chopped
½ teaspoon *each* chili powder, ground cumin, and ground coriander
2 tablespoons soy sauce
1 tablespoon ketchup
1 cup diced cooked ham
Salt and pepper to taste

1. Place the rice in a large mixing bowl and separate the grains with a fork or your fingertips. Set aside.

2. Heat the oil in a large nonstick skillet or wok over high heat and stir-fry the onion until slightly softened, about 2 minutes. Add the garlic, jalapeño, and spices, and cook, stirring constantly, for 1 minute.

3. Add the rice and the remaining ingredients and cook, stirring, over medium-high heat until heated through, about 5 minutes. Taste for the addition of salt and pepper and serve immediately.

Variation: Replace the ham with diced cooked chicken or baby shrimp for variety and consider adding ½ cup diced cooked vegetables such as carrots or zucchini for color and texture. Cooked peas are also a great addition.

Asian Ingredients
Getting to Know Your *Char Siu* from Your *Kimchee*

With the popularity of Asian cooking and dining on the rise (no longer just Chinese and Japanese, but Thai, Korean, and Vietnamese), many larger U.S. cities now boast authentic Asian grocery stores, where every possible ingredient you may require can be easily purchased (provided you can read the labels!). The first time I ventured into one of these amazing stores, I was like a kid in a candy shop, wide-eyed and uncontainable, yet frustrated at not being able to recognize the many items I was sure I wanted to buy for cooking. Now, I always take along my trusty guide to Asian ingredients (with pictures) to help me along. Even if you don't have access to one of these types of markets, your local supermarket has surely expanded its Asian-ingredient repertoire and you may still need a little guidance in your journey down the aisle. Usually situated somewhere between the Mexican and Indian products, these ingredients can be a huge help to you in preparing quick stir-fry dinners, so it's worth getting to know them a little better.

SOY SAUCE: Who knew there were so many to choose from? Actually, the Chinese (the first to invent soy sauce, which was later adapted by the Japanese) use only one of two types—light or dark. Both are made from soybeans and wheat, while the latter has been enhanced with molasses and results in a darker, more caramel-like color. Light soy sauce is good for dipping and cooking with milder flavored ingredients such as fish, vegetables, and poultry. The darker version is better suited to red meat and more intensely flavored dishes. Japanese soy sauce, also called *shoyu*, has additional wheat added during the fermentation process (see page 99 for a discussion on fermented foods) and is slightly sweeter and saltier than Chinese varieties. Mixed with wasabi, it is the perfect soy sauce for sushi dipping. Tamari is simply soy sauce without wheat and consequently is preferred by many macrobiotic eaters and gluten avoiders. It is also the version that will often have alcohol added as a preservative, so be sure to read labels carefully. And don't confuse light soy sauce with the "light," sodium-reduced varieties, catering to the American market. Some Asian chefs scoff at their use, but for many dishes, particularly those that may be quite salty to begin with, it is useful in the kitchen.

HOISIN SAUCE: A popular condiment in Chinese-American restaurants, particularly with Peking-style duck, this soybean sauce, which has the licorice flavor of five-spice powder and is quite sweet, is more often used by Asian cooks as part of a marinade for meats before grilling. However, a small amount added to a stir-fry can wake up the dish and add a delicious flavor to the final sauce.

CHAR SIU SAUCE: This is a delicious barbecue sauce made with hoisin and other ingredients, usually chili sauce and vinegar. You can replicate it somewhat by mixing together ketchup and hoisin sauce, and brush it on chicken or ribs while roasting or grilling for a deliciously sweet glaze.

PONZU SAUCE: This Japanese condiment is a popular dipping sauce for sashimi (raw fish slices) and can be a tasty and light dressing for oriental noodles. It is a mixture of soy sauce, citrus juice or rice vinegar, and dried fish flakes. However, sometimes Japanese wines, such as sake or mirin, are added to *ponzu* sauce, so check for these on the ingredient label. Fish sauce and oyster sauce are close relatives and can be added to dishes for authentic flavor.

TERIYAKI SAUCE: Probably one of the most popular sauce preparations in Asian-American cooking, making your own teriyaki is quite easy to do (page 357), but in a pinch, a bottled version can add fast flavor to stir-fries and pan-glazed fillets. Some commercial brands add white wine (totally unnecessary), but in general, the better quality brands will not.

CHILI SAUCE: This red condiment can add a quick dose of heat to any dish you are preparing. Generally Szechuan in origin, chili sauce should not be confused with chili paste, a far more potent ingredient popular in Thai cooking. If you particularly like spice, red chili paste with garlic will definitely knock your socks off. In a similar vein, chili oil is simply cooking oil that has been steeped with chili peppers and can be used as a flavoring ingredient in many dishes.

RICE VINEGAR: Mildly acidic, this popular Asian vinegar can be added to many dishes, as well as salad dressings, for a subtle flavor. Sushi vinegar is rice vinegar that has had sugar added and is an excellent substitute for sake or mirin, providing the proper balance of sweet and acid that these alcoholic beverages would normally provide.

SESAME OIL: Delicious and fragrant, this oil is reserved for final embellishments of stir-fries and in cold noodle dishes, such as the popular sesame noodles. Toasted sesame oil has the best flavor and should be refrigerated once opened to prevent a rancid taste from developing.

FISH SAUCE: A common condiment in Thai and other Southeast Asian cuisines, this salty, strong-flavored liquid, often derived from anchovies, can be useful for adding quick flavor to stir-fries. Although more pungent than soy sauce, fish sauce can be used in the same way to dress everything from noodles to salads.

In addition to the above ingredients, there are many prepared sauces you can choose from, including kung pao, peanut satay, and sweet and sour. All of these are fine to use when time is limited, as long as you read the label for ingredients. Sometimes these products will contain the addition of sherry, white wine, or sake as a flavor enhancer or preservative.

Finally, most supermarkets will also provide a small Asian section in the produce aisle, where refrigerated items such as tofu, udon noodles, and gingerroot can be found. Depending upon the extent of your supermarket's inventory, you may also find fresh bean sprouts, snow peas, and shiitake mushrooms in this section. One of my favorite condiments, which is also kept refrigerated here, is the hot and spicy Korean *kimchee*, a type of pickled cabbage with lots of very visible red pepper flakes. It is served at nearly every Korean dinner table and is extremely pungent, but for those of us who enjoy our "heat," it's a great addition to a repertoire of Asian products.

Spanish Red Beans and Rice

MAKES 2 TO 3 SERVINGS The combination of rice with beans is a popular one, and not only with vegetarians. Mediterranean, American, and Caribbean cuisines all appreciate the delicious joining of these two nutritious ingredients, usually spiced up a bit with tomatoes, chiles, and garlic and served with roasted meats and chicken. As a main course or side dish, this delicious concoction, served with a sprinkling of shredded cheddar cheese and a dollop of sour cream, is sure to satisfy any Phase One hunger at dinnertime. And it couldn't be easier to make, since both the rice and beans are already cooked. Try this with black or pinto beans and experiment with different rice varieties. Any way you serve up this hearty dish, you will not go away hungry!

3 cups cooked white or brown rice, chilled

1 tablespoon canola oil

1 small onion, peeled and diced

½ medium-size green bell pepper, seeded and diced

Salt and pepper to taste

2 garlic cloves, peeled and minced

1 tablespoon chili powder

1 teaspoon paprika

1 teaspoon ground cumin

1 cup tomato sauce

¼ cup water

One 15-ounce can red kidney beans, drained and rinsed

2 tablespoons roughly chopped fresh cilantro leaves

Shredded cheddar or Monterey Jack cheese and sour cream to serve (optional)

1. Place the rice in a large mixing bowl and separate the grains with a fork or your fingertips. Set aside.

2. Heat the oil in a large nonstick skillet over medium-high heat, add the onion and green pepper, sprinkle with salt and pepper, and cook, stirring often, until softened, about 5 minutes. Add the garlic and cook another minute. Add the chili powder, paprika, cumin, tomato sauce, and water and bring to a simmer. Reduce the heat to medium, add the beans and rice, and toss well to coat and heat through, 3 to 4 minutes. Taste for seasoning and serve immediately sprinkled with the cilantro. Top with cheese and sour cream, if desired.

Smoked Salmon Kedgeree

MAKES 2 SERVINGS This British dish with Indian influences started out in the 1800s as a popular breakfast offering, but is now often served as a quick and satisfying supper. Traditionally, smoked whitefish or haddock is used and if you come across these in your local deli, feel free to use them. For American palates, I have instead incorporated smoked salmon, which not only requires little preparation, but also is more readily found in supermarkets. Often served with sliced hard-boiled eggs, you can add these as well, if you happen to have any on hand.

I always use white basmati rice for this dish, as it is light and fragrant, but any long-grain variety would do nicely. Fresh herbs really make this dish, so don't skimp on the dill and parsley. Some sliced cucumbers and a toasted bagel or pita bread will round this out perfectly and make for a satisfying supper.

2 cups cooked white basmati rice, chilled

2 tablespoons unsalted butter

1 small onion, peeled and finely diced

Salt and pepper to taste

1 teaspoon mild curry powder

4 ounces smoked salmon, cut into ½-inch-wide strips

2 tablespoons chopped fresh parsley leaves

1 tablespoon chopped fresh dill

Juice of ½ lemon

1. Place the rice in a large mixing bowl and separate the grains with a fork or your fingertips. Set aside.

2. In a large nonstick skillet, melt the butter over medium heat without browning. Add the onion, sprinkle with salt and pepper, and cook, stirring, until softened, about 5 minutes. Add the curry powder and stir well to coat the onion. Add the rice, smoked salmon, parsley, and dill and toss gently to combine and heat through. Sprinkle the lemon juice over all and serve immediately.

Variation: Make a 4-ounce portion of Seven-Minute Salmon (page 144) and flake into the rice in place of the smoked salmon. Try substituting fresh cilantro or basil leaves for the dill.

An Easy Way with Fillets

A fillet cut is simply a boneless piece of meat, usually quite thin (except for the luxuriously thick beef filet mignon), and always best when quickly cooked. This means they are a natural choice for fast and easy dinners, requiring little effort and time on your part to get them out of the pan and into your mouth. Other names for fillets you may encounter are "cutlets," "scaloppini," (usually referring to veal), and simply "thin, boneless chops" or "pan steaks" (as in the case of pork and sometimes lamb and beef). Chicken or turkey "tenders" would also fall into

Demystifying Deglazing
Delicious Flavor Without Fuss or Fear

The culinary term "deglaze" is heard on many television cooking shows and referred to in numerous cookbooks. It is simply the act of scraping up the browned bits of food (generally meat) that have accumulated on the bottom of the pan after sautéing. It is accomplished with the addition of a little liquid to help loosen those delicious morsels that often become the essential flavor of a future sauce or glaze. It is also where you will see the addition of alcohol as the choice of liquid, usually wine, and sometimes either intentionally or accidentally, the alcohol is "flamed" in the process. Since we know that "flambéing" leaves at least 75 percent of the original alcohol content and since we are, by necessity, choosing to keep a "sober" kitchen, using wine to deglaze is not an option. So, where do we turn for substitutions?

Many chefs will deglaze with stock and water. And happily, I can report that these days many chefs are actually *choosing* to deglaze with water only, in order to allow the pure flavors of their ingredients to shine through. Yet, sometimes another layer of flavor is desired. Since alcohol in cooking provides a combination of sweet and acid to the dish, we can easily replicate that role by using fruit juices and vinegars. In general, a three to one ratio of juice to vinegar will fill in nicely. For example, ¼ cup white wine can be replaced with 3 tablespoons white grape juice and 1 tablespoon white wine vinegar. The result will provide the right balance of this category. Fish fillets, of course, are also generally quick cooking and very well suited to broiling, grilling, and some types of pan-frying. We'll be looking at their versatility later in this chapter in "Fish in a Flash" on page 137.

Another advantage of choosing fillet-type cuts is that they are generally very lean (one of the reasons why longer cooking times are not recommended) and consequently make for a healthy protein choice. Whether chicken, turkey, pork, or veal, we can treat them just about the same, incorporating some simple techniques that add fast flavor and excellent taste.

Sautéing is by far the easiest method to prepare fillets and one that anyone can master. Sauté is the French word for frying, although it is generally accepted to be quicker and requires much less fat than other types of frying that you may be familiar with, such as deep-frying. All you need is a skillet (nonstick is always a good choice) or a frying pan (also called a sauté pan) and some tongs or a metal spatula. Medium to high heat quickly cooks the contents of the pan, usually with some browning, which in turn, is *deglazed* and becomes part of the delicious preparation. (See below for a discussion of deglazing and wine substitutions.) When sautéed, most fillets will take no more than 2 to 3 minutes to cook per side—a time that is hard to beat! Let's take a look at the technique in the master recipe that follows and then explore some easy variations that will never fail to make dinnertime interesting and delicious.

flavor for enhancing the final dish. You can experiment with different combinations for different recipes, if you like. I usually use white grape juice and lemon juice for fish dishes, while I have found that apple juice and cider vinegar do well with chicken and pork dishes. Red wine deglazing can be substituted with unsweetened red grape juice and red wine vinegar. Unsweetened cranberry juice is also a possibility, as is the use of balsamic or raspberry vinegars, depending upon the flavor you are shooting for. Provided the wine is playing only a supporting role and is not required in excess of ½ cup or so, these types of substitutions work beautifully. For recipes that are dominated by alcohol ingredients, a little more creativity is needed. We'll be looking at some sober makeovers of classic dishes in Phase Three.

Keeping bottles of grape, apple, and other fruit juices on hand will encourage you to use these substitutions when called for. My preferred choice of grape juice is the unsweetened Kedem brand, usually found in the kosher section of your grocer. Under refrigeration, most juices will keep quite well until needed. Vinegars should be kept at room temperature and have an extremely long shelf life. Once opened, however, they will last only about six months.

A word about commercial "cooking wines"—not only do they contain up to 17 percent alcohol, they also have a great deal of added sodium and other chemicals, which for *any* gourmet, sober or not, is a definite turnoff in the flavor department. And no, the alcohol *still* doesn't "burn off." I advise every aspiring cook, in recovery or not, to run in the opposite direction of these horrid products. Centuries ago, cooking wine had salt added to it, not only as a preservative, but also so the kitchen staff would refrain from helping themselves to the supply.

Basic Sautéed Fillets

MAKES 2 TO 4 SERVINGS This technique is so simple and quick you will welcome it more than a couple of nights a week when time and energy are limited. In this recipe we're using thin chicken fillets, but turkey, veal, or pork would also do nicely. In general, depending on their size, one fillet is an adequate portion per person, although sometimes, especially with chicken and veal, the cuts may be a bit skimpy, so two pieces per person may be a better choice. If leftovers are a result, then all the better. Having a cooked fillet on hand to slice and add to tomorrow's lunch salad or sandwich wrap is always a welcome shortcut.

Having your ingredients ready to go is the only key to this fast preparation. First, to ensure even cooking time, you may want to flatten any part of the fillet that appears too thick. This is simply done by placing the fillet between two pieces of waxed paper or parchment paper and, using the smooth side of a tenderizing mallet or a rolling pin, pounding until it is of even thickness. This has the added benefit of tenderizing the meat, which, in the case of some veal cuts, is a welcome result.

Next, choose your frying or sauté pan, one big enough to hold the number of fillets you are sautéing without them overlapping. A 10- to 12-inch skillet is ideal. Even if using a nonstick pan, you will need a little fat to promote browning. I usually use a combination of oil and butter, which provides peak flavor without burning. If using another type of skillet, you will need to add a bit more oil to prevent sticking. Salt and pepper are the only seasonings you will need, although any number of herbs and spices can be sprinkled on the fillets to add flavor and interest. Lastly, a liquid that will help you to create a quick glaze or sauce should be chosen and ready to go (see "Demystifying Deglazing," page 134). In this case, I've chosen a simple white wine substitute. It couldn't be easier!

3 tablespoons olive oil
1 tablespoon unsalted butter
Salt and pepper to taste
4 thin chicken fillets
¼ cup deglazing liquid: 3 tablespoons unsweetened white grape juice mixed with 1 tablespoon white wine vinegar

1. Heat the olive oil and butter together in a large nonstick skillet over medium to high heat until the butter just begins to brown. Sprinkle salt and pepper on both sides of the fillets and sauté them in the pan until lightly browned, 2 to 3 minutes per side. Transfer the cooked fillets to a warm platter and set aside.

2. Drain any excess fat from the skillet, leaving about 1 tablespoon. Immediately add the grape juice and vinegar and bring to a boil over high heat, using a wooden spoon to scrape up any browned bits left on the bottom from the sautéing. Boil for 1 minute, pour over the cooked fillets, and serve immediately.

Sautéed Fillets with Sesame Seeds and Lemon: Add 2 tablespoons sesame seeds to the pan before sautéing the fillets. Deglaze with ¼ cup fresh lemon juice and a pinch of sugar. Particularly good with chicken or pork.

Sautéed Fillets with Balsamic Glaze: Season the fillets with 1 teaspoon dried oregano in addition to the salt and pepper. Deglaze with ¼ cup balsamic vinegar and 2 teaspoons brown sugar. A delicious preparation for chicken or turkey.

Sautéed Fillets with Honey Mustard Apple Glaze: Add ½ apple, left unpeeled, cored, and diced, to the pan after removing the cooked fillets and cook, stirring constantly, for 1 minute. Deglaze with ¼ cup apple juice and 2 teaspoons honey mustard. Great for pork.

Sautéed Fillets with Chinese Garlic Sauce:
Add 2 garlic cloves, minced, to the pan after removing the cooked fillets and cook, stirring constantly, for 1 minute. Deglaze with ¼ cup low-sodium chicken broth mixed with 1 table-spoon Chinese duck sauce. Perfect for chicken, pork, or even tofu (see Chef's Note below).

Sautéed Fillets with Creamy Mushroom Sauce:
Do not drain the excess fat from the pan and add 1 cup thinly sliced mushrooms after remov-ing the cooked fillets. Cook, stirring a few times, until lightly browned, about 2 minutes. Deglaze with ¼ cup white wine substitute (3 tablespoons unsweetened white grape juice mixed with 1 tablespoon white wine vinegar), then whisk in ¼ cup heavy cream. Simmer until somewhat reduced, 1 minute, and taste for additional salt and pepper before serving over the fillets. Garnish with 1 tablespoon finely chopped fresh parsley leaves, if desired. Ideal for veal or chicken.

Sautéed Fillets with Spicy Pan Salsa: Season the fillets with a pinch of cayenne pepper and salt. Deglaze with the juice of 1 lime and a pinch of sugar. Add ½ cup undrained prepared salsa and heat through, stirring for 1 minute. Serve the fillets topped with a dollop of sour cream or guacamole, if desired. Excellent with chicken.

Chef's Note: Half-inch-thick slices cut from a block of extra firm tofu can fill in nicely for fil-lets. Pat them dry with paper towels before sautéing.

Fish in a Flash

As a healthy protein source, fish is unbeatable, especially when compared to red meat and poul-try, containing much less saturated fat while providing some rather healthy fatty acids in the process. We'll be looking at these beneficial fats, specifically omega-3, in more detail during Phase Three, but for now, be assured that adding some fish to your dinner menu is one of the best things you can do for yourself during this time.

In the Phase One kitchen, the greatest advan-tage that fish offers is its quick cooking. Whether you are working with shellfish, such as shrimp or scallops, or fillets of fresh or saltwater fish, hardly any time at all is required to dish up a main course. Pan searing, broiling, grilling, or roasting will all produce delicious results with very little effort. Rounded out with some quickly prepared veggies (see pages 140–141 for instruc-tions) or a frozen prepared side dish, you'll be enjoying a wholesome, nutritious dinner in record time.

Whether buying your fish from a local super-market or a specialty fish store, be sure that there is a fast turnover of sales, as fresh fish can turn bad quickly. Contrary to what you may assume, fish should never smell "fishy"; it is a sign that it is beginning to go. Cook your fish the day of purchase or, at the latest, the following day, or ask your friendly fishmonger if freezing is a possibility. Many supermarket fish department workers are surprisingly knowledgeable about cooking methods as well, so if you are unsure whether your fillets will do well grilled as opposed to under the broiler, don't hesitate to ask. To save effort and time, buy shrimp that is already shelled and deveined (a bit more costly) and select fish fillets over steaks, as they are generally boneless and often skinless.

Finally, you may be surprised to discover that much of the fish you buy is from frozen, mean-

Want Fries with That?

Quick Sides for Phase One Dinner Making

If you are making the effort to cook at least one component of your dinner, you are doing extremely well, considering the ups and downs of Phase One recovery. "Post-acute withdrawal" is no joke. If you are having difficulty grasping concepts and concentrating on details, and occasionally feel as though your mind is made of mush, then join the club. Symptoms like these can persist for weeks, months, or even sometimes years after quitting alcohol and drugs, depending on your individual makeup. So, congratulate yourself if you have been puttering around the kitchen during the early stages of recovery, especially at dinnertime after a long day.

In Phase One, making use of prepared side dishes will help you tremendously when attempting to get dinner on the table. Decide to make only one part of the meal, such as chicken fillets or a broiled steak, and supplement with good quality purchased selections that require little or no preparation. Here are a few suggestions:

- BAGGED SALADS PROVIDE A HUGE INCENTIVE TO INCLUDE SOMETHING GREEN AT DINNER. Some bags even come with their own dressings and fixings. To keep the contents fresh after opening, slip a folded paper towel into the bag to absorb excess moisture. Keep a selection of your favorite bottled dressings in the fridge or place cruets of olive oil and vinegar on the table for easy access.

- FROZEN SIDE DISHES THAT CAN BE HEATED IN THE MICROWAVE ARE INDISPENSABLE. Whether you prefer mashed potatoes, macaroni and cheese, or the many possible vegetables and their combinations like broccoli with cheese or peas and carrots, keep a supply on hand to supplement your dinner. Leaf spinach, peas, and sweet corn are particularly good in their frozen versions and many companies now make a huge array of frozen vegetable medleys to choose from. For quick oven heating, opt for shoestring French fries (they take less time than steak fries) and onion rings. Canned vegetables are also an option, although some contain a good deal of added sodium. Baby beets, lima beans, and creamed corn are good choices and can be heated in the microwave or stove-top.

- BOXED GRAIN SIDE DISHES ARE FAST AND EASY. Try out couscous, quinoa, and wild rice varieties. There are also a number of quick-cooking and tasty pilafs made with different grains and spices available at your local supermarket.

- VISIT YOUR SALAD BAR OR DELI FOR SOME COLD SALADS TO ROUND OUT YOUR MEAL. Warm evenings welcome sides of pasta or potato salad to complement burgers or chicken, and fresh cut-up fruit will provide a sweet, refreshing finish.

ing it has been "frozen at sea," but is still referred to as "fresh." Shrimp, tuna, and swordfish, among others, usually come this way and should not be refrozen without cooking. Again, your fishmonger can advise you. I don't recommend buying those big blocks of frozen fillets from the freezer section, however, as they tend to be tasteless and generally waterlogged. If you happen to live in a place where fresh fish is a luxury, be sure that the frozen pieces you buy have been individually packaged, ensuring better quality and taste. Ideally, opt for the fish counter whenever you can and look for sales when available. Try including at least one or two fish dinners per week during this time, experimenting with different varieties and preparations. You'll be amazed at how good you feel when you include this healthy protein in your diet.

Pan-Seared Scallops with Garlic Butter

MAKES 2 SERVINGS Large, succulent sea scallops are a delicious choice for quick cooking. Appropriate for many cooking methods, pan searing is probably the easiest and fastest way to serve them on a busy night. Be sure to rinse them under cold water and pat them dry with a paper towel before seasoning and searing. This will ensure a crispy and delicious outside and a tender and moist inside.

The smaller bay scallops are also a good choice here and will cook even faster, although I tend to reserve them as additions to gumbos or pasta sauces rather than serving them on their own. Whichever you choose, the flavorful garlic butter that accompanies this dish will go beautifully with a side of plain rice or egg noodles and a vegetable or salad. This is also an excellent preparation for shrimp, as are the variations that follow.

1 tablespoon olive oil
½ pound sea scallops, rinsed and patted dry
Salt and pepper to taste
4 garlic cloves, peeled and minced
Juice of 1 lemon
¼ cup (½ stick) unsalted butter, softened and cut into 8 pieces
1 tablespoon chopped fresh parsley leaves (optional)

1. In a large nonstick skillet, heat the olive oil over medium-high heat. Season the scallops with salt and pepper and quickly sear them in the hot skillet until lightly brown, about 2 minutes per side. Remove the scallops from the pan with tongs to a warm platter.

2. Add the garlic to the skillet, reduce the heat to medium, and cook, stirring, for 1 minute without browning. Add the lemon juice and, using a wooden spoon, cook for 1 minute, stirring to loosen up any browned bits of fish and garlic from the bottom of the pan. Reduce the heat to low and add the butter pieces. Stir or swirl the pan to melt the butter and taste for the addition of salt and pepper.

3. Pour the sauce over the scallops, sprinkle the parsley on top, and serve immediately.

Pan-Seared Scallops with Creamy Lemon-Ginger Sauce: Replace the garlic with 1 tablespoon peeled and minced fresh ginger. Substitute ¼ cup heavy cream for the butter and allow the sauce to simmer for 1 minute before pouring over the scallops.

Pan-Seared Scallops with Orange-Ginger Glaze: Replace the garlic with 1 tablespoon peeled and minced fresh ginger. Substitute ½ cup orange juice for the lemon juice and add 2 teaspoons orange marmalade. Simmer for 1 minute to form a glaze, swirl in the butter, and pour over the scallops.

Nutritious Fast Food

Zapping Up Your Veggies

It's a well-known fact that Americans do not eat enough vegetables. With all that we now know about the benefits, why do people still refrain from eating their veggies? I am sure that our upbringing has much to do with our tastes as adults. If we were forced to eat mushy over-cooked broccoli as a child, we probably find the prospect of broccoli enough to run the other way. I, for one, never knew that asparagus was suppose to be green and crisp, instead of soft and brown, until I was in my twenties.

Here's a little exercise for you supposed vegetable haters. Think of three vegetables you have tried and don't like or have never tried because you are sure you won't. Then let's make a deal. Every week, for three weeks, try cooking one of them according to the directions below. Give it a fair shot without prejudice and see if you don't change your mind. At the end of the three weeks, if you still don't care for the vegetables you listed, I will personally come to your house and make you a triple chocolate mousse cake. Okay, maybe not. But when you *do* reach for that triple chocolate mousse cake (or any other delectable sweet you may desire), your body will be grateful if you have fed it something beforehand that it can use to actually nourish itself. There is no way around this. If broccoli tasted like chocolate, there would be no poor farmers in the world and every kid would be rushing to the dinner table. If your idea of vegetables is French fries with ketchup, you need to start cleaning up your act and Phase One is the perfect time to start. Try to include at least one vegetable at every meal. For those of you who already love your veggies, "keep coming back" for more and expand your horizons a bit with some new and novel choices. Your body will thank you.

Certain cooking methods are better than others for preserving those valuable vitamins and minerals that vegetables have to offer. Stir-frying is better than steaming, which is better than boiling. But by far, microwaving vegetables is the best way to retain micronutrients. Below are my recommendations for vegetables that cook well in the microwave, along with their esti-mated cooking times. Use a glass or ceramic bowl or casserole with a lid. Preparation is simply a pinch of salt and a sprinkling of water, unless otherwise noted. Power level is High. Some microwaves are different, so play around with the time until you get the result you are after. All microwaved vegetables benefit from a few minutes of standing time, also called "carry-over cooking." If you will not be serving your vegetables immediately and plan to either use them in salads or reheat them another time, run some cold water over them to stop the cooking or plunge them briefly into ice water and pat dry with a paper towel. This will help to keep them crisp and green (if applicable).

MICROWAVE VEGETABLES

VEGETABLE	AMOUNT	TIME
Asparagus	½ pound, bottoms trimmed	5 minutes
Broccoli	1 head, cut into florets	4 minutes
Carrots	2 to 3 medium-size, sliced	5 to 7 minutes
Cauliflower	½ head, cut into florets	8 to 10 minutes
Corn on the cob	Husked and wrapped in wax paper	2 minutes per side
Green beans	½ pound, ends trimmed	10 minutes
Spinach (fresh)	2 cups torn and stems removed	2 minutes
Squash (acorn)	1, halved and seeded	8 to 10 minutes
Squash (butternut)	1 medium-size, peeled and cubed	7 to 9 minutes
Zucchini and yellow summer squash	1 medium-size, sliced or diced	6 to 9 minutes

If you do not have a microwave, you can steam or boil your vegetables. Be sure to have the water salted and at a rolling boil before you add them. Test doneness with a fork. Drain immediately into a colander and serve right away or refresh for later. Steaming will take a bit longer than the above times. Boiling will take a little less time, once the water has returned to a boil.

If you like your vegetables plain, you are essentially ready to serve them. A little butter and salt and pepper will, of course, make them taste that much better. I particularly like a squeeze of lemon juice on my broccoli and maybe a teaspoon of brown sugar and butter on my acorn squash. Try embellishing with some fresh or dried herbs or, if you like, a packaged sauce of some type. Before you know it, veggies will be an integral part of your dinner, so zap 'em up and eat 'em often. Fast food was never so nutritious!

Broiled Flounder with Crispy Crumb Topping

MAKES 2 TO 3 SERVINGS Delicate flounder is perfect for this preparation, as is fillet of sole. I have also had great success using tilapia and other thin, non-oily fish fillets such as haddock and plaice. Anything thicker than ¼ to ½ inch will require an extra couple of minutes under the broiler, and it would be best to lower the rack an inch or two to prevent the crumb crust from burning before the fish is cooked.

For this method we can dispense with the cumbersome broiler pan and simply cover a baking sheet with aluminum foil, which makes clean up a snap. Spray the foil lightly with cooking oil before laying the fillets on top to ensure they do not stick. Since the flounder will cook in a matter of minutes, have the rest of your meal ready to go before heading for the broiler. Serve with a lemon wedge, scoop of purchased coleslaw, and perhaps a green salad or microwaved vegetable. About two fillets per person is an ideal amount, although sizes tend to vary. Ask your fishmonger to give you more or less equal size fillets to ensure even cooking, or cut large fillets in half crosswise to make two.

Cooking spray or butter to lightly coat the pan
½ pound flounder fillets
Salt and pepper to taste
1 tablespoon unsalted butter, cut into little bits
½ cup seasoned dry bread crumbs
Lemon wedges and fresh parsley sprigs for garnish

1. Preheat the broiler and position the oven rack 3 to 4 inches below the flame.

2. On an aluminum foil-lined baking sheet that has been lightly coated with cooking spray or butter, lay the fillets cut side up in a single layer. Sprinkle with salt and pepper, dot with the butter, and lightly sprinkle the bread crumbs over each fillet.

3. Broil for 2 to 3 minutes, moving the pan around a few times to evenly brown the crumb topping. Remove from the broiler when the tops are golden and the fish is white and beginning to release liquid. Allow to rest for 2 minutes before transferring with a metal spatula to warm serving plates. Garnish with the lemon and parsley and serve immediately.

Easy Bake "Barbecued" Shrimp

MAKES 3 TO 4 SERVINGS   This dish is so easy to make and so incredibly delicious to eat that many of my clients have asked me for the recipe so they can make it themselves when I'm not around! Similar to New Orleans-style barbecued shrimp (which is, in fact, not barbecued at all!), olive oil replaces the usual butter and the shrimp is bought shelled and deveined for simplicity of preparation and easy

eating. In addition, this dish is served oven to table-top, resulting in minimal clean up.

A big loaf of fresh French or Italian bread for soaking up this fabulous sauce is really all you need to add to this meal, although a crisp green side salad will prove refreshing as an accompaniment.

½ cup extra virgin olive oil
2 tablespoons fresh lemon juice
1 tablespoon soy sauce
1 tablespoon honey
1 tablespoon dried parsley
1 tablespoon Cajun or Creole seasoning
Freshly ground black pepper to taste
1 pound raw large shrimp, peeled and deveined

1. Preheat the oven to 450 degrees.

2. In a 9 x 13-inch glass or ceramic baking dish or casserole, combine all the ingredients, except the shrimp, and stir well with a fork or whisk to combine. Add the shrimp, stir well to coat, arrange in a single layer, and set aside for 10 minutes.

3. Bake until the shrimp are cooked through, stirring occasionally, for about 10 minutes. Bring to the table and serve immediately with lots of napkins.

Roasted Tilapia with Chile Oil and Scallions

MAKES 2 TO 3 SERVINGS   Tilapia has become a popular light-fleshed fish, well suited to just about any cooking method, but particularly good for grilling, roasting, and frying, as it holds together nicely. Mild in taste, it will absorb any flavor you care to impart, and here a spicy chile oil livens up the result. The Asian section of your supermarket should carry a hot oil, sometimes referred to as Szechuan oil, although I have also seen it alongside other flavored varieties in the oil and vinegar section.

I happen to adore the version of sesame noodles that my local Chinese take-out makes and will often serve them with this for a total spiced up experience. Although sesame noodles are usually served cold, you can heat them briefly in the microwave when using them as a side dish. There are also numerous precooked udon noodle packets available with seasonings that would make a quick and easy side dish for this tilapia. Fried rice is also a delicious accompaniment.

If you are not sure of the intensity of your chile oil, taste a little on your finger before using. You can always cut back on the heat if necessary by using half peanut or canola oil in place of the entire amount of chile oil. Scallions add a nice color and crunch to this dish, as would thinly sliced green bell peppers, if you like.

¼ cup chile oil

2 tablespoons soy sauce

1 tablespoon rice vinegar

1 teaspoon sugar

½ pound tilapia fillets

Salt and pepper to taste

1 bunch scallions, ends trimmed and cut
    into 2-inch lengths

1. Preheat the oven to 425 degrees.

2. In a small mixing bowl combine the chile oil, soy sauce, vinegar, and sugar and whisk to combine. Lay the tilapia fillets in a 9 x 13-inch glass or ceramic baking dish in a single layer and season with salt and pepper. Pour the oil mixture evenly over the fillets and scatter the scallions around them.

3. Roast in the oven until the fish is firm to the touch and no longer translucent, 10 to 12 minutes. Remove from the oven, let rest for 2 to 3 minutes, then serve straight from the baking dish.

Champion Indoor Grilling

One of the technological marvels of the twenty-first century is the surprisingly effective indoor grill—a popular and easy way to prepare meats, poultry, fish, and even vegetables in a matter of minutes with no added fat. I would imagine that toaster ovens and oven broilers are feeling a bit neglected these days as many people have discovered the ease of using a two-sided indoor grill. If this phenomenon has passed you by, you may want to look into purchasing one. This is by far the healthiest way to cook individual portions of meat such as steaks, burgers, chops, boneless chicken breasts, and fish fillets if excess fat is an issue for you. (It also makes a heck of a grilled cheese sandwich!) Clean up is also a breeze.

Broiled Scrod with Salsa

MAKES 2 TO 3 SERVINGS Scrod is essentially a young codfish with a white and delicate flesh. It is usually purchased skinned and boned, making preparation extremely easy.

Broiling and pan-frying are my favorite ways of preparing this delicious fish, but it is also well suited to roasting and baking. Here a squeeze of lime adds a little zip, and a finishing touch of purchased salsa is all you need to present this dish. Excellent sides would be a flavorful Spanish- or Mexican-style rice pilaf, warm corn muffins with jalapeño jelly, and a crisp green salad.

One ½-pound scrod fillet, cut into 3-inch pieces

Juice of 1 lime

Dash *each* ground cumin and chili powder

Salt and pepper to taste

½ cup purchased tomato salsa

1 tablespoon chopped fresh cilantro leaves

1. Preheat the broiler and position the oven rack 4 to 5 inches below the flame.

2. On an aluminum foil-lined baking sheet that has been lightly coated with cooking spray or oil, place the fish in a single layer, squeeze the lime juice over it, sprinkle with the cumin and chili powder, and season with salt and pepper.

3. Broil, shifting the pan a few times to cook evenly, until the fish is firm to the touch and golden brown around the edges, 5 to 6 minutes.

4. Remove from the broiler, transfer to warm serving plates, and spoon the salsa evenly over the pieces of fish, garnishing with the cilantro. Serve immediately.

Seven-Minute Salmon

MAKES 1 SERVING I will rarely use the microwave for cooking anything but vegetables, but this quick method has won me over. Although microwave strengths tend to vary, seven minutes seems to always be the perfect time to cook a four to six-ounce fillet. If you are on your own and in a hurry, this preparation can't be beat. If you have a dinner companion, simply double the recipe and allow two more minutes of cooking time.

Salmon's high omega-3 fatty acid content has been touted for some time now and in Phase Three we'll be looking at more ways to prepare this deli-

Omega-3 Fatty Acids
An Essential Part of Every Diet

Omega-3 fatty acids have been the focus of much discussion over recent years and, along with omega-6, they constitute what are called the essential fatty acids (EFAs). They are essential because, of all the different types of fat that exist, animals must have them in their bodies to function or else they cannot survive. The construction of hormone-like substances called prostaglandins is one of their functions, necessary for healthy cardiovascular, immune, and nervous systems. Omega-3, in particular, appears to be sorely lacking in most people's diets and this deficiency may be partly responsible for many physical as well as mental diseases, specifically coronary heart disease and possibly depression and Alzheimer's. In fact, an interesting study of northern European diets and alcoholism brings up some fascinating and relevant points regarding how truly essential EFAs may be.

Researchers looked at the diet of people in seafaring areas, specifically Scandinavia and British Columbia—people who, for many centuries, derived their EFAs from eating copious amounts of fish. As a result, their bodies may have lost the enzymes necessary to build EFAs and in turn, prostaglandins, from other fat sources, something which, under normal circumstances, we are all able to do. With modern times and a change in dietary habits, less naturally occurring EFAs were consumed and, consequently, prostaglandin production became damaged.

cious fish for a boost of this important nutrient. For now, including it in your diet whenever possible will make you that much ahead of the rest of us nutritionally.

Occasionally you will find a few pinbones that were missed in the filleting process. Run your fingers over the fillet to find them—they can be removed by hand or with tweezers by gently pulling them up and away from the flesh. Cooked in this method, any leftover salmon can be added to tomorrow's salad, Smoked Salmon Kedgeree (page 133), or a hearty fish chowder.

If you can allow the salmon to absorb the dressing, flesh side down, a bit before cooking, it will be that much more flavorful; about 15 minutes will do the trick. If not, the resulting sauce will add plenty of pizzazz. Use a ceramic or glass casserole dish with a lid or cover loosely with a paper plate or towel to prevent splattering. The skin will peel off easily when cooked, but if you prefer, you can have your fishmonger remove it for you at the store.

Serve this with a prepared rice or grain pilaf. Broccoli florets, asparagus spears, and green beans make great vegetable accompaniments. You can even spoon a little of the sauce over the veggies when serving. Since this recipe is almost *too* easy, I have offered a few more variations you can use to embellish and enhance your salmon.

(continued on page 146)

Apparently, within a decade of this change, numerous diseases became prevalent, including heart disease, diabetes, depression, and, yes, alcoholism. Why? Because alcohol has a strange effect on prostaglandin production by increasing the body's impulse to produce it, while at the same time debilitating the enzyme responsible for its production. This translates into drinking alcohol in order to alleviate symptoms of low prostaglandin production, such as depression, but only as a short-lived remedy, perhaps leaving a craving for more alcohol in its wake. It is surely an interesting theory and one that may, with the study of other genetic factors, help to explain why certain nationalities of people tend toward alcoholism more than others. It is also another potential example of how alcohol can wreak havoc on our intricate and delicately integrated bodily systems.

Although it is possible to add essential fatty acids to your system through fish oil supplements, eating sources of EFA, particularly omega-3, appears to have the greatest impact. Certain fish, which acquire their omega-3 by eating algae and other forms of sea plant life, can in turn provide us with a good amount of omega-3 if eaten on a consistent basis. These fish include salmon (especially wild salmon), sardines, herring, mackerel, bluefish, and albacore tuna. In fact, consuming two to three portions of these fish per week may be enough to make a difference. In Phase Three, we'll be looking at more specific advantages of increasing our intake of EFAs as preventive medicine and the other (very few) dietary sources that provide it. For now, adding fish to your diet a couple of times a week is a definite way to help you get back on a healthy, nutritious track.

(continued from page 145)

> One 4- to 6-ounce salmon fillet, any remaining
> pinbones removed
> Salt and pepper to taste
> ¼ cup light Italian bottled salad dressing
> 1 teaspoon unsalted butter

1. Place the fillet in a ceramic or glass casserole with a lid. Season with salt and pepper, and pour the dressing over.

2. Microwave on high power, covered, until the fish is firm to the touch and pink in color, about 7 minutes. Let rest for 1 minute and transfer the fillet to a serving plate.

3. Add the butter to the casserole and, using a wooden spoon, stir until melted. Pour the sauce over the fish and serve immediately.

Seven-Minute Salmon with Onion Garlic Ragout: Add 1 small onion, peeled and thinly sliced, and 1 garlic clove, peeled and roughly chopped, to the casserole before cooking.

Seven-Minute Salmon with Fennel: Add ½ cup trimmed and thinly sliced fennel bulb to the casserole before cooking. Add 1 teaspoon finely chopped fennel fronds to the casserole when adding the butter.

Seven-Minute Salmon with Tomato-Basil Vinaigrette: Add 1 plum tomato, seeded and diced, to the casserole before cooking. Finish with extra virgin olive oil instead of the butter and 2 teaspoons chopped fresh basil leaves.

Seven-Minute Salmon with Asian Vinaigrette: Replace the Italian dressing with an Asian-style salad dressing such as miso, ginger, or sesame vinaigrette. Omit the butter and finish with a drizzle of toasted sesame oil.

Chef's Note: *Although salmon is the ideal choice for this method, try other firm-fleshed fish, such as tuna, swordfish, or mahi mahi.*

Burgers, Steaks, and Chops

Don't assume that fast food is only available at the drive-up window. Quickly prepared hamburgers, steaks, and chops are a definite reality for the Phase One kitchen. In fact, in a matter of minutes you could be enjoying a juicy, flavorful burger with all the fixings and none of the unhealthy fats and additives that your nearby Burger King has to offer.

Oven broilers, toaster ovens (with broil settings), and stove-top grill pans are ideal for creating fast food at home, as is pan-frying. Whether they be quarter pounders, turkey burgers, sirloin steaks, or char-broiled lamb chops, you'll be glad you decided to pull out that old broiler pan or skillet and get cookin'.

The Best Burger in Town

MAKES 1 SERVING Juicy, homemade hamburgers will never fail to satisfy a hearty and impatient appetite. A far cry from those flat, fast food varieties you may be used to, these guys will definitely win hands down as the best burgers in town.

Your choice of ground beef will make a big difference in the outcome of your burger. Although leaner mixtures such as ground round or sirloin may be a healthier choice, the ideal selection for hamburgers is ground chuck, usually containing 15 to 20 percent fat, just enough to keep it flavorful and juicy without shrinking too much. You can purchase ready-formed hamburger meat but, for my liking, they tend to be a bit thin and flat. Instead, I would buy a pound of ground chuck and make four "quarter pounders," about ½ inch thick. Wrap them up in plastic wrap, then aluminum foil, and keep them in the fridge for up to two days, if not cooking right away. You can also freeze them for up to one month.

Seasoning your burger will also make a big difference. Generally, a good pinch of salt and pepper on both sides will do the trick, but you can also sprinkle on a little cayenne pepper, garlic salt, or even mix in some dried herbs. To prevent the burger from puffing up in the middle, as it always seems to do at home (which we mistakenly remedy by pushing down with a spatula and losing all the juices), gently press down the middle of the burger before cooking, making a hollow indentation. As the burger cooks, it will even out nicely.

These days we are advised to cook our burgers to well done, with an internal temperature of 150 to 160 degrees, ensuring the demise of bacteria such as *E. coli.* If you are sure of the source of your beef (freshly ground from your local butcher as opposed to supermarket mass production), you could probably safely cook your burger to a medium or medium rare temperature of 130 to 145 degrees. If you are not yet familiar with doneness from touch and look alone, you can cut into the meat to examine its progress. But remember that, even though the center may still appear pink, by the time it reaches your plate, and ultimately your mouth, a certain amount of carry-over cooking will take place and it will be perfectly done.

A toasted bun or roll is, of course, the usual partner for burgers and there are any number of styles and flavors to choose from. Try sneaking in a whole-wheat bun on occasion or substitute an English muffin or scooped out sourdough roll for variety. Tortilla wraps will also make a good receptacle, as will pocket pitas. If you enjoy the luxury of cheese on your burger, by all means add it. If broiling, watch carefully, as it melts quickly; if cooking on the stove-top, put a lid over your pan to encourage melting.

Finally, every good hamburger deserves a little condiment and flourish, so whatever your pleasure, have it ready to go. Sliced onion, tomato,

lettuce leaves, and, of course, ketchup and mustard are classic, but try experimenting with some different toppings. Below you will find some of my favorite variations.

4 ounces ground beef chuck
Salt and pepper to taste
Oil for brushing grill pan, if using
1 slice cheddar cheese
1 sesame seed bun, toasted
Toppings and condiments of your choice

1. Form the beef into a ½-inch-thick patty, rounded at the edges. Press an indent in the center and sprinkle generously with salt and pepper on both sides.

2. Preheat the broiler with a broiler pan positioned 2 inches from the flame, or lightly coat a grill pan or skillet with oil and heat it over medium-high heat until almost smoking. Broil the burger about 4 minutes per side, or pan-fry for 3 to 4 minutes per side, until medium well done and barely pink in the middle.

3. Top with the cheese and continue to broil until melted or, if cooking stove-top, cover with a lid, reduce the heat to medium-low, and cook until the cheese has melted, 30 seconds to 1 minute. Transfer to the toasted bun and serve immediately with toppings and condiments.

The Chicago Pizza Burger: Season the burger with garlic salt, oregano, and black pepper or red pepper flakes. Top with 2 tablespoons warm marinara sauce and substitute 3 tablespoons shredded mozzarella cheese for the cheddar.

The Monterey Mexican Burger: Add a dash of ground cumin and chili powder to the seasoned burger. Top with 2 tablespoons thick and chunky salsa and substitute Monterey Jack cheese for the cheddar. Serve with a dollop of guacamole (page 32).

My Favorite Mushroom and Swiss Burger:
While the burger is cooking, quickly fry 1 cup sliced mushrooms in a small skillet with 2 teaspoons olive oil and a pinch *each* of salt, pepper, and dried thyme until lightly golden. Substitute Swiss cheese for the cheddar and top the melted cheese with the mushrooms and a scoop of sour cream.

The Turkey Bacon Turkey Burger: Substitute lean ground turkey for the beef, cooking to well done. Substitute Muenster cheese for the cheddar and serve with 3 pieces of cooked turkey bacon, sliced tomato, lettuce leaves, and mayo.

The Portobello Mushroom Burger: Substitute a large portobello mushroom cap, wiped clean

Animal Protein and Your Liver

When many of us are hungry during the unpredictable days of Phase One, sometimes we want nothing more than to sink our teeth into some substantial protein. Although it is possible to be protein deficient when severely alcohol dependent, once we become abstinent and begin to eat on a regular basis, we definitely get plenty of protein from various sources including, surprisingly, many carbohydrates. In fact, too much protein can cause stress on the liver and, if we suffer from any liver damage from our drinking days, such as a fatty or enlarged liver, chronic hepatitis, or cirrhosis, a lower intake of animal protein is a must in order not to tax the liver too greatly. Your doctor can advise you on this.

Yet every once and a while the urge for a juicy steak or some succulent, meaty lamb or pork chops may hit us with a fury. I think it is merely our appetites reawakening and, no doubt, a good sign that we are feeling better. The body might be saying, "I'm ready—feed me!" after an initial period of being coddled and nursed. Or maybe we need the amino acids that only animal protein can provide. Whatever the reason, an occasional quickly broiled steak or chop is an ideal choice for a fast, mouthwatering dinner. Rounded out with a salad or vegetable and some hearty grain bread, you're well on your way to satisfying the urge.

Determining portion size can be a bit confusing, given the ridiculously huge servings we may be used to at restaurants. Similarly, packaged steaks and chops in the meat section of your supermarket usually try to dictate your portion size to you. Two steaks in a pack must mean, of course, two portions—never mind that they are each nearly half a pound each! Try to limit serving size to three or four ounces at most per person. Feel free to cut steaks in half or in threes or ask your butcher to do it for you, and save the pieces for another meal. Or share a large portion with someone else. With other healthy additions to the meal, I guarantee no one will go away starving, while that protein craving will be happily satisfied. Afterwards, your liver will thank you.

and stem removed, for the meat. Brush lightly with olive oil before seasoning. Substitute fontina cheese for the cheddar and finish with 1 tablespoon thinly sliced oil-packed sun-dried tomatoes and a handful of arugula leaves.

Chef's Note: Other ground meats that make tasty burgers include veal, lamb, chicken (not too lean), and pork (not too fatty). Ask your butcher to grind these to order if you have trouble finding them and tell him or her what you will be using it for so they can include a proper balance of fat (about 15 percent is fine). If you are feeling adventurous, try one of the new burger kids on the block, such as buffalo, ostrich, or venison. Much lower in fat than ground chuck, they boast delicious flavor and are available frozen in burger patties at many supermarkets.

The Perfect Steak

MAKES 1 SERVING Beef cuts such as sirloin (on the bone or boneless), top loin, filet mignon, and rib eye are good choices for making the perfect steak. Be sure to trim away excess fat and season well with salt and freshly ground pepper. A light coating of oil for pan-frying and stove-top grilling will prevent the meat from sticking. Broiler pans, especially those that are not nonstick, may benefit from a light coating of oil as well, but watch for flare-ups under a high flame. Depending on the thickness of your steak, the cooking method that you choose, and the desired degree of doneness, each side will take from three to nine minutes to cook. You can check the internal temperature with an instant-read meat thermometer: 120 to 125 degrees for rare, 135 to 140 degrees for medium, and 150 to 160 degrees for well done. After you have experience with this type of cooking, you will be able to check for doneness merely by touch and

look. Cutting into the meat to check for color is discouraged because you end up releasing valuable juices and hacking up your presentation. However, if this helps you to learn, by all means go ahead. Remember that foods, particularly meats, will continue to cook even after they have been removed from the heat source. A rare-looking steak could end up being medium well when served; estimate that the internal temperature will increase by at least five degrees or more after it rests. And resting time is of utmost importance in the cooking of a perfect steak. Just a few minutes of patience will result in a tender and moist steak after the juices have been reabsorbed by the meat.

Everyone has their own favorite condiment for the perfect steak, whether it be steak sauce, ketchup, horseradish, or freshly squeezed lemon juice. Very little else is needed if the quality of the steak is high and the cooking method is a good one. But some enjoy their steaks smothered in sweet fried onions or sautéed mushrooms, and there are some other rather well-known steak presentations, which you will find below. This method is for pan-frying, which allows us to whip up a quick sauce (through deglazing) while the steak is resting, but if you prefer to broil or grill, serve your steak with a bottled condiment like béarnaise or horseradish sauce that will deliciously complement the beef.

1 teaspoon olive oil

One 3- to 4-ounce 1-inch-thick steak, trimmed of excess fat

Salt and pepper to taste

2 tablespoons water

1 teaspoon unsalted butter

1. Heat the olive oil in a nonstick skillet over high heat until almost smoking. Season the steak with salt and pepper and pan-fry 3 to 4 minutes per side for rare and 7 to 9 minutes for well done, reducing the heat, if necessary, to cook evenly.

(continued on page 151)

Substituting for Brandy, Bourbon, and Other Liquors

Often a recipe will call for a small amount of brandy to deglaze a skillet or sauté pan and, when combined with a few other ingredients, its flavor will become part of a quick pan sauce for steaks and chops. Classic renditions that often use this technique are Steak au Poivre, Steak Diane, and many others. These recipes include distilled liquor, namely bourbon whiskey and flavored brandies like applejack and calvados.

Since we know that brandy is distilled from wine or other fermented fruit juices, and that wood barrels are used for infusing the distinct brandy flavor, we can easily find a comparable substitute by looking at ways to enhance our already flavorful wine substitutes. The easiest way I have found is to use balsamic vinegar for the acidic component. Balsamic vinegar is always aged in wood barrels and, consequently, will not only possess the appropriate flavor, but also the characteristic tannins (the stuff that imparts that puckery feeling in your mouth).

When substituting for an apple brandy such as applejack, start with apple juice instead of white grape juice. Other fruit-flavored brandies are usually reserved for dessert making and in Phase Three we'll be looking at some fine substitutes for framboise (from raspberries), kirsch (from cherries), and Poire William (from pears), among others. For savory dishes, sticking with a "fortified" wine substitute (from the addition of balsamic vinegar) will provide the ideal characteristics we are after without imitating too closely the actual taste and flavor of real alcoholic brandy and other distilled liquors.

Incidentally, you may find many recipes suggesting that you substitute brandy with a combination of brandy extract and water. Obviously, all alcohol-based extracts, not just vanilla, contain a good 35 percent alcohol by volume, so this is not an option worth considering. In addition, imitation flavors that are too close for comfort can trigger taste buds and olfactory senses into a state of craving, unconscious or otherwise, so steer clear of any extracts that are alcohol-based or alcohol flavored.

Finally, skillet-prepared steaks, particularly in fine restaurants, may have a splash of red wine added for a quick deglazing, not referring to it as anything more than "pan juices." As you saw in the steak recipe, water can just as easily accomplish this minimal task, so if you doubt that your steak is being prepared "alcohol-free," don't hesitate to tell the waiter to ensure there is no added alcohol of any kind. The more we request these small but important favors when dining out, the more likely our needs, as recovering alcoholics, will be recognized and respected in eating and dining circles. In turn, as the general public becomes more aware of these legitimate concerns, perhaps some of the stubborn stigma attached to our problem will begin to melt away. If folks with high blood pressure can request "no salt," why are we any different?

(continued from page 149)

2. Remove from the heat, transfer the cooked steak to a serving plate, and add the water to the hot skillet. Using a wooden spoon, scrape up the browned bits of the meat from the bottom of the pan and swirl in the butter. Pour over the steak and serve immediately.

Steak with Easy Mushroom Sauce: While the steak is cooking, quickly sauté ½ to 1 cup sliced mushrooms around the edges of the skillet. Substitute light cream for the water and omit the butter. Taste for salt.

Steak au Poivre: Press 1 teaspoon coarsely cracked black peppercorns into both sides of the steak before pan-frying. Deglaze the pan with water or light cream, whichever you prefer.

Steak Diane: After transferring the steak to rest, sauté 1 tablespoon finely chopped shallot over medium heat in the skillet for 1 to 2 minutes (you may add more oil if needed). Omit the water and add 1 tablespoon fresh lemon juice, 1 tablespoon Worcestershire sauce, and 1 teaspoon spicy brown mustard to the pan, scraping up the browned bits. Finish with 1 tablespoon unsalted butter and 1 teaspoon chopped fresh parsley leaves, if desired.

Steak Pizzaiola: After transferring the steak to rest, add 1 tablespoon olive oil to the skillet and over medium-high heat, quickly sauté ½ small onion, peeled and diced; 1 garlic clove, peeled and minced; 1 plum tomato, seeded and diced; and a pinch of dried oregano. Finish with 1 tablespoon balsamic vinegar and spoon over the steak.

Chili Rubbed Spicy Steak: Mix together 1 teaspoon chili powder, ½ teaspoon ground cumin, and ¼ teaspoon garlic powder. Rub into both sides of the steak and season well with salt and pepper. Substitute fresh lime juice for the water and serve with a dollop of prepared salsa.

Recovery Note: For Steak Diane, remember that Dijon mustard is made with white wine. Choose, instead, from the other numerous mustards available in your supermarket.

Garlic and Herb Broiled Lamb Chops

MAKES 2 TO 3 SERVINGS Rib chops and loin chops are well suited to this broiled recipe. Depending on their size, serve two or three per person. Trim away any excess fat or ask your butcher to do it, but leave a little around the edges to hold the chops together. Much of this fat will melt away during cooking.

My very favorite preparation for lamb is the simple garlic and fresh herb coating below. I am so fond of it that I will use it as a type of marinade for leg of lamb roasts, allowing an overnight infusion. Here, however, these small tender chops require no marination time and are simply brushed with the fragrant and delicious paste before broiling. Any combination of fresh herbs will do, although I like to include a little mint if available, as well as some rosemary. Use your handy dandy mini processor or the chopper attachment on your hand-held immersion blender to make the paste. Dried herbs can be used if necessary.

In my opinion, lamb should be served medium rare with an internal temperature between 140 and 145 degrees, but you may cook it to medium well (150 to 160 degrees) if you prefer. If you haven't tried lamb in a while or think you may not care for it, try this recipe and I guarantee you will be won over! Buttermilk biscuits from the store or homemade (page 254) served warm with butter and a little mint jelly will complement these chops beautifully.

2 large garlic cloves, peeled and minced

1 tablespoon *each* finely chopped fresh rosemary,
   parsley, thyme, and mint leaves

Olive oil to moisten (1 to 2 tablespoons)

Salt and pepper to taste

4 or 6 rib or loin lamb chops, trimmed of
   excess fat

1. Preheat the broiler and position the oven rack to 4 inches below the flame.

2. In a small mixing bowl combine the garlic, herbs, and olive oil to create a paste. Season the chops with salt and pepper and spread the paste evenly over each on both sides.

3. Place the chops in a broiler pan or a rack on top of a baking pan with sides and broil the chops to the desired degree of doneness, 4 to 5 minutes per side for rare, 5 to 6 minutes for medium, and 7 to 8 minutes for well done. Remove from the oven and let rest for 2 to 3 minutes before serving.

Tandoori Broiled Lamb Chops: Spread ¼ cup purchased tandoori paste over the chops in place of the garlic-and-herb mixture. Lightly coat the broiler pan with oil before cooking and serve with lemon wedges, basmati rice, and plain yogurt or raita (page 261).

Broiled Lamb Chops with Mango Mustard Glaze: Omit the garlic-and-herb paste and mix together ¼ cup mango chutney and ¼ cup honey mustard. Reserve 2 tablespoons of the glaze for serving. While the chops are broiling, brush the remaining glaze evenly over both sides every few minutes until chops are done. Serve with the reserved glaze mixture on the side.

Chef's Note: Broiled tomatoes make an excellent accompaniment to lamb. Halve a large ripe tomato, remove the seeds and juice, and drizzle with olive oil. Top with seasoned bread crumbs and broil, cut side up, alongside your chops.

Maple Pan-Glazed Pork Chops

MAKES 2 SERVINGS When buying pork chops for pan-frying, thinner cuts (about ½ inch) are ideal for fast preparations like this one. Loin and rib chops, as well as boneless cuts from the loin, are perfect choices. Trim away any obvious excess fat, leaving a bit to hold the chop together and provide flavor.

A lot of discussion has gone on over the years about checking for doneness when cooking pork. If you follow many recommendations of cooking to an internal temperature of 170 degrees, the result will be overcooked, dry, and unpleasantly chewy. These guidelines were introduced when the danger of trichinosis was a real possibility, but today it is rarely an issue. In fact, we now know that simply cooking pork to an internal temperature of 137 degrees kills any traces of trichinae, if they are there in the first place. I generally recommend cooking pork to 150 to 165 degrees, except for the tenderloin cut, which should be about 145 degrees and still slightly pink in the middle.

Maple syrup and thiamine-rich pork are happy companions in this easy-to-prepare dish that provides a delicious sweet glaze. Try rounding this out with a side of candied sweet potatoes (page 238) and string beans or a salad for something green.

1 tablespoon canola oil

1 tablespoon unsalted butter

Two ½- to ¾-inch-thick center-cut pork chops,
   trimmed of excess fat

Salt and pepper to taste

¼ cup all-purpose flour for dredging

2 tablespoons cider vinegar

½ cup apple juice

⅓ cup pure maple syrup

1. Heat the oil and butter together in a medium-size nonstick skillet over medium-high heat until the butter is melted. Season the chops with salt and pepper and lightly coat them in the

flour, tapping off any excess. Fry the chops until nicely browned, 2 to 3 minutes per side. Remove the pork chops and set aside.

2. Add the vinegar to the hot skillet, scraping up any browned bits left from frying. Add the apple juice and maple syrup and bring to a simmer. Return the chops to the skillet and cook, covered, over low heat until the pork is just barely pink and the sauce has formed a nice glaze, about 8 minutes. Turn each chop in the glaze to coat well and serve immediately.

Pork Chops with Sour Cream Dill Sauce: Replace the vinegar with water, substitute low-sodium chicken broth for the apple juice, and omit the maple syrup. Remove the chops when they are cooked and add ⅓ cup sour cream and 1 tablespoon chopped fresh dill to the pan, whisking well to combine. Cook at a low simmer until thickened, 2 to 3 minutes, and pour over the chops to serve.

Honey Soy Glazed Pork Chops: Substitute soy sauce for ¼ cup of the apple juice and honey for the maple syrup.

Pork Chops with Balsamic Cherry Glaze: Substitute balsamic vinegar for the cider vinegar. Replace the maple syrup with cherry preserves.

Chef's Note: Fruit is always a natural partner for pork. Try adding apricot or peach preserves as a sweetener, or brush the chops with orange marmalade and mustard before grilling or broiling. In addition, apples are always a welcome accompaniment. Open a jar of naturally sweetened chunky applesauce as a condiment or make Cinnamon Apple Compote (page 181) when time allows.

The Espresso Lane

Ham Steaks with Redeye Gravy for Quick Comfort

Fully cooked ham steaks offer a quick solution for a comforting dinner on energy-sapped nights. Look for them in the refrigerated, cooked meat section of your grocer or ask your deli counter to cut you a ½-inch-thick slab of store-baked ham. When pan-fried, these can be ready in seconds and will provide some excellent lean protein as well as thiamine. Deglaze your skillet with leftover morning coffee or espresso and a pinch of brown sugar and you have the traditional redeye gravy. Canned pineapple rings make for a great garnish. Serve up some purchased cornbread and coleslaw on the side and dinner is ready in record time.

Getting Comfortable and Feeding Your Inner Child

By Phase Two, what has changed is nearly everything! Cravings are fewer and farther between. Time away from home to attend programs or meetings has lessened. We're hopefully feeling a lot more confident and healthier by having removed alcohol from our lives and are discovering the satisfying and happy life of sobriety. This isn't to say that we feel great every day of the week, but it does get better. When the occasional Phase One day rears its head, we can take the early recovery lessons we've learned and use them to cope—by talking to someone who can help, attending support meetings, and knowing that as difficult as the day may seem, "this too shall pass."

In terms of food, reexamine your Phase One goals and make sure they are all still in play. Get back on track if you've found yourself skipping breakfast or neglecting to eat regularly. No one is perfect. Remember that old unhealthy habits took a long time to become routine and that new and better habits may take some time to stick. Be patient with yourself, continue to pat yourself on the back, and keep at it. Remind yourself how much better your life is now and how much better it will become as you progress in your recovery.

Enjoying the Comfort of Good Food

Eating and cooking "comfort food" is one of the best ways to rediscover yourself. With more time available, as well as energy and inclination, now is the time to really enjoy the pleasures of comfort-food cooking. Try to remember what you loved most about certain foods when you were a child and reintroduce yourself to some old favorites. Bring happy memories back to the front burner by making and enjoying "feel good" dishes, from heart-warming breakfasts to old-fashioned desserts. Believe it or not, memories of good meals from our childhood can encourage some healthy neurochemical activity by helping us regain a positive sense of who we are. When my Italian grandmother prepared her weekly pot of sauce and meatballs, she always gave me the first cooked meatball (when no one was looking) ladled with a bit of sauce in a small dish to be eaten with a teaspoon. Since I was only three or four years old at the time, she probably thought a fork was too precarious a utensil to put in my hands. But to this day, when I eagerly taste the "first meatball," I always eat it out of a small bowl with a spoon. That's because it makes me feel good. Whatever foods conjure up those comforting feelings for you, by all means enjoy them.

Sharing the Pleasures of the Table

Share your memories and favorite foods with your family and friends and begin to create new, happy, and fulfilling memories for the future. We have the ability to change who we are by what we see, think, and do every day, so start creating positive associations to replace those that are worn out and negative. Homestyle meals that warm your heart and bring you closer to others help to encourage an atmosphere of love and support. Food has an amazing ability to heal and can be one of the best ways to repair and rebuild the damage of the past.

When Comfort Calls, Open the Door to Your Inner Child

The recipes in Phase Two address many of the issues we now may face during this time, such as the rediscovery of ourselves, our likes, our loves, and the value of family and friends who have supported us along the way. Make a point of cooking up a delicious full-blown breakfast on the weekend and enlist the help of those around you in the entire process. "Weekend Breakfasts and Brunches: Welcoming Starts to Leisurely Days" (page 159) offers a number of tasty ideas for those mornings when time allows for a little extra effort and fun in the kitchen. Comfort food and all its fixings can be found in the chapters "Old-Fashioned Entrées That Feed the Soul" (page 186) and "Supportive Sides, Vegetables, and Complements" (page 225). Reacquaint yourself with the classic meals and traditional dishes that once helped to mold who you are. Those same meals can now remind you of what you love and can contribute to the positive future that lies ahead. At the same time, try some unfamiliar dishes to expand your cooking talents; experiment with making and tasting meals that can offer insight into what others find comforting. As an added incentive to tie on the apron, "Cozy Conclusions: Desserts to Live For" (page 265) provides perfect sweet endings that will send your taste buds soaring and put a smile on the face of every inner child.

Simple Goals for Phase Two

BEGIN TO MAKE FUNDAMENTAL CHANGES IN YOUR DIET. If Phase One found you eating one too many chocolate chip cookies, start grabbing an apple or an oatmeal cookie instead. If you pour whole milk on your cereal and in your coffee, think about switching to 2 percent. Make small, incremental positive changes, which will be more likely to stick. A quick jump to skim or soy milk, for instance, may be too much change too soon, causing you to lose your resolve to improve your eating and find you quickly back at square one. With cravings lessening, think more about what you are eating on a regular basis and stop bad habits before they become problems.

STRIKE A BALANCE. If you know you'll be going out to eat and will probably order that delicious cheesecake for dessert, choose a lighter lunch to balance out your daily calories and fat. Keep a mental tally of what you're eating throughout the day and try not to overindulge too often. Enjoy making and eating your favorite dishes, just stick to reasonable portions. Otherwise, when Phase Three rolls around, you'll have more work ahead of you to drop the added weight you've likely gained. Now is the time to seek balance—an often unknown factor in the lives of addicts and alcoholics.

INVITE FAMILY AND FRIENDS OVER TO SHARE A MEAL. Let good food be the focal point of get-togethers with those you are close to, sharing the pleasures of cooking and eating with friends and family. Consider throwing your first sober party (see page 184) to get your feet wet and build your confidence as a sober host. Celebrate your sobriety and let others share in the progress you've made.

CHECK IN ON PHASE ONE GOALS. Periodically, we all get a bit lackadaisical, especially as we begin to feel better and our lives improve. Be mindful that this is a time when many of us get stuck in a rut. Check back with your Phase One goals to make sure they are well in place and that you are continuing to eat regularly, wisely, and are avoiding food prepared with alcohol. At the same time, foods with "trigger effects" may be happily losing their power. Test out the waters first, keeping an eye on how you react and feel; if there are any hints of unwanted associations and cravings, wait a bit longer. Take your time—Phase Two can often require more than a year, and sometimes even two or three, before many of us feel truly comfortable with our sobriety.

5

Weekend Breakfasts and Brunches

Welcoming Starts to Leisurely Days

During *Phase One, we learned to appreciate the value* of a nutritious breakfast; even simple meals such as cereal, fruit, and toast start our day off in the right direction. Often, especially during busy weekdays, this is all we realistically have time to prepare for others and ourselves before we race off to our daily obligations and meet the demands of our hectic schedules.

By the time Phase Two rolls around, you'll probably be pretty comfortable with the idea of eating in the morning and may even wish for something with a little more substance every once and a while. Pancakes, French toast, omelets—weekends are perfect for attempting these more lavish and hearty dishes, when there is ample time to both prepare and enjoy a delicious morning meal. Include your family in the preparation or consider inviting friends over for a small brunch to kick off the weekend in style.

In terms of health, eating a heavier breakfast only a day or two per week also makes sense if you are watching your calorie intake. An occasional splurge on pancakes or French toast is certainly justified if you have been monitoring your diet during the week and exercising regularly. Home-cooked, comforting breakfasts can be wonderfully satisfying at this time and should be included as part of your Phase Two routine whenever possible. Hearty breakfasts bring people together, soothe the soul, and nourish our bodies after a demanding workweek.

As a personal chef, I don't generally have the opportunity to cook breakfast for clients, although I do make healthy recommendations when appropriate. But when I worked as a live-in private chef, it was a different story. Although weekday breakfasts were simple and required little or no preparation, weekends allowed me the opportunity to pull out all the stops and create a wonderful array of dishes, from Blueberry Madness Pancakes (page 161) to Baked Asparagus Frittata with Roasted Peppers and Ham (page 175). One of the most popular catering requests I receive is for a brunch party, including everything from muffins to omelets to fresh fruit platters and always accompanied by copious amounts of nonalcoholic beverages, such as regular and flavored coffees, a variety of teas or hot cocoa, fruit juices, and sometimes smoothies. Indeed, if you are planning to host your first "sober" party, you may want to make it a brunch for this very reason. Mid-morning get-togethers tend to be associated less with drinking than other types of parties, such as those that take place at the "cocktail hour," so you can easily serve a wonderful variety of beverages without the anticipation of alcohol. Since social occasions often create a certain amount of stress for those of us in recovery, even during Phase Two, it's important to do everything you can to make for a more comfortable and sobriety-safe atmosphere when entertaining.

Let's get started by cooking some old favorites with a few new twists and exploring the many nutritious and delicious breakfast and brunch offerings that can contribute to our Phase Two recovery.

Pancakes, Waffles, and French Toast

Who doesn't enjoy these delectable breakfast treats served with a pat of butter and pure maple syrup? No one, according to manufacturers of pancake mixes, syrups, frozen waffles, ready-to-eat French toast, and even ready-to-microwave pancakes! A quick jaunt through your grocery store will prove the point. But when was the last time you pulled out grandma's pancake griddle from the pantry or dusted off the old waffle iron? Making homemade pancakes, waffles, and French toast is really quite simple and far more delicious than any prepared product you might find in the store, contrary to what Aunt Jemima or Mrs. Butterworth may tell you. So tie on your apron, grab your spatula, and let's start flipping!

Golden Medallion Pancakes

MAKES 36 PANCAKES We're all familiar with those delectable silver dollar pancakes served up at diners and pancake houses. Well, here's a recipe to celebrate your sobriety—whip up a stack of these luscious little medallions and start counting your blessings! Better make a lot of these to go around, as they'll disappear while your back is turned. Enjoy with a side of crispy bacon and some excellent quality maple syrup.

1 cup all-purpose flour
1 tablespoon sugar
2 teaspoons baking powder
¼ teaspoon salt
1 large egg, slightly beaten
1 cup low-fat milk
2 tablespoons unsalted butter, melted
Canola oil for coating the griddle

1. In a medium-size mixing bowl, whisk together the flour, sugar, baking powder, and salt.

2. In another medium-size mixing bowl, combine the egg, milk, and melted butter. Add the flour mixture to the wet ingredients and mix with a fork until blended but still a bit lumpy. Allow to rest for 15 to 20 minutes; this brief wait will activate the baking powder, making your pancakes light and fluffy.

3. Heat a large griddle or skillet over medium heat and brush with a little canola oil. Test for readiness by dropping a bit of the batter on the surface; it should sizzle and begin to brown almost immediately. Pour a tablespoon of batter for each pancake onto the hot griddle and cook until bubbly. Adjust the heat as necessary. The edges will begin to look dry while the middle is still wet but bubbling. Turn the pancakes over with a metal spatula and cook until golden. (Refrain from flattening them with the back of your spatula!) Work in batches and transfer to a heated platter to keep warm. Brush the griddle or pan with more oil as necessary.

4. Serve hot with butter and maple syrup.

Chef's Note: Make larger pancakes if you like from this same batter, which will yield 8 to 10 standard-size pancakes. This recipe can be doubled or tripled for a hungry crowd.

Variations:

- Substitute ½ cup of the all-purpose flour with whole wheat pastry flour for a nutritional boost.

- Sprinkle any of the following on the pancakes before flipping: mini chocolate chips, thin slices of banana, chopped walnuts or pecans, blueberries, raspberries, or hulled and sliced strawberries.

- Instead of maple syrup, serve with fruit jellies or preserves or dust lightly with confectioners' sugar.

The Price of Silver and Gold

Silver dollar pancakes were named after the 1½- to 2-inch-diameter coins they resemble, first minted in Philadelphia in 1794. Silver dollars were kept in circulation until 1965, when the price of their silver content began to exceed their face value.

The first golden AA medallions originated with Sister Ignatia, who nursed alcoholics at St. Thomas Hospital in Akron, Ohio, in the 1930s. She gave each released patient a religious medal with the symbol of the Sacred Heart on it. Then she insisted that they return the medal to her before they took their first drink. There are millions of sobriety medallions in "circulation" today with the same original face value—*priceless*.

Blueberry Madness Pancakes

MAKES 12 TO 15 PANCAKES If you like traditional blueberry pancakes, you will love this incredible concoction consisting of hearty pancakes oozing with blueberries, blueberry butter, and a drizzle of sweet blueberry syrup. Throw in a Blueberry Passion Yogurt Smoothie (page 24) and your friends and family will think you've gone over the edge! No problem. You'll be way ahead of them in the antioxidant department and, since blueberries also have been shown to improve memory, you'll be sharper and more alert, too!

I've added some whole wheat flour and wheat germ to the batter, which holds up nicely with the strong concentration of berries, as well as providing a few more nutrients. If the blueberries are not particularly sweet or affordable, feel free to use a frozen package or even a well-drained jar of them. If you were able to find blueberry juice at your local health or specialty food store for your smoothie, it will come in handy here, but could easily be replaced with red grape juice. If time does not allow, use purchased blueberry pancake syrup (usually found next to the maple syrup in the supermarket) and add a few fresh berries for a thicker consistency. The blueberry syrup recipe below is also delicious over waffles and ice cream.

BLUEBERRY SYRUP

1 cup blueberry preserves

½ cup blueberry juice or red grape juice

1 teaspoon fresh lemon juice

½ cup fresh blueberries, picked over for stems

BLUEBERRY BUTTER

½ cup whipped unsalted butter, softened

2 tablespoons blueberry preserves

PANCAKES

¾ cup all-purpose flour

½ cup whole wheat flour

¼ cup toasted wheat germ

1 teaspoon salt

2 teaspoons baking powder

1½ teaspoons baking soda

3 tablespoons sugar

2 cups buttermilk

3 large eggs, slightly beaten

¾ cup (1½ sticks) unsalted butter (not whipped), melted

Canola oil for coating the griddle

1½ cups fresh blueberries, picked over for stems

1. To make the blueberry syrup (if not using purchased), whisk together the blueberry preserves, blueberry juice, and lemon juice in a small, heavy-bottomed saucepan over medium heat until smooth and pourable, about 10 minutes. Remove from the heat and stir in the blueberries. Set aside and keep warm.

2. To make the blueberry butter, mix together the blueberry preserves and whipped butter in a small mixing bowl until well combined and purple throughout. Transfer to a small serving dish and chill until ready to use.

3. To make the pancake batter, combine the flours, wheat germ, salt, baking powder, baking soda, and sugar together in a medium-size mixing bowl and whisk until well blended. In a large mixing bowl, mix together the buttermilk, beaten eggs, and melted butter. Add the dry ingredients to the wet and, using a fork, combine until well moistened and blended. Allow to rest for 10 minutes to activate the leaveners before using.

4. Heat a griddle or skillet over medium heat and brush with some canola oil. Test for readiness by dropping a small bit of batter on the skillet; it should sizzle and almost immediately turn brown. Working in batches, allow about ⅓ cup batter for each pancake and pour onto the griddle. Sprinkle some of the blueberries on top of the wet, bubbly pancake and flip it over with a metal spatula when the edges are dry and beginning to brown. Cook a further minute or two until the other side is golden and transfer to a heated platter.

The Morning After

Think Aunt Jemima and Eggo have a monopoly on ready-made or frozen pancakes and waffles? Think again. Before you toss out those uneaten blueberry pancakes or buttermilk waffles, consider saving them to enjoy as a repeat performance another morning when cooking time may be limited. Wrap them tightly in plastic and store in the fridge for up to three days or freeze them for up to one month. When there's no time for pancake production, simply warm your stack on a serving plate in the microwave. Waffles will fare better in a hot oven (400 degrees) or toaster oven and will come back to life as crispy as ever. So, happily save the fruits of your labor and look forward to the morning after!

5. To serve, stack 2 or 3 pancakes on a plate, top each with 1 teaspoon of the blueberry butter, and drizzle the warm blueberry syrup over all.

Chef's Note: Dried blueberries are deliciously flavorful and would make a nice addition to either the blueberry butter or the pancakes themselves, if you happen to find them. Generally, when freshly packed, they are moist enough to cook with. If, however, your dried blueberries seem overly dry, they will require a little reconstituting. Simply allow the blueberries to soak in enough warm water to cover for 20 minutes. Drain and use as directed above. Dried blueberries also make an excellent addition to Blueberry Lemon Buttermilk Muffins (page 55).

Old-Fashioned Buckwheat Pancakes

MAKES 10 TO 12 PANCAKES Buckwheat is not really a cereal or grain, as its name suggests, but a type of herb that produces seeds or kernels, which in turn are ground into flour or hulled (groats) and toasted into the familiar kasha. Nutritionally, it is an excellent source of B vitamins and magnesium. Buckwheat flour's heavier, assertive flavor makes for a satisfying pancake and pairs well with fruit and sour cream. If not available in your local supermarket, look for buckwheat flour at a health food store or specialty grocer.

A little dollop of crème fraîche or sour cream and a spoonful of healthy apricot preserves rounds out this delicious breakfast treat, but the usual maple syrup would also work nicely.

½ cup buckwheat flour
½ cup all-purpose flour
2 teaspoons baking powder
2 teaspoons sugar

½ teaspoon salt
¼ cup (½ stick) cold unsalted butter, cut into
   small pieces
2 large eggs, slightly beaten
1 cup low-fat milk
Canola oil for the griddle
Apricot preserves and crème fraîche or
   sour cream for serving

1. In a medium-size mixing bowl, whisk together both flours, the baking powder, sugar, and salt. Add the cold pieces of butter and, with a pastry blender or fork, work the butter into the flour mixture until it resembles fine meal.

2. In another medium-size mixing bowl, beat together the eggs and milk, then add this to the dry ingredients, mixing only until moistened and blended. Allow the mixture to rest for 10 minutes to let the baking powder activate.

3. Heat a griddle or skillet over medium heat and brush with a little canola oil. Spoon the batter onto the griddle to form 3-inch pancakes. Cook for 1 to 2 minutes per side, until golden brown, and transfer to a heated platter. Work in batches and brush the pan with more oil as necessary.

4. To serve, spread a teaspoon of apricot preserves over the entire pancake, top with a dollop of crème fraîche, and serve immediately.

Variation: Try making these in small "medallion" shapes as in Golden Medallion Pancakes (page 160) and top with a piece of smoked salmon and 1 teaspoon sour cream with a dill sprig or caviar garnish for an elegant brunch hors d'oeuvre.

Dad's Cornmeal Hotcakes

MAKES 10 TO 12 PANCAKES On some Sunday mornings when I was little, my father would orchestrate a huge family breakfast like the ones he ate as a boy growing up in the Midwest. There would be piles of bacon, sausages, fried eggs, and hotcakes, with warm maple syrup poured over everything! I remember him saying it didn't matter that everything was kind of mixed up together because it would eventually end up that way in my stomach. With hindsight, I am more convinced that his presentation was due to inadequately sized plates that couldn't accommodate those huge Midwest portions, rather than any aesthetic concern. But to this day, I still love to eat these toasty cornmeal hotcakes, topped with an egg, alongside some delicious breakfast sausages, all smothered in warm syrup!

¾ cup all-purpose flour

¾ cup yellow cornmeal

3 tablespoons sugar

½ teaspoon baking powder

½ teaspoon baking soda

½ teaspoon salt

1 to 1¼ cups buttermilk, as needed

2 large eggs, slightly beaten

3 tablespoons unsalted butter, melted

Canola oil to coat the skillet

1. In a medium-size mixing bowl, combine the flour, cornmeal, sugar, baking powder, baking soda, and salt with a whisk.

2. In another medium-size mixing bowl, combine the buttermilk (start with 1 cup), eggs, and melted butter. Add the dry ingredients to the wet mixture and, using a fork, stir to just moisten and blend. This batter is very thick and is spooned rather than poured, but, if necessary, you may add the remaining ¼ cup buttermilk to thin the consistency somewhat.

3. Heat a griddle or skillet over medium heat and coat lightly with canola oil. Spoon about ⅓ cup of the batter onto the skillet, helping it to spread somewhat with the back of the spoon to about 3 inches wide. Cook until the bottom is golden and the top is a little dry but bubbling. Flip over and cook for another minute or two, until golden on the bottom. Repeat with the remaining batter,

transfer the hotcakes to a heated platter, and coat the griddle with more oil as necessary.

4. Serve stacked with a fried or poached egg on top and breakfast sausage links or bacon on the side. Drizzle with warm maple syrup.

Mexican Cornmeal Hotcakes: If you like a little "heat" in the morning, try this variation to get your engine started. Add 1 small jalapeño, seeded and minced, and ½ cup cooked corn kernels, drained, to the hotcake batter. When serving, top with the egg, but serve red or green jalapeño jelly and some spicy chicken sausages or chorizos on the side.

Easy Buttermilk Waffles

MAKES 6 TO 8 WAFFLES These days waffle irons are usually nonstick coated and have timers to tell you when to add the batter and when your waffles are cooked. Nothing could be simpler. Years ago, however, cooks took care to oil the iron and "sense" when the waffles were done to perfection, by smell and color. Much has been written about how to make the perfect waffle—golden and crispy on the outside while moist and chewy on the inside. Tips like adding extra oil to the batter for crispiness, separating the eggs, or substituting club soda for some of the liquid for fluffiness have been suggested. And, of course, there are the famous Fanny Farmer yeasted raised waffles, which require that the batter be prepared the night before.

I have found that a simple light spray of cooking oil, such as canola or even butter-flavored, on both sides of the nonstick iron will result in the desired crispiness without all the added fuss. Fluffiness is really a result of not overcooking the waffles, which we tend to do when we are shooting for that extra crispiness, so by helping along the crisping process, we can still get a moist and fluffy waffle. Try this method and see if your result is not waffle perfection!

1½ cups all-purpose flour

¼ cup sugar

1½ teaspoons baking powder

1 teaspoon baking soda

¼ teaspoon salt

3 large eggs, slightly beaten

1¼ cups buttermilk

¼ cup (½ stick) unsalted butter, melted

Nonstick cooking spray to coat the
   waffle iron

1. In a medium-size mixing bowl, whisk together the flour, sugar, baking powder, baking soda, and salt.

2. In another medium-size mixing bowl, whisk together the eggs, buttermilk, and melted butter. Add the flour mixture to the wet ingredients and combine until just blended. Allow the waffle batter to rest for 15 minutes to activate the leaveners.

3. Preheat your waffle iron according to the manufacturer's directions and coat each side very

Choosing Sides

A stack of pancakes or a couple of fried eggs can appear a bit lonely on your plate without a little something on the side. Traditionally, our choices were limited to fried bacon, sausages, or the occasional mound of hash brown potatoes, but no more! Today, healthy alternatives to fat-laden side orders are becoming more and more popular. Here are a few smarter decisions you can make when choosing sides:

- CANADIAN BACON: Many people have already discovered this delicious and lean alternative to traditional strip bacon. Taken from the tender eye of the loin, back bacon, as it is also known, is really closer in taste and appearance to ham. It is packaged precooked in cylindrical slices and shrinks very little when heated, so it provides more servings per pound than its side-derived counterpart.

- TURKEY BACON: Consumption of this lower-fat alternative to classic pork bacon is definitely on the rise. Flavorful and crispy when cooked up, turkey bacon fills in nicely as a side dish to pancakes and omelets. And consider using it whenever regular bacon is called for in soup and entrée recipes. It also makes a delicious BLT!

- CHICKEN SAUSAGE: Available in breakfast link or dinner size in the meat department of your grocer, chicken sausages seasoned with aromatic herbs such as sage and fennel are great choices for side dishes at brunch or breakfast. Try oven roasting them instead of pan-frying and serve with pancakes and maple syrup for a tasty lower-fat treat.

- SOY BREAKFAST PATTIES: Usually found in the frozen breakfast sausage section of your supermarket, this choice is perfect for vegetarians who crave the savory taste of bacon or sausages. They cook up quickly and will add a good dose of protein and calcium to your plate.

lightly with cooking spray just before adding the batter. Spoon the batter onto the waffle iron, close, and cook until golden brown. This may take anywhere from 4 to 9 minutes, depending upon the waffle iron you are using. Transfer the cooked waffles to a heated platter and repeat with the remaining batter. Serve immediately.

Variations: Substitute ½ cup of the flour with whole wheat pastry flour or even buckwheat flour for added nutrition. Although you may add small pieces of fruit or chopped nuts to the batter as with pancakes, I recommend using these additions as toppings instead. Try a mixture of sliced bananas, chopped walnuts, and honey or sugared sliced strawberries with a dollop of yogurt or whipped cream.

Chocolate Waffles: Substitute ¼ cup of the flour with unsweetened cocoa powder and increase the sugar to ⅓ cup. These are particularly good as dessert waffles with a scoop of ice cream and a drizzle of hot fudge.

Cinnamon Bun Waffles

MAKES 8 WAFFLES Here is my own favorite take on Marion Cunningham's excellent raised waffles of *Fanny Farmer Cookbook* fame, which require an overnight rise for the batter, but are well worth the result, especially if you love cinnamon buns as much as I do. My only alteration to the batter is the addition of cinnamon and a touch more sugar, but the topping is what turns this delicious waffle into a gloriously gooey treat.

WAFFLES
½ cup warm water
1 package active dry yeast
2 cups warm (not hot) milk

½ cup (1 stick) unsalted butter, melted
1 tablespoon granulated sugar
1 teaspoon ground cinnamon
1 teaspoon salt
2 cups all-purpose flour
2 large eggs
¼ teaspoon baking soda

TOPPING
One 8-ounce package Neufchâtel cheese
2 tablespoons confectioners' sugar
½ teaspoon ground cinnamon
½ cup chopped pecans or walnuts
½ cup dark corn syrup
1 tablespoon unsalted butter
2 tablespoons firmly packed dark brown sugar

1. To make the batter for an overnight rise, mix together the warm water and yeast in a large mixing bowl and allow it to stand for 5 minutes until dissolved. If it doesn't start to bubble and froth, that means the yeast is no good and you'll need to start again with fresh yeast. Add the milk, melted butter, granulated sugar, cinnamon, salt, and flour and beat with an electric mixer or wooden spoon until well blended. Cover the bowl with plastic wrap and allow to sit overnight at room temperature.

2. To make the topping, combine the softened Neufchâtel cheese with the confectioners' sugar and cinnamon in a medium-size mixing bowl. With an electric mixer, whip to combine and set in the refrigerator until ready to use.

3. In a medium-size saucepan, combine the pecans, corn syrup, butter, and brown sugar and bring to a simmer over medium heat, stirring well to blend. Keep warm for serving or refrigerate and warm again later before serving.

4. When you are ready to prepare the waffles, add the eggs and baking soda to the overnight batter and beat well to combine. Heat your waffle iron according to the manufacturer's directions and, when hot, pour ½ cup to ¾ cup of batter into the iron and bake until the waffle is golden and crispy, 2 to 4 minutes. Repeat with the remaining batter.

5. To serve, place one or two waffles on a plate, spread the sugar cinnamon cheese over the top (about 2 tablespoons per waffle) and drizzle the gooey pecan syrup over all. Serve immediately.

Classic French Toast with Vanilla Sugared Fruits

MAKES 4 SERVINGS Traditionally, French toast is made from stale or "lost bread," called *pain perdu*, and it was invented to make use of day-old baguettes. Consequently, the best French toast is usually derived from bread that has seen better days or will never on any day be enjoyed as a good-quality eating bread. I discovered the latter one summer when I worked as a private chef on a remote island that had little to offer in the way of crusty French or Italian bread. The little general store stocked mostly a "heat and serve" variety of baguettes because the shelf life was longer. Although it was a disappointing eating bread, it was the perfect bread for French toast.

Day-old egg-based breads are also good choices for making French toast and many will swear by the Jewish challah or French brioche loaf as being the ultimate choice. Vienna bread and soft Italian bread also does quite well. Here, I recommend a soft baguette, either of the "heat and serve" variety or a simple soft loaf. You can speed up the "stale" process a bit by slicing it the night before and exposing it to the air. A soft whole-grain will also do well.

It's always best to work with thicker slices that you cut yourself rather than thin presliced bread. If you choose to use a presliced commercial loaf, be sure it has become somewhat dry and stale so that it can hold up to the egg mixture better. Some flavored commercial presliced breads make delicious French toast, such as cinnamon swirl, cinnamon raisin, or banana, but I think you will happily enjoy the "lost bread" version once you give it a try.

Although maple syrup is always a welcome finish to French toast, here a garnish of berries starts the morning off on a healthy note. Feel free to substitute any other seasonal fruit combination, such as peaches, nectarines, kiwi, or plums. Having a canister of vanilla sugar (see page 168) is particularly handy for this recipe and really enhances the flavor of your French toast and fruit; however, plain granulated sugar will certainly work in this recipe.

FRENCH TOAST
  3 large eggs
  1 cup milk (whole, 2 percent, or 1 percent)
  1 teaspoon vanilla sugar (see page 168), or
      1 teaspoon sugar and 1 teaspoon nonalcohol
      vanilla extract
  Pinch of salt
  Twelve ½-inch-thick slices day-old soft French
      bread (see headnote)

SUGARED FRUIT TOPPING
  2 cups hulled and sliced strawberries
  1 cup raspberries, blueberries, or blackberries
  2 tablespoons vanilla sugar or regular
      granulated sugar
  Confectioners' sugar for dusting
  3 tablespoons unsalted butter and canola oil
      for the skillet

1. To make the French toast, whisk together the eggs, milk, vanilla sugar, and salt in a medium-size mixing bowl. Arrange the sliced bread in a single layer in a 9 x 13-inch glass or ceramic baking dish and pour the egg mixture over them. Allow to soak for 8 to 10 minutes, turning them over to absorb the egg mixture well.

2. To make the sugared fruits, combine the berries in a medium-size mixing bowl and sprinkle

(continued on page 168)

Extracting Flavor

How to Make Vanilla Sugar

Infused granulated sugar can take on any number of flavors, making it a perfect alternative to traditional extracts, which contain at least 35 percent alcohol by volume. Vanilla sugar is probably the best known of this type and makes a wonderful sweetener for fruit, coffee, or tea, as well as an alternative ingredient to regular sugar in many baking recipes. The secret is the aromatic vanilla bean, which infuses the essence of pure vanilla into anything it comes in contact with, minus the added alcohol.

To make vanilla sugar, pour a one-pound box of granulated sugar into an airtight canister and insert one or two whole vanilla beans. Close tightly and leave to infuse for about a week, occasionally shaking the container. After that, you will have ready-made vanilla sugar; as you use the contents of the canister, add more granulated sugar to replace it, because the vanilla bean will continue to flavor the sugar for up to six months. You can also add any used vanilla bean pods to this canister for additional flavor or consider starting a confectioners' vanilla sugar canister for delicious dusting of cakes, tarts, and cookies. Be sure the used bean pod has dried completely, however, before inserting it into the sugar.

Although initially expensive to buy, vanilla beans are far more intense in flavor than extracts and can be used and reused in a multitude of dishes. Once you experience its delicious and fragrant essence, the vanilla bean will become a welcome addition to your recovery cooking.

See page 444 for more flavored-sugar recipes and check out the "Resources" section (page 455) for information on ordering unusual flavored sugars online.

(continued from page 167)

the vanilla sugar over them. Fold carefully to coat and refrigerate until ready to use.

3. Heat a heavy skillet or griddle over medium heat and melt 1 tablespoon of the butter with a drop or two of canola oil. When the butter is melted and hot, place 4 of the soaked bread slices in the skillet and cook until golden brown, 1 to 2 minutes per side. Continue with the remaining butter and soaked bread, transferring each batch to a warmed platter and adding another tablespoon of butter and a bit of canola oil.

4. When ready to serve, spoon the sugared fruits over the French toast, dust generously with confectioners' sugar, and serve immediately.

Baked Whole Wheat French Toast with Orange Maple Glaze

MAKES 4 SERVINGS This easy baked version of French toast is a snap to prepare and can even be assembled the night before. Whole wheat bread holds up nicely to the intense flavor of orange zest. You can also make this with presliced whole wheat or whole-grain bread, which will eliminate an overnight soak and require only a few minutes of absorption time before baking.

Use a good quality maple syrup and allow the zest to flavor it as it reduces. Wait to add the orange sections until ready to serve. You can also use a can of mandarin orange slices in a pinch.

FRENCH TOAST

4 large eggs
½ cup orange juice
½ cup evaporated skim milk
1 teaspoon grated orange rind
8 thick slices whole wheat bread

ORANGE MAPLE GLAZE

1 cup pure maple syrup

1 teaspoon grated orange rind

1 cup orange segments, cut in half

1 tablespoon unsalted butter

Confectioners' sugar (optional)

1. To make the French toast, whisk together the eggs, orange juice, evaporated milk, and orange rind in a medium-size mixing bowl. Arrange the bread slices in a single layer in a 9 x 13-inch glass or ceramic baking dish (or use two baking dishes if you are using presliced wider cuts of whole wheat bread). Pour the egg mixture over the bread, turn once to allow absorption, and cover with plastic wrap. Refrigerate for 1 hour or overnight. (Again, if using presliced commercial bread, allow only a few minutes of soaking or the bread will fall apart.)

2. To make the glaze, combine the maple syrup and orange rind in a small saucepan. Over medium to low heat allow to simmer and reduce almost by half until thickened into a glaze, about 20 minutes.

3. Meanwhile, preheat the oven to 400 degrees and coat a large baking sheet with the butter. Place the soaked pieces of bread on the sheet, leaving some space between each, and bake for 10 minutes. Turn the bread slices over and continue to bake until golden brown, about 5 more minutes.

4. When the syrup has reduced to a glaze, add the orange segments and stir to combine. To serve, spread 1 tablespoon of the glaze, including some of the orange pieces, over each slice of French toast and dust lightly with confectioners' sugar if, desired.

Variation: Try substituting vanilla soymilk for the evaporated milk for added flavor and protein.

Ways with Eggs

Whether scrambled, fried, poached, or boiled, eggs are an excellent addition to a weekend breakfast or brunch. Thankfully, they have survived the cholesterol hysteria of the last few decades and are now considered to be part of a healthy diet, containing virtually every vitamin and mineral our bodies require. Scientists have finally agreed that high dietary cholesterol (as found in egg yolks) has only a slight effect on high plasma cholesterol (as found in blood levels, known as LDL). Saturated fat and refined sugars and starches play a far more important role in raising our cholesterol. Even consuming an egg or two per day has shown to have no detrimental effect on long-term health. So, by all means, serve up an egg dish or two on the weekends at the very least and enjoy the benefits of this powerful protein.

Creamy Scrambled Eggs

MAKES 2 TO 4 SERVINGS What constitutes great scrambled eggs is determined by individual taste. If you like a "tighter," chewy consistency (what some people might consider rubbery!), your eggs will require additional cooking time. If, however, your idea of the perfect scrambled egg is creamy, tender and "loose," your eggs will be cooked in no time at all. For scrambled eggs with plenty of flavor, you'll want to use butter and season well with salt and pepper. The amount of butter you use is really up to you. I once saw Martha Stewart insist upon a whopping 1 tablespoon of butter per egg! Although surely creamy and flavorful, I would rather allot my butter calories and fat to a side dish or buttered toast. Another way cooks suggest making scrambled eggs creamy is by adding, of all things, cream to the beaten eggs or, on occasion, a dollop of sour cream. Again, this is a luxury I would rather pass on for another dish and certainly is not at all necessary.

In my view, the keys to creamy scrambled eggs are a little butter, a little water, and a low, slow heat source, with constant but light scrambling with a rubber spatula or wooden spoon. The eggs should always be removed from the heat when they still appear to be too runny. As in other recipes, such as roasted chicken, we see the effects of "carry-over heat," because by the time they arrive on your plate, they are cooked to perfection. If they look done while still in the frying pan, they are essentially overcooked. Keeping these tips in mind will result in the creamiest and most delicious scrambled eggs you can make. Once you get the technique down, you can start to add little things to your scramble, like grated cheese, herbs, or smoked salmon, for example. Below you will find some of my favorite variations.

1 tablespoon unsalted butter
4 large eggs
1 tablespoon water
Pinch of salt and pepper

1. Melt the butter in a medium-size frying pan, preferably nonstick, over medium-high heat.

2. Whisk together the eggs, water, salt, and pepper until combined. When the butter has melted, pour the egg mixture immediately into the frying pan all at once and reduce the heat to medium-low. Using a rubber spatula or wooden spoon, gently stir and "scramble" the eggs, working from the edges of the pan into the center. Remove from the heat when thickened but still moist, transfer to a heated dish or platter, and serve immediately.

Ham and Cheddar Scramble: Add ¼ cup *each* diced cooked ham and shredded cheddar cheese after you have poured the eggs into the pan. Continue as directed.

Smoked Salmon Scramble: Reduce the amount of salt to a dash and add ½ cup smoked salmon cut into small pieces and 1 teaspoon chopped fresh dill after you have poured the eggs into the pan. Continue as directed.

Cream Cheese and Chive Scramble: Cut 2 ounces light cream cheese into small cubes and add to the egg mixture as it begins to thicken. Sprinkle with 1 tablespoon chopped fresh chives right before serving.

Scrambled Egg Burrito: Place the finished eggs in the center of a warmed flour tortilla, add a little salsa, shredded cheese of your choice, and/or guacamole, and roll up your eggs in delicious Mexican style!

Skillet Pepper and Egg Sandwich with Sun-Dried Tomatoes

MAKES 4 SERVINGS This preparation is a happy medium between a scramble and an omelet and a great alternative to the fat-laden, take-out breakfast sandwiches of the fast food world. In fact, my grandmother was whipping these up years before anyone heard of a McMuffin! Sometimes she would add slices of Italian sausage (left from her famous sausage and peppers) or add a bit of diced ham or pepperoni. I've added sun-dried tomatoes here for an interesting twist.

I particularly like this served on a whole wheat roll or baguette that has been scooped out in order to hold more of this delicious skillet creation. It would be equally as tasty on a whole wheat sandwich bun or English muffin, if you prefer. As a final condiment, a splash of good old ketchup is what I love, but you could also try a spoonful of spicy salsa or zesty tomato sauce.

1 tablespoon olive oil

2 teaspoons unsalted butter

1 medium-size green bell pepper, seeded and cut into thin strips

1 medium-size onion, peeled and cut into thin strips

Salt and pepper to taste

½ cup chopped oil-packed sun-dried tomatoes

6 large eggs

2 tablespoons water

4 whole wheat rolls, soft insides scooped out

1. In a large nonstick skillet, heat the olive oil with the butter over medium heat until the butter melts. Add the bell pepper and onion, sprinkle with salt and pepper, and cook, stirring, until soft, about 8 minutes. Add the tomatoes and stir.

2. Whisk the eggs and water together in a medium-size mixing bowl and pour all at once into the skillet. Cook over medium heat, stirring occasionally with a wooden spoon, but allowing the eggs to set and brown a little. Switch to a rubber

(continued on page 173)

Making Sense of the Egg Hunt

If you are confused by the myriad egg choices available in your supermarket, you're definitely not alone. These days there are more colors, sizes, and varieties of eggs than ever before. White, brown, free-range, organic, small to jumbo, graded, pasteurized, and stabilized—it's enough to ruffle anyone's feathers just shopping for a dozen eggs! Here are some egg-ssentials to help you in your hunt:

• *WHITE OR BROWN?* Contrary to popular belief, an eggshell's color is not a determinant of taste or nutritious value, but rather the breed of hen that laid the egg. The choice is purely individual preference, although brown eggs tend to cost a bit more.

• *AA, A, OR B?* This classification was created by the USDA to indicate both the interior and exterior quality of the egg. AA is considered the best, while B is the least desirable. Cleanliness, good shape, and texture contribute to a high-quality exterior, while interiors are judged by the amount of air present inside the shell, with less being more favorable, making for a denser, better-proportioned egg.

• *DOES SIZE MATTER?* Egg size is determined according to minimum weight per dozen and is designated as jumbo, extra large, large, small, or peewee. Large-size eggs are the most popular ones called for in cooking, but extra large and jumbo may make for a more satisfying fried, boiled, or poached egg. Small and peewee sizes are ideal for babies and children, as well as smaller appetizer portions and salad platters, when hard boiled.

• *PAPER, PLASTIC, OR BASKET?* Egg cartons are generally made of corrugated cardboard or Styrofoam, although some are now packaged in clear plastic containers. The original carton type is less important than where you store them after purchasing. Keep eggs refrigerated in the carton they came in; exposure to air and odors when transferred to baskets or so-called egg keepers will lessen their quality in no time. And, of course, don't be bashful about opening up the carton while in the store to check for broken shells or leakage before buying, as well as reading the expiration date stamped on the side of the lid.

- *WHAT ARE ORGANIC AND FREE-RANGE EGGS?* In general, organic means the hens have been fed organic grain, while free-range indicates that the birds have been allowed to wander around and peck the ground instead of being confined to a cage. In fact, the color of the yolk is an indication of what the hens have been eating; for example, dark yolks reveal a wheat diet, while lighter yolks are the result of corn, grass, and alfalfa. A new type of egg, which is high in omega-3 content, is a great way to increase your consumption of this essential fatty acid, especially if you are not a fish eater. Farmers fortify chicken feed with algae meal to attain this result. The label on the egg carton will indicate if the eggs are a good provider of omega-3.

- *WHAT ABOUT SALMONELLA?* We have heard a lot in the news about the dangers of eating uncooked eggs. The strain of bacteria called salmonella can be found in eggs with cracked shells, so any damaged eggs should be immediately discarded. However, modern commercial food technology has found ways to work around this potential danger by lightly pasteurizing eggs and sometimes adding stabilizers. As a result, the white appears somewhat milky in color, but is safe to use in recipes that call for raw eggs such as mousses and some salad dressings. It is not unlike the result of gently coddling, or dipping into boiling water briefly, to partially cook whole eggs in the shell. Still, pregnant women, infants, and the elderly should not consume raw or partially cooked eggs as a necessary precaution, while those of us in early recovery with compromised immune systems should also steer clear for a while. Pasteurized liquid eggs, found in the refrigerator section of your grocer, are sold in cartons and have the yolk and white already mixed together before exposure to bacteria-killing heat. Interestingly enough, products called egg substitutes actually have egg whites in their list of ingredients (although the yolks are omitted) and are combined with food starch and other somewhat undesirable additives to create an "eggy" consistency.

Incidentally, eating raw eggs, or drinking the infamous hangover remedy of a whole raw egg floating in tomato juice and Tabasco or some other dreadful combination, regardless of salmonella danger, has never proved to have any scientific basis for relieving distress and bolstering constitution. And in the case of the prairie oyster, it was no doubt the jigger of brandy or other "hair of the dog" it contained that usually eased hangover symptoms by reintroducing alcohol in our systems.

(continued from page 171)

spatula and cut the egg mixture into four equal portions. Continue to cook the egg patties, flipping them over and lightly browning each side. The middle should still be moist.

3. Scoop each patty into a roll and serve immediately with your choice of condiment.

Cheese-y Egg Sandwich: If you can't resist a little melted cheese on your breakfast sandwich, when the eggs are nearly cooked, top each patty with a slice of quick-melting cheese such as fontina, Monterey Jack, or American, cover the skillet with a lid, reduce the heat to low, and allow the cheese to melt for 20 to 30 seconds before scooping and serving.

Mushroom, Swiss, and Sour Cream Omelet

MAKES 2 SERVINGS Omelet making is often considered to be a challenge to home cooks, who may find that all their hard work results in broken pieces of overcooked and tasteless eggs with the filling everywhere except where it belongs! Do not despair if your first few tries are not up to your standards. Many culinary school students spend hours learning to prepare the perfect omelet and still have trouble. Along with roasting a chicken, making a classic French omelet is one of those traditional tests of a true chef, and I know many professionals who struggle with this technique.

American omelets tend to be a bit easier to make because they consist of only one fold, as opposed to the double-fold French-style omelette. A helpful place to start is with a good pan designed for the job, but not necessarily an "omelet pan"— one of those double-sided contraptions that you ceremoniously flip over and hope that the other side stays in one piece! A 10- or 12-inch nonstick skillet or frying pan—the size depending on the

number of eggs you are using—and a large spatula for flipping is all you need to turn out the perfect omelet. Low heat and a lid for the pan will also make your efforts easier, as well as having all your ingredients ready to go.

I prefer to cook any filling contents separately and add them with the cheese rather than cook them first in the skillet (as we will see, this works much better for frittatas). Here, we sauté the mushrooms first in a small skillet and keep them on the side until called for.

Using too many eggs and overstuffing are common reasons why omelets break when they are flipped. Once you get the feel for omelet making, there will be no stopping you as far as creative fillings and flavors are concerned.

FILLING

1 tablespoon olive oil

1 teaspoon unsalted butter

8 ounces mushrooms, wiped clean, stems removed, and caps sliced

Salt and pepper to taste

½ cup shredded Swiss cheese

2 tablespoons reduced-fat sour cream

OMELET

4 large eggs

¼ cup milk

Pinch of salt and pepper to taste

1 tablespoon unsalted butter

1. To make the filling, heat the olive oil and butter together in a medium-size skillet over medium to high heat until the butter is melted. Add the mushrooms, sprinkle with salt and pepper, and cook until nicely browned, 8 to 10 minutes, stirring only occasionally. Remove the skillet from the heat and set aside. Have the Swiss cheese and sour cream ready.

2. To make the omelet, whisk together the eggs and milk with the salt and pepper in a medium-size mixing bowl. Melt the butter in a 10- or 12-inch

nonstick skillet over medium heat, being sure to coat the entire bottom and edges. Add the egg mixture, reduce the heat to medium-low, and cook gently, tilting the pan occasionally to spread the uncooked eggs to the edges and moving the cooked areas to the center with a rubber spatula. While the eggs are still wet and uncooked but somewhat set, cover the pan, reduce the heat to low, and allow to cook a further minute or two, until the surface of the omelet is nearly dry and the bottom is lightly golden. If the eggs puff up, poke them gently with a fork to release the air.

3. Spoon the sautéed mushrooms onto one side of the omelet and sprinkle with the shredded cheese. Cover again for about 45 seconds, allowing the cheese to melt. Just before flipping, dollop the sour cream on top of the mushroom-cheese side. Using a large spatula, carefully lift up the plain side of the omelet and flip it over onto the filled side. Slide the entire omelet onto a heated platter and serve immediately.

Spinach, Tomato, and Feta Cheese Omelet: Substitute well-drained cooked spinach for the mushrooms, add ½ tomato, diced, and use crumbled feta cheese in place of the Swiss, omitting the sour cream.

Ranchero Cheddar Omelet: Substitute ½ cup drained chunky salsa for the spinach, replace the Swiss cheese with cheddar, and add ½ ripe avocado, peeled, pitted, and sliced.

Ham and Garden Vegetable Omelet: Reduce the mushrooms by half and substitute ½ red bell pepper, seeded and diced, and 2 scallions, ends trimmed and thinly sliced, sautéing as directed above. Add 3 ounces cooked ham, diced. Omit the cheese and sour cream, if desired, and sprinkle with chopped fresh parsley leaves for garnish.

Sweet Strawberry Omelet: Omit the mushrooms, Swiss cheese, and sour cream. Add 1 teaspoon *each* sugar and nonalcohol vanilla extract (or 1 teaspoon vanilla sugar, see page 168) to the egg mixture. Fill with ¼ cup thick strawberry yogurt and ½ cup hulled and sliced strawberries mixed together. Serve with a dollop of strawberry preserves on top.

Skillet Frittata with Red Potatoes, Artichokes, and Swiss Chard

MAKES 4 TO 6 SERVINGS Frittatas are different from omelets in their method of preparation as well as the ingredients that are generally included (or excluded). Firstly, they usually have more eggs and consequently are much bigger (flat, not folded) and thicker. They also usually include potatoes of some sort, while excluding shredded cheeses like cheddar and Swiss in favor of adding grated Parmesan or Romano to the egg mixture. Frittatas will take a bit longer to cook and there is no stress of flipping or folding over! Usually finished under a broiler, the top and bottom will be nicely browned, while the inside remains a moist and creamy delight. They are impressive to serve at brunches and are easily divided up into pie-shaped wedges for serving. The recipe calls for drained canned or frozen artichoke hearts, but if you are feeling up to a little more work and would like to substitute fresh cooked and diced artichoke hearts, the result will truly be an unforgettable gourmet treat.

3 tablespoons olive oil
3 small red potatoes, boiled in water to cover
    until fork tender, drained, and sliced, with
    skin left on (about 1 cup)

Salt and pepper to taste

2 cups roughly chopped Swiss chard leaves

1 cup diced artichoke hearts, fresh, frozen
     (thawed), or canned (drained)

6 large eggs

¼ cup freshly grated Pecorino Romano cheese

2 teaspoons chopped fresh thyme leaves

2 teaspoons chopped fresh parsley leaves

1. Heat 2 tablespoons of the olive oil in a heavy 12-inch skillet and layer the slices of boiled potatoes around the bottom, sprinkling with salt and pepper. Fry over medium to high heat until lightly browned, turning once. Add the Swiss chard and gently stir in. Reduce the heat to low, cover, and allow to cook until the leaves are tender, about 5 minutes. Remove the lid, add the remaining 1 tablespoon olive oil and the artichoke hearts, and stir gently to combine.

2. In a medium-size mixing bowl, whisk together the eggs, cheese, thyme, parsley, and a small pinch of salt and pepper and pour all at once into the skillet. Using a fork, quickly distribute the vegetables around evenly. Cook, covered, over medium heat until the eggs are just set, but the top is still of liquid consistency, 10 to 15 minutes. Check the bottom of the frittata to be sure it is not browning too quickly and reduce the heat if necessary.

3. Place the skillet under a preheated broiler to finish cooking the top of the frittata, about 2 minutes, moving the skillet around to cook evenly. Remove the frittata from the skillet by loosening the edges with a knife or metal spatula and sliding it onto a warm platter. If you are feeling brave, you can also flip this out onto a round platter. Let rest for 5 minutes before slicing and serving.

Chef's Note: If your skillet does not have an oven-proof handle, wrap a few layers of aluminum foil around the handle to protect it when broiling. Remember to grab it with an oven mitt on.

Baked Asparagus Frittata with Roasted Peppers and Ham

MAKES 6 TO 8 SERVINGS Frittata making can't get much easier than this. Requiring no flipping, sliding, or even broiling, everything is just mixed together in one big bowl and poured into a glass casserole dish to bake. There are only a couple of things to keep in mind when opting for this method. First, the addition of more fat, in the form of cream, provides necessary moisture. Secondly, the frittata must contain a lot of ingredients to weigh it down, so to speak, so it doesn't balloon into a hollow egg puff. Plentiful and evenly distributed vegetables in the form of asparagus and roasted peppers, as well as the addition of diced ham, help to achieve this end.

What I love about this frittata is how it holds together so nicely and comes out of the dish with no trouble at all. Cut into squares, it is perfect for a fancy brunch or can be enjoyed by the family on Saturday morning and then easily reheated in the microwave (if there's any left!) for Sunday breakfast. Try experimenting with other cooked vegetables to make your own variety of baked frittata. Just remember to keep the proportions the same for a smooth and delicious outcome every time.

You may use prepared roasted bell peppers or see page 120 for instructions on roasting peppers.

1 pound thin asparagus

1 tablespoon unsalted butter

10 large eggs

½ cup light cream

Pinch of salt and pepper

1 red bell pepper, roasted, peeled, seeded, and sliced

1 yellow or orange bell pepper, roasted, peeled,
     seeded, and sliced

4 scallions, ends trimmed and sliced ¼ inch thick

4 ounces cooked ham, diced

2 tablespoons chopped fresh parsley leaves

1. Trim the woody bottoms from the asparagus and cut into ¼-inch pieces. Cook in boiling salted water until slightly tender, 2 to 3 minutes. Drain, rinse under cold running water, and set aside on a paper towel to dry.

2. Preheat the oven to 350 degrees and butter a 13 x 9-inch glass baking dish.

3. In a large mixing bowl, whisk together the eggs, cream, salt, and pepper. Add the cooked asparagus, roasted peppers, scallions, ham, and parsley and stir to combine. Pour the entire bowl into the buttered dish, distribute the ingredient pieces evenly with a fork, and bake until lightly golden and set, 30 to 40 minutes. Cut into squares and serve.

Poached Eggs and Breakfast Bruschetta

MAKES 4 SERVINGS Poaching is one of the healthiest ways to prepare eggs. It is the basis of Eggs Benedict, a delicious but rich concoction topped with Hollandaise sauce, which tends to negate the health benefits of poaching. But poached eggs are equally delicious in their own right, served on toast or alongside it.

Here I've combined the popularity of bruschetta with poached eggs to create a happy and healthy union. Sourdough bread, excellent glycemically because of its vinegar content, which helps slow carbohydrate absorption, is ideal in this dish. Lightly toasted and served with a tomato, mushroom, and sage-scented topping, these bruschetta will become regulars at your weekend breakfast table.

Poaching eggs is really quite simple. There are even microwave egg poachers available to assist in the process, although do be careful not to overcook your yolk when zapping. There are also stovetop poachers, which work quite well, although the eggs are technically steamed this way. Traditionally,

poached eggs are prepared in a swirl of vinegared and salted water, which helps to instantly coagulate the runny white while keeping the yolk moist. The instructions for this method follow.

BRUSCHETTA
2 tablespoons olive oil
10 ounces fresh mushrooms, such as portobello, baby bella, cremini, or white button (or a combination), wiped clean, stems trimmed, and roughly chopped
Salt and pepper to taste
2 garlic cloves, peeled and minced
1 teaspoon chopped fresh sage leaves
2 large ripe tomatoes, seeded and cut into ¼-inch dice
Splash of balsamic vinegar
8 thick slices sourdough bread

POACHED EGGS
2 tablespoons white wine vinegar
Pinch of salt
4 large eggs

1. To make the bruschetta, heat the olive oil in a large skillet or frying pan over medium to high heat. Add the mushrooms, sprinkle with salt and pepper, and cook, stirring occasionally, allowing the mushrooms to lose their water. Continue to cook until the water evaporates and the mushrooms are lightly browned and softened, about 8 minutes total. Add the garlic and sage, reduce the heat to medium-low, and cook for another 2 minutes. Add the tomatoes, turn off the heat, and stir gently to combine. Season with the balsamic vinegar and taste for salt and pepper. Set aside.

2. To make the poached eggs, bring a shallow pan or a skillet (with a lid) with about 3 inches of water in it to a low simmer. Add the white vinegar and a good pinch of salt. When the water is ready, give it a swirl with a wooden spoon and carefully break the eggs directly into the water one at a

time. Turn off the heat and immediately cover the poaching pan, allowing the eggs to cook undisturbed for 3 minutes or so. When the whites are opaque and the yolks have a thin covering of white, remove them from the liquid using a slotted spoon. Place them to drain on paper towels.

3. Toast the sourdough slices, either in a toaster or under a broiler, until both sides are lightly golden. You may also grill them if you have a stovetop grill. Trim the eggs of any extraneous white to round off the edges and immediately place them on top of the sourdough toast (one per person). Serve the tomato-and-mushroom topping on the side with the remaining sourdough toasts.

Chef's Note: *If you are preparing your poached eggs in advance, plunge them into a bowl of cold water to stop the yolks from hardening. Store them in the cold water in the refrigerator until you need them. Reheat them just before serving by returning them briefly to the poaching liquid, which has been kept warm on the stove. Be sure to pat them dry before placing them on the toasts.*

Recovery Note: *At fine restaurants, eggs are sometimes poached in a white wine liquid, which may become the final sauce. Be sure to ask before ordering.*

Cereals and Fruit

If the most you've explored in Phase One is instant oatmeal and Cheerios, you're in for a real treat! Homemade cereals, cold and hot, are not only fabulous to eat but also inexpensive to make, compared to buying the ready-made stuff. A batch of homemade granola is far cheaper than the fancy store-bought varieties and has the added attraction of being your own personal creation with all the ingredients you like and none of the ones you don't. How many times have you looked closely at the bag and thought, "Oooh, I'd like that . . . if it weren't for the chopped dates!" Well, here's your chance to become the chef of cereals—granola, muesli, multigrain, old-fashioned oatmeal—the choice is yours.

In addition to the pleasure of making and eating your own cereals, you can pat yourself on the back for including the healthiest foods on the planet in your morning breakfast bowl. Oatmeal, barley, wheat berries, wheat germ, and all those delicious dried fruits and nuts are so glycemically perfect, they will see you through the day with a steady flow of energy and a positive, healthy attitude to whatever life chooses to "dish out" for you! As you remember from our discussion of complex carbohydrates and the glycemic index ("Getting the Basics Straight: Understanding Macronutrients and the Glycemic Index," page 28), it's like revving up your engine with a powerful, time-released energy elixir to start the day and sustain you throughout. Once you master making these cereals, you may want to allow a little extra time in the morning on weekdays to prepare them and reap their wonderfully nutritious benefits.

Fruit for breakfast is always a great addition and can be presented in a number of attractive ways. Whether added to cereal, yogurt, or on its own, fruit is something we should make a point of including in our diet on a regular basis for much needed vitamins, minerals, and fiber. Keep a plentiful supply of seasonal fruit on hand to help start your day on a healthy note.

Easy Homemade Granola

MAKES ABOUT 6 CUPS Since granola will keep in an airtight container for two weeks or more, spending the time to make a batch every once in a while will pay off in terms of time and money in the long run and you'll have some on hand during the week when you're in more of a rush. Granola, generally a sweet and crunchy cereal, goes well with yogurt and fresh fruit and makes a good addition to a cold breakfast spread that may include muffins, bagels, or toast. It's also great on ice cream!

3 cups old-fashioned rolled oats (not the quick-cooking kind)
¼ cup toasted or raw wheat germ or bran
¼ cup sesame seeds
¼ cup sweetened flaked coconut
½ cup canola oil
¼ cup honey
¼ cup firmly packed light brown sugar
Pinch of salt
1 cup chopped dried fruit and/or nuts of your choice (optional)

1. Preheat the oven to 325 degrees.
2. In a large mixing bowl, combine the oats, wheat germ, sesame seeds, and coconut and mix well.
3. In a small saucepan, heat the oil with the honey, brown sugar, and salt over medium to low heat, stirring, until the sugar has dissolved. Pour this into the dry ingredients and mix well to coat.
4. Transfer the mixture to a large baking sheet with a rim and spread out evenly. Bake until golden

and crisp, about 30 minutes, occasionally shaking the pan and redistributing the granola to evenly brown.
5. Transfer to a clean mixing bowl and add the dried fruit and/or nuts, if desired. Let cool completely and store in an airtight container.

Ginger Granola with Almonds: Add 1 teaspoon ground ginger and ½ teaspoon ground cinnamon to the dry ingredients. Finish with ½ cup sliced almonds and ½ cup crystallized ginger cut into ¼-inch dice.

Maple Pecan Granola: Substitute pure maple syrup for the honey. Finish with ½ cup chopped pecans and ½ cup golden raisins.

Orange Spice Granola: Add 1 teaspoon *each* grated orange rind and ground cinnamon and ¼ teaspoon *each* ground nutmeg and allspice to the dry ingredients. Finish with ½ cup orange-scented dried cranberries and ¼ cup cinnamon raisins (available in packets in most supermarkets).

Apricot and Sunflower Seed Granola: Add ¼ cup apricot nectar to the honey mixture. Finish with ⅔ cup chopped dried apricots and ⅓ cup hulled sunflower seeds.

Marvelous Muesli

MAKES 6 TO 8 SERVINGS A Swiss nutritionist developed muesli in the nineteenth century as a health food for the nation. The traditional preparation, which requires an overnight soaking of oats and dried fruit, has been somewhat lost in the translation and in most grocery stores, the muesli you find is in actuality a variety of granola. Real packaged Swiss muesli, when eaten straight with a little milk, leaves most people thinking they have just been chomping on shredded cardboard, and unless you take the time to soak the cereal, much of the nutritional value will be unavailable to your body as it cannot be absorbed through normal digestion. Needless to say, in order for muesli to become "marvelous," both nutritionally and taste wise, I will be taking a few liberties here and stray from the original recipe. That does not at all mean that it is any less healthy, since the ingredients of oats, bran, and dried fruits are still included. I've just sweetened and toasted it up a bit to tempt any early morning riser into pouring a hearty bowl!

Flax cereal flakes are available at most health food stores and are a good source of omega–3 fatty acids. If you can't find them, plain bran flakes or even raisin bran (omitting the extra raisins in the recipe) is a fine addition.

MUESLI

2 cups quick-cooking rolled oats
1 cup flax cereal flakes or bran flakes
½ cup toasted wheat germ or bran
½ cup Grape Nuts cereal
¼ cup seedless raisins or dried currants
¼ cup dried blueberries, cranberries, or cherries

TO SERVE

Milk, soymilk, or yogurt
½ cup cored and diced apple per serving

1. Preheat the oven to 350 degrees.
2. To make the muesli, spread the oats out over a large baking sheet with a rim and toast in the oven, stirring occasionally, until lightly golden and fragrant, about 20 minutes. Transfer to a large mixing bowl, combine with the remaining ingredients, and let cool completely.
3. To serve, scoop ½ to ¾ cup muesli into a bowl, moisten with milk, soymilk, or yogurt, and top with the diced apple. Keep extra muesli in an airtight container at room temperature for 2 weeks.

Cereal, Fruit, and Fiber

Are You Eating Enough?

Many of the foods that provide the greatest amount of fiber in our diets, such as whole grains, fruits, and vegetables, were probably carelessly ignored during our active addictions. Fiber itself does not directly provide vitamins and minerals, but it can greatly contribute to overall health and should be included as an important part of our diet in recovery. Although recent studies have rendered the correlation between fiber and colon cancer debatable, there is little dispute that a diet rich in fiber can lower serum cholesterol and help in our fight against heart disease and diabetes.

Initially, increasing fiber in your diet may upset your system with bloating, as the friendly bacteria in the gut attack and digest these complex carbohydrates. Eventually, with increased digestive health after Phase One, our bodies will become more efficient at regularly handling fiber intake, and breakfast time is the perfect occasion to make a point of including it in your daily routine.

Fiber, also known as roughage or bulk, is categorized by its ability to become soluble in water. Insoluble fiber cannot be digested by our enzymes, but it protects the intestinal tract by moving waste through our system. It is found in whole grains, especially the bran, or outer layer, of the grain, as well as in nuts, seeds, and fruit. Water-soluble fiber can prevent the reabsorption of cholesterol in our digestive tract and ultimately helps to lower blood cholesterol. It is found in oats, beans, and many fruits.

The USDA recommends consuming 20 to 35 grams of fiber daily, while other fiber advocates suggest shooting for 40 grams per day. Although this may sound like a lot, increasing the amount of whole grain cereals and fruit you eat will easily help you attain these levels. For example, a bowl of oatmeal with ½ cup raspberries contains about 25 grams!

Usually the greater the fiber content in a carbohydrate, the lower it is on the Glycemic Index, which makes it a better choice for overall health. However, when whole grains are finely ground, such as in whole wheat bread flours, much of the fiber benefit is reduced and its glycemic rating rises. Of course, whole-grain flours contain more nutrients and are certainly wiser choices than highly processed white flours, but glycemically it makes little difference. A more effective method of adding fiber is to simply increase your consumption of whole grains, fruit, and vegetables. Here are some easy ways to boost your fiber intake at breakfast time:

- Choose orange juice with pulp rather than without, or try a glass of pineapple or unsweetened grapefruit juice.

- Serve a whole-grain roll or bagel with your scrambled eggs, instead of a croissant or white toast.

- Add ½ cup fruit, such as raspberries, strawberries, blueberries, or bananas, to your cereal bowl.

- Fill your omelet with leftover cooked vegetables such as sautéed broccoli or zucchini or steamed or roasted asparagus.

- Have a British-style breakfast by serving ½ cup baked beans with your eggs, bacon, and toast.

- Add ¼ cup oat bran to your hot cereal or pancake and waffle batter for 4 grams of soluble fiber or add 1 tablespoon psyllium husks to your fruit smoothie for a whopping 8 grams.

Old-Fashioned Oatmeal with Cinnamon Apple Compote

MAKES 3 TO 4 SERVINGS Old-fashioned oats, unlike steel-cut oats, really take little time to cook—a mere five minutes—but many people find anything beyond the "instant" realm a little too much work during the week. Try this version on the weekend and, before long, you'll be making time in the morning on other days to fit it into your breakfast schedule! Because they are less processed than quick-cooking oats, old-fashioned oats have more to offer in the nutrition department. Cook them in a nonstick pot to avoid scorching and sticking.

Apples make a great companion to creamy oatmeal and both the apple juice and apple compote are excellent low-glycemic choices, adding to the energy-sustaining value of oats. You can make the compote another time if you like and reheat it when serving your oatmeal. It also goes well with pork dinners and is the basis for Ellen's Baked Stuffed Apples on page 413, so whipping up a little Cinnamon Apple Compote when your apple supply is plentiful is a great idea. It will keep refrigerated for up to five days.

Classically, a big bowl of old-fashioned oatmeal is undeniably delicious served with a pat of butter, a spoonful of brown sugar, and a quick pouring of cream. If you can afford the calories, enjoy yourself! Otherwise, the compote topping, along with a little milk (or even vanilla soymilk), will finish off this creamy oatmeal in style.

CINNAMON APPLE COMPOTE

1 tablespoon unsalted butter
4 Golden Delicious apples, peeled, cored, and diced
1 tablespoon sugar
¼ teaspoon ground cinnamon
¼ cup water

OATMEAL

2 cups apple juice
1 cup water
1½ cups old-fashioned rolled oats (not the quick-cooking kind)
Pinch of salt
Milk for serving (optional)

1. To make the compote, melt the butter in a large skillet (preferably not nonstick) over medium heat, then add the apples, sugar, and cinnamon. Stir well to coat, add a little of the water, and allow to cook until the apples are fork tender but not mushy and all the liquid has evaporated, leaving little browned bits of apple and sugar on the bottom of the pan. Use a wooden spoon to scrape up these caramelized bits with the help of the remaining water, then swirl the pan to coat the apples, and remove from the heat. Keep warm if going to serve immediately.

2. To make the oatmeal, bring the apple juice and water to a boil in a medium-size nonstick saucepan. Add the oats and salt and stir to combine. Bring back to a boil, reduce the heat to a simmer, and cook for 5 minutes, stirring occasionally to prevent sticking.

3. When the oatmeal has reached the desired consistency, remove from the stove and spoon into individual bowls. Serve with a spoonful of the apple compote and a splash of milk, if desired.

Variation: Add 2 tablespoons golden raisins to the saucepan when cooking the oatmeal for more sweetness and flavor. Top the compote with chopped walnuts, if desired.

Multigrain Morning Blend

MAKES ABOUT 4 CUPS DRY (1 CUP DRY MAKES 3 TO 4 SERVINGS, COOKED) This delicious multifaceted, multigrain blend wins hands down as the most nutritious and healthiest addition you can make to your diet in Phase Two. The extra time it takes to prepare is well worth the final energy-boosting result. To keep things simple, as I always like to do, I've measured out a batch quantity so you needn't measure small amounts each time. Simply take one cup of the blend and cook it according to the directions below. You'll recognize many of the grains listed as ingredients for savory dishes or grain salads or soups. They also work equally beautifully as a creamy breakfast cereal, with each grain enhancing the texture and flavor of the other. Look for them in your local supermarket or health food store. Wheat berries can often be found in Italian delis and be sure to seek out steel-cut oats (also called Scotch oats), which are minimally processed and will hold up to the longer required cooking time.

You can serve this unadorned, except for a small drizzle of honey or maple syrup or a pat of butter and spoonful of brown sugar. But this cereal blend is even better with the flavored variations, which are easy to prepare and especially delicious when the dried fruit has a chance to plump up during the cooking process and flavor the grains naturally.

MULTIGRAIN BLEND

1 cup steel-cut oats
1 cup wheat berries
1 cup cracked wheat (bulgur)
½ cup pearl barley
½ cup whole kasha
¼ cup sesame seeds

TO COOK

1 cup of Multigrain Blend
1 teaspoon canola oil
2 cups water
1 tablespoon sugar
Pinch of salt

1. To make the multigrain blend, combine all the ingredients in an airtight container and store at room temperature.

2. To cook 1 cup of the blend, heat the canola oil in a medium-size nonstick saucepan over medium-high heat and add the dry blend. Stir well to coat and toast the grains for 2 minutes. Add the water, sugar, and salt and stir to combine. Bring to a boil, reduce the heat to a simmer, and cook, covered, stirring often, until the grains are tender, 30 to 35 minutes. Keep the heat low and add a little water if the grains begin to stick before they are done. Taste for doneness; the grains should be soft, but chewy. Serve immediately.

Cherry Vanilla Multigrain Blend: Substitute vanilla sugar (or add 1 teaspoon nonalcohol vanilla extract) for the sugar and add ½ cup dried cherries to the saucepan during the final 15 minutes of cooking. Serve with a drizzle of cherry juice and cream. (A splash of vanilla soymilk really makes this perfect!)

Banana Bread Multigrain Blend: Add ½ teaspoon ground cinnamon to the dry blend and ½ cup golden raisins during the final 15 minutes of cooking. Top with slices of banana, toasted walnuts, and a drizzle of honey.

Cranberry Raspberry Blend: Substitute 1 cup cran-raspberry or cranberry juice for 1 cup of the water (the cereal will turn a lovely color). Add ⅓ cup dried cranberries during the final 15 minutes of cooking and top with a spoonful of raspberry yogurt.

Caramelized Grapefruit Halves

MAKES 4 SERVINGS This has become a popular way to serve grapefruit at fancy brunches and restaurants. I am always looking for an excuse to utilize my lonely kitchen torch that only seems to come out for crème brûlée, but you can easily prepare this under the broiler with the same result. Pink grapefruit makes a nice presentation, but white grapefruit will be fine, too. This has won over many people who dislike the tartness of grapefruit and may be a way to get them, especially kids, to enjoy grapefruit and the nutrition they have to offer, including vitamin C and soluble fiber.

Raw sugar is the residue left after sugarcane has been processed. It is usually found under the names of Demerara, Barbados, or Turbinado. Its flavor is similar to that of light brown sugar, which could be substituted here.

2 large pink or white grapefruit, cut in half
4 teaspoons raw or light brown sugar

1. Take each grapefruit half and cut a small piece from the bottom of the rind in order for it to sit without wobbling on a baking sheet. With a sharp paring or grapefruit knife, section the grapefruit as you would for serving with a spoon, carefully cutting between the membranes.

2. Sprinkle each prepared grapefruit half evenly with 1 teaspoon of the sugar and set under a preheated broiler for a few minutes only, shifting the pan to evenly melt and caramelize the sugar. If using a kitchen torch, caramelize the grapefruit tops, being careful not to set the flame too near the rind. Let rest a minute and serve.

Fresh Fruit Salad with Raspberry Vinegar Honey Glaze

MAKES 4 TO 6 SERVINGS A side dish of fresh seasonal fruit is always welcome in the morning, but most people have little time to devote to preparation on a busy weekday. Let weekends be the time to serve a refreshing fruit salad with flair, and use it as an excuse to clean out the fridge compartments and fruit bowls by gathering together all the fruit you may have forgotten about during the week. Making fruit salad is a great way to salvage any bruised or discolored fruit by simply discarding the undesirable parts and dicing up the still sweet and ripe portions. Any seasonal combination will do and your on-hand supply will usually dictate the ingredients. For those starting from scratch or planning a brunch presentation, below is one of my favorite combinations and it can be easily doubled for a bigger crowd.

½ **cantaloupe, seeded, flesh removed from**
    rind, and diced or shaped with a melon
    baller
½ **honeydew melon, seeded, flesh removed**
    from rind, and diced or shaped with a
    melon baller
1 cup fresh pineapple chunks
1 cup fresh strawberries, hulled and halved
1 cup fresh blueberries, picked over for stems
2 kiwi fruits, peeled and diced
1 ripe mango, peeled, seeded, and diced
¼ **cup honey**
1 tablespoon raspberry vinegar
1 teaspoon chopped fresh mint leaves

1. Prepare all the fruit and combine gently with a rubber spatula in a large mixing bowl.

2. Whisk together the honey, vinegar, and mint and pour over the fruit, folding gently to coat. Cover with plastic wrap and allow to chill at least 30 minutes before serving and up to 2 hours in advance.

Recovery Note: *Fancy brunches sometimes serve fruit salads that have been doused in alcohol. Brandy, fruit-flavored liqueurs, and champagne are often used. Ask if you're not sure.*

Lemon Yogurt Blueberry Parfait

MAKES 4 SERVINGS Think those ice cream glasses are just for dessert? Think again. How about starting your breakfast with a delicious and nutritious creamy parfait? Blueberries and lemon are natural partners and both are refreshing as a morning treat. Serve with a toasted Blueberry Lemon Buttermilk Muffin (page 55) and you've got the perfect summer breakfast to satisfy anyone's sweet tooth without too much damage! You also can try this with strawberries and raspberries (paired with strawberry or raspberry yogurt, if you like).

2 cups lemon yogurt
1 pint fresh blueberries, picked over for stems
1 cup granola (plain or flavored) of your choice
¼ cup crème fraîche or reduced-fat sour cream
4 sprigs fresh mint (optional)

1. Using 4 ice cream parfait or sundae glasses, layer the lemon yogurt, blueberries, and granola in them decoratively, repeating each layer until all the ingredients are used.

2. Top with 1 tablespoon of crème fraîche and a mint sprig, if desired. Serve immediately or cover with plastic wrap and chill until ready to serve.

Planning a Brunch Party
Sober Suggestions for a Super Bash

If you feel like doing a little entertaining, but are worried about the atmosphere of a potential drinking party, throwing a brunch is a great way to ease into a newly sober social life. Here are some tips for making your brunch a success, as well as some delicious menu suggestions to get you started:

- **SMALL IS BEST:** Don't overwhelm yourself with more than eight or ten guests. Only invite as many people as you feel comfortably able to handle. If three or four is your limit, begin there. Be sure each guest knows that you are not drinking any longer, so they do not suddenly appear at the door with a bottle for the host. Your nearest and dearest friends and family will respect your tremendous effort at recovery and will not want to jeopardize your health, so don't be afraid to tell them that booze will not be served.

- **SPECIFY THE HOURS:** On your invitation or in verbal communication, state the exact time of the party, for example, 11:00 A.M. until 2:00 P.M. This not only helps you organize your serving, but narrows the time frame for what might initially be a somewhat stressful endeavor for you, especially if this is your first time entertaining sober. Short but sweet is a good place to start.

- **CHOOSE AN EASY THEME:** Don't take on big celebration events like birthdays or Christmas, particularly those that are associated with alcohol, unless you are ready. Instead, choose a generic theme like a Celebration of Spring Brunch or I Just Got Promoted at Work Brunch. Even better, think about celebrating a milestone of your sobriety—six months, one year, two years—let everyone know how far you've come and let them congratulate you on your success.

- STICK TO PAPER AND PLASTIC: Make clean-up easier by using disposable plates, napkins, utensils, and cups, perhaps coordinating designs and colors with your theme. Remove all drinking glasses related to alcohol from your cupboard, if you haven't already, in case someone unknowingly grabs one to pour a drink. A sudden visual trigger, especially during a stressful event, could pose a problem.

- PROVIDE PLENTY OF NONALCOHOLIC BEVERAGES: Have available individual cans or bottles of fruit juices, sparkling water, and, of course, coffee—both regular and decaf. Borrow a coffee urn or rent one from a party supply shop and make the coffee half an hour before arrival time. If it's cold out, consider adding hot teas or cocoa to your menu or, in the summertime, make a pitcher of citrus punch or iced tea.

- DON'T ATTEMPT TO COOK EVERYTHING: Supplement your cooking with store-bought selections. Buy bagels and croissants if you are busy making frittatas or omelets. Or, if you enjoy baking muffins and scones, consider buying ready-made quiches or heat-and-serve hors d'oeuvres to supplement. Choose a menu that can be prepared ahead, with little left to do before people arrive.

- ENLIST SOME HELP: Ask a close friend or spouse to help you along during the party, by bringing out food platters or clearing empty plates and cups, to lessen your job and allow you to mingle and relax with your guests. An occasional check-in to see how you're coping can be invaluable from someone close who understands your trepidations. Don't be afraid to ask for emotional support.

- ENJOY YOURSELF!: Parties were designed for fun, so be sure to enjoy your own. If you've never "partied" without the alcohol, this will be a great way to convince yourself that good times don't depend on it. And don't forget to give yourself a huge pat on the back when it's over for a job well done!

SAMPLE BRUNCH MENU FOR 8

Old-Fashioned Buckwheat Pancakes with Smoked Salmon and Sour Cream (page 163)
Baked Asparagus Frittata with Roasted Peppers and Ham (page 175)
Baked Whole Wheat French Toast with Orange Maple Glaze (page 168)
Fresh Fruit Salad with Raspberry Vinegar Honey Glaze (page 183)
Irish Tea Bread (page 60) and Whole Wheat Brown Sugar Scones (page 57)
Butter and Assorted Jams
Citrus Fruit Cooler (page 12) or Green Tea Punch (page 16)
Coffee, Tea, Juices, and Sparkling Water

6 | *Old-Fashioned Entrées That Feed the Soul*

Comfort food can mean different things to different people. Often a fond memory is wrapped up in a dish we think of as homey or consoling. Maybe a particular person is associated with that dish, like a grandmother. Or maybe it is our bodies telling us what we need to eat to "feel good" nutritionally. Whatever the source of the message, it's a good idea to pay attention to it and try to reestablish a positive relationship with food at this time. This is not the same thing as relying on food to make us feel good, as is common in many food addictions. Rather, it is a way of welcoming food back into your life after, perhaps, years of it sitting on the back burner in deference to your addiction.

Are "soul food" and "comfort food" one and the same? Since we know that the body, mind, and soul are inextricably joined, the answer is a resounding "yes" But what kinds of meals nourish the soul? Depending on your cultural background and family traditions, "soul food" for you may be different from what your good friend considers comforting and soulful. However, there are a few commonalities that tend to ring true for everyone.

In the savory department, as opposed to the sweet, which we'll be getting to shortly (be patient, all you sweet tooth folks out there!), adjectives like "creamy," "rich," and "hearty" can be heard, while descriptions such as "meat and potatoes," "like Mom used to make," or "old fashioned" are popular. Ingredients such as cream, butter, potatoes, and cheese are often found lurking in "comfort food" recipes, while techniques like "fried," "creamed," and "slow roasted" are mentioned in the instructions. Many of the comforting dishes in this chapter require a little more love and attention than were needed in the recipes we saw in "Keeping It Simple," but the results are worth every bit of effort. And, by Phase Two, we are certainly ready for a little more of a challenge.

Many traditional comfort foods contain more fat and calories than we may normally want to consume, but, in moderation, there is no reason why we shouldn't enjoy the benefits and soul-healing properties of home-cooked comfort. Still, you will notice suggestions here and there throughout this chapter that offer small but significant adjustments to lower fat and increase health content. If we make little changes as we go, we are less likely to notice that anything is missing and more apt to incorporate those changes in the long term. As we reestablish our relationship with food, we come to know ourselves again and can begin to create a solid foundation in Phase Two to build upon for the rest of our lives. Step by step, block by block, the life we have saved in Phase One can be strengthened and encouraged to grow with the choices we make every day, especially regarding what we cook and eat.

So, to help you start building, here are some basic recipes that spell "comfort" for many and "delicious" for all!

A Bird's Eye View of Favorite Fowl and Popular Poultry

Both domestic and wild bird species have been popular main courses for centuries, from ancient times through the first Thanksgiving, and are still served on a regular basis today. Whether roasted, fried, skinned, or stuffed, in the words of Brillat-Savarin, the nineteenth-century epicure, "poultry has been for the cook what canvas is to the painter." Although some of the more unusual fowl selections he may have had the pleasure of eating, such as pigeon and woodcock, are less commonly cooked in our day, the host of techniques and presentations that can be used in preparing poultry are still quite remarkable in number. But how do we know what type of poultry is best suited to specific preparations? And what about seeking out some unusual fowl for special occasions? Here's a brief guide to assist you in your poultry picking.

The ubiquitous chicken is by far the most popular choice for home cooks and for good reason. It is an easy size to prepare whole, it can be quartered or boned quite readily (especially by your butcher) for a myriad of cooking methods, and, in general, takes little time to cook. Mild in taste, as opposed to game-flavored fowl, it is the main poultry choice of children and most adults as well, blending well with the flavors of nearly all ethnic cuisines. Fryers and broilers (sometimes referred to as broiler-fryers, without differentiation), weighing between two and four pounds, are the youngest and most tender of common domestic-raised chickens and are best suited to sautéing, broiling, and roasting. The slightly older and larger roasters (up to five pounds) have a higher fat content and, as their name suggests, are ideal for roasting and rotisserie cooking. Also good for roasting are capons, not actually hens, but roosters that have been castrated and fed a high-caloric diet in order to produce oversized breasts and a thick layer of fat just under the breast skin, which melts and naturally bastes the capon during cooking. This rather barbaric procedure, called "caponizing," was developed by the ancient Greeks and perfected by the Romans when force-feeding hens (to the same end) became illegal and threatened to diminish the quantity of hens, which were valuable egg layers. Although it produces an extraordinarily succulent roast, capons have become somewhat less popular in America than in Europe, and are consequently more difficult and expensive to obtain.

Stewing hens, quite inexpensive but sometimes difficult to find (also called fowl or boiling fowl), are older still and, as a result, are much less tender, although better in flavor than broiler-fryers and roasters. For this reason, they are best cooked with a moist heat such as that which stewing, poaching, and braising would provide. Little Rock Cornish game hens, weighing only one to two pounds, are actually a special hybrid of Cornish and White Rock chickens and do best when roasted, broiled, or grilled. A squab chicken, also called a French *poussin*, is quite small as well and can be cooked in the same manner as Rock Cornish game hens. It is not really a squab (or pigeon, as the French refer to them), in the wild game sense, but rather a domesticated, milder relative that can often be found fresh or frozen in gourmet meat markets.

Brillat-Savarin also described the turkey as "one of the finest gifts given to the Old World by the New," and it was indeed here, in the Americas, that turkeys lived for two million years, long before European explorers discovered our continent. Benjamin Franklin took a particular liking to the turkey as a symbol, suggesting it should be the official bird of the United States, replacing what he thought was the less-respectable bald eagle. But turkeys had already been associated with delicious standard fare at American tables, beginning perhaps with the four wild turkeys that graced the harvest feast of the Pilgrims in 1621 and it was at those tables, much to Franklin's disappointment, that its reputation grew. Although smaller turkeys are now available, weighing between 5 and 8 pounds, the standard holiday bird will be either 8 to 16 pounds (female) or upwards of 25 pounds (toms). Since turkey meat is subject to drying out when cooked (or overcooked, which is often the case), self-basting varieties are injected with butter or oil to add adequate moisture, but the real trick to a tender bird lies in persistent, manual basting by the cook. Roasting is by far the most popular method of cooking a turkey, but deep frying, in a large outdoor vat, is gaining popularity with chefs across America, because the result is a perfectly moist and tender inside, enveloped by a super crispy, delectable skin.

A golden and crispy skin is also the hallmark of a perfectly roasted duck, a favorite in Asian cooking and made classic in the alcohol-laced French recipe *canard a l'orange* (see Chapter Twelve, "Sober Makeovers," for a sobered-up version of duck with orange sauce). It is said that the duck varieties now available to us in the United States (primarily the Long Island and White Pekin) all descended from three ducks and a drake that found their way from China to New York on a clipper ship in 1873. Usually purchased frozen, although sometimes available fresh in certain parts of the country, duck poses a difficult task for the average cook because, when roasted whole, the breast meat generally overcooks before the dark meat is done. The best way around this is to have the duck quartered and to roast the thighs, legs, and wings at a high oven temperature until golden and crisp, reserving the breasts for a much shorter stove-top sauté, keeping them medium-rare and deliciously moist. The somewhat larger and meatier Muscovy duck breasts are often sold separately, boned, trimmed, and ready to cook, ideal for sautéing to a tender conclusion. Duck and its fat are highly prized in French cooking, contributing to many fabulous dishes such as duck confit (duck stewed and preserved in its own fat) and the classic cassoulet, a mixture of several meats, including duck, and slow-cooked white beans, baked together in a casserole.

Similar to duck in fat content and preparation is the goose, a bird more popularly served in Britain and Europe, but sometimes available in American meat markets, usually around the Christmas holidays. Goose is probably most famous for *foie gras*, an extremely rich, gourmet delicacy made from the goose's enlarged force-fed liver, often prepared on its own as an appetizer or made into a spreadable pâté.

Other less commonly seen fowl selections are pheasant, guinea hen, grouse, and quail, all particularly gamy in flavor and suited to any number of cooking methods depending on the age of the bird. They are usually sold frozen and sometimes partially boned. The tiny quail is especially delicious deep-fried or stuffed and is a popular offering in many gourmet restaurants.

Free-range chickens, as opposed to the mass-produced birds, are usually fed a vegetarian diet, free of antibiotics and hormones, and are allowed slightly more space to maneuver (about one square foot) than the cramped conditions of the average commercially bred chickens. Some prefer this more expensive variety and feel that the taste is more flavorful.

When selecting any type of poultry to buy, whether fresh or frozen, it should not have any hint of an off odor and both the skin and flesh should look smooth and absent of discoloration. Defrost frozen poultry in the refrigerator or microwave. Large whole birds can be submerged (still wrapped) in a pot of cold water to help speed up the process a bit, but do not leave any poultry out of the fridge for an extended period of time. Raw, defrosted chicken in the fridge should be cooked within two days. You can, of course, freeze any fresh chicken you purchase, provided it is well wrapped. I recommend first wrapping it in freezer paper, then enclosing in an airtight plastic bag, clearly labeling the date and contents. Try to use any frozen uncooked chicken within two to three months of purchase for maximum safety as well as flavor.

Salmonella and other bacterial growth are a danger in all types of raw poultry so always wash any knives, cutting boards, plates, and utensils that have come in contact with uncooked skin and flesh. Hot, sudsy water (with an antibacterial soap) is best for decontaminating all kitchen tools. In addition, your hands are also subject to spreading any bacteria, so wash them frequently when handling raw meat of any type.

Simple Roast Chicken

Roasting a chicken has been called one of the true tests of a good cook. To keep the breast meat succulent while ensuring that the dark meat is cooked through is not always an easy task. If you have ever purchased a precooked rotisserie chicken from the supermarket, which is a popular offering these days, you will know what I mean.

There are a couple of tips I can offer. First, use a hot oven. Many people tend to roast their chickens at temperatures lower than 400 degrees. This means that the bird will be in the oven a lot longer and has a greater chance of drying out. Another tip is to raise the chicken up off the surface of the roasting pan by using a small rack or even some rolled up and coiled aluminum foil. This way the heat can circulate more evenly. Lastly, do not be afraid to move your chicken from face up to face down. I recommend turning over the chicken halfway through the cooking so that the back and dark meat are well roasted and the juices flow down into the breast. Succulent, juicy breast meat and well-cooked legs and thighs will be the result.

1 tablespoon canola oil
One 3- to 4-pound chicken, giblets and excess fat removed, washed, and patted dry with paper towels
Salt and pepper

1. Preheat the oven to 425 degrees. Rub the canola oil all over the chicken skin, then season generously with salt and pepper on the outside and also inside the cavity.

2. Place the chicken breast side up in a shallow roasting pan fitted with a small rack or rolled up aluminum foil and roast in the middle of the oven for 30 minutes.

3. Using tongs or 2 large serving forks, turn the chicken over, breast side down, onto the rack or foil and continue to roast for another 20 to 25 minutes. Test for doneness by inserting an instant-read meat thermometer into the fleshiest part of the thigh. Remove from the oven when the temperature reaches 175 degrees, or when the juices run clear after piercing the thigh with a fork and no blood appears when the joints are cut. Allow to rest for 10 to 15 minutes to let the juices settle before carving.

Lemon Rosemary Roast Chicken: Squeeze the juice of ½ lemon over the chicken before roasting and insert the squeezed-out rind into the cavity along with 2 or 3 sprigs fresh rosemary.

Orange and Thyme Roast Chicken: Squeeze the juice of ½ orange over the chicken before roasting and insert the squeezed-out rind into the cavity along with 3 or 4 sprigs fresh thyme.

Chili Lime Roast Chicken: Rub the outside of the chicken with 1 tablespoon chili powder before roasting. When the chicken is done and resting, pour the juice of 2 limes all over. Serve with the pan juices.

Double Garlic Roast Chicken: Place 1 head garlic, lightly smashed (skin still attached is okay) into the cavity of the chicken and season the outside with 1 teaspoon garlic powder and a dash of paprika. Serve with the roasted garlic cloves.

Onion and Herb Roast Chicken: Peel and slice a small onion into thin circles and insert under the skin over the breasts and thighs. Do this by inserting your fingers between the skin and the flesh to loosen the thin membrane that attaches them, beginning at the breast cavity and working out towards the thighs and legs. Sprinkle 1 tablespoon dried herbs such as thyme, oregano, or marjoram and 1 teaspoon onion powder over the outside of the chicken before roasting. Serve slices of the chicken with the cooked onion rounds.

Chef's Note: *If you like a little "jus" with your chicken, deglaze the roasting pan with ½ cup wine substitute (see page 134) or chicken broth. Pour out any excess fat from the pan, add the liquid, and, over medium heat on top of the stove, use a wooden spoon to scrape up the browned flavorful bits. Let cook a minute or two and serve along with your chicken.*

Crispy Fried Chicken with Biscuits and Gravy

MAKES 4 SERVINGS Southern fried chicken is, without a doubt, comfort food for many. Unfortunately, traditional methods of skillet frying can be heavily laden with fat, which may, even during Phase Two, present a rough task to our digestive systems. This recipe, however, is a happy compromise between pan-frying and oven-frying and even allows for a quick pan gravy, which is surely the best of both worlds!

Try making the buttermilk biscuits on page 254 or purchase some store-baked ones from your supermarket. Round this out with buttered peas, carrots, or string beans and you've got a finger-lickin' good meal that satisfies body and soul.

CRISPY-FRIED CHICKEN
   8 chicken thighs and/or breasts, on the bone or
      boneless and skinless, if desired
   Salt and pepper to taste
   ½ cup all-purpose flour
   2 large eggs, beaten
   2 cups dry or fresh bread crumbs
   ½ cup canola oil, or enough to cover bottom of
      skillet with ¼ inch oil

GRAVY
   3 tablespoons all-purpose flour
   2 cups half-and-half or milk
   Salt and pepper to taste

   1. To make the chicken, preheat the oven to 400 degrees. Trim the fat off chicken pieces and remove the skin, if desired. Season each piece with salt and pepper.

   2. Have ready an assembly line of one dish containing the flour, another with the beaten eggs, and another with the bread crumbs. Heat the canola oil in a large nonstick skillet over medium-high heat.

3. Dip the chicken pieces in the flour first, shake off the excess, dip in the egg to coat all over, then dredge in the bread crumbs to coat evenly. When the oil is hot enough, place the chicken in the skillet (it should sizzle immediately) and allow to brown on each side, about 3 minutes, over medium to high heat. You are not trying to cook the chicken through at this point, only to make a crisp

coating. Drain the browned chicken pieces on paper towels to remove the excess oil, then transfer to a baking sheet that has been lined with parchment paper. Bake until an instant-read meat thermometer registers 165 degrees when inserted into the thickest part and the chicken is crispy and golden, 30 to 40 minutes. (Note: If you are using boneless chicken pieces, reduce the cooking time to 20 to 30 minutes.)

4. To make the gravy, pour out all but about 3 tablespoons of the oil in the skillet, add the flour, and cook over medium heat 2 to 3 minutes, scraping up the browned chicken bits from the bottom of the pan. Add the half-and-half and, using a wire whisk, combine and stir until thickened and bubbly. Season with salt and pepper.

5. When the chicken is done, slice warm buttermilk biscuits in half and place face up on each plate with a serving of chicken. Pour the creamy gravy over all and serve.

Variation: For a lighter gravy, you can substitute 1½ cups chicken broth and ½ cup milk for the half-and-half.

Family Matters

Creating Comfort in Your Home

Too often, the fast pace of American life does not allow for the family to dine together as it once did. Leisurely family meals, unfortunately, are turning out to be a thing of the past, while fast food consumption is on the rise. Even kids have hectic schedules these days, which take them away from the house and interfere, more often than not, with the dinner hour. Yet research by the National Center on Addictions and Substance Abuse at Columbia University has consistently shown that the more often a child eats dinner with his or her family, the less likely that child is to smoke, drink, or use illegal drugs later on. Powerful statistics like this should be sending us all back to the table. But how do we fit it in?

Setting aside at least one night a week when the whole family will be together is a good place to start. Create a comfortable atmosphere and serve something you know will please everyone. Roast chicken is always a winner, as are mashed potatoes or macaroni and cheese. Select a special dessert to entice everyone to linger at the table. Phase Two is when we need to reconnect with our family and assure them they have not lost us to our recovery, as they did with our addiction. A little planning in anticipation of the dinner hour will reap tremendous awards at this time and help to create a home of comfort and love.

Farmhouse Chicken Stew with Dumplings

MAKES 4 SERVINGS This delicious meal will satisfy everyone's craving for comfort. Who can resist tender pieces of chicken, flavorful stewed vegetables, and plump, hearty dumplings, all napped in a creamy easy-to-make sauce?

A classic Dutch oven (usually made of cast iron and named after the Pennsylvania Dutch immigrants who introduced it to American cuisine) is the ideal cooking receptacle for this type of stew. A heavy-bottomed pot with a tight fitting lid would also do the job.

Traditionally, hens and other tough old birds

were used for stewing, but the average cut-up broiler-fryer will fill in nicely here. Leaving the skin on is purely a matter of choice—I tend to retain the skin while cooking to ensure flavor and juiciness and give diners the choice of removing it before eating. I happen to love potatoes in this dish, so I usually add quite a few, and have found that baby Yukon Golds are perfect. However, larger red-skinned potatoes that have been quartered are excellent as well. Steer clear of the starchy Idaho baking types, as they will fall apart too readily.

Spooned dumplings are one of the easiest things to make and one of the most appreciated additions to stews like this. "Oooh, you made dumplings!" is the usual reaction you will get. Always associated with comfort, they also help to soak up the delicious sauce.

CHICKEN STEW

¼ cup (½ stick) unsalted butter

2 tablespoons canola oil

One 2½- to 3-pound broiler-fryer chicken, quartered

Salt and pepper to taste

All-purpose flour for dredging

1 medium-size onion, peeled and chopped

1 celery stalk, ends trimmed and cut into ½-inch-thick slices

3 medium-size carrots, peeled and cut into 2-inch pieces

2 cups low-sodium chicken or vegetable broth

2 cups water

16 to 20 baby Yukon Gold potatoes, or 4 medium-size red potatoes, quartered

½ cup light or heavy cream

DUMPLINGS

2 cups all-purpose flour

1 tablespoon baking powder

1 teaspoon salt

1 tablespoon chopped fresh parsley leaves

2 large eggs

¾ cup buttermilk

1. To make the stew, heat together the butter and oil in a Dutch oven or stewing pot over medium-high heat until the butter melts. Season the chicken pieces with salt and pepper, dredge well in the flour, tap off any excess, and fry until nicely golden and crisp on both sides, about 10 minutes. You may need to do this in several batches. Transfer to a plate and set aside.

2. Add the onion and celery to the pot and cook, stirring, over medium heat until slightly softened, 3 to 4 minutes, scraping up the browned bits from the bottom of the pot. Add the carrots, stir to coat, and cook for 1 minute. Add the broth and water, increase the heat to high, and bring to a simmer. Return the chicken to the pot, reduce the heat to low, and cook, covered, until the chicken and vegetables are tender, 35 to 40 minutes. Add the potatoes after the first 20 minutes of cooking time.

3. To make the dumplings, whisk together the flour, baking powder, salt, and parsley in a medium-size mixing bowl. In another medium-size mixing bowl, combine the eggs and buttermilk using a whisk or fork. Add the liquid mixture to the dry ingredients all at once and stir quickly with a fork to combine. You can add a touch more buttermilk if necessary to moisten, but do not overmix.

4. When the chicken and vegetables are cooked, add the cream to the pot, increase the heat to medium and bring to a simmer, stirring occasionally. Drop heaping tablespoons of the dumpling batter into the simmering pot, covering the top of the surface without crowding. Reduce the heat to low, cover, and cook until the dumplings are firm and puffy, 10 to 12 minutes. Serve straight from the pot.

One-Crust Chicken Pot Pie

MAKES 4 SERVINGS Pot pies have "comfort" written all over them. It's no wonder that these hearty, homemade, one-dish meals are a popular request of my personal chef clients. They simply can't compare to store-bought, frozen versions. Here, a golden puff pastry top replaces the usual doughy double piecrust, while a light velouté sauce (a stock-based white sauce) flavors the vegetables and chicken to perfection.

This is an ideal way to use leftover chicken that has been either roasted or simmered. If you are able to plan ahead, consider adding an extra chicken or chicken pieces when making Basic Broth for Chicken Soup (page 78) to ensure there will be plenty of leftovers for a dish like this. You can also use leftover turkey. If, however, there is no leftover poultry to be had, and you are *really* craving a pot pie, see the Chef's Note below for instructions on quick cooking boneless chicken breasts.

Leftover cooked vegetables may also be included—this is a great "clean out the fridge" dish—but the directions that follow assume you'll be using uncooked. If not, simply add any pre-cooked vegetables to the casserole at the end, prior to baking.

1 sheet frozen puff pastry, defrosted

1 large egg, beaten

3 tablespoons unsalted butter

1 small onion, peeled and chopped

1 medium-size celery stalk, ends trimmed
　　and chopped

Salt and pepper to taste

3 tablespoons all-purpose flour

3 cups low-sodium chicken broth

1 cup water

2 medium-size carrots, peeled and sliced into
　　½ inch-thick rounds

1 medium-size red potato, peeled and diced

½ cup frozen peas

2 to 3 cups diced cooked chicken or turkey

1. Puncture the puff pastry sheet with a fork several times and place on an ungreased baking sheet. Brush with the beaten egg and bake in a preheated 400 degree oven until golden, 20 to 25

minutes. Remove from the oven and allow to cool for a few minutes. Reduce the oven temperature to 325 degrees. Take the casserole dish you will be using (a round or oblong 1-quart glass or ceramic casserole is ideal) and turn it upside down over the baked puff pastry, pressing down. With a sharp knife, cut around the dish like a stencil to make a lid for your pot pie. Set aside.

2. In a heavy-bottomed, wide pot, melt the butter over low to medium heat. Add the onion and celery, sprinkle with salt and pepper, and cook, stirring, until softened, 3 to 5 minutes. Do not allow the butter or vegetables to brown. Add the flour and combine with a wooden spoon, cooking over medium heat until bubbly, but not brown. Add the chicken broth and water, increase the heat to medium-high, and bring to a simmer. Add the carrots, potato, and peas and cook until tender at a low simmer, about 15 minutes. Remove the vegetables with a slotted spoon and transfer to the casserole, leaving the sauce in the pot. Add the cooked chicken and any other cooked vegetables you may be using to the casserole as well and stir to combine.

3. Check to see if the sauce is thick enough; it should just coat the back of a spoon. If too thin, allow to boil down slowly, uncovered. If too thick, you may add a little water. Taste for seasoning and adjust accordingly. When the sauce is ready, pour it over the chicken and vegetables and stir lightly to combine. Top with the baked puff pastry lid. Warm the pot pie in the oven for 15 to 20 minutes, then serve.

Chef's Note: When leftover chicken is not available, cook 3 to 4 boneless, skinless chicken breasts, cut into bite-size pieces, in the simmering velouté sauce along with the vegetables. When the chicken is no longer pink and the vegetables are tender, about 15 minutes later, remove them with a slotted spoon and transfer to the casse-

role. Proceed with the recipe as directed above.

Variation: Try adding any of the following cooked vegetables to the casserole at the end: broccoli florets, cut-up string beans, peeled pearl onions, or lima beans.

Zia Jenny's Chicken Cacciatore

MAKES 4 SERVINGS When my great-aunt Jenny arrived at our house when I was a child, she would usually come prepared to create a delicious feast with my grandmother, her sister. Together, they used to whip up comforting Italian dishes in the kitchen while gossiping in dialect about the family and friends they knew. Before long, there were alluring aromas filling the house and everyone knew not to be late for dinner that night!

Chicken cacciatore was one of Jenny's specialties; tender succulent chicken fell off the bone and was enveloped in a rich and zesty tomato sauce, indicative of her Sicilian upbringing. She often served it over creamy polenta (page 379) instead of the more commonly used spaghetti or linguine. A crisp green salad, often composed of dandelion greens from the yard, rounded out the meal, along with some delicious semolina Italian bread for dipping into the hearty sauce. I now use dried porcini mushrooms in this dish to impart a rich, woodsy flavor. Allow them to soak in warm water for at least 20 minutes. Lift the mushrooms out of the infused liquid, then pour the liquid through a fine sieve to remove bits of dirt and grit. This wonderfully fragrant mushroom "juice" is then added to the sauce to reinforce the mushroom flavor.

¼ cup olive oil
One 3½-pound chicken, cut into 8 serving pieces
Salt and pepper to taste
1 medium-size onion, peeled and chopped

3 garlic cloves, peeled and minced
¾ to 1 ounce dried porcini mushrooms, reconstituted in 1 cup warm water, drained (liquid reserved), and roughly chopped
One 28-ounce can tomato puree
¼ cup tomato paste
One 16-ounce can diced tomatoes in juice
2 cups low-sodium chicken or vegetable broth or water
2 tablespoons red wine vinegar
2 teaspoons dried oregano
1 teaspoon fennel seeds
1 bay leaf
1 teaspoon sugar
Dash of red pepper flakes

1. Heat the oil in a large heavy-bottomed skillet or Dutch oven over medium-high heat. Season the chicken pieces with salt and pepper and fry them in the hot oil until browned, about 4 minutes per side. Transfer the chicken to a plate and set aside.

2. Add the onion to the skillet and cook, stirring, until softened, 2 to 3 minutes. Add the garlic and porcini mushrooms and continue to cook, stirring, for 1 to 2 minutes. Add the remaining ingredients, including the strained liquid from the mushrooms, and stirring occasionally, bring to a low simmer. Return the chicken and its juices to the skillet, submerge them in the sauce, and cook, covered, over medium-low heat for 1 hour, stirring occasionally to prevent sticking. You may add a touch of water if necessary.

3. When the chicken is tender and falling off the bone, remove it from the skillet with a slotted spoon and set aside to keep warm. Allow the sauce to boil, if necessary, to thicken slightly. Taste for the addition of salt and pepper and spoon half the sauce over the chicken to serve. Offer the remaining sauce on the side to spoon over polenta or pasta. Pass grated Pecorino Romano cheese for sprinkling.

The Magic of Mushrooms
Familiarizing Yourself with Fungi

Now that I have your attention . . . did you know there are thousands of different mushroom varieties growing in the world today? No longer is our culinary choice limited to the common white variety. More and more fresh, as well as dried, types of this fungus are available in local supermarkets, creating a bit of confusion about their uses, taste differences, and methods of preparation. Here's a brief guide to the types of mushrooms you are likely to encounter in your produce aisle:

- **FRESH CULTIVATED COMMON MUSHROOMS:** In addition to the prolific white version we are typically used to, cremini mushrooms, a slightly darker variety of this type, are also commonly seen these days, usually packaged in 8- or 10-ounce cartons. They can be used in place of white mushrooms in just about any recipe, providing a fuller flavor. Portobellos are simply the mature cremini mushrooms, which are also called baby bellas, grown into meaty, flavorful adults. The tough stem of the portobello is normally removed and sometimes the black gills, located on the underside of the cap, are scraped off, so as not to "stain" certain dishes, particularly light-colored sauces. Common mushrooms are versatile in their uses; they can be sautéed, stuffed, eaten raw in salads, and even grilled. For mild flavor in soups, stews, and pasta sauces, they are ideal.

- **FRESH WILD MUSHROOMS:** Here we separate the men from the boys—mushroom gourmets prize these intensely flavored varieties and will even seek them out in the woods. However, numerous wild mushrooms are poisonous and, unless you are an expert in the field, you should stick to the produce aisle when choosing these exotic varieties. Chanterelle, wood ear, oyster, and hen-of-the-woods are just some of the fresh wild selections you will find packaged in small three- to four-ounce containers. They are also sometimes a bit costly, but if your budget allows, experiment by using them in dishes where you would normally use common mushrooms. The flavor will be far more assertive, but definitely enjoyable. Asian varieties such as shiitake, maitake, and enoki are now available fresh and add a wonderful flavor to stir-fries and Asian-style broths. In addition, they hold tremendous medicinal value—something the East has known for centuries—by enhancing the immune system and even possessing anticancer and cholesterol-lowering properties. I particularly adore fresh maitake and will buy them whenever I see them available, often adding them to a simple sauté of scallops, along with fresh ginger and scallions. Morels and fresh porcini mushrooms, the elite of the wild mushroom category, are prized by chefs, but usually are far too costly and difficult to find for the average cook. The dried versions, although not as alluring, can be found more readily and will not break the budget.

- **DRIED AND CANNED MUSHROOMS:** Nearly all of the above wild mushroom varieties can be found dried, either whole or sliced, in little packets in or near your produce section. A little reconstitution with warm water will bring them back to life and, at the same time, provide a delicious liquid that can be added to soups, sauces, and other recipes. Be sure to strain the resulting "liquor," as it is called, to remove all the grit before using. Dried porcinis are frequently available these days and will add a delicious, woodsy flavor to pasta sauces and stews. As far as canned mushrooms are concerned, the only variety I will generally purchase is the Chinese straw mushroom, which makes a great addition to stir-fries and is very often used by your neighborhood Chinese restaurant in many of their selections. Marinated mushrooms would be another exception, although they sometimes will contain wine or vermouth. Read the labels to be sure.

Cultivated white mushrooms, the most common variety, are composed primarily of water—nearly 90 percent!—which is why they tend to shrink up so pitifully when cooked. Try to visualize this when you are purchasing them, especially for sautéing a batch to accompany a steak or burger, so there is enough to go around. One 10-ounce box will yield only about one cup when cooked. Wild varieties are much less water-filled and will not shrink so dramatically. To clean your mushrooms, never soak them in water, which will inevitably make them mushy. Simply wipe away dirt with a damp paper towel, trim the stems with a sharp paring knife, and proceed with your recipe. When purchasing, look for perky and vibrant fungi and avoid tired and bruised-looking ones. Mushrooms should always feel firm and not smushy, a sign that they may be past their prime. Similarly, look for tightly closed caps when buying cultivated common varieties, which indicates freshness, with the exception of portobellos. Always keep your fresh mushrooms refrigerated and use them within a few days of purchase.

Finally, if you have been browsing around your local health food store, you may have come across supplements, teas, and tonics that utilize the healing power of some mushrooms. Reishi, a popular mushroom that is cultivated purely for medicinal purposes in China and Japan (it is too hard and bitter to be eaten), boasts anti-inflammatory and immune-enhancing properties as well as possible liver protection. I have tried a green tea variety that is mixed with reishi, which was particularly good. Incidentally, magic mushrooms contain a substance with psychoactive properties called psilocybin, a hallucinogen. They seem to work their "magic" because of psilocybin's similarity in structure to the neurotransmitter serotonin. Excessive use is believed to result in chronic psychosis and symptoms similar to those of schizophrenia.

Mediterranean Chicken with Garlic and Olives

MAKES 4 SERVINGS Further down the Mediterranean from Italy, in places like Greece and Morocco, comforting chicken dishes are prepared with tangy local ingredients and often the addition of dried fruit. This recipe is inspired by that cuisine and is also a perfect example of how a flavorful vinegar can replace wine to both tenderize and enhance a dish when used as part of a marinade and incorporated into the final result. Good ingredients abound here, with flavorful olives, sweet prunes, plenty of garlic, and extra virgin olive oil, all of which contribute to the delicious sauce.

You could use chicken breasts instead of the recommended dark meat, but I like the way the chicken thighs hold their own with the other assertive ingredients. If possible, marinate the chicken overnight or at least a few hours before cooking for maximum intensity of flavor. The ideal accompaniment for this dish is plenty of cooked orzo.

½ cup extra virgin olive oil

½ cup balsamic vinegar

8 garlic cloves, smashed and skin removed

2 bay leaves

1 teaspoon dried oregano

8 chicken thighs on the bone, skin removed

1 cup pitted prunes

½ cup pitted Mediterranean olives, such as
  Kalamata, Gaeta, or green Spanish, drained

¼ cup pine nuts

¼ cup capers, drained

Salt and pepper to taste

1 cup apple juice

¼ cup packed dark brown sugar

1 tablespoon chopped fresh parsley leaves for
  garnish

1. In a 9 x 13-inch glass casserole or roasting pan, combine the olive oil, vinegar, garlic, bay leaves, and oregano, stirring together with a fork. Add the chicken pieces, flesh side down, and distribute the prunes, olives, pine nuts, and capers around them. Cover with aluminum foil and allow to marinate in the refrigerator for at least 2 hours and preferably overnight.

2. When ready to cook the chicken, preheat the oven to 375 degrees. Season the chicken casserole with salt and pepper. Add the apple juice and brown sugar, stirring lightly just to combine. Cover again with the foil.

3. Bake on the center rack of the oven, covered, until the chicken is cooked through, about 45 minutes. Turn the thighs over halfway through the cooking. Test for doneness by piercing with a fork or inserting an instant-read thermometer in the fleshiest part of the thigh. The chicken is done when the internal temperature reaches 165 to 175 degrees.

4. With a slotted spoon, remove the chicken, prunes, and olives and transfer them to a warm serving platter. Pour the remaining liquid into a medium-size saucepan and boil over high heat to reduce and thicken the sauce, about 10 minutes. When the sauce is thick enough to lightly coat the back of a spoon, taste for seasoning and pour over the chicken. Sprinkle with the chopped parsley and serve immediately.

Roast Turkey Breast

Loaded with tryptophan for serotonin production and relaxation, roast turkey is truly medicinal soul food, as well as the hands-down choice for home-cooked comfort. Roasting an entire bird is, of course, time consuming and leaves little room in the fridge for anything else. So, consider purchasing the breast only, available either unsplit on the bone (essentially a turkey without legs) or a smaller boneless breast often called a London broil cut. It is easy to prepare and ready in no time, allowing you to enjoy the comfort of a roast turkey dinner without all the added holiday fuss. Served with supportive side dishes like Classic Mashed Potatoes (page 226) and My Favorite Cornbread Stuffing (page 258), you'll wonder why you waited until Thanksgiving for this wonderfully soothing meal! And, like your Thanksgiving bird, leftovers will make for great sandwiches and terrific dishes like Turkey Tetrazzini with Wild Mushrooms and Sage (below) or One-Crust Chicken Pot Pie (page 193).

If you are particularly fond of the dark meat from the turkey, you can also purchase legs and thighs in most grocery stores. Roast them along with the turkey breast if you like, but be sure they reach an internal temperature of 175 degrees (or the juices run clear when pierced with a fork), which will require a little extra cooking time.

1 tablespoon unsalted butter, softened
One 1½- to 3-pound turkey breast, boneless
   cut or partially boned
Salt and pepper to taste
4 sprigs fresh sage

1. Preheat the oven to 400 degrees. Rub the butter over the skin of the turkey breast and season both sides with salt and pepper.

2. Place the breast in a shallow roasting pan and tuck the sage under the breast. Roast until an instant-read meat thermometer inserted into the thickest part registers 165 degrees or, when cut into, the turkey is no longer pink and the juices run clear, 30 to 55 minutes, depending on the weight. Remove from the oven and let rest for 10 minutes before slicing on the diagonal.

Honey-Glazed Turkey Breast: In a small saucepan, melt 2 tablespoons unsalted butter with ¼ cup honey. Brush or spoon the glaze over the turkey every 10 minutes while roasting.

Maple-Glazed Turkey Breast: In a small saucepan, heat 2 tablespoons unsalted butter with ¼ cup pure maple syrup until the butter melts. Brush or spoon the glaze over the turkey every 10 minutes while roasting.

Italian Roast Turkey Breast: Rub the outside of the turkey with 2 tablespoons olive oil in place of the butter and sprinkle evenly with 1 teaspoon *each* dried oregano, basil, and garlic powder. Once the turkey is done, pour off the fat from the roasting pan and deglaze the pan over medium heat with the juice of 1 lemon, scraping up the browned bits from the bottom of the pan. Serve with the pan juices.

Turkey Tetrazzini with Wild Mushrooms and Sage

MAKES 4 SERVINGS This creamy casserole with tryptophan-rich turkey is sure to bring on a good night's sleep after dinner! Tetrazzini is a popular way to make use of leftover Thanksgiving turkey, but should really be enjoyed a lot more often. You can purchase a boneless split breast of turkey, often called a London broil cut, and roast or poach it before starting. If you have leftover roasted turkey breast (previous page) on hand, this recipe will be a snap. In a pinch, your supermarket deli may have store-roasted turkey breast; ask for a one-pound chunk and dice it when you get home.

I use a variety of wild mushrooms for a gourmet touch, but you can substitute the common white button ones if you prefer. Fresh sage is a natural companion for this dish but you may use dried rubbed sage as a substitute.

Spaghetti is traditionally used in this dish but other forms of pasta would work equally well. Also traditional in most recipes is the making of what's called a velouté, which is simply stock or broth that has been thickened with a butter-and-flour roux. However, here we are making a white sauce, or béchamel, for added richness.

(continued on page 202)

Genetics and Alcoholism
Understanding the Family Connection

Between 35 and 40 percent of alcoholics have a genetic component that predisposes them to their disease. This is not to say that genetics assured the development of alcohol dependence; there are many ways to reach this unwanted goal, not the least of which is through prolonged and chronic use. However, the majority of this percentage of people can point to other family members, from grandparents on down the line, who have suffered from the same illness. Often there are "related" addictions in the family as well, such as gambling, eating disorders, and sometimes depression or other mental illnesses. The intricate connection between these addictions, their relation to brain chemistry, biological factors, and possible inheritance, is still being discovered.

We know that alcoholics are considered to be one of two types: Type I, the most common type, is often characterized by later onset of alcohol dependence and, in general, tends to be the most amenable to treatment. Type II, on the other hand, appears to hold a strong genetic correlation, in particular, between fathers and sons. The onset is early and resistance to treatment is often high. These people tend to claim an instant attraction to alcohol. Why is this so and can genetics explain why some people become addicted while others do not? The way in which we metabolize alcohol when it is first ingested may hold the key to understanding our inherited tendencies, as well as the possible *unlikelihood* of becoming addicted. Here's how it works.

There are two major metabolic pathways for the metabolism of alcohol. The first, called the alcohol dehydrogenase (ADH) pathway, determines the rate at which we metabolize alcohol in the liver and stomach. Alcohol is broken down into acetaldehyde, and although the speed at which this takes place is different for everyone, on average, it has been shown to equate to one drink per hour, hence the rule-of-thumb advice of sticking to one drink per hour to keep from getting drunk. However, genetic variants of the metabolic enzymes that are involved in this process, also called isozymes, influence this rate, causing metabolism of alcohol to be sometimes faster or slower in different people. The amount of ADH we are born with does not change—we can never metabolize any faster than that. Researchers have categorized these isozymes as ADH 1–5, with many variant subcategories, to explain these metabolic differences. Similarities in the ADH pathway exist in "collective families," like races and those from common hereditary backgrounds, accounting for the notion that, for example, the Irish tend to be able to drink heavily (as their ADH-metabolizing rate may be faster), while others, say from more southern climates, cannot (because they have less ADH available). Some may lack the ability to metabolize at all. To illustrate this, a recent study found that Polynesians have inherited a gene from their Asian ancestors, ADH2*2, which makes drinking alcohol less pleasant for them and consequently will make them less likely to become alcoholics. This genetic marker is common in 50 percent of Asian peoples and affects the way in which they break down acetaldehyde. Extremely toxic, acetaldehyde must be quickly disposed of by the body, but since many Asians possess a genetic mutation—one tiny amino acid that inactivates the necessary enzyme—they cannot rid themselves of this harmful substance. Unable to be metabolized by the liver, it pours out into the bloodstream, resulting in what is known as the "flush reaction," characterized by the dilation of blood vessels, a rise in body temperature, palpitations, and nausea. This can happen with less than one drink. Obviously, people who experience negative effects like these will probably not become alcoholics.

Yet, just as there are individuals who have negative reactions from alcohol, there are also those who appear to have an abnormally *positive* response. Improved performance, better eye-hand coordination, and a lesser feeling of drunkenness are some of these positive reactions, which brings us back to Type II alcoholics. It was once thought that sons of alcoholics became drinkers because they learned the behavior from their fathers. But famous twin studies have shown that, regardless of upbringing, a similar tendency toward the disease existed between these genetically identical children of alcoholic parents. Researchers believe that when Type II alcoholics experience positive effects from drinking, in part dictated by the genetic variants of their isozymes, it seems natural that they will continue to drink and increase their consumption, which in turn will speed up the biochemical process of alcohol dependence. Ultimately, genetics ends up playing a strong role in these instances.

The second major pathway, called the microsomal ethanol oxidizing system (MEOS), is only activated when consumption is long-term and constant. Here tolerance is developed and, in fact, alcohol is now *necessary* in order to maintain the system. Addiction is the result. There are also genetic variants at play in the MEOS pathway, which brings us back to the more common Type I alcoholics. They may need to "work" at becoming addicted. Instead of an instant reaction, they must increase their use over time in a chronic, progressive way. Consequently, they are the ones who will suddenly realize that an alcohol problem has "crept up" on them, after years of consuming it without many consequences. Genetically, the tendency may be there, but without the addition of nongenetic factors to encourage use, it could go completely "untapped," never becoming an issue at all.

Finally, why do some children of Type II alcoholics become complete teetotalers? This seems to be, for the most part, a conscious decision, which unknowingly or not, could end up saving their lives. By avoiding that first "love affair" with drink, they don't experience the positive reactions that their siblings who drink may feel. In such cases, the idea of alcoholism "skipping" a generation is often played out, with the grandchildren of the alcoholic becoming alcoholics themselves, yet without a father or mother possessing any sign of the disease.

(continued from page 199)

Tetrazzini can also be made with chicken and fresh parsley can replace the sage, if you desire.

8 ounces spaghetti, broken in half

10 ounces mixed wild mushrooms, such as shiitake, oyster, and/or chanterelle

1 tablespoon unsalted butter

1 tablespoon olive oil

Salt and pepper to taste

1 teaspoon finely chopped fresh sage leaves

2 cups diced cooked turkey

SAUCE

¼ cup (½ stick) unsalted butter

¼ cup plus 1 tablespoon all-purpose flour

1 quart milk (whole, 2 percent, or 1 percent)

Dash of ground nutmeg

Salt and pepper to taste

TOPPING

2 tablespoons unsalted butter, melted

¼ cup freshly grated Parmesan cheese

¾ cup plain dry bread crumbs

Salt and pepper to taste

1. Cook the spaghetti according to the package directions. Drain and rinse under cold running water. Set aside to drain well.

2. To prepare the mushrooms, remove any dirt specks with a moistened paper towel, cut away any hard stems, and cut them into ¼-inch-thick slices. Melt the butter with the olive oil in a medium-size skillet over medium to high heat, add the mushrooms, sprinkle with salt and pepper, and cook, stirring, until the mushrooms are tinged golden and their volume has reduced in size, about 10 minutes. Remove from the heat, mix in the sage, and set aside.

3. Preheat the oven to 350 degrees. Lightly butter a 9 x 13-inch baking dish.

4. To make the sauce, in a large saucepan, melt the butter over medium heat, then add the flour. Using a wire whisk, stir and cook for a minute or two, until well combined and bubbly but not brown. Add the milk, increase the heat to medium-high, and continue to whisk until thickened. Add the nutmeg and season with salt and pepper. Immediately combine with the diced turkey, cooked spaghetti, and sautéed mushrooms and pour into the prepared baking dish.

5. To make the topping, add the Parmesan cheese and bread crumbs to the melted butter, stirring to moisten. Add a pinch of salt and pepper and evenly spread the mixture over the top of the casserole. Bake until the edges are bubbly and the topping is golden, 30 to 40 minutes. Allow to rest for 5 to 10 minutes before serving.

Chef's Note: You can toast the topping even more by placing the casserole under a broiler for a minute or two.

Recovery Note: Some tetrazzinis call for "cameo" roles of sherry and white wine (see page 439), especially when making the traditional velouté. If you happen to be visiting Aunt Mabel over Thanksgiving weekend and she is serving tetrazzini, be sure to ask about her recipe.

Turkey Loaf with Sage and Onion

MAKES 6 TO 8 SERVINGS A moist and flavorful turkey loaf can provide some much needed comfort by enhancing our natural brain chemistry with "feel good" tryptophan. Finding ways to include turkey in our cooking is always a welcome endeavor, but if you have tried turkey loaf in the past and found it to be dry and less than flavorful, don't dismiss it yet. This recipe will change your mind!

Making a turkey loaf is a little different than traditional meatloaf making (page 212) because of

(continued on page 204)

Too Close For Comfort

Do You Know What's on Your Plate?

Think that gourmet chefs hold the monopoly on cooking with alcohol? Think again. Beer-battered fish, sherry-laden she-crab soup, and frogmore stew may provide comfort for some, but they could also conjure up some unwanted neurochemical activity. Southern cooks love to add a splash of bourbon to many a skillet concoction or barbecue sauce, Jewish mothers like to add a touch of brandy extract to their hamantaschen, while little Italian grandmothers often have a bottle of Chianti lurking nearby for the occasional addition to the pot. When someone else is doing the cooking, don't be afraid to ask about what you're eating—it's not impolite, it's imperative.

The best story I've heard in this regard is about an incident that took place at a local out-patient treatment center. It was family night, when husbands, wives, and significant others attend a group meeting with their addicted spouses to work through recovery issues and open up the lines of communication. One spouse decided to prepare a special treat for break time—her famously delicious bread pudding. What recovering alcoholic or addict could resist a dessert like that—sweet, creamy, and loaded with fat and calories! As the group began to dig into this seemingly innocuous pleasure, one person asked about the ingredients, because he thought there was a familiar taste. The cook announced that she knew she couldn't make this with the usual Bailey's Irish Cream Whiskey because of the alcohol, so she substituted Irish Cream–flavored coffee creamer instead. As silence filled the room, except for the clang of a few forks hitting the table, the questioner's jaw dropped to the floor. "That was my absolute *favorite* drink!" he finally said. "I *love* Bailey's. I mean . . . I *loved* Bailey's." Oops.

For the remaining two hours of group, Bailey's Irish Cream became the main topic of discussion. Everyone talked about when they had first tried it, or how they had a good friend who always drank it, or that whiskey should never be sweetened up like that—it's much better unadulterated, and on and on and on, until the counselor finally stepped in and put a halt to the excitement. One simple mistake led to a night of dangerous reminiscing and it wasn't even the real thing! If you think your brain chemicals don't possess a super-human memory, think again. And be sure to watch what other people are pouring on your plate. As food critic Marian Burros so aptly put it, "Someone is putting brandy in your bonbons, Grand Marnier in your breakfast jam, Kahlua in your ice cream, Scotch in your mustard, and Wild Turkey in your cake. Americans may be drinking fewer alcoholic beverages, but they are certainly eating more of them than ever before."

(continued from page 202)

its extra-lean quality and subtler flavor. Be sure to use a combination of white and dark meat, generally called lean ground turkey, for fuller flavor and moistness. Fresh sage really perks up this loaf and adds a lovely aroma to the final outcome. I like to serve this with the usual turkey "fixin's," like cornbread stuffing, sweet potatoes, and cranberry sauce, but, just like its traditional counterpart, turkey loaf makes a great hot "meatloaf" sandwich when you're in a hurry and also goes well with any type of side dish and vegetable.

- **2 pounds lean ground turkey**
- **2 large eggs, beaten**
- **1 cup seasoned dry bread crumbs**
- **1 small onion, peeled and finely chopped**
- **1 tablespoon prepared mustard**
- **1 tablespoon finely chopped fresh sage leaves or**
  - **2 teaspoons rubbed dried sage**

1. Preheat the oven to 325 degrees. In a large mixing bowl, combine all the ingredients and mix well with your hands or a wooden spoon.

2. Transfer mixture to a buttered 9 x 4-inch glass, ceramic, or nonstick loaf pan and pat down well to remove any empty spots or air pockets. Smooth the top with the tines of a fork and cover with a sheet of aluminum foil. Bake until an instant-read meat thermometer inserted in the middle registers 165 degrees, or the juices run clear when the middle is pierced with a fork, about $1\frac{1}{4}$ hours. Do not uncover the turkey loaf during baking except to check for doneness.

3. Remove from the oven and allow to rest for 10 to 15 minutes. Using a knife, loosen the edges of the loaf and turn out onto a warm serving platter. You may also carefully lift up with two metal spatulas and transfer to your platter. Slice and serve.

Turkey Loaf Italian Style: Add 2 large garlic cloves, peeled and minced, and 1 teaspoon *each* dried oregano, basil, and marjoram to the meat mixture. Top with one 8-ounce can tomato sauce before baking and do not cover the loaf with foil while baking.

Turkey Loaf Tex-Mex: Add $\frac{1}{2}$ medium-size red bell pepper, seeded and finely chopped; 1 small jalapeño, seeded and minced; 1 teaspoon chili powder; and $\frac{1}{2}$ teaspoon ground cumin to the meat mixture. Cook as directed above and serve with store-bought enchilada sauce.

Golden Croquettes with Creamy Cheese Sauce

MAKES 3 TO 4 SERVINGS (8 CROQUETTES TOTAL) Crispy fried and golden croquettes, whether made from chicken or turkey, are an excellent way to use up leftovers, while adding a bit of comfort to the dinner table. Pan-frying, as opposed to deep-frying, is my method of choice here, which will lessen somewhat the saturated fat content. Be sure the croquettes are well chilled before frying, so they will hold together while cooking. Fresh bread crumbs are particularly good here, but dry will fill in nicely.

A basic white sauce serves as both a binder for the croquettes and the creamy sauce accompaniment. Make it ahead when you can, to give it a chance to cool; even the day before is fine. Served up with any number of comforting side dishes, this meal will please everyone's taste buds—try canned hominy, fresh corn, or rice. In the green department, broccoli florets, peas, and asparagus are just a few vegetables that will welcome a drizzle of this delicious creamy cheese sauce on the side.

CROQUETTES
- **1 cup Easy White Sauce (page 243)**
- **2½ cups finely chopped cooked chicken or turkey**
- **1 tablespoon grated onion**
- **1 tablespoon chopped fresh parsley leaves**
- **1 teaspoon fresh lemon juice**

Salt and pepper to taste

All-purpose flour for dredging

1 large egg, beaten with 1 tablespoon water

2 cups plain dry bread crumbs or 3 cups fresh
    bread crumbs

CHEESE SAUCE

1 cup Easy White Sauce (page 243)

$2/3$ cup shredded cheddar cheese

Dash of paprika

Canola or light olive oil for frying

1. In a large mixing bowl, combine the white sauce, chicken, onion, parsley, lemon juice, and salt and pepper to taste. Fold together to blend, cover with plastic wrap, and refrigerate until well chilled, 1 to 2 hours.

2. To make the croquettes, set up an assembly line of flour for dredging, a shallow bowl containing the beaten egg and water, and the bread crumbs. Have ready a baking sheet lined with waxed or parchment paper. Form the chicken or turkey mixture into 8 oval-shaped patties and dredge each in the flour, dip into the egg mixture, and coat evenly with the bread crumbs. Set on the baking sheet as they are done.

3. To make the cheese sauce, heat the white sauce in a medium-size saucepan over medium-low heat, stirring constantly, until hot and slightly bubbly. Remove from the heat and stir in the cheddar cheese and paprika until the cheese is melted. Set aside in a warm place.

3. Pour enough oil into a skillet to come halfway up the thickness of the croquettes. Heat the oil over medium heat to 365 degrees or until a cube of bread dropped into the oil quickly fries up golden.

4. Fry the croquettes in the oil until golden and crisp, about 3 minutes per side. Do not crowd the skillet, working in batches if necessary. Transfer the croquettes to a plate lined with paper towels to drain. Serve on a warm platter with the cheese sauce spooned over or on the side.

Curried Croquettes with Creamy Sauce:
Replace the parsley with 2 teaspoons curry powder. Omit the cheese from the sauce and add $1/2$ teaspoon curry powder with the paprika.

Tarragon Croquettes with Creamy Mustard Sauce: Substitute chopped fresh tarragon leaves for the parsley. Omit the cheese from the sauce and add $1/2$ teaspoon dry mustard with the paprika.

Salmon Croquettes with Creamy Jarlsberg Dill Sauce: Substitute fresh-cooked or flaked, canned salmon that has been well drained for the chicken or turkey. Use Jarlsberg instead of cheddar cheese and add 2 teaspoons chopped fresh dill leaves.

Stuffed Cornish Game Hens with Apricot Glaze

MAKES 2 TO 4 SERVINGS Game hens, or rock Cornish hens as they are also known, are basically miniature-sized chickens that may weigh up to $2\frac{1}{2}$ pounds at most. Since eating them tends to be a bit labor intensive and the ratio of meat to bone is pretty small, one bird per person is the usual serving size. However, if you are serving numerous side dishes, one larger hen can feed two people, especially when stuffed.

In days when we see people refraining from stuffing poultry because of health and fat concerns, Cornish hens are still popularly prepared this way. Any type of stuffing will do, but I particularly like one that is fruit based, as it complements the flavor of the hen so well. The pan juices make for a luscious yet light sauce. Serve with Herb Roasted Potatoes (page 230) or one of the sweet potato recipes (pages 238–240). Watercress Salad (page 324) would be a good choice as an accompaniment or first course.

APRICOT CORNBREAD STUFFING

1 tablespoon unsalted butter

¼ cup diced red onion

¼ cup diced celery

½ apple, left unpeeled, cored and diced

4 dried apricots, diced

Salt and pepper to taste

¼ teaspoon dried thyme

1 large corn muffin, crumbled

¼ cup orange juice

APRICOT GLAZE

¼ cup (½ stick) unsalted butter

1 tablespoon canola oil

3 tablespoons apricot preserves or jam

2 Cornish game hens, giblets and fat deposits
   removed, rinsed, and patted dry

Salt and pepper to taste

Splash of orange juice for deglazing

1. Preheat the oven to 400 degrees.

2. To make the stuffing, melt the butter in a medium-size skillet over medium heat until foamy. Add the onion, celery, apple, and apricots and season with salt, pepper, and thyme. Cook over medium-high heat until softened, about 5 minutes. Remove from the heat and gently stir in the crumbled corn muffin. Drizzle with the orange juice and stir to moisten. Set aside.

3. To make the glaze, melt together the butter, oil, and apricot preserves in a small saucepan over medium-low heat. Stir to combine and set aside.

4. Season the hens with salt and pepper and fill the cavities loosely with the stuffing. (There is no need to skewer or truss.) Place on a wire rack set in a roasting pan, making sure the hens don't touch each other, and brush each hen with the glaze. Roast on the center rack of the oven for 15 minutes, then carefully turn them breast side down so as not to disturb the stuffing, brush again with the glaze, and roast for 20 minutes, basting occasionally. Turn the hens breast side up, brush with the remaining glaze, and roast, basting often, until the skin is crisp and golden and the juices run clear when the thigh is pierced with a fork, another 15 to 20 minutes.

5. Transfer the hens to a platter and cover with aluminum foil to rest. Remove the rack from the roasting pan, pour out all but 1 tablespoon of the fat, and deglaze over medium heat on the stovetop with a splash of orange juice, scraping to loosen up the browned bits from the bottom of the pan. Serve the hens drizzled with the pan sauce or on the side.

Roasting Up a Comforting Dinner

Cooking Tips, Times, and Temperatures

Classic roast dinners, with traditional sides of potatoes, veggies, gravy, and other delicious complements, spell comfort for everyone. So, don't wait for the holidays to create these wonderfully satisfying meals. Weekends are the perfect time to prepare an old-fashioned dinner with all the fixings for family and friends and bring a bit of festivity to the dining table. Here are some cooking tips to get you started, followed by cooking directions for common roasts:

- Remove the roast from the refrigerator one to two hours before cooking in order to allow it to come to room temperature. A roast taken straight from the fridge will take much longer to cook.

- Roasts should be cooked uncovered and without moisture; don't add liquid or you may end up boiling your meat.

- The right size roasting pan is key—not too deep, which will encourage steaming, and neither large nor small, to discourage burning and encourage air circulation.

- Roast fat side up to allow for natural basting and season with salt and pepper.

- Add cut-up potatoes and other vegetables to the roasting pan during the final 30 to 40 minutes for delicious accompaniments.

- Test for doneness with an instant-read thermometer by inserting it into the thickest part, avoiding bone and fat, and remember that the roast will continue to cook once it is removed from the oven (an additional 5 to 10 degrees).

- Always let the roast rest at least 15 minutes before slicing to allow the juices to be reabsorbed by the meat. Use this time to deglaze the pan (see page 134 for nonalcohol deglazing suggestions) and make your pan sauce or gravy.

CUTS OF BEEF

EYE ROUND ROAST, SIRLOIN, AND ROUND TIP: These back cuts, although flavorful and economical, can be extremely tough if overcooked. They are part of the hard-working muscles of the animal and may look like tender cuts, but in general, they require moist-heat cooking (like pot roast) for the best results. However, as along as you enjoy medium-rare or rare beef, these are good choices. Slow roasting is the best method.

Roasting temperature: 325 degrees
Minutes per pound: 18 (rare), 20 (medium-rare)
Servings: 3 to 4 per pound

RIB EYE, STANDING RIB ROAST, AND PRIME RIB: These are the elite of the roast beef choices and will produce delicious and tender results from slow roasting or a combination of initial high-heat searing followed by slow cooking. They are generally too cumbersome to sear on top of the stove (bone-in or not), so begin with a hot oven (about 500 degrees) for the first 15 minutes to create a crusty brown exterior and those desirable browned bits in the roasting pan, which will contribute to a flavorful gravy.

Roasting temperature: 500 degrees (first 15 minutes), 350 degrees (remainder)
Minutes per pound: 15 (rare), 20 (medium)
Servings: About 3 per pound

TENDERLOIN OR WHOLE FILLET: Because it is the least-used muscle, this cut is by far the most tender. Not inexpensive, a whole tenderloin will require quite a bit of trimming, which can be tricky for the inexperienced. If you are spending the money for this special piece (filet mignon is cut from here), have your butcher trim it properly and get it ready for cooking. Half fillets are also available. Stove-top searing (in a roasting pan) is my preferred method here, as is a hot oven to finish. Rare to medium-rare is the best way to serve this, but for finicky eaters, the tapered tail ends up medium-well, if it has not been tied. Two half pieces may be the best solution if more than one or two of your diners prefer well-cooked meat. That way you can simply cook one half for a longer period of time or get it into the oven first.

Roasting temperature: 425 degrees (may sear stove-top first)
Minutes per pound: 7 to 8 (rare), 10 (medium)
Servings: 3 to 4 per pound

CUTS OF VEAL

LOIN, RUMP, OR ROUND ROAST: A perfectly cooked veal roast is a wonderful delicacy, but often hard to achieve. One of the reasons is that veal needs to be cooked thoroughly in order to bring out its unique flavor, but by the time this happens, this extremely lean cut of meat will dry out. The solution is to provide plenty of extra fat by smearing butter or wrapping the roast in pork fat or bacon and roasting at a low temperature. Breast of veal, often stuffed and rolled, is also a treat, although it requires a somewhat different cooking method. After an initial searing to brown the outside, braise in a little liquid while covered to produce a succulent and tender result, not to mention a presentation splash at the table. Have your butcher bone the breast and create a pocket for stuffing to help you along.

Roasting temperature: 325 degrees
Minutes per pound: 25 (medium-well)
Servings: 3 to 4 per pound

CUTS OF PORK

LOIN ROAST, CENTER CUT, SIRLOIN, OR SHOULDER ROAST: Pork roasts are extremely economical, as well as delicious. Boned, rolled, and tied by the butcher, loin roasts can be one of the easiest things to prepare. Searing first on the stove or in a hot oven will make for some delectable crispy bits, while ensuring a tender and moist interior. Other cuts, primarily with bone-in, do well either slow roasted or at high temperatures, depending on your preference. Pork is adequately cooked at an internal temperature of 145 degrees (see page 152 for a discussion of safely cooking pork), although some prefer no traces of pink, which will necessitate a temperature of 160 degrees. The small pork tenderloin requires very little cooking and is a good choice for a small audience. For instructions, see Roasted Pork Tenderloin with Quick Roasted Apples (page 214).

> Roasting temperature: 350 degrees
> Minutes per pound: 20 to 25 (medium-well)
> Servings: 2 to 3 per pound

CUTS OF LAMB

WHOLE LEG, HALF LEG SIRLOIN OR SHANK, ROLLED SHOULDER: Roasted lamb indicates festivity whenever it is served and should really be enjoyed on a regular basis. Garlic and fresh herbs bring out the best that lamb has to offer (see the recipe for lamb chops on page 151 for the ideal marinade) and can be rubbed on the outside or inserted into a rolled roast. When not too large to handle, a lamb roast should be seared stove-top first, then cooked to medium-rare or medium in the oven. Some people refuse to eat lamb unless it is well done, so you may be better off with a bone-in leg cut, which can provide for different degrees of doneness. Have the butcher trim away the fell, or thin outer membrane, as well as any inordinate amount of fat that is present.

> Roasting temperature: 425 degrees (first 15 minutes, if not searing), 350 (remainder)
> Minutes per pound: 12 (medium-rare), 15 (medium), 20 (well done)
> Servings: About 3 per pound

Meat Temperature Chart, Using an Instant-Read Thermometer:

BEEF
Rare . . . . 120° to 125° F
Medium-rare . . . . 130° to 135° F
Medium . . . . 140° to 145° F
Medium-well . . . . 150° to 155° F
Well done . . . . 160° F and above

VEAL
Medium-well . . . . 165° F

PORK
Medium-well . . . . 150° F

LAMB
Rare . . . . 135° F
Medium-rare . . . . 140° to 150° F
Medium . . . . 160° F
Well done . . . . 165° F and above

Old-Fashioned Pot Roast Dinner

MAKES 6 SERVINGS A chapter on comfort food wouldn't be complete without a recipe for pot roast. This flavorful dish owes its name, of course, to its method of "roasting." In actuality, this popular method of cooking is really a braise, in which the outside of the meat is seared in hot oil, then liquid is added for slow cooking. It is often used for tougher and less expensive cuts of meat that require a little time to become tender, but it is well worth the effort in the end. I generally use a bottom round rump roast, but you will have equal success with a chuck roast or shoulder.

Yankee pot roast simply means that there are vegetables added, usually potatoes and carrots, during the final stages of braising. Most pot roasts in general are made this way, however, sometimes mashed potatoes and other types of vegetables prepared separately are equally tasty as accompaniments. I particularly like the flavor that the cooking liquid imparts to the potatoes and carrots, so I always add them. Sometimes I will add string beans just to get something green into the meal. Peas and lima beans are also a good addition, as are turnips.

This is one of those dishes that gets tastier the longer it sits and does not suffer in the least from reheating. If you are taking the time to prepare pot roast, you may as well make a large one, as leftovers are great to have on hand. Serve with some horseradish sauce (page 260) on the side to complement the beef.

One 3- to 4-pound bottom round rump roast
Salt and pepper to taste
2 tablespoons canola oil
1 large onion, peeled and roughly chopped
1 celery stalk, ends trimmed and roughly chopped
2 tablespoons all-purpose flour
½ cup apple juice
4 cups low-sodium beef broth
1 bay leaf

1 sprig fresh thyme or ½ teaspoon dried thyme
3 or 4 medium-size carrots, peeled and cut into
    1-inch-thick rounds
3 or 4 medium-size red potatoes, peeled and cubed

1. Trim the roast of visible fat. Season it generously with salt and pepper. In a 6- to 8-quart Dutch oven, heat the canola oil to almost smoking over high heat. Add the roast and brown well on all sides. Remove it from the pan, add the onion and celery, and cook, stirring and scraping up the browned bits from the bottom, for about 5 minutes. Add the flour and stir to coat. Cook another 1 to 2 minutes. Add the apple juice and, as it sizzles and boils, scrape up any remaining bits from the bottom. Immediately add the beef broth and herbs and bring to a simmer. Return the roast to the pan, cover, and allow to braise over very low heat until nearly fork tender; depending on the size of your roast, this may take anywhere from 1½ to 2½ hours. You want the meat to be cooking at a very slow simmer; if the liquid is really churning, then turn the heat down—you don't want boiled beef. Occasionally turn the roast over in the liquid and be sure there is enough to keep about two-thirds of the roast submerged. If not, add a little water and keep simmering, covered.

2. When the pot roast is just about fork tender, add the carrots and potatoes and allow to cook, covered, until the meat and vegetables are perfectly tender, about an additional 30 minutes. If necessary, you may add a little water while the vegetables are cooking to prevent sticking. The final liquid should have a gravy-like consistency and not be watery. It is better to add a little water as needed rather than have to thicken the gravy later with more flour or cornstarch.

3. Remove the pot roast from the pan and let it rest for 5 to 10 minutes before slicing. Taste the gravy for seasoning and adjust if necessary. Serve the roast on a platter with the vegetables around it and the gravy and horseradish sauce, if using, on the side.

The Best Beef Brisket

MAKES 6 SERVINGS If tender beef is your choice, this brisket recipe will surely satisfy. Although it requires lengthy slow cooking, there is really nothing for you to do while it's in the oven. Try this on a day when you know you will be around, just to keep an eye out and enjoy the aroma wafting from the kitchen. Brisket cuts come from the breast section and are usually available in flat cut, which is quite lean, and point cut, a fatter piece considered to be more flavorful. Either would be fine to use here, but be sure to trim well of excess fat. The popular St. Patrick's Day offering of corned beef (cured in a seasoned brine) is most often a beef brisket cut.

One 3- to 4-pound brisket cut of beef, trimmed of fat
4 garlic cloves, peeled and minced
1 teaspoon dried thyme
Salt and pepper to taste
3 medium-size onions, peeled and sliced
One 28-ounce can whole plum tomatoes, drained and chopped
1 cup low-sodium beef broth or water
1 tablespoon chopped fresh parsley leaves (optional)

1. Preheat the oven to 325 degrees. Place the trimmed brisket in a roasting pan or Dutch oven. Rub the garlic and thyme over the meat and sprinkle with salt and pepper. Cover the brisket with the onions and tomatoes and pour the beef broth around. Cover the pan with aluminum foil and allow to slow cook until tender. Depending upon the size of the brisket, this may take anywhere from 2 to 4 hours. Occasionally, turn over the brisket and spoon the onion-and-tomato mixture over it, recover with the foil, and continue until done.

2. When the brisket is fork tender, remove from the oven and let rest in the liquid for 10 minutes.

Transfer the brisket to a serving platter, pour the liquid mixture into a large saucepan, and simmer, if necessary, to reduce somewhat. It should be the consistency of a thick soup. Taste this sauce for the addition of salt and pepper and pour all over the brisket, which has been sliced on the diagonal. Sprinkle with the parsley, if desired, and serve.

Chef's Note: When storing your cooked brisket, be sure to submerge the pieces in the sauce. If you are not serving immediately, you can store the brisket whole directly in the tomato-onion mixture. In fact, you will be able to slice thinner pieces if the brisket has been chilled in this way. To reheat, simply microwave or heat on top of the stove with the sauce in a large skillet, covered, over low heat.

Salisbury Steak with Mushroom Gravy

MAKES 4 SERVINGS This dish is a real favorite with kids and adults alike, especially when served with buttered egg noodles or creamy mashed potatoes. Not really a steak in the true sense of the word, seasoned ground beef is formed into patties and cooked in a hearty gravy to make this classic comfort food. Dr. J.H. Salisbury, a nineteenth-century English physician, inspired its creation; he encouraged his weak patients to eat plenty of beef as often as possible. We have surely come a long way since then in our dietary recommendations (we are now encouraged by doctors and nutritionists to drastically *reduce* our intake of red meat), but there is still a place for this delicious meal at the Phase Two dinner table. Lean ground beef will reduce the saturated fat intake without sacrificing taste, as the patties will gain much moisture and flavor from the gravy.

By using some prepared ingredients in this recipe, Salisbury steak can be whipped up in no time, providing some quick comfort on a hungry night. Baby carrots make a nice side dish, while starting with a crisp green salad will provide some necessary micronutrients and fiber.

- 1 pound lean ground beef
- 1 small onion, peeled and minced
- Salt and pepper to taste
- 2 tablespoons olive oil
- One 10-ounce package white or cremini mushrooms, wiped clean and sliced
- 1 dry packet mushroom gravy (found in the soup section of the supermarket)
- 2 cups cold water
- One 16-ounce can low-sodium beef broth
- 2 tablespoons chopped fresh parsley leaves

1. In a medium-size mixing bowl, combine the beef, onion, and salt and pepper. Form 8 oval-shaped patties from the mixture and season the outside again with salt and pepper.

2. Heat the olive oil in a large nonstick skillet over medium-high heat and fry the patties until browned, about 3 minutes per side. Transfer to a plate and set aside.

3. Add the mushrooms to the skillet and cook, stirring occasionally, over medium heat until softened and lightly brown around the edges, about 5 minutes. Add the dry gravy packet and stir with a wooden spoon to coat the mushrooms. Add the water slowly, stirring with a fork to combine, and increase the heat to high. Add the beef broth and bring to a low simmer. Return the patties to the skillet and cook, covered, over low heat until no longer pink and firm to the touch, about 20 minutes. Stir occasionally to prevent sticking.

4. Transfer the patties to a warm serving platter and simmer the mushroom gravy, if necessary, to reduce and thicken until it coats the back of a spoon. Pour half the gravy over the patties and sprinkle with the chopped parsley. Serve the remaining gravy on the side.

My Favorite Meatloaf

MAKES 6 TO 8 SERVINGS The humble meatloaf has been a staple of the American dinner table for decades. It is also one of the most popular orders at local diners. Making a juicy, flavorful meatloaf is really not too difficult, but many home cooks say they are disappointed in the result because it is often dry and tasteless and nothing like what "Mom used to make." I prefer using the beef, veal, and pork combination, often sold as (what else?) meatloaf mix, for flavor and moistness, but you may use a lean ground beef if you like.

Everybody I know has a "secret ingredient" for meatloaf, from minced garlic to maple syrup; below you will find mine.

- 2 pounds lean ground beef or a combination of beef, veal, and pork
- 2 large eggs, beaten
- 1½ cups seasoned dry bread crumbs
- 1 small onion, peeled and finely chopped
- ½ cup ketchup
- 1 tablespoon Worcestershire sauce
- 1 teaspoon prepared mustard
- Salt and pepper to taste
- Secret ingredient: ½ cup hickory smoked BBQ sauce

1. Preheat the oven to 350 degrees. Lightly grease a 9 x 5-inch glass, ceramic, or metal loaf pan.

2. In a large mixing bowl, combine all the ingredients. Mix together well with a fork, wooden spoon, or, preferably, your hands.

3. Transfer the meatloaf mixture to the prepared loaf pan. Pat down well to eliminate any air pockets and empty spaces. Smooth the top with the tines of a fork. Cover with a sheet of aluminum foil and bake for 1 hour. During the last 20 minutes, remove the foil, drain a bit of the excess fat away, if necessary, and continue to bake until browned on

top and an instant-read thermometer inserted in the center registers 155 to 160 degrees.

4. Remove from the oven and allow to rest for 10 minutes. Using a knife, loosen the edges by sliding the blade around the inside of the loaf pan. Either flip over onto a warmed serving platter or remove using two metal spatulas and lift out onto your platter. Slice and serve.

Peter's Favorite Meatloaf: Substitute soy sauce for the Worcestershire sauce and omit the mustard. Use Chinese hoisin or *char siu* sauce as the secret ingredient.

Mom's Favorite Beefloaf: Use lean ground beef only, omit the ketchup, and add 1 cup minced white button mushrooms. Use Italian-style tomato sauce as the secret ingredient.

Old-Fashioned Glazed Meatloaf: Instead of using a loaf pan, shape the meatloaf mixture into an oval-shaped cylinder and place on a rimmed baking sheet lined with parchment paper. Bake, uncovered, for 30 minutes, then coat with a glaze made of ½ cup ketchup, 1 tablespoon honey, and 1 teaspoon ground cumin. Continue to cook a further 20 to 30 minutes, until done.

British Shepherd's Pie

MAKES 4 SERVINGS Ask anyone who lives across the "pond" what his idea of comfort is and you will hear a resounding "Shepherd's pie like mum used to make!" Here in America, we are slowly being introduced to this dish through gourmet frozen food companies, but, in reality, shepherd's pie is not gourmet at all. It is true, down-home British fare. Its cousin, "cottage pie," is very similar, except that it almost always will use leftover roasts as its starting point.

This British "casserole" consists of a layer of flavorful gravy-coated ground beef or lamb, topped with everyone's absolute favorite—mashed potatoes. You can use leftovers or whip up a batch especially for this dish.

1 tablespoon canola oil
1 medium-size onion, peeled and chopped
1 medium-size carrot, peeled and chopped
1 pound lean ground beef or lamb
Salt and pepper to taste
1 tablespoon all-purpose flour
½ teaspoon dried thyme
¼ teaspoon ground cinnamon
2 cups low-sodium beef broth
1 tablespoon tomato paste
1 recipe Classic Mashed Potatoes (page 226)
1 cup shredded cheddar cheese

1. Preheat the oven to 375 degrees.
2. In a heavy-bottomed pot, heat the canola oil over medium heat, add the onion and carrot, and cook, stirring, for 3 to 4 minutes. Add the ground beef, sprinkle with salt and pepper, and cook until lightly browned all over. Break up clumps of beef if necessary with a fork. Add the flour, thyme, and cinnamon, stir to combine, and cook a further 2 minutes. Add the beef broth and tomato paste and bring to a low simmer. Allow to cook until most of the liquid has evaporated, stirring occasionally, leaving only a coating of gravy that clings to the beef. This will take 15 to 20 minutes. Transfer to a 1-quart casserole and spread evenly over the bottom.
3. Combine the mashed potatoes (2 to 3 cups) with the cheddar cheese. Spread this over the beef layer evenly. Use a fork to pat it down and make decorative lines and patterns across the top. Bake until the edges are bubbly, 25 to 30 minutes. Remove from the oven and let rest for 5 minutes before serving.

Chef's Note: Try making individual shepherd's pies in small pie tins or ceramic portion-sized casseroles. They freeze exceedingly well and are easily reheated for a quick meal.

Roasted Pork Tenderloin with Quick Roasted Apples

MAKES 4 TO 6 SERVINGS Pork roasts and chops are often found on comfort food menus, especially in the South. Juicy and flavorful, this "other white meat" can actually be a healthy choice too, since modern American pork is about 50 percent leaner than it was years ago. By far, the tenderloin cut is the leanest and most tender part, if not overcooked. It is also the easiest to prepare, while requiring very little cooking time for a delicious roasted result.

Many packaged pork tenderloins come already marinated with various flavorings, such as teriyaki or lemon herb. These are certainly fine to use, as long as they do not contain alcohol. This recipe calls for an unseasoned pork tenderloin, usually less expensive than the prepared ones. They generally weigh between 1 and 2 pounds and have a long tapered end.

I have always loved the combination of pork and apples. Fortunately, for those of us in recovery, apples are one of the best fruit choices, both glycemically and nutritionally, so serve your pork tenderloin with Quick Roasted Apples or, in a pinch, a jar of prepared applesauce (chunky-style). If you are feeling ambitious, make Cinnamon Apple Compote (page 181), which goes beautifully with this tenderloin. Pair up with any of the sweet potato recipes (pages 238–240) and you'll be in the true "southern comfort" zone in no time.

One 1- to 2-pound unseasoned pork tenderloin
Salt and pepper to taste
1 teaspoon ground cumin
1 tablespoon canola oil

QUICK ROASTED APPLES
2 large Golden Delicious apples, left unpeeled, quartered and cored
½ teaspoon ground cinnamon

1. Preheat the oven to 400 degrees. Have ready a shallow roasting pan.

2. Season the pork tenderloin with salt, pepper, and the cumin. In a large skillet, heat the canola oil over medium-high heat. When it begins to smoke, add the pork tenderloin and brown quickly on all sides, about 1 minute per side. Turn off the heat and transfer the tenderloin to the roasting pan.

3. To make the roasted apples, add the quartered apples and cinnamon to the hot skillet and, without turning on the heat, stir quickly to coat the apples with the drippings. Transfer the skillet contents to the roasting pan, distributing the apples around the tenderloin. Roast until an instant-read thermometer inserted in the center registers 140 degrees and the tenderloin and apples are golden, 20 to 25 minutes, turning the tenderloin and apples over halfway through.

4. Remove the tenderloin from the oven, transfer to a cutting board, and allow to rest 10 to 15 minutes for the juices to settle, covered with a sheet of aluminum foil.

5. Slice thin pieces of the tenderloin on a diagonal slant. It should be just barely pink and juicy in the center. Transfer with the apples to a warm serving platter and serve.

Melt-in-Your-Mouth Country-Style Pork Ribs

MAKES 4 SERVINGS This dish is a real favorite for many of my clients who wish for some "finger-lickin'" good ribs when the weather does not allow for outdoor grilling. The sauce itself is worth making and any extra you may have will end up being a favorite barbecue sauce for other cuts of meat as well. Slow cooking is the key here, but not much attention needs to be paid once the cooking begins. After a couple of hours, these tender pieces of pork will fall off the bone and melt in your mouth, a result that will truly reward your patience and care.

2 to 3 pounds country-style pork ribs on the bone
Salt and pepper to taste
2 teaspoons canola oil
1 medium-size onion, peeled and finely chopped
2 garlic cloves, peeled and minced
1 tablespoon peeled and minced fresh ginger
One 12-ounce bottle tomato ketchup
One 9-ounce bottle chili sauce
1 cup water
¼ cup cider vinegar
¼ cup fresh lemon juice
¼ cup firmly packed dark brown sugar
1 tablespoon Worcestershire sauce
1 teaspoon chili powder
1 teaspoon ground coriander
½ teaspoon *each* ground cumin, paprika, and curry powder
Dash of cayenne pepper or more to taste

1. Preheat the oven to 425 degrees. Sprinkle the ribs with salt and pepper and brown them in a roasting pan in the oven until most of the fat has been rendered, about 30 minutes. Shake the pan occasionally to brown evenly.

2. Meanwhile, in an 8- or 10-quart heavy-bottomed pot, heat the canola oil over medium heat, add the onion, and cook, stirring, until softened and lightly browned, 2 to 3 minutes. Add the garlic and ginger and cook, stirring, for another minute. Add the remaining ingredients and stir well to combine. Bring to a low simmer and cook, covered, for 10 to 15 minutes in order to marry the flavors.

3. Place the browned ribs in the pot with the sauce, submerging them as well as possible. Bring back to a slow simmer and cook, covered, until the pork is fork tender, 1½ to 2 hours. Stir occasionally and add water, if necessary, to prevent sticking.

4. To serve, transfer the ribs to a warm serving platter and provide the sauce on the side.

Country Cured Glazed Ham

Delicious country-style glazed hams grace many American holiday tables, as well as Sunday dinners. Large, fully cooked hams on the bone are ideal for glazing and, economically, a good choice as well, for leftovers are always eagerly eaten up during the week. In order for a ham to be classified as "country cured," also known as "country-style," it must meet certain standards of preparation in its curing, seasoning, smoking, and aging. These standards produce a ham of high quality of which Smithfield hams, hailing from the Virginia town of the same name, are probably the best known.

There are many ways to glaze a ham and any number of ingredients will do very well, but something sweet is always used, whether it is brown sugar, molasses, maple syrup, or a fruit-based component like jam or marmalade. Often a sweet fortified wine, such as Madeira, is used for basting, as is hard cider, beer, and bourbon. Here we can substitute a liquid that will provide adequate sweetness and acidity—cherry cola—an old standby with new potential for recovery cooking! It will also result in a lovely caramel-colored glaze.

My mother always made her famous Raisin Sauce (page 260) to serve with baked ham, and sweet potatoes were also a favorite accompaniment at my house. Of course, you can present your ham in the traditional fashion, studded with whole cloves and covered with pineapple rings and maraschino cherries if you like. Just watch out for those booze-marinated cherries!

One 6- to 7-pound fully cooked butt portion ham
½ cup whole-grain mustard
½ cup honey
½ teaspoon ground allspice
One 10.5-ounce can cherry cola (*not* diet)

1. Preheat the oven to 350 degrees.

2. Trim the rind and any excess fat from the ham, leaving a ¼-inch layer of fat. Using a sharp knife, score the fat layer, creating a parallel grid pattern, about 1 inch between scores. Place the ham on a wire rack in a large roasting pan.

3. In a small mixing bowl, combine the mustard, honey, and allspice and brush the scored fat layer of the ham with the mixture. Pour the cherry cola into the pan and bake for 30 minutes. Now begin basting with the pan liquid every 10 minutes, until the ham is completely heated through and nicely glazed, 1 to 1½ hours. Remove from the oven, reserve the pan juices, if desired, and allow the ham to rest for 15 minutes before carving.

Chef's Note: If you are using a pre-sliced, spiral-cut ham, be sure to keep it covered with aluminum foil while baking to ensure moistness, and check directions for shorter heating times. If using a partially cooked ham, make sure the internal temperature has reached 170 degrees so that it is safely cooked through.

Recovery Note: Don't let anyone convince you that beer basting is a safe preparation. Former beer drinkers, most especially, have a keen sense of recognition for the smell and taste of their drink of choice, which could trigger some unwanted cravings.

Irish Lamb Stew

MAKES 4 SERVINGS One of the most comforting types of dishes around, slow cooked, stewed lamb with plenty of potatoes and carrots can conjure up those "feel good" chemicals in no time. Traditionally, the cheaper and tougher mutton was used in Ireland, where this dish originated, but today, stewing lamb is quite readily available and not at all costly. Lamb pieces on the bone generally cut from the neck and packaged as "stewing lamb" will provide the best flavor, although it may require a bit of trimming. You will need a good two pounds for four people, as the bone-to-meat ratio is quite high. I will sometimes add a lamb shank or two for some extra meat, when my grocer has them available. Since most of the resulting gravy's flavor is derived purely from the lamb (no broth is called for here), it will be necessary to season with salt and pepper more than usual. Taste as you go, and add a bit as needed.

Although most cooks will refrain from using a starchy potato, such as Idaho or russet, in stews as they tend to disintegrate, I particularly like them here, and by cooking them after the lamb is done, we can remove them just at the exact moment of fork tenderness. They also help to thicken the flavorful resulting gravy. I also like adding turnips, and because some folks don't care too much for their taste, I always cut them in a different shape from the potatoes so everyone knows what they're getting!

This is definitely a one-dish meal, apart from biscuits or bread on the side for soaking up the gravy, and a refreshing salad of crisp greens dressed with a little olive oil and vinegar.

2 tablespoons light olive oil

2 pounds stewing lamb on the bone, trimmed
   of excess fat

Salt and pepper to taste

All-purpose flour for dredging

1 large onion, peeled and diced

1 large celery stalk, ends trimmed and diced

3 sprigs fresh thyme

2 bay leaves

½ teaspoon dried rosemary

2 tablespoons unsweetened red grape juice

Splash of red wine vinegar

4 medium-size carrots, peeled and cut into
   1-inch-thick rounds

4 small turnips, peeled and quartered

4 medium-size Idaho or russet potatoes,
   peeled and cut into 1-inch cubes

1. Heat the olive oil in a large, heavy-bottomed skillet or Dutch oven over medium-high heat. Season the lamb with salt and pepper, lightly dredge in the flour, knocking off any excess, and pan-fry in a single layer until nicely browned on both sides, 8 to 10 minutes total. Remove the lamb from the skillet and set aside.

2. Add the onion and celery to the skillet, sprinkle with salt and pepper, and cook over medium heat, stirring, until softened, about 6 minutes. You may add a touch more oil if necessary. Add the herbs, grape juice, and vinegar and stir with a wooden spoon to loosen any browned bits of meat from the bottom of the pan. Return the lamb to the skillet, add enough water to cover, stir to combine, and bring to a simmer. Cook, covered, over medium-low heat, keeping the liquid at a low simmer, until the meat is fork tender and falling off the bone, 1½ to 2 hours. Check periodically for the addition of more water to prevent sticking. Remove the lamb with a slotted spoon and set aside in a serving dish to keep warm.

3. Add the carrots and turnips to the gravy and cook, covered, at a low simmer until fork tender, 10 to 12 minutes. Transfer with a slotted spoon to the lamb dish and cover to keep warm.

4. Add the potatoes to the gravy and cook, covered, at a low simmer, until just fork tender, 6 to 8 minutes. Add a little more water if necessary to keep the gravy at a simmer, but keeping it thick enough to coat a spoon. Transfer the potatoes to the serving dish and taste the final gravy for salt and pepper. Pour over all and serve immediately.

Tender Ragout of Veal

MAKES 4 SERVINGS Lean veal takes center stage in this surprisingly rich, thick, and satisfying stew, enhanced with aromatic rosemary and saffron. Ragout is derived from the French word *ragoûter*, which means "to stimulate the appetite," and there is no question that this dish will do just that.

Simply cooked fresh egg noodles, like fettuccine, make the perfect bed for this dish and cling to the well-seasoned sauce exceptionally well.

Plain white button mushrooms and pearl onions absorb the delicious flavor of the ragout and add to its heartiness. Frozen pearl onions, sometimes called small whole onions, are already blanched and peeled and will make this recipe a lot easier. If you are using fresh, you will need to soak them briefly in hot water to help loosen the skin before removing with a paring knife.

This recipe is also a great study in alcohol substitution. Here we deglaze with fruit juice and vinegar, adding the proper acidity and sweetness that a wine might normally provide.

3 tablespoons olive oil
1½ pounds lean stewing veal (like boneless shoulder), trimmed of any fat and cubed
Salt and pepper to taste
¼ cup all-purpose flour
1 small onion, peeled and chopped
1 medium-size celery stalk, ends trimmed and diced
1 small carrot, peeled and diced
4 garlic cloves, peeled and chopped
10 ounces small white button mushrooms, wiped clean and hard stems removed
1½ cups fresh or frozen pearl onions, peeled
¼ cup apple juice
1 tablespoon red wine vinegar
2 cups low-sodium chicken broth
One 15-ounce can diced tomatoes, drained
Pinch of saffron threads
2 small sprigs fresh rosemary
1 bay leaf

1. Heat the olive oil in a heavy-bottomed stewing pot over medium-high heat. Season the veal cubes with salt and pepper, lightly dredge them in the flour, tapping off any excess, and brown in the hot oil in a single layer. You may need to do this in batches. Transfer the browned veal to a plate and set aside.

2. Add the chopped onion, celery, and carrot to the stewing pot and cook, stirring, over medium heat until softened, about 8 minutes. Add the garlic and cook a further minute. Pour in the apple juice and vinegar and over medium high heat scrape up the browned bits on the bottom of the pot while the liquid reduces. Immediately add the mushrooms and whole onions and stir well to coat. Add the chicken broth, tomatoes, saffron, rosemary, and bay leaf and bring to a simmer.

Saffron Spice

Removing the Stigma

Saffron is, by far, the most expensive spice in the world. The amount of labor required to produce one ounce is responsible for its luxury. The tiny yellow-orange stigma, of which there are only three per flower, must be carefully removed by hand from the center of a small purple crocus. After it is dried, it will require about 14,000 more stigmas in order to make just one ounce. Yet cooks all over the world are willing to pay well for this remarkable spice, which is highly aromatic and pungent, imparting a bright yellow color to everything it touches. Saffron is an essential ingredient in dishes like paella, risotto Milanese, and bouillabaisse, just to name a few, and, since a little bit goes a long way, in the end it is well worth the expense. Sometimes you will see ground or powdered saffron available, but too often it may be "cut" with an inferior spice, such as turmeric, which boasts the same brilliant color but doesn't have the flavor. The stigmas, or threads, as they are also known, are the saffron of choice and can be purchased in many supermarkets and gourmet food stores, often in airtight packets or jars. Keep saffron in a cool, dark place and crush the threads between your fingers before using to release its powerful flavor.

3. Return the veal cubes to the pot with any drippings that may have accumulated on the plate. Reduce the heat to low, cover, and cook at a low simmer until the veal is fork tender, 1¼ to 1½ hours. Stir occasionally and add a little water, if necessary, to prevent sticking.

4. When the veal is done, discard the rosemary sprigs and bay leaf. If the liquid is too thin, transfer the veal, mushrooms, and pearl onions with a slotted spoon to a warm serving bowl and allow the sauce to boil down a few minutes until it is rich and thick. Taste for seasoning, adjust if necessary, and pour the sauce over the veal mixture. Serve immediately.

Larry's Friday Night Fish Fry

MAKES 4 SERVINGS Okay, Larry—this one's for you! If fish and chips sound like comfort food to you, it will be hard to resist these delicious fried fillets. Catfish is the fish of choice here, but any firm white-fleshed variety will do, such as cod, scrod, hake, or halibut. Many fishmongers now carry catfish nuggets, neat little bites that are ideal for this preparation. Larry, my literary agent and friend of undying loyalty and immense tenacity, says you must be patient with the buttermilk marinade—don't try to rush this—and rightly so, as the acidic qualities of buttermilk will provide for moistness and flavor by breaking down the enzymes of the fish protein, not unlike the way that alcohol helps to tenderize meat in a marinade. White, not yellow, cornmeal is a must too, as is Cavender's All-Purpose Greek Seasoning. If you have trouble finding either, you can substitute fine ground yellow cornmeal and a generic seasoned salt-and-pepper blend.

If you happen to own a deep fryer, this would be the time to pull it down from the shelf and make use of it. If not, you can pan-fry in about ½ inch of oil, brought to a temperature of 370 degrees. Use the bread cube test if you do not have

(continued on page 220)

More Than One Way to Fry a Fish

A Collection of Crispy Coatings

Although cornmeal is a traditional American coating for fish, and particularly delicious with catfish, it is only one way to obtain a tasty outside crust. One of the easiest coatings to make is with all-purpose flour, enhanced with the addition of salt, pepper, cayenne pepper, or a flavorful seasoning blend. Dip fillets into milk or water and dredge in the seasoned flour, shaking off any excess. Pan- or deep-fry until golden. Small whole fish, such as smelts, or whitebait, or the classic Italian *fritto misto*, a medley of bite-size pieces and tiny fish, do well in just a light coating of plain flour. They can then be seasoned and squirted with lemon juice when they emerge from the deep fryer.

Batter frying is a popular technique that provides a protective coating that will seal in the moistness of the fish while becoming deliciously crispy and tasty on the outside. Batters are usually made by combining flour and eggs with another liquid, such as water, milk, or beer (see page 439 for a sobered-up beer battered shrimp). They can also be lightened with beaten egg whites and the addition of baking powder. Japanese tempura is probably the lightest and most delicate batter, made from cornstarch, flour, ice water, and egg, and is an excellent choice for shrimp and vegetables.

Classic bread crumb coatings are perfect for pan-frying fish fillets, especially those that are tender and delicate. A light dusting of flour is followed by a dip in beaten eggs and then a dredge in seasoned bread crumbs. Fresh, homemade bread crumbs will provide a particularly crispy result, as will the Japanese *panko* crumbs, available in Asian specialty markets. For an ultimate buttery bread crumb coating, do as the French do: cut strips of sole or flounder fillet (called *goujonnette*, or "little fish"), moisten them with melted butter, season well, dip in fresh bread crumbs, and fry in clarified butter for two minutes per side. Decadent, yes, but very delicious!

Chef's Note: Make clarified butter by slowly melting unsalted butter, allowing the milk solids to sink to the bottom. Skim off the top foam and carefully pour or ladle out the golden liquid. Without its milk solids, butter can safely reach a higher smoke point without burning, which makes it ideal for frying. You can keep clarified butter (also called *ghee*), tightly covered, in the refrigerator for up to one month.

(continued from page 218)

a frying thermometer: just drop a cube into the hot oil and if it immediately turns golden brown, the oil is hot enough. Try not to crowd the fryer or pan and work in batches if necessary, to keep the temperature from dropping below 360 degrees.

Crispy Oven Fries (page 230) are the perfect partner here. Serve with some coleslaw, tartar sauce, and lemon wedges for squeezing.

1½ pounds catfish fillets, cut into 2-inch pieces or
    bite-size nuggets
2 cups buttermilk
Canola oil for frying
2 cups white cornmeal
2 tablespoons Cavender's All-Purpose Greek
    Seasoning

1. Place the catfish in a shallow glass or ceramic baking dish and pour the buttermilk over. Move the fillets around to coat, cover the dish with aluminum foil, and allow to marinate in the refrigerator for at least 1 hour, preferably 2 or 3 hours.

2. Heat ½ inch of canola oil in a deep fryer or deep-sided skillet over medium-high heat to 370 degrees. Meanwhile, drain the fillets into a large colander, shake gently, and allow them to continue draining naturally without patting dry. In a rectangular baking dish, mix together the cornmeal and seasoning and set aside.

3. When the oil is ready, dredge the fillets in the cornmeal coating and fry until golden and crispy, 3 to 4 minutes. Drain briefly on brown paper bags and serve immediately.

Super Special Crab Cakes

MAKES 4 SERVINGS Crab cakes are too often filled with more bread or potatoes than actual crab meat. This special recipe is nearly 100 percent crab, well worth the additional expense. Delicately fla-vored with cilantro and the standard Old Bay Seasoning, a quick browning in canola oil and a final bake in the oven helps to crisp up these cakes to perfection. A dab of prepared tartar sauce when serving is certainly a must.

Surprisingly, these crab cakes freeze well and can be reheated in a hot oven to crisp up the outside coating for a quick and easy meal. Consider making some extras and keeping a small supply in the freezer. They can also be made mini-sized for variety or hors d'oeuvres.

1 pound jumbo lump crabmeat, picked over for
    shells and cartilage
3 cups fresh bread crumbs
½ cup low-fat mayonnaise
2 large egg whites, slightly beaten
2 tablespoons finely chopped fresh cilantro leaves
1 teaspoon Old Bay seasoning
Salt and pepper to taste
Canola oil for frying

1. Preheat the oven to 375 degrees. Line a baking sheet with parchment paper.

2. In a medium-size mixing bowl, gently combine the crabmeat, ½ cup of the bread crumbs, the mayonnaise, egg whites, cilantro, Old Bay, and a little salt and pepper with a rubber spatula. Try not to break up the lumps of crab. Form the crab mixture into 8 balls of equal size and place them on the prepared baking sheet. Flatten each ball slightly with the palm of your hand to form a cake, cover with plastic wrap, and refrigerate until ready to fry. (You can make the crab cakes to this point a few hours ahead, if desired.)

3. Pour enough canola oil in a large, heavy, non-stick skillet to reach a ¼-inch depth and heat to 360 degrees over medium-high heat. Alternatively, you can test the oil by dropping a cube of bread into the skillet. If it immediately sizzles and browns, the oil is ready.

4. Meanwhile, dredge the crab cakes in the remaining 2½ cups bread crumbs and, using your

hands, press gently to adhere the bread crumbs and reshape, if necessary. Fry in the hot oil until golden brown, about 2 minutes per side. Transfer to paper towels to soak up any excess oil and place on a baking sheet lined with fresh parchment paper. Bake until heated through and very crispy, 10 to 12 minutes. Serve hot or at room temperature.

Chef's Note: Make fresh bread crumbs from stale or day-old bread by pulsing in the food processor or blender. If using prepared dry bread crumbs, be sure they are plain, not seasoned, and reduce the amount to 2 cups.

Spicy Creole Shrimp

MAKES 4 SERVINGS This will surely wake up those taste buds for you spice fans out there, while providing a nice dose of Louisiana comfort. Any level of "heat" is perfectly fine here and can be adjusted to your liking.

  White long-grain rice is the traditional accompaniment to this dish, but a brown basmati rice would be an excellent choice for extra fiber and flavor.

  1 pound large shrimp, shelled and deveined
  Creole or Cajun seasoning blend (such as Emeril's
    Essence) to taste
  2 tablespoons canola oil
  1 medium-size onion, peeled and chopped
  1 medium-size green bell pepper, seeded and
    chopped
  1 celery stalk, ends trimmed and chopped
  Pinch of salt and pepper
  2 garlic cloves, peeled and minced
  One 28-ounce can whole plum tomatoes, drained
    and roughly chopped
  One 4.5-ounce can tomato sauce
  1 cup water

  ½ teaspoon dried oregano
  1 teaspoon sugar
  1 cup long-grain white rice, cooked according to
    package directions

  1. Sprinkle the shrimp generously with the Creole seasoning. Set aside.

  2. In a large, heavy-bottomed pot, heat the canola oil over medium heat, then add the onion, bell pepper, celery, salt, pepper, and a sprinkling of Creole seasoning and cook, stirring, until soft, 8 to 10 minutes. Add the garlic and cook an additional minute. Add the chopped tomatoes, tomato sauce, water, oregano, and sugar, bring to a simmer, and let cook for about 10 minutes to marry the flavors.

  3. Add the seasoned shrimp and cook only until they begin to stiffen and change color, which will take no more than 3 minutes at a simmer. Remove with a slotted spoon and transfer to a warm serving bowl.

  4. Allow the Creole sauce to cook down until somewhat thick, 5 to 10 minutes, and taste for additional Creole seasoning and salt and pepper. Be careful not to add too much salt, as most of the seasoning blends contain some sodium. When the sauce is done, pour over the cooked shrimp, stir to coat, and serve with the cooked rice.

Simple Seafood Oven Paella

MAKES 4 SERVINGS Spanish comfort is often spelled "paella," traditionally a delicious blend of spicy chorizo sausage (a coarse-ground pork sausage spiced with chili powder), chicken, and shellfish, all cooked in a flavorful saffron-scented rice pilaf. Here the focus is on the shellfish and the emphasis is on simple. Stove-top paella making can be a bit tricky for the inexperienced, but this easy oven method is truly a snap to make and always a winner at the dinner table. If you can't find fresh chorizo (now available in many supermarkets and always seen in Hispanic grocery stores), you can substitute any other spicy fresh sausage you wish, such as an Italian variety. Even a spicy turkey or chicken sausage would be fine.

Your choice of shellfish is really up to you, as well as your fishmonger's availability, but be sure to include squid, or calamari, as it is familiarly known, which is always accessible in the frozen seafood department. It can be purchased already cleaned, but be sure that some of the delectable tentacles are included, which are often snubbed by squeamish seafood eaters and consequently absent from the box or bag.

Clams and mussels should be well scrubbed under cold running water to remove all sand and grit, as well as the mussel's "beard," which you remove by firmly pulling away from the shell. Stubborn beards can be helped along with a wire brush or scrubber. If you like, buy shrimp that is shelled and deveined so you can save a bit of time in the overall preparation.

Arborio rice, the Italian-grown short-grain variety famous for its use in risotto, works surprisingly well here, rather than the usual medium- or long-grain rice. The result is, in fact, almost risotto-like; the rice is creamy and the overall consistency of the paella rich and hearty.

1 tablespoon olive oil
1 fresh chorizo (or other spicy) sausage link, casing removed and meat crumbled
1 medium-size onion, peeled and chopped
½ medium-size green bell pepper, seeded and diced
3 garlic cloves, peeled and minced
1 cup Arborio rice
½ teaspoon crushed saffron threads
1 cup bottled clam juice
1 cup low-sodium chicken or vegetable broth
½ cup water
½ pound large shrimp, shelled and deveined
1 dozen clams, scrubbed

1 dozen mussels, scrubbed and debearded (see headnote for instructions)
½ pound cleaned squid, tubes cut into rings and several tentacles included
½ cup frozen green peas, thawed
Lime wedges for serving

1. Preheat the oven to 450 degrees.

2. Heat the olive oil in a large nonstick skillet over medium heat and add the crumbled sausage. Cook and stir for 1 minute. Add the onion, bell pepper, and garlic and continue to cook over medium heat until somewhat softened, about 3 minutes. Add the rice and saffron and, using a wooden spoon, stir to coat the rice with the contents of the pan. Add the clam juice, broth, and water, increase the heat to medium-high, and bring to a simmer, stirring occasionally. Transfer the entire contents of the skillet to a 9 x 13-inch glass casserole dish and spread out evenly.

3. Add the uncooked shrimp, clams, and mussels to the rice mixture. Cover the casserole with a sheet of aluminum foil and bake in the oven for 30 minutes. Add the squid and peas, stir once, and return to the oven, covered, until the rice has absorbed all the liquid, a further 15 minutes. Taste several rice grains for doneness and seasoning. If the rice is not yet tender, add a touch more water and return to the oven, covered, for a further 5 to 10 minutes. Season with salt and pepper if required. When the rice is cooked (remember that Arborio rice will retain a bit of bite even when it is fully cooked), bring the casserole to the table and serve with the lime wedges.

Midwestern Salmon Loaf

MAKES 8 SERVINGS In homage to my Missouri-born grandmother, Ella James, as well as all my midwestern readers, I am including this dish, which I have enjoyed since a child, thanks to my father's insistence that my East Coast mother learn the recipe. Smothered in creamed hominy (page 243), based on a simple white sauce, and served with a side of cooked greens, usually spinach, I always looked forward to this comforting meal, which my mother still, to this day, in spite of her Italian upbringing, makes on a regular basis. Given what we now know about the health benefits of eating salmon, whether fresh or canned, salmon loaf definitely deserves a hearty welcome back to the table.

This recipe hasn't changed much since its heyday in the 1950s, except that fresh dill is far more available these days, so I am substituting it for the usual dried. Crushed soda crackers or saltines are the usual binder here, but dry, or even fresh, plain bread crumbs could be used. Whatever you do, don't forget the white sauce, even if you must make it from a packet. It is the essential "comforting" finish for this classic American dish from the heartland.

Two 15-ounce cans pink salmon, drained (liquid
  reserved) and picked over for skin and bones
1 cup crushed saltine crackers
1 cup whole or 2 percent milk
2 large eggs, beaten
¼ cup (½ stick) unsalted butter, melted
1 tablespoon chopped fresh dill leaves
1 teaspoon fresh lemon juice
Dash of Tabasco sauce
Freshly ground pepper to taste

1. Preheat the oven to 350 degrees. Lightly butter a 9 x 5-inch loaf pan.

2. In a large mixing bowl, combine all the ingredients, mixing thoroughly. You may add a little of the reserved salmon liquid to moisten, if necessary, so that the mixture holds together.

3. Pat down the mixture firmly into the prepared loaf pan and smooth the top with the tines of a fork. Bake on the center rack of the oven until golden around the edges and firm to the touch,

about 45 minutes. Remove from the oven and allow to rest for 5 to 10 minutes, then loosen the edges with the blade of a knife and transfer the loaf, using two metal spatulas, to a warm serving plate. Slice and serve.

The Best Tuna Noodle Casserole

MAKES 4 TO 6 SERVINGS If childhood comfort food appeals to you, this creamy classic will definitely bring back fond memories. If, on the other hand, your recollection of tuna casserole is dry and tasteless, you are in for a big surprise. In the words of celebrity chef Emeril Lagasse, this version is "kicked up" to comfort zones unknown to man.

I first started making this embellished version in, of all places, England, where cream tends to reign supreme, but the usual red label canned cream of mushroom soup was unavailable. Out of necessity, I had to improvise and this recipe was the result. This is by no means a low-fat dish, but on occasion, a piping hot, heaping plateful of an ultra creamy casserole is a comfort-food must. If the guilt is overwhelming, you can substitute light cream.

2 tablespoons unsalted butter
One 10-ounce package white button mushrooms,
  wiped clean, hard stems removed, and sliced
Salt and pepper to taste
2 cups heavy cream
Dash of cayenne pepper
Two 6-ounce cans solid white tuna packed in water
  or oil, well drained and flaked
½ cup frozen peas
2 teaspoons fresh lemon juice
8 ounces medium-size egg noodles, cooked
  according to package directions, drained, and
  rinsed under cold running water
1 cup crushed lightly salted potato chips

1. Preheat the oven to 350 degrees. Lightly butter a 10-inch round casserole dish.

2. Melt the butter in a medium-size skillet over medium heat and cook the mushrooms, sprinkled with salt and pepper, stirring occasionally, until somewhat softened, about 6 minutes. Set aside.

3. In a large saucepan, heat the cream with a pinch of salt and pepper over medium heat, whisking occasionally to prevent boiling over and reducing the heat as necessary. Cook until somewhat thickened, about 10 minutes, then add the cayenne, cooked mushrooms, tuna, and peas and stir well to combine. Taste for seasoning, adjust if necessary, and remove from the heat. Stir in the lemon juice.

4. Add the cooked noodles to the sauce mixture, stir well to coat, and pour into the prepared casserole. Top evenly with the potato chips and bake until the edges are bubbly and the topping is toasted, 30 to 40 minutes. Serve piping hot.

7 | Supportive Sides, Vegetables, and Complements

Wﾍﾞ hat would meatloaf be without mashed potatoes? Or roast turkey without candied yams? Some old-fashioned entrées are unimaginable without their classic side dishes and in this chapter we'll be filling in the gaps to finish off those fabulous dishes we cooked in Chapter Six, "Old-Fashioned Entrées That Feed the Soul."

Hearty potato side dishes have always been popular accompaniments to many meat and poultry dishes—hence, the old "meat and potatoes" pairing that promises to "stick to your ribs." But potatoes are only the beginning. Other classics, such as macaroni and cheese, oven-baked beans, and creamed spinach, are certainly indispensable in rounding out a meal that is rooted in comfort and tradition. They're all here—those old-time favorites we all remember that can now provide the perfect prescription for culinary happiness and spiritual health when comfort calls. You'll also find a few newer and healthier versions of some of these classics, as we inch our way towards Phase Three and healthy alternatives in eating.

I've also included some traditional condiments and complements that always finish off a classic meal in style. So, get comfortable, have fun, and make a good old-fashioned time of it!

Classic Mashed Potatoes

MAKES 4 TO 6 SERVINGS Making mashed potatoes is easy, but making *great* mashed potatoes requires attention to a couple of details. First, your choice of potato is important; russets, Idahos, and red-skinned potatoes are all good selections. Yukon Gold potatoes also work well, but stay away from long whites and the so-called all-purpose potatoes, which tend to produce gummy results. Second, always allow your cooked potatoes to "dry out" a bit before mashing (the less moisture they hold, the fluffier they will be). Many chefs will dry out their boiled potatoes in a low oven. I usually just let them sit in the strainer until their edges begin to look fluffy and dry. Lastly, don't be afraid to add plenty of sweet cream butter and make sure your milk or cream is warm when mashing.

What should you mash them with? This is really a matter of choice. An old-fashioned potato masher will certainly do the trick, although it may leave a lump or two. A potato ricer will make your potatoes smoother, as will a food mill. Never use a food processor, because you will turn your lovely mashed potatoes into glue. My preference is a plastic potato ricer with the larger-holed disc; I have always had the best results with this.

A debatable point is how to cook your potatoes for mashing. Some people prefer to bake them. I always boil them in salted water to cover, beginning them in cold, not hot water, and adding a good dose of kosher salt. Bring to a simmer and cook until fork tender, not mushy and falling apart.

There are, of course, many ways to lighten up or flavor your mashed potatoes. Start with the basic recipe, then try some of the delicious variations that follow.

2 pounds potatoes (red, russet, Idaho, or
  Yukon Gold), peeled and cut into 1-inch cubes
Salt
¼ cup (½ stick) unsalted butter, cut into small
  pieces
⅓ cup heavy cream, warmed
Pepper to taste

1. Place the diced potatoes in a large pot, then add a generous pinch of salt and enough cold water to cover. Bring to a boil, reduce the heat to a simmer, and cook until fork tender, 10 to 15 minutes. Pour into a colander and allow to drain until dry but still warm, about 20 minutes.

2. In a large mixing bowl, combine the potatoes, butter, and warm cream and mash with a potato masher to the desired smoothness. If using a potato ricer, put the diced butter in the bottom of the mixing bowl and, working in batches, rice the potatoes over the butter. Add the cream and blend well with a wooden spoon. Taste for the addition of salt and pepper and serve immediately.

Variations: For fluffier mashed potatoes, use a little less cream. This is a good idea if you will be using them as a topping for another dish, such as British Shepherd's Pie (page 213). For creamier mashed potatoes, add a touch more liquid. You can also substitute light cream, milk, or buttermilk for the heavy cream, if desired.

Garlic Mashed Potatoes: Add 4 large peeled and smashed garlic cloves to the pot when boiling the potatoes. Drain as directed above. A potato ricer or food mill will work best to break down the garlic cloves. If you are using a hand masher, you can leave the larger pieces of garlic as they are or press them through a strainer and return them to the potato mixture.

Mashed Potatoes Italian Style: Make Garlic Mashed Potatoes, substituting extra-virgin olive oil for the butter. Omit the heavy cream.

(continued on page 228)

Are You Getting the Support You Need?

Advice for Family and Friends

You have probably heard a lot about how addiction is a family disease. Every person who lives with or is intimately involved with an active alcoholic or addict knows this to be true. Marriages suffer and parent-child relationships crumble under the strain of daily life with someone who is addicted. Myriad feelings—from anger to resentment to complete confusion or depression—all can take place and usually in the same day. However, now that your alcoholic no longer drinks and has begun a healthy recovery plan, why haven't these feelings gone away? Shouldn't everything be better now that the problem is behind you?

Codependency, a term coined in the 1970s to describe the clinical condition of people who are directly affected by the behavior of addicts, may be a familiar one to you by now. Although many different definitions exist, it is sometimes best described by its symptoms: low self-worth, obsessive thinking, a need to control, and erratic, self-defeating behavior are just a few. Often these behaviors are rooted in life experiences that occurred long before the alcoholic's problem, and sometimes can even be part of the reason why you may find yourself sharing your life with an addict. Many wives of alcoholics were daughters of alcoholics, and many mothers of alcoholics were alcoholics once themselves. None of these problems go away just because the drink was put down. And, just as there are phases of recovery from addiction, there are necessary stages of recovery for significant others and family members. Fortunately, much has been written about these issues and thankfully there are numerous support groups available for those who need to heal (see the "Resources" section for more information on support groups, page 456).

Getting support during this typically difficult time is just as important for you as it is for your alcoholic. Just as you both have suffered greatly, so you both must heal in order for any recovery to be successful and long lasting. Learning about the disease, understanding that improvement comes in small steps, and sharing your thoughts, fears, and hope are a good place to start. Working at creating a comfortable atmosphere at home by sharing the cooking and eating of meals together as a family can also assist in healing wounds and help you to rediscover each other. Every day of recovery is one to be proud of, so don't neglect to praise yourself as well as your alcoholic for solid progress. Step by step, you will both find your way out of the darkness and welcome the light and love that is there waiting for you in a new, sober lifestyle.

(continued from page 226)

Mashed Potatoes with Celery Root: This wonderful combination is popular in French cuisine. Substitute half of the potatoes with peeled and diced celeriac and proceed as directed above.

Mashed Potatoes and Turnips: A Midwestern favorite, substitute half of the potatoes with peeled and diced white turnips and proceed as directed above. A potato ricer or food mill will work better in this instance. You can also use yellow turnips (called rutabagas or Swedes). In this case, I would also add a dash of nutmeg.

Smashed Potatoes with Sour Cream and Chives: In this case, baby red-skinned potatoes are actually preferred. Substitute them for the usual starchy variety and cook them whole and unpeeled. Use an old-fashioned potato masher and keep the mixture lumpy. Reduce the butter to 2 tablespoons, omit the heavy cream, and stir in $2/3$ cup sour cream and 1 tablespoon chopped fresh chives.

Lightened-Up Mashed Potatoes: Reduce the butter to 2 tablespoons and substitute chicken or vegetable broth for the cream.

Mashed Potatoes to the Rescue!

Why is it that mashed potatoes are on everyone's top 10 list of comfort foods, especially those of us in recovery? Is it the creaminess? The buttery flavor? The fond memories of a time gone by? Yes, probably all those things, and more because it also works to activate those "feel good" brain chemicals. I can't tell you how many stories I have heard about the comforting effect that mashed potatoes have had on people in recovery, sometimes even coming to the rescue when cravings hit for alcohol and drugs.

The reasons are clear. Potatoes happen to be very high in satiety, or the level of feeling satisfied after eating, as well as having an immediate effect on blood glucose. Starchy types of potatoes such as Idahos and russets rank high on the Glycemic Index, which indicates their quick conversion to glucose (although the addition of fat, in the form of butter and cream, may lower its rating somewhat). Add that to their ability to boost serotonin and you have a top-notch dish for providing ultimate comfort.

Stories abound about mashed potatoes, but one in particular has struck me as most interesting. I had a client in recovery whose daughter of 11 was being treated for depression and attention deficit disorder. While the doctors were unsuccessfully experimenting with different medication combinations and doses, she was, unknowingly, self-medicating with food, particularly mashed potatoes. Every time I went to their house to cook, she requested more and more mashed potatoes. It appeared to be the only food she was eating on a regular basis.

One day I asked her mother how she was feeling and she informed me that the doctors had settled on a medication regimen that seemed to be good for her; she had been following this

Easy Potato Pancakes: Shape leftover mashed potatoes (any flavored variation or plain is fine) into ¾-inch-thick patties and coat in plain or seasoned dry bread crumbs. In a skillet over medium-high heat, fry them in hot canola oil (enough to come halfway up the patties) until golden brown, about 3 minutes per side. Drain on brown paper bags and serve immediately.

Chef's Note: *Consider adding any of the following to your final product for variety and flavor: 1 tablespoon prepared horseradish,*

1 teaspoon wasabi powder, 1 cup shredded Swiss or pepper jack cheese, ½ cup minced scallions, 1 cup chopped cooked spinach or collard greens, well drained.

When reheating mashed potatoes on the stove-top, add a little milk and keep over low heat, stirring often. If microwaving, reheat on half power and stir once or twice at one-minute intervals.

new course for a few weeks. It occurred to me that I had not been asked for mashed potatoes for a couple of weeks and the answer why was plain. She no longer "needed" to eat them. Her brain chemistry had "settled down" and the craving was gone.

I have encountered similar "settling down" instances of people in recovery who, during the first year or two, tend to crave certain foods. Eventually, either through medication or a natural healing process, their brain chemistry readjusts to normal levels. But while in the throes of these food cravings, it is often a "must have" feeling, not unlike that felt in addiction. I know there are some out there who claim that if we give in to our food cravings, we are simply swapping one addiction for another. Indeed, there are many alcoholics and addicts who eventually join Overeaters Anonymous to deal with food issues as a direct result of their recovery. But the reality is that giving in to our alcohol or drug craving instead is a far worse prospect. As our recovery progresses, we can slowly incorporate changes in our diet to reflect our growing interest in health and nutrition. It would be folly to attempt big changes early on. By the time we reach Phase Three, these changes will become far easier to make and are more likely to stick.

The story of my client and her daughter taught me much about the power of food. It also clearly pointed to a genetic factor at work; similarities in brain chemistry can sometimes manifest themselves as different disorders. One family member may be an alcoholic, another a compulsive gambler, yet another an overeater. Scientists are coming very close to pinpointing these genetic factors, which will inevitably help practitioners to diagnose patients more accurately. The more we learn, the better equipped we will be to find solutions that provide better individual treatment for what appears to be a growing frequency of mental and neurological disorders.

Herb Roasted Potatoes

MAKES 4 TO 6 SERVINGS Crispy and savory roasted potatoes are often the perfect partner for a simple roasted chicken, a flavorful brisket, or deliciously broiled chops and steaks. Golden brown and fragrant from the addition of fresh herbs, they add a comforting touch to any plate. The ideal potatoes for the job are baby red- or white-skinned varieties; baby Yukon Golds are most delicious. Simply cut them in half, to provide plenty of roasting surface, and proceed with the recipe. You could also use larger red-skinned potatoes or Yukon Golds that have been quartered or cut into eighths, depending on their size. Starchier varieties of potatoes are generally not well suited for this method, but could certainly be used in a pinch. Fingerlings—baby potatoes of the long variety and named for their thumb-size appearance—are also delicious roasted. Try a combination of baby red, white, and purple for a stellar performance.

Any combination of fresh herbs will add a wonderful flavor, but rosemary and thyme tend to be the ones most often used. Dried herbs could also fill in, as could a commercial spice blend that contains a variety of dried herbs, salt, pepper, and garlic powder. Experiment with different potatoes and flavors until you find your favorite version.

> 1½ to 2 pounds baby red, Yukon Gold, or fingerling potatoes (or any combination), left unpeeled and halved
> 3 tablespoons canola oil
> Salt and pepper to taste
> ¼ cup roughly chopped fresh herbs, such as rosemary, thyme, or marjoram or a combination

1. Preheat the oven to 425 degrees.

2. Place the potatoes in a roasting pan or glass casserole dish large enough to hold them in a single layer and drizzle the oil over them. Sprinkle with salt, pepper, and the herbs, lightly toss with a rubber spatula to coat evenly with the oil and herbs, and roast in the oven until crispy, brown, and fork tender, shaking the pan occasionally to distribute, about 45 minutes.

3. Place the cooked potatoes on a layer of paper towels to absorb the extra oil, season again with salt to taste, and serve immediately.

Herb Roasted Potatoes with Whole Garlic Cloves: Add peeled whole garlic cloves from 1 head of garlic to the pan before roasting.

Herb Roasted Potatoes with Onions and Peppers: Add 1 onion, peeled and cut into medium-size chunks, and 1 green bell pepper, seeded and sliced into strips, to the pan before roasting.

Roasted Potatoes with Sun-dried Tomato Pesto and Basil: Omit the fresh herbs and add ½ cup store-bought sun-dried tomato pesto to the pan during the final 5 minutes of roasting, tossing well to coat the potatoes with it. Sprinkle with 1 tablespoon chopped fresh basil leaves to serve.

Crispy Oven Fries

MAKES 4 SERVINGS Here's a great alternative to the often heavy oil-laden French fries we are used to. Crisped to perfection with the help of a cooking spray or mister (see page 48 for details), these guys will quickly turn your deep fryer green with envy. Idaho or russet potatoes are the spud of choice, and they can either be peeled or left au natural, depending on your preference.

A nonstick baking sheet is preferred here, but you can improvise with a piece of parchment paper on your usual baking sheet. Not too different looking from classic steak fries, be sure to cut the potatoes by first halving them lengthwise, through the narrowest side. Lay each half flat on the cutting board and cut ½-inch wedges straight down. You should yield 4 to 5 wedges per half of a medium-size Idaho or russet. Apart from the usual salt and pepper, no other seasoning is needed, although for my favorite spicy fries, see the variation below.

4 medium-size Idaho or russet potatoes, peeled or unpeeled and cut into wedges
Cooking oil spray
Salt and pepper to taste

1. Preheat the oven to 450 degrees.
2. Lightly spray a nonstick baking sheet or one that has been covered with a piece of parchment paper and place the potatoes in a single layer, side by side. Lightly spray the potatoes, sprinkle with salt and pepper, and bake in the oven until crisp, brown, and fork tender, about 20 minutes per side. Season again with salt, if desired, and serve immediately.

Spicy Oven Fries: Substitute cayenne pepper for the black pepper and add a dash of paprika.

American Scalloped Potatoes

MAKES 4 TO 6 SERVINGS This is a classic dish that is always popular at the dinner table. Perfect as a side for meatloaf, chicken, or pork chops, scalloped potatoes will bring back memories for almost all of us. Somewhat tedious in preparation, scalloped potatoes become much easier with the help of a food processor fitted with a slicing blade, or a manual slicer, called a mandolin. Inexpensive plastic versions of this highly prized French piece of cooking equipment can be found under the label of Japanese mandolin, and you may find it to be helpful in many of your other kitchen duties as well. (It can make perfectly thin waffle chips, which is an added plus.) However you slice them, the potatoes must be thin to create the proper layered effect. Use a sharp slicing knife if you are doing this by hand.

Although gratins are generally associated with the addition of cheese, a gratin dish, which is shallow and wide, is the perfect receptacle for scalloped potatoes, ensuring plenty of crispy surface area for each serving. A 9 x 13-inch glass casserole dish will fill in nicely too.

The choice of potato for this American-style classic is not limited to russet or baking type potatoes. All-purpose white potatoes will do well also, because of the addition of flour to the recipe, which will help thicken the excess water they exude. Yukon Gold is another great variety to use.

Patience is a virtue here—good scalloped potatoes cannot be rushed, especially if you are anticipating a crispy, golden top. Season liberally with salt as you layer—the potatoes will happily absorb it, resulting in a perfectly seasoned outcome.

3 tablespoons unsalted butter, softened
2 pounds Idaho, russet, white, or Yukon Gold
** potatoes, peeled and thinly sliced (⅛ to ¹⁄₁₆ inch)**
Salt and pepper to taste
2 tablespoons all-purpose flour
2 cups milk (whole, 2 percent, or 1 percent)

1. Preheat the oven to 350 degrees.
2. Using 1 tablespoon of the butter, lightly grease the bottom and sides of a 2-quart gratin dish or 9 x 13-inch glass casserole. Layer half the potato slices, slightly overlapping, in the dish, season well with salt and pepper, and sprinkle half the flour evenly over the slices. Dot with 1 tablespoon of the butter, cut into bits. Repeat with the remaining potatoes and flour, finishing with the remaining 1 tablespoon butter. Pour the milk over the top.
3. Cover with a sheet of aluminum foil and bake for 45 minutes. Remove the foil and bake until the top is crispy and golden, about 30 minutes more. Remove from the oven and let rest 5 to 10 minutes, then serve.

Cheese Scalloped Potatoes: Sprinkle each potato layer with ½ cup shredded cheddar, Swiss, Fontina, or Monterey Jack cheese.

Are You a Potato Head?

Getting to Know Your Taters and Tubers

Hardy root vegetables, potatoes, and tubers compose many traditional comfort-food side dishes, so it pays to get to know them a little if you'll be inviting them into your kitchen. But can you tell the difference between a parsnip and salsify, a yam and a sweet potato? Most checkers at your local supermarket can't either, which can add to the confusion. Not to worry. The next time your checker looks blankly at your produce bag, asking, "What's this?" you'll be able to rattle off an intelligent and fascinating description to make even the produce manager jealous.

Vegetables that grow under the ground are called roots and tubers. They have dense flesh that can either be sugar-filled, when immature, or starchy, when older. Root vegetables include carrots, beets, turnips, parsnips, celeriac, and salsify and are, in essence, just that—roots belonging to a plant growing above the ground. The plant helps to locate the root vegetable and pull it up from the ground. In some cases, such as beets and turnips, the "tops" or "greens" are prized as well and can be cooked like spinach or other leafy greens. Tubers include potatoes, sweet potatoes, yams, and Jerusalem artichokes (which have nothing to do with Jerusalem or with artichokes, for that matter—recently they have been dubbed sunchokes, to eliminate the confusion).

The most popular tuber is, of course, the potato and, in simplest terms, a potato is either waxy or starchy. A little less simply, potatoes fall into one of four categories: russet, long white, round white, and round red. Russets, of which Idahos are just one type, are particularly starchy, which makes them best for baking, French-fry making, and, some would argue, mashed potatoes. Long whites, also called California or white rose, have a thin, pale skin, and are more often boiled, as they have less starch, but can also be baked or fried. Round whites and reds, essentially "boiling potatoes," are considered to be of the waxy variety, containing quite a bit of moisture and not much starch. This is one of the reasons that, glycemically speaking, boiling potatoes, in particular baby reds, have a low Glycemic Index (GI) rating (see page 28 for a complete discussion of the GI rating system) compared to russets, their composition being slower to break down when eaten, thus having less of an effect on blood sugar. The best way to lower the GI rating of a baked potato is to eat the skin as well as the flesh, which will greatly slow down the metabolism.

Today, of course, there are numerous gourmet potatoes available—Yukon Golds used to be considered such but are now quite popular and widely available. Bintje, Desiree, and Ratte, a Delicate little gem adored by French cooks, are starting to find their way into our local produce sections. It's worth trying any of these more unfamiliar types for variety, particularly if you happen to enjoy potatoes as part of a home-cooked meal. Little "new" potatoes, which can be any variety provided they are young, are a delight to eat (page 238)—they have yet to convert their sugar into much starch and, as a result, are crisp, tasty, and a little sweet to boot.

Fingerlings, which are baby long whites, are also delicious and can be boiled, steamed, or roasted. Purple or blue potatoes, cultivated for centuries in South America but only now gaining popularity in the U.S. (particularly as potato chips), are fun to serve and can be boiled or roasted. Some have pretty lavender streaks throughout the flesh, while others are primarily colored on the outside only.

Yams and sweet potatoes, often referred to interchangeably, are not identical. Some sweet potatoes are, in fact, pale fleshed and dry, while others, usually those with darker skins, can have moist, bright orange flesh. The latter are the ones people are generally referring to when speaking about yams, and they are the ones I will be referring to in the recipes. But pale-skinned sweet potatoes are definitely worth a try—baked and eaten with butter, they resemble russets in texture and taste. True yams, of which there are over 150 different species grown in the world, are not really grown or marketed in the United States, so when you see those big boxes of Louisiana yams for sale at Thanksgiving time, know that they are really sweet potatoes. Frankly, it doesn't matter much recipe-wise and, in fact, sweet potatoes actually have more nutritive value than yams—in particular vitamins A and C. Occasionally you'll find real yams in the produce section—taste them and see if you prefer one over the other.

When choosing your potatoes, look for firm, eyeless, and bruise-free spuds. Keep them in a cool, dry place and use them, particularly sweet potatoes, sooner rather than later. Refrigeration will, unfortunately, encourage an unpleasant sweet taste and browning of the flesh, so avoid this whenever possible. If you come across any green tinges, indicating that the potatoes have been exposed to prolonged periods of light, remove them, as they can be toxic when consumed in large quantities. The rest of the potato is fine to use. Incidentally, the humble potato was not accepted for culinary use for many centuries, as it was believed to be poisonous, like other members of the nightshade family to which it belongs, such as eggplants and tomatoes. But once Sir Walter Raleigh courageously planted them on his property in Ireland in the sixteenth century, the myth was quickly debunked and the Irish embraced the potato wholeheartedly. The rest is culinary history.

French Scalloped Potatoes

MAKES 6 SERVINGS Also called *pommes Dauphinoise*, here the French take scalloped potatoes to heights beyond decadence! Never mind milk; heavy cream is the name of the game. These delicious potatoes are an excellent accompaniment to meats, such as beef and lamb, and are always a special treat, especially at holiday time. Enjoy them now, before we cut back on our saturated fat in Phase Three!

For this recipe I prefer using the Idaho or russet variety of potato and will slice them by hand into rather generously thick pieces, at least ¼ inch, nearly ½ inch. Garlic is an important element in this dish, as is seasoning well with salt. Warming the cream beforehand will help to speed up the process a bit, but again, as in American Scalloped Potatoes, they cannot be rushed. Hiking up the temperature will only result in bubbling over, as well as causing the cream to break and curdle, quite the opposite of our deliciously creamy intention. These are extremely rich, so a little bit goes a long way here—four medium-size potatoes will easily satisfy six people.

    1 tablespoon unsalted butter, softened
    4 medium-size Idaho or russet potatoes, peeled
        and cut into about ⅓-inch-thick slices
    2 cups heavy cream
    4 garlic cloves, peeled and minced
    Salt and pepper to taste

1. Preheat the oven to 325 degrees. Butter the bottom and sides of a 9 x 13-inch glass casserole or 2-quart gratin dish. Layer the potatoes evenly in the casserole.

2. In a medium-size saucepan, heat the cream with the minced garlic, a generous amount of salt (about 1 teaspoon), and freshly ground pepper over medium heat until bubbles form around the edge of the pan. Pour this over the potatoes and cover the dish with a sheet of aluminum foil.

3. Bake for 45 minutes, then remove the foil and bake until the potatoes are fork tender, most of the liquid has been absorbed, and the top is slightly golden, another 20 to 30 minutes. Remove from the oven and let rest 10 minutes before serving.

Chef's Note: It is important to add enough salt to the cream in order to flavor the potatoes. The best way to test this is to taste the warm cream before you pour it over the potatoes. If it seems just a bit too salty, then it is exactly the right amount.

Potato and Onion Casserole

MAKES 4 TO 6 SERVINGS This preparation is derived from the French *pommes boulangère*, meaning that the method is "baker's style." At one time, French cooks would bring their earthenware pots of meat and vegetables to the local baker, where he would slow cook the concoction in his stone oven. At the end of the day, folks would pick up their cooked meal to take home for dinner—sort of a slow-cooked fast food convenience. After many hours in the oven, the flavors would be deliciously married and the ingredients tender and succulent. A flavorful broth (from the addition of water at the beginning) would result and be enjoyed along with the cooked vegetables and meat. From this idea, potatoes and onions cooked in broth became known as *boulangère* style.

Here we add prepared broth to sautéed onions and thinly sliced potatoes and bake them in the oven (for a lot less time!), deriving peak flavor. No cream or milk is needed in this recipe, so the fat content is reasonably low, except for the butter. To make this even lighter, simply reduce the amount of butter, or leave it out all together, but expect a little less browning. You can use chicken, beef, or vegetable broth, depending on what you'll be serving them with—a low-sodium chicken broth is always a good neutral choice.

¼ cup (½ stick) unsalted butter

1 tablespoon olive oil

2 medium-size onions, peeled and thinly sliced

Salt and pepper to taste

1 teaspoon chopped fresh thyme leaves

2 pounds Yukon Gold or red- or white-skinned potatoes, peeled and cut into ⅛-inch-thick slices

2 cups low-sodium chicken, beef, or vegetable broth

1. Preheat the oven to 400 degrees.

2. Melt 1 tablespoon of the butter with the olive oil in a medium-size skillet and cook the onions, sprinkled with salt and pepper, over medium-low heat until softened, about 8 minutes, stirring a few times. Add the thyme and cook a further minute.

3. Transfer the mixture to a 2-quart casserole dish and spread evenly over the bottom. Layer the potato slices on top of the onions, pour the hot broth over, and dot with the remaining 3 tablespoons butter, cut into bits.

4. Cover with a lid or a sheet of aluminum foil, and bake for 30 minutes. Remove the cover and continue to cook, occasionally basting the top with the liquid, until golden brown, 25 to 30 minutes more. Remove from the oven and let rest for 5 minutes, then serve.

Twice-Baked Potatoes

MAKES 4 SERVINGS In essence, twice-baked potatoes are just the topping for a plain baked potato (see "This Spud's for You," page 236) and the potato pulp all mixed up together and baked again.

Bearing that in mind, there are any number of ways to prepare these super-stuffed taters, so the recipe below is simply a guideline.

Usually a lengthwise sliver of the skin of a baked potato is removed, in order to scoop out the pulp. You can, however, simply cut them in half and scoop, making for a smaller serving size. But since this is comfort food at its best, we'll make it the traditional way; well-stuffed, these potatoes can become a meal in itself.

Twice-baked potatoes can also be prepared ahead and popped in the oven to heat through and crisp up the skin. Consider this when the other parts of your meal may require a bit more of your attention.

4 medium-size Idaho or russet potatoes, baked (see headnote) and still hot

2 tablespoons unsalted butter

½ cup sour cream

Salt and pepper to taste

½ cup shredded cheddar cheese

1. Preheat the oven to 425 degrees.

2. Using a sharp paring knife, cut out a long, narrow opening on top of each potato, big enough to insert a teaspoon for scooping. Discard the top and scoop the pulp into a medium-size mixing bowl. Add the butter and sour cream, season with salt and pepper, and mash together with a fork or potato masher.

3. Spoon the potato mixture back into the skins, and place the potatoes in an ungreased 8-inch-square baking pan. Bake until lightly browned, 20 to 25 minutes. Top each potato with 2 tablespoons of the cheese and return the dish to the oven until the cheese has melted, about 5 minutes. Serve immediately.

Yogurt and Dill Twice-Baked Potatoes: Substitute plain low-fat yogurt for the sour cream and add 2 teaspoons chopped fresh dill to the mixture. Omit the cheese or top instead with dill havarti or Swiss.

Horseradish Bacon Twice-Baked Potatoes: Add 1 tablespoon prepared horseradish and 4 bacon strips that have been crisp fried, drained, and crumbled to the mixture.

Roasted Pepper and Garlic Twice-Baked Potatoes: Add ½ of a roasted pepper, diced, and 4 roasted garlic cloves (page 120), roughly chopped, to the mixture. Substitute mozzarella for the cheddar cheese.

Portobello Surprise Twice-Baked Potatoes: Spoon half the mixture into the skins, then insert slices of sautéed or grilled portobello mushrooms (about 2 slices each) before adding the remaining mixture.

Goat Cheese Herb Twice-Baked Potatoes: Reduce the sour cream to ¼ cup and stir it together with 3 ounces crumbled goat cheese before adding it to the pulp. Add 1 tablespoon chopped fresh basil leaves and 1 teaspoon *each* chopped fresh parley leaves and chives. Omit the cheese topping.

Chef's Note: If the potatoes have been stuffed ahead of time and are straight from the refrigerator, allow an additional 10 to 15 minutes of heating before adding the cheese topping.

This Spud's for You!

The Perfect Baked Potato

Like mashed potatoes, baked potatoes seem to conjure up all kinds of comfort. Recently they have even been touted as the "alternative medicine" for antidepressants such as Prozac because of their ability to temporarily increase serotonin production. Whether you serve them alongside a succulent steak or on their own, a perfectly baked potato will please any appetite for comfort food.

Ideal baking potatoes have low moisture and high starch content, resulting in a fluffy baked interior and crisp skin. For this reason, choose russets, Idahos, or the buttery texture of Yukon Gold, which although higher in moisture, ends up just as fluffy and delicious as its classic baking counterparts.

Many people never eat the skin of their baked potato, which has baffled me in light of the popularity of potato skins as appetizers at restaurants. I can only guess that it's because most baked potatoes served to us, especially in restaurants, have been either wrapped in foil, so the skin has not had a chance to crisp up as it should, or because they often look like they were baked early that day (and usually they are). Frankly, I can't blame them. Unfortunately, not only are you missing out on the most delicious part of the potato, you are depriving yourself of essential fiber and nutrients, including vitamin C, B_6, and a whole host of minerals.

The best method for baking your potatoes does not involve the microwave, nor does it have

Buttery Parsley Potatoes

MAKES 4 SERVINGS Ideal as a side dish for fish of any kind, these classically prepared potatoes are easy to make too. Waxy-type spuds are the ones to choose for this job—baby reds or whites are ideal here. I will usually peel them for appearance sake, but you can leave them unpeeled, if you like, or opt for a larger red-skinned potato to peel and quarter.

Italian parsley is the more flavorful of the two common varieties (the other being curly), and should be used here when available. Speaking of Italian, this is the only potato dish I ever remember my Italian grandmother making. Not a popular item in the Italian repertoire (unless transformed into gnocchi), the potato is often snubbed in favor of pasta as a starch at dinner. I think the method (boiling, draining, and adding butter) somehow seemed familiar to her, so she would make these with reasonable regularity.

You can start these ahead by boiling the potatoes to fork tender and cooling them down in very cold water until you are ready. After cooking the potatoes, drain most of the liquid from the pot, add some cold water and a few ice cubes, and set them aside. When dinnertime approaches, quickly heat them in a little of the water, drain, and proceed with the recipe.

you greasing up the potato or wrapping it in foil. The best way to bake a potato is to put it in a hot oven (at least 400 degrees and up to 450 degrees) and do nothing to it except poke a couple of holes in it with the tines of a fork. (Yes, they do explode from time to time if you don't take this precaution!) Depending on its size, after 45 minutes to an hour, you will have a perfect baked potato, crispy skinned and soft and fluffy on the inside, ready to receive a myriad of garnishes. Here are a few familiar (and some unfamiliar) suggestions:

- Butter, salt, and freshly ground pepper
- Sour cream, chopped fresh chives, and crumbled crisp-fried bacon
- Shredded cheddar, Swiss, or Fontina cheese
- Salsa and guacamole
- Chili with beans
- Nacho cheese and sliced jalapeño peppers
- Sautéed mushrooms and sour cream
- And for all you gourmets out there . . . crème fraîche and lumpfish caviar!

Be creative with your favorite toppings and design a meal around your perfectly baked potato. British diners have been doing this famously for years; "jacket potatoes," as they are called across the Atlantic, are often the center of a hearty lunch or dinner with a simple side of canned beans and a light salad. However you choose to dress them up, just remember to eat your "jacket."

1½ pounds medium-size red or baby red or
   white potatoes, peeled or unpeeled
Salt
¼ cup (½ stick) unsalted butter
2 tablespoons chopped fresh Italian parsley leaves
Pepper to taste

1. Place the potatoes in a large saucepan, add a good pinch of salt and enough cold water to cover. Bring to a boil and cook over medium heat until fork tender, 10 to 15 minutes.

2. Drain in a colander and return the potatoes to the saucepan. Add the butter and parsley, stirring gently to coat. Season with salt and pepper and serve immediately.

Steamed New Potatoes with Fresh Mint

MAKES 4 SERVINGS When I lived in England, I remember everyone waiting with mouth-watering anticipation for the first appearance of new potatoes. Grown on the island of Jersey in the English Channel, they boasted the best flavor in the world, and I can agree that they were definitely worth waiting for. Here in America, we can now happily find similar tiny new potatoes at our local farmer's markets, so I have begun to make them in this simple way once again.

Very little embellishment is needed—fresh, fragrant mint is the only enhancer—while steaming will retain maximum flavor and nutrition. An ideal accompaniment for any type of roast or fish, these little gems are delicious with just a sprinkle of sea salt for a taste of new potato heaven.

1½ pounds tiny new potatoes, unpeeled
1 handful fresh mint sprigs
Kosher or sea salt

1. Place a steamer basket or metal colander over a pot of simmering water. Do not submerge. Place the potatoes and mint sprigs in the basket, cover with a lid, and steam until fork tender, about 10 minutes, depending on size.

2. Serve immediately with a sprinkle of salt.

Old-Fashioned Candied Sweet Potatoes

MAKES 4 TO 6 SERVINGS I have known so many people over the years (myself, included!), who have struggled with this classic dish. Thankful that we generally only serve it at Thanksgiving time, most of us, out of pure exasperation, have purchased ready-made frozen varieties or simply opened a can. Well, I am happy to announce that I have finally cracked this one and once you see how fabulous the result is, you too will be enjoying candied sweet potatoes on a regular basis.

The secret is to bake the potatoes before hand. Not only does it make this dish a snap, but the flavor from a bit of caramelization in the oven will add to the final outcome. Boiling or adding the sweet potatoes raw to the syrup (the usual methods) only seems to invite either a soggy, mushed-up mess or an uncooked, inedible result. This method will also cut down on overall cooking time, often an issue when the usual things like turkey, stuffing, and other delectable dishes require oven space. But don't wait until the holidays to enjoy these delicious sweet potatoes—they are perfect as a side dish for roast chicken, ham steak, turkey loaf, or even brisket. Although not necessary, you can top with the usual marshmallows, if you like, during the final minutes of baking. Those of us with a sweet tooth will surely appreciate the addition!

4 to 6 medium-size sweet potatoes
¼ cup (½ stick) unsalted butter
½ cup dark corn syrup
¼ cup firmly packed dark brown sugar
Salt and pepper to taste

1. Preheat the oven to 375 degrees. Butter the bottom and sides of a 9 x 13-inch glass or ceramic baking dish.

2. Place the sweet potatoes on an aluminum foil-lined baking sheet and bake until fork tender, turning once, 35 to 45 minutes, depending upon their size. Some of the skin may blacken and liquid may begin to ooze. This is perfectly fine and part of the caramelization process. Remove from the oven and allow to cool slightly on the baking sheet.

3. Meanwhile, in a small saucepan over medium heat, melt together the butter, corn syrup, and brown sugar, stirring well to combine. Simmer until the sugar has dissolved, 1 to 2 minutes.

4. Using a sharp paring knife, carefully remove the skin from the sweet potatoes and cut them into quarters. Place them flat side down in a single layer in the prepared baking dish. Sprinkle with salt and pepper and pour the syrup mixture over them evenly. Bake, basting occasionally, until nicely glazed and bubbly, about 45 minutes. Remove from the oven and allow to rest for 5 to 10 minutes, then serve.

Easy Whipped Sweets

MAKES 4 SERVINGS Baked sweet potatoes, as prepared in the candied sweet potato recipe, are only a hop, skip, and a little jump to this easy and delicious dish. They will whip up beautifully with just a tad of butter and honey for flavor, making a great accompaniment for any poultry or meat entree. It's another way to include this tremendously healthy, nutrient-rich tuber in your diet, while the result is creamy and comforting.

3 to 4 medium-size sweet potatoes, baked according to the directions in step 2 above
2 tablespoons unsalted butter, softened
2 tablespoons honey
Dash of ground nutmeg
Salt and pepper to taste

1. Using a sharp paring knife, carefully remove the skin from the hot potatoes and cut into chunks.

2. In a medium-size mixing bowl, using a hand blender or electric mixer, whip the potatoes together with the butter, honey, nutmeg, salt, and pepper until smooth. Serve immediately.

Maple Cinnamon Whipped Sweets: Substitute maple syrup for the honey and cinnamon for the nutmeg.

Double Ginger Whipped Sweets: Substitute ¼ teaspoon ground ginger for the nutmeg and stir in ¼ cup finely minced crystallized ginger.

Whipped Sweets and Carrots: Make Honey Roasted Baby Carrots (page 241) and process in a food processor until smooth. Whip together with the prepared sweet potatoes as above, reducing the honey to 1 tablespoon.

Sweet Potato Casserole with Pecan Topping

MAKES 6 TO 8 SERVINGS Follow the directions for baking sweet potatoes and you've halfway completed this delicious and creamy casserole. The eggs will make this almost soufflé-like in texture, while the topping adds a crunchy finish.

CASSEROLE
4 to 6 medium-size sweet potatoes, baked according to the directions in step 2 of Old-Fashioned Candied Sweet Potatoes, above
2 large eggs, lightly beaten
2 tablespoons unsalted butter, melted
2 tablespoons firmly packed light brown sugar
½ teaspoon *each* ground cinnamon, ginger, and salt
¼ teaspoon ground nutmeg
Pepper to taste

1 cup coarsely chopped pecans
1 tablespoon granulated sugar
½ teaspoon ground cinnamon

1. Preheat the oven to 350 degrees. Lightly butter the bottom and sides of a 9 x 13-inch glass casserole dish.

2. Scoop out the pulp of the baked sweet potatoes into a large mixing bowl. Add the remaining casserole ingredients and, using a hand-held blender or electric mixer, beat together until smooth. Transfer the mixture to the prepared casserole and use a rubber spatula to spread evenly.

3. Combine the topping ingredients in a small mixing bowl. Sprinkle the topping evenly over the surface of the sweet potato mixture and bake until puffed up and slightly golden around the edges, 30 to 40 minutes. Serve immediately.

Roasted Sliced Sweet Potatoes with Cinnamon Sugar

MAKES 4 SERVINGS These little sugar-roasted medallions are sure to add the perfect touch to any main course poultry or meat dish. Hard to eat just a few, I usually make plenty of extras when kids are around who love the sweet and crispy outside and the creamy, tempting inside. You may have to keep the family at bay, if you hope to have any left for the dinner table! Nutritional finger food at its best, these guys are low in fat and high in antioxidants. Serve them with meatloaf, brisket, or roast chicken or turkey.

4 medium-size sweet potatoes, ends trimmed, peeled, and cut into ½-inch-thick rounds
Cooking oil spray
Salt and pepper to taste
1 tablespoon cinnamon sugar (see Chef's Note)

1. Preheat the oven to 400 degrees. Coat a baking sheet lightly with cooking oil spray.

2. Place the sweet potato rounds in a single layer on the prepared baking sheet. Spray the tops of the rounds with the oil and sprinkle with salt and pepper and half the cinnamon sugar.

3. Roast for 15 minutes. Turn the circles over and sprinkle with the remaining cinnamon sugar. Roast until the edges are crispy and brown and the insides are fork tender, another 10 to 15 minutes. Serve immediately.

Chef's Note: Although you can buy prepared cinnamon sugar, making your own is easy to do. Simply combine 3 parts granulated white sugar and 1 part ground cinnamon. To make ¼ cup, combine 3 tablespoons sugar with 1 tablespoon ground cinnamon. Extra cinnamon sugar can be stored in a jar with your other spices.

The Ultimate Baked Sweet Potato

MAKES 1 SERVING Recently, the baked sweet potato has enjoyed a bit of popularity, thanks to our friends "down under," who have inspired a string of restaurants throughout America. The preparation I am about to show you is so sweet and delicious that I dare say it will satisfy any sweet craving you may have, hands down. Try it on its own sometime and you will see what I mean.

The method we used to bake the sweet potatoes for the previous recipes will not do here. Instead of a dry, withered-looking skin that is removed, we are shooting for a soft and delicious edible one—this is accomplished with a little butter and an aluminum foil wrap. A tasty result is not the only benefit—we'll be getting some important nutrients and fiber, as well.

1 large sweet potato

1 teaspoon unsalted butter, softened

Salt and pepper to taste

½ teaspoon cinnamon sugar (see Chef's Note on page 240)

1 tablespoon Honey Nut Butter (see Chef's Note following)

1. Preheat the oven to 400 degrees. Using a fork, poke a few holes in the sweet potato and rub the outside with the butter. Wrap it in aluminum foil and bake on a baking sheet until fork tender, 40 to 50 minutes.

2. To serve, remove from the foil and cut an opening down the long end of the sweet potato. Squeeze the ends together to open up. Season with a little salt and pepper, sprinkle the cinnamon sugar over, and top with the honey nut butter. Serve immediately.

Chef's Note: To make Honey Nut Butter, combine ¼ cup softened unsalted whipped butter, 1 tablespoon chopped pecan pralines (or any other sugar-coated nuts you may prefer), and 1 tablespoon honey. Mix well and chill until ready to use.

Broccoli Bake with Crumb Topping

MAKES 4 SERVINGS The nutritionally packed broccoli gets dressed up here with a smooth sour cream sauce and savory crumb topping. Rich and delicious, even broccoli nonenthusiasts will take a second look when you bring this to the table. You can use frozen broccoli florets if you like, but fresh is always better and easy to prepare, especially in the microwave (see page 140). Serve this with turkey, chicken, or pork that has been simply prepared to allow this dish to shine.

1 pound broccoli florets, cooked to crisp tender

½ cup sour cream

¼ cup (½ stick) unsalted butter

½ teaspoon prepared mustard

Salt and pepper to taste

CRUMB TOPPING

1 tablespoon olive oil

2 tablespoons unsalted butter

⅔ cup seasoned dry bread crumbs

1. Preheat the oven to 350 degrees. Lightly grease a 9-inch square glass baking dish.

2. Place the cooked broccoli florets in a single layer in the prepared baking dish. In a small saucepan over medium heat, combine the sour cream, butter, and mustard, season with salt and pepper, and cook, stirring, until the butter has melted and the sauce is smooth, about 5 minutes. Pour evenly over the broccoli.

3. Make the crumb topping by melting together the olive oil and butter in a small saucepan. Remove from the heat and stir in the bread crumbs until moistened. Sprinkle the topping evenly over the broccoli and bake until the topping is golden and the sauce is bubbly, about 25 minutes. Remove from the oven and allow to rest for 5 minutes, then serve.

Honey-Roasted Baby Carrots

MAKES 4 SERVINGS This is an excellent accompaniment to pork, chicken, or turkey and is easy to prepare. Packaged baby carrots, peeled and ready to go, make this dish a snap, although, if you like, you can use medium-size carrots, peeled and cut into 1-inch pieces. The honey adds a lovely glaze and sweetness towards the end. Try substituting maple syrup for the honey, which works equally well.

One 16-ounce bag peeled baby carrots

1 tablespoon canola oil

Salt and pepper to taste

1 tablespoon honey

1. Preheat the oven to 375 degrees.

2. In a medium-size mixing bowl, coat the baby carrots with the canola oil and a pinch of salt and pepper and place them in a single layer on a rimmed baking sheet or in a shallow roasting pan. Roast for 25 to 30 minutes, shaking the pan occasionally, to brown evenly.

3. During the last 5 minutes, drizzle the honey over the carrots and stir to coat. When the carrots are fork tender, serve immediately.

Honey-Roasted Carrots with Ginger and Sesame Seeds: Add 2 teaspoons peeled and finely chopped fresh ginger and 1 teaspoon sesame seeds when coating the carrots with the canola oil. If you wish, add 1 teaspoon soy sauce when you add the honey.

Cauliflower with Cheese Sauce

MAKES 4 SERVINGS This member of the cabbage family was first introduced to America in the seventeenth century by European settlers and has been part of our cuisine ever since. Many of us have rarely eaten cauliflower any other way than smothered in a rich cheese sauce and baked to a delicious bubbly finish. In Phase Three we'll be looking at a terrific roasted version (page 348), but until then, enjoy the comfort that this creamy dish can provide.

Some cooks will prepare the cauliflower whole, pouring the sauce over before bringing it to the table, but I like the idea of each floret getting a good dousing of cheese sauce, while baking will enhance the final flavor. You can cook your cauliflower to crisp tender in the microwave or by boiling (see page 140), but be aware that just a tad too much cooking time will result in a mushy mess. It's always best to err on the side of crunchy.

1 medium-size head cauliflower, trimmed, cut into florets, and cooked to crisp tender

2 tablespoons unsalted butter

1 small onion, peeled and finely chopped

2 tablespoons all-purpose flour

2 cups milk (whole, 2 percent, or 1 percent)

Salt and pepper to taste

½ pound processed cheese (such as Velveeta or American), cut into pieces

Dash of paprika

1. Preheat the oven to 350 degrees. Lightly grease a 9-inch square glass casserole dish.

2. Place the cooked cauliflower florets in a single layer in the prepared dish.

3. In a medium-size saucepan over medium heat, melt the butter and cook the onion, stirring, until soft but not browned, about 3 minutes. Add the flour, stir well, and cook for 1 minute. Add the milk, season with salt and pepper, increase the heat to medium-high, and, stirring constantly, cook until bubbly and thickened. Reduce the heat, if necessary, to prevent sticking.

4. Add the cheese to the saucepan and, over low heat, stir until completely melted and smooth. Taste for additional seasoning and pour evenly over the cauliflower florets. Sprinkle the top with a dash of paprika and bake until the edges are slightly golden and bubbly, about 25 minutes. Remove from the oven and allow to rest 5 to 10 minutes, then serve.

Corn and Okra Succotash

MAKES 4 SERVINGS Traditional succotash includes lima beans, but here I've substituted that southern favorite, okra, to make a delicious and easy-to-prepare side dish that is especially good with Melt-in-Your-Mouth Country-Style Ribs (page 214). During the summer months, when corn is sweet and plentiful, I will take it right off the cob for this dish, but frozen or canned varieties work equally well. Similarly, fresh okra is ideal, but frozen pieces will make your job a lot easier and do not detract from the outcome.

1 tablespoon olive oil
1 tablespoon unsalted butter
½ medium-size onion, peeled and chopped
½ medium-size green bell pepper, seeded and
   chopped
½ pound fresh or frozen small okra, bottoms
   trimmed and cut into ½-inch-thick rounds
2 cups fresh, frozen, or canned corn kernels, drained
One 8-ounce can tomato sauce
1 cup water
½ teaspoon ground coriander
¼ teaspoon paprika
Dash of cayenne pepper
Salt and pepper to taste

1. Melt the butter with the olive oil in a large skillet over medium heat, add the onion and green pepper, and cook, stirring occasionally, until soft, about 5 minutes. Add the sliced okra, stir well, and cook for 3 minutes.

2. Add the remaining ingredients, stir well to combine, and bring to a simmer. Reduce the heat to low and cook uncovered, stirring often, until the vegetables are tender and most of the liquid has evaporated, about 15 minutes. Taste for seasoning and serve.

Corn and Lima Bean Succotash: Substitute ½ pound frozen lima beans for the okra.

Hominy with Easy White Sauce

MAKES 4 SERVINGS White sauce, also called béchamel, is simply a butter-and-flour roux, or thickener, with the addition of milk and seasoning. Depending upon the amount of roux that is used, the sauce can be thin, medium, or quite thick. In general, a medium white sauce will suit most dishes and can be easily embellished with other ingredients to create numerous variations (page 245).

Creamed vegetables, or those that are served in a medium white sauce, are always associated with comfort. Particularly popular in the Midwest, creamy versions of peas and onions, spinach, and mixed vegetables are often found alongside home-cooked entrees, providing a rich aspect to what would normally be a simple square meal.

One of my very favorite ways to use a simple white sauce is to make creamed hominy, a delicious accompaniment to croquettes (page 204), salmon loaf (page 222), crab cakes (page 220), and many other classic poultry and fish entrees. Hominy is simply dried white or yellow corn kernels that have had their hull and germ removed. It is the basis of the more popularly known grits when ground to a meal. Hominy can be found dried whole, in which case it must be reconstituted and cooked, similar in method to that of dried beans and other grains. It is also found precooked and in cans, ready to heat and serve. This is by far the easiest way to use it and the best choice for this dish. Also called pozole, hominy can be added to casseroles and stews and is often used in Mexican and Spanish cuisine. It is not only delicious, but also boasts more soluble fiber than brown rice.

EASY WHITE SAUCE
   3 tablespoons unsalted butter
   3 tablespoons all-purpose flour
   2 cups milk
   Salt and pepper to taste
   Dash of ground nutmeg

Two 15-ounce cans white or yellow hominy, drained
Dash of paprika

1. Melt the butter in a medium-size saucepan over medium-low heat, stir in the flour, and cook,

(continued on page 245)

Getting Sauced

Easy Ways to Dress Up Your Veggies

If you like to serve your vegetables in creamy, comforting sauces, Easy White Sauce is the perfect place to start. Gourmet chefs have been dressing up this simple béchamel for ages with everything from cheese to herbs and spices. Below are some easy variations and recommendations on ways to "sauce up" your plain vegetable sides:

MORNAY SAUCE: Here's the classic cheese sauce in gourmet form. Simply add ¼ cup *each* grated Gruyère cheese and Parmesan to your finished Easy White Sauce. Stir in off the heat to prevent the sauce from breaking. A dash of cayenne pepper is traditionally added. Serve as is or pour it over your cooked vegetables, add a sprinkling of Parmesan cheese, and lightly brown under the broiler for a delicious finish.

TOMATO PARMESAN SAUCE: Stir in 1 tablespoon tomato paste and 2 tablespoons freshly grated Parmesan cheese off the heat. Layer grilled zucchini or eggplant in a gratin dish, spoon the sauce over the vegetables, sprinkle with additional Parmesan cheese, and brown lightly under the broiler. Serve extra sauce with cooked pasta.

ROASTED GARLIC SAUCE: This is my take on the classic *sauce soubise*, which traditionally adds onion puree. Here, a heaping tablespoon of roasted garlic puree (page 120) adds great flavor and interest. Try it with cauliflower, pearl onions, or even mashed potatoes!

HERB SAUCE: Stir in 1 tablespoon finely chopped fresh herbs; choose from parsley, basil, dill, tarragon, or a combination. Excellent with peas, carrots, or potatoes, especially when served alongside poached, baked, or grilled fish.

MOCK HOLLANDAISE SAUCE: Here, Easy White Sauce fills in for the traditional melted butter for a lower calorie and more stable result. In a small bowl, beat 2 large egg yolks and add a little of the hot Easy White Sauce, whisking well. Slowly pour the egg mixture into the saucepan and return to the stove over low heat for 1 to 2 minutes to cook the eggs but not scramble them, stirring constantly. Add 1 tablespoon fresh lemon juice off the heat. Delicious with any vegetable, particularly steamed asparagus. Sprinkle with paprika before serving.

Recovery Note: For those of us who are now "off the sauce," watch for embellished white sauces that contain alcohol, usually in the form of wine or sherry. Typically these are anything à la king, Newburg, and Cardinal, among others. These days, not everyone makes these sauces in the classic "sauced up" way, so ask, if you are not sure, when eating out.

(continued from page 243)

stirring constantly, until bubbly but not browned, about 2 minutes. Add the milk and a good pinch of salt and pepper, increase the heat to medium, and, using a wire whisk, stir constantly until thickened and bubbling. Add the nutmeg, cook a further minute, taste for seasoning, and remove from heat.

2. Add the drained hominy, stir well to combine, and heat through. If necessary, you may reheat the creamed hominy over a very low flame, stirring often. Transfer to a warm serving dish, sprinkle the paprika on top, and serve.

Lightened-Up Easy White Sauce: Use 2 percent, 1 percent, or skim milk. You may also reduce the butter by 1 tablespoon. Plain soymilk could also be used.

Chef's Note: Other cooked vegetables (from frozen, canned, or fresh) that could be added to your finished white sauce are peas, peas and pearl onions, peas and carrots, mixed vegetables, string beans, Brussels sprouts, or baby potatoes.

Buttery Three-Pea Medley

MAKES 4 SERVINGS Peas are no doubt the most common vegetable side dish in America. Combined with carrots or onions, dressed in a cream sauce, or served just with butter, they are a popular choice for filling the "something green" gap we know we need to provide for on our dinner plates. Fresh shelled peas, sweet and tender, are a true luxury, but are becoming more and more available in areas where they used to be hard to come by. If you can find them, they would be delicious to use here. Frozen versions are the next best thing (canned peas are too mushy and sodium packed) and are handy when time is limited.

Here I've joined the garden-variety pea we all

know and love with two of its pod pea cousins, namely the snow pea and the sugar snap pea. As a trio, they can't be beat for excellent fiber content as well as protein and vitamin C. Meatloaf and mashed potatoes are the perfect venue for this buttery dish.

¼ cup (½ stick) unsalted butter
1 tablespoon shallot, peeled and finely chopped
One 10-ounce package frozen peas, thawed
1 cup sugar snap peas, ends and tough strings
     removed
1 cup snow peas, ends and tough strings
     removed
½ cup low-sodium chicken or vegetable
     broth, hot
Salt and pepper to taste

1. Melt 2 tablespoons of the butter in a large nonstick skillet over medium heat until foamy but not brown. Add the shallot and cook, stirring, for 2 minutes. Add the peas and sugar snap peas, sprinkle with salt and pepper, and stir to coat with the butter. Continue cooking over medium heat for 2 minutes, stirring often. Add the snow peas, stir and cook a further minute. Pour in the broth, cover, reduce the heat to medium-low, and cook until all the peas are crisp tender, 2 to 3 minutes.

2. Remove from the heat, add the remaining 2 tablespoons butter, and swirl the pan until melted, coating the peas well. Taste for seasoning, add if necessary, and serve immediately.

Creole-Style Green Beans

MAKES 4 SERVINGS Here's a side dish to wake up your palate and add some zip to your entrée. Spiced up and classically Creole, these comforting green beans go well with roasted or barbecued poultry or meat and do nicely as a side dish for Spicy Creole Shrimp (page 221) as well.

Pinch of salt

1 pound fresh green beans, ends trimmed

6 strips bacon

1 small onion, peeled and chopped

1 small celery stalk, ends trimmed and diced

1 garlic clove, peeled and minced

1 small fresh chili pepper, seeded and minced

One 15-ounce can diced tomatoes, undrained

1 cup water

Pepper to taste

1. Bring a medium-size pot of water to a boil, add the salt, and cook the green beans until crisp tender, 10 to 12 minutes. Drain and set aside.

2. Fry the bacon in a large skillet until crispy, let drain on a paper towel, and crumble into bits. Set aside.

3. Drain all but 2 tablespoons of the bacon fat from the skillet, add the onion and celery and cook, stirring, over medium-high heat until softened, 6 to 8 minutes. Add the garlic and chili pepper, and cook a further minute. Add the green beans, tomatoes, and water, bring to a simmer, and cook, stirring occasionally, until much of the liquid has been absorbed and the beans are fork tender.

4. Taste for the addition of salt and pepper, adjust if necessary, and serve topped with the crumbled bacon bits.

Keeping Your Fresh Herbs Fresh

Hints on Buying and Storing

The addition of freshly chopped herbs to your cooking can make a big difference in the final flavor and presentation. These days we are fortunate to be able to purchase many unusual herbs that were not available to us years ago, unless we grew them ourselves. No longer faced with a mere choice between curly and flat-leaf parsley, we now have the pleasure of bringing home numerous little packets of fragrant fresh-picked herbs to enhance our dishes and provide color and interest to a variety of meals from breakfast omelets to dinnertime stews, roasts, and salads.

Often, herbs may be sold in rather large bunches, which inevitably become yellow, withered, and even slimy after only a brief few days in the fridge. As we reach for them to add as a final flourish to our carefully prepared dishes, we are disappointed to suddenly find them unusable. What can be done to keep our fresh herbs as fresh as possible, so they are there for us when we need them? Here are a few helpful tips to remember when buying and storing your fresh herbs:

- If at all possible, buy the smallest quantity available, even if doing so appears to be uneconomical. A large bunch of dill for a dollar will be wasted if you only need a tablespoon or two chopped. Although most common herbs, like parsley, nearly always come in large bunches, others, such as dill, cilantro, and basil, are sometimes also offered in smaller packages, like plastic boxes or wrapping, for about the same price. These may provide the exact amount you need and not take over your fridge space, as is often the case with large, bulky bunches. Some herb suppliers even package small amounts of herb combinations for specific flavor results, such as poultry mix or Italian blend, providing you with just the amount you may require. Also check the organic herb section, where you will sometimes find smaller bunches of commonly large bunched herb varieties.

- When buying your fresh herbs, look for signs of life—any bunches with dying, withered, and yellow leaves should be avoided. They should appear as if they were just fresh picked, and if your produce manager is a good one, he or she will keep large bunches submerged in cold water, occasionally misting the tops to quench their thirst. Small boxes usually contain a damp paper cloth to keep the herbs hydrated. All fresh herbs should smell fragrant and clean, even through the packaging.

- If you will be using your herbs immediately, or within a day or so, you won't need to repackage them. The exception to this rule is fresh basil, which tends to deteriorate rapidly and will benefit by being kept in a glass of cold water, about an inch or two up the stem, in a very cool place (even the refrigerator), with a plastic bag enveloping its leaves. Change the water every other day. Alternatively, you can wrap fresh basil as you would other bunches of delicate herbs you may not be using right away, by dampening a paper towel or cloth and securing it around the stems to provide moisture, while placing the whole bunch in a loose-fitting plastic bag. Sturdy-stemmed herbs such as thyme, rosemary, and bay leaves can be completely wrapped in a damp towel to avoid drying out. With appropriate moisture, fresh herbs can keep anywhere from 5 to 10 days when properly wrapped and stored in the refrigerator.

- Always wait until you are ready to use your fresh herbs before washing them. Depending on the amount of grit and dirt that is present, you can either run them under a stream of cold water or douse them briefly in a bowl of water, allowing the dirt to settle to the bottom. Gently pat them dry with a paper towel before chopping.

- If you are an avid fresh herb fan, you might want to consider growing a kitchen herb garden in containers near your kitchen door for easy access. Or if your kitchen windowsill is sunlit, some herbs will do quite well indoors. Having them handy for snipping and chopping will encourage you to use them more frequently and enjoy the pleasure and flavor they offer.

Creamy Dilled Lima Beans

MAKES 3 TO 4 SERVINGS Lima beans, named after the city of Lima in Peru because fifteenth-century explorers discovered them there, seem to be one of those bean varieties that people either love or hate. For myself, it has always been a favorite and, more often than not, a little salt and butter is all I will use when serving them, especially if they are freshly shelled. But lima bean casseroles are immensely popular, particularly in the Midwest, where cream and cheese sauces reign supreme when it comes to dressing up vegetables.

This recipe is equally creamy, but prepared totally on the stove-top for a quick and comforting side dish that will please even lima bean skeptics. Frozen limas would be my choice over canned, and fresh dill is a must for peak flavor. This preparation is also well suited to green or yellow wax beans.

> 1 tablespoon unsalted butter
> 1 tablespoon all-purpose flour
> ¾ cup low-sodium chicken broth
> ½ cup heavy cream
> 2 teaspoons chopped fresh dill leaves
> Drop of fresh lemon juice
> Salt and pepper to taste
> One 10-ounce package frozen lima beans (Fordhook or baby), cooked according to package directions and drained

1. In a medium-size saucepan, melt the butter over medium heat and stir in the flour. Cook for 1 minute. Slowly whisk in the chicken broth and, when well combined, add the cream, dill, and lemon juice and season with salt and pepper, whisking to combine. Reduce the heat to low and, stirring often, cook the sauce until it is slightly bubbling and thickened, about 5 minutes.

2. Add the lima beans, stir well to coat, and cook until heated through, 2 to 3 minutes. Taste for seasoning and serve immediately.

Rich's Best Baked Beans

MAKES 4 TO 6 SERVINGS Everyone has a family member who makes the "best" baked beans and, in my family, my brother Rich has earned this distinction. Slow-cooked and superbly flavorful, these oven-baked beans are a comforting side dish for every barbecue menu or summer celebration. Although some claim that good baked beans must be made from dried, the appropriate canned variety for the job will not only provide the perfect bean, but also save a bit of time in the process. Rich prefers using B&M-brand beans as his jumping-off point, because they use the small pea bean, the classic variety in Boston baked beans, which holds up to the long cooking time without getting mushy. I agree that, of all the brands I have tried for this recipe, B&M win hands down in the final cook-off. Oddly enough, for eating "out of can," they are not my favorite, but the size, texture, and bite of these beans make them ideal for this method of cooking.

Patience is required for an excellent result—the longer the beans are in the oven, immersed in the flavorful sauce, the more delicious they will be. Frequent stirring is also required, as is a heavy, earthenware casserole dish, which holds the heat without burning. You probably have one around, hiding behind the meatloaf pan—now is the time to bring it into daylight! If not, use a deep round or oval ceramic or glass casserole (Rich has used a glass loaf pan for the amount below with excellent success), but avoid metal, including stainless steel, which will encourage a too-rapid browning of the edges.

Once baked to perfection, baked beans should be allowed to rest for at least 15 minutes. This will continue to thicken the sauce and keep diners from burning their tongues!

> Two 16-ounce cans B&M Original Baked Beans
> ⅓ pound sliced bacon, cut crosswise into ½-inch-wide strips

1 medium-size Spanish onion, peeled and diced

2 garlic cloves, peeled and minced

1¼ cups ketchup

⅓ cup firmly packed dark brown sugar

⅓ cup dark molasses (not blackstrap)

1 tablespoon chili powder

1 teaspoon dry mustard

1 teaspoon Liquid Smoke

Freshly ground black pepper to taste

1. Preheat the oven to 325 degrees. Pour the beans into an ungreased 2-quart casserole dish.

2. In a large nonstick skillet, fry the bacon over medium-high heat until nearly crisp and most of the fat has been rendered. Using a slotted spoon, transfer the bacon to the casserole dish. Fry the onion in the bacon fat in the skillet over medium heat, stirring, until soft but not browned, about 10 minutes. Add the garlic and cook a further minute. Transfer the skillet contents to the casserole dish, along with the remaining ingredients. Stir well to combine.

3. Place the dish in the oven. As the beans begin to bubble and a crust begins to form, start stirring every 15 minutes until the mixture is reduced and thickened, being careful to scrape the sides of the casserole each time. It will take at least 1 hour, and up to 2 hours, to reach the desired consistency. Remove from the oven and allow to rest for 15 minutes, then serve.

Rich's Best Vegetarian Baked Beans: Use vegetarian style B&M Baked Beans, omit the bacon, and fry the onion and garlic in ¼ cup olive oil. Increase the Liquid Smoke to 2 teaspoons and taste for the addition of salt.

Hoppin' John with Steamin' Greens

MAKES 6 SERVINGS Real "southern comfort" can be summed up in a dish of hoppin' John and a "mess o' greens." Traditionally eaten on New Year's Day for good luck, this dish is overflowing with vitamins and minerals our bodies crave, such as A, C, thiamine, riboflavin, calcium, magnesium, and iron. Maybe the luck comes from the fact we are starting off the year with one of the healthiest meals around!

Just as in many traditional recipes, there are a number of variations, depending on what part of the South you are from. Being a Yankee myself, I will beg forgiveness of my fellow recovering southern brothers and sisters if I have "messed" with the original too much to their liking. However, I will say that this recipe has prompted many of my Yankee clients to consider taking a second look at southern cooking. If you have never tried this dish, do yourself a favor and find out what real "soul food" is all about. Excellent with chicken, turkey, or pork, this is a hearty side dish that is sure to please. Hot buttermilk biscuits (page 254) or corn muffins (page 255) would make the perfect complement.

2 cups dried black-eyed peas, picked over and rinsed

6 cups water

1 smoked ham hock or smoked turkey wing

2 sprigs fresh thyme

1 bay leaf

Pepper to taste

¼ pound bacon or salt pork, rind removed, if necessary, and diced

1 medium-size onion, peeled and chopped

3 garlic cloves, peeled and minced

2 large bunches fresh greens (about 2 pounds), such as collards, mustard greens, turnip greens, Swiss chard, or kale (or a combination), washed well to remove all grit, stems removed, and leaves cut into 1-inch-wide ribbons

1 cup white long-grain rice

Salt to taste

1. In a large saucepan, combine the black-eyed peas, water, ham hock, thyme, bay leaf, and some fresh ground pepper. Bring to a boil, reduce the heat to a simmer, and cook, covered, until the peas are tender but not mushy, 45 minutes to 1 hour. Drain and save the cooking liquid. Set both aside. (At this point, you can refrigerate the beans and the cooking liquid and continue with the recipe at another time or the next day.)

2. In a large skillet or heavy-bottomed pot, fry the bacon with the onion over medium heat until most of the fat is rendered and the onion is soft. Add the garlic and cook another minute. Carefully (watch for splattering grease) add the slightly wet greens to the pot and stir well. Reduce the heat to medium-low, cover, and cook until the greens are tender and most of the liquid has evaporated, 20 to 30 minutes.

3. Meanwhile, pour the reserved black-eyed pea cooking liquid into a measuring cup. Add enough water to equal a total of 2¼ cups. Pour this into a saucepan and bring to a boil. Add the rice, stir, reduce the heat to low, and cook, covered, until the rice is done and the liquid is absorbed, 20 to 25 minutes. Remove from the heat and let stand for 5 minutes, then taste for salt and pepper and add if necessary.

4. When the greens are cooked, add the cooked black-eyed peas and heat through. Serve on a large warmed platter with the cooked rice on one side and the beans and greens on the other.

Chef's Note: If time is limited, you can use two 14.5-ounce cans black-eyed peas, or the equivalent amount from frozen. However, a lot of extra flavor will be lost, so cook your rice in chicken broth instead of water and be sure to season the entire dish well.

Creamed Baby Spinach

MAKES 4 SERVINGS No one needs reminding that spinach is one of the most nutritious leafy greens on the planet, chock full of iron and vitamins A and C. Fortunately, there are many ways to include spinach on our menu, from adding it to soups and stews, to enjoying it in salads. Creamed spinach, a popular comforting dish, is another delicious spinach option.

Although many creamed spinach recipes call for frozen, I much prefer using fresh leaves. Unfortunately, many folks lack the patience to properly trim and wash fresh spinach, which often contains a good amount of grit that must be removed through successive soakings. As a happy compromise, I've come up with this easy preparation, which takes advantage of prewashed, ready-to-cook baby spinach, usually available in your packaged salad section. Some bags are even microwaveable and could be used here. Otherwise, steaming or sautéing is a good way to quickly cook your spinach, while retaining maximum nutritional value.

Spinach, like many other greens, can virtually cook down to nothing, or so it seems. One package of fresh will barely yield 2 servings, so although it may seem like a huge amount, do not be tempted to cut back on the indicated quantity. You may even want to double the recipe, as hearty appetites can easily eat up this delicious side dish. Excellent with any type of fish, steak, or chop, creamed baby spinach will quickly become a favorite comfort at the dinner table.

1 pound fresh baby spinach leaves
½ cup water
2 tablespoons unsalted butter
½ small onion, peeled and finely chopped
½ cup heavy cream
Dash of nutmeg
Salt and pepper to taste

1. In a large pot with a lid, cook the spinach and water together, covered, over medium-high heat until just wilted, 3 to 5 minutes. Transfer to a colander and allow to cool until comfortable to handle. Squeeze out any remaining liquid and set aside.

2. In a medium-size saucepan, melt the butter

over medium heat, add the onion, and cook, stirring, until softened, but not browned, about 3 minutes. Add the prepared spinach, heavy cream, and nutmeg, season with salt and pepper, and stir well to combine. Cook over medium-low heat until most of the cream is absorbed. Taste for seasoning and serve immediately.

Chef's Note: You can also make creamed spinach by utilizing any leftover Easy White Sauce (page 243) you may have on hand. About $1/2$ cup will be sufficient for 1 pound spinach. Adjust the seasonings, as necessary.

Brown Sugar–Glazed Acorn Squash

MAKES 4 SERVINGS The winter squash family, which includes varieties such as acorn, butternut, buttercup, and turban, are now usually available year round, although their peak season is the autumn through the winter. They are often prepared with some kind of sugar glaze or sweet type of sauce, because their flavor and texture welcomes this kind of flavor combination. Their cousin, the pumpkin, a member of the gourd family, exemplifies this pairing.

Many cooks shy away from these interesting looking, often colorful specimens in the supermarket, baffled as to how to attack them and get at the inside pulp. Acorn squash is one of the easier types to prepare, as it can simply be cut in half and cooked in its skin, providing a type of shell for its presentation, which is why it is often found stuffed with some type of filling such as fruit or hearty grains (page 378). Here, butter and brown sugar provide the only necessary addition, resulting in a delicious and sweet caramel-like glaze, while quartered pieces allow for more glazed surface area, always a good thing. Although acorn squash can be cooked in the microwave, cut side down in a lit-

tle water, for about 8 minutes, this method encourages the browning process that is essential to the tasty conclusion.

Choose acorn squash that are heavy and whose skin is hard, dark colored, and free of bruises or blemishes. Good nutrition abounds here, offering a source of iron, as well as vitamins A and C, two powerful antioxidants whose presence are announced by the squash's bright yellow pulp.

2 medium-size acorn squash, quartered and seeded
Cooking oil spray
Salt and pepper to taste
8 teaspoons unsalted butter
8 teaspoons dark brown sugar

1. Preheat the oven to 375 degrees. Cover a baking sheet with aluminum foil and spray lightly with the oil.

2. Sprinkle the acorn squash with salt and pepper, place them cut side down on the prepared baking sheet, and bake for 25 minutes, turning once to the other cut side, halfway through the cooking time.

3. Now position the squash cut sides up, place 1 teaspoon of the butter and brown sugar in each pulp cavity, and bake for 10 minutes. Use a pastry brush to coat each wedge with the melted butter and sugar and continue to cook, brushing occasionally, until the squash is fork tender and nicely glazed, about 25 more minutes. You can shift the wedges around onto their sides to encourage uniform glazing during the cooking process. Carefully remove from the foil and serve immediately.

Creamiest Macaroni and Cheese

MAKES 4 TO 6 SERVINGS Although numerous versions of this American classic can be found in the frozen food department as well as in a box or even microwaveable pouch, none can compare to home-made. Simple to prepare and great to have on hand, especially with kids at home, mac 'n' cheese just may be the most comforting side dish (next to mashed potatoes, of course!) around.

The complaint I most often hear from home cooks when making their own macaroni and cheese is its lack of creaminess. This is simply the result of too much macaroni combined with too little cheese sauce and is usually the fault of the recipe, which fails to account for additional evaporation and absorption during baking time. The end result is too often a solid cake of dry macaroni. If you follow the proportions and directions below, I guarantee you a great result!

For the creamiest of consistency, nothing really matches the processed cheeses we Americans are all too familiar with. You can, of course, use just about any type of cheese, and many chefs have been known to add gourmet flair to this simple classic by including anything from goat cheese to blue cheese (see Chef's Note below). If you are a purist of old-fashioned macaroni and cheese, however, this recipe will definitely strike a chord of familiarity and provide immense comfort to your taste buds.

10 ounces elbow macaroni or small shells
    (about 2½ cups dry)
3 tablespoons unsalted butter
3 tablespoons all-purpose flour
1 quart milk (whole, 2 percent, or 1 percent)
Dash of paprika
Dash of ground nutmeg
1 pound processed cheese (such as Velveeta
    or American), diced
Salt and pepper to taste

1. Cook the macaroni according to the package directions. Drain, rinse under cold running water, and set aside to drain well.

2. Preheat the oven to 350 degrees. Butter the bottom and sides of a 9 x 13-inch glass baking dish.

3. In a large saucepan, melt the butter over medium heat, then add the flour. Using a wire whisk, stir and cook for a minute or two, until well combined and bubbly but not brown. Add the milk, increase the heat to medium-high, continue to whisk as the mixture comes to a boil, and let boil, whisking, until somewhat thickened. Add the paprika, nutmeg, and a pinch of salt and pepper and whisk a further minute.

4. Reduce the heat to low. Switch to a wooden spoon and, stirring constantly, add the cheese in two batches, stirring constantly until melted. Watch for sticking or scorching on the bottom of the pot, reducing the heat even more, if necessary. When well combined and thick, taste for seasoning, adjust as desired, and remove from the heat.

5. Add the well-drained macaroni to the pot and stir to combine. Pour the entire mixture into the prepared baking dish and bake until the edges are bubbly and the top begins to brown, 25 to 30 minutes. Remove from the oven and let rest 10 minutes before serving.

Creamiest Macaroni and Nacho Cheese: Add 2 tablespoons drained and chopped canned jalapeño slices to your cheese sauce. Top the casserole with thin slices of tomato during the final 5 minutes of baking.

Chef's Note: Try a variety or combination of Monterey Jack, fontina, Swiss, cheddar, Gruyère, or blue cheese; however, be sure to add and stir these cheeses into the sauce off the heat. Unlike processed cheeses, there is the danger of the proteins separating if boiled, resulting in a curdled and unappetizing appearance that can't be fixed.

Noodles Romanoff

MAKES 4 SERVINGS Noodles themselves can conjure up comfort in no time and this creamy preparation will help to speed up the process. Named after one of the Russian royal families, many of which, like the Stroganoffs, had a predilection for rich dishes, this is a side dish that goes with just about anything and is always a crowd pleaser for sour cream lovers. Mildly flavored, with a crispy crouton topping, this classic will have everyone coming back for seconds.

> 8 ounces medium-size egg noodles (1/2 box)
> One 8-ounce package cream cheese, softened
> 1 cup sour cream
> 1/2 cup milk
> 2 tablespoons unsalted butter
> 1 small onion, peeled and finely chopped
> Salt and pepper to taste
> 1 large garlic clove, peeled and minced
> 1/2 teaspoon Worcestershire sauce
> Dash of Tabasco sauce
> 2 cups seasoned croutons, crushed

1. Bring a pot of water to a boil and cook the egg noodles according to the package directions. Drain and set aside in the colander. Butter the bottom and sides of a 1 1/2-quart baking dish.

2. In a large mixing bowl, beat together the cream cheese, sour cream, and milk until smooth. Set aside.

3. In a small skillet, melt the butter over medium heat and cook the onion, sprinkled with salt and pepper, until softened, about 3 minutes, stirring. Add the garlic and cook a further minute. Transfer the onion and garlic to the sour cream mixture, add the Worcestershire and Tabasco, and stir to combine. Fold in the drained egg noodles to coat well. Taste for additional seasoning and pour into the prepared baking dish.

4. Top evenly with the crushed croutons and bake until the edges begin to bubble and the top is slightly golden, 25 to 35 minutes. Remove from the oven and allow to rest for 5 minutes, then serve.

Noodles Romanoff with Mushrooms: Sauté 1/2 pound white or wild mushrooms, sliced, with the onion until soft and lightly golden. Continue as directed above.

Lightened-Up Noodles Romanoff: Use Neufchâtel cheese instead of the cream cheese, reduced-fat sour cream, and 1 or 2 percent milk.

Chef's Note: Thin egg noodles are also a good choice for this dish and very popular with kids. Consider sneaking in some veggies by adding 1/2 cup cooked frozen green peas or 1 cup cooked frozen mixed vegetables.

Upside-Down Noodle Kugel

MAKES 4 TO 6 SERVINGS Baked puddings with a potato, vegetable, or noodle base are called kugel and are a popular side dish in Jewish cooking. I have my dear friend and client, Janet, to thank for opening up my culinary repertoire to the delicious pleasures of Jewish cuisine, when, on many occasions, she has entrusted me with preparing special holiday dishes for her family and friends, despite my initial lack of experience. Thanks to her, over the years, I have come to add many traditional Jewish dishes to my list of favorite preparations and kugel is definitely way up at the top.

This recipe is borrowed from Janet's own repertoire, with a few minor embellishments, and is deliciously sweet and comforting. Served as a side dish with anything from roast chicken to beef brisket, it is indicative of the popular Jewish pairing of sweet and savory. The upside-down presentation is part of what makes this dish so enticing and attractive when brought to the table. I guarantee it will be the star of the show.

8 ounces medium-size egg noodles (½ box),
    cooked according to package directions
    and drained well
¼ cup (½ stick) unsalted butter, softened
¼ cup loosely packed dark brown sugar
8 slices canned pineapple rings, drained
1 large maraschino cherry, stem removed
2 large eggs, beaten
¼ cup canola oil
¼ cup granulated sugar
Pinch of salt
¼ teaspoon ground cinnamon
1 tablespoon fresh lemon juice
1 teaspoon grated lemon zest
¾ cup diced mixed dried fruit (including raisins,
    apricots, apples, and plums)
¼ cup coarsely chopped walnuts

1. Preheat the oven to 350 degrees. Generously butter the bottom and sides of a 9-inch square baking dish and sprinkle the brown sugar evenly over the bottom. Place 1 pineapple ring in the center of the dish, filling the hole with the cherry. Cut the remaining pineapple rings in half and arrange them around the edge, cut side facing out. Set aside.

2. In a large mixing bowl, whisk together the eggs, oil, granulated sugar, salt, cinnamon, lemon juice, and zest until well combined. Stir in the drained noodles, fruit, and nuts and pour the entire mixture into the prepared baking dish.

3. Bake until set and lightly golden, 40 to 50 minutes. Remove from the oven and let stand for 5 minutes, then loosen the edges with a knife and invert the kugel onto a serving platter. Serve immediately.

Chef's Note: Prediced and packaged dried fruit medleys are available in a number of varieties, any of which could be used here, including tropical versions that include mango and papaya. Otherwise, you can create your own combination. The unhappily named prune has found new life under its proper name, dried plum, resulting in greater popularity. Consequently, citrus-scented dried plums are also popular. Pitted and diced, they could be used here as well.

Old-Fashioned Buttermilk Biscuits

MAKES 10 TO 12 BISCUITS These easy drop biscuits will complement any good old-fashioned meal and make everyone hum with pleasure. Served warm from the oven, slathered in butter, no one can resist these delicious additions to the main meal. The inclusion of a little cake flour provides a delicacy to the texture, but in a pinch you could substitute all-purpose flour without noticing much.

1½ cups all-purpose flour
½ cup cake flour (not self-rising)
1 tablespoon sugar
1 tablespoon baking powder
½ teaspoon baking soda
½ teaspoon salt
6 tablespoons (¾ stick) unsalted butter,
    diced and softened
1 cup buttermilk

1. Preheat the oven to 375 degrees.

2. In a large mixing bowl, whisk together the dry ingredients. Using a pastry blender, the on/off pulse of a food processor, or your fingertips, work the butter into the flour mixture until the mixture resembles small peas. Add the buttermilk and, using a wooden spoon, stir quickly to combine, without overmixing. Let the dough rest for 5 minutes.

3. Using 2 tablespoons, spoon the dough onto a

nonstick or lightly greased baking pan about 2 inches apart. You can use your fingers to help shape them into more uniform rounds. Bake until the bottoms are golden and a toothpick inserted in the center comes out clean, 15 to 20 minutes. Serve immediately.

Whole Wheat Buttermilk Biscuits: Substitute ¾ cup of the all-purpose flour with whole wheat flour.

Cornmeal Buttermilk Biscuits: Substitute ½ cup cornmeal for ½ cup of the all-purpose flour.

Cheese and Herb Biscuits: Stir in ½ cup diced or shredded cheese (cheddar, Swiss, or Monterey Jack) and 1 tablespoon finely chopped fresh herbs (such as parsley, cilantro, or basil) when adding the buttermilk.

Mini Yorkshire Puddings

MAKES 4 SERVINGS (2 PUDDINGS EACH—YES, EVERYONE WILL WANT SECONDS) I learned to perfect these during my time in England, and I dare say that my British friends were quite amazed at the outcome produced by a Yank. Because they are similar to our American popovers with a slight variation, my friends didn't realize that I already had a head start. After tasting many mushy-centered large-sized Yorkshire puddings, I decided that they really needed to be smaller to prevent this unwanted outcome. A standard muffin tin provides the perfect size.

Light, golden, and puffy, these complement any type of roast, although traditionally they are served with roast beef. The flavor will be heightened if you can use the pan drippings from your roasted meat. If not, a little oil will do the trick. Make the batter ahead and let it sit in the fridge until the roast is ready. While the meat rests, you

can quickly bake these up in no time. Be sure to serve them immediately while they are still hot and poofed for maximum oohs and aahs.

1 cup all-purpose flour
½ teaspoon salt
2 large eggs, slightly beaten
1¼ cups milk
1 tablespoon cold water
2 to 3 tablespoons pan drippings or canola oil

1. In a medium-size mixing bowl, whisk together the flour and salt. Add the eggs and, using an electric mixer, beat to combine. Slowly add half the milk and continue beating at low speed until the batter is smooth. Add the remaining milk slowly, increase the mixer speed to medium, and beat well. Stir in the water and set aside in the fridge, covered with plastic wrap, until ready to use.

2. Remove the cooked roast you may be preparing from the oven and hike up the oven temperature to 425 degrees. Distribute the pan drippings among 8 of the 12 muffin cups of a standard-size muffin tin and place in the oven. After 2 to 3 minutes, the drippings will begin to sizzle and nearly smoke. Remove the tin, immediately pour about ¼ cup of the batter into each of the 8 muffin cups, and bake until puffy and golden, about 15 minutes. Flip out or use a fork to remove and serve immediately.

Classic Corn Bread

MAKES 9 TO 12 SQUARES OR 12 STANDARD-SIZE MUFFINS Making basic homemade corn bread is extremely easy to do and it's a shame more of us don't bother baking it at home anymore. We have been spoiled by the convenience of ready-made versions available in supermarkets, delis, and coffee shops. But there is much to be gained by making your own. Not only do store-bought versions often contain heavy amounts of partially hydrogenated oils and sugar as well as food additives, canceling, somewhat, the nutritious value that authentic corn bread made with stone-ground meal can offer, they cause us to miss out on the pleasure of simple baking, delicious aromas, and eating it warm straight from the oven. If baking is a touch intimidating to you at first, simple corn bread is a great place to start.

Leftover corn bread or muffins can become an instant sweet snack. Toasted and topped with a bit of jam or jelly, any sweet tooth will be readily satisfied. One of my favorite ways to serve corn muffins as a snack is to halve and pan-toast them, cut side down, with a little butter in a skillet until golden and crisp, then drizzle a little maple syrup over the result.

Always look for the term "stone ground" on the label when buying cornmeal because it means that the nutritional content is higher—stone grinding as opposed to steel grinding retains some of the hull and germ of the corn. Keep this type of cornmeal in the refrigerator, as it tends to spoil quicker than the more refined versions.

Below is a classic corn bread recipe that will provide you with a starting point. Use this as the basis for the variations that follow.

1 cup stone-ground cornmeal
1 cup all-purpose flour
2 tablespoons sugar
1 tablespoon baking powder
1 teaspoon salt
1 cup milk
2 tablespoons unsalted butter, melted
2 large eggs, beaten

1. Preheat the oven to 400 degrees. Lightly oil or butter an 8- or 9-inch square baking pan or standard 12-cup muffin tin.

2. Whisk together the dry ingredients in a medium-size mixing bowl. Beat the milk and melted butter together in a small mixing bowl. Add the milk mixture and beaten eggs to the dry ingredients and stir well with a fork to just moisten (it's okay if there are some lumps).

3. Pour the batter into the prepared pan and bake until the edges are golden and a toothpick inserted in the middle comes out clean, 20 to 25 minutes. Allow to cool for 5 minutes before cutting into squares or popping out of the muffin tins.

Sweet Mini Corn Muffins: Reduce the flour and cornmeal to ¾ cup each and increase the sugar

(continued on page 258)

Bread and Butter

Comforting Companions that Complement Your Table

Warm bread dripping with melted sweet cream butter can sometimes be a whole meal to those who adore these classic comforting companions. When we sit down at a restaurant and feel the warmth emanating from the bread basket and a dish of soft spreadable butter nearby, we know we are in a good place. And when we offer these enticing staples at our own dinner table, our family and friends know we have taken that little extra step to make for a cozy and heart-warming meal.

Bread and butter have been natural companions practically since time began, and they still hold an important place in our hearts as well as our stomachs. Choosing a good quality bread and offering something smooth and creamy to spread on it can go a long way in helping to create an old-fashioned, homestyle atmosphere when the dinner bell rings. Get adventurous and try serving some unusual breads and spreads as an integral part of your menu and round out your meal with style. Even supermarket bakeries now offer a huge variety of loaves to choose from, including French batons, sourdoughs, and multigrains. Surprise everyone with a special bread and even a flavored butter for an extra-special complementary touch. Here are some ideas to get you started:

BUTTERY GARLIC BREAD: Who doesn't adore this perfect accompaniment to an Italian-style meal? Try making it with a whole-grain or multigrain Italian or French loaf from your supermarket or local bakery for a delicious and nutritious alternative to the plain white loaf. Use a serrated knife to cut the bread horizontally and bake the halves briefly in a preheated 350 degree oven to toast the surface. Then slather with butter and sprinkle with minced garlic, kosher salt, and chopped fresh parsley leaves. Sandwich the halves back together, wrap in aluminum foil, and keep warm until ready to serve.

SWEET SODA BREAD AND ORANGE BUTTER: The next time you are serving a hearty stew or roast, offer slices of purchased Irish soda bread or make Irish Barm Brack (page 60), both slightly sweet and studded with morsels of dried fruit. Whip up some orange butter for slathering by softening 1 cup whipped unsalted butter and stirring in 1 teaspoon grated orange rind and a drop or two of orange oil.

SPICED UP TEXAS TOAST: Cut 1-inch-thick slices from a round or oblong French or sourdough loaf and grill or toast both sides. Serve with chilled spicy chili butter made by softening ½ cup (1 stick) unsalted butter and adding 1 teaspoon chili powder, ⅛ teaspoon cayenne pepper, and ¼ teaspoon garlic salt. Great with steaks, meatloaf, or anything barbecued.

MINI MUFFINS WITH FRUIT BUTTER: Make mini corn muffins (previous page) or serve a variety of small muffins and croissants, lightly warmed, with apple, pumpkin, or other purchased fruit butters on the side. Delicious with pork entrees and roast chicken.

SEMOLINA LOAF WITH DIPPING OIL: Let butter take the night off and serve a fresh baked Italian semolina loaf with dipping herbs and a fine quality extra virgin olive oil. Make your dried herb mix by combining 1 tablespoon *each* dried oregano, rosemary, basil, thyme, parsley, and garlic powder in a small mixing bowl. Add salt and pepper to taste and transfer to a small decorative jar or ramekin. Provide shallow bowls or saucers for diners to combine a pinch of herbs with olive oil poured from a cruet and happily dip away. Delicious with anything, but particularly satisfying while waiting for the pasta to arrive!

(continued from page 256)
to ¼ cup. Sprinkle with sugar and bake at 350 degrees in 2 mini-muffin tins for 20 minutes.

Savory Corn and Rye Muffins: Eliminate the sugar and substitute ¼ cup rye flour for ¼ cup of the all-purpose flour. Sprinkle with caraway seeds before baking. These are particularly good as a dinner accompaniment.

Low-Fat Corn Bread: Use equivalent amount of egg substitute or egg whites for the whole eggs, use skim or 1 percent milk, and substitute canola oil for the butter. This type is great for toasting.

Mexican Roasted Corn Bread: Lightly brush one large husked cob of corn with canola oil and roast in the oven in a small baking pan at 400 degrees until most of the kernels are golden, 20 to 25 minutes. (You could also add ⅔ cup drained canned corn kernels in place of the roasted corn, if you prefer.) When cool enough to handle, use a sharp knife to remove the corn from the cob and add this to the batter. Add 1 seeded and minced jalapeño; 2 teaspoons chopped fresh cilantro leaves; 3 scallions, ends trimmed and finely chopped; and ½ cup shredded sharp cheddar cheese.

My Favorite Cornbread Stuffing

MAKES 10 TO 12 SERVINGS Everyone has a favorite stuffing and this one is definitely mine. Although I grew up with a more traditional white bread and sausage type of stuffing, eventually I learned to love the distinct flavor of a cornbread-based version. I like to add lots of ingredients (e.g., nuts, dried fruit, and mushrooms) to provide a variety of tastes and textures, many of which you could elimi-

nate for particularly fussy eaters. Whatever you decide, be sure to use a combination of fresh and dried sage, along with fresh thyme, which really enhances the outcome.

Many people prefer not to cook the stuffing inside the bird cavity and this recipe is ideal for such cooks. It bakes perfectly well in a covered baking dish, keeping moist and delicious. The Classic Corn Bread recipe (page 255) will provide the perfect start. Otherwise, purchased corn muffins or bread will be fine if you are in a hurry. Refrain from using seasoned dry corn bread cubes from a package, as they will not offer the richness or moistness we are after. Makes enough for an 18-pound turkey; for smaller birds or to serve as a side dish, you can make half the amount.

1 recipe Classic Corn Bread, cut into 1-inch cubes, or
    8 to 10 cups cubed corn bread or muffins
One 16-ounce package bulk pork sausage
¼ cup (½ stick) unsalted butter
1 large onion, peeled and chopped
1 large celery stalk, ends trimmed and chopped
10 ounces white mushrooms, stems trimmed
    and sliced
Pinch of salt
1 Red Delicious apple, left unpeeled, cored and
    cut into ½-inch dice
1 tablespoon chopped fresh sage leaves
1 teaspoon rubbed dried sage
1 teaspoon chopped fresh thyme leaves
Freshly ground pepper to taste
⅓ cup dried cranberries
⅓ cup coarsely chopped pecans
2 large eggs, slightly beaten
1 to 1 ½ cups low-sodium chicken broth, as needed

1. Preheat the oven to 325 degrees. Butter a 9 x 13-inch baking pan.
2. Place the cubed cornbread on a baking sheet and toast in the oven until the outside is dry but the inside is still moist, 12 to 15 minutes. Transfer to a large mixing bowl and set aside.

3. In a large skillet, fry the sausage over medium-high heat, breaking it up with a fork as it cooks, until no longer pink. Transfer with a slotted spoon to the mixing bowl. Add the butter to the skillet and melt with the drippings from the sausage over medium heat, scraping up any bits of remaining sausage from the bottom of the pan. Add the onion and celery and cook, stirring often, until somewhat softened, 2 to 3 minutes. Add the mushrooms and salt and continue to cook, stirring a few times, until soft and the mushrooms have released their liquid, about 5 minutes. Add the apple, herbs, and pepper and cook until the mixture is lightly golden, a further 2 minutes, stirring often. Transfer the contents of the skillet to the mixing bowl and gently fold into the cornbread and sausage.

4. Fold in the cranberries, pecans, and eggs. Starting with ½ cup of the broth, add to the mixture to moisten, folding gently. Continue adding a little broth (up to 1½ cups total) until the stuffing holds together without appearing mushy. Transfer to the prepared baking pan, cover with aluminum foil, and bake until firm and heated through, 30 to 40 minutes. Alternatively, place the stuffing inside the rinsed and dried cavity of a turkey or chicken (stuff it in loosely, don't pack it in or it won't cook properly), and cook according to roasting directions.

Quick Brown Pan Gravy

MAKES 2 TO 3 CUPS If your idea of comfort includes gravy, here's an easy way to prepare it from the pan drippings of your roast or turkey. Purchasing a fat-separating measuring cup will help immensely—excess fat rises to the top, while the delicious juices remain below, to be added to the gravy. Otherwise, pour the drippings into a regular measuring cup and, after a few minutes, you will be able to spoon off most of the fat.

You can use canned or homemade broth. If I am roasting a turkey, I will put the giblets in a saucepan, cover with water, and let it sit at a low simmer on the back burner to make a flavorful turkey broth for gravy making. Use the recommended alcohol substitutes for deglazing (see page 134) for optimal flavor.

Pan drippings from a roast, turkey, or chicken
½ cup deglazing liquid
⅓ cup all-purpose flour
1½ cups low-sodium beef, chicken, turkey, or
    vegetable broth
Salt and pepper to taste

1. Pour the pan drippings into a fat separator or measuring cup. When settled, transfer ⅓ cup of the fat to a medium-size saucepan and discard the rest, if not using a separator.

2. Deglaze the roasting pan with the deglazing liquid, using a wooden spoon to scrape up the bottom bits. If using a metal roasting pan, you can deglaze over low heat on top of the stove. Pour the liquid into the fat separator or measuring cup and set aside.

3. Add the flour to the fat in the saucepan and, over medium-high heat, cook until bubbly, whisking constantly, 1 to 2 minutes. Slowly pour in the separated pan juices, continuing to whisk, followed by 1 cup of the broth. Bring to a simmer and allow to cook, stirring constantly, for 2 minutes. If too thick, add a little more broth. Taste for the addition of salt and pepper, transfer to a warm gravy boat, and serve hot.

Giblet Gravy: Coarsely chop the neck meat and giblets that have been cooked in a saucepan with water or broth and stir into the gravy before serving.

Chef's Note: If you have seasoned your roast, chicken, or turkey generously, the flavored pan drippings, plus a broth that contains salt, may provide adequate seasoning. Be sure to taste the gravy before adding more salt and pepper.

Recovery Note: Enlighten the family member who makes the gravy at holiday time about the delicious alternative deglazing liquids they can use in place of alcohol, if they normally reach for an open bottle.

Mom's Raisin Sauce for Ham

MAKES ABOUT 1½ CUPS A glazed baked ham was unthinkable without Mom's Raisin Sauce when I grew up and even today, she will meticulously prepare this special complement when family and friends come for a traditional ham dinner. I recall her patiently cutting each little raisin in half and this careful, loving attention, no doubt, contributed somehow to the final outcome. Fortunately, a food processor fitted with a blade and aided by a sprinkling of flour to prevent sticking can accomplish this task in seconds, although I sometimes wonder if by taking this shortcut, I am leaving out some essential, intangible ingredient!

These kinds of sweet sauces, such as Cumberland sauce (be aware that port is generally used), and a variety of chutneys that are paired with meat dishes are rooted in the medieval culinary practice of combining many different flavors or "humors" in one dish, to create a balanced meal that nourishes the psyche as well as the body. To this day, numerous sweet condiments continue to complement savory dishes, from turkey with cranberry sauce to pork with applesauce and, in essence, even ketchup with hotdogs! There is something about their sweetness that brings out the best in cooked meats and poultry and this sauce is no exception. Enjoy it served warm and lightly spooned over your sliced ham.

1 cup seedless dark raisins
1 teaspoon all-purpose flour
1¾ cups water
½ cup firmly packed dark brown sugar
¼ cup granulated sugar
3 tablespoons cider vinegar
2 teaspoons prepared mustard
¼ teaspoon ground cloves
Dash of ground mace
½ cup grape jelly
2 to 3 drops red food coloring
1 teaspoon Worcestershire sauce
1 tablespoon unsalted butter

1. In a small bowl, mix together the raisins and the flour. Transfer to a food processor and coarsely chop using the on/off pulse. Alternatively, place the floured raisins on a cutting board and chop with a knife.

2. Pour the water into a medium-size saucepan, add the raisins, and bring to a boil over high heat. Reduce the heat to low, cover, and allow to simmer for 15 minutes. Add the sugars, vinegar, mustard, cloves, and mace, stir to combine, and cook, uncovered, over medium-low heat, stirring often, until somewhat reduced and syrupy, about 20 minutes. Stir in the jelly, food coloring, and Worcestershire and continue to cook until nicely thickened and able to coat the back of a spoon, about 10 minutes more.

3. Remove from the heat, swirl in the butter, and serve warm.

Hot Horseradish Sauce

MAKES ABOUT 1 CUP Although many condiments can be readily purchased in the supermarket, horseradish sauce being one of them, the authentic and somewhat forgotten version of true horseradish sauce can really liven up a meal with piquancy and pleasure. An odd-looking fellow, to say the least, fresh horseradish root can always be found around Passover time, as it is one of the five bitter herbs used in the celebration. If you have trouble finding it, you can make the shortcut version below, which makes use of prepared horseradish in a bottle and already includes the necessary vinegar. Serve this sauce cold with brisket, pot roast, or good old-fashioned roast beef.

½ cup whipping or heavy cream
One 3-inch piece fresh horseradish root, peeled and grated
1 teaspoon sugar
½ teaspoon dry mustard
2 teaspoons white wine vinegar
Pinch of salt and pepper

1. In a medium-size mixing bowl, using a wire whisk or electric mixer, whip the cream until stiff peaks form.

2. Add the remaining ingredients and gently fold into the whipped cream. Transfer to a serving bowl and refrigerate until ready to serve, up to 3 hours.

Shortcut Horseradish Sauce: Fold 2 to 3 tablespoons prepared horseradish, to your taste, into the whipped cream and omit the remaining ingredients.

Cucumber Yogurt Raita

MAKES ABOUT 2 CUPS This is my favorite condiment for spicy curry dishes; it is tremendously creamy and cooling when the "heat" level gets high. Try it with *Nasi Goreng* (page 130) or as a complement to any type of tandoori cooked meat or poultry.

One 16-ounce container plain low-fat yogurt
1 Kirby cucumber, peeled and cut into ½-inch dice
1 teaspoon sugar
1 teaspoon fresh lime juice
1 tablespoon *each* chopped fresh cilantro and mint leaves
Salt and pepper to taste

1. Empty the yogurt container into a medium-size mixing bowl and stir to a smooth consistency.

2. Fold in the remaining ingredients, transfer to a serving bowl, and chill until ready to serve. Raita will keep refrigerated for several days. Stir well, if necessary, before serving.

Gingered Mango Chutney

MAKES ABOUT 1 CUP Chutneys originated in East India and are meant to accompany curry-flavored dishes, providing a hot yet sweet complement on the side. Many different fruits can be used, but mangoes are by far the most popular and are used in the famous Major Grey's version. I like to throw in plenty of fresh ginger for added bite and for its medicinal properties (see page 11)—it may help you digest those super-hot curry dishes! This chutney tastes amazingly fresh and vibrant and is a far cry from bottled versions. Try it also as a condiment with a sharp cheddar cheese and crackers.

½ cup sugar
½ cup cider vinegar
¼ cup water
One 2-inch piece fresh ginger, peeled and chopped
1 small jalapeño pepper, seeded and chopped
2 ripe mangoes, peeled, pitted, and cut into rough ½-inch dice
2 teaspoons chopped fresh cilantro leaves
1 teaspoon chopped fresh mint leaves

1. Combine the sugar, vinegar, and water in a medium-size saucepan over medium-high heat, bring to a simmer, and cook, stirring a few times, until the sugar has dissolved. Add the ginger and jalapeño, reduce the heat to a low simmer, and cook for 2 minutes. Add the mangoes, stir well to combine, cover, reduce the heat to very low, and cook, stirring occasionally, until the mango is fork tender, 12 to 15 minutes. Remove the cover, stir in the

herbs, and cook until most of the liquid has evaporated, about 3 minutes more.

2. Transfer to a serving bowl, let cool to room temperature, then chill in the refrigerator until ready to serve. It will keep for up to 2 weeks.

Gingered Peach Chutney: Substitute 4 large, ripe yet firm peaches, peeled, pitted, and cut into rough ½-inch dice, for the mangoes. Omit the cilantro.

Bread and Butter Pickles

MAKES 3 PINTS Pickling, preserving, and canning used to be common practices in late nineteenth-century America. It allowed people to enjoy the fruits (and vegetables) of their labor, particularly during the off-season, when gardens were dormant and fresh produce was a mere memory until springtime arrived again. By the early twentieth century, commercial canning became a big business and, with the advent of the freezer, home canning and preserving declined rapidly. Still, there was always someone who could be found diligently "putting up" their tomatoes for the winter or pick-

ling their cucumbers for the neighbors, keeping the tradition alive.

Today, with the return to comfort food, coupled with a concern about preservatives and chemical additives, people are once again beginning to experience the joy of making their own pickles, preserves, and canned goods. Local farmers' markets and food fairs will usually provide the venue for numerous homemade, sweetly decorated jars of strawberry preserves, pickled vegetables, and even pasta sauces.

Although I am not an avid preserver, I do happen to love bread and butter pickles, and so I started to make my own with a certain regularity. When I was growing up, my grandmother and I used to pickle peppers, and with this knowledge and technique, I taught myself to make these delicious cucumber delights. The best part is that the traditional method of carefully processing jars and sealing the contents is unnecessary here, as these pickles require only a brief period under refrigeration and are meant to be eaten within a couple of weeks. Obviously, without the usual boiling and sealing, you can't store these on the shelf for eating months later. But, if you happen to be an expe-

(continued on page 264)

Making Pickles
A Mindful Exercise for a Grateful Recovery

Many years ago, I first heard the so-called pickle theory of addiction and, being that it was loosely related to food, I never forgot the story. It is said that, once we alcoholics and addicts go from being cucumbers to pickles, there is no turning back. Since our brain chemistry has been forever changed from the incessant ingestion of alcohol and chemicals, just as one cannot return a cucumber to its normal state, we cannot return to a normal drinking life. You can squeeze all the vinegar out, soak them with water, bake them in the sun, whatever you think will work, but you will never again have the cucumber you started with. It is probably the example I give most when trying to explain to those who do not understand the necessity of abstinence, why alcohol is not an option for me any longer. I am forever changed. I am forever a "pickle."

"Pickled" is, of course, just one of the many euphemistic ways we describe drunkenness, but it struck me that this particular one might provide a great reminder for those of us who, in moments of wishful thinking, hope against hope to drink normally once again, if indeed we ever did. In reality, addiction specialists believe that our disease actually progresses quietly during abstinence, so that if we were to "pick up" again, not only would we pick up where we left off, we also would rapidly find ourselves further down the abyss of addiction than we could have possibly imagined. People who have slipped into a full-blown relapse after years of abstinence can attest to this phenomenon, with the pickle theory, no doubt, weighing heavily on their minds.

Early on in my recovery, I discovered a meditation technique called mindfulness. Based on Buddhist practices, being "mindful," or keeping your thoughts in the present moment, can help in keeping you focused and destressed. It is not unlike the "one day at a time" philosophy that we know so well and has become an additional valuable tool for many who struggle to stay sober during the early phases of recovery. It also provides enormous insight into the way we approach our lives, while teaching us to appreciate what we have, here and now, at this moment.

Mindful cooking, a common practice in Buddhist temples, in which the state of mind and spiritual awareness of the cook are as important as the food he or she is preparing for the others, is the application of this technique in the kitchen. It can be demonstrated in as simple a practice as appreciating the taste and texture of a raisin or the patient attention given to a pot of steaming rice. It is an exercise meant to create a greater understanding—an understanding of the universe as a whole and how you, at this moment, and even the food you are preparing and eating, are part of that greater whole. Where you are, what you have become, and what you are doing at this moment are exactly where you need to be.

What does all this have to do with pickles and cucumbers? Every summer when my local farmer's market is in full swing, I will purchase several pounds of firm, solid, and crispy cucumbers, take them home, and turn them into pickles. While I make them, I think about the process—in a short time, they will be bread and butter pickles. Forever. Then I pack them up and give them out to all my friends to enjoy, keeping, of course, one jar for myself. And every time I bite into one, I smile—because I am mindful that, although these once fresh and crispy cucumbers have now become pickles, for the here and now, in this moment, they are delicious, perfect, and just as they should be.

(continued from page 262)

rienced canner, you can use this recipe to preserve the pickles in the traditional, longer-lasting way. For this technique, however, I have found that empty marinara sauce jars and their screw-top lids, when run through the dishwasher on a high heat wash-and-dry setting, are excellent containers to use, while ending up adequately sterilized for our purposes.

The smaller Kirby cucumbers are ideal for pickling, because they do not have large and bitter seeds, as do the more common mature varieties. You will recognize them as the cucumbers used for whole dill pickles by their shape and size. Unwaxed, they do not require peeling, just like their English hothouse cousin, which could also be used here, although its cost is normally prohibitive in comparison. Having said that, I have tasted some delicious bread and butters made from thinly shaved common cucumbers, although they are less popularly used.

Enjoy making and eating these sweet and crisp complements to sandwiches, salads, and meats. They are sure to become an annually anticipated treat in your house.

2 pounds Kirby cucumbers, washed well and cut into ¼-inch-thick rounds (about 8 cups)
½ pound Bermuda, Spanish, or Vidalia onions, peeled, halved, and thinly sliced into half moons (2 to 3 cups)
¼ cup coarse kosher salt
Ice cubes
2 cups cider vinegar
1½ cups sugar
1 tablespoon yellow mustard seeds
1 teaspoon turmeric
1 teaspoon celery seeds
1 teaspoon black peppercorns
½ teaspoon ground ginger

1. In a large mixing bowl, combine the cucumbers, onions, and salt, toss well to coat, and cover the surface with ice cubes. Let stand for 2 hours, then drain, rinse well under cold running water, and drain again.

2. In a large stainless steel pot, combine the remaining ingredients over medium heat, bring to a boil, and cook, stirring a few times, until the sugar has dissolved. Add the drained cucumbers and onions, stir well, and return to a boil, cooking for 1 to 2 minutes. Remove from the heat and let stand for 10 minutes, gently stirring once or twice.

3. Using a slotted spoon, distribute the cucumbers and onions among three 1-pint clean jars with lids. Pour the syrup, including the spices, into each jar, leaving ¼ to ½ inch of space below the top. Put on the lids and allow to cool somewhat before transferring to the refrigerator.

4. Keep in the refrigerator for at least 10 days before opening. Every few days, gently shake the jars to distribute the spices. Once opened, eat within 2 weeks. Unopened, you many store them in the refrigerator up to 1 month.

8 *Cozy Conclusions*

Desserts to Live For

Comfort food doesn't always appear as the main course. In fact, many would argue that the best comfort food arrives after the entrée. Homemade desserts like puddings, pies, and cobblers often remind us of an era when life was less stressful and people took more time to prepare a sweet conclusion to every meal. Fresh seasonal fruit became delicious homemade pies in the hands of grandma, or leftover rice was transformed into a warm creamy dessert and topped with a dollop of real whipped cream. Classic, homemade cakes—from devil's food to pound cake—sat on the kitchen table ready for the nearest appetite, while fruit and frozen desserts provided sweet refreshment when temperatures soared.

Restaurant chefs have picked up on this trend by offering us generous portions of homey desserts such as bread puddings and warm chocolate cake. But part of the delight in these dishes is the actual watching and anticipation of the final product and, unfortunately, most restaurants cannot supply that kind of comfort. Without Aunt Sally to serve the warm peach cobbler, a restaurant version can easily lack the "soul" it was intended to have. Too often, a pretty presentation replaces the comfort of rustic familiarity. No one can truly recreate that feeling, but you can come awfully close in your own kitchen.

These recipes offer a comforting "feel good" sensation, not just in the tasting, but in the entire process of becoming. Enjoying the making, as well as the eating, of these dishes can do wonders for the healing process and help us to get back in touch with our inner child who so enjoyed the anticipation of simple pleasures. Since recovery, like addiction, is a family affair, preparing and eating delicious desserts together are a way of helping to heal the collective spirit. Although some of the recipes are too luxuriously rich to be indulged in every night, when following a balanced and healthy diet, they can certainly be enjoyed by everyone on occasion. Remember that balance is something we are striving for in our lives at this time and that includes having one slice of cake, not three! Still, you will find many dessert recipes in this chapter that allow you to leave nearly all your guilt behind, as we begin to incorporate some healthier ingredients and techniques. Enjoy these when a sweet tooth after dinner requires a bit of attention.

I have tried to include as many "comfort" desserts as I can to cover every taste and regional background. If you don't find what you're looking for here, ask your aunt for that strudel recipe you used to love or grandma for the secret she always used in making her fresh fruit pies. Bring back the joy of dessert making and baking into your life and you will be well on your way to healing your spirit, as well as your mind and body.

Puddings, Pies, and Cobblers

Some of the most comforting desserts we know fall into the category of puddings, pies, and cob-blers. Traditional dishes such as these can conjure up all kinds of good memories and homemade pleasures, from butterscotch pudding to peach cobbler.

Puddings, whether served warm or chilled, usually make us think of the more common varieties such as chocolate, vanilla, or butterscotch. But actually a lot of other desserts are technically called puddings, many of which are made from fruit, bread, rice, or other grains. Surprisingly, some savory dishes are also referred to by this name, such as Yorkshire pudding or black pudding (the Irish name for blood sausage, made from oatmeal, suet, and pig's blood). In fact, originally the English word "pudding" meant sausage, from the French word *boudin*, and later was used to describe anything boiled or steamed in a sausage-shaped bag. Eventually, pudding came to mean food of soft consistency and in England it is now used to refer to any type of dessert, from crumbles to cakes to ice creams. In this chapter you will find familiar classic sweet puddings from Cinnamon Bread Pudding (next page) to Easy Lemon Meringue Pudding Cups (page 270), a fun cross between a pudding and pie.

Similarly, pies have also been used to describe both sweet and savory dishes, generally those that have a bottom crust and sometimes a top crust. With regard to piecrust making, for the most part, I have recommended using purchased premade piecrusts, either frozen or refrigerated (in the case of traditional dough) or premolded from crackers or crumbs (available in the bakery aisle of your supermarket). Although many of these products contain partially hydrogenated oils, something I recommend avoiding, the ease of preparation they provide at this stage of our baking outweighs somewhat their unhealthy characteristics. For those who would like to venture into piecrust making, the whole wheat recipe accompanying Sun-Dried Tomato and Pepper Jack Quiche (page 349) will be perfect to use for the recipes in this section. Happily, all of the pies are extremely easy to make, not to mention delicious to eat.

Cobblers, crumbles, buckles, grunts, and slumps are primarily baked fruit desserts with a top crust of some sort, from biscuits to streusel-like crumbs. They may indeed be the true essence of American comfort food desserts, rustic in appearance, warm and sweet from the oven, and doubly delicious topped with ice cream or whipped cream. Enjoy baking and eating these classic desserts, while making them a part of your family tradition.

Cinnamon Bread Pudding

MAKES 6 SERVINGS Warm bread pudding with a scoop of ice cream or a spoonful of whipped cream can be wonderfully comforting and delicious. Originally, bread puddings utilized leftover stale bread to make an inexpensive, yet hearty, dessert. Nowadays, chefs will often bake a specific type of bread to use in the pudding, such as sweet challah or Italian panettone. Here, regular store-bought sliced cinnamon bread fills in nicely and adds the right amount of sugar and spice to the outcome. You can add raisins or fruit, or use a cinnamon raisin loaf or any other type of "breakfast" bread normally used for toasting. There are many on the market these days, from banana nut to maple flavored.

Bread pudding keeps extremely well in the refrigerator and can be quickly warmed in the oven or microwave to replicate a "just-baked" presentation. A good quality vanilla ice cream is the usual accompaniment, while sweetened whipped cream is also a popular topping.

1 loaf sliced cinnamon or cinnamon raisin bread
4 large eggs
2 cups milk

1 cup heavy cream
¾ cup sugar
1 teaspoon ground cinnamon

1. Preheat the oven to 350 degrees. Lightly butter a 9 x 13-inch glass baking dish or nonstick baking pan.

2. Using a serrated bread knife, cut the slices of bread into ½-inch cubes. You can stack 4 or 5 slices at a time and cut through the pile at once. Transfer to a large mixing bowl and set aside.

3. Whisk together the eggs, milk, heavy cream, sugar, and cinnamon in another large mixing bowl until well combined, then pour over the bread cubes. Stir lightly and let soak for 10 minutes, allowing the bread to absorb most of the liquid.

4. Transfer this mixture to the prepared baking dish, smooth out the surface, and bake until the top is lightly golden and a toothpick inserted in the middle comes out clean, 30 to 40 minutes. Let rest for 10 to 15 minutes before cutting and serving.

Apple Cinnamon Bread Pudding: Before baking, add to the mixture 2 Golden Delicious apples that have been peeled, cored, sliced, and sautéed in 1 tablespoon unsalted butter and 1 teaspoon sugar in a large skillet over medium heat until fork tender.

Cherry Vanilla Bread Pudding: Use a loaf of buttermilk or country white sliced bread in place of the cinnamon bread. Increase the sugar to 1 cup. Use vanilla sugar (see page 168) or add 1 tablespoon nonalcohol vanilla extract. Omit the cinnamon and add a dash of nutmeg. Drain a 15-ounce can of pitted cherries and stir into the mixture before baking.

Chocolate Chocolate Chip Bread Pudding: Use a loaf of country white sliced bread instead of the cinnamon bread. Substitute purchased chocolate milk or chocolate soymilk for the regular milk and reduce the sugar to ½ cup. Stir in ¾ cup mini semisweet chocolate chips just before baking.

Recovery Note: Beware that many restaurants often add bourbon or rum to bread pudding, either in the mix or in an accompanying sauce. If the latter is the case, ask them to "hold the sauce" and bring some whipped cream instead.

Granny Smith Brown Betty

MAKES 6 SERVINGS Here's another rustic baked dessert that makes use of bread, this time the crumbs. Classic brown betty, always a comforting end to a meal, particularly when hot from the oven and drizzled with the traditional hard sauce, may just be the oldest American dessert, according to culinary historians. Here I use the crisp and tart Granny Smith apple as a base, although other types, such as Red or Golden Delicious, would work well too. I particularly like the taste of ginger here and have added crushed gingersnaps to the fresh bread crumbs for even more flavor.

Classic brown betty recipes will sometimes call for sherry as a moistener, but a little apple juice will be just fine as a replacement. Serve hot with lemon hard sauce or a drizzle of cream.

BROWN BETTY

3 cups fresh bread crumbs

1 cup crushed gingersnaps

½ cup (1 stick) unsalted butter, melted

4 Granny Smith apples, peeled, cored, and thinly sliced

½ cup firmly packed dark brown sugar

1 teaspoon ground ginger

1 teaspoon ground cinnamon

2 tablespoons apple juice

LEMON HARD SAUCE

1½ cups confectioners' sugar

½ cup (1 stick) unsalted butter, softened

2 tablespoons fresh lemon juice

1 teaspoon grated lemon rind

1. Preheat the oven to 375 degrees. Lightly butter a 9-inch square baking dish.

2. To make the brown betty, combine the bread crumbs, gingersnaps, and melted butter in a medium-size mixing bowl and stir well to combine. In a large mixing bowl, combine the apples, brown sugar, ginger, and cinnamon and toss to coat.

3. Begin assembling by spreading one-third of the crumb mixture over the bottom of the baking dish and topping with half of the apple mixture. Sprinkle 1 tablespoon of the apple juice over the apple layer and continue layering as directed above, finishing with a final layer of bread crumbs.

4. Cover tightly with a sheet of aluminum foil and bake for 30 minutes. Remove the foil and bake until the top is golden and crisp, a further 30 minutes. Remove from the oven and let cool at least 10 minutes before serving.

5. While the brown betty is baking, make the hard sauce by combining the ingredients in a small mixing bowl and stirring until smooth. Cover and refrigerate, bringing to room temperature just before serving.

6. To serve, spoon the still hot brown betty into a serving dish and top with 1 tablespoon of the hard sauce.

Recovery Note: Traditional hard sauce might as well be called brandy sauce, as it is more often than not made with this distilled liquor. Check when buying jars of ready-made hard sauce at specialty food stores and ask when it appears on the dessert menu at restaurants.

Uncle Bill's Rice Pudding

MAKES 6 SERVINGS Rice pudding is definitely on everyone's list of comfort food, whether served slightly warm or perfectly chilled. Leftover rice is a great stand-in and saves loads of time in the preparation. Otherwise, cook up a small amount of rice beforehand and allow to cool somewhat before using. My Uncle Bill was a cook in the army, where I am sure there was plenty of leftover rice to utilize. Desserts, particularly puddings, were his specialty. His secret was to separate the eggs for a light and creamy result. This is his classic recipe, which we've been making in our family for years, although I've added the super fragrant vanilla bean for additional flavor. Cut a long slit down half a vanilla bean pod to open it up and use a paring knife to scrape the little seeds into the saucepan. You can also plop the scraped pod into the saucepan for even more intense vanilla flavor, but remember to remove it before adding the eggs. And be sure to dry out the pod and use it to make vanilla sugar (page 168) for future baking.

These days, chefs make rice pudding with basmati rice, brown rice, and even "risotto" versions with Arborio rice. I like the old-fashioned version below, but you can experiment with other types of rice if you like. Traditionally, plump raisins and cinnamon are the usual additions. Try adding other dried fruit, such as cranberries or cherries. For an added cinnamon sensation, use the new cinnamon-flavored raisins that are now available. Any way you serve it, rice pudding is truly comfort in a bowl.

> 2 cups whole milk
> ⅓ cup sugar
> ½ cup Thompson seedless or golden raisins (optional)
> ¼ teaspoon ground cinnamon, plus more for sprinkling
> ½ vanilla bean pod, slit open
> 3 cups cooked white long-grain rice
> 2 large eggs, separated
> 1 tablespoon unsalted butter

1. In a medium-size saucepan, combine 1½ cups of the milk, the sugar, raisins, if using, and cinnamon, then scrape the seeds from the vanilla bean into the mixture, add the pod itself, and bring to a simmer over medium heat, stirring often. Stir in the cooked rice, reduce the heat to medium-low, and cook slowly until somewhat thickened and creamy, about 15 minutes, being careful not to scorch the bottom of the pot by reducing the heat to low, if necessary.

2. Whisk together the egg yolks and the remaining ½ cup milk in a small mixing bowl. In a medium-size mixing bowl, beat the egg whites with an electric mixer until stiff peaks form.

3. Remove the vanilla pod from the rice mixture, if necessary. While stirring constantly, slowly add the beaten yolk mixture and butter to the saucepan and cook over very low heat, continuing to stir, for 2 minutes. Remove from the heat, add the beaten egg whites, and fold in gently with a rubber spatula to blend. Pour into individual pudding dishes or one large casserole and sprinkle lightly with cinnamon. Serve warm or chilled.

Chef's Note: If vanilla bean pods are not handy, use the same amount of vanilla sugar in place of the regular sugar, or add 2 teaspoons nonalcohol vanilla extract.

Old-Fashioned Butterscotch Pudding

MAKES 6 SERVINGS My favorite childhood pudding was butterscotch, the one my mother made from the box. (Yes, I admit it!) I loved to eat it still warm and usually helped clean up by licking the spoon and scraping the bottom of the pot. As an adult, I have enjoyed making and eating a traditional homemade butterscotch pudding, wonderfully creamy and, dare I say, even tastier than my childhood favorite. Butterscotch sauce has always been a favorite of mine as well, and here the first step results in a super delicious one, which can be used as a topping for ice cream, bread pudding, brown betty, or even apple pie. Consider making just this part of the recipe when you feel like enjoying a little warm butterscotch sauce.

Here we make use of that old kitchen staple, the double boiler. If you don't happen to have one, you can easily rig one up by placing a medium-size stainless steel bowl over a pot of simmering water. Just be sure that the bowl does not touch the water, as too much heat can cause burning and scorching. I like to serve this warm with a dollop of whipped cream and some dark chocolate shavings.

BUTTERSCOTCH SAUCE
1½ cups firmly packed light brown sugar
½ cup (1 stick) unsalted butter
1 cup heavy cream, warmed

PUDDING
2½ cups milk (whole, 2 percent, or 1 percent)
3 large egg yolks
¼ cup cornstarch
Pinch of salt

1. To make the butterscotch sauce, combine the brown sugar and butter in a medium-size saucepan over medium heat. Stir while the butter melts and continue to cook, stirring occasionally, until bubbly and smooth, 5 to 10 minutes. When the sugar mixture is ready (you will smell a distinct fragrance of caramel), remove from the heat and slowly add the warm cream, being careful not to splatter yourself, stirring constantly until well combined. Set aside.

2. To make the pudding, in the top of a double boiler over simmering water, whisk together the milk, egg yolks, cornstarch, and salt until warm to the touch. Add the butterscotch sauce, whisking

constantly, and cook until the pudding begins to thicken and is just boiling, about 10 minutes.

3. Remove the pan from the double boiler and pour the pudding into a dessert bowl or individual custard dishes or ramekins. Cover with plastic wrap to prevent a skin from forming or leave uncovered. Serve warm or chilled.

Easy Lemon Meringue Pudding Cups

MAKES 6 SERVINGS If you like classic lemon meringue pie, you will love these little pudding cups, which closely resemble the real thing. They're easy to make and delicious to eat, and you'll find yourself whipping them up for dessert on a regular basis. Two ingredients from childhood make an appearance in this recipe, graham crackers and Marshmallow Fluff. I don't know any kid—big or small—who doesn't enjoy this sweet combination.

In essence, this tangy filling is just another type of cornstarch pudding, without the milk, enhanced with the flavor of fresh lemon zest and juice. Make it ahead of time to give it a chance to cool before assembling the cups. Be sure to use clear glass custard cups in order to see the nicely layered effect.

1½ cups plus 1 tablespoon sugar
⅓ cup cornstarch
1½ cups water
3 large egg yolks, slightly beaten
3 tablespoons unsalted butter, softened
¼ cup fresh lemon juice
Grated rind of 1 medium-size lemon
¾ cup graham cracker crumbs (about 10 crackers crushed)
3 tablespoons unsalted butter, melted
1¼ cups marshmallow creme (such as Marshmallow Fluff)
2 tablespoons cold water

(continued on page 272)

Minute Tapioca Parfaits

Quick and Comfy Pudding Desserts

Years ago, every kitchen pantry had a box of minute tapioca lurking somewhere, ready for instant pudding making. Most cooks just followed the recipe on the box and whipped up a quick dessert when there was an oversupply of milk in the fridge. In addition to instant versions, pearl tapioca is also available in its regular form, requiring an overnight soak before turning into classic tapioca pudding. Many cooks prefer this to the minute variety, as it produces larger, "pearly" results. Tapioca, extracted from the root of the cassava plant, is also made into flour and is useful as a thickening agent in pies and soups, much as cornstarch is often used. This is one of the reasons that tapioca is so well suited to pudding making.

Today, tapioca pudding is readily available in tubs, although the consistency is a bit different from that of homemade, resembling more a vanilla pudding than a light custard. Still, it can be readily transformed into parfaits with the addition of plain or macerated fruit (see page 61) or fruit preserves, an excellent way to add nutrition and fiber to your diet while enjoying a sweet conclusion. If you would like to make your tapioca from scratch, just follow the recipe on the box, allow it to cool, and use it to create your layered tapioca parfait. Here are some ideas to get you started.

If your old wine glasses no longer pose a trigger for you, they can be the perfect receptacle for a layered pudding parfait. Otherwise, water goblets or ice cream sundae glasses are great to use. When layering, shoot for at least four tiers to create interest. And be sure to provide long spoons for eating (like sundae or iced tea spoons), if your parfait is particularly tall!

To sweeten up fresh-cut strawberries, mix in a little strawberry jam or preserves and a touch of water to create a glazed effect and use this to layer with your tapioca. Delicate raspberries and blackberries do best on their own, sprinkled throughout, although a spoonful of raspberry preserves in the middle of the parfait will provide a nice sweet surprise. Drained canned cherries would also make a good addition.

Experiment with less common fruits such as fresh figs, kiwis, starfruit, or prickly pears, for a colorful and healthy presentation. Place the cut up or sliced fruit in the glass facing out while spooning in the tapioca for a dramatic display. Sweet ripe bananas make an excellent partner for tapioca. Make a mock banana split by inserting long slices of banana into the tapioca pudding and topping with a little strawberry syrup.

Most parfaits have a final flourish of whipped cream and even a maraschino cherry. For something different, top instead with a dollop of vanilla yogurt and a sprinkling of your favorite granola. Finish with a ripe, long-stem Bing cherry.

(continued from page 270)

1. In a medium-size saucepan, combine 1½ cups of the sugar, the cornstarch, and water and cook, stirring constantly, over medium-high heat, until thickened and bubbly. Continue to stir and cook for 1 minute. Remove from the heat.

2. Have ready the beaten eggs in a small mixing bowl. Slowly pour half the cooked sugar mixture into the eggs, stirring constantly to combine. Pour the egg mixture back into the saucepan, return to the heat, and boil, stirring constantly, for 1 minute. Remove from the heat, add the butter, lemon juice, and grated rind, and stir until smooth. Transfer to a clean bowl, let cool somewhat, then refrigerate, covered, until cool.

3. In a small mixing bowl, combine the graham cracker crumbs, the remaining 1 tablespoon sugar, and the melted butter. Stir with a fork until moistened and set aside. in another small bowl, mix together the Fluff and water until smooth.

4. To assemble the pudding cups, place 1 tablespoon of the crumb mixture in the bottom of each custard cup, lightly pressing down. Distribute half of the lemon filling over the crumbs, spread to the edges, and top each with 1 tablespoon of Fluff, spreading evenly. Sprinkle the remaining crumbs over the marshmallow layer, distribute the remaining lemon filling, and top each with 2 tablespoons of Fluff. Use the back of a spoon to decoratively create meringue-like peaks. Refrigerate for at least 30 minutes before serving.

Easy Key Lime Meringue Pudding Cups:
Substitute Key limes, or regular limes, for the lemon juice and grated rind. You may add a few drops of green food coloring to the filling at the end of cooking to create a lime green color, if desired.

Mom's Deep Dish Apple Crumb Pie

MAKES ONE 9-INCH DEEP-DISH PIE; 8 SERVINGS   The wonderful aroma of an apple pie baking in the oven is sometimes enough to conjure up comforting memories for anyone. Served warm "à la mode" or with a sliver of sharp cheddar cheese, a truly good apple pie is perhaps the definition of comfort food.

For easy, no-sweat baking, I am all for utilizing prepared piecrusts. I have found that refrigerated crusts that you mold yourself into a pie pan are better than frozen crusts, which tend to crack easily, but either one is fine here. This shortcut takes a lot of the tension and stress away from home pie baking. And although these types of products *do* contain some undesirable fats, for an occasional pie, especially at this time of our recovery, they often encourage us to take that sometimes scary leap into the unfamiliar world of baking. If, however, your trepidation is minimal, Chapter Ten offers a recipe for a whole wheat piecrust (page 349) that works beautifully here.

Granny Smith is usually the apple of choice for pie baking, as it holds up nicely without becoming too soft and mushy. However, during the autumn season, there are numerous apple varieties that could also be used, including Cortland, Braeburn, Empire, and Gala. In general, the Red Delicious and Macintosh eating apples are not suited for pies. Usually, the sign above the apple display in your supermarket will explain the difference between the varieties they carry, recommending those that are best for eating or baking. Try them out and see which you like best.

Taking the few extra minutes to layer your apple slices, rather than dumping them into the pie shell, will result in a lovely slice of pie that holds together better and looks professional. Try sprinkling some golden raisins or dried cranberries into the filling for a delicious variation.

1 frozen deep-dish piecrust, thawed,
    or 1 unbaked piecrust in a 9-inch deep-dish
    pie pan

FILLING

8 Granny Smith apples, peeled, cored, and
    cut into ¼-inch-thick slices

⅔ cup sugar

1 teaspoon fresh lemon juice

1 teaspoon ground cinnamon

1 tablespoon all-purpose flour

CRUMB TOPPING

1 cup all-purpose flour

½ cup sugar

½ cup (1 stick) unsalted butter, softened

¼ teaspoon ground cinnamon

1. Preheat the oven to 375 degrees. Have the unbaked piecrust ready for filling.

2. To make the filling, in a large mixing bowl toss the apple slices with the sugar, lemon juice, cinnamon, and flour until evenly coated.

3. To make the crumb topping, combine the ingredients in a medium-size mixing bowl with your fingers or a fork to resemble a coarse meal.

4. Begin assembling the pie by layering the apple slices in the prepared piecrust in a circular pattern. Continue layering until all the slices have been used and the filling forms a small mound in the middle. Do not worry that it is way above the edge of the crust, as the apples will cook down considerably. Now, take the crumb topping and, using a handful at a time, press the mixture firmly onto the apple filling, being sure to cover any gaps.

5. Bake for 50 minutes to 1 hour on the center rack of the oven. You may want to place a baking sheet on the rack below to catch any drips. The pie is done when the topping is golden and a fork inserted in the center of the apples can be removed easily. If the edges of the crust begin to brown too much before the pie is done, cover them loosely with aluminum foil to protect from burning. Let

cool at room temperature for at least 1 hour before slicing, so that the juices will not weep out. Serve warm or chilled.

Chef's Note: *For a wonderfully fragrant pie, substitute vanilla sugar (page 168) for the regular sugar in the filling.*

Easy Banana Cream Pie

MAKES ONE 9-INCH PIE; 8 SERVINGS Cream pies are a hallmark of American baking and belong on any comfort food list. However, diner versions tend to be mile-high servings of sugar and saturated fat. Here, the healthy vitamin C- and potassium-packed banana takes center stage instead, resulting in a satisfyingly sweet pie without too much guilt.

Making use of commercially prepared piecrusts, like the graham cracker crust here, helps to speed up the process. There are also ready-made cookie crumb crusts available to use and a vanilla or shortbread version would be a delicious complement to the bananas in this recipe.

A quick cornstarch pudding filling is really all we need to prepare, while a little sweetened whipped cream will top this pie off in style. Be sure to allow your pie ample time to chill before slicing.

1 ready-made 9-inch graham cracker crumb crust

FILLING

⅔ cup granulated sugar or substitute vanilla sugar
    (see page 168) and omit the vanilla extract

⅓ cup cornstarch

Pinch of salt

3 cups milk (whole or 2 percent)

2 large egg yolks, slightly beaten

2 teaspoons unsalted butter

2 teaspoons nonalcohol vanilla extract

3 medium-size ripe bananas

½ cup heavy or whipping cream

1 tablespoon confectioners' sugar

1. To make the filling, in a medium-size saucepan, combine the granulated or vanilla sugar, cornstarch, and salt. Slowly whisk in the milk and, over medium heat, cook, stirring constantly, until bubbly and thickened. In a small mixing bowl, have ready the beaten egg yolks. Slowly stir half of the hot milk mixture into the yolks, combine well, then return this to the saucepan, whisking constantly, and bring to a low boil. Cook for 1 minute, then remove from the heat. Immediately add the butter and vanilla (if using) and stir well. Transfer to a clean bowl, allow to cool somewhat, then cover and refrigerate until chilled but not set.

2. When ready to assemble the pie, peel the bananas and cut into ¼-inch-thick slices. Line the bottom of the crumb crust with half of the sliced bananas and spoon half of the filling over them, spreading evenly. Repeat with the remaining bananas and filling.

3. To make the topping, in a small mixing bowl with an electric mixer, beat the cream and confectioners' sugar together until soft peaks form. Spoon the whipped cream topping over the pie filling and spread decoratively. Chill at least 1 hour before serving.

Strawberry Banana Cream Pie: Replace half the bananas with 1 cup hulled and sliced strawberries and layer them together. Decorate the top with 8 to 10 whole small or medium-size strawberries and serve with a drizzle of strawberry syrup.

Black Bottom Banana Cream Pie: Use a ready-made 9-inch chocolate wafer crumb piecrust or make your own by combining 1½ cups crushed chocolate wafers and ⅓ cup melted unsalted butter. Press evenly into the bottom and sides of the pie pan and chill in the refrigerator for

30 minutes. In a small heavy saucepan, combine 4 ounces dark or bittersweet chocolate, ¼ cup heavy cream, and 2 tablespoons unsalted butter and stir together over low heat until the chocolate and butter have melted and the mixture is smooth. Pour all but 2 tablespoons of the chocolate into the bottom of the crust, spread evenly, and chill for 15 minutes. Now layer half the bananas, pressing them gently into the soft chocolate layer. Continue layering as directed above, with the filling and bananas, and top with the whipped cream. Use the remaining warm chocolate to decorate the top by dipping a fork into the mixture and shaking it over the top of the pie in a zigzag fashion. Chill well before serving.

Chef's Note: *To make your own graham cracker crust, mix together 1½ cups crumbs (from about 20 crackers); ¼ cup sugar; 5 tablespoons unsalted butter, melted; and a pinch of salt. Press the mixture firmly into the bottom and up the side of a 9-inch pie pan and chill for 10 minutes before filling. For a firmer crust, bake in a preheated 375 degree oven for 6 to 8 minutes.*

Triple-Chocolate Pecan Pie

MAKES ONE 9-INCH PIE; 10 SERVINGS Even though I happen to love both pecan pie and chocolate, I always thought this to be an odd combination until I finally tried it. Really a chocolate *chip* pecan pie, since the filling itself is more like a traditional pecan pie with the chips oozing throughout, this pie will satisfy any sweet or chocolate craving you may experience, but try to reserve it for dessert (if you can) and cut a small sliver when serving—it's very rich.

Once again, using a prepared piecrust will make this recipe easier. For the pecans, rather than buy chopped pieces, purchase the halves, then break them roughly into large pieces, as we are after a coarse consistency. Chocolate chips will work nicely, although a combination of chunks and chips will create a pie with varied texture and visual appeal. If the edges of the piecrust begin to brown too quickly before the filling is set, you can cover them loosely with a sheet of aluminum foil that has a circle cut out of the middle to expose the filling. Pecan pie of any type should be served at room temperature, or briefly warmed by the slice in the microwave, and topped with whipped cream.

1¼ cups pecan halves, broken
¼ cup *each* semisweet, milk, and white chocolate chips, chunks, or ¼-inch pieces
One 9-inch frozen piecrust, thawed, or 1 ready-made unbaked piecrust in a 9-inch pie pan
3 large eggs
1 cup light corn syrup
1 cup firmly packed dark brown sugar
⅓ cup unsalted butter, melted
Pinch of salt

1. Preheat the oven to 350 degrees. Sprinkle 1 cup of the pecans and half the chocolate over the bottom of the prepared piecrust and set aside.

2. In a medium-size mixing bowl, beat the eggs until well combined. Add the corn syrup, brown sugar, melted butter, and salt and continue to beat until smooth, 1 to 2 minutes. Pour the mixture into the piecrust and sprinkle the remaining ½ cup pecans and chocolate over the top.

3. Bake on the center rack of the oven until the filling is set and the top is golden, about 1 hour. Test by inserting a sharp knife in the center; it should come out clean, except for bits of melted chocolate. Let cool on a wire rack and serve at room temperature.

Sour Cream Pumpkin Pie with Gingersnap Crust

MAKES ONE 9-INCH DEEP DISH PIE; 8 SERVINGS This recipe brings together all the flavor of a traditional pumpkin pie with the lightness of a chiffon-style pie. When I lived in England, I introduced my British friends to this version of pumpkin pie at Thanksgiving time, since most of them who had tasted pumpkin pie in the States found it too heavy, dense, and, consequently, unappealing. They were won over by this recipe and were delighted to eat it any time of year! Pumpkin is high in antioxidants and should be enjoyed a lot more frequently than once a year.

Once again, cookie crumbs, this time from gingersnaps, provide a quick and easy crust. The sharpness of the gingersnaps is a beautiful complement to the pumpkin filling, all tied together with a fragrant array of aromatic spices. Surprise everyone with this delightful and delicious dessert.

GINGERSNAP CRUST
1½ cups crushed gingersnaps (about 24 cookies)
⅓ cup unsalted butter, melted

FILLING
One 16-ounce can unsweetened pumpkin puree (about 2 cups)
2 large eggs, separated
¾ cup sugar
1 cup reduced-fat sour cream
1 teaspoon ground cinnamon
1 teaspoon ground ginger
¼ teaspoon *each* ground nutmeg, ground cloves, and salt

1. To make the crust, combine the cookie crumbs and butter in a small mixing bowl. Stir with a fork to moisten and press the mixture firmly, with your fingertips, into the bottom and sides of a 9-inch deep-dish pie pan. Refrigerate until ready to use.

2. Preheat the oven to 350 degrees. To make the filling, beat together the pumpkin, egg yolks, sugar, sour cream, spices, and salt in a medium-size mixing bowl until well combined. Wash and dry the beaters and, in another medium-size bowl, beat the egg whites until they form stiff peaks. Gently fold the beaten egg whites into the pumpkin mixture with a rubber spatula. (A few streaks of egg white are okay.)

3. Pour the filling into the chilled piecrust and bake on the center rack of the oven for 1 hour and 10 minutes. Test to see if a knife inserted in the middle of the pie comes out clean. If not, return to the oven and bake until the filling is set, about another 10 minutes. Let cool on a wire rack, then refrigerate. Serve well chilled.

Recovery Note: In many recipes, pumpkin pie and bourbon are common bedfellows, probably a direct result of "southern comfort" cooking influences. Watch when ordering out and be mindful of the accompanying whipped cream, which is often spiked with a potent potable.

Roasted Peach and Cinnamon Sugar Cobbler

MAKES 4 TO 6 SERVINGS Fruit cobblers, crisps, and crumbles are definitely comfy desserts, especially in the summer. Peaches at the height of their season are traditionally the fruit of choice, although berries, apples, pears, and rhubarb are marvelous alternatives. Here the classic peach cobbler gets an interesting twist by roasting the peaches first, which results in a naturally sweeter taste, as well as a beautiful rosy hue on the fruit itself.

Classic cobbler biscuit topping can be rolled out and laid flat on top of the fruit (creating a bumpy or "cobbled" look) or is sometimes dropped by spoonfuls (when less firm) over the fruit mixture. Here, we quickly roll out the cinnamon sugar biscuit to cover the surface of the peaches, which helps to prevent too much of the delicious liquid from evaporating. Try this recipe with nectarines when they are in season, for a change of pace.

FRUIT MIXTURE
- 2 pounds ripe peaches
- 2 teaspoons canola oil
- ½ cup granulated sugar, or more to taste
- 1 tablespoon cornstarch
- ½ cup water
- Dash of ground cinnamon
- Dash of ground nutmeg
- 1 tablespoon unsalted butter, cut into pieces

BISCUIT TOPPING
- 1½ cups all-purpose flour
- ¼ cup granulated sugar
- 1½ teaspoons baking powder
- 1 teaspoon baking soda
- 1 teaspoon salt
- ¼ teaspoon ground cinnamon
- 3 tablespoons cold unsalted butter, diced
- ⅔ cup buttermilk
- 1 tablespoon cinnamon sugar (page 240)

1. Preheat the oven to 400 degrees. To prepare the fruit, coat the peaches lightly with the canola oil and place in a roasting pan. Roast for 45 minutes, occasionally shaking the pan to brown all the sides of the peaches. Remove from the oven and let cool until easily handled. Leave the oven on.

2. With the aid of a paring knife, skin the peaches. They should be soft and caramelized on the outside, but still firm on the inside. Remove the pit and slice into chunks. Transfer to a buttered baking dish (9-inch round or 8-inch square). Set aside.

3. In a small saucepan, combine the granulated

sugar, cornstarch, and water. Heat until warm and dissolved and pour over the peaches. Sprinkle with the cinnamon and nutmeg and dot with the pieces of butter.

4. To make the biscuit topping, combine the flour, granulated sugar, baking powder, baking soda, salt, and cinnamon in a medium-size mixing bowl. Using a pastry blender or your fingers, work in the cold butter to form a coarse, sand-like consistency. Add the buttermilk and stir to moisten with a fork. Turn out onto a floured board and roll or pat the dough out to roughly the size of the baking pan. Using two metal spatulas, carefully lift the biscuit topping and lay it over the peach mixture. Press down slightly to create a "cobbled" look. Sprinkle the top with the cinnamon sugar and bake until the crust is golden and the edges are bubbly, 30 to 40 minutes. Let cool for 10 minutes before serving.

Shortcut Blackberry Cobbler

MAKES 4 SERVINGS Cobblers that are made from fresh berries, particularly blackberries, are a delicious treat, but unless you have access to someone's blackberry bush, you will end up spending a fortune in the grocery store just on one dessert, not to mention emptying out the sugar canister to compensate for their usual tartness. Here's a great economical solution, and a quick one at that. Look in the frozen fruit section for bags of blackberries, or even mixed berries, which will sometimes include raspberries and marion berries, a type of blackberry developed and grown in Oregon with a delicious, sweet flavor. If they happen to include some strawberries or blueberries, that's okay too, but avoid those packaged in syrup. These products, once we enhance them with blackberry preserves, can quickly become a base for your cobbler. Top

with a quick drop biscuit, and you will be enjoying a super cobbler in no time flat. Serve warm with a good quality vanilla ice cream, and splurge on a small container of fresh blackberries as a garnish with mint leaves.

COBBLER TOPPING

1¼ cups buttermilk baking mix, such as Bisquick

1 tablespoon sugar, plus additional for sprinkling

¼ cup milk

¼ cup sour cream

FRUIT FILLING

⅔ cup blackberry jam or preserves

½ cup water

1 teaspoon fresh lemon juice

One 16-ounce bag frozen blackberries or mixed berries (about 4 cups), thawed

1 tablespoon unsalted butter, cut into pieces

1. Preheat the oven to 350 degrees. Lightly butter a 9-inch square baking pan.

2. To make the topping, combine the baking mix and sugar in a medium-size mixing bowl. Add the milk and sour cream and, using a fork, combine just until moistened. Set aside.

3. To make the fruit filling, combine the jam, water, and lemon juice in a medium-size saucepan and cook over medium heat, stirring with a whisk, until bubbly. Remove from the heat and gently stir in the berries. Pour the mixture into the prepared baking pan and spread evenly. Dot with the pieces of butter.

4. Spoon the cobbler batter in 4 mounds over the fruit and sprinkle a little sugar over each. Bake until bubbly and a toothpick inserted in the crust comes out clean, 30 to 40 minutes. Serve warm.

Shortcut Apricot Blackberry Cobbler:
Add one 15-ounce can apricot halves packed in light syrup to the fruit filling, including the syrup.

Healthy Fruit Choices
Low Ratings for High Marks

We already know that fruit is a healthy part of every diet, but do certain fruits contain more nutrients than others and are some better glycemically (less able to spike up blood sugar), particularly when combined with sugar and refined carbohydrates? The answer is yes, most definitely.

Nutritionally, many fruits contain important essential vitamins, as well as an assortment of necessary minerals. But powerful antioxidant polyphenols are also present in many fruits, which have been shown to have cancer-fighting properties, as well as the ability to protect against heart disease. These pigments, as they are classified, are what give color to the vibrant fruits we enjoy, from bright red strawberries to intensely orange-colored mangoes. In addition, fruits can be a tremendously important source of fiber in our diet. The pectins (natural substances that are gelatinous in makeup and extracted for their thickening power) and seeds found in fruit such as raspberries, strawberries, and kiwis, for example, are excellent for providing water-soluble fiber, necessary for preventing the reabsorption of cholesterol in the digestive tract. It is this type of fiber that is responsible, in part, for the lower Glycemic Index (GI) rating of many fruits. Including these in your diet, even at dessert time, is a good idea because their lower absorption rate will help to slow down the overall absorption of a dish that may contain sugar and high glycemic-rated carboyhydrates, such as refined flour. So go ahead and dig into that peach cobbler!

Here's the top ten list of low glycemic-rated fruits:

Prickly (cactus) pear	7	Pear	38
Bing cherry	22	Plum	39
Grapefruit	25	Strawberry	40
Peach	30	Green grape	46
Apple	38	Orange	48

NOTE: Surprisingly, GI ratings for raspberries, blueberries, and blackberries have yet to be determined, but judging by their extremely high fiber content, one would guess they would surely rank in the top ten.

Blueberry Crumb Buckle

MAKES 6 SERVINGS The buckle is the first cousin of the cobbler, with the fruit mixed into a batter and baked like a cake. I've added a crumb topping here to add some texture and interest and the result is not unlike a crumb cake studded with berries.

Blueberries, like all seasonal fruit, are best used in baking when their natural sweetness is at its height. I have had experience with tart blueberries that no amount of sugar seemed to be able to improve. Here in New Jersey, local summer blueberries are succulent, large, and full of sweet flavor. Be sure to taste the berries before deciding how much sugar is needed. Frozen or even jarred blueberries in a light syrup will also work here, but need to be well drained of excess liquid first.

CRUMB TOPPING
¼ cup (½ stick) unsalted butter, diced
½ cup sugar
⅓ cup all-purpose flour
½ teaspoon ground cinnamon

BUCKLE
¾ up (1½ sticks) unsalted butter, softened
¾ cup sugar
1 teaspoon nonalcohol vanilla, or substitute vanilla
    sugar (page 168) for ¼ cup of the sugar above
¼ teaspoon baking powder
1⅓ cups all-purpose flour
½ teaspoon salt
3 large eggs
2 cups fresh blueberries, picked over for stems

1. Preheat the oven to 350 degrees. Butter a 9 x 13-inch glass baking dish.

2. To make the crumb topping, combine the butter, sugar, flour, and cinnamon in a small mixing bowl, using a pastry blender, fork, or your fingers to form a crumb-like consistency. Set aside.

3. To make the buckle batter, with an electric mixer beat together the butter and sugar in a large mixing bowl until light and creamy. Beat in the vanilla. In a medium-size mixing bowl, whisk together the dry ingredients. With the mixer on low speed, add the eggs to the butter mixture, one at a time, then the dry mixture in batches, beating well to combine. Fold in the blueberries and spread the batter evenly in the prepared baking dish. Sprinkle the crumb topping evenly over the batter and bake on the center rack of the oven until a toothpick inserted in the center comes out clean, 40 to 50 minutes. The top should be crisp and golden. Let cool for at least 10 minutes before serving with whipped cream or ice cream.

Fruit and Nut Crumble

MAKES 6 SERVINGS British crumbles end many a Sunday meal, served warm from the oven with a drizzle of cream. Not unlike our American crumb pie, without the bottom crust, these dishes are easy to make and comforting and delicious to eat.

I have always appreciated the English taste for dried fruit, which is eaten far more often in Britain than in the States. Mincemeat pies and fruitcakes have always been popular there, even outside the Christmas holiday season. Since dried fruit and nuts are such excellent additions to our diet, I've included both in this recipe, but don't worry, the result is amazing. Intensely flavored and satisfying, this crumble will have you reaching for seconds, which in this case is certainly allowed!

FRUIT FILLING
1 pound mixed dried whole fruit, such as apricots,
    pitted prunes, figs, dates, and raisins
Juice and grated rind of 1 large orange
¼ cup firmly packed light brown sugar

CRUMBLE TOPPING

1 cup whole wheat flour

½ cup chopped walnuts

⅓ cup firmly packed light brown sugar

⅓ cup unsalted butter, softened

1. Butter a 9-inch glass pie dish. To make the fruit filling, place the dried fruit in a medium-size saucepan, add enough cold water to cover, bring to a simmer, and cook, stirring occasionally, until the fruits are plump and soft but not falling apart, about 20 minutes. Pour out half of the water remaining, add the orange juice, rind, and brown sugar, and cook another 10 minutes, stirring often. Pour the mixture into the prepared pie dish and set aside.

2. Preheat the oven to 350 degrees. To make the crumble, in a medium-size mixing bowl, combine the crumble ingredients and, using a fork or your fingers, work the mixture until well combined and crumbly. Sprinkle the topping evenly over the fruit, but do not press down. Bake on the center rack of the oven until the edges are bubbly and the top is golden, 30 to 40 minutes. Serve warm.

What's in Your Strudel?

Questions to Ask When Lurking Around Your Local Bakery

If you are at all like many of us in recovery, you are probably spending a bit more time than you used to browsing through the bakery section of your supermarket. Or maybe the neighborhood corner bakery that you thought had closed years ago has suddenly caught your eye. Yes, sometimes those goodies can seem awfully tempting occasionally and we may want to succumb to their allure, especially when we are too busy and drained to bake something ourselves. But are you sure about what's been added (or not added) to your Napoleon or drizzled into that delectable-looking strudel?

I talk to bakers on a regular basis and have found that if you sound even a tad knowledgeable, they will happily discuss the ingredients of their wares. And if the counterperson doesn't know, they'll usually head back to inquire of the pastry chef. So, instead of just asking, "Is there alcohol in that?" try some of these clever questions the next time you stroll into the bakery for a purchase and see how much respect and information you'll gain!

"DO YOU ADD RUM TO YOUR NAPOLEONS OR IS THAT JUST VANILLA PASTRY CREAM?" Fine bakeries will often add a splash of rum to their pastry fillings, while not so fine bakeries may add rum extract, both of which are things to avoid. A good, flavorful pastry cream generally doesn't need either and will contain simply vanilla extract or, when particularly good, even specks of vanilla beans.

"IS THERE ANY OTHER FLAVOR IN THE CHOCOLATE MOUSSE TART?" Here, you're trying to find out if they have added any brandy or another type of liqueur. Pure chocolate is what you want.

"OOOH, BLACK FOREST CAKE. THAT DOESN'T REALLY HAVE KIRSCH IN IT, DOES IT?" In classic Black Forest cake, the cherries are flavored with a good dousing of Kirsch, a brandy made from the juice and pits of cherries. You'll be able to find out if the cherries are simply in a sugar syrup glaze or have had any alcohol added to them. (See Chapter Twelve, "Sober Makeovers," for New Black Forest Cake, page 440.)

"THAT TIRAMISU MUST HAVE LOTS OF BRANDY, RIGHT?" Usually, the ladyfingers of classic tiramisu are saturated with espresso, and sometimes brandy, while the filling also may contain brandy or brandy extract. However, some bakeries refrain from adding brandy at all, so find out right away what the main ingredient really is. (See page 445 for a sobered-up tiramisu.)

"IS THAT AN AUTHENTIC PECAN PIE, OR HAS IT BEEN KICKED UP WITH BOURBON OR WHISKEY?" Most bakeries, unless they are cutting-edge gourmet, will not add alcohol to pies, but you never know.

Of course, some goodies are completely self-explanatory and don't require any questions at all—rum baba, Amaretto cheesecake, Kahlua layer cake—but a few items could be deceptive, depending upon the preference of the chef. They include cannoli, *sfogliatelle*, and even cream puffs, which have been known to contain crème chantilly, whipped cream that is sometimes spiked with liqueur. If you're not sure, just ask.

Baked goods that are mass-produced and prepackaged by the supermarket are easy to investigate by reading the label. By law, the ingredients must be listed in order of greatest quantity, so check for flavorings further down the list, past all the usual stabilizers, preservatives, additives, and partially hydrogenated gunk. In fact, once you do this, you may even be tempted to go home and bake your own goodies—now that you know what's *really* in that strudel!

Classic Cakes

What could be more comfortingly familiar than a classic layer cake with homemade frosting? Betty Crocker and Duncan Hines have been supplying us for decades with the easy fixings required for homemade cakes. And some folks have even found ways to enhance these mixes and turn them into myriad quick and tasty cake varieties. With all these modern-day conveniences, do people really bother anymore to make cakes from scratch? In a time when comfort food and family traditions have experienced a resurgence and concerns about unhealthy fats and preservatives grow, many home bakers are once again turning to grandma's old cookbook for inspiration. If it has been a long time since you tasted a real homemade cake, now is a great time to reacquaint yourself with this truly delicious American tradition.

Ring, tube, and Bundt cakes are classic homey preparations and can satisfy any after-dinner sweet tooth. For special occasions, layer cakes can't be beat, and the devilish Chocolate Blackout Cake (page 296) will provide the perfect conclusion for those times when the chocolate monster arrives for dessert!

Easy One-Layer Carrot Cake

MAKES 9 SERVINGS Studded with nuts and raisins and topped with just enough light cream cheese frosting to provide sweet satisfaction after any meal, this carrot cake couldn't be simpler to make. Lower saturated fat and vitamin-rich carrots highlight this deliciously moist cake, certain to please any traditional carrot cake fan. Be sure to cool the cake completely before frosting to prevent the cream cheese frosting from melting. You can deco-rate the top with additional chopped walnuts, if you like, or pipe the frosting into a lattice design (see Chef's Note following).

CARROT CAKE

2 large eggs
¾ cup canola oil
½ cup granulated sugar
1 cup all-purpose flour
1 teaspoon baking soda
1 teaspoon ground cinnamon
½ teaspoon ground ginger
½ teaspoon salt
1 cup grated carrots
½ cup golden raisins
½ cup chopped walnuts

NEUFCHÂTEL FROSTING

One 3-ounce package Neufchâtel cheese
2 teaspoons milk
1 teaspoon fresh lemon juice
1 cup confectioners' sugar

1. Preheat the oven to 350 degrees. Lightly butter and flour a 9-inch square baking pan, knocking out the excess flour.

2. To make the carrot cake, combine the eggs, oil, and granulated sugar in a large mixing bowl and beat with an electric mixer on medium speed for 2 minutes. In a medium-size mixing bowl, whisk together the flour, baking soda, cinnamon, ginger, and salt. On low speed, add half the flour mixture to the oil mixture and beat until combined. Add the remaining flour and beat again for 2 minutes. Stir in the carrots, raisins, and walnuts.

3. Pour the batter into the prepared pan. Bake on the center rack of the oven until a toothpick inserted in the middle comes out clean, 30 to 40 minutes. Let cool completely on a wire rack before frosting.

4. To make the frosting, beat together the Neuf-châtel cheese, milk, and lemon juice in a medium-size mixing bowl until well softened and smooth.

Add the confectioners' sugar a little at a time and beat on medium-high speed until all lumps are gone and the frosting is thick and smooth. You may add more confectioners' sugar, if necessary, to attain good spreading consistency. Evenly frost the top of the cake and serve chilled or at room temperature.

Two-Layer Carrot Cake: For a larger cake to serve 12, double the quantity of ingredients for both the cake and frosting. Bake the cakes in two 9-inch round pans that are well greased, floured, and fitted with parchment paper circles. Be sure the cake is absolutely cool before icing.

Chef's Note: For a decorative lattice effect, transfer the frosting to a pastry bag fitted with a medium-size star tip and pipe a zigzag design on the top of the cake. Disposable pastry bags are available in cake decorating stores and many supermarkets, making cleanup quick and easy.

Tropical Gingerbread Upside-Down Cake

MAKES 8 SERVINGS Here's a take on traditional gingerbread, as well as the popular pineapple upside-down cake, both of which drum up old-fashioned, home-baked memories. Instead of the usual pineapple, however, a combination of tropical fruits and macadamia nuts, delicious complements for the gingerbread, provides the topping. Classic upside-downs are made in heavy cast-iron skillets, always a tricky endeavor to turn out without a few extra hands to assist. Here a regular 9-inch round cake pan, preferably nonstick, will enable you to do the flipping on your own with a lot less trepidation.

Since ginger is the star of the show here, I've included it in a triple dose for a sharp-flavored outcome. Fresh, ground, and crystallized ginger all add to the gingery taste, while molasses provides a rich, dark texture to the cake. Enjoy this warm with a little whipped cream or vanilla ice cream on the side.

TOPPING

¼ cup (½ stick) unsalted butter
⅔ cup firmly packed light brown sugar
One 15-ounce can tropical fruit salad in syrup, well drained
½ cup roughly chopped macadamia nuts
2 tablespoons diced crystallized ginger

CAKE

2 cups all-purpose flour
2 teaspoons baking powder
2 teaspoons ground ginger
1 teaspoon ground cinnamon
½ teaspoon salt
¼ teaspoon *each* baking soda, freshly ground black pepper, ground cloves, and ground allspice
½ cup (1 stick) unsalted butter, softened
½ cup firmly packed light brown sugar
2 large eggs
¾ cup dark molasses (not blackstrap)
1 tablespoon peeled and grated fresh ginger
¾ cup whole milk

1. Preheat the oven to 350 degrees. Lightly butter a 9-inch round cake pan.

2. To make the topping, melt the butter in a small saucepan. Add the brown sugar and cook, stirring, over medium heat until bubbly, about 3 minutes. Pour into the prepared cake pan, tilt the pan to coat the bottom with the melted sugar, and distribute the fruit, nuts, and crystallized ginger over it evenly. Set aside.

3. To make the cake, whisk together the flour, baking powder, ground ginger, cinnamon, salt, baking soda, pepper, cloves, and allspice in a large mixing bowl. In a medium-size mixing bowl, beat together the butter and brown sugar until light and fluffy. Add the eggs and beat until well combined. Add the molasses and fresh ginger and beat well. Mix in half the dry ingredients, then the milk, then the remaining dry ingredients, beating well after each addition. Pour and spread the batter evenly over the fruit and nuts. Bake until a toothpick inserted in the center comes out clean, about 40 minutes.

4. Let the cake cool on a wire rack for 5 minutes, then run a sharp knife around the edges and place a cake platter over the top. Invert onto the platter, carefully lifting up the baking pan. Allow to cool for 40 minutes before serving.

Old-Fashioned Applesauce Spice Cake

MAKES ONE 10-INCH RING CAKE; 10 TO 12 SERVINGS
Tube or ring cakes are often associated with home baking, and today supermarket bakeries often display a variety of these cakes, from lemon poppy seed to rocky road. But probably one of the earliest versions of this type of cake was the good old-fashioned applesauce spice cake. Long before recipe developers learned that applesauce could help replace fat, and even sugar, in many desserts, providing necessary moisture and flavor, moms were whipping up this classic cake as a delicious, yet simple, dessert. It is definitely worth reviving as a comforting addition to your baking repertoire.

SPICE CAKE
  1 cup seedless raisins
  ½ cup apple juice
  ½ cup (1 stick) unsalted butter, softened
  1⅔ cups granulated sugar
  1 large egg
  1½ cups plain unsweetened applesauce
  2½ cups all-purpose flour
  1½ teaspoons baking soda

  1 teaspoon ground cinnamon
  ½ teaspoon *each* ground cloves, ground allspice, and salt

ICING
  ½ cup confectioners' sugar
  1 tablespoon apple juice

1. Preheat the oven to 350 degrees. Lightly butter and flour a 10-inch tube pan, knocking out the excess flour. In a small bowl, combine the raisins and apple juice and set aside.

2. To make the spice cake, beat together the butter and granulated sugar in a medium-size mixing bowl until light and fluffy. Add the egg and applesauce and beat until well combined. In another medium-size mixing bowl, whisk together the dry ingredients and add to the butter mixture in 2 batches, beating each time to incorporate. Add the raisin-and-juice mixture and stir well with a wooden spoon to combine. Pour into the prepared pan and bake on the center rack of the oven until the cake begins to pull away from the sides of the pan and a toothpick inserted in the middle comes out clean, 45 to 50 minutes. Let cool for 10 minutes, then run a knife around the edge of the pan and lift the tube portion out onto a wire rack to cool completely.

3. To make the icing, mix together the confectioners' sugar and apple juice in a small mixing bowl. When the cake is cooled, loosen the bottom by running a knife under it, then lift the cake up off the tube section using two metal spatulas, transferring it to a cake platter. Use a teaspoon to drizzle the icing evenly over the top.

Orange Sunshine Cake

MAKES ONE 10-INCH TUBE CAKE; 10 TO 12 SERVINGS
The taste of fresh oranges makes this cake a refreshing conclusion to any meal. Traditional sun-

shine cakes are really sponge cakes, a close relative of the angel food cake, with egg yolks included. Also traditional is the separating of the yolks and whites, but this recipe does not require this additional step, resulting in a denser and, I think, more pound cake–like texture. Here, we use cake flour, which has a higher starch content than all-purpose, resulting in a tender, fine texture, but feel free to substitute all-purpose in a pinch. The crumb, or texture, will just be a bit coarser. The deliciously tangy glaze finishes off this cake beautifully.

CAKE
- 1 cup (2 sticks) unsalted butter, softened
- 2 cups granulated sugar
- 5 large eggs, at room temperature
- 3 cups cake flour (not self-rising) or 2¾ cups all-purpose flour
- 1 tablespoon baking powder
- ¼ teaspoon salt
- ¾ cup fresh-squeezed orange juice (from 3 to 4 medium-size oranges)
- Grated rind of 1 medium-size orange

ORANGE GLAZE
- 1½ cups confectioners' sugar
- 3 tablespoons fresh squeezed orange juice
- 1 teaspoon grated orange rind

1. Preheat the oven to 350 degrees. Butter and flour a 10-inch tube pan, knocking out excess flour.

2. To make the cake, beat together the butter and granulated sugar in a large mixing bowl until light and fluffy. Add the eggs, one at a time, beating well after each addition to combine. In a medium-size mixing bowl, whisk together the flour, baking powder, and salt. Add this mixture alternately with the orange juice to the butter, sugar, and egg mixture, beating well to combine.

(continued on page 287)

Picking Flours

Most supermarkets now carry a variety of flours, meals, and starches in addition to old-reliable—all-purpose—as people become more health conscious and home bakers expand their repertoires. Here's a quick guide to these alternative ingredients, as well as some hints on buying and storing:

ALL-PURPOSE FLOUR: More often than not, you will see this as an ingredient in nearly all basic baking recipes, even those that call for alternative flours, so it is worth understanding its general composition. Made from a blend of hard wheat and soft wheat, all-purpose flour is highly refined and does not, unfortunately, contain any of the healthier parts of the wheat kernel, such as the germ and bran. Consequently, you will find, because of government regulations, that all-purpose flour is necessarily "enriched" with vitamins and minerals. It is sometimes bleached (naturally or chemically), but also sold unbleached, in addition to being presifted.

BREAD FLOUR: Since gluten is desirable for bread baking, these flours contain a high percentage of gluten-forming proteins, as well as small amounts of additives to encourage yeast activity. Bread bakers will often make use of specialty flours and additives, such as gluten flour and dough enhancers, that increase both the texture and rise of their products.

WHOLE WHEAT FLOUR: Heavier in texture than all-purpose flour, this alternative has a stronger wheat flavor because it contains the wheat germ. Nutritionally, it is a better choice than all-purpose, although glycemically it makes little difference because it is still quite refined and processed. Used alone in baking, traditional whole wheat flour tends to be a bit heavy. Most health-conscious recipes acknowledge this fact and will call for a combination of whole wheat and all-purpose. However, King Arthur Flour now makes a 100 percent white whole wheat flour that is ground from hard white winter wheat berries, but identical nutritionally to traditional red whole wheat. It is much milder in taste and can be substituted whenever all-purpose or whole wheat flour is called for.

CAKE FLOUR: Very refined and soft, this flour is reserved for delicate cakes and pastries and will sometimes already contain rising additives. Similarly, pastry flour, although generally not self-rising, is soft-textured and ideal for baking, and is also available in a whole wheat variety.

SELF-RISING FLOUR: This popular version used profusely in Europe is essentially a time saver, as it is simply all-purpose flour with the addition of baking powder and salt. If you remember to omit these additions in your quick bread recipes, you can use it in place of all-purpose flour.

RYE, OAT, BUCKWHEAT, AND OTHER GRAIN FLOURS: Just about any grain can be milled into flour and used in baking recipes for added texture and nutrition. In general, these flours are less processed and fuller flavored and are usually combined with all-purpose flour in bread and dessert baking, with the exception of corn and rice flours (also known as starches), which are highly refined and more often used as thickeners.

When buying alternative flours, it is usually possible to find smaller two-pound bags and I would recommend purchasing these because of their shorter shelf life. In general, any flour that is less processed and contains part of the germ will tend to go rancid because of the oil that is present. Refrigerating or freezing these types of flours will help to keep them fresh. Wrapping the bags tightly or putting the flour in an airtight container will also sustain their shelf life at cooler temperatures. All-purpose, bread, and cake flours will keep at room temperature for up to six months and should be stored in a dry, dark place to discourage mold and bugs.

Unless a recipe specifically requires it, sifting flour is more or less a thing of the past. To measure flour accurately, gently scoop with a measuring cup and use a blunt knife to scrape away the excess. Be sure not to pack or press down.

(continued from page 285)

Add the orange rind and mix well. Pour the batter into the prepared pan and bake on the center rack of the oven until the cake begins to pull away from the sides of the pan and a toothpick inserted in the middle comes out clean, about 1 hour. Transfer to a wire rack to cool for 15 minutes.

3. To make the glaze, beat together the confectioners' sugar and orange juice and rind until well combined. Loosen the edges of the pan with a sharp knife and remove the tube portion with the cake, transferring it to a wire rack. Let cool a further 10 minutes before carefully removing the cake with two metal spatulas onto a cake platter. While the cake is still warm, drizzle the glaze over the top. Let cool completely before slicing.

Lemon Sunshine Cake: Substitute ½ cup fresh lemon juice and ¼ cup water for the orange juice in the cake and grated lemon rind for the orange rind. For the glaze, substitute lemon juice and grated rind where orange is called for.

Pink Grapefruit Sunshine Cake: Substitute pink grapefruit juice and grated rind where called for in the cake and glaze. You can also add a few drops of red food coloring to the cake batter for a pink shade.

Recovery Note: Sponge and pound cakes often have liqueurs added to them after they are baked, since they are such excellent absorbers. In particular, orange-flavored cakes may have Cointreau or Grand Marnier drizzled over the top, much like a whiskey cake might have bourbon. Watch for these when ordering out.

Poppy Seed Bundt Cake

MAKES ONE 8-INCH BUNDT CAKE; 8 TO 10 SERVINGS
This is a light, yet flavorful, cake that will make a satisfying dessert for any night of the week. Bundt cakes are classic, old-fashioned baking at its best, reminiscent of bake sales and country fairs. Bundt is actually the trade name of a type of tube pan with fluted edges. You can also find mini Bundt pans, which are usually attached to each other on one large tin. These are particularly tricky to unmold, but are worth the effort because of the fabulous presentation. Unless your pan is nonstick, it is important to grease every nook and cranny of the pan in order to prevent sticking. The dusting of confectioners' sugar will help you to see if you missed any spots.

Not unlike a light angel food, this cake incorporates beaten egg whites for rising purposes, creating a lovely texture. Almond extract (nonalcohol) provides a nice flavor enhancement, although vanilla or lemon would be equally delicious.

Unsalted butter, softened, for greasing pan
Confectioners' sugar for dusting pan
¼ cup poppy seeds
¾ cup milk
¼ cup (½ stick) unsalted butter, softened
½ cup granulated sugar
¼ cup canola oil
2 teaspoons nonalcohol almond extract
1 tablespoon baking powder
1½ cups all-purpose flour
5 large egg whites, at room temperature

1. Preheat the oven to 350 degrees. Generously butter an 8-inch Bundt pan, preferably nonstick, and dust with the confectioners' sugar, knocking out the excess.

2. In a small saucepan, combine the poppy seeds and milk and bring to a boil over medium heat. Reduce the heat to low and cook, stirring a few times, for about 5 minutes. Remove from the heat, cover (to prevent a skin from forming), and set aside to cool.

3. In a large mixing bowl, beat together the butter and granulated sugar until light and fluffy. Add the oil and extract and continue to beat until

well combined. Stir in the poppy seeds and milk, then add the baking powder and flour gradually, beating on low speed until well mixed.

4. Wash and dry the beaters and, in a large mixing bowl, beat the egg whites until soft peaks form. Gently fold them into the batter using a rubber spatula until all traces of white are gone. Evenly spoon the batter into the prepared pan and bake on the center rack of the oven until the cake begins to pull away from the sides of the pan and a toothpick inserted in the middle comes out clean, 40 to 50 minutes.

5. Transfer to a wire rack and let cool to nearly room temperature before loosening slightly with a knife and inverting onto a cake platter. Let cool completely before serving.

Perfect Marble Pound Cake

MAKES ONE 9-INCH LOAF; 8 TO 10 SERVINGS Of all the different flavors of pound cake that can be conjured up, my most favorite version, by far, is an old-fashioned chocolate marble pound cake. Store-bought varieties just don't seem to possess the delicious moistness and flavor that a home-baked pound cake provides, particularly in the marble category. Why this is the case, I'm not really sure, except that perhaps butter, as well as other high-quality ingredients, is foregone in favor of those that are cheaper and have a longer shelf life.

Originally, pound cakes were simply composed of a pound each of butter, flour, sugar, and eggs. Over the years, many variations have been developed and numerous flavorings have been added, from lemon to almond to coconut. Loaf pans are the traditional baking receptacle, although tube pans are also often utilized. Here, a standard loaf pan will work nicely—nonstick metal will produce the best results.

For a sweet tooth with a bit of chocolate craving, a slice of this cake will truly satisfy. Be sure to use unsweetened Dutch-processed cocoa powder for an intense chocolate experience.

1 cup (2 sticks) unsalted butter, softened
1 cup sugar
1 teaspoon nonalcohol vanilla extract, or
    substitute vanilla sugar (see page 168) for
    ¼ cup of the sugar above
4 large eggs, at room temperature
2 cups all-purpose flour
1 teaspoon baking powder
2 tablespoons unsweetened Dutch-processed
    cocoa powder
1½ tablespoons canola oil

1. Preheat the oven to 325 degrees. Generously butter and flour a 9 x 5-inch loaf pan, knocking out the excess flour.

2. In a medium-size mixing bowl, beat the butter for 1 minute. Gradually add the sugar, beating well on medium-high speed until the mixture is light and fluffy, about 5 minutes. Add the vanilla. Beat in the eggs, one at a time, scraping the bowl down well after each addition. In another medium-size mixing bowl, whisk together the flour and baking powder. Add this slowly to the batter, beating on medium-low speed, just until combined.

3. Clean and dry the beaters and, in a small mixing bowl, beat together the cocoa powder and oil to a paste. Add a third of the batter to the chocolate and beat until well combined, about 1 minute.

4. Pour half the white batter into the loaf pan. Top with the chocolate batter and spoon the remaining white batter on top. Use a knife to create a marble look by cutting a zigzag through the batter. Do not overwork with the knife. Bake on the center rack of the oven until the cake begins to pull away from the sides of the pan and a toothpick inserted in the middle comes out clean, 55 to 65 minutes. Let cool on a wire rack for 15 minutes, then run a sharp knife around the edges and remove the loaf to cool completely before serving.

Orange Chocolate Marble Pound Cake: After removing a third of the batter from the mixing bowl, add 1 teaspoon grated orange rind and ½ teaspoon nonalcohol orange extract to the white batter and continue as directed. A few drops of pure orange oil could be substituted instead. Orange, as well as lemon oil, is extremely strong, but does not contain alcohol. It is available in specialty food stores or can be ordered online.

Coconut Chocolate Marble Pound Cake: After removing one-third of the batter from the mixing bowl, stir in ⅓ cup sweetened flaked coconut to the white batter and continue as directed.

Strawberry Cheesecake Bites

MAKES 32 CHEESECAKE BITES Who can resist the smooth and creamy sensation of a delicious cheesecake? Very few of us, I'm sure. Although numerous excellent quality, ready-made cheesecakes that can be doctored up with a little creativity (see page 294) are easily found in your supermarket bakery, freezer section, or by mail-order, these little bites are so easy to make and satisfying to eat, you may just decide to make them on a regular basis. And one of the best things about bite-size desserts is that they can calm a sweet tooth without breaking the calorie budget, provided you limit your intake!

Here, lower fat Neufchâtel cheese lightens up this classic, as does a reduced-fat sour cream topping. Fresh strawberries add a colorful and nutritious finish, although other berries would work just as well, including blueberries, raspberries, blackberries, or even a combination.

Mini muffin tins and paper liners are all you need to create these little gems. Be sure to cool them completely before adding the strawberries and glaze.

CHEESECAKE

Two 8-ounce packages Neufchâtel cheese, softened

3 large eggs

1 large egg yolk

⅔ cup sugar

2 teaspoons nonalcohol vanilla extract, or substitute vanilla sugar (see page 168) for ⅓ cup of the sugar above

TOPPING

1½ cups reduced-fat sour cream

⅓ cup sugar

1 teaspoon nonalcohol vanilla extract, or substitute vanilla sugar for the sugar above

TO FINISH

½ cup seedless strawberry or raspberry jelly or jam

1 tablespoon water

32 medium-size fresh strawberries, hulled and cut in half

1. Preheat the oven to 300 degrees. Fill 32 mini-muffin cups (or bake in batches) with paper liners and set aside.

2. To make the cheesecake, beat the cheese until smooth in a medium-size mixing bowl with an electric mixer. Add the eggs and egg yolk, one at a time, beating well between each addition. Add the sugar and vanilla and beat until well combined.

3. Fill the muffin cups, leaving about ⅛-inch space from the top. Bake on the center rack of the oven until the tops begin to crack and the edges begin to brown, about 30 minutes. Remove from the oven and place the muffin tins on a wire rack, leaving the oven on.

4. To make the topping, beat together the sour cream, sugar, and vanilla in a small bowl. Once the tops of the cakes have dropped slightly, 5 to 10 minutes, top each one with the sour cream mixture and return them to the oven for 5 minutes. Remove from the oven, allow the cakes to cool in the tins for 10 minutes, then carefully remove them while

(continued on page 292)

Poppy Seeds and Drug Screening
A Case for False Positives?

Do you enjoy a morning poppy seed bagel or poppy seed dressing on your dinner salad? If so, you may be wondering if there is any truth to the notion that eating foods containing poppy seeds could result in a positive drug test for opiates. Popularized by the infamous *Seinfeld* episode in which Elaine fails her drug test after eating her favorite poppy seed muffin, this debate has prompted several laboratory studies to determine if eating products made with poppy seeds could create a false positive.

Many treatment centers, particularly out-patient programs that continue for several months, may be required to conduct random drug screenings for various substances. Some workplaces may also require testing. (Even if you only partook of alcohol, you may be tested for other substances, as people often turn to substitutes when their drug of choice is taken away.) These types of tests are regulated by the National Institute on Drug Abuse, which sets the minimum concentration levels to a point which, some believe, may be too low, resulting in a positive test after poppy-seed ingestion. But how many poppy seeds must you eat to get a positive result? Some tests have shown that two or three bagels could cause a positive reading. Other laboratory results have found that larger quantities, such as the amounts found in a densely filled poppy seed Danish or hamantaschen (a Jewish pastry), might cause readings that test positive for opiates. Why is this so? Here's a little background.

The opium poppy has been cultivated for centuries and has long been known to have both analgesic and euphoric properties. After the flowers have begun to wither, the pod containing the tiny seeds starts to swell and ripen. Once completely ripened, the seeds can be gathered for cooking and eating. But if the pod is cut before it ripens, a milky juice can be collected and, once dried, becomes crude opium. This crude form contains many different drugs, morphine being the best known. In the early nineteenth century, it was discovered that morphine could be isolated from opium, dried into a powder, and, by 1853 and the invention of the hypodermic needle, mixed with water and injected into the body. (It is said that the first morphine addict on record was the wife of the man who invented the hypodermic.) Today it is used in hospitals as a powerful pain reliever, where it can be monitored because of its strong tendency to create dependency. Some recent studies have shown that if Naltrexone, the FDA-approved drug that blocks parts of the opioid-reward pathway and has been successful in reducing craving in some abstinent alcoholics, is administered with morphine for pain, the patient is less likely to become dependent. This is a promising discovery for people in recovery who must be mindful of pain-relieving substances and the possibility of relapse.

Codeine, often found in cough syrups or prescribed along with aspirin or acetaminophen (as in Tylenol), is also from the crude opium, but is a less powerful analgesic, although still highly addictive. Heroin, which is derived from morphine, is actually more powerful than its derivative because it produces the same effect in smaller doses. Although the poppy seeds themselves contain traces of morphine, they do not have a clinical effect on the body, as do the opium derivatives.

When drug screening is conducted for opiate use, it is the presence of morphine and codeine that is being sought in urinary samples. Heroin (diacetylmorphine), codeine (methlymorphine), and some varieties of poppy seeds can cause a positive morphine result. Fortunately, scientists have developed a confirmatory test that can be conducted on the specimen when an initial positive result is attained. The gas chromatography-mass spectrometry (GC/MS) test can identify the specific substance ingested by recognizing its molecular structure as well as its pattern of metabolites. This is particularly helpful in heroin detection, as it is rapidly metabolized by the human system and thus rarely turns up in initial testing.

So should you forego your favorite muffin or bagel if you are subject to drug screening? Although small amounts of poppy seeds are not likely to skew your results, the debate is still on whether avoidance of these tiny seeds is necessary, and whether, for former opiate addicts, they could pose any sort of trigger. Probably more important an issue would be any medications you might be taking that could result in skewing other drug tests, besides opiate detectors. Some prescription medications have been known to create false positives for illegal substances, so it is always best to be up front about what you are taking.

Incidentally, tests for alcohol are still primarily done through the breath, and although various parameters influence the level of impairment, its presence is usually easily detected. Saliva tests, now becoming more popular, can also test for the presence of alcohol and are comparable to blood alcohol concentration (BAC) tests. The question must be asked, can eating something prepared with alcohol cause a positive test result? In the Alcohol Retention in Food Preparation study (see page 92), the researchers determined that eating a slice of their brandy Alexander pie was the equivalent of drinking about one-third of a glass of wine. This would result in something negligible on a BAC test, about .002 percent, certainly not legally intoxicated and probably not even obtainable on a breath test. But some saliva tests are able to detect levels beginning at 0.00 and on those, perhaps, an ever so slight positive could appear. Maybe your friendly local police officer couldn't care less, but your neurochemicals just might stand up and take notice.

(continued from page 289)

still in their paper cups and transfer to a wire rack to cool completely. Refrigerate until ready to finish.

5. In a small saucepan over medium heat, combine the jelly and water, whisking just until melted and smooth. Let cool for 5 minutes. Place 2 strawberry halves decoratively on top of each chilled cake and, using a pastry brush, lightly glaze the berries with the jelly mixture. Return to the fridge to set. Serve well chilled.

Chef's Note: Consider flavoring your cheesecake bites with another nonalcohol extract in place of the vanilla, such as lemon, orange, or almond, and finish with a decoration of sliced kiwi; mandarin orange segments, glazed as above; or sliced almonds, dusted with powdered sugar.

Recovery Note: Some restaurant cheesecakes are embellished with liqueurs. Amaretto, in particular, is a favorite addition, so check before you order.

Devil's Food Cake with No-Boil Fluffy White Frosting

MAKES ONE 2-LAYER CAKE; 10 SERVINGS This classic combination of dark, moist chocolate cake with a marshmallow-like frosting has been a favorite for as long as most of us can remember. In the early twentieth century, devil's food cake began its popularity and was probably named as a contrast to the also popular angel food cake. What usually distinguishes devil's food from a regular chocolate cake is the greater amount of cocoa powder, although today there are numerous recipes for devil's food cake that don't even include it. I prefer one that is even a little heavy-handed in the cocoa powder department, and once you make this cake, you will know why.

Boiled icing, seven-minute frosting, white mountain frosting—all of these refer to the light and fluffy frosting we know and love made from egg whites and sugar syrup. It is the perfect complement to devil's food cake and one that I am sure will bring back comforting memories in no time. But the technique of boiling sugar and water together to what is called, in culinary terms, the soft ball stage, has frightened off many a fan of this delicious frosting, who prefers not to fiddle with candy thermometers and boiling hot sugar syrup. No more, my friends! The amazingly easy no-boil technique below will have you whipping up this frosting on a regular basis. Once you learn to make it, you'll have the basis for the upcoming Fabulous Whipped Buttercream (page 295), as well as Pink Cloud Sorbet (page 304), a deliciously light frozen concoction I have named in honor of what all of us know only too well—the "pink cloud" of early recovery (see page 306 for a discussion of pink cloud bursts, ruts, and other familiar Phase Two phenomena). So, jump in, start baking, and watch everyone hum with pleasure at the sight and taste of this classic comforting cake.

DEVIL'S FOOD CAKE
⅔ **cup unsalted butter, softened**
1⅔ **cups sugar**
3 **large eggs**
2 **cups all-purpose flour**
1¼ **teaspoons baking soda**
1 **teaspoon salt**
⅓ **teaspoon baking powder**
¾ **cup unsweetened Dutch processed cocoa powder**
1⅓ **cups cold water**

NO-BOIL FLUFFY WHITE FROSTING
2 **large egg whites**
¼ **teaspoon cream of tartar**
⅓ **cup sugar**
1 **teaspoon nonalcohol vanilla extract, or substitute**
   vanilla sugar (see page 168) for the sugar above
½ **cup light corn syrup**

1. Preheat the oven to 350 degrees. Cut 2 circles of waxed or parchment paper to fit the bottom of two 9-inch round cake pans. Butter and flour the pans, knocking out the excess flour, and place a paper circle in the bottom of each pan. Set aside.

2. To make the cake, beat together the butter and sugar in a medium-size mixing bowl until light and fluffy. Add the eggs, one at a time, beating well after each addition. In another medium-size bowl, whisk together the flour, baking soda, salt, and baking powder. In a small mixing bowl, whisk together the cocoa powder and water. Beating on medium-low speed, alternate adding the flour and cocoa mixtures to the egg mixture, combining well, but not overbeating. Pour the batter into the prepared pans and bake on the center rack until a toothpick inserted in the middle comes out clean, 30 to 35 minutes. Transfer to wire racks to cool for 15 minutes. Remove from the pan, peel off the paper, and place the cakes on the rack to cool completely.

3. Clean and dry the mixer beaters. To make the frosting, beat together the egg whites and cream of tartar in a medium-size mixing bowl at medium speed until the whites begin to form soft peaks, about 1 minute. Gradually beat in the sugar and continue to beat until stiff peaks have formed, about 2 minutes. Beat in the vanilla, if using. While beating at high speed, slowly pour the corn syrup into the egg white mixture, beating well and scraping down the sides of the bowl, until the frosting is thick and spreadable, about 3 minutes.

4. To finish the cake, place one cake round on a cake plate and spread with a third of the frosting. Place the other cake layer on top and frost the top and sides with the remaining frosting.

Chef's Note: *This cake is best stored at room temperature in a covered cake holder.*

Golden Layer Cake with Fabulous Whipped Buttercream

MAKES ONE 9-INCH TWO-LAYER CAKE, ONE 9 X 13-INCH SHEET CAKE, OR 20 CUPCAKES A simple golden yellow cake recipe can provide the base for any number of different cakes, so this will be just what you need to get you going on the road to super cake baking. Along with the devil's food cake recipe on the previous page, which would pair up nicely with some of the buttercream versions that follow, this recipe is one you will want to have in your baking repertoire.

As in the Orange Sunshine Cake (page 284), using cake flour will make for a soft and tender result, but all-purpose flour can be substituted.

Sharing the baking, frosting, and decorating (as well as eating) of classic layer cakes, whether for birthdays or just for fun, will help to bring back the art of dessert making into your family and kitchen.

2/3 cup unsalted butter, softened

1½ cups sugar

3 large eggs, at room temperature

2 teaspoons nonalcohol vanilla extract, or substitute vanilla sugar (page 168) for ½ cup of the sugar above

2½ cups cake flour (not self-rising) or 2¼ cups all-purpose flour

2½ teaspoons baking powder

1 teaspoon salt

1 cup milk (whole or 2 percent), at room temperature

1 recipe Fabulous Whipped Buttercream (page 295)

1. Preheat the oven to 350 degrees. Cut 2 circles of waxed or parchment paper to fit the bottom of two 9-inch round cake pans. Butter and flour the pans, knocking out the excess flour, and place a paper circle in the bottom of each one. Set aside.

2. In a medium-size mixing bowl, beat together

(continued on page 295)

Playing Dress Up with Cheesecake and Other Creative Ideas for Fast Desserts

When you feel like serving a knockout dessert but lack the time to make it from scratch, take advantage of the many ready-made components your local supermarket has to offer. Here are some ideas on how to dress up those store-made desserts with a little flair and creativity:

GOURMET CHEESECAKE: A plain cheesecake has the potential to become an elegant dessert in no time. Visit the fruit section and grab a box of red, succulent strawberries, then zip down the baking aisle and reach for a bottle of strawberry syrup. Whole strawberries—washed, dried, and hulled—can be used to decorate the top of the cheesecake. Lay them flat side down, covering the surface, drizzle strawberry syrup over all, and refrigerate until dessert time. Serve with more squiggled syrup on the plate. Or, if time allows, slice assorted fruit and create a mosaic topping that can be quickly glazed. How about a chocolate-covered cheesecake? Make the chocolate icing on page 297 and, depending on the size of your cheesecake, use half or all of the recipe while still slightly warm and pourable to coat the whole cake. Place it on a wire rack set on a baking sheet with rims to collect the chocolate overflow and chill well before serving.

SHORTCAKE SHORTCUTS: Plain sliced pound cake, angel food cake, buttermilk biscuits, and traditional ready-made sponge cakes can be dressed up with sweetened whipped cream and sliced fresh strawberries or a combination of seasonal berries. Add 1 tablespoon sugar to the berries and refrigerate about 30 minutes to create a natural syrup that will soak into the cake, or drizzle purchased syrup. Warm cut buttermilk biscuits briefly in the microwave before piling them up with berries, syrup, and whipped cream for a particularly comforting dessert. Try other seasonal fruits for shortcake, like peeled and pitted peaches or nectarines.

INSTANT BROWNIE SUNDAES: Purchased brownies provide the base for this chocolate lover's delight. Scoop vanilla ice cream on top, heat hot fudge in the microwave, pour over, and top with whipped cream and sprinkles. (Heat the brownie briefly before adding the ice cream for a totally decadent experience.) Don't forget the cherry!

WAFFLES WITH FROZEN YOGURT: Pick up a pack of ready-made waffles in the bread aisle or frozen food section and serve warm with your choice of frozen yogurt and fresh fruit. Blueberry waffles with frozen raspberry yogurt and fresh blueberries are particularly tasty. A drizzle of raspberry or blueberry syrup wouldn't hurt, either.

Chef's Dress-Up Tip: Add a dusting of confectioners' sugar and a mint sprig to any dessert plate to add that certain something and make your guests feel special.

(continued from page 293)

the butter and sugar together with an electric mixer on medium speed until light and fluffy. Add the eggs, one at a time, beating well after each addition. Beat in the vanilla.

3. In another medium-size mixing bowl, whisk together the flour, baking powder, and salt. On medium-low speed, beat half the flour mixture into the egg mixture, then half the milk, then the remaining flour, followed by the remaining milk, to combine. Try not to overbeat. Divide the batter evenly between the prepared pans and bake on the center rack of the oven until the tops are lightly golden and a toothpick inserted in the middle comes out clean, 25 to 30 minutes. Let cool on wire racks for 10 minutes, then remove the cakes from the pans, peel off the paper, and let cool completely on wire racks before frosting.

4. Place one cake round on a cake plate and frost with a third of the buttercream (mocha or chocolate would make for a delicious combination). Place the other cake layer on top and frost the top and sides with the remaining buttercream.

Chef's Note: For a 9 x 13-inch sheet cake, bake 35 to 40 minutes. For cupcakes, bake 18 to 22 minutes.

Lemon Yellow Cake: Substitute ½ cup fresh lemon juice and ½ cup water for the milk and add 1 teaspoon grated lemon rind with the vanilla. Tangy Lemon Buttercream (page 296) is the perfect companion.

Simple Coconut Cake: Substitute unsweetened light coconut milk (available in the Asian section of your supermarket) for the regular milk. Frost with No-Boil Fluffy White Frosting (page 292) for a super finish.

Peanut Butter Cake: Substitute ⅓ cup smooth peanut butter (not natural) for ⅓ cup of the butter. For a double whammy of peanut butter, make Peanut Buttercream (page 296) or, if you prefer, stir ½ cup mini semisweet chocolate chips into the cake batter and finish with Rich Chocolate Icing (page 297).

Chocolate Chip Cake: Stir in ⅔ cup mini semisweet chocolate chips before pouring into the cake pans. Chocolate Buttercream (page 296) is a great choice for frosting.

Fabulous Whipped Buttercream

MAKES ABOUT 2 CUPS, ENOUGH TO FROST TWO 9-INCH CAKE LAYERS, ONE 9 X 13-INCH SHEET CAKE, OR ABOUT 20 CUPCAKES. This whipped buttercream frosting is simply the easy no-boil fluffy white frosting taken a step further with the addition of butter, although slightly more sugar is required to compensate for this. Although I have seen several cookbooks use the corn syrup trick for the basic no-boil frosting, I have never seen anyone turn it into a buttercream, which, to me, seems the logical next step, since traditional boiled icings (essentially Italian meringues) are often transformed into these types of frostings, also called mousseline buttercreams. For the amateur cook, this method is surely a godsend and, once tasted, will quickly replace those tub frostings we too often reach for, which tend to be overly sweet and absent of any butter flavor. Similarly, the traditional so-called buttercream recipe one finds on the back of the confectioners' sugar box has always been rather disappointing, as it is often granular, too sweet, and subject to cracking. Fabulous Whipped Buttercream, on the other hand, is soft, creamy, pleasantly sweet, and buttery in flavor. It welcomes any number of flavorings, which should be added after the frosting has been prepared. Be sure that whatever you are adding, whether it is melted chocolate, coffee, or fruit puree, is cool and not hot, so as not to melt the butter.

1 recipe No-Boil Fluffy White Frosting (page 292), except increase the sugar to ½ cup
1 cup (2 sticks) unsalted butter, softened but still cool
Choice of flavoring (see variations below)

1. Have ready the no-boil frosting, whipped to stiff peaks. On medium-high speed, begin to add the butter by the tablespoon every 15 seconds or so, until all the butter has been used. At first, the frosting will appear thin and even somewhat curdled, but continue to beat, increasing the speed to high, until the frosting becomes smooth and firm.

2. Beat in your choice of flavoring. If the frosting seems a little soft for spreading, refrigerate for 10 minutes, then frost the cooled cakes.

Vanilla Buttercream: Beat in 2 teaspoons nonalcohol vanilla extract at the end. Or, you could substitute any nonalcohol extract, such as almond or coconut, for a different flavor.

Chocolate Buttercream: Beat in 4 ounces melted and cooled bittersweet or semisweet chocolate.

Mocha Buttercream: Beat in 2 ounces melted and cooled milk chocolate and 1 tablespoon instant coffee dissolved in 1 teaspoon warm water. Wait until cool to add.

Espresso Buttercream: Beat in 1 tablespoon instant espresso dissolved in 1 teaspoon warm water once it has cooled.

Lemon Buttercream: Beat in 1 tablespoon fresh lemon juice and the grated rind of 1 lemon. Or add several drops of pure lemon oil. Orange oil would also be a good choice of flavoring. Use food coloring to make the frosting yellow or orange, if desired.

Peanut Buttercream: Beat in ⅓ cup smooth peanut butter (not natural).

Strawberry Buttercream: Beat in ⅓ to ½ cup chilled strawberry puree (see page 304). If you do not mind speckled frosting, leave in some of the seeds, otherwise, strain the puree first through a fine sieve.

Chef's Note: Buttercream should be refrigerated, especially in warm weather. However, 30 to 40 minutes before slicing your cake, remove it from the fridge and let it stand at room temperature to soften a bit. If your kitchen is cool, you can keep a buttercream-frosted cake out of refrigeration for up to 2 days.

Chocolate Blackout Cake

MAKES ONE 3-LAYER CAKE; 10 TO 12 SERVINGS I can't resist including this amazingly rich and decadent cake for obvious reasons, even though it requires a little more effort. The blackout cake, characterized by its intense chocolate flavor, pudding filling, and chocolate cake crumb exterior, was made famous at Ebinger's bakery in Brooklyn during the 1950s. Although many restaurants have tried to duplicate the original, I understand from die-hard fans that nothing they have experienced comes close. Hopefully, this recipe will change their minds.

Devil's food cake is the perfect base for this heavenly concoction, because it is dark and dense. The pudding filling takes us back to Phase One, specifically the recipe for Dark Chocolate Pudding. (About half the pudding recipe will be sufficient, so you can either adjust the quantities or save the extra for another time.) In fact, this is an ideal dessert to make if the chocolate monster happens to be coming to dinner! Even though we have journeyed towards Phase Three, making great strides in our recovery each day, every one of us will have a Phase One day now and again. A little self-indulgence (and a whole lot of chocolate) won't steer us off track by much. So, give yourself a break and enjoy!

CAKE

1 recipe Devil's Food Cake (page 292), baked and cooled

FILLING

½ recipe Dark Chocolate Pudding (page 72), well chilled

RICH CHOCOLATE ICING

One 12-ounce bag semisweet chocolate chips
¾ cup (1½ sticks) unsalted butter, cut into pieces
½ cup hot water
1 tablespoon light corn syrup

1. Have ready the cake and filling and begin making the icing. In a medium-size saucepan over low heat, melt the chocolate and butter together, stirring occasionally. Remove from the heat and add the water. Immediately whisk thoroughly until the mixture becomes smooth and glossy. Add the corn syrup, whisk well, and set aside to cool and thicken for about 30 minutes, occasionally whisking the mixture. You can refrigerate the icing to help speed up the thickening process, but watch that it doesn't become too hard to spread.

2. To assemble the cake, use a long serrated knife to cut each round horizontally into 2 layers. Keeping the knife parallel to the counter, use a gentle sawing motion to cut through from one side to the other. You could also use a long strand of dental floss with a similar gentle motion, keeping an eye on the side of the cake to ensure that the floss remains in the middle.

3. Place 1 layer on a cake plate. Spoon half the pudding filling over the layer and spread evenly. Top with another cake layer, spoon the remaining filling over, and spread evenly. Place a third cake layer on top, saving the fourth layer for making crumbs for the topping. Use half of the icing to apply a layer to the sides and top of the cake. Refrigerate for about 10 minutes. Crumble the remaining cake layer finely into a medium-size mixing bowl, discarding any hard edges.

4. Spread the remaining icing on the top and sides of the cake. Sprinkle the cake crumbs on the top and sides, pressing lightly so they stick to the icing. Be sure to cover all areas so that only crumbs are visible. Return to the fridge and chill for at least 1 hour before slicing and serving.

The Facts about Blackouts

Blackouts may actually be one of the least-studied aspects of addiction. Yet between 30 to 40 percent of men, both alcoholic and nonalcoholic, have experienced this phenomenon at one time or another after the consumption of alcohol. Although little is known genetically, it is believed that some people, men in particular, may be more predisposed to blackouts than others. Surely anyone that has experienced them knows the terror that blackouts can leave in their wake.

This frightening phenomenon occurs when information processing is disrupted by alcohol in several brain regions, particularly the hippocampus, which plays a central role in memory formation. Damage to even a single region of cells in the hippocampus can result in the inability to form new event memories. So, when alcohol is consumed, usually in large quantities but not always, it affects this area, allowing the person to continue to appear lucid and operational, but not able to create any sort of memory of the incident, as is later evident. Some periods of blackout last for minutes, while others can last up to days. Some people have actually found themselves hundreds of miles away in a strange place, unable to recall how they got there or what transpired over an extended period of time. Obviously, they were able to function well enough to accomplish these feats, but memories of their actions were not "recorded," as it were, so they cannot recall any details, large or small.

Originally, the occurrence of alcoholic blackouts was associated with severe progression of the disease, but it has now been found that it may be a poor indicator of alcoholism, when taken as a single symptom, since many nonalcoholics have also experienced blackouts without being dependent. In general, nonalcoholic blackouts occur when there is heavy, episodic drinking, resulting in a rapid rise in blood alcohol levels. There also seems to be a connection between alcoholic blackouts and a prior history of head injury, perhaps exacerbating the disturbances of the hippocampus. Again, much more study is needed to determine the actual mechanism by which these memory losses occur. Although sometimes compared to amnesia, blackouts are often quite different. In amnesia, particularly temporary lack of recall caused by trauma, the retrieval of memories can sometimes occur through the administration of cues, particularly those that were present at the time of memory encoding. However, since there is no encoding taking place during blackouts, it is impossible to retrieve anything at all. Blackouts are also sometimes confused with passing out, or a state of unconsciousness, which in actuality is the total opposite of what occurs. The person is usually 100 percent functional and often quite capable of participating in activities, including those that are highly emotionally charged.

The closest comparison to the experience of blackouts may be what is known as conscious sedation—a state produced by sedative, "hypnotic" drugs, including tranquilizers, that are administered in surgery so that the patient can be "awake" during some types of operations. While the procedure takes place, the patient may appear alert and even calm, but afterward is unable to recall the events. This similarity is not all that surprising when we note that these anxiety-reducing drugs, also known as benzodiazepines, exert their sedative effects through the GABA system (gamma-aminobutyric acid neurotransmitters), similar to the way alcohol acts in several areas of the brain including the hippocampus.

Fresh Fruit and Frozen Desserts

Light, refreshing fruit desserts can be just as satisfying as a slice of cake and sometimes preferable, especially when the weather is warm and local fruits are at their sweetest peak. Easy to make and requiring little or no baking, these dishes, from Very Berry Gratin (right) to Kiwi Fruit Fool (page 301), can offer just the right amount of sweetness to finish off a meal in a healthy style. For many of the recipes, a food processor will come in handy, although success can also be found with a standard blender. Similarly, a hand-held immersion blender is a quick way to instantly break down fresh fruit when required. Consider using any of these tools to make your preparation that much easier.

Frozen desserts have always been a popular choice and these days many cooks are making their own ices and ice creams, thanks to easy-to-use ice cream makers designed for the home. Not all of the frozen delicacies in this section will require one, however, so if you don't own one yet, don't refrain from exploring the pleasures of making frozen desserts. Granitas and sorbets, particularly Pink Cloud Sorbet (page 304), a fun and noteworthy addition to every recovery dessert menu, can be whipped up easily and enjoyed before you know it. So, have fun and eat up!

Very Berry Gratin

MAKES 4 SERVINGS Here, a super easy preparation leads to a delicious and soothing conclusion to any meal. Berries take the spotlight, topped with a creamy gratin that you can whip up from sour cream or crème fraîche, now available in many supermarkets. A thickened cream with a rich and tangy taste, crème fraîche is often used as an addition to soups and creamy gravies, as well as desserts, because it can be boiled without curdling. It can actually be made at home by adding 2 tablespoons buttermilk to 1 cup whipping cream and allowing it to stand at room temperature, covered, for up to 24 hours, until it develops a rather thick consistency. After a good stir, it can be refrigerated up to 10 days.

Since this dish will be going under the broiler, a traditional gratin dish is ideal, although any type of shallow, flameproof dish will work just as well. Little individual gratin dishes make for a nice presentation if entertaining dinner guests. Use only fresh berries, as frozen or jarred versions, even when drained, will exude too much liquid.

1½ cups fresh raspberries
½ cup fresh blackberries
½ cup fresh blueberries, picked over for stems
1 cup crème fraîche or sour cream (don't use reduced-fat or nonfat)
½ cup firmly packed light brown sugar

1. Place the berries in the bottom of an ungreased 8- or 9-inch gratin dish, spreading them out decoratively. Refrigerate until well chilled and nearly ready to serve.

2. Preheat the broiler to high and set the oven rack 3 to 4 inches below the flame. In a medium-size mixing bowl, whisk the crème fraîche until smooth and a bit fluffy. Spoon the crème fraîche over the chilled berries to coat. Sprinkle the brown sugar evenly over the top. Broil until the sugar caramelizes, moving the dish around, if necessary, to lightly brown all the topping, about 4 minutes. Carefully remove from the oven and serve immediately.

Recovery Note: Restaurant fruit gratin desserts will often be topped with sabayon, a light, foamy custard made with Marsala wine, white wine, or champagne. See page 446 for a nonalcohol version of sabayon (the French name) or zabaglione (the Italian name).

Sautéed Plums with Ginger Syrup

MAKES 4 SERVINGS This easy stove-top dessert is particularly good with a scoop of vanilla ice cream. Just about any fruit could be used, although I like the combination of plums and ginger, not only because they are natural partners but also due to the healthy aspects of both—plums are quite low on the Glycemic Index and ginger, of course, is truly medicinal (see page 11) and an excellent aid to digestion, particularly after a heavy meal.

In the summertime, there are oodles of plum varieties to choose from, including red, purple, black, and green. Select plums that are not too soft, so they can hold up to the sautéing, but are ripe enough to be sweet. Chinese plum sauce, available in the Asian section of your supermarket, will add a lovely sweetness to the final dish, as will the tangy ginger preserves, available in the jam and jelly section.

3 tablespoons unsalted butter
1 tablespoon sugar
4 medium-size plums, pitted and cut into ½-inch-thick slices

¼ cup finely chopped crystallized ginger
¾ cup white grape juice
1 tablespoon Chinese plum sauce
1 tablespoon ginger preserves

1. Melt the butter in a large skillet over medium heat, add the sugar, and stir until it has melted. Add the plum slices in a single layer and cook, shaking the pan occasionally and turning the fruit over, until somewhat browned and softened, but not mushy, about 5 minutes. Carefully transfer the plums to a serving bowl and set aside.

2. Add the chopped ginger and grape juice to the skillet and, over medium-high heat, scrape up any browned bits of fruit from the bottom and boil until the liquid has reduced by about a third. Whisk in the plum sauce and ginger preserves and continue to cook and stir until the liquid becomes syrupy. Immediately pour over the plums and serve warm with ice cream or whipped cream.

Chef's Note: In the wintertime, canned plums will fill in nicely for fresh. Drain the syrup and use it in place of the grape juice and plum sauce.

Recovery Note: Sautéed fruit is very often flambéed with alcohol, so watch for restaurant versions that may include brandy or another type of distilled liquor or fortified wine.

Baked Bananas with Maple Walnut Glaze

MAKES 4 SERVINGS Ripe, sweet bananas are the key to this wonderful dish that is great on its own or even better with ice cream—maple walnut ice cream will definitely take it over the top. I have served this with Ben and Jerry's The Full VerMonty (maple ice cream with roasted pecans and a caramel swirl) to rave reviews, topped with a dollop of whipped cream!

Not unlike the classic Bananas Foster, a traditional New Orleans dessert made by caramelizing bananas and flaming them in cognac, this preparation is done in the oven and orange juice provides the necessary acidity to balance the super sweet glaze. Serve while still warm, but not straight from the oven, as the hot glaze may burn a few tongues.

4 medium-size ripe bananas, peeled and cut
   in half lengthwise
½ cup chopped walnuts
3 tablespoons unsalted butter
¼ cup firmly packed light brown sugar
½ cup pure maple syrup
2 tablespoons orange juice

1. Preheat the oven to 375 degrees. Butter a 9 x 13-inch glass baking dish and lay the bananas, flat side down, in a single layer. Sprinkle the walnuts evenly over the top and set aside.

2. Melt the butter in a small saucepan over medium heat and add the remaining ingredients, stirring well to combine. Cook, stirring, until all the sugar is dissolved and the mixture begins to bubble. Pour evenly over the bananas and walnuts and bake until the bananas are soft and nicely glazed, occasionally spooning the syrup over the bananas to coat, about 20 minutes. Let cool 10 to 15 minutes before serving.

Kiwi Fruit Fool

MAKES 4 TO 6 SERVINGS One of my very favorite desserts from England is gooseberry fool, a lovely pale green, sweet, yet slightly tart, whipped dessert that is perfect for warm summer nights. Gooseberries are, of course, a bit hard to come by here in America, but I have found that the colorful and nutritious kiwi fruit is perfect for the job. Fools are old-fashioned desserts that consist of only two things—a fruit puree and whipped cream. Depending on the fruit, no cooking is necessary, only brief periods of chilling—a welcome idea when summer temperatures in the kitchen may soar.

A food processor is a plus here, although I have known English cooks who will mash fruits into a puree by hand, then tediously strain them through a sieve. I prefer not to strain out the tiny black seeds of the kiwi, as they are a great source of fiber and add a pretty speckled look to the final dessert. Try making this with fresh strawberries, blackberries, or raspberries, all of which you may want to strain, although remember that it is the tiny seeds that, in part, make these berries so healthy. I will usually strain only half and keep the rest unstrained.

The addition of sugar, in this case superfine sugar, which will dissolve instantly, will be dependent upon the tartness of the fruit. It's best to start with 1 or 2 tablespoons, then taste and add more as necessary. Since the whipped cream is unsweetened, all the sugar in the dish will be from the fruit mixture, so it's okay to oversweeten the puree a bit.

6 to 8 kiwi fruits, peeled and cut in half
Superfine sugar to taste
2 cups whipping or heavy cream

GARNISH
1 kiwi fruit, peeled and cut into rounds
Fresh mint sprigs

1. Process the halved fruits in a food processor until smooth. You should have about 2 cups of puree. Transfer to a medium-size mixing bowl and sweeten to taste with the sugar, stirring well to dissolve. Cover with plastic wrap and chill for 1 hour.

2. In another medium-size mixing bowl, beat the cream to soft peaks with an electric mixer on high speed. Gently stir in the chilled fruit puree until the mixture is even colored and no streaks appear. Spoon the fool into 4 or 6 goblets or pudding

(continued on page 304)

To Everything There Is a Season

Finding Your Passion Fruit

I can always tell that Thanksgiving is around the corner when I spot my favorite little seckel pears in the supermarket—toy-sized, tan-skinned pears that I love to peel and poach for delicate desserts. The persimmons are also arriving at this time, plump, bright orange-colored fruits with a floral aroma and succulent, sweet flesh. As the year progresses and our produce section transforms itself from one season to the next, it is almost like greeting old friends we haven't seen in quite some time, with all the surprise and elation that goes along with it. Sometimes we don't realize how much we missed them until they appear once again.

I have a friend whose father would travel to Italy only in August—a time when most cities are void of people and activity, as the Italians travel elsewhere for their vacations. It's not a terribly good time for sightseeing because many places are closed for the end of the summer. But, he still went every August for one reason and one reason only—the fruit. Peaches and figs, as I recall, were his passion, and it was as if all the planning, traveling, and a year full of anticipation came down to that first heavenly bite of a ripe Italian August peach. I remember my friend and her parents visiting Florence when I was there as a student and witnessing the twinkle in her father's eye as we entered the San Lorenzo market to go fruit shopping. I think he may have actually dashed to the peach stand, leaving us in a cloud of dust. Later that week they invited me to tag along to a small village outside of Venice where we stayed with relatives, and under the orchard trees, we ate figs that we picked from the trees ourselves. To this day, when I see fresh figs in the supermarket, I think back on that lovely time and inevitably return home with a few figs to enjoy. You see, fresh figs are just one of my many passion fruits.

Buying produce and planning your menu seasonally is considered the sign of a good cook, someone who knows how to take advantage of flavors at peak season. Doing so will increase your passion for your ingredients as well, since you'll anticipate the arrival of certain fruits and vegetables, knowing, like my friend's father, that this is the time to enjoy them to their fullest. Here are a few suggestions to help you find your own fruits of passion.

SUMMER PLEASURES

The summer fruit displays in our local supermarkets are perhaps the brightest and most colorful of the four seasons, offering succulent berries of all descriptions, peaches, nectarines, and the mouthwatering, sweet red watermelon. Early summer (June and July) is when the Bing cherries arrive, however, and for an all too brief time, we can enjoy their unmatched flavor and sweetness. For an even briefer period, small light red, tart cherries may make an appearance as well—excellent for including in savory dishes and particularly suited to pork. Of course, figs are at their finest, as well as the unusual looking lychee nuts, which contain a moist, floral fruit, once you get beyond its prickly exterior. Mangoes are also at their finest. Late summer brings the unusual plucot—a California hybrid of the plum and apricot, fancifully speckled and sometimes referred to as dinosaur egg plums, bursting with sweetness and flavor.

AUTUMN SPECIALTIES

We know that fall is on its way when room is made for apples and pears, which reflect the deep earthy colors of autumn leaves. Cravings for fruit pies, crumbles, and crisps abound, as days get shorter and nights turn chilly. Pomegranates, those beautiful crimson-colored oddities, arrive during this time as well. Used in many Mediterranean and Middle Eastern dishes, the seeds of the pomegranate are removed and eaten whole, or made into juice or syrup. Its high antioxidant content is three times that of green tea and red wine.

WINTER WONDER FRUITS

Citrus fruits take center stage during the winter months with surprising variety: everything from little sweet/sour kumquats to the red-fleshed blood oranges so popular in Europe. Minneola tangelos, a tangerine and grapefruit hybrid, are seedless and super sweet, while clementines, satsumas, and tangerines, all of the mandarin orange family, arrive in large quantities to grace our holiday tables, along with winter grapes and unshelled nuts of all varieties. For a taste of the tropics during the cold winter months, papayas come to us at peak season with brightly colored flesh and a reminder of warmer days gone by.

SPRING SURPRISES

We know it is springtime when the first baskets of sweet strawberries arrive, giving us a glimpse of the summer berry abundance yet to come. Apricots, which have an all too short growing season of 10 weeks, are at their peak now, while fresh pineapples, best beginning in March, find their way to our supermarkets with their sweet fragrance breathing life into a winter-worn display. It is also at this time that the *real* passion fruit, a dimpled, dark purple-skinned, unusual fruit with a seductive sweet, yet tart, golden flesh, is in abundance. Eaten plain or transformed into ice cream, sorbet, or drinkable nectar, the passion fruit (so named because of its flower's resemblance to the symbol of Christ's passion, the crown of thorns) reminds us that, as the seasons come and go, there is always a surprise awaiting us just around the corner, if we are passionate enough with anticipation and patient enough for the perfect peach.

(continued from page 301)
cups, making a decorative swirl on the top. Chill for 2 to 3 hours before serving with the kiwi slices and mint sprigs decoratively placed on top.

Pink Cloud Sorbet

MAKES ABOUT 1½ QUARTS I have been making this frozen dessert for many years, but it wasn't until my own recovery that I made the connection between its pink and fluffy appearance and the recovery term "pink cloud" (see page 306). Ever since then, I have referred to this creamy and delicious dessert as my pink cloud sorbet, with, of course, several other "colorful" variations.

Technically not really a sorbet, this dessert is closer to what is known as a frozen soufflé, without the egg yolks. Its base is simply the recipe for No-Boil Fluffy White Frosting, which is really a shortcut type of Italian meringue. Mixed together with a fruit puree, in this case, strawberry, it can be frozen as is or in an ice cream maker, resulting in a slightly fluffier outcome. I have made it both ways numerous times and it is not at all necessary to enlist the aid of an ice cream maker, unless you would like to. Try it both ways and see which you prefer.

Frozen fruit actually is preferred here to make the puree, but certainly fresh strawberries, or the fresh version of whatever fruit you decide to use, will work as well. The frozen fruits, when pureed and added to the meringue, will help to speed up the overall freezing time, but again, this is not a necessity. Two cups of fruit puree is what you are after—generally a one-pound package of frozen fruit will accomplish this, but sometimes 12-ounce packages are all you can find. This will be okay to use, as the recipe is equally good with more or less fruit. The exactness of the quantities is less important than the quality of the ingredients.

I will generally not strain the fruit puree, because I like the appearance and health benefits of the tiny seeds from strawberries, raspberries, and other types of berries and fruit. You can, of course, strain the puree if you prefer, but you will need to start out with more fruit, as you will lose about a third of the volume. Simply process the fruit (fresh or straight from frozen) in a food processor for a few minutes until smooth, then transfer to a large measuring cup to check the resulting amount of puree. Have your No-Boil Fluffy White Frosting ready to go, as well as a container in which to freeze the sorbet, if you are not using an ice cream maker—a stainless steel bowl is a good choice. This sorbet is a particularly delicious accompaniment to chocolate cake and would be especially fun to serve with Chocolate Blackout Cake (page 296), for a truly unique recovery dessert!

1 recipe No-Boil Fluffy White Frosting (page 292)
2 cups pureed frozen or fresh strawberries

1. Have ready the prepared frosting in a large mixing bowl. Fold in the strawberry puree until the mixture is of uniform color and no streaks appear. Do not be concerned if the mixture loses some of its fluffiness.

2. Pour into a clean stainless steel bowl, smooth over the top with a rubber spatula, and freeze, covered with a sheet of aluminum foil, until firm yet still soft and creamy, 2 to 3 hours, or overnight. When firm and set, remove the foil, and place a piece of plastic wrap directly over the surface to prevent ice crystals from forming. Alternatively, pour the mixture into an ice cream maker and follow the manufacturer's instructions. Use an ice cream scoop to serve. Pink cloud sorbet will keep frozen for up to 2 weeks.

Purple Cloud Sorbet: Substitute 2 cups pureed mixed berries (such as raspberries, blueberries, blackberries, and strawberries) for the strawberries and continue as directed above.

Variations: Try any of the following pureed fruits for a different flavor and color, peeled and pitted where necessary: mangoes (fresh or frozen), kiwi (fresh), pineapple (fresh or canned, drained), apricot or peach (canned and drained).

Chef's Note: You can make a rainbow presentation of sorbet colors by layering a few variations, such as strawberry, mango, and kiwi. Divide 1 recipe of the frosting into 3, and add $1/2$ to $2/3$ cup different fruit puree to each. Use a Jell-O mold and allow about 30 minutes in the freezer before adding the next layer. Right before serving, submerge the mold in hot water for 2 seconds and flip over onto a serving platter. For individual rainbow sorbets, layer as above in parfait or sundae glasses kept in the freezer. No flipping required.

Honeydew Granita

MAKES ABOUT 1 QUART If Italian ices and sno-cones take you back to childhood, this granita, or water ice, will produce the same refreshing and comforting results. Not unlike the previous fool recipe, ices start with a base of pureed fruit and, in place of the cream, incorporate a simple syrup made from sugar and water. A close relative of the popular sorbet, you could actually transform an ice such as this into a sorbet version by freezing it in an ice cream maker. Traditional granita, however, is coarser in texture and usually stirred by hand once ice crystals begin to form. However, if you prefer, the granita can be allowed to freeze into a solid slab, which can then be broken into pieces and grated in the food processor for tinier crystals. This is handy to know in case you happen to overfreeze your granita or have any leftover that is too solid to slush with a fork.

Old metal ice cube trays (without the inserts) are actually the best receptacles for making granita, so if you have a few in the basement, bring them on up. Otherwise, a metal baking pan that is *not* nonstick coated will work well too; scraping the ice crystals with a fork as outlined below would scratch up a nonstick coating and ultimately ruin your pan. If you are opting for the food processor grating of solid pieces, *do* use the ice tray inserts, as this will help you remove the granita later.

1 large ripe honeydew melon, halved, seeded, and flesh scooped out
2 cups simple syrup (page 16), chilled
1 teaspoon fresh lemon juice

1. In a food processor, process the melon flesh until smooth. Transfer to a large mixing bowl, add the simple syrup and lemon juice, and stir well to combine. Pour into a metal tray or baking dish and put in the freezer.

2. After about 45 minutes, remove from the freezer and, using a fork, scrape the ice crystals from around the edges into the center, stirring and mashing the partially frozen mixture into the liquid. Do this again 2 or 3 times or more over the next 3 hours, until the consistency is firm, yet still slightly slushy. The more often you stir the mixture, the smoother it will become. Spoon into goblets or custard cups and serve immediately.

Variations: There are numerous exotic melons available these days, from Persian to casaba, all with distinctly fragrant and delicious flesh. Try substituting any of these, or even the common cantaloupe, for the honeydew.

Pineapple Orange Granita: Substitute 1 cup pineapple puree and 1 cup orange juice for the honeydew puree. Proceed as directed above.

Peach Granita: Substitute peach puree for the honeydew, using two 15-ounce cans cling

(continued on page 308)

Feel You're Getting Your Just Desserts?

Pink Cloud Bursts, Ruts, and Other Phase Two Concerns

During the ups and downs of Phase One, something miraculous will usually happen to us. Suddenly we feel incredibly good—our confidence is up, our health has improved, and we are happy in our sobriety. This phenomenon, called the "pink cloud" by those who, from their greater experience, know only too well the transience of this feeling, must unfortunately give way to the imminent cloud burst that is just around the corner.

Research and treatment professionals have found that this period of time can be the most critical stage of our recovery, for when the pink cloud shifts and reality sets in, usually during Phase Two, we may become overwhelmed by what we see and feel. If you have ever asked yourself, "Is this all there is?" or "Where's my piece of the pie?" you can rest assured that you are experiencing this common phenomenon. It is now that we run the risk of getting stuck in our sobriety, without moving forward. We have created a comfortable rut, and by doing so, ceased to grow and improve. We face our situation with a shrug and may even keep sober by "white knuckling," another common phenomenon, which indicates we may be staying away from drink out of sheer will power and nothing else. These types of feelings can often lead to the thing we fear most—the dreaded relapse.

I remember my treatment counselor taking me aside one day and telling me I would hear, usually from fellow recoverers, a lot about how relapse is a normal part of the disease and that you can expect it to happen at some time or another. "This is not at all true," he said emphatically and I have never forgotten that. Yes, many people who face this disease may need to try surmounting it more than once. And sometimes it seems there are those who just can't stay clean and sober. But for others, it seems they just put down the drink and never looked back. How can we all be so different when battling the same disease?

For those of us who have struggled with relapse, we know how debilitating and even humiliating it can be. By far the best thing we can do is simply jump right back on the wagon and not look back, except to learn from our mistakes, as well as the accomplishments of others. However, any amount of recovery that we attain, even for a short period of time, is valuable to us and can never be taken away. This is because recovery skills are developmental, with each one making the next skill possible. It is not like starting from scratch again—we need to find out where we took that wrong turn on the last lap, not the whole race, and our positive recovery experiences will help us to get back on track.

How can we avoid relapse from happening in the first place? This is, of course, the $25,000 question and, unfortunately, there is no definitive answer. Our recovery is by necessity an interactive process that must be worked at. Each of us must examine what we are doing or not doing to aid our ongoing recovery or enlist the help of someone who can see a bit clearer than we can at this moment, like a sponsor or a therapist. For instance, you may feel you've done all the right things. You don't drink or use anymore and in fact, you don't even think about it much these days, but still there is a lingering doubt in your mind that maybe there should be something more to this sobriety thing. What were once new and interesting strategies for staying sober have become dull and lifeless routines, performed without enthusiasm or pleasure. You wait for the really good things to start happening—the things that everybody told you would happen—your life would be wonderful and healthy, your relationships would be back on track, and your problems would pretty much be solved. So, what happened and why do you feel so awful? When this type of thinking sets in, we know it is time to act. But how?

It helps to understand much of what research has discovered about the recovery process. When we become addicted, essentially we cease to grow. For the months, years, even decades of active addiction, our personality sort of hibernates, and we create a false sense of identity for ourselves—a façade with buried emotions. When recovery takes place, and after the pink cloud disappears, we are essentially back to where we started—our preaddictive personality with all its potential defects and undesirable traits. We do not suddenly become healthy psychological specimens just because we quit our addiction; we need to start growing again. And sometimes what we must face in this growth process, whether it be accepting the horrible things we have done while actively using or coping with hidden family background issues, is too much to bear and we sabotage our recovery by refusing to accept and deal with our own personal reality. And, if we become lackadaisical about protecting our sobriety by associating with old drinking acquaintances, or visiting old haunts, or not watching our diet and denying potential triggers, we set ourselves up for relapse. Before you know it, we wake up with a hangover and feel worse about ourselves than ever before.

It takes courage and dedication to confront trying times like these. Identifying difficult periods is half the battle. Resolving to do something about it is the answer. Ask for help if you need it and remember that everyone goes through these tough times, which, in the end, will help us to grow. Make a conscious effort to change negative habits and find the support that you need. Rising up and moving forward when it seems the hardest and most challenging will lead us toward what may be the best part of recovery that awaits—Phase Three—when we can actually use our own experiences and lessons to support and help someone else.

(continued from page 305)

peaches in heavy syrup, drained and processed until smooth. Use the drained heavy syrup and enough simple syrup to equal 2 cups of liquid, and continue as directed above.

Classic Lemon Ice: Substitute 1 cup fresh lemon juice and 1 cup cold water for the honeydew puree. Add the grated rind from 1 lemon if you like a particularly tangy lemon ice or a drop or two of pure lemon oil.

Bittersweet Chocolate Ice Cream

MAKES ABOUT 1½ PINTS Ice cream makers are fast becoming one of the most popular appliances of the twenty-first century kitchen, thanks to modern technological freezing mechanics and the easy-to-follow directions that are always included in each box. If ice cream is quickly becoming one of your passions, you might want to look into purchasing one of these fun machines. The inside drum, where all the action will take place, can be kept in the freezer, ready to go. Once you make your ice cream base, or liquid, you simply pour it into the cold drum and attach it to the machine, which will result in some of the best ice cream you have ever tasted within 20 to 30 minutes.

Many bases for homemade ice cream are made from eggs and often require delicate custard making, which can sometimes be a bit tricky for the first-time churner. Instead, this recipe requires only the melting of chocolate, in this case, a fine quality bittersweet variety, heated with milk, cream, and sugar. It is then slowly added to beaten egg yolks to cook them enough to avoid any bacterial growth, then simply chilled. This ice cream is delectably rich and deep chocolate in flavor—remember that darker chocolate can actually provide healthy phytochemicals (see page 70)—so it is something we can certainly enjoy in small doses without too

much guilt. Since Ben and Jerry have enlightened us to the idea of adding everything short of the kitchen sink to our ice cream, feel free to concoct your own crazy combinations from some of the suggestions below.

1¼ cups heavy cream
1 cup whole milk
⅓ cup sugar
6 ounces bittersweet chocolate, broken into
  pieces (about 1 cup)
2 large egg yolks
Pinch of salt

1. In a medium-size saucepan, combine the cream, milk, sugar, and chocolate and, over low heat, whisk constantly until all the chocolate is melted and the mixture is completely smooth. Set aside.

2. In a medium-size mixing bowl, beat together the egg yolks and salt with an electric mixer on medium-high speed until thick. Beating on low speed, slowly pour the chocolate mixture into the eggs and beat until well combined. Cover with plastic wrap and chill until the mixture is cool to the touch, about 1 hour or more.

3. Pour the mixture into an ice cream maker, following the manufacturer's instructions. Cover and freeze until ready to serve.

Variations: During the final 3 minutes or so of churning, add ½ to 1 cup of any of the following or a combination: chopped nuts (plain or chocolate covered), chocolate chips or chunks, mini marshmallows, or cut-up pieces of brownies, cookies, or cake. Or stir in by hand, after churning but before transferring to the freezer, marshmallow, caramel, or fudge topping, fresh raspberries, or peanut butter.

Double Chocolate Mint Ice Cream: Substitute 1 cup mint chocolate chips for the bittersweet chocolate. Stir in ½ cup broken chocolate mint cookies (like Girl Scout brand or Keebler Grasshopper cookies).

Milk Chocolate Almond Ice Cream: Substitute 1 cup milk chocolate chips for the bittersweet and stir in ½ cup slivered almonds after churning. Add 1 teaspoon nonalcohol almond extract to the egg mixture.

Dark Chocolate Cherry Ice Cream: Substitute 1 cup semi-sweet chocolate chips for the bittersweet and stir in ½ cup chocolate-covered cherries, cut in half, including the liquid centers (watch for alcohol-laced candies!) after churning.

Cappuccino Gelato

MAKES ABOUT 1 QUART; ABOUT 10 SERVINGS Here's a great finish for an Italian-style meal. Served up in coffee cups and decorated to look like cappuccino, this delicious *gelato* will fill in for after-dinner coffee *and* dessert at the same time. *Gelato* is simply the Italian name for ice cream, but it differs from American versions because it is usually denser and richer in flavor, while being surprisingly lower in butterfat. *Gelaterias* (Italian ice cream parlors) have become quite popular in the States these days and many of them boast authentic consistency and taste. Often, in Italy, *gelato* is served in a hollowed-out brioche bun, the counterpart to our American ice cream sandwich. People stroll along the streets in the evening enjoying their *gelato* after a light supper.

If you have never tried *gelato*, you are in for a delicious treat. Although some would maintain that any *gelato* outside of Italy is a mere, faint replica, this recipe comes pretty close in texture and flavor. And the presentation is unbeatable! Have fun and serve up this dessert when friends and family are visiting for a perfectly sweet conclusion.

GELATO
 5 cups whole milk
 ⅓ cup instant espresso powder
 ¼ cup cornstarch
 1½ cups sugar

TO SERVE
 Heavy cream, whipped to soft peaks
  and chilled
 Ground cinnamon
 Chocolate-covered espresso beans
 Pirouette cookies

1. In a small saucepan, heat ½ cup of the milk to scalding (when bubbles are forming around the edge of the pan), then add the instant espresso and whisk until it is dissolved. In a small mixing bowl, combine another ½ cup of cold milk with the cornstarch and stir until it is dissolved. Set both aside.

2. In a large saucepan, combine the remaining 4 cups milk with the sugar and cook over medium heat, stirring constantly, until the mixture just comes to a boil and the sugar is dissolved. Whisk in the cornstarch mixture and simmer over low heat, whisking continuously until the milk thickens, about 2 minutes. Remove from the heat and whisk in the espresso mixture.

3. Transfer to a bowl and allow to come to nearly room temperature. Cover with plastic wrap and chill until cool to the touch, at least 40 minutes. Pour into an ice cream maker and follow the manufacturer's instructions to freeze. Transfer the *gelato* to the freezer until ready to serve.

4. To compose the cappuccino desserts, place a scoop of the *gelato* in a coffee cup with a saucer and smooth over the top with the back of a spoon. Place a dollop of the whipped cream over the *gelato*, spreading it to the edges of the cup, sprinkle with a little cinnamon, top with 3 or 4 chocolate espresso beans, and insert a pirouette cookie to the side. Serve immediately.

Finding Your Way Around the Ice Cream Parlor

These days there are enough choices of ices and ice creams to make your head spin before you even decide on a flavor. Here are a few helpful definitions to guide you in your selections:

WATER ICE: This is essentially the Italian ice we grew up with—simply a combination of water, sugar, and some kind of flavoring. The French call it *granité* and the Italians refer to it as *granita*, basically because its consistency is granular, from the formation of ice crystals. It can be made easily at home without an ice cream maker.

SORBET: Just a fancy name for an ice that is smooth rather than granular, sorbet can be made by freezing the same liquid base used for water ice in an ice cream maker. They have become particularly popular lately, as they are completely fat free, containing no eggs, milk, or milk solids. However, without any added fat, protein, or fiber, it is more likely to spike blood sugar, which is why I usually recommend retaining the seeds in the fruit puree, which provides some fiber and helps to slow down the metabolic reaction.

SHERBET: Okay, here's where a little bit of confusion enters the ice cream parlor. Sherbet, as we know it, generally contains milk—a kind of sorbet made with dairy—so it is richer than an ice but lighter than an ice cream. Unfortunately, the derivation of the word sherbet comes from the Middle East term *charbet*, which is simply sweetened fruit and water, without any milk. Because of this word origin, French sherbet means sorbet and Italian sherbet is *sorbetto*, neither of which contain dairy. Then there is, of course, ice milk, less popular today than it once was, which is closer to ice cream, but contains less milk fat and milk solids and is generally a lot less creamy.

ICE CREAM: Here, we can rest assured that cream is probably on the ingredient list, although poorer quality ice creams will replace some of it with starches and milk solids. French ice cream is made from an egg custard base and is similar in taste and texture to those you may find called "custard-style." "Light" ice cream means that it is reduced in fat by at least 50 percent, while "fat free" is made from nonfat milk. There is also "no sugar added," which may be sweetened artificially. *Gelato*, the Italian ice cream, actually has no cream (I did say *probably*), so it is lower in butterfat, but still rich and intense in flavor because less air has been incorporated into the mixture.

FROZEN YOGURT: Popular with those who are minding their fat intake, frozen yogurt is not necessarily lower in calories or sugar, other important considerations for dieters. It is a good choice for those who have difficulty digesting ice cream made from real cream, but the other benefit of friendly bacteria that yogurt normally boasts is believed to be lost once it is frozen. Soft-serve frozen yogurt is quite creamy and delicious and gives soft-serve ice cream a real run for its money, as opposed to the hard frozen yogurt varieties.

FROZEN SOY DESSERTS: With the increased interest in adding healthy soy to everyone's diet, frozen soy products have begun to appear in the ice cream section. Particularly attractive to those who are dairy intolerant, these "ice creams," either made from soymilk or tofu, are debatably healthy, at least glycemic-wise. Believe it or not, frozen tofu desserts such as those made by Tofutti were tested for their Glycemic Index (GI) rating and were found to be a whopping 115—way over the rating for glucose tablets! Why this is the case can only be due to the fact that the main ingredients are water, sugar, and high-fructose corn syrup. Tofu is way down in the ingredient list, indicating that there is much less of it in the final product than one may assume. Frozen soymilk products, on the other hand, appear to be better (regular soymilk has a GI rating of 30), probably because soymilk is generally the main ingredient, although a proper rating has not yet been determined.

Enhancing Your Health and Becoming a Sober Gourmet

B y Phase Three, generally reached by the third or fourth year of sobriety, we have come to an important point in our recovery when, more often than not, life is good, physical and mental health is greatly improved, and we are easily able to face the trials of life without reaching for a chemical substance to get us through them. We've made great strides, but in some ways, there are more mountains to climb. With the days of Phases One and Two comfortably behind us (although they will inevitably pop up, now and again), we first need to acknowledge where we are in our recovery before we can determine how much further we need to go. Think about overcoming any remaining obstacles to healthy living and make a plan of action. It is during this time that many of us decide to face the final addiction—nicotine—and begin exercising on a regular basis if we haven't started already. If weight has become an issue, or illnesses such as diabetes or cardiovascular disease have come upon us, we can apply what we know through our achievement of sobriety to these concerns by making the necessary changes and improvements needed to keep us as healthy as possible. And food still has an important role to play, perhaps more important than ever.

Increasing the Quality of Recovery

Phase Three, which, in essence, includes the rest of our lives, will determine the direction of our future and predict the quality of our lives and our recovery for years to come. Now is the time to deal directly with problems that may jeopardize or reduce the quality of our lifelong sobriety, such as family-of-origin issues and self-defeating bad habits that are still difficult to overcome, as well as health issues that may be a direct result of our addiction. In a way, we have now caught up with the rest of the world and may even have begun instituting healthy lifestyle habits that many others lack. But don't stop there. Moving forward and continually improving is an important key to our overall success. Not drinking, not thinking about drinking, and remaining comfortably sober are merely scratching the surface.

Continuing to Grow and Learn

If we have been educating ourselves about the disease of addiction, we know that as former alcoholics and addicts we may be susceptible to certain illnesses and diseases. Lingering bad health habits should be faced directly and preventive measures should be utilized to increase our chances of living a long and healthy life. What we eat (and don't eat) can make a difference and keeping abreast of health and nutritional research will empower us to make wise choices that could affect us directly in the future. Taking a strong interest in your health and the health of your loved ones is one way to make great strides during Phase Three. Encouraging others through example is another. The recipes in Phase Three will help you to enhance your health through sensible eating and deli-

Simple Goals for Phase Three

CONTINUE TO MAKE POSITIVE CHANGES IN YOUR DIET. With small steps, we were able to incorporate positive changes in our diet during Phase Two. Continue this process by trying new cooking styles and ingredients, while increasing your consumption of nutritionally packed foods, which may ward off future illness and keep you feeling healthy and at your best.

OPEN YOUR MIND AND APPRECIATE THE POWER OF KNOWLEDGE. In order to continually make positive changes, we need to be open to suggestion and become aware of new developments in research pertaining to our disease and general health. Seek out information to empower yourself and adopt new and sensible habits to increase the quality of your recovery and your life.

BE PROUD OF YOUR ACCOMPLISHMENTS. Too often we forget how far we've actually come in our recovery process. Becoming sober is no doubt the hardest thing you have ever done and should be given the recognition it deserves, particularly from you. Be proud of your recovery and celebrate important milestones with your favorite foods, shared in the company of those friends and family who are also proud of what you have achieved.

REACH OUT AND MAKE A DIFFERENCE IN THE LIVES OF OTHERS. We have the power to make a positive difference in the lives of addicts and alcoholics who still suffer, as well as those who are new to recovery. Advocating for accessible treatment, telling your story, and educating the public are ways in which we can help to remove the stigma that addiction still carries and pave the way for greater understanding and compassion. By reaching out, we help ourselves as well, reminding us of the struggles of the past and how the miracle of healing found its way into our lives. Spreading the facts, offering an example, and providing much-needed hope to others is perhaps the greatest thing we can achieve in our recovery journey.

cious alternatives. "Salads: The Mainstay of a Healthy Diet" (page 316) contains many ways to lighten up your eating and enjoy the benefits of side and main course salads. "Vegetarian Cooking: Expanding Your Culinary Horizons" (page 344) will provide you with many new and tasty ideas for increasing the amount of healthy plant-based foods in your diet, while "When Food Is Your Preventive Medicine: Discovering the Functionality of Cooking and Eating" (page 382) will teach you that what you eat can increase the likelihood of living a long and healthy life. Finally, in "Sober Makeovers: A New Look at Some Old Devils" (page 421), we'll come full circle by renovating classic alcohol-laden dishes with sensational and sober results, celebrating our sobriety in the process and enjoying the best of what life has to offer.

9 | *Salads*
The Mainstay of a Healthy Diet

*S*alads are, no doubt, the most versatile course on any menu. They can be served at the beginning of a meal to whet the appetite or as a side dish to accompany a heavy entrée by providing refreshment. They may even become the meal itself, especially when the weather is oppressively warm. The French will serve salads towards the end of a meal, as a palate cleanser, while in America, we often find ourselves at the infamous salad bar, piling up our plates as we wait for our entrée.

Whether simple and casual or a creative orchestration of diverse ingredients, salads are a definite must as part of a healthy diet. Crisp greens can provide a good dose of vitamins A and C, as well as calcium, while being high in fiber and low in calories. Add to that a plentiful array of raw vegetables, such as tomatoes, cucumbers, bell peppers, and onions, and we are well on our way to eating a super-nutritious meal. Often, it is not the salad ingredients themselves that pose dietary hazards, but rather the choice of dressing that can upset the balance of a healthy course. We're talking about those creamy, high-calorie, and, yes, often delicious, salad dressings we buy in bottles and jars. Although some boast fewer calories and fat grams, most are still loaded with undesirable ingredients, ranging from numerous starches, preservatives, and stabilizers to unhealthy oils that are partially hydrogenated. One solution to this dilemma is to make your own dressings, and in this chapter you will find many recipes that are easy to prepare and great to have on hand for any variety of tossed greens. Thankfully, we are also starting to see healthier varieties of bottled dressings in our supermarkets that actually taste pretty good! Look for those that contain olive or canola oil, with a minimal amount of additives. Keep a couple of these on hand as well, so there is always something available to dress up your greens.

Of course, salads do not always mean just lettuce and vegetables, and we'll be looking at some fabulous pasta and grain versions that make for delicious side dishes as well as light lunches. And if salad is your main course of choice, the variety of recipes in this chapter will satisfy any hungry appetite, while providing substantial nutrition. So, let's step into the salad garden and get acquainted with the mainstay of our new and healthy prescription for Phase Three eating.

Side and First Course Salads

One of the healthiest ways to round out a meal is with a fresh green salad, either served before the main dish or alongside it. Eating a variety of lettuces and raw greens is a great way to consume important nutrients and add fiber to your diet. For the weight conscious, salads are an indispensable addition to your daily menu.

Try to eat at least one small salad a day and choose a variety of vegetables to add to your bowl. Traditional additions such as tomatoes,

cucumbers, bell peppers, onions, broccoli florets, and carrots are excellent choices. Also try other ingredients like chickpeas and beans, alfalfa and broccoli sprouts (see page 417, "Broccoli Sprouts: The Functional Super Food"), or nuts and seeds such as walnuts and sunflower seeds. Dress the salad with a drizzle of olive oil and a splash of vinegar or lemon juice for the simplest of preparations, or try some of the salad dressing recipes in this chapter.

There are particular salad combinations that work really well together, generally categorized by chefs as "composed salads," and these are perfect accompaniments for specific meals. Let the produce section of your market inspire you when choosing greens and vegetables. Fresh, crisp, and healthy-looking ingredients will always make for a delicious salad combination. If you begin with the best ingredients, you can't go wrong.

Arugula, Red Onion, and Cherry Tomato Salad with Parmesan Curls

MAKES 4 SERVINGS Arugula, also known as rocket or roquette, is a rich source of iron as well as vitamins A and C. Its lively, peppery taste makes it a favorite addition to Italian salads. It is also easy to grow and is actually classified as an herb, so add some to your kitchen herb garden if you like its flavor. You'll want to make several sowings over a few week's period to keep it coming.

If you find arugula too assertive on its own, you can replace half the amount below with romaine lettuce or a curly leaf variety. This salad makes an excellent first course or side for pasta or pizza. Be sure to use a good quality extra virgin olive oil and serve with plenty of crusty whole-grain bread to dip into the olive oil.

8 cups arugula

¼ cup finely chopped red onion

Juice of ½ lemon

⅓ cup extra virgin olive oil

Kosher salt and pepper to taste

12 cherry tomatoes

Small chunk of Parmesan cheese

1. Arugula must be washed well, as it tends to be gritty with sand. Cut off the ends and wash in a bowl of cold water, lifting out the greens with your hands and transferring them to a colander. Do this 2 or 3 times, until there is no longer an accumulation of grit at the bottom of the bowl. Dry well in a salad spinner or gently press between paper towels. Set aside in a clean salad bowl.

2. In a small mixing bowl, combine the onion, lemon juice, and olive oil. Add a good pinch of kosher salt and a generous grinding of black pepper. Whisk together and set aside.

3. Cut the cherry tomatoes into quarters. With a vegetable peeler, make Parmesan curls for garnish (about ½ cup).

4. When ready to serve, add the tomatoes to the olive oil dressing and gently fold. Then add this to the bowl of arugula and toss well to coat. Taste for seasoning and add a pinch of salt if needed. Transfer the salad to 4 serving plates and garnish each with some Parmesan curls.

Easy Greek Salad

MAKES 4 SERVINGS Greek salads have been popular for a long time as a luncheon salad at restaurants and diners. They are also excellent side or first course salads for dishes of Mediterranean origin, such as Mediterranean Chicken with Garlic and Olives (page 198) or Garlic and Herb Broiled Lamb Chops (page 151).

Feta cheese is traditionally used in this salad and is readily available packed in brine or vacuum sealed. You can even buy packages of crumbled feta that are plain or flavored with herbs, garlic, or sun-dried tomatoes. Any of these could be used in this salad, although I particularly like the creaminess of a chunk of plain feta cheese broken into bite-size pieces as a smooth complement to the texture of the raw vegetables. If you find feta cheese too strong, you might want to try this salad with goat cheese, which is a little less assertive. *Ricotta salata*, a firm version of Italian ricotta cheese, is also a good choice.

Choose a crisp and compact head of romaine lettuce, the only real green that can stand up to this bold and tangy flavor combination.

GREEK SALAD DRESSING

1 garlic clove, peeled and minced

2 teaspoons dried oregano

Juice of ½ lemon

3 tablespoons red wine vinegar

⅔ cup olive oil

Salt and pepper to taste

1 heaping tablespoon grated Pecorino Romano cheese (optional)

SALAD

½ head romaine lettuce, leaves washed and dried

1 large ripe tomato, cut into wedges

½ cucumber, sliced

½ red onion, peeled, thinly sliced, and separated into rings

½ green bell pepper, seeded and cut into thin strips

4 ounces feta cheese, broken into bite-size pieces

½ cup Kalamata or other marinated olives, drained

1. To make the dressing, whisk together the ingredients in a small mixing bowl and chill until ready to serve.

2. To make the salad, tear the cleaned and dried romaine lettuce leaves into bite-size pieces and place in a large salad bowl. Add the remaining salad ingredients and toss lightly. Drizzle some of the dressing over the salad (you will have extra) or serve on the side.

Lettuces and Greens

Solid Salad Foundations

Years ago the only lettuces we saw in our local grocers were the common head of iceberg, romaine, Boston, and maybe escarole and watercress. Today our choices are infinite and we are even provided with prewashed and torn selections in bags and plastic cartons for our convenience. Gourmet baby greens, frisée, and organic sprouts are just some of the myriad salad ingredients we are privileged to enjoy. So, when we are faced with salad making, where do we begin and what should we choose?

Although lettuces are often classified by categories such as butterhead, crisphead, leaf, and romaine, unless you are a lettuce gardener, it is sometimes more helpful to acquaint yourself with these greens by getting to know the characteristic taste they may contribute to a salad. In very simple terms, this will mean whether or not a lettuce is mild or assertive. More often than not, a great lettuce salad will contain a nice balance of these flavors, mixed and matched for complementary results. Many packaged salads do this by combining different lettuces and even perhaps adding shredded carrots, red cabbage, and other salad ingredients for an additional contrast of texture, color, and taste. But doing this yourself is quite easy and will drastically cut down on the cost of buying bagged salads on a regular basis. As we saw in Phase One, conveniences such as these were readily welcomed for energy-sapped days and certainly if time is not on your side, buying these prepackaged products will certainly help you along. But for those who would like to expand their salad making, here is some helpful information to guide you in your green picking.

MILD-FLAVORED LETTUCES AND GREENS

ICEBERG: This classic standby was, for a time, shunned in favor of darker-leaf lettuces because it was believed to contain far less nutrients than its cousins. However, recent research has shown that iceberg provides many of the same benefits that romaine lettuce has to offer, while its advantage is that it will keep quite a long time under refrigeration. Look for heads that are heavy for their size without blemishes and tear apart the leaves with your hands to prevent the usual brown oxidation "rust" that occurs from cutting with a knife. Iceberg is always a good starting point for any mixed salad and handy to keep around for sandwiches and shredding.

ROMAINE: This is the classic ingredient in Caesar salad and a lettuce preferred by most salad eaters as the foundation for many tossed green salads. The leaves are less tightly packed than those of iceberg and oblong in shape. They will often contain quite a bit of dirt and grit, however, and must be washed well before eating. Packages of romaine hearts (simply the inner leaves stripped of any outer blemished and tough ones) are popular these days and provide a good compromise between the prepared bag salad and the whole, untrimmed head. Romaine boasts good flavor and crispness.

BOSTON AND BIBB: These lettuces are soft in texture with a particularly mild sweetness of flavor. Because of their delicacy, they are often preferred by those who have difficulty digesting anything raw. The inner leaves are often yellow and white and very tender, hence their appropriate categorization of butterhead. Very light dressings should be used with these types of lettuces so as not to mask their subtle flavor.

LOOSE-LEAVED LETTUCES: By this we mean varieties such as green leaf and red oak leaf, which are delicate in flavor and soft in texture. However, like romaine lettuce, and perhaps even more so, they require several washings in cold water to remove grit and dirt. Do this by separating the leaves from the stem and placing them in a large pot or bowl of cold water. Gently circulate the leaves with your hands to help loosen the dirt, then lift out. Repeat with fresh cold water until no grit appears in the bottom of the bowl, then drain in a colander and dry carefully.

SPINACH: Depending on whether you buy baby spinach leaves or the larger, more mature stalks, spinach can range from mild to slightly pungent in flavor. Unless you are making a spinach salad, it is usually combined with other greens, because it tends to cause a bit of mouth puckering from the oxalic acid it contains. Although always considered a good source of iron (as Popeye always said!), it is this same oxalic acid that unfortunately blocks the body's absorption of much of the iron as well as calcium that is present, making spinach less nutritious in this regard than previously thought. However, some studies have shown that when eaten with acidic foods, such as citrus or vinegar, our bodies are better able to access the iron present in spinach, as well as other iron-rich greens.

ASSERTIVE AND TANGY LETTUCES AND GREENS

ESCAROLE AND CHICORY: These sharp-tasting leaves will add a nice tang to any salad. They are particularly popular with Italian salad makers and perfectly suited to a drizzle of olive oil and a splash of balsamic vinegar. Escarole is actually a type of chicory, although a little less curly, so they are really very similar in their bitterness and texture. When cooked, they also make a delicious side dish, especially with garlic and olive oil. Both need to be well washed, and it is usual to cut them into smallish pieces rather than to serve the whole leaf.

ENDIVE AND RADICCHIO: Although a bit confusing, these are also members of the chicory family, despite their quite different-looking appearance. Belgian endive is the most common type found in supermarkets and is characterized by a small torpedo shape with large white ribs and minimal yellow-green leaves. Radicchio leaves, on the other hand, are reddish purple with a bit less white rib, especially towards the more tender center. Both make fine additions to salad for varied texture and color, as well as being good for grilling, roasting, and braising.

ARUGULA: Also called rocket, this is definitely an assertive green because of its peppery flavor, but it is highly tender and soft in texture. It grows in sandy soil and, consequently, unless you buy it prewashed, you will need to do several cold water baths (as described under "Loose-Leaved Lettuces" previous page) to remove all the granules. But any extra work is certainly worth it, because arugula is one of the tastiest salad greens available to us today. It is superbly delicious with ripe, sweet tomatoes and a drizzle of olive oil, but for those who prefer only an accent of tang, arugula mixes well with romaine and baby leaf lettuces.

WATERCRESS: Once only a garnish on a plate, watercress adds a lively touch to any salad. Both the leaves and the tender stalks can be eaten. Watercress is usually sold in bouquets, roots submerged in water, and is extremely perishable, so it should be used within a couple of days of purchase. It also makes a delicious classic soup (page 112), as well as being suited to delicate stir-fries and quick sautés.

OTHER UNCOMMON VARIETIES: Many more unusual choices are available to us in the produce section of our supermarket and when looking for something just a little different, consider a bunch of dandelion greens or a head of the decorative-looking frisée to add zip to your usual green salad. Mesclun, also called gourmet mix or spring mix, is simply a variety of small salad greens, which can be served on their own or mixed in with other types of lettuces. You'll find everything in it from baby arugula to mizuna (a petite Japanese green) to baby beet tops. A handful of mesclun will make any salad more interesting and attractive when served.

Although I own a good salad spinner, I confess that it is rarely utilized—blotting with paper towels can dry most any lettuce leaf adequately, although tender greens like arugula really do benefit from a spin or two. It is usually best to wash your lettuce as you need it, although a plastic perforated bag, with a folded paper towel inserted under the leaves, will help to keep your washed lettuce fresh and crisp.

Recovery Note: Many supermarkets now carry a vegetable wash that is purported to remove any toxic residue, bacteria, and insecticides from your salad greens, as well as other vegetables and fresh fruit. These sprays will often contain alcohol, however, so if you choose to use them, read the labels carefully.

Tomato Fennel Salad

MAKES 4 SERVINGS This incredibly simple salad relies on the ripe sweetness of summer tomatoes and the crisp flavor of fennel for its success. I first had this served to me in Italy by an Italian cook at the height of the tomato season. It was literally made in seconds and served on a leaf of escarole. As an accompaniment to a grilled steak with delicious Tuscan bread on the side, it is one of the most memorable meals I have enjoyed!

When tomatoes are not particularly at their peak, I have also made this with the addition of sliced onions, oil-cured olives, and fresh herbs to jazz it up. Hopefully, you have been enjoying the versatility of fennel since Phase One, but if you prefer, you can substitute celery hearts for a similar result.

2 large, ripe tomatoes, cut into wedges
1 medium-size fennel bulb, bottom trimmed, stalks
  discarded, and bulb cut into bite-size pieces
Pinch of salt
¼ cup extra virgin olive oil, or more to taste
Juice of ½ lemon
4 large escarole or lettuce leaves (optional)

1. In a large salad bowl, combine the tomato wedges and fennel. Sprinkle with the salt and add

Throwing Tomatoes at Free Radicals

As a member of the nightshade plant family, along with the potato and the eggplant, the tomato was once considered poisonous to eat, but today it may be just the answer to fighting off those dangerous free radicals that can make us prone to chronic disease and age-related illnesses. Lycopene is a phytochemical antioxidant found in tomatoes and is also responsible for their vibrant red color. Researchers believe there may be even more protective substances in tomatoes yet to be discovered, in addition to the excellent micronutrients they already boast, including vitamins A, B, and C, potassium, iron, and phosphorus. In addition, tomatoes offer a good amount of fiber. Sounds like the perfect vegetable, right?

Tomatoes, in actuality, are *fruits*, not vegetables. This is because a fruit is defined as the edible part of the plant that contains the seed, as opposed to the edible stems, leaves, or roots. In fact, the French first referred to tomatoes as *pommes* (apples), or specifically, *pommes d'amour* (love apples), because they were thought to possess aphrodisiac powers. Although discovered in the sixteenth century by conquistadors in Mexico and Central America, both North America and Europe shunned the tomato until much later. Eventually, French Creole cooking in Louisiana made great use of it in gumbos and jambalayas in the early nineteenth century and Italy, in particular, brought it to celebrity status as the essential sauce for pasta. Before long, the tomato became a staple cooking ingredient and heirloom varieties began to emerge.

the olive oil and lemon juice. Toss lightly to coat and let sit at room temperature until ready to serve.

2. Spoon on top of a large escarole or lettuce leaf to serve, if desired.

Fresh Herb Salad with Buttermilk Dressing

MAKES 4 SERVINGS The next time you are perusing your produce section for salad ingredients, don't overlook the fresh herb section. Not just for mincing and garnishing, herbs can add wonderful flavor and freshness to a simple green salad and pair up nicely with practically any entrée. I particularly like this salad with Simple Oven-Poached Salmon (page 386) or Simple Roast Chicken (page 190), especially when hot weather dictates lighter fare and easier preparations.

I have suggested using a mesclun salad mix but you could also use a combination of Boston or Bibb lettuce and green or red oak leaf lettuce. Any delicate green would work well here and complement the fresh herbs.

This dressing is light and slightly sweet and is also excellent with salads that include avocado slices, nuts, or fresh fruit wedges, such as apples or pears. Feel free to add ingredients such as these to

Although available year round, the summer months are when a juicy sweet tomato can almost make a meal in itself. Thickly sliced with a sprinkle of coarse salt, there is little else that can taste as good when tomatoes are at their peak season. Greenhouse-grown tomatoes and those that are not vine-ripened pale in comparison. Always sniff your tomato at the root end to detect the smell of the vine. It will be a good indicator of flavor.

Tomato varieties abound, especially for the gardener, but supermarkets have also begun to carry a significant array. Little cherry, grape, and pear tomatoes are often quite sweet and attractive in delicate salads. Italian plum tomatoes make excellent tomato sauces, while the large beefsteak is perfect when sliced for a hamburger, layered with fresh mozzarella, or eaten on its own. For those who find the acidity of raw tomatoes difficult to handle, yellow tomatoes have arrived on the scene in many forms as well, containing less acid, while tasting succulent and sweet.

When tomatoes are sun-dried, they intensify in flavor and make nice additions to salads, pizzas, pasta sauces, and a variety of other dishes. They are usually packed in oil, but can also be found dry-packed, in which case they should be marinated in a flavorful olive oil to soften their consistency. Oven-roasted tomatoes are incredibly delicious and can be made at home, sliced and laid on an oiled baking sheet and roasted for about two hours in an oven on very low temperature (about 225 degrees). The resulting slices are great on sandwiches and pizzas or as part of an antipasto salad platter.

Tomatoes should never be refrigerated, as the pulp becomes grainy and the flavor is entirely lost. Choose firm, unblemished tomatoes and store them at room temperature until ready to eat.

the recipe below for a heartier first course or side salad.

BUTTERMILK DRESSING
½ cup buttermilk
¼ cup light mayonnaise
1 teaspoon prepared mustard
2 tablespoons honey
1 tablespoon cider vinegar
Salt and pepper to taste

SALAD
8 cups mesclun or spring mix
½ cup sprigs fresh dill
½ cup sprigs fresh parsley
½ cup sprigs fresh cilantro

1. To make the dressing, whisk together the ingredients in a small mixing bowl and chill for 30 minutes before using. It will keep, tightly covered, in the refrigerator for up to 5 days.

2. To make the salad, combine all the greens in a large salad bowl. Be sure the herb sprigs are bite-size and not too large. Toss well with your hands to distribute.

3. Serve the dressing on the side or drizzle on top of each serving.

Watercress Salad with Roasted Beets and Orange Citronette Dressing

MAKES 4 SERVINGS Watercress is a delicious, somewhat peppery green, available year round and generally sold in a small bouquet bunch or sometimes prewashed in packets. Here it headlines with fresh beets that have been roasted in the oven. You may substitute canned cooked beets if you like, but the delicious flavor of fresh beets will be missed, so

I recommend this easy roasting method for a top-notch result. Beets should always be peeled *after* they are cooked to retain important nutrients. Wait for them to cool down and simply rub the thin skin off with a paper towel.

When handling beets, there is always a good chance that their beautiful color will stain your hands (not to mention your cutting board). This comes with the territory, as they say, and frankly is worth it when you taste the result. A little lemon juice and soapy water, however, will help remove any stains.

Citronette dressings, as opposed to vinaigrette dressings, incorporate the acidity of citrus fruit in place of vinegar. This makes for a lighter, fresher taste, which is especially good with a salad like this, as well as any other variations that include fruit. Orange is a perfect partner for beets as well as watercress, but you could also make this with pink grapefruit with equal success. Blood oranges, when available, are also a good choice and add an interesting color combination to your presentation.

I like to garnish this salad with a small slice from a log of goat cheese, just to round out the flavors and textures. If, however, you are watching your calorie intake during Phase Three, skip the garnish and enjoy the salad as it is.

ORANGE CITRONETTE DRESSING
1 teaspoon grated orange rind
½ teaspoon dried thyme
¼ cup orange juice
1 tablespoon fresh lemon juice
½ cup light olive oil
Salt and pepper to taste

SALAD
4 medium-size beets, tops discarded and washed
1 tablespoon olive oil
8 cups watercress, stems removed, washed, and dried

2 large navel oranges, peeled (making sure
   to remove as much of the white pith as
   possible) and sectioned
One 2-inch piece soft goat cheese (optional)

1. To make the dressing, whisk together the dressing ingredients in a small mixing bowl and chill until ready to use.

2. To make the salad, start by preheating the oven to 400 degrees. Place the beets in a roasting pan and drizzle the olive oil over them. Roast until the beets are fork tender, about 1¼ hours, shaking the pan occasionally. Allow the beets to cool until easy to handle and peel by rubbing the skin away with a paper towel or use a sharp paring knife to peel away the outside and trim the ends. Cut each beet into ½-inch-thick wedges, place in a medium-size bowl, and pour the dressing over, tossing lightly to coat. Set aside to cool completely.

3. When ready to serve, have the watercress in a large bowl, add the beets in the dressing, and toss with your hands or wooden spoons to coat. Divide this mixture among 4 salad plates, garnish with the orange segments and a slice of the goat cheese, if desired.

Crunchy Asian Slaw with Ginger Sesame Vinaigrette

MAKES 4 SERVINGS   Cole slaw gets an Eastern make-over in this delicious salad that is a perfect accompaniment for any basic stir-fry (page 126), Teriyaki Tofu (page 357), or Ginger Fried Rice (page 129). Old-fashioned cole slaw, laden with mayonnaise and calories, is replaced with this tangy and healthier version. This slaw makes an excellent filling for sandwich wraps when combined with diced cooked chicken or shrimp. The dressing is also well suited for a cold chicken or beef salad and is a good addi-

Potato Salad
Reinventing an Old Favorite

Mayonnaise-laden, old-fashioned potato salads appear at nearly every picnic table in America. Unfortunately, if you are watching your waistline, you will inevitably watch it expand after enjoying too much of a good thing. How about trying some of these new takes on an old favorite:

- Substitute light or reduced-fat mayo for the usual mayo and thin it out with lowfat milk for a less calorie- and fat-loaded classic potato salad.

- Reduced-fat sour cream or plain low-fat yogurt with chopped fresh dill sprigs and scallions can make for a deliciously creamy potato salad with far less guilt.

- Add a little Italian flair by dressing your potatoes lightly with olive oil, vinegar, and some fresh herbs and sliced oil-packed sun-dried tomatoes.

- Serve a roasted baby potato salad with the skins on, coated gently with a dollop of pesto sauce and tossed with slivers of roasted red pepper.

- Make your own German-style potato salad by adding cider vinegar, a little chicken broth, a pinch of sugar and tossing in some diced onion and crumbled crisp-fried turkey bacon.

tion to your repertoire of salad dressings. It will keep refrigerated for a week.

You can purchase shredded cabbage and carrots to speed up the preparation somewhat or use the shredding blade on your food processor. Although the common white or green cabbage is

(continued on page 327)

Have Your Cheese and Eat It Too

Tips for Enjoying High Fat in Little Nibbles

Everyone seems to love the taste of cheese, whether it be a sharp English cheddar, a mild creamy Brie, or a rich, tangy Montrachet. Unfortunately, when watching calorie and fat intake, cheese may be off the menu. Although providing a good amount of protein, most cheeses contain enough saturated fat to drastically outweigh many positive benefits. Must they be off limits when following a healthy diet plan? Not necessarily.

Since most full-fat cheeses, as opposed to reduced-fat versions, are rich and intensely flavored, a little bit can go a long way towards satisfying your taste buds. And salads just may be the best place to add those little nibbles without overdoing your calorie quota. Here are a few tips for enjoying your favorite cheeses in small doses:

- Use the coarse side of a cheese grater to shred cheddar, Swiss, Edam, and other semi-firm cheeses to sprinkle by the tablespoonful over your salad, after dressing it with oil and vinegar. Try the reduced-fat versions of Jarlsberg and cheddar, because they are still quite flavorful, without the extra fat grams.

- Keep packages of precrumbled, soft-ripened cheeses, such as blue, feta, gorgonzola, and goat cheese, on hand for sprinkling into your salad and limit yourself to a tablespoon at most, because these strong-flavored varieties will provide ample taste in little amounts.

- Create a salad around a low-fat fresh curd cheese such as cottage cheese, farmer's cheese, or ricotta by placing a mound in the middle of your greens and accompanying it with fresh or canned fruit and their juices, eliminating the need for dressing.

- Choose bite-size mozzarella balls, cut them into quarters (they'll seem like a lot more), policing yourself to one serving size, and use them as a garnish for a tomato, cucumber, and onion salad, with a little extra virgin olive oil and fresh basil leaves.

- If you are including cheese in your first course or side salad, be mindful of its fat content and reduce the amount of overall calories and fat in your entrée by opting for lean protein and fewer carbohydrates.

- Consider a dessert in European style, by pairing fresh fruit with a nibble of cheese at the end of your meal. Some classic and complementary duos include apples and cheddar, pears and gorgonzola, grapes and asiago, and figs and mascarpone.

(continued from page 325)

traditional in cole slaw making, try the more delicate Chinese Napa or the inner leaves of the Savoy for something different.

GINGER SESAME VINAIGRETTE

2 tablespoons sesame seeds

1 tablespoon peeled and minced fresh ginger

1 garlic clove, minced

1 tablespoon packed light brown sugar

1 tablespoon soy sauce

3 tablespoons unseasoned rice vinegar

¼ cup canola oil

2 tablespoons toasted sesame oil

Salt and pepper to taste

COLE SLAW

2 cups cored and shredded white, Savoy, or Napa cabbage

1 cup shredded carrots

1 cup fresh bean sprouts

½ cup snow peas, blanched in boiling water for 1 minute, drained, and cut into strips

½ red bell pepper, seeded and cut into thin strips

1. To make the vinaigrette, begin by toasting the sesame seeds in a dry skillet over medium heat, shaking frequently until lightly golden. Transfer to a small mixing bowl. Add the remaining dressing ingredients and whisk well to combine. Refrigerate until ready to use.

2. To make the cole slaw, combine the ingredients in a large mixing bowl. Pour the dressing over all and toss well to coat. Let marinate for at least 30 minutes in the refrigerator, tossing occasionally.

3. Before serving, taste for seasoning and add more sesame oil, if desired.

Spicy Asian Slaw: Add ¼ teaspoon red pepper flakes to the ginger sesame vinaigrette to spice up your slaw.

Three-Bean Salad with Sun-Dried Tomato Balsamic Vinaigrette

MAKES 4 TO 6 SERVINGS This salad takes the classic three-bean salad to new and interesting heights with a flavor-packed dressing that makes the beans stand up and demand attention. This is particularly good as part of a cold salad buffet table and is a nice accompaniment to pasta dishes when served over lettuce greens as a side salad.

Choose sun-dried tomatoes that have been marinated in olive oil or use a sun-dried tomato pesto in the dressing, available at some specialty stores, minding the addition of salt. Balsamic vinegar is naturally sweet and requires less oil in salad dressings to balance its acidity. Be sure to let this bean salad marinate as long as possible and even overnight if possible for the flavors to really become absorbed.

SUN-DRIED TOMATO BALSAMIC VINAIGRETTE

¼ cup chopped sun-dried tomatoes or sun-dried tomato pesto

2 garlic cloves, peeled and minced

1 teaspoon prepared mustard

¼ cup balsamic vinegar

½ cup extra virgin olive oil

1 teaspoon sugar

Salt and pepper to taste

SALAD

1 pound fresh green beans, ends trimmed

1 cup canned chickpeas, drained and rinsed

1 cup canned red kidney beans, drained and rinsed

1 small onion, peeled, cut in half, and thinly sliced into half moons

1 celery stalk, ends trimmed and thinly sliced

½ cup sun-dried tomatoes, cut into strips

2 tablespoons chopped fresh parsley leaves (optional)

1. To make the vinaigrette, whisk together the ingredients in a small mixing bowl and refrigerate until ready to use.

2. To make the salad, cook the fresh green beans in boiling salted water until fork tender and immediately refresh under cold running water or plunge into ice water briefly to stop the cooking. Drain well and add to a large mixing bowl containing the chickpeas, kidney beans, onion, celery, and tomato.

3. Pour the dressing over the mixture and toss to coat. Allow to marinate in the refrigerator until ready to serve, at least 45 minutes. Check for seasonings and top with the parsley, if desired.

Hearty Whole-Grain and Pasta Salads

Salads made from healthy whole grains and pasta are excellent additions to your diet at this time, especially for reducing hunger pangs if watching your waistline or cutting back on refined carbohydrates. We have already seen the power of grains, such as barley and oats, for sustaining energy and curbing cravings. Now we'll meet some other grains that offer similar benefits, as well as revamping some old reliable pasta salads.

Hearty salads like these can almost become meals in themselves and are great solutions for traveling lunches and snacks. I will often make several grain and pasta salads for my clients, who will enjoy them as a side dish all week long with everything from roast chicken to soup. Whole grains should become a part of everyone's diet, especially those of us in recovery who can benefit from the slower metabolism of these healthy ingredients. In addition, diabetics and heart patients benefit tremendously by eating whole grains because they help to maintain healthy blood glucose levels while also lowering cholesterol. Besides all that, they are delicious and satisfying. So let's get started with an old favorite—pasta—and see what new possibilities are in store.

Lemon Zesty Pasta Shells with Tuna and Artichokes

MAKES 4 TO 6 SERVINGS Remember the old summer picnic macaroni and tuna salad, smothered in mayonnaise and saturated fat? This alternative will have everyone coming back for more without the guilt as they sing your praises! Although pasta salads that have so-called Italian dressings have been around for a while, they always seem to be plagued by mushy pasta and way too pungent vinegar. This recipe has the delicious flavor of olive oil and lemon juice, and grated lemon rind is the secret ingredient that makes this salad so refreshing and unique.

Tuna that is packed in olive oil is ideal here, but a solid white in spring water, well drained, will work nicely too. Artichoke hearts that are marinated in olive oil are the best choice, but must be drained before being added to the salad. Be sure to add plenty of freshly ground black pepper and don't skimp on the lemon rind—it really enhances the flavors of this salad.

8 ounces (½ box) medium-size pasta shells
One 6-ounce can tuna packed in olive oil, drained
One 6-ounce jar artichoke hearts, drained
2 tablespoons small capers, drained
½ cup pitted black olives, drained and sliced
Juice and grated rind of 1 lemon

½ cup extra virgin olive oil

Salt and pepper to taste

2 tablespoons chopped fresh parsley leaves

1. Cook the pasta shells in boiling salted water according to the package directions. The pasta should be *al dente* (firm to the bite, not mushy). Drain well and rinse under cold running water. Set aside to drain completely.

2. In a large mixing bowl, break up the tuna slightly with a fork. Cut the artichoke hearts into small pieces and add to the bowl. Add the well-drained pasta shells, capers, olives, lemon juice and rind, and olive oil and toss carefully with a rubber spatula to combine. Sprinkle with a little salt, give a few good grindings of black pepper, and add the parsley. Again toss carefully and allow to sit for 10 minutes.

3. Taste for the addition of more salt and pepper if necessary, drizzle a touch more olive oil, and serve.

Farfalle Spinach Salad with Pancetta and Pine Nuts

MAKES 4 TO 6 SERVINGS Both pasta *and* spinach salads get a new look and taste in this delicious combination salad. Farfalle, also known as butterfly pasta or bowties, is the perfect partner for garlic-sautéed baby spinach and the flavorful Italian pancetta. You can substitute diced hickory smoked bacon if you can't find pancetta in your neck of the woods. Toasted pine nuts (also called pignoli) add texture and taste, while shredded carrots add a little color and crunch. This attractive dish is really two salads in one and makes a great addition to a picnic spread or a side salad for grilled chicken or steak.

8 ounces (½ box) farfalle pasta

3 tablespoons pine nuts

2 tablespoons olive oil

2 garlic cloves, peeled and minced

8 ounces baby spinach, washed well and dried

Salt and pepper to taste

2 ounces pancetta, cut into ¼-inch dice

1 shallot, peeled and finely chopped

½ cup cider vinegar

1 teaspoon sugar

½ teaspoon prepared mustard

1 cup sliced fresh mushrooms

½ cup shredded carrots

⅓ cup freshly grated Parmesan cheese

1. Cook the farfalle pasta in boiling salted water according to the package directions. The pasta should be *al dente* (firm to the bite, not mushy). Drain well and rinse under cold water. Set aside to drain completely.

2. In a small dry skillet over medium heat, toast the pine nuts just until lightly golden, shaking the pan to prevent burning, and set aside.

3. In a large skillet, heat the olive oil over medium heat. Add the garlic and cook only 30 seconds or so. Do not brown. Add the spinach, sprinkle with salt and pepper, and cook, stirring, until just wilted, a minute or two. Transfer to a large mixing bowl to cool.

4. In the same skillet over medium-high heat, fry the diced pancetta until crisp and brown. Transfer the pieces with a slotted spoon to a paper towel-lined plate to drain and discard all but 2 tablespoons of the accumulated fat in the skillet. Add the shallot and cook, stirring, over medium heat for 2 minutes. Add the vinegar, sugar, and mustard and bring to a boil, stirring with a wooden spoon to scrape up any browned bits on the bottom of the skillet. Remove from the heat and set aside.

5. To assemble the salad, add the drained pasta to the bowl of garlic-sautéed spinach along with the toasted pine nuts, mushrooms, carrots, and cooked pancetta. Toss well to combine. Add the vinegar dressing and toss to coat. Taste for the addition of salt and pepper, sprinkle with the grated Parmesan cheese, and serve immediately.

Asian Noodle Salad with Peanut Sauce

MAKES 4 TO 6 SERVINGS Peanut and sesame sauces, popular in Asian cuisine, are tasty ways to prepare cold noodles for appetizer salads or side dishes. Tossed with an assortment of stir-fried vegetables, they become a healthy addition to any meal and are particularly good when paired with simply prepared teriyaki chicken or grilled shrimp.

The variety of Asian noodles that exists is extensive, although not always readily available in U.S. supermarkets. Fortunately, just about every noodle from the East has a Western counterpart, so substitutions are not difficult. But if you happen to live near an Asian grocery, explore the shelves and try out the different varieties they offer. For this recipe, I generally seek out the Japanese udon noodle, a soft white wheat flour noodle, but you can use fettuccine, linguine, or the sometimes more available somen noodle.

The standard supermarket peanut butter is fine here. If you are feeling adventurous and would like to explore some alternatives, substitute soybean butter for the peanut butter and get an added boost of soy isoflavones, as well as protein. You could also add some cooked edamame beans for additional crunch, not to mention their health benefits. The addition of hot Szechuan oil is certainly optional and only if you like your noodles spicy (like I do!).

SALAD

8 ounces udon noodles

1 tablespoon canola oil

4 scallions, ends trimmed and cut into
    1-inch pieces

½ red bell pepper, seeded and thinly sliced

1 cup baby or regular bok choy leaves, sliced
    into ½-inch-wide strips

Salt and pepper to taste

½ cup shredded carrots

2 cloves garlic, peeled and minced

One 1-inch piece fresh ginger, peeled and minced

Toasted sesame oil to drizzle over the noodles

½ English or Kirby cucumber, peeled (if desired),
    halved lengthwise, and cut into ¼-inch-thick
    half moons

PEANUT SAUCE

½ cup smooth peanut butter

2 tablespoons rice vinegar

1 tablespoon toasted sesame oil

1 tablespoon soy sauce

1 heaping tablespoon light brown sugar

½ cup hot chicken or vegetable broth

1 teaspoon hot Szechuan oil (optional)

Salt and pepper to taste

GARNISH

½ cup unsalted dry-roasted peanuts

1. To make the noodle salad, start by cooking the udon noodles in boiling salted water according to the package directions. Rinse well under cold water and set aside to drain.

2. In a large skillet or wok, heat the canola oil over high heat until it begins to smoke, then add the scallions, bell pepper, and bok choy. Sprinkle with salt and black pepper and stir-fry quickly for 2 minutes. Add the carrots, garlic, and ginger and stir-fry another minute. Remove from the heat and transfer to a large mixing bowl. Drizzle the cooked and drained udon noodles with a little sesame oil to prevent sticking and add to the bowl. Also add the cucumbers and toss well to combine.

3. To make the peanut sauce, whisk together the ingredients in a small mixing bowl. Taste and add salt and pepper if necessary or more brown sugar, if desired. Pour over the noodle mixture and toss well to coat.

4. Garnish with the peanuts and serve cold or at room temperature.

Chef's Note: If the salad is prepared ahead and chilled, you may need to add a tablespoon or two of warm water just before serving to loosen up the dressing and bring back the smooth, creamy consistency.

Brown Rice, Wild Rice, and Wheat Berry Salad

MAKES 4 TO 6 SERVINGS Rice is another popular ingredient for salads, but here it is combined with both wheat berries and the misnomered wild rice (see right) to create one of the healthiest and most delicious salads I know. This is perhaps my favorite grain salad, not only to eat but to make as well, because of its easy preparation. Unlike other types of grain salads that include several different ingredients and, hence, require separate pots and individual cooking times, these three grains cook together in one pot.

The addition of dried fruit infuses a wonderful sweetness to this salad and makes it a great accompaniment to chicken and turkey. I have also served this warm as a side dish in the wintertime with great success. If you cannot find wheat berries, sold also as "shelled wheat" or "hard wheat," substitute barley, which has a similar texture. I have found it much easier to locate this wheat recently and hopefully you will too. It is a great addition to your diet and has tremendous versatility. Try to seek it out and keep a supply in your fridge. Just like other whole grain and wheat products, it keeps much better when cold.

½ cup brown long-grain rice
½ cup wild rice
½ cup wheat berries
1½ cups chicken or vegetable broth
1½ cups water
¼ cup dried cranberries

Wild About Rice

If you like the nutty flavor and chewy texture of brown rice, you will love the addition of wild rice to soups, salads, and pilafs. Technically, it is not a member of the rice family at all, but is the seed of a wild grass that grows in shallow, muddy waters in the northern United States and Canada. Native Americans have been harvesting wild rice for centuries as a staple of their diet. Nutritionally, wild rice is very similar to brown rice in fiber content and as a source of the much-needed B vitamins, while providing an even richer supply of vitamin E and protein. So, go wild and add some wild rice to your diet for a great nutritional boost and a jolt of flavor!

¼ cup chopped dried apricots
¼ cup raspberry vinegar
1 tablespoon walnut oil
½ cup chopped walnuts
1 tablespoon chopped fresh parsley leaves
Salt and pepper to taste

1. In a medium-size saucepan with a lid, combine the brown rice, wild rice, and wheat berries. Add the chicken broth and water and bring to a boil. Stir, reduce the heat to a simmer, and cook, covered, until all the liquid is absorbed and the grains are tender, 40 to 45 minutes. During the final 15 minutes, add the dried cranberries and apricots, stir to distribute, and cover. Transfer the cooked grains and fruit to a large mixing bowl to cool.

2. Whisk together the raspberry vinegar and walnut oil and add to the grain mixture, tossing to coat. Add the walnuts and parsley, stir to combine, add salt and pepper if necessary, and serve at room temperature or slightly chilled.

Barley Basil Salad with Grape Tomatoes

MAKES 4 TO 6 SERVINGS The healthy and glycemically perfect barley grain finds a delicious home with fresh basil and grape tomatoes in this satisfying salad. I like to serve this with a little sliced smoked mozzarella on a bed of lightly dressed arugula for a great flavor combination. Here, canola oil is used instead of olive oil because it interferes less with the richness of the barley. When yellow pear or grape tomatoes are in season, they make a beautiful addition by replacing half the red grape tomatoes. Cherry tomatoes can also be substituted here.

1 cup pearl barley

2 cups water

Salt

1½ cups red grape tomatoes, cut in half

2 cups fresh basil leaves, chopped

Juice of ½ lemon

1 tablespoon red wine vinegar

2 tablespoons canola oil

Pepper to taste

1. In a medium-size saucepan with a lid, combine the pearl barley, water, and a good pinch of salt and bring to a simmer. Allow to cook, covered, over low heat until tender, 35 to 40 minutes, adding more water if necessary. Rinse under cold water in a colander and set aside to drain.

2. Sprinkle the tomatoes with a little coarse salt and toss lightly in a medium-size mixing bowl. Add the cooled barley and basil and toss again to combine.

3. In a small mixing bowl, whisk together the lemon juice, vinegar, and canola oil and pour over the barley mixture. Toss to coat, add a good grinding of black pepper and salt, if necessary, and serve at room temperature.

Variation: *Edamame* (fresh soybeans) go remarkably well with this salad. Add about 1 cup cooked from frozen for a delicious and healthy Phase Three variation.

Choosing the Perfect Salad Oil

Oil and vinegar is perhaps the simplest and most popular way to dress a salad and today we are offered myriad choices of both, even at our local supermarket. In fact, olive oil, the classic choice for Italian dressings, is now available in many different varieties and flavors, making it difficult at times to make the right choice. How do we discern the best oil for the job? Here are a few hints.

Oils that we use for cooking are not as frequently used in salads, although Italian cooks will often fry in extra virgin olive oil and canola oil will sometimes find its way into the salad bowl. But in general, intensely flavored unrefined oils are reserved for cold salad dishes because they begin to break down and smoke when heated for any amount of time, ruining their taste. Oils such as walnut, hazelnut, toasted sesame, and many fine quality extra virgin olive oils fall into this category. They are wonderfully aromatic and subtly flavored and produce the best results when they are allowed to dominate on their own. For instance, walnut oil is a delicious addition to tossed salads that contain fruit, nuts, cheese, and assertive greens, as well as many grain and legume salads, particularly lentil. Deep green cold-pressed extra virgin olive oil is ideal for bread dipping and drizzling over antipasto platters of vegetables, as well as tangy greens such as arugula and escarole. Although we are lucky enough to be offered some excellent olive oils in our supermarkets and specialty food stores, I must say that I believe the Italians keep the best stuff for themselves, as I have never tasted anything close to the amazingly delicious olive oil available in Italy. Yet there are many more high quality choices these days than there were years ago, thanks in part to the discovered health benefits that olive oil has to offer.

When an oil is to be used in a salad dressing that contains several different flavors, such as herbs, cheeses, and perhaps vegetables, it's usually best to choose one that is more or less neutral in flavor so as not to mask the contribution of the other ingredients. For these types, a light olive oil or canola oil would be appropriate to use. Bottled dressings will often contain safflower oil, a completely neutral and rather tasteless oil, because it does not solidify when refrigerated. Similarly, you may find soybean oil as well as partially hydrogenated oils, which again, add no flavor but offer a longer shelf life and, perhaps most importantly to the manufacturer, are cheaper to use. When buying bottled dressings, look at the label for as few ingredients as necessary and not a laundry list of preservatives and other unpronounceable substances. The more natural (and recognizable) the ingredients, the better.

When making a vinaigrette dressing, which is essentially a mixture of oil and vinegar along with flavored ingredients, the usual ratio of oil to acid is three to one, although some prefer a more acidic taste and may add a splash more vinegar, depending on what else is in the dressing and what it is going to be used for. Vinaigrettes are easy to make and can be whisked together just before serving. Although we have all heard that oil and vinegar don't mix, they can form an emulsion (a smooth combining of otherwise noncombinative liquids) with the help of other ingredients. Xanthum gum is an emulsifier often found in commercial salad dressings. Homemade vinaigrettes do just as well with a small dab of prepared mustard. Try whisking oil and vinegar with a little mustard, honey, salt, and pepper and you will have a creamy (and extremely well-combined) honey mustard dressing that cost about 25 cents to make. You may be tempted never to buy the commercial version again!

Oils such as extra virgin and sesame, as well as nut oils, should be kept in the refrigerator so as not to become rancid, although if you have a cool, dark pantry, this would be adequate for storage. Try to buy only the amounts of oil that you will use for the next two months, since many oils tend to be highly perishable. And whatever you do, don't store them in the cabinet next to the stove for easy access, as that is the quickest way to turn your often expensive oils rancid and unusable. Instead, consider purchasing small cruets to refill when necessary if you like your salad oils within immediate reach on the table.

Bulgur Wheat Salad with Fresh Herbs

MAKES 4 TO 6 SERVINGS Tabbouleh is a classic grain salad made from cracked wheat or "bulgur" wheat and is popular at many delis and restaurants. However, I have always found that the lovely nutty flavor of the wheat is often masked by too much dressing and doctoring. I prefer a version where the grain is the star of the show.

This salad lets the wheat dominate, while aromatic fresh herbs take a supporting role and enhance the overall result. Try it as an accompaniment for grilled lamb or chicken or serve alongside hummus with some pita bread wedges for a complete vegetarian meal.

> 1 cup bulgur (cracked wheat)
> 2 cups water
> 1 tablespoon olive oil
> 1 teaspoon grated lemon rind
> 1 tablespoon *each* finely chopped fresh parsley,
>   mint, cilantro, and chives
> ½ cup diced cucumber
> ½ cup seeded and diced red bell pepper
> Salt and pepper to taste
> Bibb lettuce leaves
> ¼ cup low-fat plain yogurt (optional)

1. In a medium-size saucepan with a lid, combine the bulgur and water, bring to a boil, reduce the heat to low, and simmer, covered, until the wheat is tender, 35 to 40 minutes. Transfer to a medium-size mixing bowl and allow to cool.

2. Add the olive oil, lemon rind, herbs, cucumber, and bell pepper to the bulgur and, using a fork, toss to combine. Season with salt and pepper. Serve individual portions on a lettuce leaf topped with a dollop of yogurt, if desired.

Couscous Salad with Orange, Thyme, and Chickpeas

MAKES 4 TO 6 SERVINGS Actually a form of pasta made from semolina, couscous is a lighter choice for a salad than rice, barley, or wheat and goes particularly well with sliced roasted chicken or turkey. Israeli couscous is composed of larger, perfectly round little balls and has a texture closer to that of pasta. It requires a little longer cooking time than regular couscous, which is generally precooked and takes less than five minutes to prepare. Be sure to check the label on your package to determine the cooking time. If precooked, follow the instructions below.

Chickpeas add nice substance to this salad and go well with the thyme and orange flavors. Combined with some cold leftover diced roast chicken, this salad makes an excellent filling for wraps or can become a main course salad served on a bed of greens.

> 1 cup couscous
> 1½ cups low-sodium chicken or vegetable broth
> Juice and grated rind of 1 orange
> One 15-ounce can chickpeas, drained and rinsed
> 2 teaspoons chopped fresh thyme leaves
> 1 tablespoon extra virgin olive oil
> Salt and pepper to taste

1. Put the couscous in a medium-size mixing bowl and bring the chicken broth and orange juice to a boil in a small saucepan. Immediately pour the hot broth mixture over the couscous, stir briefly with a fork, cover, and allow to sit until all the liquid has been absorbed and the couscous is firm but tender, about 20 minutes.

2. Fluff the couscous with a fork and add the remaining ingredients, tossing to combine. Taste for seasoning and serve at room temperature.

Main Course Salads

When protein enters the salad scene, what was merely a sideshow becomes the main event. Especially welcome on hot summer evenings when turning on the oven is a definite turn-off, cold salad suppers can satisfy the hungriest of appetites, while also providing dieters with a healthy alternative to a large and heavy meal. And leftover meats and fish can find a happy home in main course salads by applying a little creativity.

Some traditional main course salads may be familiar to you, such as Salade Niçoise or Chef's Salad, but the possible combinations of greens, vegetables, and protein are endless, depending upon the contents of your fridge and your own taste. Beginning with what you already have is always a good place to start. Focus on one or two ingredients and create as you go. Some of the best meals I have enjoyed were prepared in just this way. Rounded out with some good quality bread, salad suppers can be a great choice for a quick, light respite.

Curried Chicken Salad

MAKES 4 SERVINGS This chicken salad not only makes a delicious dinner centerpiece, it is also wonderful as a sandwich filling for lunch in pita bread or a wrap. If you have leftover chicken, simply cut it into bite-size pieces before tossing it with the dressing. Otherwise, you can quickly poach some boneless, skinless chicken breasts and proceed from there. Simply simmer them in a pot of water until firm and no longer pink inside. Allow to cool before dicing. Use a mild or Madras curry powder and allow the flavors to marry for at least 30 minutes in the fridge before serving.

CHICKEN SALAD

4 cups cooked chicken, cut into small pieces
1 large celery stalk, ends trimmed and diced
1 teaspoon curry powder
½ cup light mayonnaise
2 tablespoons milk
Salt and pepper to taste

TO SERVE

8 large lettuce leaves, washed and dried
1 ripe mango, peeled, pitted, and sliced
1 green bell pepper, seeded and cut into strips
1 medium-size cucumber, sliced
Pita or Indian naan bread

1. Combine the chicken salad ingredients in a medium-size mixing bowl and allow to chill in the refrigerator for at least 30 minutes.
2. Meanwhile, decoratively arrange the lettuce leaves, mango slices, bell pepper strips, and cucumber slices on a large platter, leaving room in the middle for the chicken salad. When ready to serve, transfer the chicken to the middle of the platter and serve with the pita or naan bread.

Tropical Paradise Chicken Salad

MAKES 4 SERVINGS This is surely one of the tastiest preparations for chicken salad I know and is both light and refreshing on a hot day. If you like, purchase a whole ripe pineapple, slice it in half lengthwise, cut out the fruit, discard the core, and reserve the empty shells for your presentation.

If you are short on leftover chicken, poach three or four boneless, skinless chicken breasts and proceed from there (for poaching instructions, see headnote, page 335). I like watercress with this flavor combination to balance the sweetness of the pineapple, but you can use any greens you might prefer. This is terrific rounded out with corn muffins or banana bread.

CHICKEN SALAD
　4 cups cooked chicken, cut into small pieces
　1 cup fresh or canned pineapple chunks, drained
　½ cup sliced almonds
　½ teaspoon paprika
　½ cup light mayonnaise
　2 tablespoons pineapple juice
　Salt and pepper to taste

TO SERVE
　4 cups watercress, stems removed, washed,
　　and dried

Phase Three and Healthy Weight Loss

During Phases One and Two, we concentrated on specific goals. Staying clean and sober had to be our only true focus in Phase One, and virtually anything that helped us through that difficult period was acceptable, considering the alternative. Dealing with cravings to drink or use was not an easy task, but we saw that healthy food choices could help to keep these feelings at bay. Regular meals and snacks designed to stabilize glucose levels and control hunger pangs were indispensible. And if we reached for a few too many chocolate chip cookies at snack time, at least we were grateful that it wasn't the bottle we grabbed.

During Phase Two, we began to feel more comfortable in our sobriety and took steps in our eating and meal planning to reconnect with food, something that had long been placed on the back burner in deference to our addiction. We began to reestablish healthy relationships with family and friends and found that the pleasures of the table could assist us in healing our bodies, minds, and souls. But along the way, we may have ended up taking in more calories than we were able to burn off and, as a result, we may be looking in the mirror at a slightly larger version of ourselves. So many people in recovery experience weight gain after a time that you can rest assured you are definitely not alone. Of course, there are some folks out there who never seem to pile on any extra pounds, of whom the rest of us are eternally envious! Be that as it may, now just may be the time to think about losing any excess weight you may have accumulated by embarking on a healthy weight-loss plan.

Pineapple shells (optional)
2 kiwi fruits, peeled and sliced
1 orange, cut into wedges

1. Combine the chicken salad ingredients in a medium-size mixing bowl and allow to chill in the refrigerator for at least 30 minutes.

2. Meanwhile, arrange the watercress around the edges of a large platter. If using the pineapple shells, place them in the center, side by side. Decoratively arrange the sliced kiwis and orange wedges around the edge of the platter. Fill the pineapple shells with the chicken salad or place in a mound in the middle of the platter.

Layered Turkey Cobb Salad with Roquefort Dressing

MAKES 4 SERVINGS Created by Robert Cobb, the owner of the Brown Derby in 1920s Los Angeles, this salad has become an American classic. Usually made with slices of roasted chicken or turkey and a wonderful array of salad lettuces and vegetables, the Cobb salad will often include hard-boiled eggs, crumbled bacon, and blue cheese as well.

Here, we focus on our old friend from Phase One, tryptophan-filled turkey, for the main protein ingredient. Lean and tasty turkey bacon becomes our garnish. The healthy avocado (see page 33)

What exactly is a healthy weight-loss plan? First and foremost, any diet that guarantees rapid results with little effort must be suspect. Quick fixes and miracle cures are not the answer, as we know through our recovery experiences. For anything to be long-lasting and worthwhile, it must require effort on our part and patience in the long-term. The simple truth is that we must eat less and move more over an extended period of time. Although there are literally thousands of diet plans you could follow, they all boil down to these basic principles if we hope to achieve and maintain a healthy weight throughout our lifetimes.

Sometimes, a little bit of a jump start is necessary and here we have the advantage of knowing how support from others who are in the same boat can help to guide us when the rowing gets rough. Diet organizations, such as Weight Watchers, that meet for weekly support and record results may be a good idea for those who find going it alone a bit difficult to handle. Similarly, if eating has not only added a few pounds but become an inordinately important part of your existence, groups like Overeaters Anonymous may be appropriate and helpful. Use what you have learned about things like the Glycemic Index, fiber, and basic nutrition to find a plan that works for you. Whatever diet you choose to follow, be patient with yourself and be sure to include exercise as part of your regimen. Begin slowly and wisely. And don't expect dramatic results in record time. Most importantly, just as we may find ourselves during Phase Three having a periodic Phase One day, with cravings, temptations, and perhaps lots of chocolate, forgive yourself if you experience a "slip" in your diet. Just dust yourself off and get right back with the program. Remember that neither Rome nor your spare tire was built in a day—so it will require time and effort to reach your goals, as well as your toes!

also makes an appearance, as do lycopene-rich tomatoes, while vitamin E–packed sunflower seeds provide the finishing touch. You can use either salted or unsalted sunflower seeds depending on your preference. In addition, try to use a clear glass salad bowl in order to see the layered ingredients for optimal presentation.

The Roquefort dressing that accompanies this salad is one of my very favorites, and is, in fact, the first thing I ever made in my food processor way back when. It can also be put together in a blender or whisked by hand. In a pinch, you can substitute blue cheese or gorgonzola, but make the effort to find Roquefort, as it has such a delicious taste and creamy texture. Serve the dressing well chilled on the side for drizzling.

ROQUEFORT DRESSING

¼ pound Roquefort cheese, crumbled

1 small garlic clove, peeled

1 scallion (white part only), ends trimmed and
    roughly chopped

⅓ cup light mayonnaise

¼ cup reduced-fat sour cream

1 tablespoon tarragon vinegar

1 teaspoon prepared mustard

1 teaspoon sugar

Freshly ground black pepper

COBB SALAD

½ head romaine lettuce, washed, dried, and
    roughly torn apart (about 4 cups)

2 cups baby greens

1 medium-size Belgian endive, washed and
    sliced crosswise ½ inch thick

1 large, ripe tomato, thinly sliced

2 medium-size, ripe avocados, pitted,
    peeled, and sliced

¾ pound thinly sliced roasted turkey
    breast, cut into ½-inch-wide strips

2 large hard-boiled eggs, peeled
    and sliced

4 strips turkey bacon, crisp-fried, drained on
    paper towels, and crumbled

1 tablespoon shelled sunflower seeds

1. To make the dressing, combine the ingredients in a food processor or blender and process until smooth and creamy, about 1 minute (the blender may take a bit longer). If mixing by hand, be sure to mince the garlic and scallion first. Transfer to a serving bowl and refrigerate until ready.

2. To make the salad, toss together the lettuces and endive to combine well in a large mixing bowl and place half the mixture in the bottom of a glass salad bowl. Top with the tomatoes and avocados, arranging them close to the edges, and cover with the remaining lettuce mixture. Arrange the turkey and egg slices over the second lettuce layer and sprinkle the crumbled bacon and sunflower seeds over the top. Serve immediately with the dressing on the side.

Chef's Note: *You can prepare the layered salad up to 2 hours before serving and keep it covered in the refrigerator; the acid from the tomatoes will help to keep the avocados from turning brown. However, if prepared any further in advance, sprinkle a little lemon juice over the avocados as you layer them to keep them fresh.*

Tuna and Cannellini Bean Salad Platter

MAKES 4 SERVINGS This is a popular salad combination in Italy and is always enjoyed with an excellent quality extra virgin olive oil and crusty Italian bread on the side. I have often made this as part of an antipasti buffet spread with other Italian specialties. Served with a variety of oven-roasted vegetables (page 348) or juicy, sliced tomatoes atop a bed of spring mix greens as below, this supper salad is sure to please everyone.

TUNA AND BEAN SALAD

Two 6-ounce cans tuna packed in olive oil or spring water, well drained

One 15-ounce can cannellini beans, drained and rinsed

1 teaspoon chopped fresh sage leaves

2 tablespoons extra virgin olive oil

½ small red onion, peeled and diced

Salt and pepper to taste

TO SERVE

4 cups spring mix lettuces or mesclun

2 medium-size, ripe tomatoes, sliced

Salt and pepper to taste

Extra virgin olive oil for drizzling

½ cup oil-cured olives, drained

Crusty Italian bread such as whole wheat or semolina

1. In a medium-size mixing bowl, flake the drained tuna and add the beans, sage, olive oil, onion, and a pinch of salt and fresh ground pepper. Combine gently with a rubber spatula and allow to sit at room temperature for 10 minutes.

2. On a large platter, put the spring greens on one side and top with the tomato slices. Place the tuna and bean salad on the other side of the platter. Season the greens and tomatoes with a little salt and pepper and a drizzle of olive oil. Decorate the platter with the olives and serve with the sliced bread.

Salmon Fillet Salade Niçoise

MAKES 4 SERVINGS Here's a little bit of a twist on the traditional tuna Salade Niçoise. Salmon, another healthy fish loaded with omega-3 fatty acids, takes center stage instead. The recipe for Simple Oven-

All About Olives

Some classic composed salads would not be complete without their olives. Salade Niçoise requires the petite French gems of the same name, while Greek salads must have their Kalamatas. If your supermarket deli is extensive enough, they may have an olive bar where you will find these and numerous other varieties of green, brown, and black olives, variously flavored and all quite delicious. They are wonderful to add to just about any type of salad or antipasto platter and great to have on hand for nibbling. Here's what you need to know about this ancient revered fruit of the symbolic branch of peace.

Until olives are processed, their fresh state is rather bitter in taste and usually green in color. When they are harvested and how they are brined and cured determine their final appearance and flavor. Young green varieties produce the familiar Spanish olive, while those that are left to ripen on the tree will naturally turn dark brown or black, such as the Kalamata, Gaeta, and Niçoise. In between these, the ripe, yet still green olive is the type used to make the common black olive we usually find in cans, also called the Mission olive. Its distinct flavor, or lack thereof, comes from curing and oxygenation, without brining (a period spent in a salt solution). Dry-cured olives, also called oil cured, are dark black and wrinkly in appearance with a distinct bitterness. These are my favorites.

Unopened jars of olives have an extremely long shelf life—up to two years—but once opened, they will last several weeks only. Keep a supply of them on hand for quick additions to salads, pasta dishes, sautés, and snack trays. Although high in fat, olives boast healthy monounsaturated oils, which many believe are responsible in part for the excellent cardiovascular health of the Mediterranean people.

Poached Salmon (page 386) is perfect for this dish, but you can quickly cook salmon fillets under the broiler, grill, or even microwave them (page 144) specifically for this dish. Allow about ¼ pound per person and either arrange on individual plates or on one large platter for the table.

Instead of the usual French vinaigrette found on most Salades Niçoises, the Dill and Yogurt Dressing makes a delicious accompaniment, complementing the salmon perfectly.

DILL AND YOGURT DRESSING

1 cup low-fat plain yogurt
½ cup milk
1 teaspoon fresh lemon juice
1 teaspoon sugar
2 tablespoons chopped fresh dill
Salt and pepper to taste

SALAD

½ head romaine or green leaf lettuce, washed
    and dried
1 pound salmon fillet, cooked (see headnote)
4 large hard-boiled eggs, peeled and quartered
¼ pound green beans, ends trimmed, boiled
    in water to cover until fork tender, drained,
    and cooled completely under cold running
    water
2 medium-size, ripe tomatoes, cut into wedges
2 medium-size red potatoes, boiled in water
    to cover until fork tender, drained, cooled,
    peeled, and sliced
¼ cup Niçoise olives, drained
½ green bell pepper, seeded and cut into ¼-inch-
    thick rings
½ cup sliced cucumber
Lemon wedges for garnish

1. To make the dressing, whisk together the ingredients in a medium-size mixing bowl and chill until ready to use.

2. To make the salad, be sure all the ingredients

are cool or at room temperature. Begin to arrange a large platter or 4 individual plates with the lettuce leaves on the bottom, the cooked salmon in the middle, partially flaked, and the remaining components arranged decoratively around. Serve with lemon wedges and the dressing on the side.

Mexican Marinated Shrimp Salad

MAKES 4 SERVINGS America's favorite shellfish provides the basis for this fabulous marinated salad laced with fresh lime juice and cilantro. The minced jalapeño peppers add just the right amount of zip—use as much as you like, depending on their potency. Marinating overnight will really boost the flavor of this recipe, but it can also be enjoyed in just a couple of hours if you can't wait.

This is a favorite salad for buffet entertaining and offers a great break from the usual shrimp cocktail we always see. As a dinner salad entrée, serve with a large tossed bowl of assertive greens lightly dressed with olive oil and vinegar and accompany with some crusty French or whole grain bread. A bowl of Quickie Gazpacho (page 111) would also be delicious to include on the side.

1 pound bag frozen cooked jumbo shrimp, tail on
1 medium-size jalapeño, or more to taste, seeded
    and minced
2 tablespoons chopped fresh cilantro leaves
¼ cup light olive oil
Juice of 1 lime
1 tablespoon red wine vinegar
Salt and pepper to taste
Lime wedges for serving

1. Place the shrimp in a large colander and thaw under cold running water or spray. Pat dry and transfer to a large mixing bowl.

2. In a small mixing bowl, whisk together the jalapeño, cilantro, olive oil, lime juice, and vinegar until the mixture thickens, then pour over the shrimp. Gently toss with a rubber spatula until the shrimp are well coated. Season lightly with salt and pepper (you can add more to taste later), cover with plastic wrap, and refrigerate at least 2 hours or preferably overnight. Occasionally, give the shrimp a light tossing in the marinade to coat evenly.

3. To serve, remove the shrimp from the marinade with a slotted spoon and divide among 4 plates, garnishing each plate with a lime wedge. You can also serve family style, straight from the bowl.

Recovery Note: Marinated shrimp salads and appetizers on Mexican restaurant menus may be laced with tequila or vodka. Ask before ordering.

Remembering Your Salad Days and Telling Your Story

Ah yes. Those salad days of yore. A time of youthful inexperience, innocence, and indiscretion. Today that is how we define this euphemistic expression, but when Shakespeare coined it in *Antony and Cleopatra*, his words were less affectionate: "My salad days; when I was green in judgment, cold in blood."

If we were to ask those family members and friends who suffered through our years of addiction, it is likely they would agree more with Shakespeare than the dictionary. When we were actively seeking and using our drugs of choice, our judgment was greatly impaired, even seemingly naïve, while our actions were often cold and calculating. We would do virtually anything to get what we wanted and feed our bodies what they craved. We were consumed by a disease that had a tight hold on our entire being. Are these "salad days" really something we want to remember, or are they best left forgotten once our amends and apologies are made?

Sometimes by telling our stories to those who are newer to recovery than we are, as well as to individuals who still suffer in the darkness of addiction, we can help provide strength and hope through our experiences. If you have ever listened to someone else tell the story of their addiction and recovery, in all its startling, sometimes horrific detail, and identified with something they have said, then you know the power that you also possess to move someone else, maybe even out of that final step of denial and into the first step of acceptance.

Being of service and support to other alcoholics and addicts has always been a cornerstone of twelve-step programs, as well as many other addiction support groups. Recently, research has confirmed what we've known all along—alcoholics can help other alcoholics get and stay sober. And by helping others, we can help ourselves too, because telling our story will never fail to remind us why we are here in the first place. So, don't toss those "salad days" memories aside just yet—they might have the power to save someone's life.

Super Supper Chef's Salad

MAKES 4 TO 6 SERVINGS A main course chef's salad is traditionally made from leftovers that the chef may rescue and put to another use, such as slices of leftover roast beef or turkey. In diners, cold cuts are generally used and rolled up into those funny-looking spirals interlaced with processed American cheese. I prefer to make a chef's salad from a combination of delicious leftovers and some new and fresh ingredients as well. You are the creator here and whatever you happen to find in the fridge that can be doctored up a bit and presented in a new way is the basis for your Super Supper Chef's Salad. Adding a couple of ingredients specifically prepared for your chef's salad makes it seem less like a plate of leftovers and more like a planned orchestration of flavors and textures. Making a dressing especially for the salad also adds a special touch.

Below you will find my suggestions for a chef's salad that is sure to please everyone, but feel free to make your own additions and variations, depending on your taste and the contents of your pantry and fridge. You are the chef, so go to town and enjoy creating. Remember, too, that a beautiful presentation makes even the humblest of foods appear fancy and gourmet. Serve with warm biscuits, cornbread, or even garlic bread to round out the meal. I particularly like the poppy seed dressing below, but a plain vinaigrette or other type of dressing is certainly appropriate. (For some background on the poppy seed, check out "Poppy Seeds and Drug Screening: A Case for False Positives?" on page 290.)

POPPY SEED DRESSING
1 cup light mayonnaise
½ cup buttermilk
¼ cup honey
¼ cup cider vinegar
2 tablespoons poppy seeds
Salt and pepper to taste

SALAD
1 large red bell pepper
1 cup small broccoli florets
1 head romaine or green leaf lettuce, separated into leaves, washed, and dried
1 small head radicchio, cored and roughly chopped
1 small endive, cored and cut into ½-inch-thick strips
1 medium-size cucumber, cut in half lengthwise and cut into thin half moons
½ medium-size red onion, peeled and thinly sliced
1 cup diced cooked chicken or turkey breast meat
¼ pound sliced baked or boiled ham, cut into strips
One ¼-pound piece Swiss cheese (Emmenthaler, Jarlsberg, etc.), cut into ¼-inch cubes
One 8-ounce can (1 cup) chickpeas, drained and rinsed
¼ pound thinly sliced roast beef or a small (¼ pound) grilled steak (sirloin or filet mignon) cut into strips
1 large, ripe tomato, cut into wedges
½ cup crumbled blue cheese

1. To make the dressing, whisk together the ingredients in a small mixing bowl and allow to chill for 1 hour before using.

2. To make the salad, roast the bell pepper by placing it directly over the stove's open flame using tongs and turning it occasionally until the entire outside skin has turned black. You may also do this under the broiler or on a grill. Place the blackened pepper in a small bowl, cover with aluminum foil, and allow it to steam on its own until cool enough to handle, about 20 minutes. Rub the outside of the pepper with a paper towel or your hands, removing the blackened skin and discarding it. You may briefly run the pepper under cold water to aid the process, but some of the flavor will be lost, so do this only if necessary. Cut open the skinned pepper, remove the core and seeds, and cut into strips. Set aside.

3. Blanch the broccoli florets by plunging them into salted boiling water for 1 minute and immediately draining them and running cold water over the florets until they are cool. Lay on a paper towel to dry.

4. Reserve several whole leaves of the romaine or green leaf lettuce. Tear the remaining lettuce into medium-size pieces and place in a large mixing bowl. Add the radicchio and endive and toss lightly to combine. Add the broccoli florets, cucumber, onion, diced chicken, ham, Swiss cheese, and chick-peas and, using tongs or your hands, toss gently to distribute the ingredients throughout.

5. Arrange the whole lettuce leaves on a large serving platter and transfer the tossed salad ingredients on top of them. Place the slices of the roast beef decoratively around the platter's edge, along with the wedges of tomato. Place the roasted red bell pepper strips in a mound in the center of the platter. Sprinkle the crumbled blue cheese over all and serve with the dressing on the side, along with your choice of biscuits or bread, if desired.

10 | *Vegetarian Cooking*
Expanding Your Culinary Horizons

W hen most of us think of a vegetarian diet, we imagine plates of tasteless tofu, accompanied by mounds of salad greens or perhaps a bowl of rice and beans. Although not terribly far off in terms of ingredients, vegetarian eating is not nearly so stark and uninteresting. Years ago, when plant-based eating first became popular, there were limited food choices available for those who aimed to eat a balanced meal with plenty of nutritional impact, while avoiding animal products. But, for the nearly 16 million people in America today who call themselves vegetarians, the possibilities are now enormous and delicious.

Even if you are not inclined to restrict your diet to this extent, nutritionists now recommend that everyone should eat at least one vegetarian dinner per week. The overwhelming benefits of vegetarianism, as well as the proven healthful properties of soy, have prompted government health officials to admit that equivalent amounts of beans, tofu, and other plant-based proteins can adequately replace sources from meat, poultry, and fish. Although a strict vegetarian diet must be careful to include certain necessary nutrients not found in the animal kingdom (see page 352 for a detailed discussion of vegetarianism), opting for a meatless meal even once a week will go a long way to improving our overall health and well being. As we become more health conscious in Phase Three, we should try to welcome a few different, even unfamiliar dietary changes that may help us to enhance our recovery lifestyle and attain our health goals. Small, incremental changes, such as adding one vegetarian meal to our menu per week, will be more likely to stick in the long run than any sudden, dramatic changes, which ultimately could create inordinate stress and, even at this time, result in cravings and behavior that could jeopardize our sobriety. For those who already consider their diet to be mainly vegetarian, this chapter may become your "comfort food" set of recipes, which will provide both excellent sustenance and delicious, heart-warming pleasure.

Soy, of course, is the focus of much diet and health research these days, even though vegetarians have been consuming it routinely for years. As a powerful addition to our diets to help prevent disease, we'll be investigating a multitude of ways to increase your soy intake in both meat- and plant-based diets in "When Food Is Your Preventive Medicine." For now, however, soy will appear briefly as a healthful ingredient and tasty addition to several dishes. Similarly, the question of how to include the all-important omega-3 fatty acids in the vegetarian diet will be answered in the forthcoming chapter. Although most omega-3 found in nature is animal-derived, specifically from fish, there are several plant sources of this powerful nutrient that can be included in our diet and we'll be exploring these extensively later on.

Many of the recipes from previous chapters would make excellent choices for vegetarian meals, such as the numerous soups in Phase One (made with vegetable broth instead of chicken or beef broth), as well as the side and first course salads we prepared in Chapter 9 that contain a plentitude of greens, vegetables, and even fruit. Rounded out, if you like, with a hearty grain bread, you have a simple meatless dinner that is both filling and deliciously satisfying. But vegetarian eating has the potential of being much more creatively varied and the recipes in this chapter will prove this beyond any doubt you may have about boring veggie-based meals. For those who have yet to venture into the world of vegetarian eating, I guarantee you will be happily surprised.

Starters and Light Fare

Vegetables can provide the base for a great beginning to a meal by whetting the appetite without filling us up. They can also be the focus of a light supper or lunch, embellished with a salad of simple greens on the side, and are an excellent choice when weight watching, because they are generally lower in saturated fat and calories. These are some of my very favorite preparations and those most relished by my personal chef clients. Enjoy them as a starter to the main course selections that follow or as a light meal on their own.

Globe Artichokes with Italian Bread Crumb Stuffing

MAKES 4 SERVINGS How to eat an artichoke has baffled even some of the most sophisticated of diners, so don't feel the least bit intimidated by this unusual looking vegetable of the thistle family. It is well worth getting to know, particularly since recent research has uncovered the artichoke's amazing prebiotic ability (see "Making Friends with Bacteria: Artichokes and Digestive Health," next page). In addition, artichokes offer necessary fiber; are low in calories; contain good amounts of magnesium, potassium, and vitamin C; and provide three grams of protein as well, making them an excellent choice for vegetarian diets.

Although globe artichokes come in many sizes (globe referring to the true artichoke, as opposed to the Jerusalem or Chinese artichoke), look for large or jumbo varieties for this recipe. They will be far meatier in both the leaves and heart and make great receptacles for the bread crumb stuffing, which will be packed in between the leaves. Some stuffed artichokes are loaded with filling, often sausage- or crab-based, but this recipe is lighter and perfect as a starter since the stuffing is merely a sprinkling of flavorful bread crumbs, meant only to provide a complement to the artichoke rather than take over its starring role.

Artichokes should be washed well in between the leaves to remove any grit. Sometimes the dangerously pointy leaves should be trimmed with scissors by snipping off about ½ inch of the ends. Rub a cut lemon over any snipped areas to prevent browning. Not all artichokes will require snipping, depending upon the age they were when picked, but usually the larger varieties available in the summer months will have these prickly thorns. Since we are not really stuffing them in the true sense of the word, we needn't remove the inner fuzzy inedible center called the choke until we encounter it in our eating, so our preparation will be quite easy. Cut

off the bottom stem so that the artichoke can stand upright. To assist in filling the leaves and cooking more quickly, press any closed leaves open by turning the artichoke upside down and twisting it on a solid surface. You'll hear a squeaky sound that indicates the artichokes are fresh, as the leaves are persuaded to open.

¼ cup Italian-seasoned dry bread crumbs
2 tablespoons grated Pecorino Romano cheese
½ teaspoon garlic salt
Freshly ground black pepper to taste
4 large globe artichokes, stems removed, washed well, and leaves trimmed if necessary
4 large garlic cloves, peeled and gently smashed
Extra virgin olive oil for drizzling

1. In a small mixing bowl, stir together the bread crumbs, cheese, garlic salt, and pepper.

2. Open up the outer leaves of the artichoke and, using a teaspoon, sprinkle a little of the bread crumb mixture into the openings. Fill only the larger outer green leaves and stop when you reach the yellow-tinged ones. Continue filling each artichoke until you have used all of the bread crumbs. Place a garlic clove into the soft center of each artichoke and set them side by side in a pot big enough to hold them all comfortably.

3. Add about 1 inch of cold water to the pot and drizzle a little olive oil over the top of each artichoke. Cover and bring to a simmer, cooking over the lowest of heat until the outer leaves can be easily removed, 30 to 45 minutes. Check occasionally to see if the water level is low and add as necessary.

4. Remove the artichokes from the pot with a pair of tongs and transfer them to a plate lined with paper towels to soak up any excess water. Serve warm or at room temperature.

Making Friends with Bacteria

Artichokes and Digestive Health

Bacteria are normally present in the human digestive tract, with different strains numbering in the hundreds. But not all of them are bad to have around. Friendly bacteria, also called probiotics, are live microorganisms that can protect the body from "unfriendly bacteria," the guys we hope to eliminate when we take antibiotics. Unfortunately, antibiotics do not discriminate between the good guys and the bad guys, killing off our friends in addition to our enemies. Without these beneficial bacteria, we may become susceptible to many digestive ailments, including even colon cancer, as well as lowered immunity and a host of other health problems. And antibiotics are not the only assassins—stress, chlorinated water, anti-inflammatory drugs, chemotherapy and, yes, even alcohol can destroy the good guys in record numbers.

Eating live active cultures such as those found in yogurt and other fermented foods such as miso and pickles can help us maintain a healthy balance of bacteria throughout our gastrointestinal system (see page 99 for a discussion of fermented foods). But we can do even more for our bacterial friends. By eating foods that contain prebiotics, fiber-like substances of which inulin and fructooligosaccharide (FOS) are just two, we can enhance not only the amount but the actions of our probiotic friends, providing them with necessary food to do their job. And this is where artichokes can be of great help. In addition to the many other healthy benefits artichokes offer, they are also a great source of prebiotics, as are onions, bananas, asparagus, whole-grain breads, and some tubers.

A word or two regarding tummy upsets. If you are not used to foods containing probiotics and prebiotics, you may experience a bit of gastric discomfort at first, as the good guys go to battle with the bad. This will eventually pass and the reverse will be true; upon regular consumption, artichokes, in particular, are known to be an excellent aid to digestion. In fact, during Roman times, they were offered at the end of a meal to provide relief from overeating.

Perhaps the most famous tale of artichoke consumption is from the sixteenth century, when Catherine de Medici of Italy, having married King Henry II, was forced to relocate to France, where she found herself missing her beloved artichokes, not to mention her talented chefs. She summoned her culinary experts (and artichokes) to her new locale, single-handedly introducing many new ingredients and cooking techniques that today comprise the basics of French cooking. On one evening in particular, however, she consumed so many artichokes that she suffered severe indigestion for days, no doubt brought on by the sudden reintroduction of prebiotics to her system, as they helped the probiotics go to war with the harmful bacteria. We can guess that internal bacteria battle was probably no less fierce than the infamous war between the Huguenots and French Catholics, which also occurred under Catherine's reign.

Roasted Vegetable Melange

MAKES 4 SERVINGS This delicious platter of assorted roasted vegetables is a great start to any meal and would make a particularly good beginning as an antipasto platter with the addition of olives, tomatoes, and assorted cheeses. Healthy olive oil adds wonderful flavor, while a sprinkling of Parmesan cheese provides the finishing touch. Surprisingly, many vegetables do very well with this method, including cauliflower, which can be turned into a fabulous version of Cream of Cauliflower Soup (page 88) when the quantity below is doubled.

Asparagus makes a terrific addition to any vegetable platter. Roasting precludes the necessity of peeling—simply cut off the stalks where the woody part begins. Look for thick, firm asparagus stalks without brown blemishes and with tightly closed tips. Although some chefs consider white asparagus a special delicacy, I find them a bit tasteless and stringy and certainly not worth the usually prohibitive supermarket price. Asparagus is a good source of vitamins A, B, and C, as well as iron.

½ medium-size head cauliflower, leaves removed
1 small yellow squash, ends trimmed and cut into
  ½-inch-thick rounds
1 pound fresh asparagus, woody bottoms removed
½ medium-size red or orange bell pepper, seeded
  and cut into ½-inch-wide strips
1 cup canned chickpeas, drained and rinsed
¼ cup extra virgin olive oil
Salt and pepper to taste
2 heaping tablespoons freshly grated Parmesan
  cheese

1. Preheat the oven to 375 degrees.
2. Remove 1 inch from the cauliflower stalk, keeping the rest to hold the florets together. Using a large chef's knife, cut the cauliflower into ¼-inch-thick slices so that they will lie flat on a baking sheet. Try not to crumble the florets as you slice. Place in a single layer, along with the squash slices, on a baking sheet with a rim that has been lightly coated with olive oil. On another lightly oiled baking sheet with a rim, place the asparagus and bell pepper in a single layer and sprinkle the chickpeas around them.

3. Drizzle the ¼ cup of extra virgin olive oil over both sheets of vegetables and sprinkle with salt and pepper. Roast in the oven, occasionally shaking the pans to brown evenly, 25 to 30 minutes. Use a metal spatula halfway through to turn over the cauliflower and squash slices.

4. When the vegetables are lightly browned and fork tender, immediately remove them from the oven and sprinkle the Parmesan over them. Let rest for 5 minutes, then serve family style on a platter or make individual appetizer plates.

Caponata with Fennel and Pignoli

MAKES 6 TO 8 SERVINGS Here the classic Italian eggplant appetizer is enhanced with fragrant fennel, our old friend from Phase One that is an aid to digestion and a tackler of flatulence, which tends to be a common herbivore complaint. Pignoli, or pine nuts, add a tasty crunch and a nice dose of potassium to this dish, as well. Pignoli are available in the condiment, baking, or Italian-ingredient section of your supermarket and usually come in small jars, but are more economically purchased by the bag in specialty grocers or health food stores. They should be kept in the refrigerator or freezer, as their high fat content causes them to go rancid quickly. They are one of the classic ingredients in pesto sauce and also make delicious additions to cookies so having some on hand is not a bad idea, if you have the chance to buy them in bulk.

The longer the caponata sits, the more flavorful it will become, so making this ahead of time is a good thing to do when possible. Generally served cold or at room temperature, this delicious eggplant palate teaser is great for spreading on crusty bread and crackers or can become part of a vegetable antipasto platter.

3 tablespoons olive oil, plus more if needed
    for frying
1 large eggplant, ends trimmed, peeled,
    and cut into ½-inch cubes
Salt and pepper to taste
1 medium-size onion, peeled and diced
1 medium-size fennel bulb, fronds removed,
    rough stalks peeled before chopping, and
    bulb cut into ½-inch pieces
2 large garlic cloves, peeled and minced
⅓ cup pine nuts
½ cup chopped pitted green olives
1 cup canned diced tomatoes with juices
¼ cup small capers, drained
1 tablespoon balsamic vinegar
1 tablespoon red wine vinegar
Pinch of sugar

1. Heat the olive oil in a large nonstick skillet over medium heat and add the eggplant. Season with salt and pepper and cook, stirring often, until the eggplant is soft inside and lightly browned on the inside, about 12 minutes. You can add more olive oil if needed to prevent sticking. Remove the cooked eggplant with a slotted spoon and transfer to a bowl. Set aside.

2. Heat a touch more oil in the skillet, add the onion and fennel, season with salt and pepper, and cook over medium heat, stirring occasionally, until softened but not brown, about 8 minutes. Add the garlic and pine nuts and cook a further minute, stirring often. Add the remaining ingredients to the skillet, stir well to combine, and bring to a simmer. Stir in the cooked eggplant and continue to cook, stirring

often, until the eggplant begins to break down and the mixture appears thick, about 5 minutes.

3. Remove from the heat, taste for seasoning and let cool slightly, then cover and chill. Bring to room temperature, if desired, before serving.

Sun-Dried Tomato and Pepper Jack Quiche

MAKES 6 TO 8 SERVINGS Thankfully, quiche has survived its bad rap from the he-man population and become a staple offering in most supermarket delis and freezer sections. Homemade quiches, however, can't be beat and allow you to be creative in your choice of cheese and filling. Here we are using the intensely flavored sun-dried tomato as our vegetable, as well as roasted peppers and the pleasantly spicy pepper Jack cheese, for those of us who enjoy a little bit of kick. Plain Monterey Jack could be substituted for the pepper Jack, if you prefer. Half-and-half will make for the ultimate filling (even light cream, if you can spare the calorie and fat extravagance!). If watching your weight, substitute reduced-fat milk, but no less than 2 percent, however, as the lack of liquid fat will upset the overall consistency of the cooked quiche.

In Phase Two, we took advantage of the convenience of prepared piecrusts and if you are all thumbs in the baking department, you can certainly use them here. But, as we try to eliminate hydrogenated oils from our diet, it's not a bad idea to tackle a bit of piecrust making, especially the whole wheat version included here. A food processor really makes this a snap, but you can also use a pastry cutter or fork. After a few tries, you may decide it's not so awful a prospect and happily incorporate homemade piecrusts in your dessert making as well. Whole wheat crusts are particularly delicate, so I always roll them between two pieces of waxed or parchment paper as instructed below, which also assists in transferring the crust to the pie pan.

Quiche is delicious when warm or at room temperature and makes a terrific take-along lunch as well as an appetizer or light supper. It also freezes extremely well, so any leftovers can be wrapped tightly in plastic wrap, then aluminum foil, and kept in the freezer for up to one month.

WHOLE WHEAT PIECRUST

1¼ cups whole wheat pastry flour

¼ teaspoon salt

½ cup (1 stick) unsalted butter, very cold and cut into ½-inch dice

⅓ cup ice cold water, or more as needed

QUICHE FILLING

1 cup loosely packed shredded pepper Jack cheese

⅓ cup roughly chopped marinated sun-dried tomatoes, patted dry of excess oil

⅓ cup roughly chopped roasted peppers (see page 120 for instructions or use jarred)

3 large eggs

1 cup half-and-half (or whole or 2 percent milk)

Dash of ground nutmeg

Salt and pepper to taste

1. To make the piecrust, have ready a 9-inch deep-dish pie pan. Place all the ingredients, except the water, in a food processor and pulse until mixture resembles sand, but butter bits are still visible, 5 to 10 seconds. You may also do this step with a pastry blender or fork, if desired. Add the cold water a little at a time and process (or stir in) for several seconds until the dough forms a ball.

2. Transfer the dough onto a piece of lightly floured wax or parchment paper, sprinkle with a little more flour on the dough, flatten a bit with the palm of your hand, and place another piece of wax or parchment paper on top. Use a rolling pin to form a circle of dough slightly larger than the pie pan, adding more flour as necessary to prevent sticking. Carefully transfer the dough to the pan and press lightly to fit, reattaching any pieces that may come apart. Flute the edges with your fingers and refrigerate for 10 minutes.

3. Preheat the oven to 350 degrees. Poke a few holes in the bottom of the piecrust with the tines of a fork and bake until the crust is very lightly browned on the edges and set in the middle but still uncooked, about 12 minutes. Remove from the oven and immediately sprinkle half of the cheese over the bottom of the crust to melt and form a seal. Add the sun-dried tomatoes, roasted peppers, and the remaining cheese, sprinkling around evenly, and set aside.

4. In a medium-size mixing bowl, whisk together the eggs, half-and-half, and nutmeg and season with salt and pepper. Slowly pour the mixture into the pie shell and bake until the filling is set and lightly browned and the crust is golden, 45 to 55 minutes. Allow to cool somewhat before slicing and serving.

Broccoli and White Cheddar Quiche: Substitute ⅔ cup cooked broccoli florets for the sun-dried tomatoes and peppers and white cheddar cheese for the pepper Jack.

Spinach and Mushroom Quiche: Substitute ⅓ cup chopped cooked spinach leaves and ⅓ to ½ cup sautéed mushrooms of your choice for the sun-dried tomatoes and peppers. Use Swiss, Jarlsberg, Emmenthal, or Gruyère cheese in place of the pepper Jack.

Asparagus and Smoked Gouda Quiche: Substitute ⅔ cup cut-up cooked asparagus spears for the sun-dried tomatoes and peppers and smoked gouda for the pepper Jack.

Zucchini, Olive, and Fontina Quiche: Substitute ½ cup diced cooked zucchini and 2 tablespoons chopped pimento-stuffed olives for the sun-dried tomatoes and peppers. Use shredded Italian fontina for the pepper Jack and add 1 tablespoon finely chopped fresh basil leaves to the egg mixture.

Chef's Note: If not rolling out your piecrust immediately, gather the dough together, wrap securely in plastic wrap, and refrigerate until later, but remember to allow it to warm up a bit before attempting to roll it out, as whole-wheat pastries tend to crumble easily when cold. You can substitute plain whole-wheat flour in the crust, but your crust will be less tender and may need a touch more water. Similarly, all-purpose flour will be fine, but less nutritional and will require a little less water for the dough to come together. Consider instead a nice compromise with King Arthur's white whole-wheat flour, available in many supermarkets or through their website (see the "Resources" section, page 455, for more information). (See page 285 for a discussion of different flours and their uses.) For dessert piecrusts, add 1 tablespoon sugar to the flour with the salt.

Potato and Caramelized Onion Tart

MAKES 4 TO 8 SERVINGS This recipe is a delicious combination of sweet caramelized onions and satisfying potatoes in a light puff pastry crust, all tied together with quick-melting mozzarella cheese. I will usually make this in a rectangular fluted tart pan with a removable bottom and cut it into squares for serving, but a round tart pan would work equally well.

Purchased puff pastry, found in the freezer sec-

tion of your supermarket, will make this preparation easy. Just cut pieces to fit the tart pan and join them with a little water as paste, pressing them together. If you happen to have leftover baked or boiled potatoes (any type will do), you can skin these and slice them for the potato layer. Otherwise, quickly boil a couple of medium-size red-skinned, Yukon Gold, or another variety of potato in salted water until just fork tender. Allow to drain and let cool for 20 minutes before peeling and slicing, so that the water has a chance to evaporate.

Packets of preshredded mozzarella cheese are easily found in the dairy section of the supermarket. Some varieties have bits of tomato, peppers, and herbs mixed in, or are combined with other cheeses into what's called a "pizza" mix. Any of these would be delicious here and it is okay to opt for part-skim mozzarella. However, avoid the non-fat varieties, because they will not melt properly.

1 sheet frozen puff pastry, thawed but still cold
1 tablespoon unsalted butter
1 large onion, peeled, cut in half, and thinly sliced into half-moons
Salt and pepper to taste
1 teaspoon dried *herbes de Provence* (see page 354)
2 medium-size potatoes (any type), cooked (see headnote), peeled, and cut into ¼-inch-thick rounds
8 ounces mozzarella cheese, shredded (about 1 cup)

1. Preheat the oven to 400 degrees.
2. Roll out and cut the puff pastry dough to fit the bottom and sides of a 10 x 5-inch rectangular or 9-inch round tart pan with a removable bottom. Moisten any pieces with water to join them together, poke holes into the bottom with a fork, and bake until lightly golden but not fully cooked, about 12 minutes.
3. Meanwhile, melt the butter in a large skillet

over medium heat, add the onion, season with salt and pepper, and cook, stirring often, until soft and lightly browned, 10 to 12 minutes. Stir in the *herbes de Provence*, taste for additional seasoning, and set aside.

4. Place the potato rounds in a single layer over the partially baked pastry crust (a little overlapping is fine) and sprinkle with salt. Spread the cooked onion over the potatoes and sprinkle the mozzarella cheese evenly over the top. Bake until the cheese has melted and begun to brown and the tart crust is deep golden, about 15 minutes. Allow to cool for 5 minutes before lifting up from the pan sides and serving.

Do You Know Who's Coming to Dinner?

A Guide to Vegetarian Eaters

When someone tells you they are vegetarian, what exactly does that mean? If their only restriction is that they don't eat red meat, then they are not vegetarians at all, just red-meat abstainers. But if they are vegan, lacto-ovo eaters, or macrobiotic followers, would you know what to serve (or not to serve) if they came for dinner? Here are a few helpful definitions:

THE LACTO-OVO VEGETARIAN: Here we have the most popular type of vegetarian and perhaps the easiest to accommodate. Although they do not eat meat, fish, or poultry, they do include eggs and milk products in their diet. This means cheese is also okay, so any sort of pasta dish (without the meatballs) would certainly be fine to serve, as would dishes like omelets (filled with veggies) or bean burritos with sour cream and guacamole. Ice cream will often be a favorite dessert.

THE LACTO VEGETARIAN: This is the lacto-ovo minus the eggs, so a little more attention needs to be paid to ingredients. It all depends upon how strict their consumption of eggs is, since many breads, muffins, and other baked goods will contain them. Some lacto vegetarians will only avoid eggs staring back up at them from the plate, while happily eating products that disguise their presence. The best thing to do is ask. Dairy is perfectly acceptable, however, so cheese-based sauces (mac and cheese is a good choice) or creamed soups are usually okay.

THE OVO-VEGETARIAN: Here is the reverse of the lacto eater—eggs are eaten, but milk products are avoided. This can be a bit tricky and again depends on how strict a dairy snubber they are. Chances are these folks may be lactose intolerant as well, so be careful not to include any milk or cheese by accident. Omelets (without the cheese) are a good choice, as are hearty meatless soups and stews. Dessert may pose a small dilemma, but to get around this comfortably, when they ask if they can bring anything, have them provide the dessert. Then you'll know for sure if milk products (including chocolate) are totally off limits.

THE VEGAN: These eaters are usually quite strict in their diet, excluding all meat, poultry, eggs, dairy, and even honey, and they will often shun products such as wool, silk, and, of course, leather, in their choice of lifestyle. So, stick with the veggies, grains, and beans in this case and ask what exactly they will not be able to eat, so there are no surprises. Often, this type of vegetarian has made a serious and conscientious choice that may have moral and ethical undertones, so it would be gracious to abide by their wishes whenever possible.

Some rarer types of vegetarians we may come across on occasion are fructarians, who eat mainly fruit, nuts, and seeds and will only eat plants that can be harvested without killing the plant; macrobiotics, who practice a spiritual approach to food, balancing yin and yang, and slowly eliminating most foods apart from brown rice; and natural hygienists, who will eat only raw fruit and vegetables, plus some grains and seeds. Many of these drastic eating plans are not recommended for children, pregnant women, or anyone with a compromised immune system. In fact, if you are considering making changes in your diet towards a more vegetarian approach, it is best to do this slowly to give your digestive system a chance to adjust. It is also important to ensure that you are getting enough calcium, iron, vitamin B-12, and zinc, all nutrients that tend to be scarce in vegetarian diets.

When I was a personal chef at a local rectory, I used to prepare a sit-down committee dinner for 10 to 15 people several times a month that included a woman who was a lacto-vegetarian. Rather than serving her something completely different, I always tried to make use of the majority of ingredients I was using for the others and concoct a meal that was nearly unnoticebly different from the others. For example, in place of fried crab cakes, her plate had fried three-bean cakes, while all the other fixings and vegetables were identical to the other diners. Usually vegetarians feel awkward enough making any special requests and there is no need to add to their uneasiness by having them stand out with an obviously alternative meal. There are numerous dishes you can prepare that lend themselves to a quick vegetarian makeover, so be creative and make an effort. It will always be greatly appreciated.

Surprisingly, although many people think that vegetarians are super health conscious and more likely to eat a nutritious diet, a good amount of restrictive eaters tend to overdo it in the refined carbohydrate and saturated fat categories, particularly those who rely on dairy to supply protein. Not all vegetarians I have encountered are particularly stellar eaters, often neglecting to include enough healthy oils, protein, and low glycemic carbs. Be sure to do your research before embarking on any diet that may take you way off the mainstream and into uncharted territory to ensure that you will be satisfied eating the necessary foods to keep your body healthy and reap the benefits that a vegetarian diet can offer.

Herbes de Provence

A Medley of France's Finest

Available in the gourmet spice section of your supermarket or specialty food store, *herbes de Provence* is an assortment of dried herbs commonly used in the south of France to flavor anything from meat to fish to vegetables. It is an excellent, all-around seasoning blend to have on hand for quick additions to your cooking and will save you fumbling through several different spice jars to season your dish. Typically, it contains the following herbs: basil, fennel, lavender, marjoram, rosemary, sage, savory, and thyme. Often packaged in little clay pots, a bit of *herbes de Provence* will liven up any dish you choose. Rub a pinch between your fingers to release its flavor.

You may also find another French blend on the spice shelf called *fines herbes*, which is different in content and flavor. Generally very finely chopped, this blend is often better added towards the end of cooking to impart a lovely taste and fragrance just before serving, as its strength tends to dissipate quickly when heated. It is particularly delicious when added to omelets and sautéed vegetables, especially mushrooms, and usually includes chervil, chives, parsley, and tarragon, although sometimes marjoram and savory are also included.

Falafel Bites with Tahini Sauce

MAKES 4 TO 6 SERVINGS These scrumptious little Middle Eastern delights pack a powerful punch of protein for a meatless meal, with chickpeas as the main ingredient. In addition, tahini, a paste made from ground sesame seeds, is a super source of calcium for nondairy eaters. Most supermarkets carry tahini in the deli or condiment section and it is an essential ingredient in hummus (see Easy Homemade Hummus, page 34). Everyone seems to love falafel, usually found stuffed into pita bread and eaten sandwich-style with a yogurt dressing, such as Cucumber Yogurt Raita (page 261). You could certainly make a meal of them that way if you like, adding a little shredded lettuce and chopped tomatoes to the pita pocket. Or try them as an appetizer for one of the vegetarian main dishes coming up. If you need persuading that meatless dishes offer satiety, this recipe will happily convince you.

TAHINI SAUCE
- ⅓ cup tahini
- ¼ cup water
- ¼ cup fresh lemon juice
- 2 tablespoons fresh cilantro leaves
- 1 large garlic clove, peeled and roughly chopped
- ½ teaspoon salt
- ¼ teaspoon sugar

FALAFEL BITES
- Two 15-ounce cans chickpeas, drained and rinsed
- 2 tablespoons whole wheat flour, plus more for dusting
- ½ medium-size onion, peeled and diced
- 2 large garlic cloves, peeled and roughly chopped
- 2 teaspoons ground cumin
- ¼ teaspoon cayenne pepper
- Salt to taste
- 1 large egg white
- Canola oil for frying

1. To make the tahini sauce, combine the ingredients in a blender and process until smooth. Taste for salt and add more, if necessary. Transfer to a serving bowl and refrigerate until ready to serve.

2. To make the falafel bites, combine all the ingredients except the egg white in a food processor and process until smooth. Add the egg white and pulse until well combined. Shape the mixture into 16 walnut-size balls, pressing down lightly to form small patties, and place on a baking sheet lined with waxed or parchment paper.

3. Heat enough canola oil in a skillet to come halfway up the width of the patties over medium-high heat. Using the bread-cube test (page 220), check to see that the oil is ready. When it is, lightly dust the patties in flour and fry them until crisp and golden, 3 to 4 minutes per side.

4. Drain on paper towels and serve immediately with the tahini sauce on the side.

Crispy Tofu Salad with Peanut Coconut Dressing

MAKES 4 SERVINGS For those carnivores who require serious coaxing to try tofu, this preparation will often win them over. I believe it's partly because when tofu is breaded and fried, it vaguely resembles a cross between chicken nuggets and fried mozzarella. In addition, peanut-flavored sauces and dressings are always a popular choice and, when paired with tofu, it can turn an otherwise skeptical first tasting into something familiar.

I don't often use peanut oil for frying, but in this case it provides some necessary flavor, although canola oil could also be used. If you would like to use a deep fryer, you certainly can, but pan-frying is my usual method for this recipe. A temperature of 375 degrees is ideal for the oil if you have a thermometer; otherwise, wait until the breaded tofu sizzles nicely when added to the skillet to determine if the oil is hot enough.

A simple bed of shredded iceberg lettuce is actually a terrific choice for this salad, but other greens, particularly an Asian-style mix if you can find it, would also be excellent. Cucumber, scallions, and thinly sliced red bell peppers would make nice additions to the salad if you like.

PEANUT COCONUT DRESSING
½ cup chunky-style peanut butter
½ cup canned unsweetened coconut milk
1 tablespoon rice vinegar
1 tablespoon honey
1 teaspoon soy sauce
1 teaspoon toasted sesame oil
Dash of Tabasco sauce
3 tablespoons warm water or more to reach
  desired consistency

CRISPY FRIED TOFU
One 15-ounce block firm or extra firm tofu
¾ cup plain dry bread crumbs
2 tablespoons toasted wheat germ
1 tablespoon sesame seeds
Pinch of salt
2 large eggs, beaten
Peanut oil for frying

TO SERVE
4 cups shredded iceberg lettuce

1. To make the dressing, , whisk together the ingredients, except the water, in a small mixing bowl until well combined. Add the water by the tablespoon until the consistency is thick but pourable. Taste for the addition of salt and more Tabasco, if desired, and set aside.

2. To make the tofu, drain and cut it into 4 equal pieces, then into approximate 1-inch cubes to make 16 pieces total. Lay the cubes on a double sheet of paper towels and blot dry, pressing gently with additional towels to soak up the excess moisture. In a shallow dish, stir together the bread crumbs, wheat germ, sesame seeds, and salt. Have the beaten eggs ready in another shallow dish.

3. Heat enough peanut oil in a deep skillet over medium-high heat to come about halfway up the tofu cubes. Dip the tofu in the egg and dredge in the bread crumb mixture. When the oil is hot, carefully add the tofu cubes one at a time to the skillet (the oil should sizzle nicely) and fry until crispy and golden, about 2 minutes per side. Remove with a slotted spoon and drain on paper towels, sprinkling a little salt over each piece.

4. To serve, mound each plate with the lettuce, top with 4 tofu cubes each, and drizzle the dressing over.

Carrot, Walnut, and Edamame Salad

MAKES 4 TO 6 SERVINGS Classic carrot salad gets a new age lift in this delicious and nutritious starter or side salad. A bag of shredded carrots, usually sold next to the bagged salads in the produce section of your supermarket, will make this recipe very easy to prepare. Otherwise, use the shredder disc on your food processor to get the desired texture; you'll need three or four peeled medium-size carrots to equal a 10-ounce bag of preshredded carrots.

The walnut is one of the few plant sources that contains mighty omega-3 fatty acids, as does its oil. Walnuts are a good addition to a vegetarian diet for this reason alone, although they are also a source of vitamins C and E and plant-based protein. The flavor of the walnut combines particularly well with orange juice and honey, which provides a deliciously sweet dressing for the carrots and edamame beans. Walnut oil, like toasted sesame oil, tends to go rancid quickly and should be kept under refrigeration. Purchase the smallest bottle you can find, because it will only keep for a few months. Edamame, or fresh soybeans, are bright green in color and similar to fava beans or limas in appearance and texture. They are a great way to include soy in your diet and make a fine addition to soups and salads. Look for them in the frozen section of your supermarket either shelled or still in the pod.

I will often serve this salad on a bed of mild Bibb or Boston lettuce leaves to whet the appetite before a Japanese-style meal. Leftovers also

Eating Edamame

Healthy Before-Dinner Munchies

Instead of grabbing a handful of peanuts as you anxiously await your dinner, do as the Japanese do and reach instead for edamame. Popularly served in Japanese restaurants while you peruse your menu, edamame beans are fresh soybeans and are usually served in their pods as appetizers. Just squeeze open the shell and you will find two or three little morsels to calm those hunger pangs and keep you munching (the pods are inedible). These little gems are happily found in most supermarket freezer sections, usually with organic or vegetarian selections. They are available shelled (ideal for additions to soups and stews) or still in the pod, perfect for whipping up your own little bowl of *edamame* pod appetizers. Cook them in boiling salted water for about five minutes, drain, then plunge into ice water to keep them green and crisp. Dry on paper towels and store them, covered, in the fridge for up to three days for spontaneous nibbling urges. Like other soybean products, edamame offer a good amount of protein and fiber, and they won't ruin your appetite for dinner.

make for a great lunch with a bowl of miso soup (page 102).

One 10-ounce bag shredded carrots (about 3 cups)
⅔ cup edamame beans, cooked according to package directions, plunged into ice water, and drained
½ cup walnut pieces
⅓ cup dried currants
Juice of 1 medium-size orange
¼ cup walnut oil
1 tablespoon honey
Salt and pepper to taste

1. Bring a medium-size pot of salted water to a boil and cook the shredded carrots for 1 minute, then drain in a medium-size colander and plunge into ice water. Set aside to drain completely.

2. In a medium-size mixing bowl, combine the cooked edamame beans, walnuts, and currants, then add the drained carrots and combine gently with a rubber spatula.

3. In a small mixing bowl, whisk together the orange juice, walnut oil, and honey and season with salt and pepper, then pour over the carrot mixture and gently toss to coat. Taste for seasoning and serve well chilled.

Teriyaki Tofu with Sesame Sprouts

MAKES 4 SERVINGS One of the greatest things about cooking with tofu is that it will quickly absorb any number of flavorful marinades. Teriyaki, a delicious Japanese marinade and sauce, is quick and easy to make yourself and can be used with chicken, beef, and fish dishes, as well as tofu. For this preparation, a firm or extra-firm tofu is the one to choose so that it will hold together nicely during the pan-frying. Pat the slices dry with a paper towel before adding them to the marinade.

Stir-fried fresh bean sprouts, scallions, and shredded carrots are a wonderful accompaniment and should be cooked just barely to heat through, allowing the crunch to remain as a contrast to the dense tofu slices. Mung bean sprouts are the common variety we usually associate with Asian cooking, but soybean sprouts are also sometimes available and would make an excellent addition here. The addition of Ginger Fried Rice (page 129) would turn this into a hearty dinner.

TERIYAKI MARINADE
1 cup low-sodium soy sauce
2 tablespoons rice vinegar
1½ tablespoons dark brown sugar
1 tablespoon peeled and finely chopped fresh ginger
1 large garlic clove, peeled and minced
One 15-ounce block firm or extra-firm tofu, cut into eight 1-inch-thick triangles and patted dry
1 tablespoon canola oil
Salt and pepper to taste
1 bunch scallions, ends trimmed and cut into 1½-inch lengths
1 cup shredded carrots
2 cups mung or soy bean sprouts
Toasted sesame oil for drizzling

1. In a 9 x 13-inch glass baking dish, combine the marinade ingredients and stir well with a fork until the sugar has dissolved. Add the tofu triangles in a single layer and allow to marinate for at least 30 minutes, turning them over halfway through.

2. Heat the canola oil in a wok or large nonstick skillet over high heat. Remove the tofu from the marinade and lightly pat dry with a paper towel. Reserve the marinade. Lightly season the tofu with salt and pepper and fry it in the oil (do not stir-fry or move around in the pan) until the edges are golden and crisp, about 3 minutes per side. Transfer the tofu with a metal spatula to one side of a large heated platter.

3. Add a touch more oil to the wok or skillet and heat to nearly smoking. Add the scallions and carrots, sprinkle with salt and pepper, and stir-fry over high heat for 2 minutes. Add the bean sprouts, season again with salt and pepper, and continue to stir-fry another minute. Transfer the vegetables to the other side of the platter.

4. Pour the reserved marinade into the hot wok or skillet and allow to boil over high heat to slightly thicken, about 3 minutes. Pour the teriyaki glaze over the tofu triangles. Drizzle the sprout mixture with a little sesame oil and serve immediately.

Stocking Up on Soy

Easy Ways to Increase Your Soy Protein Intake

The FDA has stated that at least 25 grams of soy protein per day (about four servings) can lower high cholesterol and reduce the risk of heart disease. Research studies have shown that soy consumption can decrease the growth of prostate cancer, lower the risk of breast cancer, relieve menopausal symptoms, and prevent the onset of osteoporosis. If millions of people in countries such as China, Japan, and Indonesia rely on soy as their main source of protein, it would follow that they also have less incidence of the above diseases and age-related illnesses and, in fact, this has proven to be the case. In addition, it was discovered that Asian men who moved to the West and began eating like Americans began to show a greater incidence of heart disease and prostate cancer. So the facts are certainly clear—we need to decrease our animal protein consumption by replacing it with a beneficial amount of soy protein. But how do we do it, especially when we live in a society that boasts a culinary history of "meat and potatoes" and McDonald's? Believe it or not, it's quite easy to do—here are a host of simple ways to get your minimum four servings (6.25 grams each) of soy protein a day:

PRODUCT	AMOUNT	SOY PROTEIN CONTENT
Roasted soynuts	¼ cup	17 grams
Tempeh	4 ounces	16 grams
Canned soybeans	½ cup	15 grams
Tofu	4 ounces	10 grams
Edamame	¼ cup	9 grams
Miso	¼ cup	8 grams
Soy flour	¼ cup	8 grams
Soymilk	1 cup	7 grams
Soy yogurt	6 ounces	6 grams
Soy sauce	1 tablespoon	1 gram

In addition to the sources above, there are now numerous products that are made either with isolated soy protein, the powder made from nonfat soy flour, which has no bean flavor at all, or enhanced with soy isoflavones, their phytoestrogens. Soy protein powder can contain an enormous serving—nearly 84 grams. However, we can't yet assume that inordinately large quantities of soy, especially from fortified products and supplements, will necessarily be better for us. So opt for whole soy foods whenever possible. Some of the surprisingly tasty soy foods made from actual soybeans are soy chips, soy pretzels, soy pita bread, soybean hummus, and the delicious peanut butter alternative, roasted soybean butter. When you come across these in your supermarket or health food store, definitely give them a try. In addition, soymilk, now in flavors like vanilla, chocolate, and strawberry, are nutritious cow's milk alternatives, while soy ice cream consumption is definitely on the rise. Soy creamer is even available for your morning coffee. Before you know it, you'll have reached your 25 grams with no problem and will be well on your way to becoming a healthier and more soyful you!

Buddha's Burrito

MAKES 4 SERVINGS If Buddha and the Frito Bandito ever got together to cook, this might be something they would concoct. Tofu has the wondrous ability to fill in for the traditional roles normally played by meat and poultry and this dish exemplifies its versatility. Baked tofu, now readily available in supermarkets that carry soy products, has already been marinated and slow baked to remove most of its moisture. It is denser than regular tofu and contains more concentrated soy protein. There are numerous flavors to choose from as well as plain, and here one of the non-Asian flavors would obviously be best. I have seen barbecue, hickory, savory, and even Italian in local markets. If you are using a flavored variety, lessen the amount of seasoning you are adding to adjust for this.

Black beans are delicious in these burritos, but any type of chili bean such as pinto or red kidney could be used. If you see a can of black soybeans, by all means use them to boost your soy intake.

All the traditional burrito garnishes can accompany this dish, so whip up some guacamole (page 32) and serve salsa and chips to start.

2 tablespoons canola oil
1 medium-size red onion, peeled, cut in half, and thinly sliced into half moons

1 medium-size green, red, orange, or yellow bell pepper (or a combination), seeded, and cut into ¼-inch-thick strips
1 small jalapeño, seeded and minced
Salt and pepper to taste
1 teaspoon chili powder
1 teaspoon ground cumin
One 8-ounce package baked tofu, plain, barbecue, or hickory flavor, cut into 1-inch strips
One 15-ounce can black beans, drained and rinsed
1 tablespoon finely chopped fresh cilantro leaves
8 burrito-size flour tortillas
1½ cups shredded cheddar or Monterey Jack cheese
Sour cream and salsa for serving (optional)

1. Heat the canola oil in a large nonstick skillet over medium-high heat. Add the onion, bell pepper, and jalapeño, sprinkle with salt and pepper, ½ teaspoon of the chili powder, and ½ teaspoon of the cumin, and cook, stirring often, until the vegetables are softened, about 6 minutes. Add the tofu, black beans, and the remaining ½ teaspoon each chili powder and cumin, and cook another 2 minutes to heat through. Stir in the cilantro and remove from the heat.

2. Spoon the mixture down the center of each tortilla, dividing evenly. Top with equal amounts of the cheese and wrap the tortilla around the filling by folding over one end and rolling it up. Serve immediately with sour cream and salsa, if using.

Stews and Casseroles

Although hearty stews and casseroles are usually associated with meat, they are by no means restricted by its inclusion. Some of the most satisfying and tasty dishes are those that do not contain even an ounce of red meat or poultry. Vegetarian one-dish meals, such as the ones in this section, can be surprisingly satisfying, even to the die-hard meat and potatoes eater.

Most of the recipes in this section, as well as the previous section, "Starters and Light Fare," are appropriate for vegan eaters (see page 353 for a discussion of vegan eating), while a few lean heavily on dairy and eggs, such as Lentil Pastitsio (page 367) and Easy Pesto and Goat Cheese Lasagne (page 369). Today there are numerous soy substitutes available, from milk to cheese, that many vegetarian cooks utilize in place of dairy. Feel free to try any of these, if you like. I have had particular success with soymilk as an alternative ingredient in everything from soups to sauces. And when butter is called for in a nondairy white sauce, simply substitute a light olive oil or canola oil.

Eggs, on the other hand, are not always simple to replace. Egg substitutes sold in cartons actually have egg whites in them, so for the egg abstainer, they are not truly egg-free (akin to alcohol abstainers using so-called nonalcohol wines!). Since eggs are usually added to provide moisture, as well as act as a binding agent, a proper substitute would possess these same qualities. In baking, applesauce, mashed bananas, and other fruit purees will often work nicely, while soft or silken tofu can replicate, somewhat, a tender and soft consistency in custards and sauces. We'll be looking at ways to include soft tofu in dishes such as these in the next chapter.

Kale, Butternut, and Butter Bean Stew

MAKES 4 SERVINGS This dish is one of my very favorite vegetable stews and the one I have been making the longest for all types of eaters, whether vegan or carnivorous. The nutritional content really cannot be surpassed, because all the ingredients are chockful of potent vitamins and minerals. Kale is a great source of calcium, iron, and folic acid, while butternut squash, in all its vibrancy, contains the antioxidant vitamin A as well as riboflavin, an extremely important B vitamin that many alcoholics will often have in short supply, especially in early recovery. Among many things, riboflavin is necessary for proper neurochemical functioning, which it performs alongside other B vitamins and it is what gives B-complex supplements their usual orange-yellow color.

Butter beans are creamy and delicious and provide the necessary protein to make this dish nutritiously well rounded. In actuality, they are simply large yellow lima beans, but when seeking them in the canned vegetable section of your store, they will fall under the label of butter beans, the usual term for them in the South and now pretty much universally accepted, although some people will still refer to them as limagrands.

If you find butternut squash a bit intimidating to tackle, look for ready-to-cook peeled and diced packages in your produce section, an increasingly common option. Similarly, I have been seeing packages of trimmed and washed kale and collards lately for those in a hurry, as well as pitted Kalamata olives. Frozen chunks of butternut squash, as well as packages of kale or collards, could be used as well, but I would urge you whenever possible to make the fresh choice for optimal taste and nutrition.

> 2 tablespoons olive oil
> 1 large onion, peeled and diced
> Salt and pepper to taste

2 medium-size garlic cloves, peeled and minced

1 medium-size butternut squash, peeled, seeded, and cut into 1-inch cubes

1 large red bell pepper, seeded and cut into 1-inch pieces

1 large bunch kale or collards, washed well, stems removed, and leaves cut into 1-inch-wide strips

1½ cups vegetable broth

1½ tablespoons finely chopped fresh sage leaves or 2 teaspoons rubbed dried sage

Two 15-ounce cans butter beans, drained and rinsed

½ cup Kalamata olives, drained, pitted, and roughly chopped

Freshly grated Parmesan cheese

1. Heat the olive oil in a large, heavy-bottomed pot or Dutch oven over medium-high heat. Add the onion, season with salt and pepper, and cook, stirring, until softened, 6 to 8 minutes. Add the garlic and cook a further minute. Add the squash, bell pepper, and kale, season with salt and pepper, and stir well to coat with the onion mixture. Stir in the vegetable broth and sage and bring to a simmer. Reduce the heat to low, cover, and cook, stirring occasionally, until all the vegetables are tender, about 20 minutes.

2. Stir in the beans and olives and cook until heated through, about 3 minutes. Taste for seasoning and serve in bowls, passing the Parmesan cheese for sprinkling on top.

Three-Bean Eggplant Chili

MAKES 4 TO 6 SERVINGS The protein and energy potential of beans is highlighted in this delicious chili, in which the usual "carne," or meat, is replaced with an array of vegetables. Virtually any choice of beans will work here, although my preference is for red kidneys, pintos, and black beans. In fact, if you can find canned black soybeans, you can sub-

stitute them for the regular black beans and give yourself an added boost of nutritious soy isoflavones (see Chapter 11, "When Food Is Your Preventive Medicine," for more information on the benefits of adding soy to your diet). Whichever you choose, be sure the canned beans have not already been seasoned with spices or are packaged in sodium-laden chili sauce, as they will tend to overseason the final dish. You can, of course, make this as spicy as you wish by increasing the amount of cayenne pepper, but watch for the addition of salt, because your canned tomatoes and tomato sauce (unless low-sodium) will add a lot on their own.

Cook up some white or brown long-grain rice as a bed for your chili, top it with shredded cheddar or Monterey jack cheese, and add a dollop of sour cream or plain yogurt. A little guacamole on the side (see page 32) with tortilla chips and you will be in Mexican heaven!

2 tablespoons canola oil

1 medium-size onion, peeled and diced

1 medium-size green bell pepper, seeded and diced

1 medium-size carrot, peeled and diced

Salt and pepper to taste

1 medium-size eggplant, ends trimmed, peeled, and cut into ½-inch cubes

One 8-ounce can tomato sauce

One 15-ounce can diced tomatoes, with their juices

1 cup water

3 tablespoons chili powder

1 tablespoon paprika

1 teaspoon ground cumin

⅛ teaspoon cayenne pepper or more to taste

1 cup *each* canned pinto, red kidney beans, and black beans, drained and rinsed

1. Heat the canola oil in a medium-size heavy-bottomed pot over medium heat, add the onion, bell pepper, and carrot, season with salt and pepper, and cook until somewhat softened, stirring a few times, about 8 minutes. Add the eggplant and a touch more oil and continue to cook, stirring

often, until the eggplant has softened a bit, about 5 minutes. Stir in the tomato sauce, tomatoes, water, and spices and bring to a simmer. Reduce the heat to low, cover and cook, stirring occasionally, until the vegetables are tender and the sauce has thickened somewhat, about 15 minutes.

2. Stir in the beans and cook, uncovered, until they are heated through and the sauce is thick, about 5 minutes. Taste for seasoning and serve immediately.

Chef's Note: It's an old adage but true—chili tastes better the next day, because its flavors meld and intensify. Consequently, this is a great make-ahead meal and is also excellent for freezing.

Since beans usually come in 15-ounce cans, you will have some leftovers from this recipe. Store them in an airtight container in the fridge with fresh cold water and add them to salads, quesadillas (page 42), or sandwich wraps.

Eating Protein in a Vegetarian World
Twenty-Five Easy Ways to Tally Up Your Essential Aminos

The most-asked question of vegetarian eaters is, "Where are you getting your protein?" Once a major issue for meatless eaters, piling up protein grams is easy to do provided your calorie intake is adequate. At one time, nutritionists believed it was necessary to combine plant-based proteins in specific proportions and at specific times in order to reap the benefits—so-called complete protein eating. However, it has been found that a varied diet throughout the day, which includes a good variety of protein's building blocks, called amino acids, is all you need. The Recommended Dietary Allowance (RDA) of protein for adult males is about 63 grams and only about 50 for adult females. Watch how easy it is to tally up your numbers:

Potato	4 grams	1 cup soymilk	8 grams
1 cup broccoli	5 grams	1 cup green peas	9 grams
2 slices whole wheat bread	5 grams	One 3-ounce bagel	9 grams
1 cup brown rice	5 grams	1 cup quinoa	11 grams
¼ cup almonds	6 grams	1 cup baked beans	12 grams
¼ cup sunflower seeds	6 grams	½ cup soybeans	14 grams
1 large egg	6 grams	½ cup tempeh	15 grams
1 cup oatmeal	6 grams	1 cup kidney beans	15 grams
1 cup spaghetti	7 grams	1 cup chickpeas	15 grams
1 ounce cheese	7 grams	1 cup black beans	15 grams
1 cup milk	8 grams	5 ounces firm tofu	16 grams
2 tablespoons peanut butter	8 grams	1 cup lentils	18 grams
1 cup yogurt	8 grams		

Pasta e Fagioli
(Pasta and Beans)

MAKES 4 SERVINGS This classic Italian favorite is often categorized as a soup, but by far the best way to serve true *pasta e fagioli* is thick, rich, stew-like, and piping hot. Although nonvegetarian recipes will call for bacon, pancetta, or ham hocks to enhance the flavor, they are not necessary ingredients here, as the vegetable stock provides plenty of flavor.

As with many dried bean recipes, an overnight soak will decrease the overall cooking time, but it is not a required step. Since I usually use small dried white beans, such as Great Northern or navy, or even small pink beans rather than the traditional cannellini, total preparation time will be reduced anyway, but feel free to soak your beans beforehand, rinsing them well before using.

This is a heavy-loaded carbohydrate dish that will help induce relaxation; both pasta and beans aid in the production of the neurotransmitter serotonin, which calms and soothes. This is probably why *pasta e fagioli* is considered comfort food to many Italians. I know that when I was growing up, it was certainly a dish I looked forward to with anticipation and always felt happily satisfied after a bowl or two.

2 tablespoons olive oil
1 small onion, peeled and chopped
1 small carrot, peeled and chopped
1 medium-size celery stalk, ends trimmed and diced
2 garlic cloves, peeled and minced
1 cup dried small white or pink beans, picked over
    and rinsed
4 cups vegetable broth, plus water or more broth to
    be added later as needed
One 15-ounce can tomato sauce
Salt to taste
1½ cups pasta such as ditalini or small shells
Pepper to taste
Extra virgin olive oil for drizzling

1. In a large soup or stewing pot, heat the olive oil over medium heat. Add the onion, carrot, and celery and cook, stirring, until softened, about 8 minutes. Add the garlic and cook, stirring, another minute. Add the dried beans, broth, and tomato sauce and bring to a simmer. Cook at a gentle simmer over low to medium heat until the beans are soft, anywhere from 45 minutes to 1½ hours. Add water or more broth as necessary to prevent sticking and stir occasionally.

2. When the beans are tender, taste them for seasoning and add salt if necessary. Now add the dried pasta, making sure there is enough liquid in the pot to just cover all the ingredients. Keep on a low simmer and stir often. Watch that there is always enough liquid, as the pasta will quickly absorb most of it. Add only enough water or broth during this time to maintain the consistency of a very thick stew. After 10 to 12 minutes, test the pasta for doneness. If it is still too hard, add a little more liquid and continue to cook.

3. When the pasta is done, remove the pot from the heat. Add a generous grinding of black pepper, drizzle with a little extra virgin olive oil, stir briefly, and serve immediately.

Chef's Note: When Italians first came to this country, they were introduced to the many conveniences of prepared canned foods. As a result, pasta e fagioli *was sometimes made in minutes merely by adding a can of Campbell's pork and beans (beans in tomato sauce to them!) to a pot of cooked pasta. Although not terribly authentic, I will admit I was served many a pasta and bean dish by my relatives in just this fashion and certainly managed to clean the plate! Give it a try (with a can of vegetarian-style beans) when time is short. And don't forget to finish with a tasty drizzle of olive oil!*

Microwave reheating of either method is ideal, but you can also reheat this stove-top over low heat. Add a little water, stir, and cover with a lid.

Indian Curried Potato Stew

MAKES 4 SERVINGS The curry sauces of India are wonderful complements to vegetarian ingredients, from potatoes to lentils to tofu and everything in between. Ranging from mild to ferociously hot, traditional curries will often include a number of spices that, when combined, form the classic curry flavor, without the commonly seen curry powder even on the ingredient list. Indeed, curry powder is simply a mixture of as many as 20 different spices, herbs, and seeds that have been pulverized and blended together, and most Indian cooks will prepare their own unique curry blend from scratch each and every day. For our purposes, however, we will combine a commercial curry powder with several other spices and seeds in order to create layers of flavor, and we'll add a touch of *garam masala* at the end, a wonderfully fragrant spice blend that will enhance our stew's exotic flavor (see below for a discussion of curry seasonings).

Potatoes are an excellent choice for curry dishes, because they absorb color and flavor quite readily. Waxy red-skinned potatoes are the best choice for holding their shape in stews like these, but white all-purpose varieties, as well as Yukon Golds, would also work well here. The addition of a small amount of red lentils, tiny salmon-colored pulses or dried legumes popularly used in Indian cooking, helps to thicken the sauce as well as provide even more nutrition in the form of iron and protein. They will turn yellow as they cook and practically disintegrate, becoming an integral part of the sauce. Since they absorb liquid quite readily, it may be necessary to add a little more broth or

A Flurry of Curry Seasonings

Your average supermarket will probably only carry two types of curry powders: mild and hot, also called madras, but if you have the opportunity to visit an ethnic market, you will soon discover there is a lot more to curry than meets the eye. And a dinner out at an Indian restaurant will indeed prove that no two curries are at all alike. Here are a few hints to save you from the confusing flurry of spices, sauces, and preparations you might encounter.

TANDOORI Referring to the actual oven it is cooked in, tandoori dishes are flavored with a dry mild spice of brilliant red-gold. You can buy tandoori powder or paste to replicate the taste, but without the earthenware oven to cook it in a distinct taste will be missing, although barbecuing can come close. Tandoori is usually used on chicken and shrimp, and not vegetables, although firm tofu and *paneer*, an Indian compressed cheese, would be a plausible vegetarian option.

MASALA This is simply an aromatic spice blend that differs from cook to cook and is used to flavor all types of dishes. It may resemble curry powder or it may be *garam masala*, a unique mixture of cinnamon, cloves, nutmeg, and other similar spices that is usually added to a dish at the very end. Although it does contain ground peppercorns, it is not meant to be spicy as a rule. Many supermarkets now carry it in the spice section or in the ethnic food aisle.

water during the cooking to ensure that the stew does not stick to the bottom of the pot. Along with other pulses and beans, red lentils are often used to make something called *dal*, a spicy side dish for main course curries.

Curries are usually served over basmati rice and this stew can be as well. However, the potato base makes it equally satisfying on its own. Serve some delicious condiments alongside, such as Cucumber Yogurt Raita (page 261) and Gingered Mango Chutney (page 261) to cool down any "heat" and round out the flavors.

2 teaspoons yellow mustard seeds

2 tablespoons canola oil

1 medium-size onion, peeled and chopped

½ medium-size red bell pepper, seeded and diced

Salt and pepper to taste

1 tablespoon peeled and finely chopped fresh ginger

1 large garlic clove, peeled and minced

1 teaspoon turmeric

¼ teaspoon *each* ground cumin, coriander, and cardamom

Dash of cayenne pepper, or more to taste

3 cups vegetable broth or water

½ cup canned tomato sauce

1 tablespoon curry powder, mild, medium, or hot

⅓ cup dried red lentils, picked over and rinsed

4 large red potatoes, peeled and cut into 1-inch cubes

Onμe 10-ounce package fresh spinach, washed well and tough stems removed

1 cup canned chickpeas, drained and rinsed

1 teaspoon *garam masala*

TIKKA MASALA Very popular with Western diners, this is a soothing, creamy sauce created by combining yogurt with a *masala*. *Korma* sauces and *rogan josh* (not always made with lamb) are also considered mild, at least to the Indian palate, and often contain yogurt, cream, and sometimes ground nuts.

VINDALOO This is only for the most courageous of eaters. If you think a madras curry is hot, this will definitely make you sweat. I have only seen true vindaloo curries in England, where they are a little more used to Indian cooking, but even then, I am sure the heat is toned down a bit to compensate for the Western palate. Red chile peppers are what give vindaloo its kick.

Turmeric is the spice that gives common curry powder its distinct yellow-orange color and has been used for centuries in Indian cooking for flavoring as well as for medicinal purposes. Long known for its anti-inflammatory ability, recent studies indicate that it may also be beneficial in warding off Alzheimer's disease, as well as multiple sclerosis, diseases that appear to occur at a remarkably low rate in India. It is the compound called curcumin in turmeric that is responsible for these benefits. Turmeric is sometimes called the poor man's saffron, as it is often used as a cheap substitute due to its similar rich and vibrant yellow color.

Recovery Note: Alcohol rarely makes an appearance on the Indian menu as an ingredient, although Indian beer and gin are popular beverage offerings for Westerners. A far better coolant for a mouth on fire, however, would be a *lassi* yogurt drink or a bite of *naan* bread.

1. Heat a large, heavy-bottomed pot or Dutch oven over medium-high heat, add the mustard seeds, and cook, shaking the pan occasionally, until they begin to pop, about 3 minutes. Add the oil, onion, and bell pepper, season with salt and pepper, and cook over medium heat until softened and lightly browned, 6 to 8 minutes. Add the ginger and garlic and cook a further minute. Add the turmeric, cumin, coriander, cardamom, and cayenne and stir well to coat the onion mixture with the spices. Stir in the broth and tomato sauce and bring to a simmer over medium heat. Stir in the curry powder and lentils, add the potatoes, and cook, covered, at a low simmer until the potatoes are nearly fork tender, about 12 minutes.

2. Remove the cover, add the spinach and chickpeas, stir gently, and continue to cook until the spinach is wilted, the potatoes are fully cooked, and the sauce is thick. Taste for the addition of salt, stir in the *garam masala*, and serve immediately.

Farmers' Market Giambotta

MAKES 4 SERVINGS When my grandmother had leftover homemade spaghetti sauce, a few meatballs, and not much more, she always managed to stretch it into a delicious *giambotta* by adding vegetables. Also called *ciambotto*, a southern Italian word meaning "mixture," today it has come to mean just about any type of tomato-based Italian stew that includes onions, peppers, and invariably some kind of meat, whether it be pork sausage, beef, or veal, although the original *ciambotto di Apulia* made use of local seafood.

It occurred to me early on that what I loved most about this dish were the flavorful vegetables she added and cooked in the sauce. Sometimes she would even add hard-boiled eggs at the end to substitute for the limited number of meatballs in the pot. Recently I began to play around with this dish and came up with a hearty and delicious vege-

tarian version that is no less satisfying than the original. The summer farmers' market supplied the inspiration and most of the ingredients, while some shortcuts from the pantry made it easy to create.

You can serve this on its own, over pasta, or even as a side dish for carnivorous eaters. Accompanied by a crisp green salad and some Italian bread to soak up the sauce, you'll be glad you made plenty, because second helpings are irresistible.

2 tablespoons olive oil, plus a little extra
   during frying
1 medium-size red or Vidalia onion, peeled, cut in
   half, and cut into ½-inch-thick half moons
1 small green bell pepper, seeded and cut into
   1-inch pieces
Salt and pepper to taste
2 large garlic cloves, peeled and roughly chopped
2 tablespoons shelled pumpkin seeds
1 small eggplant, ends trimmed, peeled, and
   cut into ½-inch cubes
1 medium-size zucchini, ends trimmed,
   cut in half lengthwise, and cut into
   ½-inch thick half moons
One 10-ounce jar marinara sauce
⅔ cup water (used to swish out the remaining
   sauce in the jar)
1 heaping tablespoon store-bought sun-dried
   tomato pesto
1 large carrot, peeled and cut into ½-inch-thick
   rounds
1 large potato (any variety), peeled and cut into
   1-inch cubes
1 cup small cauliflower florets
2 tablespoons roughly chopped fresh Italian
   parsley leaves
2 tablespoons roughly chopped fresh basil leaves
4 hard-boiled eggs (optional), peeled
Freshly grated Parmesan cheese

1. Heat the olive oil in a large, heavy-bottomed pot or Dutch oven over medium heat and cook the onions and bell peppers, sprinkled with a little salt

and pepper, until slightly softened, stirring, about 4 minutes. Add the garlic and pumpkin seeds and cook a further minute. Add the eggplant and zucchini, drizzle a little more olive oil over the mixture, sprinkle with salt and pepper, and continue to cook, stirring occasionally, until softened somewhat, but not browned, about 5 minutes. Add the marinara sauce, water, and sun-dried tomato pesto, stir well, and bring to a simmer. Add the carrots, cover, and cook over low heat for 10 minutes. Add the potatoes and cauliflower and continue to cook, covered, until all the vegetables are fork tender, 12 to 15 minutes.

2. Stir in the parsley and basil. Cook, uncovered, another 3 minutes to thicken the sauce, if necessary, and serve immediately in bowls, topped with a warm and peeled, whole hard-boiled egg, if using, and passing Parmesan cheese for sprinkling.

Chef's Note: Boost your protein by adding ½ cup frozen soybeans along with the potatoes and cauliflower. Other delicious additions would be okra, string beans, artichoke hearts, and chickpeas.

Lentil Pastitsio

MAKES 4 TO 6 SERVINGS. Here is a terrific vegetarian version of the classic Greek casserole, normally made with ground lamb or beef. Lentils are the ideal substitute for meat in this case and provide an excellent amount of protein, along with the eggs used for thickening and the dairy-based white sauce. You'll need about three cups of white sauce for this dish (see page 243 for the Easy White Sauce recipe), so you can double the recipe and save a cup for something else, or simply make 1½ times the recipe. You can also substitute Lightened-Up Easy White Sauce (page 245) if you prefer.

The common brown lentil is the one to use for this dish. Be sure to rinse them well and pick them

over for dirt and pebbles. You can cook them in vegetable broth or water; either would be fine, but be sure they are still a little firm to the bite so they do not overcook when added to the sauce. This pastitsio is definite vegetarian comfort food—hearty, rich, and super satisfying. Moussaka, another traditional and homey Greek dish, can also be vegetarianized in this way. Serve this with Easy Greek Salad (page 318) for a perfect and nutritious meal.

LENTIL FILLING

1 tablespoon olive oil

1 tablespoon unsalted butter

1 medium-size onion, peeled and chopped

Salt and pepper to taste

1 cup tomato sauce

½ cup water

1 teaspoon sugar

¼ teaspoon ground allspice

Dash of ground cinnamon

1 cup dried lentils, cooked in generous water to cover until tender but not mushy, drained, and refreshed under cold running water (about 3 cups cooked)

WHITE SAUCE CUSTARD

1½ recipes Easy White Sauce (see headnote)

3 large eggs

1 cup grated Pecorino Romano cheese, plus more for sprinkling

8 ounces ziti, cooked according to package directions, drained, and rinsed under cold running water

1. To make the lentil filling, heat together the olive oil and butter in a large nonstick skillet over medium heat. Add the onion, season with salt and pepper, and cook, stirring, until softened, about 5 minutes. Add the remaining filling ingredients, except the lentils, stir well to combine, and bring to a simmer. Add the cooked lentils, reduce the heat to low, and cook gently, stirring often, until most

of the liquid has been absorbed and the lentils are tender. Do not overcook. Taste for the addition of salt and pepper and set aside.

2. Preheat the oven to 350 degrees. Butter a 9 x 13-inch glass baking dish.

3. Heat the white sauce in a medium-size saucepan, if not already warm. In a large mixing bowl, lightly beat the eggs, then add the warm white sauce very slowly (to avoid scrambling the eggs), whisking continuously. Add the cheese and whisk to combine. Gently stir in the drained pasta, coating well, and set aside.

4. Layer the pastitsio by transferring half of the pasta mixture to the baking dish, distributing it evenly. Spoon the lentil mixture over next, smoothing the layer with the back of a wooden spoon. Top with the remaining pasta, sprinkle with grated cheese over all, and bake until the top is very lightly golden, the edges are bubbly, and the pastitsio is hot throughout, 35 to 45 minutes. Allow to stand 5 minutes, then serve.

Going Organic
When What You're *Not* Eating Matters

As consumer demand grows, many supermarkets are now offering organic produce to their shoppers. For about 20 percent more money, fruits and vegetables are organically certified to be free of pesticides and toxic agrichemicals that might normally be added for fertilization and growth enhancement. How important is it to invest in the extra cost and what do we gain by going organic?

Although many pesticides can be washed away with soap and water, it is the other, quite toxic, chemicals that may pose the actual problem in the future. We have yet to determine to what extent these toxins could contribute to cancer and other life-threatening diseases, but it is safe to say that, given the choice, we would do much better protecting our future health by avoiding these types of chemicals. In addition, as alcoholics and addicts, we have put enormous stress on our livers already and by eliminating further toxins, whenever possible, we can do our livers a favor for a change.

If the cost of going organic is a question of affordability, we can simply try to avoid specific nonorganic produce that we know for sure poses a threat of toxic contamination. For example, strawberries, Mexican cantaloupes, and Chilean winter grapes have been known to contain methyl bromide, a cancer-causing pesticide. Whenever possible, opt for the organic version, which often will boast far better flavor, as well. If buying organic is a question of accessibility, start asking your local grocer to look into carrying a larger selection. If enough people begin to ask, consumer demand will eventually win out.

Easy Pesto and Goat Cheese Lasagne

MAKES 6 SERVINGS Lasagne as a vegetarian entrée holds a myriad of possibilities, particularly for dairy eaters. Indeed, in my house growing up, lasagne rarely contained meat, which was nearly always served on the side in the form of meatballs or sausages, if at all, no doubt reflecting my grand-mother's southern Italian origin, since meat sauces tend to be more utilized in classic northern dishes such as *lasagne verdi al forno*. Still, most lasagne recipes, meatless or not, will include the traditional filling of ricotta cheese and eggs. Here the intensely flavored and creamy goat cheese, also called *chevre*, provides an interesting break from the classic, combining nicely with purchased pesto and tomato sauces for a delicious and easy result. Look for a jarred sauce that is garden-style, or chunky vegetable, to add texture and flavor.

Although many cooks take advantage of "no boil" lasagne sheets, I am not a fan of this method, preferring the old-fashioned way of cooking the

Organic products are not limited to fruits and vegetables. Wheat, soy products, and even meats that are not laden with hormones and antibiotics are now available. If you can find them, buy them whenever affordable. The price of these types of foods has gone down drasti-cally over the last few years and is likely to continue as people become more conscious of what they are *not* eating and how it can make a difference.

At the other end of the spectrum is what's known as genetically modified (GM) foods, a topic still in hot debate. These bioengineered foods have had genetic alterations made to them in order to ensure better pest and disease resistance and herbicide tolerance, as well as the pos-sibility of greater nutrition. Soybeans are among the most common of the GM crops and many soybean derivatives are found in processed foods we consume on a regular basis, such as breakfast cereals and vegetable oils. As of yet, however, the labeling of GM-containing foods is not mandatory and many opponents of bioengineering are pushing for such required public information. Among their other criticisms is the danger these crops may pose to the environ-ment by causing harm to unintended organisms that end up consuming the by-products of GM-grown plants, such as Monarch caterpillars, which eat the pollen of GM corn crops. The unknown effects to human health are also cited, although most scientists adamantly believe that these types of foods do not present any risks to our overall health.

Still, both organic and bioengineered foods, although completely diverse in nature, seem to be the undeniable future of agriculture. As new studies are conducted, we can become more knowledgeable about the pros and cons they offer. The best you can do is try to be as well informed as possible. Reading labels, as always, is a good habit to develop to ensure we are buying what we want to eat and not something we don't.

sheets beforehand. I think it makes for a better dish overall. Keep the water at a rolling boil and stir often to prevent sticking (see page 118 on helpful tips for cooking pasta). Be sure to drain and rinse them under cold running water (this removes the starch that will cause the sheets to stick together), patting them dry before layering. This will avoid any excess moisture from ruining the consistency of your sauce and ensure that your lasagne will hold together when cut. Serve with an arugula or crisp lettuce salad. A side dish of broccoli or string beans, sautéed in garlic and olive oil, would also be a fine complement.

> 9 ounces (about 3 small logs) goat cheese
> ½ cup prepared basil pesto
> ½ cup light cream or milk
> Freshly ground black pepper to taste
> 9 curly lasagne sheets, cooked according to
>   package instructions, drained, and rinsed under
>   cold running water
> One 16-ounce jar garden vegetable pasta sauce
> 3 tablespoons freshly grated Parmesan cheese
> 2 cups shredded whole-milk or part-skim
>   mozzarella cheese

1. Preheat the oven to 350 degrees.

2. In a medium-size mixing bowl, whisk together the goat cheese, pesto, cream, and pepper to a spreadable consistency and set aside. Pat dry the lasagne sheets and cut the ends, if necessary, to fit a 9 x 13-inch baking dish. Spoon a few tablespoons of the pasta sauce, minus any vegetable pieces, into the dish and spread evenly over the bottom.

3. Begin layering the lasagne: Place 3 pasta sheets on the bottom of the baking dish, spread half the goat cheese mixture over them, spoon about ½ cup of the sauce over that, and sprinkle with 1 tablespoon of the Parmesan and ½ cup of the mozzarella. Repeat that order again.

4. On the top layer of lasagne sheets, spoon the remainder of the sauce over evenly and sprinkle

with the remaining 1 tablespoon Parmesan and 1 cup mozzarella cheese. Bake until the cheese is melted and slightly browned and the edges are bubbly, 30 to 40 minutes. Allow to rest for 10 minutes before slicing and serving.

Vegetable and Tofu Tian

MAKES 4 SERVINGS   *Tian* is simply the French term for a shallow baking dish, not unlike a gratin dish, and is used to describe the ingredients as well. Most often these will be an assortment of sliced vegetables, including tomatoes, zucchini, yellow squash, eggplant, and sometimes potatoes, all topped with bread crumbs and then baked. I have seen some wonderfully enticing *tians* made with vegetables such as sliced celery root, oven-dried tomatoes, and sweet potatoes, and recently I have added circles of firm polenta (page 379) to my own creations, which would be a good choice here as well. But for added protein, slices of tofu make a surprisingly fabulous addition, readily soaking up the flavors of the vegetable broth, olive oil, and its neighboring vegetables. A good quality homemade or purchased vegetable stock is a must in this case, so be sure to have some on hand.

The layering of a *tian* resembles that of a row of dominoes that has just fallen. A regular oval gratin or *tian* dish will hold about 3 to 4 rows comfortably, beginning at the short end and going down the long way. You can also make shorter rows beginning on the long end, if you prefer. The idea is to stagger the slices of vegetables and, in this case, tofu, to make the *tian* colorful throughout when served; a bit of creativity here is certainly welcomed and encouraged!

> 2 medium-size zucchini, ends trimmed and cut into
>   ½-inch-thick rounds
> 1 medium-size yellow squash, ends trimmed and
>   cut into ½-inch-thick rounds

1 large red bell pepper, seeded and cut into 1-inch
pieces

2 small red onions, peeled and cut into ¼-inch-thick
rounds

2 small celeriac (celery root), peeled, completely
trimmed of gnarls, and cut into ½-inch-thick
rounds

1 small eggplant, ends trimmed, left unpeeled, and
cut into ½-inch-thick rounds

One 15-ounce block extra firm tofu, drained, cut
into 12 thin slices, and patted dry

Salt and pepper to taste

2 teaspoons *herbes de Provence* (page 354)

1 cup vegetable broth

3 tablespoons extra virgin olive oil

1 cup Italian-seasoned dry bread crumbs

1. Preheat the oven to 375 degrees. Lightly coat a shallow oval or rectangular 1½-quart ceramic or glass baking dish with olive oil.

2. Layer the *tian*, domino fashion, with the vegetable slices and tofu. Season with salt and pepper (add only minimal salt if the vegetable broth is not low-sodium), sprinkle with the dried herbs, pour the vegetable broth over, and drizzle the olive oil on top. Cover the surface evenly with the bread crumbs and bake until the vegetables are fork tender, most of the liquid has evaporated, and the top is lightly golden, about 45 minutes. Allow to rest for 5 minutes before serving.

Grilled Vegetable and Tofu *Tian*: Grilling the vegetables and tofu prior to layering will make for a deliciously enhanced flavor. Brush them lightly with olive oil and grill only to mark both sides and not to cook. Assemble and cook the *tian* as directed above.

Great Grain Dishes

Healthy, delicious whole grains can provide an enormous amount of nutrition, particularly in a vegetarian-based meal. Many of them are excellent sources of protein in their own right, absent of saturated fat and full of necessary fiber. Here we'll be meeting some unusual grains, as well as using some familiar ones, to create satisfying dishes that do a body good.

Dishes such as Rustic Risotto (below) and Vegetable Brown Rice Biryani (page 373) make terrific main course meals, while simpler grain dishes, such as Dried Fruit Kasha (page 377) and Confetti Couscous (page 378), can become the perfect side for a plate of steamed or stir-fried vegetables or tofu. Try to experiment with different varieties of grains, many of which are now available in local supermarkets, and reap the benefits of adding great grains to your diet.

Rustic Risotto

MAKES 4 SERVINGS This is by far my favorite risotto dish and one that offers excellent nutrition for a vegetarian dinner night. Italian risotto is made with Arborio rice, a starchy short-grain variety that contributes to the resulting creamy texture, although recently other types of risotto rice have arrived on the scene, such as Carnaroli, and many chefs are making use of them with gusto. Arborio, however, is still the easiest to find; look for it in the rice and grain section of your supermarket or, on occasion, in the pasta section.

The addition of curly Savoy cabbage and beans gives this risotto a particularly country-style appearance, unlike many other risotto dishes, which often focus on one ingredient, such as asparagus or mushrooms. Incidentally, the classic risotto Milanese is simply prepared with one very extravagant focus: saffron. It has a lovely color and fragrance and is perhaps the most famous of all Italian rice dishes.

Although many claim that risotto making is too laborious a prospect for the average cook, I feel that as long as you have your ingredients ready to go, there is really no big feat in this preparation. You just have to accept that you will be stirring for about 22 minutes and serving immediately after. Put on some nice music and enjoy the process!

RISOTTO

Generous pinch of salt

6 large Savoy cabbage leaves, hard centers
    removed

1 quart vegetable broth

2 tablespoons unsalted butter

2 teaspoons olive oil

3 medium-size shallots, peeled and finely chopped

Pepper to taste

1½ cups Arborio rice

¼ cup white wine substitute (see Chef's Note
    below)

½ cup canned borlotti or Roman beans (or
    substitute cannellini beans), drained and rinsed

¼ cup canned chickpeas, drained and rinsed

¼ cup frozen soybeans (edamame), cooked
    according to package directions and drained

TO FINISH

2 tablespoons unsalted butter

½ cup freshly grated Parmesan cheese

¼ cup heavy cream (optional)

1. To make the risotto, bring a large pot of water to a boil, add the salt, and blanch the cabbage leaves for 5 minutes. Drain, cool under cold running water, pat dry, and roughly chop. Set aside.

2. Heat the broth in a medium-size saucepan and keep it on the back burner of the stove over the lowest level heat. Place a ½-cup ladle in the pot for adding to the risotto in step 4.

3. Melt the butter with the olive oil over medium heat in a large saucepan. Add the shallots and chopped cabbage, season with salt and pepper, and cook, stirring, until softened but not browned, 3 to 4 minutes. Add the rice and stir well to coat the grains with the fat. Add the wine substitute and cook over medium-high heat, stirring constantly, until all the liquid has evaporated.

4. Now begin to add the broth by the ladleful, stirring constantly and waiting to add the next ladleful until the previous one has been absorbed by the rice. Keep the heat at a temperature that will simmer the liquid gently and not boil it. Be patient with this process and continue, one ladleful at a time, as the rice begins to become creamy and tender. When there is about ½ cup of broth left, stir in the borlotti beans, chickpeas, and soybeans, continuing to stir constantly and finally adding the rest of the broth. This whole process should take 20 to 23 minutes.

5. When the rice is tender and creamy (but still firm to the bite), remove from the heat and finish by adding the butter, cheese, and cream, stirring until well combined. Taste for seasoning and serve immediately.

Chef's Note: See page 134 for possible wine substitutions. In this case, I would recommend 3 tablespoons white grape juice and 1 tablespoon white wine vinegar.

Recovery Note: In order to save preparation time, restaurants will normally cook their risotto up to and including step 3 and use wine to do so. This means that, inevitably, alcohol will have been added long before your order. Consequently, it is virtually impossible for them to redo the risotto without alcohol. However, always ask if wine is included, as some more adventurous chefs may occasionally depart from the traditional ingredients and incorporate other flavorful liquids.

Vegetable Brown Rice Biryani

MAKES 4 SERVINGS Created centuries ago by Moghul emperors to sustain their garrisons on the move, biryani dishes of Indian and Pakistani origin are often seen on Indian restaurant menus and are becoming a popular choice for healthy eaters of all types. Packed with a variety of excellent energy-sustaining ingredients, such as basmati rice, nuts, peas, and raisins, it is not surprising that this dish has endured for so long.

This version makes use of brown basmati rice. I think it combines well with the other ingredients, while offering a delicious and nutty flavor of its own. Any number of vegetables and dried fruit could be added, depending upon your preference, but often you will find carrots, potatoes, and sometimes small florets of broccoli and cauliflower, particularly in a vegetarian version. Biryani is, of course, also made with meat, and this is one of those adaptable dishes that can be easily transformed into a meat lover's meal by stirring in diced cooked chicken, beef, lamb, or even baby shrimp at the end. If you need to accommodate both a vegetarian and a carnivore at the dinner table, this is the perfect recipe to make.

Serve with pita bread, a green salad, and some plain lowfat yogurt (or Cucumber Yogurt Raita, page 261) on the side for a delicious and satisfying dinner. Leftover biryani also makes a terrific filling for a sandwich wrap.

RICE

1 cup brown basmati rice
1 tablespoon unsalted butter
3 tablespoons golden raisins
2 tablespoons slivered almonds
1 bay leaf
1 medium-size cinnamon stick
3 cardamom pods, gently crushed
½ teaspoon turmeric
1 teaspoon coarse salt
2 cups water

VEGETABLES

2 tablespoons unsalted butter
1 teaspoon canola oil
1 small onion, peeled and diced
Salt and pepper to taste
1 large garlic clove, peeled and minced
2 teaspoons peeled and minced fresh ginger
½ medium-size red bell pepper, seeded and diced
1 small carrot, peeled and diced
1 medium-size red potato, peeled and diced
½ cup cut-up green beans (fresh or frozen)
½ cup water
1 teaspoon mild curry powder
¼ cup frozen corn
⅓ cup frozen green peas

1. To make the rice, put it in a strainer and rinse under cold running water until the water runs clear. In a large saucepan, melt the butter over medium heat, add the raisins and almonds, and cook, stirring, for 2 minutes. Add the rice and stir well to coat the grains. Add the bay leaf, cinnamon, cardamom, and turmeric and cook, stirring constantly, for 1 minute. Stir in the salt and water, bring to a simmer, and cook, covered, over low heat until the rice is tender and the liquid has been absorbed, 25 to 35 minutes. Fluff with a fork and set aside.

2. To make the vegetables, melt the butter in the oil in another large saucepan over medium heat. Add the onion, season with salt and pepper, and cook, stirring a few times, until softened, about 3 minutes. Add the garlic and ginger and cook a further minute. Add the remaining ingredients, stir well, bring to a simmer, and cook, covered, until the vegetables are tender, 5 to 8 minutes. Remove the lid and allow the remaining liquid to evaporate over low heat, stirring to prevent sticking. Remove from the heat.

(continued on page 375)

Harvesting Some Unusual Grains and Reaping Their Benefits

More and more we are being offered accessibility to some formerly unfamiliar grains, even in our local supermarkets. There was a time, unbelievably so, that brown rice was difficult to find, but today we are faced with making the choice between several different brown rice varieties, whether they be short or long grain, basmati or Texmati, or numerous blends and mixtures. As we become more health conscious as a society (although some would argue that most American diets are far from healthy!), interest has grown over the benefits of eating whole grains and whole-grain products. We see this in our supermarket bread aisle, where labels boast of the addition of whole wheat and other lesser known grains. When you buy "nine-grain" bread, how many of the nine have you even heard of? Cereals, crackers, and even bakery goods have jumped on the bandwagon. Below are a few unusual grains you may come across during your supermarket harvesting.

AMARANTH: This was the staple food of the Aztecs, a powerhouse of protein, iron, and calcium. It has a slightly sweet flavor and is often ground into flour for making crackers and bread. It is one of the tiniest grains around and can be used as a thickener in soups and stews.

MILLET: Resembling couscous in size and color, this lesser-known grain in America is still the staple of poorer populations in Asia and Africa. It is an excellent source of protein and can be cooked like rice. If it looks familiar to you, that's because we use a type of millet in packages of wild birdseed. It's often found in seeded breads and cereals.

QUINOA: A staple of the Incas, this grain is still prepared extensively in South American cuisine. It is highly nutritious and can be used like rice, even in dessert puddings. It has a delicate flavor and an ivory-white color and is delicious on its own or combined with other grains or pasta.

SPELT: This grain has been used since ancient times and is highly digestible, although when used whole it is generally combined with other grains. It is a great alternative for those who are wheat intolerant and makes for a tasty high-protein bread. You can substitute spelt flour for wheat flour when baking.

TRITICALE: A hybrid of wheat and rye, this nutty-flavored grain is high in protein and contains less gluten than wheat. As a whole kernel, it can be used to make breakfast cereals, pilafs, and stews. Triticale flour is sometimes found low-gluten breads, combined with regular whole wheat flour.

(continued from page 373)

3. Add the hot rice to the vegetable mixture pot and gently fold in. Remove the bay leaf, cinnamon stick, and cardamom pods. Taste for seasoning, transfer to a large bowl or platter, and serve.

Sweet-and-Sour Tempeh

MAKES 2 SERVINGS Tempeh is a high-protein soy food, which comes to us from Indonesian cuisine. It is made from cooked soybeans that are fermented to form a dense and chewy cake, often including other grains, such as millet, brown rice, and barley. One serving alone can contain more fiber than most people consume in a day, while its protein content is high and concentrated, rivaling that of meat protein, and much more than other soy foods. It is also iron rich and an excellent source of many B vitamins.

Unlike smooth tofu, tempeh has a texture that reflects the grains it contains and because of this trait, it makes an excellent meat substitute in many dishes, particularly those that call for ground meats. Traditionally, however, it is usually prepared to highlight its own unique flavor and properties, and this recipe is a good example.

Most tempeh we buy today is ready to be eaten and does not require presteaming. However, a brief simmer in a flavorful liquid, or a light steaming once marinated, will make it easier to handle, especially if you will be crumbling it and using it like ground meat. In addition, preparing it in one of these fashions will also bring out its full flavor and remove the initial tang that is usually present straight from the packet.

Sweet-and-sour sauce is a popular preparation in Chinese cooking and one well suited to tempeh. You could also use tofu, or the more traditional pork or chicken, with this recipe, but refrain from the initial simmering and simply stir-fry as directed below. Serve over a bed of plain steamed rice or lo mein noodles.

TEMPEH

One 8-ounce package tempeh (preferably three grain), cut into 1-inch cubes
1 cup low-sodium vegetable broth
2 tablespoons soy sauce
Dash of Tabasco sauce

SWEET-AND-SOUR SAUCE

¼ cup ketchup
¼ cup low-sodium vegetable broth
3 tablespoons rice vinegar
3 tablespoons sugar
1 tablespoon soy sauce
1 teaspoon cornstarch

TO STIR FRY

2 tablespoons canola oil
Salt and pepper to taste
4 scallions, ends trimmed and cut into 2-inch long pieces
½ medium-size green bell pepper, seeded and cut into 1-inch squares
½ medium-size carrot, peeled and sliced into thin rounds
1 large garlic clove, peeled and minced
2 teaspoons peeled and minced fresh ginger

1. To make the tempeh, combine it with the broth, soy sauce, and Tabasco in a medium-size saucepan and bring to a simmer. Allow to cook, covered, on the lowest of heat until all the liquid is absorbed, about 30 minutes. Remove from the heat and set aside.

2. To make the sweet-and-sour sauce, whisk together the ingredients in a small mixing bowl. Set aside.

3. Heat 1 tablespoon of the canola oil in a wok or large nonstick skillet over high heat, and stir-fry the tempeh cubes, sprinkled with a little salt and pepper, until golden brown, about 3 minutes. Remove with a slotted spoon to a clean plate.

4. Heat the remaining 1 tablespoon canola oil over high heat, add the scallions, bell pepper, carrot,

and a sprinkling of salt and pepper, and stir-fry until slightly softened, about 2 minutes. Add the garlic and ginger and stir-fry a further minute. Reduce the heat to medium, add the sweet-and-sour sauce and the browned tempeh, stir well, and cook until all the ingredients are hot and well combined and the sauce has thickened. Serve immediately.

Persian Polow with Caramelized Cabbage and Chickpeas

MAKES 4 SERVINGS When I lived in England, I had the pleasure of working for an Iranian family, who introduced me to the joys of Persian cooking. Unlike Indian curried rice dishes, Persian renditions are much less spicy, subtly aromatic, and involve the making of a *tahdeeg*, a crunchy rice layer removed from the bottom of the pot at the very end and considered quite a delicacy in Iran. The closest comparison I have found, when describing it to my American clients, is a perfectly crisp and golden patty of hash brown potatoes, just made with rice instead.

There are many different types of these *polow*, or rice, dishes, but this one has been a favorite of mine and many of my clients for a long time. For meat eaters, I will make tiny lamb meatballs to sprinkle throughout, while roasted chickpeas replace the meat in this vegetarian version. In addition, the healthy but humble cabbage transforms itself into a cinnamon-scented marvel, which blends well with the mildly seasoned, aromatic white basmati rice.

Don't be discouraged if your *tahdeeg* is not perfect the first time you make this, as it is an accomplished art among Persian women. Much depends on the pot you are using, the intensity of your flame, and the layering of the rice. It is well worth learning to make, however, because, once

tasted, it will be relished and reached for by everyone at the table before they even begin to dig into the rice. You will need a heavy-bottomed pot with a tight-fitting lid to ensure that the bottom layer crisps nicely and the rice is properly steamed.

As is the case with many Middle Eastern rice dishes, pita bread, a plain green salad, and Cucumber Yogurt Raita (page 261) are perfect accompaniments, while yogurt lassi drinks (page 25) make the ideal beverage.

RICE
2 cups white basmati rice, rinsed under cold running water until the water runs clear

CABBAGE MIXTURE
3 tablespoons canola oil
1 to 1½ pounds white cabbage, cored and thinly shredded
1 large onion, peeled, halved, and thinly sliced into half-moons
Salt and pepper to taste
½ teaspoon ground cinnamon

ROASTED CHICKPEAS
1 tablespoon canola oil
2 cups canned chickpeas, drained and rinsed
½ teaspoon mild curry powder
Salt and pepper to taste

TO COMPOSE THE POLOW
½ of a large beaten egg
1 heaping tablespoon plain low-fat yogurt
2 tablespoons water
Pinch of saffron threads
2 tablespoons canola oil
Ground cinnamon and mild curry powder for sprinkling

1. To make the rice, bring a large, heavy-bottomed pot of water to a boil. Add a generous amount of salt and boil the rice just until the grains begin to break down, 3 to 4 minutes. Immediately drain into a colander and rinse with cold water. Set aside.

2. To make the cabbage mixture, heat the oil in a large pot or Dutch oven over medium-high heat, add the cabbage and onion, season with salt and pepper, stir well, and cook, covered, stirring occasionally to prevent sticking, until somewhat soft and just beginning to brown, about 20 minutes. Remove the lid, stir in the cinnamon, and continue to cook, uncovered, stirring often, until the cabbage and onion are completely tender and golden in color, another 6 to 8 minutes. Taste for seasoning and set aside.

3. To make the chickpeas, heat the oil in a large skillet over high heat. Add the chickpeas and curry powder, season with salt and pepper, and pan roast the chickpeas, shaking the skillet occasionally, until they are lightly browned, about 10 minutes. Set aside.

4. In a small mixing bowl, whisk together the partial egg, yogurt, and 1 tablespoon of water. Crush the saffron between your fingers and add it to the bowl, stirring well to combine. Stir in about ½ cup of the parboiled rice and set aside.

5. To begin composing the *polow*, add the oil and the remaining tablespoon of water to the pot that you cooked the rice in and set over high heat. When the oil begins to spatter, pour in the egg-and-rice mixture and distribute it evenly over the bottom of the pot just shy of the edges. Sprinkle an additional ½ cup of parcooked rice over this to cover any empty spots and proceed with the layering: a third of the cabbage mixture, then a third of the chickpeas, then a third of the rice. Sprinkle with a little salt, cinnamon, and curry powder and repeat two more times. Do not spread out the ingredients but rather pile them into a mountain shape, finishing with the rice at the top and a last sprinkle of cinnamon and curry powder. Using the end of a wooden spoon, poke 3 or 4 holes down into the mountain of ingredients. Take a dry dishtowel, wrap the pot lid tightly, securely twisting the towel over the handle, and firmly press the covered lid down onto the pot to seal. This will encourage steam without the dripping of water on the inside of the lid, which could make your rice soggy. Immediately turn the flame to very low and allow to steam this way for at least 30 minutes and up to 45 minutes. Do not remove the lid during this time.

6. When ready to serve, drench a dishtowel with cold water, wring it out, fold it in half, and lay it flat on a cutting board. Remove the pot, lid and all, from the stove and place it directly on the wet towel. You will hear a loud hiss. Leave for 5 minutes, then remove the lid and, using a large serving spoon, scoop out the rice mixture and transfer to a warm platter. When you have gotten down to the crispy *tahdeeg*, use a metal spatula to scrape up the browned layer. It's okay if it is not in one piece. Place the golden *tahdeeg* on the platter with the rice and serve immediately.

Dried Fruit Kasha

MAKES 4 TO 6 SERVINGS Buckwheat groats, or kasha, as it is also known, is a popular ingredient in Jewish cooking, most often seen in the delicious kasha varnishkes, where it is combined with bowtie pasta as a main dish or used as a side dish for brisket or roasted chicken. See the variation that follows for whipping up this easy, classic dish.

Kasha comes toasted in a variety of grinds, from fine to whole. The smaller cuts are often used to make cereal for children, while the large cuts are ideal for dishes such as this one and when combined with other grains (see page 181 for the use of kasha in Multigrain Morning Blend). It also makes an ideal stuffing for vegetables such as acorn squash or cabbage and is great as a side dish for such vegetarian fare as Roasted Vegetable Melange (page 348) or fried falafel or tofu.

Containing all of the necessary B vitamins, kasha is an excellent grain choice for meatless eating, while its hearty consistency and nutty flavor make it super satisfying for hungry appetites.

1 cup coarse or whole kasha
1 large egg or 2 large egg whites, slightly beaten
1 tablespoon unsalted butter
1 tablespoon canola oil
1 medium-size onion, peeled and diced
1 medium-size carrot, peeled and diced
Salt and pepper to taste
$\frac{2}{3}$ cup chopped mixed dried fruit
$1\frac{1}{2}$ cups vegetable broth or water

1. In a small mixing bowl, combine the kasha and beaten egg and mix well to coat the grains.

2. Melt the butter in the oil in a large nonstick skillet over medium heat, add the onion and carrot, season with salt and pepper, and cook, stirring often, until softened, about 4 minutes. Add the chopped dried fruit and stir to combine, cooking a further minute. Increase the heat to medium-high and add the egg-coated kasha, stirring and breaking up the lumps of grains as they toast and release a nutty fragrance, about 3 minutes. Add the broth, stir well, reduce the heat to low, and cook, covered, until the kasha is tender and the liquid has been absorbed, about 15 minutes.

3. Allow the pot to rest off the heat for 5 minutes, then fluff the kasha with a fork, transfer to a large bowl, and serve immediately.

Kasha Varnishkes: Omit the dried fruit and prepare as directed above. Meanwhile, cook 2 cups bowtie or farfalle pasta according to package directions. Add the drained pasta to the cooked kasha, season with additional salt and freshly ground pepper, and serve.

Kasha-Stuffed Acorn Squash: Microwave, steam, or bake 2 large acorn squash that have been halved and seeded. Scoop out all but $\frac{1}{4}$ inch of the pulp next to the skin, and combine it with a $\frac{1}{2}$ recipe of Dried Fruit Kasha.

Spoon the mixture back into the acorn squash halves, sprinkle lightly with freshly grated Parmesan cheese, and set under the broiler until lightly golden on top, about 4 minutes.

Chef's Note: *Consider adding any of the following to your kasha preparation in step 1 for extra nutrition and flavor: $\frac{1}{2}$ cup chopped walnuts, hazelnuts, or roasted soynuts or $\frac{1}{4}$ cup shelled sunflower seeds, pumpkin seeds, or pignoli nuts.*

Confetti Couscous

MAKES 4 SERVINGS Not really a grain by definition, couscous is a type of pasta made from semolina and formed into tiny granular-looking pieces. Most of the couscous that is available to us is instant cooking, requiring very little time to prepare, and consequently a good choice for a quick meal. Here we'll be adding some colorful vegetables for texture and taste, turning a plain dish of couscous into something special. The smaller the dice of vegetables (about $\frac{1}{4}$ inch) that you have patience to create will add to the beautiful confetti appearance.

You may also come across Israeli couscous, a bigger variety resembling large pearl tapioca. When cooked, it tastes more like a pasta than its smaller counterpart and is fun to use on occasion. Whole wheat couscous is also becoming more readily available and is usually my preferred choice for that little bit of extra nutrition, especially for vegetarian eaters. Cubes of baked tofu or cooked soybeans can be mixed in to make a main course dish, if you like. Otherwise, you can serve this on the side with a vegetable stew or casserole such as Farmers' Market *Giambotta* (page 366) or Vegetable and Tofu *Tian* (page 370).

2 tablespoons olive oil or unsalted butter
1 small carrot, peeled and diced

4 scallions, ends trimmed and cut into ¼-inch pieces
1 small celery stalk, ends trimmed and diced
½ small red bell pepper, seeded and diced
Salt and pepper to taste
3 cups vegetable broth
1½ cups instant couscous
1 tablespoon finely chopped fresh parsley, basil,
    cilantro, dill, or a combination

1. Heat the oil or melt the butter in a large saucepan over medium heat. Add the carrot, scallions, celery, and bell pepper, season with salt and pepper, and cook, stirring often, until the vegetables are tender, 5 to 8 minutes. Add the broth and bring to a boil.

2. Stir in the couscous, remove from the heat, cover, and set aside until the liquid is absorbed, about 10 minutes. Add the chopped herbs, fluff the couscous with a fork, and serve immediately.

Quinoa and Vermicelli Pilaf

MAKES 4 SERVINGS A rather unusual grain, but one well worth getting to know, is quinoa, which contains more protein than any other grain and includes the eight essential amino acids required by the body. In addition, it boasts unsaturated fat, high fiber, a lower carbohydrate content than other grains, and a plethora of nutrients, including iron, magnesium, and calcium. When cooked, quinoa expands like rice, three to four times its original volume, and takes no more than 15 minutes to prepare. It definitely comes close to being the perfect food, something the Incas knew centuries ago, referring to it as the sacred mother grain. It is becoming increasingly available in supermarkets and can always be found in health food stores.

This preparation, with broken pieces of vermicelli pasta, is a popular one with eaters who are new to quinoa, as it reminds them, I suppose, of Rice a Roni. Pan toasting both the vermicelli and quinoa before cooking them in broth helps to bring out the flavors and keep the grains and pasta separated. Be sure to rinse the quinoa under cold running water to remove any traces of saponin, a natural coating that may add a slightly bitter taste.

1 tablespoon unsalted butter
1 tablespoon canola oil
½ medium-size onion, peeled and finely chopped
Salt and pepper to taste
1 teaspoon *herbes de Provence* (see page 354)
¼ cup sliced almonds
1 cup quinoa, rinsed well until water runs clear
3 to 4 ounces dry vermicelli pasta, broken into
    1-inch pieces
2½ cups vegetable broth or water

1. Melt the butter in the oil in a large saucepan over medium heat. Add the onion, season with salt and pepper, and cook, stirring, until softened but not browned, about 4 minutes. Add the herbs, almonds, quinoa, and vermicelli pieces and stir occasionally over medium-high heat until the grains and pasta begin to brown, about 5 minutes. Pour in the broth, stir well, and bring to a simmer. Cover lid, reduce the heat to low, and cook until the liquid has been absorbed and the grains and pasta are cooked, 15 minutes.

3. Remove from the heat, allow to rest for 3 minutes, then fluff with a fork and serve immediately.

Cheese-Baked Polenta Slices

MAKES 4 SERVINGS Italian polenta, or "cornmeal mush," as we Americans call it, is a delicious accompaniment for any type of vegetable or meat stew, particularly those that are tomato based. It can be served soft and creamy, resembling southern-style grits, or firm, cut into shapes, then baked, broiled, or grilled. Both ways are equally appealing and tasty.

(continued on page 381)

Wholesome Grains of Wisdom

Gratitude and Food for Thought

When we begin recovery, we are usually encouraged to read a daily meditation from any number of inspiring books written by people who, either through their own experience of addiction or codependence, have eloquently and succinctly put into words what many of us are feeling during this difficult time. These daily grains of insight and wisdom can often offer us hope and strength when we are feeling particularly low and defeated, while planting a seed of gratitude for our new life of recovery. As is too often the case, however, once we begin to regain our strength and become occupied with the reality of living, we tend to put down our books and neglect to take advantage of the "food for thought" they provide.

If it's been awhile since you last dusted off your first daily meditation book, it may be time to take a second or even third look. Sometimes a particular saying or message can have quite a different impact when read with knowledge and hindsight. I know some people who have read the same ragged-paged books over and over, year after year, and are still able to reap new grains of wisdom. Others, eager to glean even more insight from a new book as each year comes to a close.

Whichever approach works for you, reacquainting yourself with daily readings can be a great reminder in the later stages of recovery of how far you have come in your healing process and keep you focused on the positive changes in your life since you began this road to wellness.

Although there are a vast number of authors who write these inspirational messages, Melody Beattie is one with whom most people are familiar, particularly those who have struggled with codependency as she has. Her groundbreaking book, *Codependent No More*, changed thousands of lives by giving hope and strength to family members of alcoholics and addicts as they tried to come to terms with the devastating existence of living with an addicted loved one. Since then, she has provided the daily meditation reader with a number of excellent books of encouragement and inspiration. Here are her thoughts on gratitude:

> "Gratitude unlocks the fullness of life. It turns what we have into enough, and more. It turns denial into acceptance, chaos to order, confusion to clarity. It can turn a meal into a feast, a house into a home, a stranger into a friend. It turns problems into gifts, failures into successes, the unexpected into perfect timing, and mistakes into important events. It can turn an existence into a real life, and disconnected situations into important and beneficial lessons. Gratitude makes sense of our past, brings peace for today, and creates a vision for tomorrow."*

*From *The Language of Letting Go* by Melody Beattie. ©1990 by HAZELDEN FOUNDATION. Reprinted by permission of Hazelden Foundation, Center City, MN.

(continued from page 379)

Cornmeal (polenta) comes in a few different grinds and varieties, from fine to coarse, and yellow to blue, and depending upon which one you are using, its cooking time can vary from 5 to 30 minutes or more. I tend to use a finer meal, usually bought as "polenta" as opposed to "cornmeal," which is rather quick cooking, so the time estimate below is on the shorter side. The best thing to do is consult the packaging to find out suggested cooking times and directions, but in general a ratio of three parts water to one part cornmeal will be accurate for firm, while four parts to one will be better for a softer version. In this recipe we are looking for a solid result so that we can cut the polenta into pie-shaped slices and bake them with olive oil and cheese. See the variations below for a soft version, as well as some delicious additions.

3 cups water
½ teaspoon salt, plus more to taste
1 cup polenta (fine yellow cornmeal)
2 tablespoons unsalted butter
Freshly ground black pepper
¼ cup olive oil
¼ cup freshly grated Parmesan cheese

1. In a large saucepan, bring the water to a boil. Add the salt and gradually whisk in the polenta, reducing the heat to low. Switch to a wooden spoon and stir constantly as the polenta cooks, 5 to 8 minutes. The mixture will bubble vigorously and you may need to reduce the heat a bit further to avoid splattering (you can also wrap your hand in a dishtowel for protection).

2. Remove from the heat, stir in the butter and pepper, and taste for the addition of salt. Immediately spread the mixture into a lightly greased 9-inch round cake pan or a deep dish pie plate, smooth the surface with the back of a spoon, and set aside to cool and firm for 30 minutes. You may prepare the polenta to this step several hours or even a day ahead, covering with plastic wrap and refrigerating until ready to bake.

3. Preheat the oven to 400 degrees. Using a sharp knife, cut the polenta into 8 pie-shaped slices. Place the slices ½ inch apart on a baking sheet coated with 1 tablespoon of the olive oil, and use the remaining 3 tablespoons olive oil to generously coat the top and sides of each slice. Sprinkle the cheese evenly over each slice and bake until lightly golden, about 15 minutes. Serve immediately.

Creamy Polenta: Increase the water to 4 cups, or use 3 cups water and 1 cup milk or soymilk, to make the polenta, serving immediately from the pot. Consider adding any of the following: 1 to 2 tablespoons finely chopped fresh herbs, ½ cup shredded cheddar cheese, ½ cup mascarpone cheese, ½ cup crumbled gorgonzola cheese and ¼ cup chopped walnuts, or 3 tablespoons basil or sun-dried tomato pesto.

11

When Food Is Your Preventive Medicine

Discovering the Functionality of Cooking and Eating

We already know that food has the power to heal. In Phase One, we saw the well-known adage of Hippocrates, the ancient Greek physician, at work as we fed and nourished our tired and neglected bodies. "Let food be your medicine," he insisted, and we did just that. We also know that food can comfort us when we require emotional healing. In Phase Two, the familiarity of old-fashioned, heart-warming dishes helped us find our way back to a place we'd almost forgotten as we began to feel comfortable with our sober selves and rediscovered the pleasures of the child within. Now, as we embark on the exciting journey called the rest of our lives, food can offer yet another service. And I am sure Hippocrates would have approved wholeheartedly.

In this chapter we'll discover how what you eat can make a difference in your future health by warding off disease and age-related illnesses. We have taken the first step toward reducing our chances of developing many diseases by putting our addiction behind us. However, depending upon how long and to what extent we abused our health in the past, we may still be at risk for alcohol- and substance dependence–related illnesses in the future. And this is where food may help.

Much research has been done in the recent past that highlights the importance of diet and specific foods that may have an enormous impact on our ability to live long and healthy lives. These foods, which provide particular health benefits beyond the traditional nutrients they contain, are called "functional" and we will be exploring their benefits in detail, as well as coming up with easy ways to include these important and potent ingredients in our everyday menus. Some will be familiar, like salmon, soy products, and many antioxidant-rich fruits and vegetables, while others may be new, such as flaxseed. All of them are just waiting to be utilized by our bodies to build up a strong resistance, while delaying and even stopping potential disease in its tracks. Be assured, however, that taste and functionality are not mutually exclusive; every recipe in this chapter is both delicious *and* healthy. So let's start reaping the benefits that fabulous-tasting, functional food has to offer!

Getting Your Omega-3: When Fat Is Essential

In Phase One, we briefly looked at the importance of including omega-3 fatty acids in our diet (page 144) and cooked up some quick and delicious salmon fare that got us started on the right path to good health. But we were only scratching the surface when it came to the amazing benefits of adding this essential fat to our diet. Omega-3 has been shown to reduce the risk of heart disease and stroke by checking the tendency of blood to clot, discouraging plaque build-up in our arteries, and reducing triglyceride levels (blood-thickening lipids which, incidentally, can be raised by excessive alcohol and

sugar consumption). They may delay the onset of diabetes (common in many alcoholics, particularly men) by improving insulin function in individuals who are vulnerable to Type 2, or adult-onset, diabetes. Lack of omega-3 fatty acids in the diet can contribute to the development of high blood pressure, depression, Alzheimer's disease, and many inflammatory diseases, such as rheumatoid arthritis and bowel diseases. The list goes on and on as each year yet another benefit of omega-3 becomes clear to researchers.

So, how do we increase our intake of this super essential fatty acid (EFA) in our diet? Salmon is a great source, particularly wild Alaskan salmon, a slightly stronger-tasting fish with less of a bright orange hue. Because it is able to feed in the wild on its own, as opposed to being fed in a farm-raised environment, Alaskan salmon tends to offer more omega-3 from the higher levels of EFAs it consumes and stores as body fat. Oddly, wild salmon tends to be less expensive at the supermarket fish counter than the farm-raised variety, perhaps due, in part, to its appearance. Don't let the darker color put you off—the wild salmon is a far better choice.

In addition to salmon, sardines are another excellent choice for omega-3 intake. Although sometimes difficult to find fresh, they are worth purchasing when they become available because they make delicious quick pan-fries and are well suited to grilling and roasting. However, if canned sardines are all that you can find, these too are just as good a source—look for those packaged in fish oil, olive oil, or in tomato sauce for maximum benefit. Other fish that boast omega-3 content are mackerel, bluefish, herring, albacore tuna, swordfish, and anchovy.

Getting your omega-3 from the fish world is really the best way because it provides both docosahexaenoic acid (DHA) and eicosapentaenoic acid (EPA), two fatty acids that do not need to be converted by our bodies to be useful. However, for vegetarians and those who crave a little variety, there are also plant sources that contain the essential fatty acid called alpha linolenic acid (ALA) that your body can convert to the more accessible DHA and EPA. These plant sources include flaxseed, walnuts, walnut oil, soybeans, and a wonderful little-known plant that is actually a weed, but is highly cherished by Mediterranean and Hispanic cultures, called purslane. We'll be meeting many of these ingredients in this section and whipping up some super dishes full of omega-3 that are sure to tempt any appetite into a healthy-eating mode.

Ten Functional Foods You're Probably Already Eating

Just because a food is functional doesn't mean it's unusual or far-fetched. Here are 10 nutritionally powerful foods you're most likely already enjoying on a regular basis, with their additional functional benefits.

1. AVOCADOS: We already know that this creamy component of guacamole is a good source of monounsaturated fat, which is linked to lower cholesterol levels (see "The Avocado Advantage," page 33). But avocados also contain glutathione, an antioxidant that fights free radicals and is particularly important in battling lung diseases caused by chronic drinking, as well as beta-sitosterol, an important plant sterol that can reduce the discomfort of BPH (benign prostatic hyperplasia) or enlarged prostate. In addition, studies are underway to determine if avocados have the potential to prevent breast cancer.

2. CHILI PEPPERS: Many of us love our hot peppers, perhaps because they can raise endorphin levels (see "Craving Spicy Foods?" page 35), but the same compound that gives them their heat, capsaicin, contains an anticoagulant that may prevent heart attack and stroke caused by blood clots. They also have an excellent supply of free radical–fighting antioxidants.

3. CHOCOLATE: Believe it or not, the chocolate monster may actually be far more of a friend than fiend, since chocolate, particularly dark and bittersweet versions, contains phenolic compounds, the same type of antioxidants touted in red wine. These, along with a good amount of flavonoids, may ward off heart disease by protecting the fats in our bloodstream from oxidation.

4. CORN: An excellent source of the B vitamin thiamin, often in short supply in alcoholics, corn also has functionality in its chemical compounds, including lutein and zeaxanthin, carotenoids that protect our eyes from age-related conditions, such as macular degeneration. Corn also provides protease inhibitors, similar to those found in soy foods, which can fight cancerous tumors by halting uncontrolled cell growth.

5. GARLIC: A medicinal star since ancient Egypt, today garlic is being studied for its ability to block the effects of cancer-causing toxins. However, garlic's prowess at fighting infection, as well as its antifungal activity, has long been acknowledged by researchers. A host of phytochemicals join together to make garlic a super healer for everything from blood clots to headaches. The sulfur compounds, including ajoenes and allyl sulfides, which are released when garlic is crushed and are responsible for its pungent smell, may be helpful in warding off bacteria and, as the legend goes, hungry vampires.

6 ORANGES: Already known as a great source of vitamin C and fiber, oranges also contain many flavonoids such as hesperidin, particularly concentrated in its rind, which may be a natural anti-inflammatory as well as a cholesterol-lowering compound. Nobiletin, found in the flesh, also has anti-inflammatory action, while the carotenoid beta-cryptoxanthin may help to prevent colon cancer.

7. PEANUTS: Once dismissed as a good protein source but too high in fat, peanuts are back on the scene, boasting heart-healthy monounsaturated fat and a host of phytochemicals. One in particular, resveratrol, the same compound found in red wine, may prevent cancer, high cholesterol, and stroke, while healthy saponins have been shown to boost immunity and encourage stable blood sugar levels.

8. PINEAPPLE: In addition to valuable fiber and vitamin C, pineapples contain a unique anti-inflammatory enzyme called bromelain, which helps to control tissue swelling and reduce pain. Bromelain has been linked to the alleviation of symptoms associated with bronchitis, osteoarthritis, varicose veins, and ordinary strains and sprains. In addition, its inflammation-reducing properties may lower the risk of stroke and heart attack.

9. TUNA FISH: Tuna is just one of the fish varieties associated with the important omega-3 fatty acids. A tuna sandwich or salad made from just four ounces of canned albacore tuna will provide you with one-third of the American Heart Association's recommended weekly intake. Not enough can be said about the benefits of adding omega-3-rich foods to your diet, while tuna also provides a good amount of tyrosine, an amino acid that aids neurotransmission and promotes good mental health.

10. WATERMELON: Surprisingly, juicy and refreshing watermelon contains more of the antioxidant lycopene than any other fruit or vegetable. This powerful phytochemical has been linked to reduced risk of prostate cancer, as well as other types of cancer, by disarming free radicals before they get a chance to create havoc in our cells. Lycopene is also associated with helping to lower the risk for heart disease and macular degeneration.

Simple Oven-Poached Salmon

MAKES 4 SERVINGS One of the best ways to include salmon in your everyday meal planning is by having it prepared and ready to eat at a moment's notice. For that reason, this poached version is ideal. It can be eaten cold as part of a lunch or dinner salad (see Salmon Fillet Salade Niçoise on page 339) or briefly heated for a quick meal. Cooked this way, the fillet is incredibly moist and does not lose any of its tenderness or flavor when served more than once or twice. I make this on a weekly basis for many of my clients, who are thrilled to have it on hand for a variety of purposes, such as adding to soups and chowders, pasta dishes, or omelets. And it is perfect for the fresh salmon variation of Smoked Salmon Kedgeree (page 133) that we made in Phase One.

Fish poaching is one of the cooking methods in which we traditionally find the use of wine, vermouth, or both when preparing the poaching liquid, also called a court bouillon. Here, a simple combination of fruit juice and lemon fills in nicely, providing the necessary acidity and sweetness to subtly flavor the fish and vegetables while they are cooking.

You can use either the tail end of the salmon or the thickest part of the fillet, in which case you will need to add two to three minutes to the cooking time for the latter. Leave the skin on, as it will help to hold the fillet together after it has been cooked. The skin will easily pull off when you are ready to serve it.

Omega-3 Fatty Acids
Not Quite the Final Word

In addition to the essential fatty acids (EFAs) known as omega-3, there are two other omegas that are worth getting to know. These are the omega-6 and omega-9 fatty acids, also available to us through diet. Unless the balance of these fatty acids in our bodies, particularly omega-3 and omega-6, is in good stead, we may not be able to take advantage of the EFAs we ingest. For example, when in excess, omega-6 seems to interfere with the efficiency of omega-3, particularly in the production of prostaglandins—important hormones that influence cell growth, immune function, and inflammation—because they are competing for the same enzymes. In order to keep this from happening, researchers have determined that a ratio of two to one, or twice the amount of omega-6 to omega-3, is really the ideal balance to shoot for. Unfortunately, our modern diet of highly processed foods ends up giving us a huge imbalance, where omega-6 becomes excessively predominant. Where do these other omegas come from?

Polyunsaturated oils such as corn, safflower, and sunflower oil and products made from them, like snack food and junk food, are the main dietary sources of omega-6 in our society. Cutting back on these types of "foods" and increasing our intake of omega-3, will go a long way in improving the ratio. In addition, when polyunsaturated oils become hydrogenated, the method so widely used in mass-produced foods in which the temperature of the oil is raised

1¼ cups water

½ cup unsweetened white grape or
   apple juice

¼ cup fresh lemon juice

1 medium-size carrot, peeled and cut into
   ½-inch-thick rounds

1 medium-size parsnip, peeled and cut into
   ½-inch-thick rounds

1 medium-size celery stalk, ends trimmed
   and cut into 1-inch pieces

1 small onion, peeled and quartered

1 bay leaf

Few sprigs *each* fresh dill and parsley

One 1- to 1¼-pound salmon fillet (preferably
   wild Alaskan), skin on and any remaining
   pinbones removed

Salt and pepper to taste

Handful of fresh dill sprigs

1 teaspoon unsalted butter, softened

1. Preheat the oven to 400 degrees. To make the poaching liquid, combine the ingredients in a medium-size saucepan and bring to a boil over medium-high heat. Stir, reduce the heat to medium-low, and simmer for 10 minutes.

2. Lay the salmon skin-side down in a lightly greased 9 x 13-inch glass, ceramic, or stainless steel baking dish. Sprinkle with salt and pepper, place the dill sprigs over the flesh, and slowly pour the

---

with the presence of hydrogen gas to make it harder and extend its shelf life ("partially hydrogenated oil" is what you will read on a food label), they end up with a high content of trans fatty acids, the villainous fat that we now know can increase the risk of cardiovascular disease, diabetes, and possibly cancer. Margarines, solid shortenings, and products that contain partially hydrogenated anything should be shunned whenever possible, although its widespread prevalence is sometimes hard to avoid. Ironically, cholesterol-lowering margarines, which contain plant compounds known as stanol esters, also contain partially hydrogenated oil, but because the amount is less than .5 gram per serving, the manufacturers are allowed to claim that their product is trans fat free. If consuming these margarines on a regular basis, one wonders if the advantages ultimately outweigh the disadvantages, since trans fats are definitely an unhealthy addition to any diet.

On the bright side, omega-9, also called oleic acid, is mostly monounsaturated and by increasing fats such as these, we can improve heart and artery health, glucose maintenance, immune function, and even protect ourselves from some types of cancer. It is the oleic acid, or olive oil consumption, that some believe is the primary contributor to the healthy Mediterranean diet, although recent research has also pointed to greater fish (omega-3), whole grain (fiber), and fruit and vegetable (phytochemicals) consumption as other important aspects of this diet. Although wine consumption may also be a factor in improved Mediterranean health, it appears to be the phytochemicals and not so much the alcohol that is the main advantage (see "The Abstinent Approach: Wine-Free Ways to Increase Your Polyphenols," page 411).

poaching liquid into the baking dish around the fish, distributing and submerging the vegetables and herbs around the edges in the liquid. Cover with a sheet of waxed paper or parchment that has been coated with the butter, directly placing the buttered side on top of the fillet. Carefully transfer to the oven and poach until the fish loses its translucency and feels somewhat firm to the touch, about 18 minutes.

3. Remove from the oven, lift off the parchment, and transfer the fillet to a shallow platter. Using a slotted spoon remove the vegetables from the cooking liquid and place around the fish. Serve immediately or cover well, refrigerate, and serve chilled.

Roasted Salmon with Sweet Mustard Dill Glaze

MAKES 4 SERVINGS This oven-roasted salmon, which is easy to prepare, is always a hit at the dinner table, even with the most finicky of seafood eaters. The outside of the fillets and the red-skinned potatoes develop a sweet and crusty flavor and texture that complements beautifully the moist and creamy inside of the salmon. In this recipe, it pays to use skinless salmon fillets so that the flavorful sauce will have a chance to penetrate the entire piece. You can remove the skin yourself using a sharp knife or ask your fishmonger to do it for you.

An excellent accompaniment for this dish would be a simply prepared vegetable such as steamed spinach or asparagus, although a more assertive bitter green such as collards or turnip or mustard greens would also be delicious, as they blend nicely with the mustard and brown sugar glaze.

¼ cup honey mustard
¼ cup canola oil
¼ cup chopped fresh dill sprigs
2 tablespoons dark brown sugar

4 medium-size red potatoes, left unpeeled and cut into ¼-inch-thick rounds
Salt and pepper to taste
Four 4-ounce salmon fillets, skin and any remaining pinbones removed

1. Preheat the oven to 375 degrees.

2. In a small mixing bowl, whisk together the mustard, canola oil, dill, and brown sugar. In a medium-size mixing bowl, toss together the potatoes, salt and pepper, and one-third of the mustard sauce to coat well. Place the salmon fillets in a zippered-top plastic bag, add the remaining mustard sauce, seal, and turn to coat the the fillets with the sauce. Set aside.

3. Spread the potatoes out evenly in a lightly greased 9 x 13-inch roasting pan or baking dish and roast for 30 minutes, turning them over with a metal spatula halfway through.

4. Shift the potato slices to the outer edges of the roasting pan and place the salmon fillets in a single layer in the middle of the pan, pouring the marinade over to coat. Return to the oven and roast until the potatoes and salmon are lightly crisp

Omega-3-Rich Fish

	Content per 4-ounce serving
Wild Alaskan salmon	3.6 grams
Albacore tuna	2.6 grams
Mackerel	1.8 to 2.6 grams
Sardines	1.7 grams
Farm-raised salmon	1.6 to 2.3 grams
Anchovy	1.5 grams
Herring	1.2 to 2.7 grams
Bluefish	0.7 gram

and browned around the edges and the fish is firm to the touch, about 25 minutes, turning the potatoes occasionally to roast evenly. Transfer to a platter or serve immediately from the pan.

Fresh Pan-Fried Sardines

MAKES 3 TO 4 SERVINGS If you have never tasted fresh sardines, you are definitely in for a culinary surprise. Much larger than the little guys we are normally used to seeing in tiny tins, these power-houses of omega-3 are fabulous when grilled, roasted, or pan-fried, as this simple recipe will show. Not always easy to come by, fresh sardines are usually plentiful in the summer months, especially near coastal areas. Originially, these little silver-skinned fish were caught off the coast of Sardinia, hence the name, although they were probably a type of pilchard or sprat. They are particularly enjoyed in the southern parts of Italy, including Sardinia and Sicily, as we will see in the recipe on page 391.

You can have your fishmonger clean and gut the sardines, if you are unfamiliar with this tedious process. The heads are also usually removed, but not always, especially when grilled. The tiny bones can be lifted out in one piece once the sardine has been cooked by opening up the cavity and pulling up from the tail end. Eating sardines is definitely a hands-on sport, but well worth the effort. Enjoy them with a simple squirt of fresh lemon juice as an appetizer before pasta or as part of a main meal.

½ cup extra virgin olive oil
1 pound fresh sardines, cleaned, gutted, and rinsed
    well under cold running water
Salt and pepper to taste
Flour for dredging
Lemon wedges for serving

1. Heat the olive oil in a large skillet over medium-high heat until it reaches 360 degrees. Do the bread-cube test if you're unsure whether the oil is hot enough (page 220).

2. Pat dry the sardines with paper towels, season them with salt and pepper, and lightly dredge in the flour, tapping off any excess. Fry in the oil until lightly browned and crisp, about 3 minutes per side. Drain on brown paper and serve immediately with the lemon wedges.

Broiled Bluefish with Green Peppercorn Mayonnaise

MAKES 4 SERVINGS Ever since bluefish, the "bull-dog of the ocean," as it is affectionately referred to by East Coast anglers, was discovered to be an excellent source of omega-3 fatty acids, it has become more prevalent in supermarket fish displays. Here in New Jersey, bluefish has a reputation of being nearly as plentiful in the summer as zucchini is in New England. Folks can't wait to proudly give it away, supposedly to show off their fishing expertise, but in reality hoping to unload this strong-tasting, dark-fleshed, and often unpopular fish. I think the reason most people shun the bluefish is because they have yet to taste it prepared at its best and I dare say that this recipe just might do the trick.

Most importantly, the dark, oily strip that runs down the center of the fillet, not unlike that seen in tuna and swordfish, must be removed completely in order to prevent the flesh from absorbing its strong smell. Once done, the bluefish fillet is far milder than most folks imagine. Have your fishmonger do this for you (he can also skin the fillet for this recipe, if you like) or suggest that your bluefish angler neighbor do it.

This doctored-up mayonnaise recipe is simple to prepare and can be whipped up in the blender or with the chopper attachment of a hand-held immersion blender. Green peppercorns are deliciously mild, as they are the underripe berry, softer

(continued on page 391)

Boning Up on Functional Fish

Easy Tips for Boosting Omega-3 in Your Diet

Many of the recipes we prepared in Phases One and Two are perfect omega-3-filled meals, including Salmon and Corn Chowder with Dill (page 107), Midwestern Salmon Loaf (page 222), and Lemon Zesty Pasta Shells with Tuna and Artichokes (page 328). Make a point of enjoying dishes like these a few times a week to get the recommended fatty fish serving of 12 ounces (8 to 10 grams of omega-3) per week. Here's how easy it is to do:

- Add drained, rinsed, and chopped anchovies or canned albacore tuna to pasta dishes like Linguine with Garlic and Olive Oil (page 117) for a delicious and healthy variation. Canned sardines in olive oil or tomato sauce also make excellent additions to tomato-based pasta dishes—add them at the end to just heat through.

- Have a good old tuna salad sandwich for lunch, or make the classic Salade Niçoise from canned albacore tuna, following the directions for Salmon Fillet Salade Niçoise (page 339), which is also a great choice.

- Top your bagel and cream cheese with smoked salmon for breakfast or add pieces of smoked or poached salmon to scrambled eggs, omelets, or frittatas (using omega-3-enriched eggs!).

- Add sardines, tuna, or flaked canned salmon to an antipasto platter and serve with whole-grain crackers or crusty bread. Canned salmon is usually of the wild variety, providing an extra good amount of omega-3 fatty acids. And for those who love a bit of "heat," sardines can now be found packed in hot sauce!

- Nibble on pickled herring tidbits with pumpernickel bread as an appetizer. Watch for herring in white wine sauce, however, and opt instead for the delicious sour cream sauce version.

- Instead of throwing a beefsteak on the grill, opt for swordfish steak, a meaty and satisfying alternative.

- Order anchovies on your pizza!

(continued from page 389)

and less pungent than their black counterparts. They are sold in small jars with brine, usually next to the jars of capers, which they visually resemble.

Fresh mackerel could be used here in place of the bluefish for an even bigger omega-3 boost. You may grill the fillets if you choose, but in that case I would leave the skin on to hold it together and refrain from flipping; simply leave it to cook skin side down over a moderately hot flame with the grill cover closed until it is firm to the touch.

GREEN PEPPERCORN MAYONNAISE

½ cup mayonnaise

3 tablespoons brine-packed green peppercorns, drained and rinsed

1 tablespoon fennel or anise seeds

1 large garlic clove, peeled

2 tablespoons fresh lemon juice

Four 4-ounce bluefish or mackerel fillets, skinned, boned, and dark oily strip removed

Salt and pepper to taste

1. To make the peppercorn mayonnaise, combine the ingredients in a blender, reserving 1 tablespoon of the peppercorns, and process until smooth and most of the seeds and peppercorns have broken down. Transfer to a small bowl and refrigerate until ready to use.

2. Preheat the broiler and set the rack to 3 inches below the flame. Place the fish fillets in a lightly oiled flameproof pan, sprinkle with salt and pepper, and use half the mayonnaise to evenly spread over the top of the fillets. Add the reserved peppercorns to the remaining mayonnaise and set aside.

3. Broil the fillets until lightly browned and firm to the touch, 5 to 8 minutes. Serve immediately with the remaining peppercorn mayonnaise.

Chef's Note: Soybean mayonnaise, contains a modest amount of omega-3 fatty acids. Try using it here for an additional dose of this important nutrient.

Southern Italian Pasta with Sardines and Fennel

MAKES 2 TO 3 SERVINGS This traditional dish makes use of canned sardines in olive oil for a delicious and hearty treat. The unusual combination of ingredients, from golden raisins to toasted bread crumbs, is what makes this dish stand out from nearly all other classic Italian pasta dishes with which you may be familiar. However, all the elements come together wonderfully in the end and I guarantee you will be whipping up this healthy omega-3-filled pasta on a regular basis.

Good quality ingredients always make the difference; extra virgin olive oil is a must, while the sardines should be packed in olive oil as well. You can buy boneless, skinless, oil-packed sardines, but traditionally the whole small sardine, bones and all, is used. I like to use a thick spaghetti for this dish to reflect the robustness of the ingredients. Save the fennel bulb to make Tomato Fennel Salad (page 322), an excellent accompaniment or first-course salad served with crusty Italian bread.

1 large fennel bulb, fronds roughly chopped, stalks cut off and left whole, bulb reserved for another use

Generous pinch of salt

8 ounces thick spaghetti or perciatelli

¼ cup white wine substitute (page 134)

¼ cup golden raisins

1 tablespoon unsalted butter

½ cup fresh bread crumbs

Pepper to taste

¼ cup extra virgin olive oil, and more for drizzling

4 medium-size garlic cloves, peeled and minced

One 3- to 4-ounce can sardines packed in olive oil, left undrained

¼ cup chopped fresh Italian parsley leaves

1. Bring a large pot of water to a boil. Add the chopped fennel fronds, whole fennel stalks, salt,

and spaghetti and cook according to the package directions. Drain, discard the fennel stalks, leaving the fronds with the spaghetti, and set aside.

2. In a small bowl, combine the wine substitute and raisins and allow to sit for 15 minutes. In a medium-size nonstick skillet, melt the butter, add the bread crumbs, season with salt and pepper, and toast, stirring often, until golden brown. Set aside.

3. In a large skillet, heat the olive oil over medium heat, add the garlic and a pinch of salt, and cook until slightly soft and fragrant but not brown, about 2 minutes. Add the sardines and stir, breaking them up somewhat, and cook a further minute. Add the raisin mixture, stir to combine, and heat through. Add the hot cooked pasta, drizzle with more olive oil, and toss well to coat with the sardine sauce. Toss in the parsley and toasted bread crumbs, taste for salt and pepper, and serve immediately.

Chef's Note: Sometimes a few tablespoons of toasted pine nuts are added for flavor and texture. Try the addition of roughly chopped toasted walnuts instead for an omega-3 boost.

Recovery Note: Not all versions of this classic dish include wine. If you happen to see it on the menu, ask how it is prepared.

Grilled Swordfish with Sweet Tomato Salsa

MAKES 4 SERVINGS Swordfish, a meaty and mild-flavored sport fish, is one of the most popular fish eaten in America. Even people who dislike fish in general seem to enjoy it, especially when grilled. Dense and firm fleshed, it holds together beautifully regardless of cooking method and lends itself to a variety of ethnic flavors, Mexican being one of the best. Here a quick and easy tomato salsa, with both a sweet and hot kick, complements the grilled flavor.

Serve guacamole (page 32) with chips to start and finish with grilled slices of fresh pineapple, topped with vanilla ice cream.

SWEET TOMATO SALSA

One 16-ounce can diced tomatoes, drained

3 scallions, ends trimmed and thinly sliced

1 medium-size jalapeño, seeded and minced

2 tablespoons extra virgin olive oil

1 tablespoon balsamic vinegar

2 teaspoons light brown sugar

Salt and pepper to taste

Oil for coating the grill

Four 4-ounce swordfish steaks, $\frac{3}{4}$ inch thick

Salt and pepper

1. To make the salsa, combine the ingredients in a medium-size mixing bowl and stir well to combine. Let stand at room temperature for at least 30 minutes to let the flavors develop.

2. Prepare the grill or preheat a broiler. Brush the grill slats with oil to prevent sticking or lightly coat a broiler pan with cooking spray and set the oven rack 3 to 4 inches below the broiler element. Season the swordfish with salt and pepper and grill or broil until cooked through (slightly pink in the center is ideal), 4 to 5 minutes per side. Serve immediately with a heaping spoonful of the salsa.

Variation: Tuna or halibut steaks would also be delicious grilled and served with this salsa.

Chef's Note: Swordfish makes excellent kebabs because of its firm flesh. Cut into $1\frac{1}{2}$-inch cubes and thread on a metal skewer for grilling.

Peppered Smoked Mackerel Pâté

MAKES ABOUT 8 APPETIZER SERVINGS Far more commonly enjoyed in Europe, pâtés tend to be under-appreciated by most of us. They are excellent appetizers for parties, large or small, and, when served with a delicious crusty bread, they can be extremely satisfying and tasty.

Smoke-curing is just one of many ways to treat and preserve food, and always adds a delicious woodsy aroma and flavor to many meats and fish. Smoked salmon and mackerel have become more popular since the omega-3 phenomenon, although they have actually been used for ages to make flavorful spreads and pâtés. Peppered smoked mackerel, available in most supermarket deli sections, is my choice here because I particularly like peppercorn pâtés in general, but you could substitute a regular smoked mackerel or even smoked trout if you prefer. Be sure to carefully remove the skin and any bones you may come across.

Use an electric mixer to blend, rather than a food processor, which will break down the nice bits of onion and bell pepper a little too much. They add a textural as well as a visual contrast to the smooth cream cheese. For a nice presentation, chill the pâté in a bowl lined with plastic wrap; this will help you to release the perfect mound from the bowl, turning it out onto the center of your serving platter. Surround with crackers and crusty French bread.

> 7 to 8 ounces peppered smoked mackerel, skin and bones removed
> Two 8-ounce packages cream cheese, softened
> 2 tablespoons sour cream
> 2 tablespoons fresh lemon juice
> 3 tablespoons finely diced red onion
> 3 tablespoons seeded and finely diced red bell pepper
> 2 tablespoons finely chopped fresh parsley leaves
> 1 teaspoon stoneground mustard
> 1 teaspoon prepared horseradish

1. Break the fillets apart, checking for any remaining bones.

2. In a medium-size mixing bowl, combine the mackerel, cream cheese, sour cream, and lemon juice. Using an electric mixer, beat together on medium speed until well combined, about 1 minute. Add the remaining ingredients and beat just to mix in. Transfer to a plastic wrap–lined bowl (see headnote), cover, and chill for at least 2 hours before serving.

Linguine with Purslane and Asiago

MAKES 2 TO 3 SERVINGS Purslane is a uniquely delicious plant-based source of omega-3 fatty acids (see page 394 for a full description of this weedy wonder). One of my favorite ways to prepare it is with pasta, particularly with garlic, olive oil, and tomatoes. Asiago cheese, preferably the younger semi-hard variety, which tastes like a soft Parmesan, provides the perfect piquancy and contrasting texture to this dish. Look for it in the gourmet cheese section of your grocer.

Fresh tomatoes in season will add wonderful flavor, but canned may also be used.

> ¼ cup extra virgin olive oil, plus more for drizzling
> 2 medium-size garlic cloves, peeled and roughly chopped
> 1 bunch purslane (about ½ pound), tough stems removed, washed well, and drained
> Salt and pepper to taste
> 8 ounces linguine, cooked according to package directions and drained
> 3 large, ripe tomatoes, peeled, seeded (see Chef's Note on page 395), and roughly chopped, or 2 cups drained canned tomatoes, roughly chopped
> 1 tablespoon red wine vinegar
> Pinch of sugar
> ½ cup finely diced Asiago cheese

(continued on page 395)

The Power of Purslane

This weed of the succulent plant family has been both a medicinal and culinary treat for many since ancient times, but only recently in the United States have we discovered its true healing power. Purslane, which grows wild in many sunny climates and is now sought out by gourmet chefs, is one of the only plant sources of mighty omega-3 fatty acids. Like flax seeds, it contains alpha linolenic acid (ALA), which our bodies convert to the important omega-3 nutrients of docosahexaenoic acid (DHA) and eicosapentaenoic acid (EPA), essential fatty acids required for life. Its power as a functional food was not lost on early Greek, Chinese, and Central American healers, who used it as a remedy for arthritis, inflammation, respiratory ailments, and improved circulation. Today it is being touted, along with the other sources of omega-3, as a potential reducer of cholesterol and blood pressure, and promises many other benefits.

Preparing purslane for eating is the easy part. Finding it may prove more difficult. Many Mexican and Hispanic dishes call for it, where it is known as *verdolaga* and is considered a comfort food, added to omelets, soups, stews, or eaten raw as a salad. Therefore, a good place to start would be a local ethnic market. I was able to find it at my nearby farmer's market for a short time this summer. You can, of course, grow your own, in which case you will be sure to have a plentiful supply from late spring through summer (see the "Resources" section, page 455, for information on ordering seed packets). No green thumb is required for this weed to take off once sowed. You might also want to persuade your local market to start carrying it and spread the word to your neighbors about its powerful nutritional content.

The tender stems and leaves are eaten, while the thicker, tougher stems are discarded. Purslane bunches, as they are sold, often have a good amount of sand and grit, which you can get rid of through several cold water soakings. It has a mild, lemony taste and plumpish leaves, which can be blanched or sautéed like spinach, or simply eaten raw. Here are just a few ways to add purslane to your everyday menu:

- Mix into a bowl of variety salad greens as you would watercress or arugula.

- Make Watercress Vichyssoise (page 112) using purslane instead.

- Have ham and purslane on rye.

- Add it to pasta sauces and stir-fries.

- Include it in omelets and frittatas.

- Add it chopped to Cucumber Yogurt Raita (page 261) for a traditional Middle Eastern delight.

(continued from page 393)

1. Heat the olive oil in a large nonstick skillet over medium heat, add the garlic, and cook just to soften, about 1 minute. Add the purslane, sprinkle with salt and pepper, and cook, stirring often, until the leaves are wilted, 2 to 3 minutes.

2. Add the hot cooked linguine, tomatoes, vinegar, and sugar and continue to cook over medium heat until the tomatoes are warmed through. Taste for the addition of salt and pepper and transfer to a heated serving platter. Sprinkle with the Asiago and serve immediately.

Chef's Note: To remove the skin from fresh tomatoes, core them first, cut a shallow X through the bottom of each with a sharp paring knife, and plunge them into boiling water for 30 seconds. Immediately transfer to a bowl of ice water. The skins will peel off easily. Cut in half and squeeze out the seeds, then chop.

Orange Flax Muffins with Dried Cranberries

MAKES 12 MUFFINS These delicious and moist muffins have a lot going for them besides flavor. Flax meal (see page 396 for a description of flax seeds and flax meal) provides a good dose of important omega-3 fatty acids, while orange juice and dried cranberries offer excellent nutritional oomph.

Allow the cranberries ample time to marinate in the juice and sugar to plump them up and bring them to full sweetness. Served warm, these muffins are wonderfully comforting with a bit of butter.

1½ cups orange juice
¾ cup sugar
¾ cup dried cranberries (look for them where
    raisins are sold in supermarkets)
1 cup whole wheat flour
1¾ cups all-purpose flour

½ cup flax meal
1 tablespoon baking powder
1 teaspoon baking soda
1 large egg, slightly beaten
½ cup canola oil
1½ tablespoons whole flax seeds

1. Preheat the oven to 375 degrees. Line a 12-cup standard muffin tin with paper liners or grease lightly.

2. In a small mixing bowl, combine ½ cup of the orange juice, ¼ cup of the sugar, and all of the cranberries. Allow to marinate for 15 to 20 minutes.

3. In a large mixing bowl, whisk together the remaining ½ cup sugar, the flours, flax meal, baking powder, and baking soda until well combined. In a medium-size mixing bowl, whisk together the egg, oil, and remaining 1 cup orange juice. Add the liquid ingredients to the dry and stir just until moistened. Fold in the cranberries with the soaking juice and flax seeds.

4. Fill the muffin cups three-quarters full and bake until lightly golden and a toothpick inserted in the center comes out clean, 30 to 35 minutes. Let cool briefly on a wire rack before turning out.

Toasted Flax Cinnamon Bread

MAKES 1 LOAF It's hard to get much healthier than this recipe, which boasts not only omega-3-rich flax, but oats and wheat bran to boot. Here we start out with whole flax seeds and toast them ourselves along with the oats and bran for a nutty, flavorful, slightly sweet bread that is a perfect companion to a cup of tea. Toasting your slices before serving will bring out all the wonderful taste and aroma it has to offer. And who can argue with cinnamon, that old favorite. Treat yourself and serve this with a smear of butter and a sprinkling of cinnamon sugar (page 240). Who knew functional foods could be so comforting?

1½ cups old-fashioned rolled oats (not the quick-cooking kind)

½ cup wheat bran

½ cup flax seeds

1 cup all-purpose flour

½ cup firmly packed light brown sugar

2 teaspoons baking powder

1½ teaspoons ground cinnamon

¾ teaspoon salt

1½ cups low-fat plain yogurt

⅔ cup honey

1 large egg, slightly beaten

1. Preheat the oven to 350 degrees. Grease and flour a 5 x 9-inch loaf pan, knocking out the excess flour.

2. Spread the oats, bran, and flax seeds on a baking sheet with a rim and toast in the oven, occasionally shaking the pan, until the oats have turned lightly golden, about 10 minutes. Transfer to a food processor and pulse until finely ground. Leave the oven on.

3. In a large mixing bowl, whisk together the ground mixture, flour, brown sugar, baking powder, cinnamon, and salt until well combined. In a medium-size mixing bowl, whisk together the yogurt, honey, and egg until well blended. Add the yogurt mixture to the dry ingredients and stir to combine. Do not overmix.

4. Spoon the batter into the prepared pan, smooth over the top, and bake until golden and a toothpick inserted in the center comes out clean, about 1 hour and 15 minutes. Let cool for 10 minutes on a wire rack before inverting onto the rack to cool completely.

The Facts on Flax

These ancient seeds, once used by Hippocrates to relieve gastrointestinal ailments, have become a modern day star in functional-food circles. Cultivated since 4000 B.C., today flax seeds are being studied for the prevention and management of numerous diseases and illnesses that are prevalent in modern society, such as heart disease and cancer. A recent study showed that eating a daily muffin made from ground flaxseeds dramatically lowered cholesterol in both men and women, while a similar study showed particular advantages for postmenopausal women and heart disease.

How exactly flax works its magic is not fully understood, although its high concentration of alpha linolenic acid (ALA), which our bodies convert to the healthy omega-3 fatty acids docosahexaenoic acid (DHA) and eicosapentaenoic acid (EPA), seems to be at the root of much of the flaxseed's benefit. What adds to its power is the presence of lignans, or phytoestrogens, which seem to play a protective role in many autoimmune diseases as well as hormone-related cancers, such as breast, endometrial, and prostate. In addition, flax is a good source of both soluble and insoluble fiber, necessary additions to the diet for keeping a healthy digestive track running as smoothly as possible, while ushering out "bad" cholesterol particles from the intestines.

Flaxseed is a particularly important addition to a vegetarian diet, along with soybeans, walnuts, and purslane, the other few plant sources of omega-3 fatty acids. However, the body must activate the ALA that these plant sources contain before it can convert it and utilize any resulting DHA and EPA, so larger dietary amounts may be necessary to compensate for this drawback. Additionally, ovo-vegetarians (see page 352 for a discussion of different types of vegetarians) should take advantage of omega-3-enriched eggs in their diet in order to obtain a good dose of this essential fatty acid.

In order to reap the benefits of flaxseeds, these tiny little brown fleck-like seeds should be ground up (preferably in a coffee grinder), otherwise they will simply pass through the body as roughage. Happily, packages of ground flaxseed, also called flax meal, are now available in many specialty food stores (see the "Resources" section, page 455, for ordering information), which makes it easy to add this super-functional food to our diet. Bags of flax meal, as well as the seeds themselves, should be stored in the refrigerator once opened, and will last for up to six months. Another flax product that is an enormously rich source of ALA but unfortunately lacks the lignans is its oil, which can be used on salads and in smoothies. However, it should not be cooked with, like canola or olive oil, as its delicate makeup will become rancid quickly, not unlike other pressed oils, such as sesame and walnut. Its distinct smell, reminiscent of oil painting class, will become even more evident, as flaxseeds are the primary ingredient in linseed oil-containing paints and varnishes. I prefer to use the ground flax seeds, as they provide much better flavor—nutty and sweet—without the off-putting aroma.

When grinding whole flaxseeds, bear in mind that the quantity will be nearly doubled. For example, ¼ cup of flaxseeds will yield seven tablespoons (just shy of ½ cup) of flax meal. Flax meal is perfect for adding to your baking recipes. Because of its high oil content, it provides a good substitute for canola oil or butter at a ratio of three to one. If your recipe requires ⅓ cup canola oil, substitute one cup flax meal. Baked goods that contain a large amount of flax will brown quickly, so keep an eye on the oven and lower the temperature somewhat, if necessary. You can also use flax meal as a substitute for dry ingredients by reducing the amount of flour called for by 25 percent and replacing it with an equal amount of flax meal.

Here are some easy ways to add ground flax to your everyday menus:

- Sprinkle over cold and hot cereals or yogurt and fruit.

- Add to your next smoothie.

- Sprinkle into waffle, pancake, muffin, cookie, and bread recipes.

- Add to meatloaf and meatball mixes for a super-moist result.

Hemp, Omega-3, and THC

Whole Food or Hype?

Hemp has been around since ancient China, where it was grown as a major grain crop. Since then, nearly every civilization has documented their use of the hemp plant as food, fiber for cloth and ropes, and paper made from the stalk. But as we all know, hemp, also called *cannabis sativa*, contains the same psychoactive chemical, tetrahydrocannabinol (THC), found in marijuana. In 2001, the United States Drug Enforcement Administration (DEA), in conjunction with its new marijuana rules, banned food products with even trace amounts of THC under the Controlled Substances Act. Up until that time, many health food stores carried hemp food products, many with traces of THC, such as oil, nuts, and various foods made from them because, among other things, hemp happens to be an excellent source of omega-3 fatty acids. Similar to flax, hemp contains a substantial amount of alpha linolenic acid (ALA), which the body can use to make essential fatty acids. For vegetarians who do not eat fish, their primary source of omega-3 may be limited to plant sources such as flax or hemp.

Confusion over hemp products and how they fit into the new regulations has caused a mild uproar amongst hemp advocates, but in reality, it is not the hemp itself that is being banned, but the THC it contains. Therefore, if manufacturers can show that their products are free of THC, they are not in danger of being discontinued. In fact, since the new regulation was announced, many hemp companies have already advertised products that are free of THC, emphatically stating that consumers cannot get "high" by eating them, so it appears the hemp market is not in jeopardy of disappearing. Just recently, I came across a new hemp granola, which offered a long explanation on the back of the package of how their hemp was THC-free according to government requirements and that all the nutritional value was still intact. This is good to know. It's also good to know that eating products that meet the DEA regulations will not affect drug testing for THC. So, feel free to enjoy a handful of hemp nuts to boost your omega-3 consumption. Just be sure to look for the THC-free symbol on the label, in case a few preregulation products still happen to be on the shelf.

Super Walnut Shortbread

MAKES 12 COOKIES These cookies combine the goodness of walnuts and their oil, providing omega-3, while allowing us to reduce the normal amount of butter usually found in traditional shortbread, and consequently the saturated fat along with it. Shortbread is a classic Scottish cookie, originally served at Christmas and New Year's, but it has definitely become a year-round, international treat.

If you happen to have one of those pretty clay shortbread molds, but never seem to use it, this recipe will bring it up from the basement for good! The decorations and indentations will show you where to cut once the shortbread is baked and turned out. A long bread knife is the best tool for the job. For making shortbread without a mold, an 8- or 9-inch tart pan with a removable bottom will do the trick.

2/3 cup walnuts
1 1/4 cups all-purpose flour
1/2 cup confectioners' sugar
Pinch of salt
1/4 cup (1/2 stick) unsalted butter, softened
1/4 cup walnut oil
1 teaspoon nonalcohol vanilla (optional)

1. Preheat the oven to 350 degrees. Spread out the walnuts evenly on a baking sheet with a rim and toast until lightly golden and fragrant, about 8 minutes. Remove from the oven and allow to cool. Reduce the oven temperature to 325 degrees.

2. Transfer the walnuts to a food processor, add half the flour, and process until finely ground. In a medium-size mixing bowl, whisk together the walnut mixture, remaining flour, the confectioners' sugar, and salt. Add the butter, oil, and vanilla, if using, and stir well to combine.

3. Press the dough into a shortbread mold, following manufacturer's directions, or into a lightly greased tart pan, firmly and evenly. Use the tines of a fork to lightly prick the dough. If not using a mold, score the dough 1/4 inch deep with a sharp paring knife into 12 pie wedges.

4. Bake until the shortbread is lightly golden around the edges and firm in the middle, 20 to 25 minutes. Let cool briefly, then cut at the score marks with a sharp knife and allow to cool on brown paper.

Variation: Add 1 teaspoon grated lemon or orange rind to the dough for additional flavor.

Super Hazelnut Shortbread: Substitute hazelnuts and hazelnut oil for the walnuts and walnut oil.

Chocolate Chip Shortbread: Stir in 1/4 cup mini semisweet chocolate chips before pressing into the pan.

Spotlight on Soy: Function at Its Finest

Adding soy to your diet is not a new idea, but it continues to attract enormous attention as a functional food. Soy foods like tofu, tempeh, miso, and soymilk continue to grow in sales in a country that not long ago shunned these Asian products, convinced they were bland and uninteresting. But today, more and more studies are being conducted that point to the benefits of adding soy to our diets and, as a result, people are listening and finally discovering that much delicious food awaits for those who are willing to try.

Soy is a high-quality plant protein, with lots of soluble fiber and a host of phytonutrients that include isoflavones, a class of phytoestrogens, which are plant chemicals with mild estrogen activity. All soy products are derived from the humble soybean, which has long been grown in the United States, mostly for export. It is high in protein and low in carbohydrates, quite different from its legume relatives and far more versatile for producing a variety of products, from tofu (soybean curd) to soy sauce.

Studies have linked soy consumption to myr-

The Nuts Have It!
More Ways to Get Your Omega-3

We saw in Phase One how a handful of nuts could provide us with nourishment and sustained energy. But who knew they could be functional too! Specifically, walnuts and hazelnuts possess excellent amounts of alpha linolenic acid (ALA), which converts to docosahexaenoic acid (DHA) and eicosapentaenoic acid (EPA) omega-3 fatty acids. And that goes for their oils as well. Walnut and hazelnut oil can add a delicious nutty flavor to salads and baked goods. The common black walnut (also called Persian) and English walnut weigh in at between 3.5 and 6.8 grams of ALA per 3½-ounce serving, not a shabby show. Hazelnuts, also called hickory nuts or filberts, are not too far behind. Roasted soybean kernels are also an excellent source, as are pumpkin seeds.

Here are some ideas for adding these functional nuts to your diet:

- The Road to Recovery Trail Mix (page 49), which already includes roasted soybeans and pumpkin seeds, can be enhanced with a handful of walnuts or hazelnuts.

- A sprinkling of chopped nuts makes an excellent addition to salads, particularly those that contain fruit and cheese.

- Pumpkin seeds are a traditional addition to many tomato-based pasta sauces and can be tossed in before serving.

- Ice cream sundaes can always use a bit of crunch from a variety of nuts, including glazed walnuts or walnuts in syrup.

- Yogurts and puddings can benefit from the addition of chopped nuts. Hazelnuts, in particular, are delicious with dark chocolate and would make a great sprinkled topping for Dark Chocolate Pudding (page 72).

- Add roasted chopped hazelnuts in addition to the walnuts called for in The Ultimate Chocolate Chip Cookie (page 66) for a double whammy of omega-3.

iad benefits, including decreased risk of heart disease, prostate cancer, and colon cancer. Its ability to reduce cholesterol has even prompted the United States Food and Drug Administration to allow soy products that contain at least 6.25 grams of soy protein per serving to state on their labels that "daily consumption of soy protein (at least 25 grams), in conjunction with a low-fat diet, can lower cholesterol levels in people with high cholesterol." Here we have functional food at its finest. And the story doesn't end there. Studies are underway to determine the beneficial role soy may play in skin care, thyroid cancer prevention, bone density loss reduction, and even memory improvement.

If you have yet to reap the benefits of adding soy to your diet, not to mention the delicious ways that soy can be prepared, you are definitely in for a surprise. Even carnivorous folks will find their palates happily pleased by these recipes, so start shining the spotlight on soy in your kitchen!

Tempeh Bolognese with Fettuccine

MAKES 4 SERVINGS Bolognese sauce, also referred to as meat *ragu*, is known for its richness, reflecting the heartiness and full-bodied cooking style of Bologna, Italy, and its region, Emilia-Romagna. It is a perfect venue for the versatility of tempeh, which makes for a surprisingly "meaty" sauce, replacing the usual beef and more traditional fatty cuts of meat often used. Steaming the tempeh beforehand will make it that much easier to crumble. Simply place in a colander over a pot of simmering water and steam the cakes whole, covered, until heated through, about 20 minutes. While still hot, but cool enough to handle, crumble the cakes into a bowl and it will be ready to add when needed.

For traditional Bolognese sauces, much flavor is normally added by sautéeing pancetta, or Italian bacon, with the vegetables, but in this case I have substituted turkey bacon as a slightly healthier alternative. To make this entirely vegetarian, however, you may want to use a soy-based bacon product instead, and substitute vegetable broth for the beef broth.

Red wine is often used here to "develop" the flavors, but the use of red grape juice and vinegar as our wine substitute will provide the expected piquancy. Between the bacon and broth, quite a bit of sodium will already be incorporated into the dish, so, except for seasoning with fresh ground pepper, refrain from adding salt until the end, after tasting for adjustment. Finishing with a traditional, yet optional, drizzle of cream will smooth out the final sauce and bring out its full richness.

4 slices turkey bacon, cut into strips and diced

1 tablespoon olive oil

1 medium-size onion, peeled and diced

1 medium-size celery stalk, ends trimmed and diced

1 medium-size carrot, peeled and diced

Freshly ground black pepper

Two 8-ounce packages tempeh, steamed and crumbled (see headnote)

¼ cup unsweetened red grape juice

2 tablespoons red wine vinegar

2 cups low-sodium beef broth

¼ cup tomato paste

2 tablespoons light or heavy cream

Salt to taste

8 ounces fettuccine, cooked according to package directions and drained

Freshly grated Parmesan cheese

1. In a medium-size heavy-bottomed pot or Dutch oven, fry the turkey bacon in the olive oil over medium-high heat until lightly browned but not crisp, about 3 minutes. Add the onion, celery, carrot, and black pepper and cook, stirring occasionally, until soft, about 6 minutes. Add the tempeh and cook, stirring often, until browned, about 3 minutes. Pour in the grape juice and vinegar,

reduce the heat to medium-low, and simmer until the vegetables and tempeh have absorbed the liquid, 4 to 6 minutes. Add the beef broth and tomato paste, stir well to combine, and cook, uncovered, stirring occasionally to prevent sticking, until the tempeh mixture has thickened and much of the liquid has evaporated, 30 to 40 minutes.

2. Stir in the cream and continue to cook at a low simmer for a further 5 minutes, stirring often. Taste now for the addition of salt, adjust if necessary, and serve immediately over the hot cooked fettucine with a sprinkling of freshly grated Parmesan cheese.

Recovery Note: Not all recipes for Bolognese sauce contain wine, but many Italian restaurants will add it. Usually the menu will reveal "slowly cooked in red wine and broth," but if you are in doubt, be sure to ask, especially if ordering the lasagne, where Bolognese ragu will often make an appearance.

Miso Chicken with Spinach and Udon Noodles

MAKES 3 TO 4 SERVINGS In "The Serenity of Soup," we met miso for the first time, prepared the classic and comforting Japanese Miso Soup (page 102), and learned how this fermented soybean paste is produced. Shiro miso (white, sweet miso) is the most commonly used variety by non-Asian cooks, but red and brown miso, saltier and more intensely flavored, can also be found.

Japanese mythology has referred to miso as a gift from the gods. Given the amount of healthy benefits it has to offer, there can be no doubt it is at least a gift from nature. As a fermented soy product, like tempeh, miso is one of the best soy sources we have to cook with, containing an excellent amount of isoflavones, as well as probiotic benefits (see page 347 for a discussion on probi-

otics and prebiotics). And for the vegetarian diet, it is one of the few sources of the necessary, and often lacking, vitamin B12. Because miso contains live, natural enzymes, it must not be overcooked or many of its benefits will be destroyed. For this reason, it is added to soups at the end of cooking and is ideal for sauces and dressings that will only be briefly heated. Open packages of miso should be stored in the refrigerator and essentially have no real date of expiration, although you should follow the recommendations on the package for optimal use. Again, as mentioned in our discussion of fermented foods (see page 99), it is important to seek out miso that does not contain alcohol as a preservative, an addition often used in inferior products.

Chicken is a delicious partner for miso sauces and dressings and this recipe is no exception. *Ponzu* sauce, a Japanese condiment consisting of soybeans, citrus juice, and dried fish flakes, adds a nice flavor dimension. Although now often found in the Asian section of the supermarket, you can substitute a combination of soy sauce and lemon juice instead. If you can find udon, the thick Japanese noodles made from buckwheat, they will be best here. If not, lo mein or even an egg-enriched spaghetti will fill in nicely. You can enjoy this dish hot or cold, depending on your seasonal preference.

MISO MARINADE
½ cup shiro miso (white soybean paste)
½ cup water
3 medium-size garlic cloves, peeled and minced
One 1-inch-long piece fresh ginger, peeled and minced

3 boneless, skinless chicken breast halves, trimmed of any fat and cut into thin slices
2 tablespoons canola oil
One 4-ounce package baby spinach leaves
8 ounces udon noodles, cooked according to package directions and drained

3 tablespoons *ponzu* sauce or low-sodium
   soy sauce mixed with 1 teaspoon fresh
   lemon juice
½ cup unsalted raw or dry-roasted cashews
Salt and pepper to taste
Toasted sesame oil for drizzling

1. Combine the marinade ingredients in a shallow baking dish, stirring well to combine. Add the chicken, coat well, and marinate, covered, in the refrigerator, for at least 1 hour and up to 3 hours.

2. Heat the canola oil in a wok or large nonstick skillet over high heat. Remove the chicken from the marinade, add to the wok, and stir-fry until just cooked and no longer pink inside, about 4 minutes. Transfer with a slotted spoon to a clean plate and set aside.

3. Add the spinach to the wok or skillet and cook just to wilting, 1 to 2 minutes. Add the cooked noodles, the chicken with its accumulated juices, *ponzu* sauce, and cashews and stir-fry until well combined and heated through. Taste for the addition of salt and pepper, drizzle a little sesame oil over all, and serve immediately or let cool to room temperature and serve.

Miso Salad Dressing

MAKES ABOUT 1 CUP One of the very first introductions to miso that most of us have experienced, apart from a bowl of miso soup at our local Japanese restaurant, is the complimentary lettuce salad topped with miso dressing that usually follows. There are numerous variations on this theme and all of them are tasty in their own right, but I have settled on this one because it reminds me most of my first delicious encounter with it.

There are many packaged salad varieties available to us these days and if you happen to find what is called an Asian Mix, including the piquant mizuna leaf, it would be perfect with this dressing.

Otherwise, miso dressing often tops a simple bowl of shredded iceberg lettuce and a couple of slivers of ripe tomatoes, and it is delicious in this ordinary way as well. You can keep the dressing refrigerated in an airtight jar for up to 2 weeks.

2½ tablespoons shiro miso (white soybean
   paste)
3 tablespoons rice vinegar
⅓ cup water
1½ tablespoons honey
Pinch *each* of dry mustard and ground ginger
¼ cup canola oil

In a medium-size mixing bowl, whisk together the miso, vinegar, water, honey, mustard, and ginger until well blended. Slowly pour in the oil while whisking to combine. You may add a touch more miso or honey, depending on your preference.

Soy Almond Cookies

MAKES ABOUT 5 DOZEN COOKIES The addition of soy flour to any baking recipe will add a nice boost of protein, about twice that of wheat flour. However, because its presence will result in a denser texture, it is usually combined with other flours to prevent any unwanted heaviness in the dough. That is one of the reasons soy works so beautifully in this recipe, which contains beaten egg whites for lightness and air, helping to compensate for soy flour's consistency. Also, almonds and soy seem to be natural flavor companions, so any difference in taste that might be more noticeable in, say, a chocolate chip cookie, will not be present here. Having said that, soy flour can readily be substituted for one-quarter of the flour called for in just about any recipe, including muffins, pancakes, layer cakes, and breads, without much detection even by the most discriminating palate.

These cookies are a variation on the traditional

Italian almond cookies served on All Soul's Day called *fave dei morti*, or "beans of the dead." The name comes from the long time practice of ceremonially offering beans to Pluto and Proserpina, the gods of the underworld. Consequently, many recipes for this type of cookie will suggest that they be shaped to resemble a large fava bean, but here a whole blanched almond decorating the top will suffice for the symbol. It is important not to overbake these cookies in order to retain a moist and chewy center. Remove them from the oven after the allotted time, or once they begin to brown around the edges even if they appear underdone. Once cooled, they will be the perfect consistency.

1¼ cups blanched whole almonds, plus more for
    decorating
⅔ cup pine nuts
1¼ cups sugar
¼ cup soy flour
1 teaspoon baking powder
2 large egg whites

1. Preheat the oven to 375 degrees. Lightly grease a baking sheet and set aside.

2. Grind together the almonds, pine nuts, and ¼ cup of the sugar in a food processor until it reaches a fine, flour-like consistency. Transfer to a large mixing bowl.

3. Add ¾ cup of the remaining sugar, the flour, and baking powder and whisk well to combine. In a medium-size mixing bowl with an electric mixer, beat the egg whites with the remaining ¼ cup sugar to stiff peaks. Add the egg whites to the dry mixture and fold to combine without overmixing, just until the dough sticks together.

4. Carefully form small teaspoon-sized balls and place on the prepared baking sheet about 2 inches apart. Press a whole blanched almond into the top to flatten the cookie slightly. Bake until the edges are slightly browned, about 11 minutes. Allow to cool somewhat before transferring to a wire rack or brown paper to cool completely.

Silken Raspberry Cream Custard

MAKES 4 SERVINGS I will admit that when I first heard of chefs using tofu to create mock desserts such as cheesecake and pudding, I was not eager to try it myself. Although I enjoyed tofu in traditional savory recipes, I found the idea of making desserts with it a bit too much. But, as we all know, good things happen that we least expect and in the recovery spirit of accepting new ideas, I decided these were worth a second look. Just about the same time, a line of tofu pudding desserts appeared in my local supermarket. My skepticism did not keep me from trying them and as I tasted a spoonful, there was a familiar, even comforting recall. They were not at all unlike the traditional custard puddings called junket that I had eaten as a child. With this in mind, I decided to try something new and the result is this recipe.

Silken tofu is the softest of all the tofus and is sometimes used as a substitute for cream or sour cream in savory dishes. If it is drained well, then processed to a creamy consistency, it becomes surprisingly soft and palate pleasing in texture. With the addition of pureed fruit and honey, it comes pretty darn close to tasting pretty darn good. So, for the majority of skeptics out there who have taken an oath of greater acceptance and open-minded thinking, this one is for you. Don't be surprised if you end up going back for seconds!

One 10-ounce package frozen raspberries in syrup,
    thawed
One 10.5-ounce package silken tofu, drained well
    and cut into large cubes
2 tablespoons honey
Fresh raspberries and whipped cream for garnish

1. Strain the raspberries in a colander and reserve the syrup in a medium-size mixing bowl. Transfer the berries to a fine mesh sieve and, working over the syrup bowl, use the back of a wooden spoon to force the raspberry pulp through the sieve, leaving the seeds behind.

2. Process the strained raspberries and syrup, tofu cubes, and honey together in a blender until smooth and creamy. Divide between 4 custard dishes, cover with plastic wrap, and chill for at least 1 hour. Serve with a dollop of whipped cream and a few fresh raspberries.

The Lingering Effects of Alcohol
How Healthy Are We?

By eliminating alcohol and other addictive chemicals from our lives, we have greatly reduced our risk of contracting many serious diseases from fatty liver to cancer. But what about the years we spent drinking? Doesn't that matter? Unfortunately, the answer is yes. Although the long-term effects of drinking in abstinent alcoholics have not been extensively studied, it is clear that a history of abuse and dependence can increase our chances of suffering some time in the future from an alcohol-related disease. Certain types of cancer, for instance, can take many years to develop before we are aware of their invasion in our bodies. Although not considered a carcinogen (cancer-causing substance), ethyl alcohol is what is called a cocarcinogen, or a pro-moter of cancer growth. It apparently operates by interacting with certain enzymes that would normally detoxify carcinogenic substances and, consequently, enhances the effects of toxic chemicals to which we are exposed. For instance, we know that drinking and smoking together can be more destructive than either activity on its own. And since it is estimated that up to 90 percent of active alcoholics and addicts smoke cigarettes, we are at greater risk for smoking-related diseases and cancers, such as emphysema, heart disease, and lung, mouth, and esophageal cancers. Long-term drinking also puts us at high risk for the development of dia-betes, particularly in men; osteoporosis, especially in women; and cancers of the colon, breast, pancreas, and liver. Recent studies have also shown a connection between chronic drinking and age-related eye and muscle conditions.

On the bright side, other recent studies have shown that much of the damage that alcohol causes to our brains is reversible. And it appears that the longer we are sober, the more the damage is repaired. We already know that brain function improves over a period of several months to a year, but a recent study of alcoholics with longer periods of sobriety (over four years) showed continued improvement in blood flow to the frontal lobes, the area associated with impulse inhibition and executive function. This may explain why many alcoholics say that after several years of abstinence, it somehow "feels easier" to stay sober. Hopefully, encouraging results like these will prompt further study concerning long-term sobriety and brain function, as well as overall health. It has even been suggested by Dr. Nancy C. Andreasen, in her excellent book, *Brave New Brain*, that tracking our brain improvement through the use of imaging techniques could serve as a powerful motivator to remain abstinent. Perhaps one day this will be a standard strategy for ongoing addiction treatment.

For the most part, the brain and liver are the most susceptible organs to the effects of alcohol, but as long as extensive damage has not occurred, the liver has an amazing ability to rejuvenate itself. If, however, cirrhosis or scarring sets in, reversibility is not possible, although the damage can be kept from getting worse. Any liver problems that you may be experiencing should be treated under the supervision of a medical professional. If you have been lucky enough to escape without dire consequences, then it would be wise to keep your liver as healthy as possible. Here, diet can play a major role. Researchers also believe that diet is responsible for 20 to 40 percent of all cancers, and perhaps even as much as 70 percent. Since the process of carcinogenesis can take anywhere from 10 to 30 years, starting with the initial onset and then promotion of existing cells, diet can be particularly important, especially early on, by increasing enzyme activity to prevent growth and progression. And it is not just what we don't eat that makes a difference. Including nutrient-rich functional food in our diet may end up being the deciding factor of whether we develop a disease or not. This section will provide you with a truckload of information about reducing the risk of heart disease, cancer, and other potential illnesses through the use of food as preventive medicine. Here are a few other ways we can help ourselves:

STOP SMOKING: If you still smoke, think very seriously about quitting. Cigarette smoke is both a carcinogen and a cocarcinogen and can kill you and the people and pets around you, without question. For most of us, this is the hardest habit to kick, but our bodies will be forever grateful. In addition, studies have shown that smoking can encourage cravings to drink, as well as increase the desire for other drugs, such as cocaine and heroin, jeopardizing our hard-earned sobriety. And women smokers, in particular, are rapidly becoming a depressing statistic, with emphysema and lung cancer deaths on the rise. Find a support group and go back to Phase One eating for a while to help you stay on track, and include lots of fruits and vegetables to get vital phytochemicals. Chronic drinking causes a serious deficiency in the antioxidant glutathione, which can be deadly to the lungs as well as the liver. Eat plenty of apples, asparagus, and avocados, all excellent sources of this important nutrient. We have all heard at least a dozen abstinent alcoholics proclaim that they "never really got sober" until they quit smoking and that it was "harder to give up than booze." Now is the time and there can be no more excuses. Phase Three is the beginning of the rest of your life, so let's make sure you have one to look forward to.

BE KIND TO YOUR LIVER: If your liver has survived repeated abuse, then be kind to it by feeding it what it needs. Continue to drink plenty of water to flush out toxins and limit your unhealthy fat intake. Dark leafy greens such as dandelion are particularly cleansing to the liver, as is dandelion root tea. Milk thistle, a plant native to the Mediterranean, has been shown to stimulate regeneration of liver cells and protect them from toxic substances; check with your medical professional about taking supplements. Omega-3-rich flax seeds (see page 396) are restorative, while your liver will also enjoy the benefits of eating beets, beet tops, artichokes, whole grains, and lemons. Steer clear of toxic substances as much as possible so your liver has less work to do. And remember that even after years of sobriety, returning to drinking can damage your liver as though the drinking had never stopped.

FEED YOUR BRAIN: Help encourage reversible brain damage by eating omega-3-rich foods such as fish and flax. Eat flavonoid-rich fruit, particularly blueberries, which have been shown to increase memory potential. Follow a balanced diet and exercise your brain. Reading, learning new skills, and doing crossword puzzles have been shown to reduce the risk of dementia, particularly Alzheimer's disease. And be mindful of ingesting even small amounts of alcohol, which can trigger unwanted neurochemical reactions. Your brain remembers even if you don't.

Phytochemicals: Nature's Protective Gift

Phytochemicals, also called phytonutrients, are specific plant-based chemicals that protect the plants in which they are found from environmental threats such as bacteria, viruses, insects, and UV rays. They act as a shield or barrier against harm, giving the plant a better chance of survival, even in life-threatening situations. Research has indicated that when we eat these plants and consume their phytochemicals, we also gain an advantage against many harmful environmental agents that could damage our DNA and trigger the onslaught of disease. Consequently, much of the functional food studies being done today involve phytochemicals and their potential medicinal behavior in the human body.

There are literally hundreds of phytochemicals in the plant world that are available to us and, interestingly enough, it appears that no single one in particular or in isolation (such as in supplements) has the same potential effect on its own. Phytochemicals somehow need each other to perform their functions. And it appears they also need the help of vitamins, minerals, fiber, and other substances naturally found in the foods in which they are present in order to work as a winning team. Therefore, eating whole foods—such as fruits, vegetables, and unrefined, minimally processed grains and other plant foods—appears to be the key to gaining the benefits of phytochemicals in our diet. Although eating whole, natural food is not a new idea, we now have yet another reason to do so.

Phytochemicals perform any number of activities. We are already familiar with the particular vitamins and minerals categorized as antioxidants (see page 7), the good guys that help to neutralize free radicals (unstable oxygen molecules) by scavenging and destroying them before they have a chance to cause too much disruption to DNA and increase our risk for cancer, cardiovascular disease, and compromised immunity. They include vitamins A, C, and E and the mineral selenium, available to us through our diet when we eat plants, and animal and fish protein. But many phytochemicals also appear to act as powerful antioxidants in their own way, and we'll be looking at some of these in greater detail. Others work by helping the body dispose of harmful cancer-causing substances called carcinogens, making them vital for warding off deadly diseases. Some phytochemicals, such as soy isoflavones, which we met in the last section, help to balance hormone levels and reduce the risk of related cancers and illnesses. Still others can stimulate our body's immune cells and infection-fighting enzymes to keep us healthy and better able to fight off disease on our own.

There are probably myriad phytochemicals we have yet to discover, as researchers continue their quest for life-saving natural substances to enhance human existence. What is most important to know, however, is that by adding these powerful nutrients to our diet through food, we can take a large step toward preventing health problems. In this section, we'll look at some specific phytochemicals found in functional foods that may make a big difference in our future health as recovering alcoholics and addicts and see how diet just might be the answer to extending our lifetime of sobriety and wellness.

Fruits That Fight Back

Plant polyphenols are a large class of phytochemicals that are powerful antioxidants, found abundantly in fruits of all descriptions. Citrus flavonoids, a category of polyphenols, have shown the ability to act as an anti-inflammatory as well, bolstering blood vessels and, in turn, battling heart disease. They also appear to improve the absorption of vitamin C, another important antioxidant. Oranges, tangerines, and grapefruit are particularly good sources. Other flavonoids, such as those found in apples and berries, are also powerful free-radical fighters and are believed to have the ability to alter the direction of cancerous cell growth. The flavonoids found in grapes contain a high level of antioxidant pigments and can prevent blood from clotting by reducing the amount of bad cholesterol that attaches itself to artery walls, just like flavonoid-rich red wine (see page 411).

Another class of plant polyphenols is phenolic acids, also found in citrus fruits, apples, and berries, as well as plums, peaches, and pears. They have the added potential to neutralize the genetic damage caused by carcinogens and cancer promoters like tobacco. And the list goes on and on. Doesn't it sound like we should be enjoying lots of fruit on a regular basis? Here are some delicious recipes for creatively including them in your diet, while highlighting their powerful nutritional content.

Chicken Breasts with Grapefruit Jus

MAKES 4 SERVINGS Roasted chicken breasts are always a welcome meal at the dinner table, but here, instead of a deglazed sauce made with broth or a wine substitute, we make use of the nutritionally powerful grapefruit for a quick and easy light *jus*, or sauce, as well as a refreshing fruit garnish. Grapefruit contains important citrus flavonoids, which fight off free radicals and reduce our risk of cancer. In addition, white grapefruit contains naringen, a flavonoid compound found in the pulp and pith, which can protect the lungs against environmental toxins, including tobacco smoke and pollution. For this reason, we'll be keeping our grapefruit segments intact and not removing the membrane, which is customary in classic presentations. Grapefruit is also a low glycemic fruit, weighing in on the Glycemic Index at a mere 25, and is an excellent source of fiber and vitamin C.

I would recommend leaving the skin on the chicken breasts to retain moistness while cooking; remove it later if you are watching your saturated fat intake. Be sure to take the breasts from the oven when they reach an internal temperature of 165 degrees to ensure a perfectly cooked and juicy result. Serve with Confetti Couscous (page 378) and a tossed salad for an eye-catching presentation and a deliciously rounded-out meal.

> 4 split bone-in chicken breast halves, skin left on
>   and trimmed of excess fat
> 2 teaspoons canola oil
> Salt and pepper to taste
> 3 white grapefruit
> Pinch of sugar
> 1 tablespoon chopped fresh parsley leaves

1. Preheat the oven to 400 degrees.
2. Place the chicken breasts in a roasting pan and brush the skins with the oil. Season with salt and pepper and roast until the skin is golden and an instant-read thermometer inserted at the thickest part registers 165 degrees, 25 to 35 minutes.
3. Juice two of the grapefruit and pour into a small bowl. Remove the rind from the remaining grapefruit and divide it into sections, removing any seeds with a sharp paring knife. Set both aside.
4. When the chicken is cooked, transfer the breasts to a heated platter. Drain off most of the accumulated oil from the roasting pan and immediately add the grapefruit juice and sugar. Using a wooden spoon, scrape up any of the browned roasting bits from the pan and stir well. Pour the *jus* over the chicken breasts, arrange the grapefruit segments decoratively around, and sprinkle with the chopped parsley. Serve immediately.

Chicken Breasts with Tangerine *Jus*: Replace the grapefruits with 4 tangerines, juicing 3 and segmenting 1. Tangerines are rich in beta-cryptoxanthin, which may help prevent colon cancer, as well as tangeretin, a flavonoid that has been linked to reduced growth of tumor cells.

Fillet of Sole with Grapes and Tarragon

MAKES 4 SERVINGS This updated version of the French classic Sole Veronique is an easy and deliciously creative way to include the powerful phytonutrients of grapes in a savory meal. Generally poached in white wine and finished with a cream sauce, here we use tarragon vinegar and white grape juice to add the necessary acidity and sweetness, while lightening up the resulting sauce by adding a mere touch of butter. The final dish pairs nicely with a simple side of steamed vegetables. Little fingerling or new potatoes, boiled or steamed, would also make a perfect accompaniment.

Grapes and their juice contain high levels of

antioxidant flavonoids, associated with a healthy heart and reduced risk of cardiovascular disease. In addition, the skin of grapes, particularly the red and purple varieties, contains resveratrol, an important cholesterol-lowering chemical that may also fight cancer. The pigments, also called anthocyanins, have been shown in laboratory studies to suppress tumor growth, while ellagic acid, a phenolic acid also found in berries, can protect the lungs from toxins. And as if that's not enough, tarragon, a traditional fine French herb with a faint anise flavor, contains cancer-preventive terpene phytochemicals, shown to stimulate protective enzymes in the body. Both tarragon and grapes complement the mild and delicious white flesh of sole fillets. You could also, however, use flounder, halibut, or grouper for an excellent result.

½ cup unsweetened white grape juice
2 tablespoons tarragon vinegar
1 tablespoon fresh lemon juice
⅔ cup red seedless grapes, cut in half
1 pound fillet of sole, cut into 4 pieces
Salt and pepper to taste
2 teaspoons unsalted butter
1 teaspoon finely chopped fresh tarragon leaves.

1. In a small saucepan, combine the grape juice, vinegar, and lemon juice and bring to a simmer. Add the grapes and cook over low heat for 10 minutes. Remove the grapes with a slotted spoon, transfer to a small bowl, and set aside.

2. Transfer the liquid from the saucepan to a medium-size nonstick skillet and return to a simmer. Season the sole with salt and pepper and carefully place in the liquid in a single layer. Cover, reduce the heat to low, and gently cook until the fish is white and firm to the touch, about 10 minutes. Carefully transfer the fish with a metal spatula to a heated platter and set aside.

3. Add the grapes to the liquid, increase the heat to medium, and cook for 2 minutes at a low boil. Remove the pan from the heat, add the butter

and tarragon, and stir well to combine. Taste for the addition of salt and pepper, adjust if necessary, and spoon the sauce and grapes over the cooked sole. Serve immediately.

Waldorf Salad with Asian Pears, Grapes, and Walnuts

MAKES 4 SERVINGS The famous Waldorf salad was created at the Waldorf-Astoria Hotel in New York City back in 1896 by the maitre d'hotel and instantly became a classic. Traditionally containing only apples, celery, and mayonnaise, this salad has prompted many variations, all of which seem to be classics in themselves. Here the crispness of Asian pears, an interestingly flavored fruit that tastes of both pear and apple, and the important phytonutrient-containing grapes make a delicious combination, topped off with omega-3-rich walnuts. Asian pears, also called Chinese pears or apple pears, should be available in your supermarket produce section, abundantly so from late summer to early fall, but also to a lesser degree year round.

Celery, as in the original creation, still makes an appearance and surprisingly contains its own unique phytonutrient in the form of phthalide, believed to lower blood pressure by reducing the levels of certain hormones that constrict blood vessels. Although high in sodium, an unwanted nutrient for those watching hypertension levels, somehow the phthalide outweighs sodium's disadvantage. This phytonutrient is also found in celery seeds, long believed to alleviate gout and rheumatoid arthritis, and now being investigated for anti-inflammatory ability. For good measure, therefore, we're including a sprinkling of these tiny, flavorful seeds.

2 Asian pears, cored and cut into ½-inch dice
½ cup red seedless grapes, cut in half
½ cup green seedless grapes, cut in half

2 medium-size celery stalks, ends trimmed and
thinly sliced

⅓ cup roughly chopped walnuts

½ cup light mayonnaise

¼ cup reduced-fat sour cream

2 tablespoons fresh lemon juice

2 teaspoons sugar

1 teaspoon celery seeds

Salt and pepper to taste

1. In a medium-size mixing bowl, combine the Asian pears, grapes, celery, and walnuts and toss together with a rubber spatula.

2. In a small mixing bowl, whisk together the mayonnaise, sour cream, lemon juice, sugar, and celery seeds until well combined. Add to the fruit mixture and toss to coat well. Taste and season with salt and pepper and refrigerate for 1 hour before serving.

The Abstinent Approach

Wine-Free Ways to Increase Your Polyphenols

No doubt since you put down that last drink, you have noticed that nearly every day researchers appear to be discovering good and healthy things about drinking, particularly red wine. The truth is, it's not all good and, frankly, most research is still unable to pinpoint the exact source of alcohol's benefit on health, if any. A recent study called heart-healthy wine an "illusion," because it appears that it is healthy people to begin with—those who exercise, eat fiber-rich diets, and do not smoke—who choose to drink wine. Still, many studies have indicated that moderate consumption (defined as one drink per day for women and two drinks per day for men) may reduce the risk of cardiovascular disease and stroke, some even pointing to beer as a healthy alternative to wine (although it appears to be the barley and hops that make a difference). Other studies indicate that moderate drinking of any alcoholic beverage may decrease the risk of heart disease, particularly in older adults. So, what's the bottom line?

Alcohol itself is a toxic substance, as we know. Even small amounts are associated with an increased risk of breast and colon cancer. And the risk of many other types of cancer goes up with increased alcohol consumption. Recommendations by nutritionists are always couched in a discussion of the dangers of potential addiction and the need to weigh alcohol's benefits against its drawbacks. But for those of us who know only too well what the drawbacks are, is there a healthy alternative? And what about people who just don't want to drink alcohol (yes, there are quite a few)? Let's get back to phytochemicals and try to put it all in perspective.

Most studies have been conducted with red wine drinkers, so it seems apparent that any benefits involved most likely stem from the phytonutrients present in a glass of red wine. Polyphenols, including flavonoids, in the form of quercetin, and phenolic acids are found in wine, as is resveratrol, a compound actually linked to cancer prevention. If we substitute other food and beverages that contain these same compounds, we can reap the identical benefits. Here are some ideas for getting your polyphenols, wine-free:

- DRINK RED GRAPE JUICE: 10 to 12 ounces per day has shown to substantially reduce the risk for heart disease. Mull with spices and drink warm on a cold evening.

- MUNCH ON GRAPES: The skins are particularly rich in resveratrol.

- EAT CHOCOLATE: No arguments here! Just 1½ ounces of milk chocolate contain the same amount of phenolics as a five-ounce glass of Cabernet Sauvignon, while dark chocolate contains even more.

- SHELL SOME PEANUTS: Another excellent source of resveratrol.

- PUT BERRIES ON YOUR CEREAL: All types of berries are rich in ellagic acid and quercetin, while blueberries in particular will help you to remember where you put your keys (a non-benefit, by the way, of wine drinking!).

- ADD RED ONIONS TO YOUR SALAD: They contain a large amount of quercetin.

- CRACK OPEN A POMEGRANATE: The edible seeds and the attached red pulp of this unusual fruit are rich in the same flavonoids as red wine. Look for pomegranate juice and molasses to include in your cooking, common additions in Middle Eastern cuisine.

- HAVE A CUP OF TEA: Green and black teas contain quercetin, along with a host of some mighty powerful antioxidants.

- SPRINKLE WALNUTS: Just like chocolate, walnuts contain phenolics, in the form of ellagic acid, in addition to their excellent omega-3 content.

- BOB FOR APPLES: Still the best way to keep the doctor away, they're loaded with flavonoids and phenolics. Better yet, enjoy a Chocolate-Dipped Caramel Apple (page 71) dredged in chopped walnuts and get a triple whammy of wine-free phytochemicals!

Ellen's Baked Stuffed Apples

MAKES ABOUT 4 SERVINGS While my dear friend and client Ellen was undergoing testing and subsequent treatment for thyroid cancer, I would make her favorite baked apples, which she loved to eat (and still does!) for breakfast, dessert, or as a sweet afternoon snack. At the time we needed to avoid the addition of dried fruit, as iodine-containing foods were off the accepted diet list, but now I add raisins and, occasionally, other chopped dried fruit for additional sweetness and nutrition whenever I have the pleasure of making them for her. I always select, whenever possible, large Rome Beauty apples, sometimes available nearly as big as a softball and always bright red in pigment. If you can find them, use them here; otherwise, choose twice the amount of baseball-sized apples of a variety that is slightly tart and firm, such as Cortland, Northern Spy, or Jonathan.

Prepare a recipe for Cinnamon Apple Compote (page 181), of which you'll need about half for stuffing the apples. The crumb topping is a basic one made with butter, flour, sugar, and cinnamon, but nuts could also be added, as well as oats or wheat germ. Incidentally, cinnamon, our popular Phase One medicinal spice, appears to have its own phytonutritional value. Cinnamaldehyde in cinnamon can ward off bacteria such as *H. pylori*, the rascal implicated in the formation of stomach ulcers, and may enhance insulin's ability to metabolize glucose.

Apples are quickly becoming the star of many functional-food lists, surpassing even green tea in some nutritional standards, as the old adage of an apple a day appears to ring true. In addition to vitamin C and fiber, there are phytonutrients galore contained in both the pulp and skin of apples. Quercetin, a flavonoid also found in green tea and associated with reduced risk of cancer, may also aid respiratory ailments by protecting the lungs from toxins. To gain the most vitamin C and glutathione,

an antioxidant enzyme, apples should be eaten raw; however, cooking them, especially with the skins on, will release the all-important pectin fiber and provide excellent free radical-fighting activity from the pigment-based anthocyanins. It appears whichever way you slice it, the apple offers amazing preventive medicine for future wellness.

Enjoy these baked apples warm with a little vanilla ice cream or frozen yogurt. One large Rome Beauty baked apple can be shared by two people.

2 large Rome Beauty apples or 4 medium-size baking apples
2 teaspoons unsalted butter
2 teaspoons light brown sugar

CRUMB TOPPING
¼ cup all-purpose flour
¼ cup firmly packed light brown sugar
3 tablespoons unsalted butter, softened
½ teaspoon ground cinnamon

FILLING
2 tablespoons dark or golden seedless raisins
½ recipe Cinnamon Apple Compote (see headnote)

1. Preheat the oven to 375 degrees.

2. Using a sharp paring knife, cut a small piece from the bottom of each apple so that they will sit flat on the cutting board. Positioning the knife at a 45 degree angle, cut into the top of the apple about one-quarter of the way down from the stem, and, with a sawing motion, cut a circle completely around the top. Remove and discard. Use a melon baller to scoop out the seeds and core, being careful not to cut too deep.

3. Place the apples, flat side down, in a small baking dish or pan, dot the insides with the butter and brown sugar, and bake for 40 minutes, using a pastry brush every 10 minutes or so to coat the inside of the apples with the butter-and-sugar mixture inside.

4. To make the crumb topping, combine the ingredients in a small mixing bowl with a pastry blender or fork. Set aside.

5. When the apples are mostly softened, but still firmly shaped, sprinkle the raisins in the cavity, stuff with the compote, and press the crumb topping firmly on top. Bake until the crumbs are browned and the apples are softened and bubbly around the edges, another 20 to 25 minutes. Serve warm or chilled.

Chef's Note: If you are using smaller apples than the giant Rome Beauties, the initial baking time will be 10 to 20 minutes less. Check the inside cavity with the tines of a fork to see if the apple pulp has softened somewhat before adding the stuffing and topping.

Lemony Plum Coffee Cake

MAKES 6 TO 8 SERVINGS Plum cakes or tortes are usually made at the beginning of fall when little Italian prune plums are abundant, but it has always seemed a shame to wait until then to enjoy them. Traditionally, these plums, cut in half and placed to completely cover the top of the cake batter, sinking ever so slightly during the baking process, are the only "correct" plums to use. However, earlier in the summer and at other times of the year when available, I have had success with many other varieties by simply quartering them to lessen their weight. I figure this also lessens *my* wait to dive into this delicious cake!

Plums contain a number of important phytochemicals, including anthocyanin, which is reflected in their reddish-blue pigment and is protective against cancer and heart disease through its destruction of free radicals. They are also a good source of chlorogenic acid, a type of phenolic acid that battles carcinogens, as well as quercetin, another antioxidant particularly helpful in preventing estrogen-dependent cancer and lung-related diseases. Sorbitol, a naturally occurring sugar, is also highly present and is what gives the plum's dried and concentrated counterpart, the prune, its well-known laxative effect.

Instead of a hint of the usual added cinnamon, I opt for the tang of fresh lemons, including the juice and grated rind, or zest, as I like the way it balances the rich, buttery texture of the cake. Citrus fruit zest, particularly from lemons, limes, and tangerines, contain a phytonutrient called limonene, which has shown promise in preventing cancer, so it's always a great idea to add it to baking recipes when appropriate. The intense and delicious flavor it adds can really wake up the entire dish, not to mention your immune system!

½ cup (1 stick) unsalted butter, slightly softened
⅔ cup granulated sugar
2 large eggs
2 teaspoons fresh lemon juice
½ teaspoon grated lemon rind
1 cup all-purpose flour
1 teaspoon baking powder
Pinch of salt
12 Italian prune plums, cut in half and pitted,
    or 6 small red or purple plums, quartered
    and pitted
Confectioners' sugar for dusting

1. Preheat the oven to 350 degrees. Lightly butter an 8- or 9-inch springform pan.

2. In a medium-size mixing bowl, combine the butter and granulated sugar and, with an electric mixer at medium-high speed, beat until light and fluffy. Add the eggs, lemon juice, and lemon rind and beat until well combined, about 2 minutes.

3. In another medium-size mixing bowl, whisk together the flour, baking powder, and salt. Add the dry ingredients to the butter-and-egg mixture in two additions and beat on medium speed until smooth, 1 to 2 minutes.

4. Pour the batter into the prepared pan and

place the plum halves, skin side up, on top of the batter in a single layer. If using quartered plums, place sideways. Bake until the top is very lightly browned and a toothpick inserted in the center comes out clean, about 40 minutes. Let cool for 10 minutes on a wire rack before unlocking the spring and removing the side of the pan. Serve warm or at room temperature, dusted with confectioners' sugar.

Super Vital Vegetables

How many times do we need to be told to eat our veggies? It seems we are forever being admonished for not including enough fresh vegetables, particularly greens, in our diet. Foods such as broccoli, spinach, and cabbage are definitely always on the "to eat" list, but some other less likely vegetables may surprise you with their powerful phytochemical composition. Did you know that red onions are one of the best sources of quercetin, one of the antioxidants bragged about in green tea and red wine? In fact, the entire onion family is overflowing with phytonutrients and we'll be looking at them in greater detail.

How about mushrooms? Did you know that eritadenine, found in shiitake mushrooms, can reduce the risk of heart disease by promoting the excretion of cholesterol? And, of course, tomatoes are rapidly becoming the darling of functional food, because they contain an abundance of lycopene, believed to be an even stronger antioxidant than beta-carotene. Surprised yet? Let's take a look at a few unusual ways to stock up on some vitally important phytonutrients that the vegetable world has to offer.

The Wonder of Onions

Did you know that when onions are eaten regularly they can lower cholesterol and may also aid in dissolving blood clots? Additionally, they are excellent providers of potassium and vitamins A, B_1, B_2, and C. The Georgia Vidalia is a particularly good source of vitamin C, as are the other sweet varieties, such as Maui, Walla Walla, and Oso Sweet. Look for firm, heavy onions when purchasing them, as well as dry, papery skin. Stored in a cool, dry place, onions will keep nicely for up to two months. Dice or slice them and add as a garnish to soups, salads, and sandwiches. If onion chopping brings you to tears (caused by the release of protective sulfuric compounds), use a very sharp knife and a minimal number of chops to avoid excessive bruising and consequential release of this tear-jerking substance.

Five-Onion Gratin

MAKES ABOUT 6 SERVINGS   Onions and garlic belong to a class of phytochemicals, different from polyphenols, called allium compounds. People who consume foods rich in allium have shown a decreased risk of stomach and colon cancer, believed to be a result of the presence of diallyl sulfide, an allium compound particularly abundant in onions. In fact, in Vidalia, Georgia, home of the famously sweet Vidalia onions, there is a marked reduction in stomach cancer compared to the rest of the country. But each member of the onion family appears to offer its own magical healing power.

Shallots are an excellent source of fructo-oligosaccharides (FOS), a prebiotic that encourages the growth of healthy bacteria in the colon (see page 347 to learn more about probiotics and prebiotics). Leeks contain an anticancer substance called kaempferol, while quercetin-rich red onions significantly reduce the risk of lung cancer and appear to contain a better form of quercetin that is more efficiently absorbed from the onions than through any other quercetin-containing foods. Garlic, of course, is always a healthy addition to any diet, boasting antibacterial activity, as well as the ability to promote cell death in cancer cells (apoptosis).

This recipe is one of my very favorites for serving at holiday meals such as Thanksgiving or Christmas. Creamy and full of flavor, this onion gratin is the perfect accompaniment to turkey, chicken, and large roasts. Whip up a recipe for Easy White Sauce (page 243) before you begin to prepare the onions. The dish can be made a few hours in advance and then heated in a hot oven just before serving.

¼ cup (½ stick) unsalted butter

1 medium-size Vidalia or sweet onion, peeled, halved, and thinly sliced into half moons

1 medium-size red onion, peeled, cut in half, and thinly sliced into half moons

5 shallots, peeled and roughly chopped

1 large leek (white part only), ends trimmed, washed well, and cut into ½-inch-thick rounds

2 medium-size garlic cloves, peeled and minced

Salt and pepper to taste

One 1-pound bag frozen pearl onions, thawed and drained

1 recipe Easy White Sauce (see headnote)

2 tablespoons finely chopped fresh parsley leaves

1. Preheat the oven to 400 degrees. Butter a 1-quart casserole or gratin dish.

2. Melt the butter in a large nonstick skillet over medium-low heat, add the Vidalia, red onion, shallots, leek, and garlic, sprinkle with salt and pepper, and cook, stirring often, until softened, about 10 minutes. Do not brown. Stir in the pearl onions and continue to cook until they are just tender, about 5 minutes.

3. Pour in the hot prepared white sauce, stir well to coat the onions, and taste for the addition of salt and pepper. Stir in the parsley and transfer the entire mixture to the prepared baking dish. Bake until the edges are bubbly and the top begins to brown, 20 to 25 minutes. Allow to rest for 5 minutes before serving.

Broccoli Cheese Soufflé

MAKES 3 TO 4 SERVINGS Broccoli is a vegetable that our bodies just can't get enough of and has probably been studied more than any other vegetable around. Amazingly, the findings just keep getting better. It contains an enormous amount of phytochemicals, which appear to work together to mobilize the body's own natural disease-fighting resources, perhaps its most important function.

Members of the cruciferous family include broccoli, cauliflower, cabbage, Brussels sprouts, kale, and other assertive greens. They belong to a phytochemical group called glucosinolates, which studies have consistently shown to reduce the risk of cancer, particularly lung, stomach, and colon. In the body, these nutrients break down into further beneficial nutrients, including indoles and isothiocyanates, which, in their own right, are powerful cancer fighters and may be instrumental in combating the carcinogens in tobacco smoke. A recent Chinese study showed that regularly eating broccoli reduced smokers' risk of lung cancer by 36 percent, believed to be due to the high concentration of isothiocyanates. And an American team of researchers found that eating at least two servings of cruciferous vegetables a week can lower the risk of getting any number of smoking-related cancers. Clearly, broccoli should be at the top of our recovery functional food list for those of us still battling the final addiction of smoking and nicotine.

This recipe offers a great way to include broccoli in your diet, especially for those who prefer it when it's presented a bit disguised. Cheese soufflés, delicious, light, and creamy on the inside, are a wonderful idea for a light supper with a crisp salad and French bread. Contrary to what you may have heard, they are not difficult to make. Similar to many other recipes that require a little organization beforehand, you will find that if you are ready to go with your ingredients, the process will be swift and easy. It has been said that the soufflé waits for no man, so have your table set and everyone ready to sit down so they can ooh and aah at its arrival and dig in at once.

1 tablespoon unsalted butter, melted
3 tablespoons Italian-seasoned dry bread crumbs

SOUFFLÉ
2½ tablespoons unsalted butter
3 tablespoons all-purpose flour
1 cup hot milk, whole or 2 percent
Salt and pepper to taste
Dash *each* paprika and ground nutmeg
4 large egg yolks
1 cup shredded Gruyère or Swiss cheese
1 medium-size head broccoli, florets and tender
    stems only, cooked in boiling water to cover
    until fork tender, drained, and chopped, or one
    10-ounce package frozen chopped broccoli,
    thawed, cooked according to package
    directions, and drained well
5 large egg whites
¼ teaspoon cream of tartar

1. Preheat the oven to 375 degrees. Using a pastry brush, coat the bottom and sides of a 1-quart soufflé dish or round baking dish with the melted butter. Use the bread crumbs as you would flour to dust the inside of the dish, knocking out any excess. Set aside.

2. To make the soufflé, begin by combining the butter and flour in a medium-size saucepan. Cook over medium heat, whisking constantly, until well combined and bubbly, but not brown. Whisk in the milk, a sprinkling of salt and pepper, the paprika,

Broccoli Sprouts
The Functional Super Food

Research scientists at Johns Hopkins University School of Medicine discovered that the antioxidant sulforaphane glucosinolate, found in broccoli, was nearly 20 times more potent in broccoli seeds that had just sprouted than in the mature head. This nutrient, which has been demonstrated to reduce the risk of cancer, may be one of the most important phytochemicals available to us through diet. Similar in look and taste to other seed sprouts such as clover, alfalfa, and radish, these broccoli sprouts, named and patented as BroccoSprouts by Johns Hopkins, are becoming widely available. Although other companies are restricted from offering BroccoSprouts, you can purchase the seeds and grow them yourself (see the "Resources" section for more information).

Products like BroccoSprouts, with high concentrations of specific phytonutrients that are naturally occurring and not bioengineered, are excellent super-functional foods to include in our everyday menus. Use them as you would other sprouts, by adding them to salads and sandwiches.

and nutmeg and whisk constantly until the mixture is thick and bubbly. Boil for 1 minute, stirring constantly. Taste for the addition of salt, adjust if necessary, and remove from the heat.

3. Whisk in the egg yolks one at a time, stirring well after each addition. Switch to a wooden spoon and add the cheese. Stir well until all the cheese has melted and the mixture is smooth and creamy. Add the chopped broccoli, which has been patted dry with paper towels, and stir to combine. Set aside.

4. Using an electric mixer in a large mixing

bowl, beat the egg whites and cream of tartar on high speed until stiff peaks form. Immediately add the egg whites to the broccoli mixture and gently fold in until nearly all traces of egg white are gone. Be sure not to overfold or your mixture may deflate. Pour the entire mixture into the prepared soufflé dish, smooth over the top with the spatula, and bake in the middle of the oven until golden and nicely puffed, 25 to 30 minutes. Serve at once.

Easy One-Pot Bigos

MAKES 4 SERVINGS If you are of Polish heritage, this traditional stew of cabbage, sauerkraut, and meat will not be unusual to you. For those who are unfamiliar, you will find a new friend in this hearty one-dish meal that makes use of phytochemical-rich cabbage as well as the sauerkraut made from it. I first learned to make *bigos* when cooking at a Polish rectory where one seminary student in particular missed his mother's *bigos* so much that he insisted I learn her recipe. Although there are probably as many different ways of making *bigos* as there are Poles, this one seemed to please everyone including myself; normally these types of stews simmer for hours and hours, but this method proved to be a real time saver.

Cabbage belongs to the cruciferous family, as does broccoli, and is similarly a terrific source of glucosinolates, compounds that have been shown to reduce the risk of cancer, such as dithiolthiones, isothiocyanates, and sulfuroaphane, all of which have powerful antioxidant qualities. Sauerkraut provides a double dose of these nutrients and, in addition, because it is a fermented food product (see page 99 for information on fermented foods and alcohol) contains live active cultures, or probiotics, which help the digestive tract remain healthy by fighting off unfriendly bacteria.

Although traditional *bigos* recipes will make use of somewhat fatty meats that are also tough and take a long time to cook, this one offers a lesser amount of saturated fat by using lean beef. Kielbasa, the classic Polish smoked sausage, although also extravagant in the fat department, is quite delicious here. As an alternative, I have had great success using turkey kielbasa instead, so you can substitute that if you like for a slightly lighter version. A thin skin surrounds kielbasa, which should be removed before dicing. It easily pulls away from the sausage if you use a sharp paring knife to begin the process at one end.

The longer this dish sits and the more often it is reheated, the more flavorful it becomes. Enjoy it with a crisp green salad and slices of seeded rye bread. Incidentally, caraway seeds, found in seeded rye bread as well as the *bigos* recipe that follows, contain limonene, the same phytochemical found in many citrus fruits and a substance that may prevent cancer!

3 tablespoons olive oil
1 pound lean stewing beef, trimmed of any
    fat and cubed
Salt and pepper to taste
1 large onion, peeled, halved, and thinly
    sliced into half moons
½ medium-size head white cabbage, cored and
    shredded
8 ounces kielbasa, skin removed and cut into
    ½-inch dice
One 15-ounce can sauerkraut, drained and
    rinsed
1 cup low-sodium beef broth
1 cup water
One 6-ounce can tomato paste
2 bay leaves
1 teaspoon caraway seeds

1. Heat 2 tablespoons of the olive oil in a large stewing pot or Dutch oven over medium-high heat. Season the beef cubes with salt and pepper and brown them in the hot oil on all sides. Remove with a slotted spoon and set aside.

2. Add the remaining 1 tablespoon olive oil to

the pot, as well as the onion, cabbage, and kielbasa, season with salt and pepper, and cook, stirring often, until the vegetables are softened, about 15 minutes.

3. Return the beef to the pot and add the remaining ingredients, stirring well to combine. Bring to a simmer, reduce the heat to low, and cook, covered, stirring occasionally, until the beef is fork tender and much of the liquid has evaporated, about 1½ hours. Add water, if necessary, to prevent sticking. Taste for salt and pepper and serve.

Shiitake Mushroom Pizza

MAKES 3 TO 4 SERVINGS Here's a delicious way to enjoy the benefits of shiitake mushrooms, which have shown to be excellent at lowering cholesterol. A Japanese study found that daily consumption (about four ounces per day) of these nutrient-rich mushrooms reduced cholesterol after only one week. In addition, shiitakes contain a compound called thioproline, which is being investigated for its ability to block the formation of cancer-causing compounds in the body, while lentinan, a polysaccharide compound also contained in shiitakes, may enhance the immune system.

Shiitake mushrooms can be found fresh or dried. If dried, they must be rehydrated in warm water for about 20 minutes. Since the price of shiitakes can sometimes be prohibitive, you can substitute half the amount required with another type of mushroom, such as crimini or the ordinary white button variety. Preferably, if you come across the medicinally powerful and extraordinarily delicious maitake mushrooms (see "The Magic of Mushrooms," page 196), substitute with some of these as well. To prepare your shiitakes, remove and discard the tough stem (or save for vegetable stock) and wipe the caps clean with a damp paper towel before slicing.

Purchased, ready-to-go pizza crusts are great time savers and perfect for this rendition. Look for a thin crust if you like your pizza crispy. A variety of cheeses will make this even more flavorful, but good old mozzarella is fine too, even a part-skim version.

2 tablespoons unsalted butter

1 tablespoon olive oil

12 ounces fresh shiitake mushrooms, wiped clean, stems removed, and caps thinly sliced (or 3 ounces dried shiitakes, rehydrated in water to cover, drained, and prepared the same way)

1 medium-size shallot, peeled and finely diced

Salt and pepper to taste

1 medium-size garlic clove, peeled and minced

1 tablespoon finely chopped fresh basil leaves

1 teaspoon dried thyme

1 tablespoon apple juice

1 teaspoon fresh lemon juice

One 10-ounce purchased full baked thin-crust pizza

2 cups mixed shredded Italian cheese such as mozzarella, fontina, and/or Parmesan

1. Preheat the oven to 450 degrees.

2. Heat the butter and olive oil together in a medium-size nonstick skillet over medium heat until the butter melts. Add the mushrooms and shallot, sprinkle with salt and pepper, and cook until the mushrooms are soft and tender, about 12 minutes, stirring a few times. Add the garlic and cook a further minute. Add the basil, thyme, apple juice, and lemon juice, stir well, and cook until no liquid remains, about 2 more minutes. Remove from the heat, taste for the addition of salt and pepper, and set aside.

3. Place the pizza crust on a baking sheet and sprinkle evenly with the cheeses. Spoon the mushrooms evenly over the top and bake until the cheese has melted and the pizza is hot throughout, 10 to 12 minutes.

4. Remove from the oven and let stand for 2 minutes before slicing into wedges with a pizza cutter and serving.

Spicy Tomato Chutney

MAKES ABOUT 2½ CUPS Fortunately, including tomatoes in our diet is an easy thing to do. From soups to pasta sauces, salads, and even ketchup, we have plenty of opportunities to get tomato's important phytonutrients, particularly lycopene, in our diets. An extremely necessary compound, lycopene has been shown to be a powerful pigment that can prevent cell damage leading to heart attacks and cancer. Lutein and zeaxanthin, two carotenoids also present in tomatoes, apparently work together to prevent vision loss, cataracts, and macular degeneration. So there is always room for more tomatoes and here is another way to gain the enormous benefits they have to offer.

Most chutneys, such as Gingered Mango Chutney (page 261), are excellent accompaniments for curry-flavored dishes, but they also can be a great condiment to serve with bread and cheese. Their sweetness and acidity complement the richness of full-fat cheeses, particularly those that are creamy and spreadable, like brie, camembert, and a number of the strong-flavored "smelly" cheeses that are so delicious spread on crusty French bread, such as raclette and my personal favorite, Saint Albray. A sharp English or Irish cheddar is also a delicious choice for chutney, served sliced with crackers.

This chutney also includes cayenne pepper, which contains the compound capsaicin, a phytonutrient that seems to thrill our neurotransmitters, while reducing congestion and performing antioxidant functions. Easy to make, great to have on hand, and long lasting when covered and refrigerated (up to two months), Spicy Tomato Chutney will become an indispensable addition to your functional food repertoire.

One 28-ounce can peeled plum tomatoes, undrained and roughly chopped
½ cup sugar
½ cup cider vinegar
⅓ cup golden raisins, roughly chopped
1 tablespoon fresh lemon juice
1 teaspoon mustard seeds
½ teaspoon salt
¼ teaspoon *each* cayenne pepper and ground allspice
One 3-inch cinnamon stick
Two 2-inch pieces lemon rind, removed with a vegetable peeler

Combine all the ingredients in a medium-size, heavy-bottomed saucepan, stir well, and bring to a boil. Reduce the heat to low and simmer, stirring occasionally, until the mixture is well thickened and reduced, about 1 hour. Remove the cinnamon stick and lemon rind, transfer to a covered container or jar with a lid, and chill. Serve cold.

12 Sober Makeovers

A New Look at Some Old Devils

I n this chapter, we take a giant step forward in our recovery cooking. We're ready to tackle making dishes of which the mere name might have set off a trigger effect in the past. Remember beer-battered shrimp and stout-braised short ribs? How about bourbon chicken or brandy-laced tiramisu? There is no denying that some dishes are inextricably associated with alcohol and although you may have forever sworn them off your list of sober-acceptable meals, you are going to discover that, given a little creativity, you can make and enjoy these previously favorite dishes alcohol-free. Up until now, recipes that called for anything beyond a simple white wine substitute or splash of sherry vinegar may have baffled you and appeared to be beyond the scope of substitution. After all, how can you make chicken marsala without the marsala or cherries jubilee without firing up the brandy? In this chapter, using some classic examples, I am going to show you how.

Of course, not every recipe we will come across in our sober kitchen will list some form of alcohol as one or more of its ingredients, but for those that do, we know we need to find an appropriate sober substitute. In the art and science of cooking, every ingredient usually has a role to play and by finding out what that role is, we can determine how best to replace it without altering the essential chemistry and taste of the final dish. At the same time, we need to be mindful of exactly replicating any alcoholic flavor too closely, as this in itself could create some unwanted associations and triggers (see "Too Close for Comfort," page 203). Just how do we accomplish this delicate balancing act, maintaining taste and flavor without compromising quality and, most importantly, our sobriety?

First of all, it's important to know that substitutions are made by chefs every day for any number of reasons, including availability of ingredients and personal taste. In fact, simple variations, as well as unusual substitutions, may wind up as future classics and often contribute to the signature style of a particular chef or restaurant. Anything can be substituted, from anchovies to zucchini, and often is. Alcohol is no exception. But, in order to decide what to use as a substitute, we first need to answer two questions:

1. How important is the role that alcohol is playing?

2. What function or taste sensation, if any, is it providing?

"The Sober Gourmet Guide to Food History 101: Why Do Chefs Cook with Alcohol?" (see page 424) tells us that alcohol mostly provides both sweet and acidic dimensions to cooking. Often it behaves as an emulsifier or thickener as well, and occasionally it is used as a tenderizer. For small amounts (up to $\frac{1}{2}$ cup), it is easy to replicate alcohol's role with a combination of fruit juice and vinegar. Together they mimic its sweet and acidic characteristics, while a quick boil can provide thickness and depth. These types of substitutions are also fine for brief marinades. We've already used many of these simple substitutions in numerous recipes throughout the book, so you are undoubtedly already familiar with the way in which they fill in perfectly for alcoholic ingredients. In these cases, the alcohol essentially plays a supporting role in the outcome of the recipe. As such, although it is an important component, it is usually less significant and certainly never more significant than the other ingredients. But sometimes the type of alcohol used, such as *kirsch* (cherry brandy), for instance, provides a specific flavor as well, which is integral to the recipe. The degree to which this specific flavor dominates, in addition to any other function it might perform, determines how important the role may be. Other times, just because of sheer quantity required, alcohol plays a very significant role in the outcome. Let's look at a couple of examples.

Coq au vin, known to us as chicken in wine sauce, typically calls for *at least* a bottle of red wine, specifically burgundy, if it is to be made in the typical Burgundian style of cooking. Traditionally, the classic version of this French dish was made from roosters (*coq*), which were inevitably tough old birds, having outlived their virility in the chicken coop. Therefore, out of necessity, a marinade of several days in wine and aromatic vegetables would take place to help tenderize the meat and mellow the flavor. Although today we do not often see roosters in *coq au vin*, the lengthy red wine marinade is still frequently used on tough, yet flavorful, old hens, in order to develop a wine flavor throughout, turning the meat and skin a distinct purplish hue in the process, revealing burgundy's role. In addition, the marinade liquid is then cooked and reduced to become the characteristic red wine sauce of classic *coq au vin*. Obviously, in this instance, the alcohol is playing an important leading role with respect to function and taste. When asked if the so-called nonalcoholic wines (see page 19 for why they are poor choices for recovery) could compete with real wine on all counts, Graham Kerr, the former Galloping Gourmet, cited *coq au vin* as one of those recipes in which any substitute, even an "alcohol-free" wine, would have difficulty matching up to the real thing. And in a case such as this, I would tend to agree. Even if we were to use one of our usual substitutions for red wine, such as red grape juice and vinegar, for example, the result, unfortunately, would be an unpalatable, poor replica at best, because the quantity of wine required in the traditional recipe for *coq au vin*, as well as the important function it performs, is too great. This isn't to say, however, that we couldn't alter the method somewhat and revise the ingredient list a bit to make a mock *coq au vin*, which draws from all the best that *coq au vin* has to offer while remaining safely sober. In doing so, we'd be creating a new kind of dish, wonderful in its own merit, and perhaps, in some respects, better tasting and possibly even healthier than the real thing. There are not many recipes such as this in which alcohol dominates so strongly, but for those that do, a little creative adjustment is all we really need to make and in this chapter I'll be showing you how, in dishes like Burgundy Style Beef Stew and Bourbonless Chicken.

For recipes in which alcohol contributes a specific, dominant flavor, regardless of quantity required, we simply need to find a substitution that is also full flavored and mimics any additional roles that the alcohol is meant to play. For example, Duck à l'Orange, a French dish known for its intensely flavored sweet yet sour orange sauce, derives much of its piquancy from the addition of Grand Marnier or Curaçao, both strong orange-flavored liqueurs. A simple substitute of orange juice can't come close to replicating the depth of flavor, but a combination of several ingredients—including orange oil and bitter orange marmalade—and a slightly different preparation style will result in a fabulous sober makeover. Other recipes that also call for intense fruit-flavored liqueurs can be prepared in a similar fashion by going straight to the source that provides the flavor for the liqueur in the first place. Cherries, raspberries, pears, and their juices can offer clean and crisp flavor, while the acidity that a liqueur provides can be easily replaced with infused vinegars, citrus, or verjuice (a sour liquid made from unripe grapes, now popularly used by many gourmet chefs). Often what people like most about these types of dishes is the way in which they actually taste like the dominant ingredient, whether it be oranges or almonds. The alcohol itself is of little importance; it is the ingredient used to make the alcohol that is the prevailing taste sensation. In New Black Forest Cake and Jubilant Raspberry Sauce, you'll see what I mean.

We'll also be looking at instances in which alcohol, in the form of beer and stout, contributes more function than taste. Beer batters are popular ways to fry shrimp and other types of fish because they result in a particularly light and crunchy crust. To a lesser degree, in terms of flavor, beer batters offer a hint of tang and a slightly bitter aftertaste. In Ginger Beer-Battered Shrimp, we'll be taking advantage of all these "beer" qualities without the alcohol. Stout, on the other hand, is often used as a marinade and is particularly associated with slow-cooking dishes, such as stews and braised short ribs or shanks. A few surprising ingredients will fill in perfectly and result in a deliciously tender and flavorful "comfort food" meal that is totally alcohol-free. And there's much, much more. So, let's roll up our sleeves and start cooking up some sensational sober makeovers!

The Sober Gourmet Guide to Food History *101*

Why Do Chefs Cook with Alcohol?

Surely, chefs haven't always reached for the bottle to pour into the stewing pot or sauté pan. What made them do it and why has alcohol become such an accepted part of fine gourmet cooking? Here's a little fun culinary history that will shed some light on the subject and may even surprise you.

CHAPTER ONE:
THE ORIGIN OF ALCOHOL AND ANCIENT ANTICS

Alcoholic beverages themselves have been around for eons. Beer came before wine and was probably discovered by chance about 10,000 years ago when someone mistakenly left a bag of grain out in the rain. When the sun came out, the mixture fermented, thanks to airborne yeast, and created a foamy liquid. Some brave soul decided to taste it, probably got a bit of a buzz, and decided it was something worth sharing with his friends. Eventually, brewing became a little more sophisticated (around 1100 A.D.) and, at that point, beer was probably used to cook with.

However, by far the preferred form of alcohol in the earliest history of cooking was wine. Winemaking, or viticulture, started in Mesopotamia at least 8,000 years ago. We know for certain that as early as 6000 B.C. the Turks were making cherry wine, followed by grape wine, although the discovery of both, like beer, was probably also an accident. By 2000 B.C. the Egyptians were using wine as payment for taxes and by the time the Greeks came along, we had a god named Dionysus, who oversaw all matters of grape cultivation, wine production, and general drunken activities. (Later he was renamed Bacchus, by the Romans, and referred to as the "lord of the vine.")

It was the Romans, in fact, who first documented their use of wine in cooking, beginning with a fellow named Apicius, born about 25 B.C., who was not only the first cookbook writer, but probably also the world's first famous gourmet. Apicius was always in search of the ultimate culinary experience and was well known for his extravagant presentations and weird ingredients, such as nightingale tongues and camel heels. But he was also quite respected for his sauces, which adorned many roasted meats, boiled fowl, and grilled fish, and it was in this context that his use of wine was most prominent.

The nature of the wine that the Romans drank and cooked with was actually a little different from wines today. It was highly concentrated, usually boiled down after fermentation and turned into a kind of syrup. It was never consumed without diluting it with water and sometimes they added honey to it; the ancients had a real taste for anything sweet. What's interesting is that the Romans, and the Greeks for that matter, renowned for their drunken revelry, appeared to be continually well intoxicated even though their wine had been boiled down (actually an early form of pasteurization). Obviously, this didn't "burn off" the alcohol, but some time between the Fall of the Roman Empire and the late twentieth century, we came to mistakenly believe that it did.

Ancient wine was called *temetum*. If you look closely, you can see the origin of abstemious, meaning abstinent (*abs* denoting "away from" and *temulentus* meaning "drunk"). The word temperance also derives from this ancient word, probably familiar to you in the context of the National Woman's Christian Temperance Union. (The most famous of these women was Carrie Nation, a lady who was known to take a hatchet to every saloon she could find and who may have started the first support group for wives of alcoholics.) Speaking of women, in ancient Rome, they were forbidden to drink wine because men thought they might become delirious (another word with an interesting origin, *delirus*, meaning crazy, from which we also get the term delirium tremens, better known as the DTs). This is also the origin of the custom of a husband kissing his wife on the lips when he came home. He could find out if his woman had been nipping at the *temetum* while he was away (no doubt nipping at his own *temetum*). The punishment was right up there with adultery. "Should you find your wife drinking wine, kill her," said Cato. Fortunately, in part thanks to Carrie Nation, we now have Al-anon meetings. But, back to our story. . . . There are two ingredients Apicius, our Roman chef, mentions quite often that bear a striking resemblance to modern-day cooking reductions of wine. One is called *caroenum*, which is made by boiling down a "must," or young wine, to about half its amount, and the other is *defritum*, which is reduced to one-third of the original wine, resembling more of a syrup. The latter was very often substituted with a thick fig puree, very sweet by itself. *Passum*, another type of wine reduction, was, most likely, almost entirely composed of honey, an ingredient which found its way into many Roman dishes and not only desserts. In fact, Apicius was best known for his honey wine sauce for fish, which was considered a Roman classic. I think it's safe to conclude here that what our ancient cooks were after was the sugar content of the wine. You must remember that actual sugar from sugar cane was a rare commodity and not readily available nor affordable until after the sixth century A.D. Fructose, the form of sugar found in most fruits including grapes, was an obvious choice for the ancient sweet tooth and that, along with honey nectar, became a common flavoring in many dishes.

In general, wine had another advantage in the kitchen because, through its fermentation and boiling process, disease-ridden germs were virtually gone. In many ways it was safer to grab the wine bottle than the water vase, and wine was certainly plentiful in Roman households of affluence. Another reason why cooking with wine became quite useful was its inherent ability to act as a preservative. Ancient civilizations learned early that meat was highly susceptible to decay and became rancid quickly if left out in the open air and light of day. Substances such as honey and oil were often poured over the surface to help delay this somewhat, preventing oxidation, but, at some point, someone must have found that wine (and vinegar as well) was also useful as a preservative with the added benefit that its acidic compounds assisted in killing off any existing bacteria. It's entirely possible that this was also discovered by accident, as was perhaps the first wine marinade, which yielded a surprisingly tender piece of meat. We can summarize, therefore, that by the time of Apicius, cooking with wine certainly had its advantages:

- Wine in general, and wine reductions in particular, provided a fruity sweetness of flavor in sauces, main dishes, and desserts.

- Reductions of wine-based liquids could serve as thickening agents because of the high sugar-syrup content.

- Wine acted as a handy preservative in unfavorable environmental conditions, and its acidity and tannins helped to tenderize meat and game when used as a marinade before cooking.

Before we leave Rome and move forward in history a bit, I must tell you about the sad demise of our friend Apicius. It seems that he spent every *dinar* he had in the pursuit of culinary pleasures. When he realized he could not maintain his extravagant lifestyle, he ended his life by poisoning his own wine goblet. On a similar note, the emperor Claudius, who was well known for his reckless drunken behavior and probably would have died as a result of his alcoholism if he had lived longer, was poisoned by his wife in the same way. Kind of gives new meaning to the expression "what's your poison?" But, it's time to say *"ave atque vale"* (hail and farewell!) to our Roman friends and step into the Middle Ages to see what role alcohol played in their culinary pursuits.

CHAPTER TWO:
BARBARIANS, SNEAKY MONKS, AND EASTERN ABSTINENCE

With the fall of the Roman Empire came the chaos and destruction of the barbarians, people who were characterized as uncivilized, lacking in taste and refinement, and, more often than not, wildly inebriated. It's true that the barbarians enjoyed their mead (a fermentation of honey and water) and had a boundless appetite for drink, but in the end they were sober enough to see a weakness in the declining Roman civilization and went in for the kill, so to speak, while Rome "fiddled" around with a wine goblet in one hand and a "Hail, Caesar" in the other. It must have been those Northern European genes that helped them hold their liquor. Unfortunately, like most Northern Europeans, they were not particularly known for their cooking expertise, unless you consider spit-roasted camel washed down with mare's milk fine dining. Consequently, we have little to explore in terms of their culinary history, except to say that after the invasions and during the early Middle Ages, alcohol production fell into quite a different domain: the realm of religion and heavenly pursuits. While the barbarians were busy invading nearby villages, medieval monasteries were quietly hiding their wine barrels underground (creating the first wine cellars) from barbaric marauders, and it is here, in the dark monastic cellars, that our history of cooking with alcohol actually begins its next chapter.

Medieval monasteries housed the largest wineries and breweries in Europe. They also contained extensive kitchen gardens and livestock farms. The diligent monks had everything they needed for a self-contained existence. They kept a good supply of communion wine on hand, provided the friars with their own daily allotments, and still had some left to sell to their neighbors at a good price. In addition to wine making, some abbeys became famous for their brewing, which was often a lucrative monastic industry.

While our brothers were busily supplying the masses with booze, the sisters were doing their part too. Convents often had small vineyards and ale was a common drink; often seven liters of ale were allotted to each nun per day. Of course, the ale of yore was more akin to O'Doul's and, as in previous centuries, a pure and clean water supply was rare. Consequently, since the sterilization process that took place in wine and ale making served as a precaution against epidemic disease, these beverages were often used in place of water. This was the era of the infamous plagues, after all, and drinking the water was a definite risk to life.

The holy fathers and brothers surreptitiously brewed something called *cerevisia* for themselves, a rather potent beer that takes its name from Ceres, the Roman god of grain and cereal which is, of course, used as the base for brewing. It is quite possible that this brew, along with wine and ale, was used in the medieval kitchen, particularly in slow-cooked stews of tough meat and game. A tenth-century manuscript from the monastery of St. Gall in Switzerland lists a few wine sauces that were made by the resident monks and it is likely that copies of Apicius's cookbook were part of some monastic libraries, which helped to carry on the cooking tradition. However, extravagances such as fine dining were not enjoyed by the majority. It was indeed the Dark Ages, with little indication of civilized progress and much global suffering and disease. For the poor, a ration of beer or ale was very often their only source of "food," providing calories in the form of carbohydrates and a smattering of protein. Beer soup was a popular peasant dish. It is no wonder that alcoholism became a huge European problem by the sixteenth century.

Still, I am sure there was a monk *somewhere* who fancied himself an aspiring chef and created culinary masterpieces for his brothers: "Friar, taste my cerevisia sauce! You will think you died and went to heaven!" (Chef personalities haven't changed much through the ages.) However, at a time when most people were just trying to survive, it is doubtful that many culinary strides were made in the kitchen, never mind written down for posterity. It would not be until the fifteenth century that cookbooks would reveal some interesting uses of alcohol (or lack thereof) and serve forth a few noteworthy dishes.

Before we turn the historical page, however, we need to take note of an important influence that was occurring at this time: Islamic civilization was bursting out of the Arabian peninsula and spreading across the Mediterranean like wild fire. By the time of the famous Crusades, an eastern wave of interest was permeating all aspects of life, especially gastronomy. The introduction of new ingredients such as exotic spices and fruits, and particularly sugar, began to shape the new cuisine, which possessed some interesting characteristics in light of our discussion:

- Sugar became used extensively in cooking and appeared as an ingredient in all courses from appetizers to desserts.

- Sour ingredients such as vinegar, verjuice (a tart liquid made from the first pressing of unfermented grapes), and Persian lemons were used to balance the sweetness of sugar and honey. And, of particular interest:

- Alcohol was neither drunk nor used in Eastern cooking, as it was forbidden by Islamic strictures.

Although old habits die hard, and I am not suggesting that alcohol disappeared from the kitchen nor that the West adopted Islamic religious protocol, it is interesting to note that as sugar and citrus became more popular ingredients, the use of alcohol, particularly wine, seemed to wane. By the fourteenth century, chefs in the West were completely enamored with the cuisine of the exotic East, not unlike American chefs of the twentieth century who looked to French cooking for inspiration. If medieval cooks had the opportunity to see Eastern cookbooks, the absence of alcohol would have been striking. Likewise, the combined use of sweet and sour tastes was extensive. By incorporating aspects of the cooking style of Islam, European cuisine inadvertently and, in some cases, intentionally, adopted these tendencies. We see this in some of the notable Western cookbooks that appeared during the late Middle Ages, such as *Le Viandier*, written by the first known French chef, Taillevent, and later with the Italian Renaissance author Platina, in his *De Honeste Voluptate*, which was the first printed cookbook and served as a serious reference for the culinary inclined for many years to come.

Many of Platina's recipes give us a good idea of how Western cooking had developed by the beginning of the sixteenth century. Although he leaned heavily on Apicius for inspiration,

Platina preached simplicity, not extravagance, and was one of the first to discuss the medicinal properties of food since antiquity. One recipe in particular from 1505 A.D. aptly illustrates this tendency, as well as the current fascination with exotic Eastern ingredients:

"A FOAMY BROTH"

4 fresh egg yolks

½ ounce cinnamon [Medieval cooks were well familiar with cinnamon and its medicinal qualities and added it to a number of dishes in very large quantities. Here, ½ ounce is about half of a modern size spice bottle you would purchase at the grocery store. Quite a lot of cinnamon, but at the time, its healing powers were believed to be unmatched.]

4 ounces sugar [Equal to ½ cup, this amount of sugar would make the concoction almost sickeningly sweet. But sugar's immense attraction during this time, as well as its supposed medicinal qualities (sugar was sold through apothecaries up through the nineteenth century) warranted the amount shown here.]

4 ounces orange juice [Probably from the sour Seville orange, which was popular, very intense in flavor, and acidic in quality. In fact, Seville oranges are still extensively used today in the Mediterranean as the preferred ingredient of marmalades and orange-flavored liqueurs such as Cointreau and Curaçao. This could explain, in part, the need for so much sugar.]

2 ounces rose water

½ teaspoon saffron [These two ingredients are direct Eastern influences that still find their way into many modern Middle Eastern-inspired dishes.]

Combine all the ingredients (except the saffron) and cook over a low flame until thick and foamy. Add the saffron (dissolved in water) at the very end for color.

Platina notes: "It is a marvelously healthy dish, especially in summer, very pleasant, and nourishes well, strengthens the liver . . . "

What's really interesting, and what may have struck you already, is the similarity of Platina's "Foamy Broth" to the Italian dessert called *zabaglione*. It is still a favorite in many old-time Italian restaurants and is made by whisking together eggs, sugar, and marsala wine (often with a dash of cinnamon) over a low flame until warm and foamy. It can be eaten on its own or used as a topping for fruit or ice cream. The French call it *sabayon* sauce and serve it exactly the same way. Marsala, a fortified wine, is considered to be the essential ingredient for an authentic *zabaglione*. In fact, I once knew an Italian chef in England who refused to include *zabaglione* on his menu unless his brother promised to cross the English Channel every month and bring back the finest marsala from Italy. By the nineteenth century, all classic recipes for *zabaglione* included marsala, although the amount of sugar was, thankfully, greatly reduced. Pellegrino Artusi, Italy's most beloved nineteenth-century chef, notes with his recipe, "add a teaspoon of ground cinnamon to make it more enervating"—an obvious throwback to Platina's "Foamy Broth" recipe and its medicinal qualities. However, what was *not* being "thrown back" in the era of Platina was the marsala wine, as it was not even invented until the late eighteenth century. Could it be that a common modern-day dessert that we have always associated with alcohol, in this case marsala, never intended to include it in the first place? It would appear so.

What exactly has the marsala taken the place of in our *zabaglione* recipe? Let's see—orange juice, rose water, a lot of sugar, and saffron. If you are at all familiar with sweet marsala (as opposed to the dry variety used in chicken and veal marsala), this is actually an excellent match since it is generally rich in sugar, fruity and fragrant, and amber in color. Ironically, thanks to Platina, we now have a possible sober replacement for sweet marsala wine through a little reverse substitution (minus all that sugar, of course!). By the way, the actual name of *zabaglione* is said to derive from a seventeenth-century monk named San Baylon who is reputed to have invented the dish accidentally. Unless he accidentally distilled marsala a hundred years before its time, he was merely making a "foamy broth" that had been prepared for centuries.

CHAPTER THREE:
FRENCH HAUTE CUISINE, RIGID RULES, AND THE RETURN OF WINE

French cooking has set the standard of Western cuisine for the last three centuries. To this day, just about every reputable culinary school in the world teaches its students the foundations of French technique. Equipped with these basics, chefs then go off on creative tangents preparing dishes in their own style, but which ultimately reflect their technical background. In a nutshell, this is the premise of modern professional cooking. Although many more influences have come into play, especially in the last few decades, such as fusion cooking, by and large the dishes of today are rooted in some form of learned technique. But this didn't happen overnight.

After the Renaissance, France slowly began distinguishing herself from the rest of Europe in the culinary arena. The seventeenth century saw the development of the first French sauces. Master chefs began documenting preparation and overall technique, and what followed was a systematized cuisine in which professional cooks were able to consistently replicate results in any kitchen. Recipes were written down with exact precision and names of dishes or sauces became common knowledge among cooking professionals.

By the eighteenth century, cookbooks were all the rage with both royal chefs and the bourgeoise, and by the late nineteenth century Antonin Carême would write down his famous "mother sauces," which would become the hallmark of classic French technique and help to crown him the father of *haute cuisine*. Carême, by the way, considered Roman cooking and the legacy of Apicius to be "essentially barbaric" and recommended dispensing with all the heavy, monotonous styles of the past, as did a fellow named George Auguste Escoffier, who arrived on the French cooking scene at the turn of the twentieth century, destined to become the true authority on classical French cooking. In addition to placing a huge emphasis on consistency through strict adherence to technique, Escoffier insisted on a code of professional conduct and order in his kitchen, which was one of the reasons he had barley water created for his staff (see page 10), to keep them sober and off the cooking wine. Professional cooking had indeed become a serious business by this time and some important ingredient changes took place, with a collection of new darlings and the elimination of some outmoded favorites:

- Butter, the new kid on the block, was embraced wholeheartedly. It replaced the "vulgarity" of lard (Carême's description) and became popular in sauce making, where it helped to "smooth out" any acidity. It was used with flour to form a *roux* for thickening and added as a final *liaison* to soften the result.

- Sugar packed its bags and moved from the domain of the savory to find its more or less permanent home in the pastry kitchen and the world of desserts. Consequently, sweet sauces and gravies were given their marching orders and, except for the occasional pinch, sugar was virtually absent from all but confection.

- Medieval spices such as ginger, cinnamon, and saffron were shown the exit sign. The only seasonings that were welcomed were those that enhanced rather than disguised the natural flavors of a dish. Pepper was allowed in moderation and the subtle flavors of fresh herbs and aromatic vegetables were beckoned with open arms.

And what of alcohol? What was the role of wine (and distilled liquors, which had become prominent) in this highly organized regime? If you are thinking that alcohol joined the cast of characters once again, you are right. Actually, it never really left, but the role that it played had sometimes been substituted with intended, as well as unintended, understudies that could provide the necessary acidity, sweetness, or thickening properties when boiled down and reduced. Indeed, wine reductions in particular made a comeback and it is surprising that Carême and Escoffier were so easy to dismiss poor Apicius. After all, he was a big fan of wine sauces, as "barbaric" as the French may have viewed his style and technique.

What is important to realize about wine and other alcoholic beverages in French *haute cuisine* is that, just like any other ingredient, they were called for in precise, exact measurements only, following a strict formula that allowed no variation or change in recipes. There were no splashes here or drizzles there. Consistency was of particular importance to Escoffier, as he eventually directed kitchen brigades of many prestigious hotels all over Europe, including The Carlton and Savoy in London, The Grand in Rome, and, in partnership with Cesar Ritz, just about every exquisite hotel in the world. As you can see, Escoffier's need for consistency was very real indeed. Chefs were to follow the recipes and techniques down to the very last drop of lemon juice. This was fine dining on a truly grand scale, so Escoffier had to be a stickler for detail and exactness if he hoped to be successful. He is said to have invented nearly 10,000 recipes within this *haute cuisine* structure and his *Guide Culinaire* of 1902 became the bible of the culinary arts, providing formulas for every possible course from soup to nuts. You only need to look at a few of his recipes to see how precise cooking techniques and ingredient measurements had become. To this day, many European chefs still follow Escoffier's recipes to a T, including any alcoholic ingredients required in precise measurements.

CHAPTER FOUR:
THE NEW CUISINE, REGIONAL CREATIVITY, AND SOBER SUBSTITUTIONS

As time went on, the French exportation of *haute cuisine* began to flourish around the world. But back in France, there was a band of innovative chefs who felt the need for a change. It was now the 1960s and although bourgeois cooking (essentially French comfort food) had been creeping into restaurants and forming a successful union with *"la technique,"* chefs began to feel dissatisfied with the heavy flour-based sauces and the somewhat disguised natural flavors. It was due to this desire for something more that the "new cooking," or *nouvelle cuisine* as it is known, came into existence. Led by such notable master chefs as Paul Bocuse, Jean and Pierre Troisgros, and Michel Guérard, the concept of fine food was about to be redefined.

The most important aspect of the *nouvelle cuisine* affected the chefs themselves even more so than the diner. For the first time in what seemed like eons, chefs could actually break away from rigid formulas and invent dishes with personal flair and creativity. Many classic dishes were lightened up, simplified, or just abandoned altogether. This was an enormous change for most chefs, who were reared in the structure of *haute cuisine,* and I am sure there was a huge, collective sigh of relief when this new trend took hold.

So, how did this trend affect the use of alcohol in cooking? Interestingly, the food scientists who conducted the USDA study on alcohol retention in food preparation (see page 92) were prompted to do so because of the growing popularity of *nouvelle cuisine* and its use of wines and spirits in cooking. *Why* were they used? Because in an attempt to lighten up the classic style, they needed to find substitutes for ingredients that might have contributed too much fat or calories in the past. Things like flour roux had to go and sauces needed to be softer and lighter in texture. As a result, chefs quite often took advantage of the properties of alcohol to bind sauces and enhance flavor. Wine reductions could eliminate the heavy use of butter and flour, while lower-fat dishes could gain interest from splashes of intensely flavored liqueurs.

What's important to note here is that by the end of the twentieth century, the use or disuse of alcohol in cooking was becoming a matter of choice. Some chefs became heavy handed with the bottle as they flambéed or finished dishes with sauces such as the Grand Marnier version in the USDA study, while others used less of just about everything and allowed the natural flavors and the fresh, crisp taste and texture of the ingredients to shine through.

The use of natural ingredients in the form of regional farm produce and locally made products became even more desirable as the century progressed. For the French in particular, just as the herbs and vegetables of the region were proudly used, so was the wine that was added to the recipe and sipped with the meal. This is a very important point to remember. In a way, the choice to use a wine in regional cooking is based more on it being "of the region" than it being alcoholic. The wine is plentiful, just as the basil is or the asparagus and all are proudly used because they are locally grown. Remember the diligent monks who established all those vineyards in the Middle Ages? They are still around today (the vineyards, that is) in every region of France, and every grape variety is different from the other, from region to region.

So what would a chef do in, say, Provence or the Napa Valley for that matter, when alcohol must be substituted? Simple. She could fill the role with a splendid array of regional vinegars, perhaps flavored with locally grown fruits or herbs, along with fresh-squeezed juices, or use a verjuice produced by the local vineyard with perhaps a pinch of sugar, to name just two. There would be numerous possibilities, but the essential point is this: there would be no need to compromise quality, flavor, or even regionality by substituting for alcohol in fine cooking. As more chefs become aware of the health concerns many of us must face while we still long to enjoy gourmet cuisine, perhaps they will delightfully explore the many creative possibilities that await them in the realm of sober substitutions.

Burgundy-Style Beef Stew

MAKES 4 TO 6 SERVINGS Dishes that are slow cooked in red wine are referred to as *à la Bourguignonne*, or in the Burgundy style of cooking. *Coq au vin* falls into this category, as well as dishes known as *daube* and *estouffade*. In general, a long marination in red wine with a variety of aromatic vegetables and herbs is required to develop flavor and tenderize the usually tougher pieces of meat or poultry that are used.

In order to create a sober rendition of a dish like this, which is characterized by tender, succulent meat in a deliciously rich sauce, often studded with pearl onions and mushrooms, it is better to begin with a cut of meat that is a bit more tender, reducing the necessity of a long marination. For traditional beef dishes done in the Burgundy style, stewing beef from the chuck, rump, or plate is often used and may need excessive fat trimming before cooking. Here, if we use a leaner cut, such as the top round or tip (often sold as tip kebabs), the marinade becomes less of an issue, while there is virtually no trimming to contend with. Still, to develop the flavor, we'll be slow cooking this in the oven, just as classic Beef Bourguignonne is done, in a little beef broth that has been enhanced with vegetables, herbs, and currant jelly, the latter providing a little sweetness and thickening power traditionally gained from the red wine and its reduction. The onions and mushrooms, as is usual, will be cooked stove-top separately and added at the end.

Burgundy stews like this rarely include potatoes and are instead often served with a side dish of fresh egg noodles or fettuccine, a fabulous accompaniment for the rich and flavorful sauce.

1 tablespoon olive oil
2 ounces pancetta or salt pork, rind cut away, if necessary, and cut into ¼-inch dice
1½ pounds lean beef (top round or tip), trimmed of any fat and cut into 2-inch chunks

Salt and pepper to taste
1 medium-size onion, peeled and finely chopped
1 medium-size celery stalk, ends trimmed and finely chopped
1 medium-size carrot, peeled and chopped
1 large garlic clove, peeled and minced
2 tablespoons currant or grape jelly
1 tablespoon tomato paste
2 tablespoons all-purpose flour
A splash of red wine vinegar
2 cups low-sodium beef broth
3 sprigs fresh thyme
1 bay leaf

ONIONS
1 tablespoon unsalted butter
8 ounces frozen pearl onions, thawed
Salt and pepper to taste
Pinch of sugar

MUSHROOMS
2 tablespoons unsalted butter
½ pound small white button mushrooms, wiped clean, stems trimmed, and left whole
Salt and pepper to taste

TO SERVE
2 tablespoons finely chopped fresh parsley leaves
10 ounces fresh egg noodles or fettuccine, cooked according to package directions, drained, and kept warm

1. Preheat the oven to 325 degrees. Heat the olive oil in a Dutch oven over medium-high heat, add the pancetta, and fry, stirring occasionally, until brown and crispy. Remove with a slotted spoon to paper towels and set aside.

2. Season the beef with salt and pepper and brown in batches on all sides in the accumulated fat (you may add a little olive oil if necessary), remove from the pan, and set aside. Add the chopped onion, celery, and carrot and cook, stirring often, until lightly browned and softened, about 4

minutes. Add the garlic and cook a further minute. Stir in the jelly and tomato paste. Add the flour and cook over medium heat until all the ingredients are well blended and bubbly, about 2 minutes. Carefully add the vinegar and beef broth, whisk to combine, and bring to a simmer. Return the beef to the pot, add only enough water to barely cover the meat, and stir in the thyme and bay leaf. Cover tightly and place the pot in the oven. Cook until the meat is fork tender, stirring occasionally, 2 to 2½ hours.

3. To make the onions, melt the butter in a medium-size skillet over medium heat, add the onions, sprinkle with salt and pepper, and lightly brown. Add the sugar and a little water, bring to a simmer, reduce the heat to low, and cook, covered, until the liquid has evaporated and the onions are tender. Set aside.

4. To make the mushrooms, melt the oil and butter together over medium-high heat. In a medium-size skillet, add the mushrooms, sprinkle with salt and pepper, and cook until nicely browned, stirring occasionally. Set aside.

5. When the beef is cooked, remove the pot from the oven and stir in the crisped pancetta and cooked onions and mushrooms. Season the sauce with salt and pepper, if necessary, and serve sprinkled with the chopped parsley, alongside the cooked egg noodles.

Bourbonless Chicken

MAKES 4 SERVINGS A popular dish named after the famous Bourbon Street in New Orleans, as well as the king of American whiskies, Bourbon Chicken is regarded as true Cajun-style cuisine in malls all over America (although genuine Cajun fare is said to be nothing of the kind!). Still, its popularity has prompted many cooks to open up a bottle of bourbon to add not an insubstantial amount to its marinade. In general, between ½ and 1 cup is suggested, although I am sure that many bourbon lovers have generously increased the amount, thinking that more must inevitably mean better.

Bourbon gets its distinctive flavor from corn, which is usually the main ingredient of the mash from which it is distilled. It is then aged in charred oak barrels to develop its flavor. In other parts of this book, we added balsamic vinegar to a simple wine substitute to provide that wood barrel flavor in recipes that call for small amounts of bourbon for quick deglazing and sauce making (see page 150). Here, balsamic vinegar will help us out again, except this time we'll be adding it to dark corn syrup in order to encourage the formation of the characteristic sweet glaze. This, with a touch of sherry vinegar and liquid smoke, will fill in beautifully for our Bourbonless Chicken, providing great depth of flavor and no lack of taste.

Instead of opting for the usual boneless chicken breasts, I have found that boneless and skinless chicken thighs are a far better choice not only for this sober rendition, but for most chicken dishes that will be cooked for an extended period of time. The darker and more flavorful meat complements the distinct flavor of the marinade much better without ever losing its own taste and tenderness.

8 skinless, boneless chicken thighs, trimmed of
    any fat and cut in half
Salt and pepper to taste
¼ cup low-sodium soy sauce
¼ cup firmly packed dark brown sugar
½ cup dark corn syrup
¼ cup balsamic vinegar
1 tablespoon sherry vinegar
½ teaspoon liquid smoke
2 tablespoons dried minced onion
1 teaspoon ground ginger
½ teaspoon garlic powder

1. Place the chicken pieces in a 9 x 13-inch baking dish in a single layer and sprinkle with salt and pepper.

2. In a medium-size mixing bowl, whisk together the remaining ingredients and pour evenly over the chicken. Cover the baking dish with aluminum foil and let marinate in the refrigerator for several hours or overnight.

3. Preheat the oven to 325 degrees. Remove the foil and bake, basting frequently, until the chicken is well browned and glazed, about 1½ hours. Serve immediately.

Chicken with Mock Marsala Sauce

MAKES 4 SERVINGS Both Chicken and Veal Marsala can be found on nearly every Italian restaurant menu. Marsala, a fortified wine with a rich and smoky flavor, comes either dry or sweet, and both variations are popular additions to dishes from entrées to desserts. In general, the dry version, similar to a dry sherry, is used in this classic preparation and, along with chicken or veal stock, is reduced to a rich brown pan sauce. Occasionally, mushrooms and even a touch of cream are added.

In order to replicate the role that marsala plays in this dish, we need to consider its task as a thickening agent as well as a flavor provider. For flavor, we can begin with a standard wine substitution of white grape juice and sherry vinegar. Combined with a dark, full-flavored broth, we'll get the consistency and color we are after. In addition, we need a subtle flavoring to wake up the sauce, and vanilla can contribute what we need.

Many chefs are discovering that the wonderfully fragrant vanilla bean actually has a place outside the pastry kitchen, infusing sauces for everything from fish to beef with marvelous results. Here, a very simple addition of a nonalcohol vanilla extract will provide that certain something to the resulting sauce. And diners will try to guess what you've substituted in your mock marsala to bring it to such delicious heights!

If you would like to add mushrooms to this dish, brown them quickly in the pan after you remove the chicken fillets and before you add the juice and stock. Thinly sliced baby bellas or even shiitake mushrooms would be excellent choices.

3 tablespoons unsalted butter
¼ cup olive oil
1 pound thin-cut chicken breast fillets
Salt and pepper to taste
All-purpose flour for dredging
½ cup low-sodium beef broth or veal stock
¼ cup white grape juice
2 tablespoons sherry vinegar
1 tablespoon nonalcohol vanilla extract

1. In a large nonstick skillet, melt the butter in the oil over medium heat. Sprinkle the chicken on both sides with salt and pepper and lightly dredge in flour, tapping off any excess. Fry the fillets, without crowding, until lightly browned, about 3 minutes per side. Transfer to a warm platter and set aside.

2. Add the broth, grape juice, and vinegar to the skillet, increase the heat to high, and stir, scraping up any browned bits from the bottom. Cook until the liquid has reduced by half, then stir in the vanilla and taste for seasoning. Pour the sauce over the chicken and serve immediately.

Duck Breasts with Bitter Orange Sauce

MAKES 4 SERVINGS Similar to the classic Duck à l'Orange, this dish is an excellent alternative to those that traditionally make use of orange-flavored liqueurs, such as Grand Marnier or Curaçao. In sauces such as these, the alcohol content can be particularly potent since it is usually added just before serving. Here, we'll be doing the same, by adding our substitute at the end for peak flavor.

Orange sauce for duck is characterized by a tangy, sour-and-sweet component called a *gastrique*, made from caramelized sugar and vinegar. Although the flavor will still be present, we can dispense with this tedious step, since the addition of bitter orange marmalade at the end will add enough tang and thickening power to the sauce. Look for English marmalade, which is distinctly bitter, without the addition of much sugar and, of course, alcohol, which is occasionally added to some gourmet brands. Orange oil can also be added at the end to heighten the flavor.

Boneless duck breasts can be purchased frozen or fresh (see "A Bird's Eye View of Favorite Fowl and Popular Poultry," page 187). Two large Muscovy breasts will serve four people adequately and will stand up to an assertive side dish without any problem. Try Brown Rice, Wild Rice, and Wheat Berry Salad served warm (page 331) or Herb Roasted Potatoes (page 230).

BITTER ORANGE SAUCE
 1 tablespoon unsalted butter
 1 medium-size shallot, peeled and finely chopped
 1 cup orange juice
 ½ cup chicken broth
 2 tablespoons sherry vinegar
 2 tablespoons honey
 2 heaping tablespoons bitter orange marmalade
 2 drops orange oil (optional)

 2 large boneless duck breasts
 Salt and pepper to taste

1. To make the orange sauce, begin by melting the butter in a medium-size saucepan over medium heat, then cooking the shallot until softened, 3 to 4 minutes. Add the orange juice, broth, vinegar, and honey, whisk well to combine, increase the heat to medium-high, and allow to boil and reduce by half, about 15 minutes. Set aside.

2. Preheat the oven to 450 degrees. Using a sharp paring knife, score the duck breast skins, making a cross-hatch pattern, being careful not to cut into the meat. Sprinkle with salt and pepper.

3. Heat a large, heavy-bottomed skillet over high heat and place the duck breasts skin side down. Fry until the skin is brown and crisp, about 8 minutes, then turn over and cook for an additional 2 minutes. Transfer the duck to a medium-size roasting pan and finish cooking in the oven to the desired degree of doneness, about 20 minutes for medium-rare. Allow to rest out of the oven for 5 to 8 minutes before slicing.

4. Finish the sauce by bringing it back to a boil and stirring in the marmalade and orange oil, if using. Taste for seasoning and spoon over the sliced duck breasts. Serve immediately.

Stout-Hearted Braised Short Ribs

MAKES ABOUT 8 SERVINGS Popularly used in slow-cooking beef dishes such as stews, briskets, and pot roasts, stout contributes richness, while also helping to tenderize tougher cuts of meat. In looking for an appropriate substitute, we want something that can accomplish these tasks and yield a flavorful gravy at the same time. Surprisingly, part of our answer lies in a simple cup of tea.

Tea has actually been used in cooking for centuries and possesses some of the same qualities found in many alcoholic beverages used in the kitchen. Tea contains tannins, compounds found in the stems, seeds, and bark of many vines and trees, which gives it the familiar astringency, or puckering quality, on the palate. Red wine naturally contains tannins, present in the skin of grapes (as does coffee, by the way), while beers have tannins added to them to clarify a cloudy appearance by causing the proteins to clump up and fall to the bottom of the vat. In fact, it is the tannins in both tea and many alcoholic beverages used as marinades that actually accomplish the tenderizing.

The essence of stout flavor is dark-roasted barley (containing tannins), which also gives these types of dark beers their distinctive color. A faint coffee flavor is usually present and derives from the barley kernels and other grains. As if made to order, the Japanese tea called *mugicha* is made from roasted barley kernels and possesses a deep color, characteristic tannins, and even a slight coffee flavor. Obviously, *mugicha* is an excellent beginning for stout substitutions, provided you can find it. Although extremely popular in Japan, second only to green tea as the most often drunk beverage in the East, it is only just becoming known in the West (see the "Resources" section for ordering information). If you are able to get it, by all means use it here. Otherwise, use either another type of dark-roasted tea or a coffee substitute made from barley and chicory. In a pinch, a cup of strong brewed coffee, which also contains the appropriate tannins, can be used instead. This, combined with a bottle of a fine quality birch or root beer with good depth of flavor, can provide the necessary sweetness and thickening power.

Beef short ribs, also referred to as flanken when cut in the opposite direction, come from the bottom section of the rib eye roast area. They are full of flavor, but require a slow braise in order to become tender. Usually two rib pieces are meaty enough for a serving, but given the amount of time and effort required for a braise, you may want to prepare a larger amount, so I have adjusted the quantities below; this is one of those dishes that is always delicious reheated. When served with mashed potatoes prepared in any style (page 226), this meal has comfort food written all over it and will melt the stoutest of hearts!

¼ cup canola oil
16 beef chuck short ribs, 3 to 4 inches long, trimmed of excess fat and membranes
Salt and pepper to taste
All-purpose flour for dredging
2 medium-size onions, peeled and chopped
2 medium-size carrots, peeled and chopped
1 large celery stalk, ends trimmed and chopped
4 large garlic cloves, peeled and minced
2 bay leaves
Two 2-inch pieces lemon rind, removed with a vegetable peeler, leaving behind the white pith
1 cup strong brewed tea or coffee (see headnote)
2 tablespoons tomato paste
One 12-ounce bottle birch or root beer
4 cups low-sodium beef broth

1. Preheat the oven to 325 degrees.
2. Heat the oil in a large skillet over medium-high heat. Sprinkle the ribs with salt and pepper, lightly dredge in the flour, and fry them in the oil, browning on all sides. Work in batches, if necessary, to keep the ribs in a single layer. Transfer with tongs to a large roasting pan or Dutch oven and set aside.
3. Add the onions, carrots, and celery to the skillet, sprinkle with salt and pepper, and cook over medium heat, stirring occasionally, until lightly browned and softened, about 10 minutes. Add the garlic, bay leaves, and lemon rind and cook 2 more minutes. Pour in the tea, stir well, scraping up any accumulated brown bits, and bring to a boil. Add the tomato paste and stir until blended, then pour the entire contents of the skillet over the ribs. Pour the birch beer and broth into the roasting pan, stir gently to combine with the ribs and vegetables, cover tightly, and bake until the meat is extremely tender when pierced with a fork, at least 2 hours and up to 3 hours. Occasionally check on the ribs during this time, moving them around in the gravy and stirring to prevent any sticking.
4. When cooked, remove the ribs from the pan and set on a warm platter. If the gravy appears slightly thin, allow it to reduce by gently boiling it on top of the stove for a few minutes. It should be thick enough to completely coat a spoon. Remove the bay leaves and lemon rind, taste for seasoning, adjust if necessary, and pour evenly over the ribs. Serve immediately.

Alcohol in Cameo Roles

When to Leave It Out

Although just about every recipe ingredient has an important role to play, sometimes its contribution is minimally required. Occasionally, alcohol is added to a dish for nothing more than glitz. Consider the use of champagne in cooking. Most skilled chefs will tell you that it is wasteful to use champagne in cooking because it contributes virtually no flavor, while its signature effervescence quickly disappears before it reaches the dining table. So why do we see menus with dishes like Salmon Roulade with a Champagne Beurre Blanc, for example? Because it is *the diner* who is impressed—usually enough to open up his wallet. Don't be fooled—often champagne vinegar is used instead, especially in sauce making. And like most "cameo" roles we see at the movies, producers hope to increase box office draw while the viewer (or diner) is left thinking, "Was that it?" Blink and you've missed it.

Still, it's always a good idea to examine the recipe a little closer. Obviously, when an ingredient is listed as "optional," it generally won't make a difference in the final outcome. But you should ask yourself if this ingredient is something that commands attention, even in small amounts. Maybe a "splash" of liquor could be substituted with a "splash" of lemon juice or a tablespoon of cognac could be substituted with a tablespoon of vinegar. Whatever the role, even small cameos, decide from the beginning whether you want to include it and substitute for it or simply leave it out. For tiny amounts and small roles, good old H_2O is sometimes the best bet. Most of the time, no one will ever notice, while the rest of the time, they may even prefer your version and ask to know the secret ingredient!

Ginger Beer–Battered Shrimp

MAKES 4 SERVINGS Like old-fashioned, nonalcoholic root beer or sarsaparilla soda, which is made from the root of the sassafras tree or sarsaparilla vine, ginger beer is made from our medicinal Phase One friend, gingerroot. Different from ginger ale because of its full and foamy consistency, nonalcoholic ginger beer has a deliciously intense flavor and possesses many of the qualities of regular beer that are sometimes desired in dishes like this one. Beer batters create a light and crispy coating for deep frying and are popularly used in many restaurants and seaside fry fests. Although most recipes for beer batters indicate you can substitute club soda for the beer, which is a great choice in many ways, I've always felt that the characteristic tang is lost. And that is where ginger beer comes to the rescue. For shrimp in particular, it is a match made in heaven. Served with the soy vinegar dipping sauce, it is a sure sober makeover winner.

In Phase Two we looked at bread and flour coatings (see page 219), which are also delicious for fish frying, but here we'll be enveloping our tender shrimp in a protective and flavorful batter. In many ways, this recipe resembles tempura, the super-light Japanese deep-fried specialty used for shrimp and vegetables. Cake flour will make this batter even lighter, although all-purpose flour is fine to use. The larger the shrimp, the more spectacular the presentation. Look for jumbo or colossal size and keep the tail on for easy dipping. To keep your shrimp from curling up when frying, cut tiny slits across the inside curve and press down gently to encourage them to lie flat.

SOY VINEGAR DIPPING SAUCE
- ½ cup soy sauce
- 2 tablespoons rice vinegar
- 1 tablespoon honey

SHRIMP

1 cup cake flour, plus more for dusting

1 teaspoon salt

1 cup nonalcoholic ginger beer

1 pound jumbo shrimp, shelled and deveined, tails
  left on

Pepper to taste

Canola oil for deep frying

1. To make the dipping sauce, whisk together
the ingredients in a small mixing bowl. Refrigerate
until ready to use.

2. In a medium-size mixing bowl, whisk together
the flour and salt. Slowly add the ginger beer,
whisking until smooth. Set aside for 20 minutes.

3. Pour enough oil in a large, deep saucepan to
come 2 inches up the sides, or follow the manufacturer's directions to fill an electric deep fryer. Heat
to 375 degrees or until a cube of bread dropped
into the oil quickly fries up golden.

4. Sprinkle the shrimp with salt and pepper and
lightly dust them in flour, tapping off any excess.
Coat with the batter, letting the excess drip off,
and fry in batches of 3 or 4, turning a few times,
until crisp and golden, 3 to 4 minutes. Remove with
a slotted spoon and drain on brown paper. Serve
immediately with the dipping sauce.

Ginger Beer–Battered Vegetables: Replace the
shrimp with assorted raw vegetables such as
peeled sweet potatoes, cut into ¼-inch-thick
rounds; red and green peppers, cored, seeded,
and cut into wedges; whole string beans; and
Vidalia onion rings.

New Black Forest Cake

MAKES ONE 9-INCH 2-LAYER CAKE; 10 SERVINGS Black
Forest Cake, or *Schwarzwalder Kirschtorte*, offers a
perfect study for sober baking. Traditionally, kirsch,
a brandy made from cherries and their pits, is used
to moisten the chocolate cake, marinate the cherry

filling, and flavor the whipped cream frosting.
Here's a good example of how a little creativity can
help us out in the makeover department.

Tortes such as these are usually made with a
very dry sponge-type cake, meant to absorb the
addition of a flavored liquid, usually some sort of
liqueur. This process is called "punching" and is frequently used by fine bakeries and specialty European cake makers. Here, however, the chocolate
cake recipe we'll be using makes a denser and
moister cake than the chocolate sponge. As a
result, "punching" is not necessary. Instead, a very
light brushing of the cake with cherry syrup and
lemon juice will be just enough to replicate the
appropriate flavor. Be sure to purchase canned
cherries in syrup and not cherry pie filling, which is
far too sweet and thick for this recipe. The canned
cherries will eliminate the marinating process
often required when fresh cherries are used, while
a light chocolate whipped cream frosting instead
of the usual spiked white whipped cream will add a
delicious and novel touch.

CHOCOLATE CAKE

½ cup milk

1 tablespoon cider vinegar

2 ounces unsweetened (baking) chocolate

½ cup (1 stick) unsalted butter

1 cup boiling water

2 cups granulated sugar

2 cups all-purpose flour

1½ teaspoons baking soda

½ teaspoon salt

2 large eggs, slightly beaten

CHERRY FILLING

One 15-ounce can dark sweet cherries in syrup

1 tablespoon fresh lemon juice

CHOCOLATE WHIPPED CREAM FROSTING

2 cups heavy or whipping cream

6 tablespoons confectioners' sugar

2 tablespoons unsweetened cocoa powder

4 ounces bittersweet chocolate

10 fresh Bing cherries, stems removed

Fresh mint leaves

1. To make the cake, preheat oven to 350 degrees. Butter and flour two 9-inch round cake pans, knocking out the excess flour. Cut two 9-inch circles out of wax or parchment paper (by tracing the cake pans) and place in the bottom of each pan. Set aside. Combine the milk and vinegar in a measuring cup and set aside.

2. Melt the unsweetened chocolate and butter together in a medium-size saucepan over medium-low heat. Add the boiling water and, using a wooden spoon, stir together until glossy. Transfer to a medium-size mixing bowl and use an electric mixer to beat in the granulated sugar on low speed. Add the remaining dry ingredients and beat until well combined, about 2 minutes. Pour in the milk-and-vinegar mixture (which should be slightly curdled) and the beaten eggs. Beat on medium-high speed for 2 minutes. The batter should appear thin.

3. Divide the cake batter evenly between the two prepared pans and bake on the center rack of the oven until a toothpick inserted in the center comes out clean, 30 to 35 minutes. Let cool on a wire rack for 10 minutes, remove the cake layers from the pans, peel off the paper, and let cool completely on a rack.

4. To make the cherry filling, drain the canned cherries, reserving the syrup. Add the lemon juice to the cherry juice and set aside.

5. To make the frosting, in a large mixing bowl whip the cream with clean beaters on the mixer to firm peaks, while adding the confectioners' sugar and cocoa a little at a time. Cover with plastic wrap and chill until ready to use.

6. To assemble the cake, place the first layer, bottom side up, on a cake platter. With a pastry brush, lightly brush the cake surface with the cherry juice. Spread about a third of the chocolate whipped cream over the layer to the edges. Arrange the cherries evenly on top of the whipped cream. After moistening the bottom of the second layer of cake with cherry juice, place it on top of the cherries and whipped cream. Spread the remaining whipped cream over the top and sides. You can reserve some of the chocolate whipped cream for decorative piping along the edges.

7. Using a vegetable peeler, make curls with the bittersweet chocolate and place in a decorative mound in the middle of the cake top. Arrange the fresh cherries evenly around the top's edge and insert a mint sprig next to each one. Refrigerate for at least 2 hours before slicing. Any remaining cake will keep refrigerated for 3 days.

Jubilant Raspberry Sauce

MAKES 4 SERVINGS Jubilee sauces, whether famously prepared with cherries or another type of fruit, are well known for the flourish they create from flambéing alcohol. For cherries, kirsch is often used, while other variations fire up cognac or orange-flavored liqueurs such as Grand Marnier. When raspberries are the focus, framboise, a raspberry-flavored brandy, is often used instead. Warm and intensely sweet, flamed jubilee sauces, normally served over scoops of vanilla ice cream, retain about 75 percent of the alcohol they initially contain, not to mention all of their distinct alcohol taste. Flamed dishes, particularly desserts, are more for show than anything else, and if you can live without the visual display, the heart of the flavor can be easily and deliciously made to be sober safe. Regardless of recovery issues, for safety reasons alone, flambéing is best left to the experienced table-side restauranteur. If you happen to be sitting near someone ordering the cherries jubilee or crepes suzettes, however, try not to take a whiff of the alcohol if it wafts your way. The nose knows, as they say!

There will be no need for the fire extinguisher

in this jubilant sauce! Raspberry syrup and jam plus a touch of raspberry vinegar help to create a deliciously flamboyant dessert sauce without the fire. It is a great example of the use of flavored vinegars, which can add zip to a dish and wake up the flavors. A touch of grated orange rind or orange oil is a splendid addition too.

½ cup seedless raspberry jam

¼ cup raspberry syrup (see Chef's Note)

⅓ cup water

2 tablespoons raspberry vinegar

¼ teaspoon grated orange rind or 2 drops orange oil (optional)

Vanilla ice cream

2 cups fresh raspberries

1. In a medium-size saucepan, whisk together the jam, syrup, water, vinegar, and orange rind or oil, if using, and bring to a simmer over medium heat.

2. Meanwhile, dish out the ice cream into dessert bowls or goblets. Remove the sauce from the heat, gently stir in the raspberries, and spoon over the ice cream. Serve immediately.

Chef's Note: *Raspberry syrup, as well as other fruit syrups, are available in the maple syrup section of your supermarket. You can also use syrup designed for flavoring coffees, found in gourmet coffee shops. Read the label, however, to be sure there is no added alcohol, either in the form of extract or as a preservative.*

Poached Pears with Chocolate Sauce

MAKES 4 SERVINGS Pears poached in red or white wine, glazed with a reduction of the poaching liquid and served with ice cream, used to be one of my prerecovery specialties. Since I knew I needed to "makeover" this often-requested dessert, I was faced with a difficult challenge. After much trial and error, my inspiration was found in a classic French pear dessert called *Poire Belle Helene*. *Poire*, or pears, prepared in this style are generally poached in a vanilla-flavored syrup, then served with ice cream, overflowing with everyone's favorite—chocolate sauce. Some recipes make use of the liqueur called Poire William, a Swiss aperitif intensely flavored with pears, adding a distinct taste sensation to the final result. When I came across a pear-infused white balsamic vinegar in my local grocer, I knew I had found my solution. Coupled with pear nectar and sugar syrup, I discovered the perfect poaching liquid. A good quality bittersweet chocolate finished the whole thing off in style.

The best pears for poaching are those that are under-ripe, as they will not become a mushy mess once cooked. My favorite variety for this is either a Forelle or the tiny Seckel pear (you'll need two or three per serving), but you can easily use a larger Bosc and simply cut it in half once it is peeled. Keep the stems on the pears for a particularly nice presentation.

½ cup sugar

½ cup water

¼ cup pear-infused vinegar (see Chef's Note)

1½ cups pear nectar

4 Forelle pears, peeled and cored, or 2 large Bosc pears, peeled, cored, and halved

4 ounces bittersweet or semisweet chocolate, roughly chopped

Vanilla ice cream

Fresh mint sprigs for garnish

1. In a medium-size saucepan, combine the sugar and water and bring to a boil over medium-high heat, stirring occasionally. When the sugar has dissolved, add the vinegar and pear nectar and return to a boil. Add the pears, cover, reduce the heat to a simmer, and poach the pears until they are tender (test with the tip of a sharp paring knife), 8 to 10

minutes. Transfer the pears with a slotted spoon to a plate and set aside.

2. Increase the heat to high and boil the poaching liquid to reduce to about ¾ cup, about 10 minutes. Remove from the heat, whisk in the chocolate until the sauce is smooth and set aside. (You can make ahead to this point and rewarm the sauce before serving, if preferred. The pears can be reheated, if necessary, in a microwave oven.)

3. To assemble, place one pear in a serving dish, put a scoop of ice cream next to it, and pour the chocolate syrup over the pear to coat. Garnish with a mint sprig and serve immediately.

Chef's Note: Fruit-infused vinegars are popular these days, particularly in salad making. If you can't find pear-infused white balsamic vinegar, use plain white balsamic vinegar, which is almost as sweet. See the "Resources" section for information on ordering infused vinegars.

Anise Almond Biscotti

MAKES ABOUT 40 BISCOTTI Licorice-flavored liqueurs, such as Anisette, Pernod, Sambuca, and Ouzo, are popular additions to many Italian and Greek desserts. Classic anise-flavored biscotti recipes will often call for up to ¼ cup or more of these types of sweet liqueurs. Other flavored recipes suggest additions like Grand Marnier, Amaretto, and Kahlua or, at the very least, alcohol-laden extracts.

Biscotti, meaning "twice baked," are great dunking cookies and well worth the effort to make at home. But, since they are, by definition, baked twice, do we really need to concern ourselves with the alcohol? Let me tell you a little story.

Janet, a good friend of mine who is an excellent baker, once asked me it it was really true about the alcohol not burning off during cooking. Athough the use of alcohol is luckily and genetically not an issue for her or her family, she was con-

cerned that the kids might be ingesting some unwanted amounts. Essentially a disbeliever, she went ahead and made her biscotti with an exorbitant amount of brandy, as the recipe required. The following day, her husband phoned from work to report he was feeling a bit funny and light-headed after lunch and was wondering if the kids were coming down with anything he might have caught. As the conversation progressed, he admitted to grabbing half a dozen of those delicious biscotti she'd made the day before and was munching on them as they spoke. Not a seasoned drinker, her husband said if he didn't know better, he'd say he felt a little tipsy. At that moment Janet remembered the ingredients of her biscotti and the discussion we had about the alcohol. Bingo! Once baked, twice baked, however you slice your biscotti, the alcohol is not going anywhere except straight towards those neurotransmitters! I love to tell this story to those who still doubt the scientific findings about cooking with alcohol.

Substituting for sweet liqueurs in cooking is actually quite an easy feat. The role that it plays is nearly always that of providing intense flavor and sweetness, whether it be almond, orange, anise, or another flavor. If we go to the source and combine its essence with sugar, we are practically there. In "Beverages," we made what is called a simple syrup from sugar and water (page 16) to add to cold drinks. We also used that same syrup to make fruit-flavored granita (page 305). If we begin, however, with a flavored sugar instead of plain sugar and make a simple syrup from that, we suddenly have an ideal substitution for sweet liqueur.

We've already seen how easy it is to make vanilla-scented sugar (page 168), but what about other flavors and varieties? Some flavored sugars we are able to purchase, such as the anise sugar used in this recipe (see the "Resources" section). In fact, many flavored sugars are now popular additions to coffee and tea, ranging in flavor from cinnamon to peppermint, and widely available on the

(continued on page 445)

Making Flavored Sugars

Super Cooking Substitutes for Taste and Tang

Infused sugars are popular with coffee and tea drinkers, as they can wake up a plain drink to create a true taste sensation. But they also can be valuable in the sober kitchen to use as substitutes for the sweet and intense flavors of many liqueurs. As we've already seen, cinnamon sugar (page 240) and vanilla-scented sugar (see page 168) are easy to make yourself and can provide instant flavor to quick desserts, beverages, and even baked goods. They are great for having on hand to sprinkle on toast, into coffee, or to fill in the flavor gap in a recipe replacing alcohol-based extracts. But there are many more possibilities. Here are some ideas for jazzing up your sugar bowl and adding interest to your cooking.

Just like making vanilla sugar, a jar of plain sugar that is allowed to sit in a cool dark place with the rind of an orange, lemon, lime, or any citrus combination will become wonderfully fragrant and full of flavor after only a few weeks. Keep adding sugar as you use it to always have a good supply on hand. Simple syrups made with citrus-flavored sugars can fill in nicely for orange-based liqueurs. Similarly, inserting the whole leaves of fragrant herbs and flowers will also make terrific sugars. Try mint leaves, lavender, geranium, or the petals from any edible flower that have not been sprayed with toxic substances. About two parts sugar to one part leaves or petals is a good ratio. Shake the jar occasionally and allow to infuse for a couple of weeks.

For instant-flavored sugar that doesn't require a wait, combine granulated sugar with mint leaves or orange rind and use a food processor to finely blend. Twice the amount of sugar to your source of flavor (for example, one cup of sugar to one-half cup orange rind) is a good proportion with which to begin. Similarly, anise seeds (about one tablespoon per cup of sugar) that have been finely ground in a spice or coffee grinder can then be processed with granulated sugar for instant anise sugar. Make an anise sugar syrup and use as a substitute for licorice-flavored liqueurs.

In a pinch, flavored teas can become strong-scented sweet alcohol substitutes when steeped in hot simple syrup (use three bags per cup of syrup). Try orange pekoe or a flavored herbal tea to use for soaking and flavoring cakes, as is done with traditional rum baba or sponge cakes. And fresh herbs like sage and tarragon steeped in simple syrup and white grape juice can become a great substitute for sweet vermouth.

(continued from page 443)
Internet and in specialty stores. Others can be easily made (see "Making Flavored Sugars," previous page), while simple syrups can also be flavored with a few drops of pure essential cooking oils, such as orange, lemon, and anise. Whichever you choose to use, it's best to keep the same liquid measurement that is called for in the recipe by using the flavored simple syrup method of substitution, so as not to alter the consistency of the dough or batter. A mere teaspoon of nonalcohol almond extract, for example, won't provide enough flavor or liquid to fill in as an appropriate substitute.

You can purchase roasted almonds, although sometimes they are difficult to find without salt or flavoring. If you can't find them, simply roast whole raw almonds in a 350 degree oven on a baking sheet until golden brown, 8 to 10 minutes.

3 tablespoons anise sugar

3 tablespoons water

½ cup (1 stick) unsalted butter, softened

¾ cup granulated sugar

2 large eggs

2¼ cups all-purpose flour

½ teaspoon baking powder

¼ teaspoon salt

¾ cup roasted almonds, chopped in half or thirds

1. Preheat the oven to 325 degrees.

2. In a small saucepan, combine the anise sugar and water, stir, and bring to a simmer over medium heat. When the sugar has dissolved, set aside and allow to cool.

3. Using an electric mixer, cream together the butter and granulated sugar in a medium-size mixing bowl until light and fluffy. Beat in the eggs and the cooled anise syrup. In another medium-size mixing bowl, whisk together the flour, baking powder, and salt. Add in two batches to the butter mixture, beating just to combine. Stir in the almonds.

4. Divide the dough in half and, on a greased and lightly floured baking sheet, shape into two flat-topped logs measuring about ½ inch high, 12 inches long, and 2 inches wide. Bake on the center rack of the oven until lightly golden, about 25 minutes. Leave the oven on, transfer the logs to a wire rack, and let cool for 10 minutes.

5. Place the logs on a cutting board and, using a serrated knife, cut at a 45 degree angle into ½-inch-thick slices. Lay the slices flat on the baking sheet and return to the oven until the biscotti are dry to the touch and lightly browned, 10 to 12 minutes. Transfer to a wire rack to cool completely and store in an airtight container for up to 2 weeks.

Chocolate Almond Tiramisu

MAKES 4 TO 6 SERVINGS Although most people consider this heavenly dessert an Italian classic, tiramisu was not invented until the 1960s in Italy, when it became an instant sensation. Literally translated to mean "pick me up" (because of the addition of espresso), the amount of alcohol generally added may end up translating as "pick me up off the floor." More often than not, brandy, marsala, or a flavored liqueur is combined with the coffee mixture in which the ladyfingers are soaked before layering. Because the espresso or coffee is more essential to this dessert than the alcohol, we can almost consider it one of those situations in which the alcohol can be left out. Still, I have found that if we replace the flavor of the alcohol with another type of interesting or contrasting flavor, the results are far better and add another dimension to the complexity of tastes that are meant to marry together. For this reason, flavored coffees offer the ideal solution.

Today there seem to be as many flavored coffees as there are teas. Whether preground or purchased by the bean, variety coffees are a delicious and easy alternative to flavoring a cup of plain coffee with syrups, sugars, or creamers. Here I've chosen a chocolate almond variety to highlight the cocoa powder dusting and add another flavor in the form of almonds. A little nonalcohol almond extract will heighten the taste, but is not necessary if the coffee is strongly brewed. Chocolate-covered almonds decorate the top and tie it all together.

Mascarpone, a buttery and ultra-rich Italian cream cheese, is available in tubs in the deli and cheese sections of most supermarkets. Be sure it is plain and not flavored. The question of using raw eggs in traditional tiramisu is often addressed in light of possible salmonella bacteria. I have always used raw eggs in this dish and now make a habit of using pasteurized eggs for added safety (see page 172 for information on eggs and safety precautions). If, however, you prefer further assurance, the egg yolks and sugar can be cooked over a double boiler, as instructed in the following recipe for *zabaglione*. Allow the mixture to cool somewhat before folding in the egg whites.

1 package soft ladyfingers (about 24)

2 large eggs, separated

¼ cup plus 1 tablespoon granulated sugar

8 ounces mascarpone cheese

1 teaspoon nonalcohol almond extract (optional)

1 cup strongly brewed chocolate almond coffee

Unsweetend cocoa powder for dusting

1 cup heavy or whipping cream

3 tablespoons confectioners' sugar

12 chocolate-covered almonds

1. Preheat the oven to 325 degrees. Place the ladyfingers in a single layer on a baking sheet and toast in the oven until dry and slightly browned around the edges, turning once, about 10 minutes. Set aside.

2. In a medium-size mixing bowl with an electric mixer, beat together the egg yolks and ¼ cup of the granulated sugar until the mixture is pale and thick. Beat in the mascarpone, almond extract, if using, and 2 tablespoons of the coffee. In another medium-size mixing bowl, beat the eggs whites with the remaining 1 tablespoon granu-

lated sugar with clean, dry beaters until stiff peaks form. Fold the egg whites into the mascarpone mixture until creamy and no white streaks appear.

3. Pour the remaining coffee into a shallow bowl and dip the ladyfingers in it briefly, one at a time, just to moisten. Line the bottom of a 2-quart glass or ceramic serving bowl or baking dish with half the ladyfingers. Cover with half the mascarpone filling, dust lightly with the cocoa powder using a tea strainer, and repeat the layering.

4. In a medium-size mixing bowl with clean, dry beaters, whip the cream with the confectioners' sugar to soft peaks. Spread on top of the tiramisu and dust again with cocoa powder. Place the almonds decoratively around the top and refrigerate for at least 2 hours before serving.

Chef's Note: *Try using any number of flavored coffees such as chocolate raspberry (garnishing with fresh raspberries), cinnamon hazelnut (dusting with ground cinnamon and garnishing with chopped roasted hazelnuts), or caramel (replacing the cocoa dusting with lightly drizzled caramel topping).*

Orange Blossom Zabaglione

MAKES 4 SERVINGS "The Sober Gourmet Guide to Food History 101" provides an interesting background to this classic Italian dessert (see page 429). Probably made for centuries as a medicinal cure-all, it wasn't until the nineteenth century that *zabaglione*, also known as *sabayon* by the French, became associated with marsala wine. Today, this warm and foamy custard is made from quite a number of alcoholic beverages besides sweet marsala wine, including champagne, Framboise, and Curaçao, to name a few. But in reality, it needn't be, and probably was never meant to be, a vehicle for a douse of after-dinner alcohol.

Depending on what you'll be serving your

zabaglione alongside, you could choose any number of flavors to focus on. For example, as a topping for fresh fruit, say peaches or apricots, you might opt for an orange spice-flavored *zabaglione* using orange juice and a dash of cinnamon. For ice cream or cake, a simple vanilla-scented topping would be delicious. But having enjoyed most *zabagliones* "straight up," as they say, I particularly like to prepare this very worthy and heavenly dessert to be served on its own without anything at all. With that in mind, the essential flavor becomes particularly important and here, thanks to Platina and his sixteenth-century recipe (page 429), I will be using the amazingly fragrant orange blossom water. We've encountered these distilled floral extracts before, namely rosewater (page 25), which are wonderful additions to recovery cooking because they do not contain alcohol as a preservative. They can be added to baked goods, ice creams, and beverages, particularly those with a Middle Eastern or Mediterranean flair. Orange blossom water is an essential ingredient in authentic baklava, the Greek layered pastry of filo dough, honey, and nuts.

Whisking your *zabaglione* requires patience and attention. The bowl should never touch the simmering water over which it sits, otherwise the eggs may become too hot and scramble before your eyes. A large balloon whisk is the appropriate tool, but feel free to enlist the aid of an electric mixer.

Zabaglione should be served immediately, while still warm and voluminous. Spoon it into tall goblets or parfait glasses for a nice presentation and serve some cookies or biscotti on the side.

4 large egg yolks
¼ cup sugar
¼ cup fresh orange juice
1 tablespoon orange blossom water

1. In a large stainless steel mixing bowl, beat together the yolks, sugar, and juice until well combined. Have ready a pot of simmering water and place the bowl over the saucepan, keeping the water level low enough so that the bottom of the bowl does not touch the surface.

2. Whisk, or beat with an electric mixer on high speed, until the mixture begins to thicken. Add the orange blossom water and continue to whisk until the mixture has tripled in volume and is thick and foamy. You can check to ensure that the eggs are cooked by inserting a candy thermometer and whisking until it registers 160 degrees.

3. Spoon the *zabaglione* into goblets or bowls, and serve immediately.

Chocolate *zabaglione*: Increase the sugar to ⅓ cup. Dissolve 1½ tablespoons unsweetened cocoa powder in ¼ cup hot water and substitute for the orange juice and orange blossom water. Top with chocolate shavings to serve.

Sober Lizzies

MAKES ABOUT 4 DOZEN At the beginning of this chapter, we talked about how chefs make any number of substitutions depending on availability and personal preferences. So when I decided to remake the classic Southern holiday cookies called lizzies as the final recipe, not only did I necessarily choose to make them sober by eliminating the usual whiskey, I also decided (since they *are* my namesake, after all) that they needed to include a few of my very favorite ingredients, not the least of which is chocolate. For those who may think they are familiar with classic holiday lizzies, don't worry that your memory is failing you; these are simply my version and I dare say you will take an intense liking to them once you bake and eat these delectable morsels yourself!

The role that whiskey usually plays in this type of recipe is basically as a marinade for dried fruit, as well as that of a "festive" ingredient. Frankly, neither role is of importance here, especially when chocolate is involved, so as a substitute, I'm merely adding a little more liquid in the form of buttermilk to retain the batter's proper consistency. In addition, although these cookies are usually baked by dropping the dough by tablespoonfuls on a cookie sheet, I like to bake them in mini muffin cups, for my own "festive" touch. Don't wait until the holidays, however, to enjoy these tasty treats. They'll keep well for a few weeks in an airtight container, ready and waiting just in case the chocolate monster decides to make an unannounced Phase Three visit for old time's sake.

1 cup dried cherries (look in the dried fruit section of the supermarket)
1 cup chopped dates
½ cup diced candied red cherries
¼ cup golden raisins
1 cup all-purpose flour
2 tablespoons unsweetened cocoa powder
3 tablespoons unsalted butter, softened
⅓ cup firmly packed light brown sugar
1 large egg
¾ teaspoon baking soda
½ teaspoon ground cinnamon

¼ cup buttermilk
1 tablespoon nonalcohol vanilla extract
2 cups chopped pecans
½ cup mini semisweet chocolate chips

1. Preheat the oven to 275 degrees. Line mini muffin tins with paper cups and lightly coat the insides of the cups with nonstick cooking spray.

2. In a medium-size mixing bowl, combine the dried cherries, dates, candied cherries, and raisins. In a small mixing bowl, whisk together the flour and cocoa. Add 2 tablespoons of the flour mixture to the fruit mixture and toss lightly to coat (this will keep them from sticking together).

3. In another medium-size mixing bowl, beat together the butter and brown sugar until smooth. Add the egg and beat well.

4. Add the baking soda and cinnamon to the remaining flour mixture, whisk to combine, and add to the egg mixture, beating until combined. Pour in the buttermilk, add the vanilla, and mix well. Stir in the flour-dredged fruit, pecans, and chocolate chips, combining well. Drop by tablespoonfuls into the prepared muffin cups and bake until lightly browned and no imprint remains when touched lightly, 18 to 20 minutes. Transfer to a wire rack to cool completely.

Bibliography

Addiction Science and Recovery

Abrous, D. N.; W. Adriani; M. F. Montaron; et al. 2002. Nicotine self-administration impairs hippocampal plasticity. *Journal of Neuroscience* 22(9): 3656–62.

Agartz, I.; R. Momenan; R. R. Rawlings; et al. 1999. Hippocampal volume in patients with alcohol dependence. *Archives of General Psychiatry* 56(4): 356–63.

Alcoholics Anonymous. *Alcoholics Anonymous* (Big Book). 3d ed. New York: AA World Services, Inc., 1976.

———. *Living Sober*. New York: AA World Services, Inc., 1989.

Alexander, William. *Cool Water: Alcoholism, Mindfulness, and Ordinary Recovery*. Boston: Shambhala, 1997.

Andreasen, Nancy C. *Brave New Brain: Conquering Mental Illness in the Era of the Genome*. New York: Oxford University Press, 2001.

Ash, Mel. *The Zen of Recovery*. New York: Penguin Putnam, Inc., 1993.

B., Hamilton. *Getting Started in AA*. Center City, MN: Hazelden, 1995.

Beasley, Joseph D., and Susan Knightly. *Food for Recovery*. New York: Crown Publishers, Inc., 1994.

Beattie, Melody. *Codependent No More*. Center City, MN: Hazelden, 1987.

———. *The Language of Letting Go*. Center City, MN: Hazelden, 1990.

Brick, John, and Carlton K. Erickson. *Drugs, the Brain, and Behavior: The Pharmacology of Abuse and Dependence*. New York: The Haworth Medical Press, 1998.

Brook, D. W.; J. S. Brook; C. Zhang; et al. 2002. Drug use and the risk of major depressive disorder, alcohol dependence, and substance use disorders. *Archives of General Psychiatry* 59(11): 1039–44.

Chopra, Deepak. *Overcoming Addiction*. New York: Three Rivers Press, 1997.

Ciccocioppo, R.; S. Angeletti; and F. Weiss. 2001. Long-lasting resistance to extinction of response reinstatement induced by ethanol-related stimuli: Role of genetic ethanol preference. *Alcoholism: Clinical & Experimental Research* 25(10): 1414–19.

Cloud, W., and R.Granfield. 2001. Natural recovery from substance dependence: Lessons for treatment providers. *Journal of Social Work Practice in the Addictions* 1: 83–104.

Conner, Steve. 7 Nov 2000. Children's sweet tooth may point to future alcoholism. London, *The Independent*. Based upon research at Mount Sinai School of Medicine presented at the November 2000 meeting of the Society for Neuroscience.

Crain, Stanley, et al. *Ultra-Low-Dose Naltrexone Can Prevent Opioid Tolerance and Dependence*. Report presented at the International Conference on Pain and Chemical Dependency, June 2002.

Daeppen, J. B.; T. L. Smith; G. P. Danko; et al. 2000. The Collaborative Study Group on the Genetics of Alcoholism: Clinical correlates of cigarette smoking and nicotine dependence in alcohol-dependent men and women. *Alcohol and Alcoholism* 35: 171–5.

Dudley, R. Evolutionary origins of human alcoholism in primate frugivory. 2000. *Quarterly Review of Biology* 75(1): 3–15.

DuPont, Robert L. *The Selfish Brain: Learning from Addiction*. Center City, MN: Hazelden, 1997.

DuWors, George Manter. *White Knuckles and Wishful Thinking: Learning from the Moment of Relapse in Alcoholism and Other Addictions.* Seattle: Hogrefe & Huber, 2000.

Fletcher, Anne M. *Sober For Good.* Boston: Houghton Mifflin Co., 2001.

Fu, Q.; A. C. Heath; K. K. Bucholz; et al. 2002. Shared genetic risk of major depression, alcohol dependence, and marijuana dependence: Contribution of antisocial personality disorder in men. *Archives of General Psychiatry* 59(12): 1125–32.

Gansler, D. A.; G. J. Harris; M. Oscar-Berman; et al. 2000. Hypoperfusion of inferior frontal brain regions in abstinent alcoholics. *Journal of Studies on Alcohol* 61: 32–7.

George, M. S.; R. F. Anton; C. Bloomer; et al. 2001. Activation of prefrontal cortex and anterior thalamus in alcoholic subjects on exposure to alcohol-specific cues. *Archives of General Psychiatry* 58(4): 345–52.

Gorski, Terence T. *Passages Through Recovery.* Center City, MN: Hazelden, 1989.

Hasin, D. S., and B. F. Grant. 2002. Major depression in 6050 former drinkers: Association with past alcohol dependence. *Archives of General Psychiatry* 59(9): 794–800.

Hommer, D. W. 1999. Functional imaging of craving. *The Journal of the NIAAA* 23(3): 187–96.

Hughes, J. R.; G. L. Rose; and P. W. Callas. 2000. Nicotine is more reinforcing in smokers with a past history of alcoholism than in smokers without this history. *Alcoholism: Clinical & Experimental Research* 24(11): 1633–8.

Johnson, Vernon E. *I'll Quit Tomorrow: A Practical Guide to Alcoholism Treatment.* San Francisco: Harper, 1990.

Kalman, D.; D. Tirch; W. Penk; et al. 2002. An investigation of predictors of nicotine abstinence in a smoking cessation treatment study of smokers with a past history of alcohol dependence. *Psychology of Addictive Behaviors* 16(4): 346–9.

Kavanaugh, Philip. *Magnificent Addiction: Discovering Addiction as Gateway to Healing.* Fairfield, CT: Aslan Publishing, 1992.

Kelley, M. L.; W. Fals-Stewart. 2002. Couples versus individual-based for alcohol and drug abuse: Effects on children's psychosocial functioning. *Journal of Consulting and Clinical Psychology* 70(2): 417–27.

Ketcham, Katherine; William F. Asbury; Mel Schulstad; et al. *Beyond the Influence: Understanding and Defeating Alcoholism.* New York: Bantam Doubleday Dell, 2000.

Kettelhack, Guy. *First Year Sobriety.* Center City, MN: Hazelden, 1992.

———. *Second Year Sobriety.* Center City, MN: Hazelden, 1992.

———. *Third Year Sobriety.* Center City, MN: Hazelden, 1992.

Koob, G. F. 2000. Animal models of craving for ethanol. *Addiction* 95(Supp 2): S73–81.

Krishnan-Sarin, S.; M. I. Rosen; and S. S. O'Malley. 1999. Naloxone challenge in smokers. Preliminary evidence of an opioid component in nicotine dependence. *Archives of General Psychiatry* 56(7): 663–8.

Kuhn, Cynthia; et al. *Buzzed: The Straight Facts About the Most Used and Abused Drugs from Alcohol to Ecstasy.* New York: W.W. Norton & Company, 1998.

Lappalainen, J.; H. R. Kranzler; R. Malison; et al. 2002. A functional neuropeptide Y Leu7Pro polymorphism associated with alcohol dependence in a large population sample from the United States. *Archives of General Psychiatry* 59(9): 825–31.

Larsen, Earnie. *Stage II Recovery: Life Beyond Addiction.* San Francisco: Harper Collins, 1985.

Leshner, Alan. 1999. Science-based views of drug addiction and its treatment. *Journal of the American Medical Association* 282(14): 1314–6.

McLellan, A. T.; D. C. Lewis; C. P. O'Brien; et al. 2000. Drug dependence, a chronic medical illness. *Journal of the American Medical Association* 284: 1689–95.

Menzies, Percy. 2001. *Why Is Recovery from Alcoholism So Difficult? And Is There Hope for Successful Treatment?* www.assistedrecovery.com/menzies.htm.

Milam, J. R., and K. Ketcham. *Under the Influence: A Guide to the Myths and Realities of Alcoholism.* New York: Bantam, 1984.

Mooney, A. J.; Arlene Eisenberg; and Howard Eisenberg. *The Recovery Book.* New York: Workman Publishing, 1992.

Moorhouse, M.; E. Loh; D. Lockett; et al. 2000. Carbohydrate craving by alcohol-dependent men during sobriety: Relationship to nutrition and serotonergic function. *Alcoholism: Clinical & Experimental Research* 24(5): 635–43.

Mueller, Ann L., and Katherine Ketcham. *Recovering: How to Get and Stay Sober.* New York: Bantam, 1987.

National Institute on Alcohol Abuse and Alcoholism (NIAAA). 1992. The genetics of alcoholism. *Alcohol Alert* No. 18.

———. 1993. Alcohol and cancer. *Alcohol Alert* No. 21.

———. 1993. Alcohol and nutrition. *Alcohol Alert* No. 22.

———. 1997. Alcohol metabolism. *Alcohol Alert* No. 35.

———. 1998. Alcohol and the liver. *Alcohol Alert* No. 42.

———. 2000. Imaging and alcoholism: A window on the brain. *Alcohol Alert* No. 47.

———. 2000. From genes to geography: The cutting edge of alcohol research. *Alcohol Alert* No. 49.

———. 2001. Cognitive impairment and recovery from alcoholism. *Alcohol Alert* No. 53.

———. 2001. Craving research: Implications for treatment. *Alcohol Alert* No. 54.

———. *10th Special Report to the U.S. Congress on Alcohol and Health*, June 2000.

National Institute on Drug Abuse. *Recovery Training and Self-Help: Relapse Prevention and Aftercare for Drug Addicts*. Rockville, MD: NIH Publication No. 93-3521.

———. Feb. 20, 2000. *Nicotine Craving and Heavy Smoking May Contribute to Increased Use of Cocaine and Heroin*. News release. www.drugabuse.gov.

Nocjar, C.; L. D. Middaugh; and M. Tavernetti. 1999. Ethanol consumption and place-preference conditioning in the alcohol-preferring C57BL/6 mouse: Relationship with motor activity patterns. *Alcoholism: Clinical & Experimental Research* 23(4): 683–92.

O'Neill, J.; V. A. Cardenas; and D. J. Meyerhoff. 2001. Effects of abstinence on the brain: Quantitative magnetic resonance imaging and magnetic resonance spectroscopic imaging in chronic alcohol abuse. *Alcoholism: Clinical & Experimental Research* 25(11): 1673–82.

Pert, Candace B. *Molecules of Emotion*. New York: Touchstone, 1997.

Peterson, Mark W. February 2002. *Are there Agents, Medications, or Behaviors that Increase Alcohol Craving and Therefore Can Trigger a Relapse?* www.alcoholmd.com/forum/.

Pluymen, Bert. *The Thinking Person's Guide to Sobriety*. New York: St. Martin's Press, 1999.

Prendergast, M. A.; B. R. Harris; S. Mayer; et al. 2000. Chronic, but not acute, nicotine exposure attenuates ethanol withdrawal-induced hippocampal damage in vitro. *Alcoholism: Clinical & Experimental Research* 24(10): 1583–92.

Ruden, Ronald A., and Marcia Byalick. *The Craving Brain*. New York: Perennial, 1997.

Simpson, D. D.; G. W. Joe; B. W. Fletcher; et al. 1999. A national evaluation of treatment outcomes for cocaine dependence. *Archives of General Psychiatry* 56(6): 507–14.

Sobell, M., et al. 1996. Recovery from alcohol problems with and without treatment: Prevalence in two population surveys. *American Journal of Public Health* 86: 966–72.

Timko, C.; R. H. Moos; J. W. Finney; et al. 2000. Long-term outcomes of alcohol use disorders: Comparing untreated individuals with those in AA and formal treatment. *Journal of Studies on Alcohol* 61: 529–40.

True, W. R.; H. Xian; J. F. Scherrer; et al. 1999. Common genetic vulnerability for nicotine and alcohol dependence in men. *Archives of General Psychiatry* 56(7): 655–61.

Twerski, Abraham J. *Addictive Thinking: Understanding Self-Deception*. Center City, MN: Hazelden, 1997.

U.S. Department of Health and Human Services. 2001. *2001 National Household Survey on Drug Abuse*. www.DrugAbuseStatistics.samhsa.gov.

———. Aug 17, 2002. *Women and Smoking: A Report of the Surgeon General*. Washington D.C.: U.S. Medicine.

Vaillant, George E. *The Natural History of Alcoholism Revisited*. Cambridge, MA: Harvard University Press, 1995.

Volpicelli, Joseph, and Maia Szalavitz. *Recovery Options: The Complete Guide*. New York: John Wiley & Sons, Inc., 2000.

Weil, Andrew, and Winifred Rosen. *From Chocolate to Morphine: Everything You Need to Know About Mind-Altering Drugs*. Boston: Houghton Mifflin, 1993.

West, James. April 2001. Alcoholism will resurface with first drink. *Insight from the Betty Ford Center and Dr. James West*. Betty Ford Center Findings 4(2): 2.

White, A. M. 2000. Alcohol-induced blackouts: What have we learned in the past 50 years? *Alcohol Research* 5: 187–88.

White, William L. *Pathways: From the Culture of Addiction to the Culture of Recovery—A Travel Guide for Addiction Professionals*. Center City, MN: Hazelden, 1996.

Whitfield, Charles L. *Healing the Child Within*. Deerfield Beach, FL: Health Communications, Inc., 1987.

———. *Co-Dependence: Healing the Human Condition*. Deerfield Beach, FL: Health Communications, Inc., 1991.

Woititz, Janet Geringer. *Adult Children of Alcoholics*. Deerfield Beach, FL: Health Communications, Inc., 1983.

Wrase, J.; S. M. Grusser; S. Klein; et al. 2002. Development of alcohol-associated cues and cue-induced brain activation in alcoholics. *European Psychiatry* 17(5): 287–91.

Cooking and Culinary History

Artusi, Pellegrino. *The Art of Eating Well*. Translated by K. M. Phillips III. New York: Random House, 1996.

Barnette, Martha. *Ladyfingers and Nun's Tummies: From Spare Ribs to Humble Pie—A Lighthearted Look at How Foods Got Their Names*. New York: Vintage Books, 1997.

Belk, Sarah. *Around the Southern Table*. New York: Simon and Schuster, 1991.

Beranbaum, Rose Levy. *The Cake Bible*. New York: William Morrow & Co., Inc., 1988.

Black, Maggie. *The Medieval Cookbook*. London: Thames and Hudson, 1996.

Bladholm, Linda. *The Asian Grocery Store Demystified*. Los Angeles: Renaissance Books, 1999.

Braudel, Fernand. *The Structures of Everyday Life: Civilization and Capitalism 15th–18th century, Volume I*. New York: Harper & Row, 1981.

Bumgarner, Marlene Anne. *The New Book of Whole Grains*. New York: St. Martin's Press, 1997.

Burros, Marian. "Alcohol, the Ultimate Additive." *New York Times*, 20 Dec 1986.

———. "The Inauguration: The Congressional Lunch: A Hot Meal is Enjoyed In a Hurry by Bush." *New York Times*, 21 Jan 2001.

Carroll, Amy, ed. *The Great Illustrated American Cookbook*. London: Dorling Kindersley. 1987.

Cost, Bruce. *Asian Ingredients*. New York: Harper Collins, 2000.

Croce, Julia Della. *Pasta: Recipes and Techniques*. New York: DK Publishing, Inc., 1997.

Cronin, Isaac. *The Mindful Cook: Finding Awareness, Simplicity, and Freedom in the Kitchen*. New York: Villard Books, 1999.

CuisineNet Café. *Graham Kerr About Your Health*. http://match.cuisinenett.com/café/cuisinenet___live/1997/00008-1.shtml.

Culinary Institute of America. *The New Professional Chef*. 5th ed. New York: Van Nostrand Reinhold, 1991.

Cunningham, Marion (ed.) *The Fannie Farmer Cookbook*. 12th ed. New York: Alfred A. Knopf, 1981.

Dalby, Andrew, and Sally Grainger. *The Classical Cookbook*. New York: Oxford University Press, J. Paul Getty Museum Publications, 1996.

Elkort, Martin. *The Secret Life of Food*. Los Angeles: Jeremy P. Tarcher, 1991.

Escoffier, Auguste. *The Escoffier Cookbook*. 1903; Reprint. New York: Crown Publishers, Inc., 1969.

Ettlinger, Steve. *The Restaurant Lover's Companion: A Handbook for Deciphering the Mysteries of Ethnic Menus*. Reading, MA: Addison-Wesley Publishing Co., 1995.

Farm Journal, Inc. *America's Best Vegetable Recipes*. New York: Harper & Row, Barnes & Noble Books Edition, 1976.

Esposito, Mary Ann. *Ciao Italia*. New York: Hearst Books, 1991.

Giacosa, Ilaria Gozzini. *A Taste of Ancient Rome*. Chicago, IL: University of Chicago Press, 1994.

Glassman, Bernard, and Rick Fields. *Instructions to the Cook: A Zen Master's Lessons in Living a Life That Matters*. New York: Bell Tower, 1996.

Good Cook Series. *Techniques and Recipes*. Chicago, IL: Time-Life Books, Inc., 1982.

Haedrich, Ken. *Country Baking*. New York: Bantam Books, 1990.

———. *Feeding the Healthy Vegetarian Family*. New York: Bantam Books, 1998.

Herbst, Sharon Tyler. *The New Food Lover's Companion*. New York: Barron's, 1995.

———. *The Ultimate Liquor-Free Drink Guide*. New York: Broadway Books, 2003.

Kafka, Barbara. *Roasting*. New York: William Morrow & Co., Inc., 1995.

Kesten, Deborah. *Feeding the Body, Nourishing the Soul*. Berkeley: Conari Press, 1997.

Lagasse, Emeril, and Jessie Tirsch. *Emeril's New New Orleans Cooking*. New York: William Morrow & Co., Inc., 1993.

Lappe, Frances Moore. *Diet for a Small Planet: 20th Anniversary Edition*. New York: Ballantine Books, 1991.

Lukins, Sheila. *USA Cookbook*. New York: Workman Publishing, 1997.

McGee, Harold. *On Food and Cooking: The Science and Lore of the Kitchen*. New York: Scribner, 1984.

McKee, Gwen. *The Little Gumbo Book*. Baton Rouge: Quail Ridge Press, 1986.

Madison, Deborah. *Vegetarian Cooking for Everyone*. New York: Broadway Books, 1997.

Marshall, Lydie. *A Passion for Potatoes*. New York: Harper Collins, 1992.

Montagne, Prosper, and Jenifer Harvey Lang (eds.). *Larousse Gastronomique*. New York: Crown Publishing, 1988.

Peterson, James. *Sauces*. New York: Van Nostrand Reinhold, 1991.

———. *Splendid Soups*. New York: Bantam Books, 1993.

Redon, Odile, et al. *The Medieval Kitchen: Recipes from France and Italy*. Chicago, IL: University of Chicago Press, 2000.

Regan, Gary. *The Bartender's Bible*. New York: Harper Collins, 1991.

Renfrow, Cindy. *Take a Thousand Eggs or More: A Translation of Medieval Recipes*. Sussex, NJ: Self-published by Cindy Renfrow, 1997.

Root, Waverley. *The Food of France*. New York: Vintage Books, 1992.

———. *The Food of Italy*. New York: Vintage Books, 1992.

Shelton, Jo-Ann. *As the Romans Did: A Sourcebook in Roman Social History*. New York: Oxford University Press, 1997.

Shimbo, Hiroko. *The Japanese Kitchen*. Boston: The Harvard Common Press, 2000.

Shulman, Martha Rose. *Provençal Light*. New York: Bantam Books, 1994.

Singh, Dharamjit. *Indian Cookery: A Practical Guide*. Harmondsworth, England: Penguin Books, Ltd., 1987.

Smith, Delia. *Complete Illustrated Cookery Course*. London: BBC Books, 1989.

Toussaint-Samat, Maguelonne. *History of Food*. Translated by Anthea Bell. Oxford, England: Blackwell Publishers, Ltd., 1998.

Vegetarian Times Editors and Lucy Moll. *Vegetarian Times Complete Cookbook*. New York: Macmillan-USA, 1995.

Weil, Andrew, and Rosie Daley. *The Healthy Kitchen*. New York: Alfred A. Knopf, 2002.

Wheaton, Barbara Ketcham. *Savoring the Past: The French Kitchen and Table from 1300 to 1789*. New York: Touchstone, 1996.

Wright, Clifford A. *A Mediterranean Feast*. New York: William Morrow & Co., Inc., 1999.

———. *Mediterranean Vegetables*. Boston: The Harvard Common Press, 2001.

Diet and Nutrition

American Dietetic Association. 1997. Position Statement of ADA: Vegetarian Diets. *Journal of the American Dietetic Association* 97(11): 1317–21.

Arts, I. C.; P. C. Hollman; E. J. Feskens; et al. 2001. Catechin intake might explain the inverse relation between tea consumption and ischemic heart disease: The Zutphen Elderly Study. *American Journal of Clinical Nutrition* 74(2): 227–32.

Augustin, J.; E. Augustin; R. Cutrufelli; et al. 1992. Alcohol retention in food preparation. *Journal of the American Dietetic Association* 92(4): 486–88.

Barclay, Laurie. June 16-17, 2002. Nuts may lower risk of diabetes. *American Diabetes Association Annual Meeting Abstract* 1644-P, 569-P.

Bardou, M.; S. Montembault; V. Giraud; et al. 2002. Excessive alcohol consumption favours high risk polyp or colorectal cancer occurrence among patients with adenomas: A case study. *Gut* 50(1); 38–42.

Barefoot, J. C.; M. Gronbaek; J. R. Feaganes; et al. 2002. Alcoholic beverage preference, diet, and health habits in the UNC Alumni Heart Study. *American Journal of Clinical Nutrition* 76(2): 466–72.

Bentzon, J. F.; E. Skovenborg; C. Hansen; et al. 2001. Red wine does not reduce mature atherosclerosis in apolipoprotein E-deficient mice. *Circulation* 103(12): 1681–7.

Brand-Miller, Jennie, et al. *The Glucose Revolution: The Authoritative Guide to the Glycemic Index*. New York: Marlowe and Company, 1999.

———. *The Glucose Revolution Life Plan*. New York: Marlowe and Company, 2001.

Carper, Jean. *Your Miracle Brain*. New York: Quill, 2000.

Christensen, J. H.; H. A. Skou; L. Fog; et al. 2001. Marine n-3 fatty acids, wine intake, and heart rate variability in patients referred for coronary angiography. *Circulation* 103(5): 651–7.

Chuen, Lam Kam, and Lam Kai Sin. *The Feng Shui Kitchen: The Philosopher's Guide to Cooking and Eating*. Boston: Journey Editions, 2000.

David, Marc. *Nourishing Wisdom: A Mind-Body Approach to Nutrition and Well-Being*. New York: Bell Tower, 1991.

DesMaisons, Kathleen. *Potatoes Not Prozac*. New York: Simon & Schuster, 1998.

Duke, James A. *Handbook of Medicinal Herbs*. Boca Raton: CRC Press, 2002.

Geleijnse, J. M.; L. J. Launer; D. A. Van der Kulp; et al. Inverse association of tea and flavonoid intakes with incident myocardial infarction: The Rotterdam Study. 2002. *American Journal of Clinical Nutrition* 75(5): 880–86.

Goldberg, I. J.; L. Mosca; M. R. Piano; et al. 2001. AHA Science Advisory: Wine and your heart: A science advisory for healthcare professionals from the Nutrition Committee, Council on Epidemiology and Prevention, and Council on Cardiovascular Nursing of the American Heart Association. *Circulation* 103(3): 472–75.

Greenwood, C. E., and G. Winocur. 2001. Glucose treatment reduces memory deficits in young adult rats fed high-fat diets. *Neurobiology of Learning and Memory* 75(2): 179–89.

Goulart, Frances Sheridan. *Super Healing Foods*. Paramus, NJ: Prentice Hall, 1985.

Guidot, David. April 2002. *Chronic Alcohol Use Causes a Significant Deficiency of the Antioxidant Glutathione in the Lungs*. Research conducted by Emory University School of Medicine and VA Hospital and presented at the Experimental Biology meeting, April 24, 2002, New Orleans, LA.

Herber, David. *The Soy Revolution: The Food of the Next Millenium*. Garden City Park, NY: Avery Publishing, 1999.

Holick, C. N.; D. S. Michaud; R. Stolzenberg-Solomon; et al. 2002. Dietary carotenoids, serum beta-carotene, and retinal and risk of lung cancer in the alpha-tocopherol, beta-carotene cohort study. *American Journal of Epidemiology* 156(6): 536–47.

Holt, R. R.; S. A. Lazarus; M. C. Sullards; et al. 2002. Procyanidin dimer B2 in human plasma after the consumption of a flavanol-rich cocoa. *American Journal of Clinical Nutrition* 76(4): 798–804.

Iannuzzi, A.; E. Celentano; S. Panico; et al. 2002. Dietary and circulating antioxidant vitamins in relation to carotid plaques in middle-aged women. *American Journal of Clinical Nutrition* 76(3): 582–7.

Ilich J.Z.; R. A. Brownbill; L. Tamborini; et al. 2002. To drink or not to drink: How are alcohol, caffeine and past smoking related to bone mineral density in elderly women? *Journal of the American College of Nutrition* 21(6): 536–44.

Jenkins, D. J.; C. W. Kendall; A. Marchie; et al. 2002. Dose response of almonds on coronary heart disease risk factors. *Circulation* 106(11): 1327–32.

Kao, W. H.; I. B. Puddey; L. L. Boland; et al. 2001. Alcohol consumption and the risk of type 2 diabetes mellitus: Atherosclerosis risk in communities study. *American Journal of Epidemiology* 154(8): 748–57.

Kawagishi, H., et al. 7 Feb 2000. *Avocados Contain Potent Liver Protectants*. Findings presented at the 2000 International Chemical Congress of Pacific Basin Societies.

Keen, C. L. 2001. Chocolate: Food as medicine/medicine as food. *Journal of the American College of Nutrition* 20(5): 436S–9S; 440S–2S.

Key T. J.; N. E. Allen; E. A. Spencer; et al. 2002. The effect of diet on risk of cancer. *Lancet* 360(9336): 861–8.

Knekt, P.; J. Kumpulainen; R. Jarvinen; et al. 2002. Flavonoid intake and risk of chronic diseases. *American Journal of Clinical Nutrition* 76(3): 560–8.

Lucas, E.A.; R. D. Wild; L. J. Hammond; et al. 2002. Flaxseed improves lipid profile without altering biomarkers of bone metabolism in postmenopausal women. *Journal of Clinical Endocrinology and Metabolism* 87(4): 1527–32.

McKeown, N. M.; J. B. Meigs; S. Liu; et al. 2002. Whole-grain intake is favorably associated with metabolic risk factors for type 2 diabetes and cardiovascular disease in the Framingham Offspring Study. *American Journal of Clinical Nutrition* 76(2): 390–8.

Martinez-Gonzalez, M. A.; E. Fernandez-Jarne; E. Martinez-Losa; et al. 2002. Role of fibre and fruit in the Mediterranean diet to protect against myocardial infarction: A case-control study in Spain. *European Journal of Clinical Nutrition* 56(8): 715–22.

Mindell, Earl. *Vitamin Bible for the 21st Century*. New York: Warner Books, 1999.

Morris, M. C.; D. A. Evans; J. L. Bienias; et al. 2002. Vitamin E and cognitive decline in older persons. *Archives of Neurology* 59(7): 1125–32.

Northrup, Christiane. *Women's Bodies, Women's Wisdom*. New York: Bantam, 1994.

O'Byrne, D. J.; S. Devaraj; S. M. Grundy; et al. 2002. Comparison of the antioxidant effects of Concord grape juice flavonoids alpha-tocopherol on markers of oxidative stress in healthy adults. *American Journal of Clinical Nutrition* 76(6): 1367–74.

Ohry, A., and J. Tsafrir. 1999. Is chicken soup an essential drug? *Canadian Medical Association Journal* 161:1532–33.

Pensiero, Laura, and Susan Oliveria with Michael Osborne. *The Strang Cookbook for Cancer Prenvention*. New York: Dutton, 1998.

Pereira, M. A.; D. R. Jacobs; J. J. Pins; et al. 2002. Effect of whole grains on insulin sensitivity in overweight hyperinsulinemic adults. *American Journal of Clinical Nutrition* 75(5): 848–55.

Reader's Digest Association, Inc. *Fight Back with Food: Use Nutrition to Heal What Ails You*. Pleasantville, NY: Reader's Digest, 2002.

Reno, Liz, and Joanna DeVrais. *Allergy Free Eating*. Berkeley: Celestial Arts, 1992.

Rios, L. Y.; R. N. Bennett; S. A. Lazarus; et al. 2002. Cocoa procyanidins are stable during gastric transit in humans. *American Journal of Clinical Nutrition* 76(5): 1106–10.

Ritchason, Jack. *The Vitamin and Health Encyclopedia, Revised*. Pleasant Grove, UT: Woodland Publishing, 1996.

Sasazuki, S.; S. Sasaki; and S. Tsugane. 2002. Cigarette smoking, alcohol consumption and subsequent gastric cancer risk by subsite and histologic type. *International Journal of Cancer* 101(6): 560–6.

Scott, Anne. *Serving Fire: Food for Thought, Body, and Soul*. Berkeley: Celestial Arts, 1994.

Seow, A.; W. T. Poh; M. The; et al. 2002. Diet, reproductive factors and lung cancer risk among Chinese women in Singapore: Evidence for a protective effect of soy in nonsmokers. *International Journal of Cancer* 97(3): 365–71.

Small, D. M.; R. J. Zatorre; A. Dagher; et al. 2001. Changes in brain activity related to eating chocolate: From pleasure to aversion. *Brain* 124: 1720–33.

Somer, Elizabeth. *Food and Mood: The Complete Guide to Eating Well and Feeling Your Best*. New York: Henry Holt & Co., 1995.

Stephenson, Gina Day, and the American Health Foundation, Valhalla, NY. 2002. *Vegetables Can Lower Smoker's Cancer Risk*. Study presented at the American Association for Cancer Research annual meeting.

Tanelian, Darren L. 2000. *Hemp: Nature's Forgotten Nutraceutical*. Natural Pharmacy Magazine. www.nutiva.com/nutrition/articles.

Terry, P.; M. Jain; A. B. Miller; et al. 2002. Dietary intake of folic acid and colorectal cancer risk in a cohort of women. *International Journal of Cancer* 97(6): 864–7.

Terry, P.; A. B. Miller; and T. E. Rohan. 2002. Prospective cohort study of cigarette smoking and colorectal cancer risk in women. *International Journal of Cancer* 99(3): 480–3.

United States Drug Enforcement Administration. 9 Oct 2001. *DEA Clarifies Status of Hemp in the Federal Register*. News Release.

Wakabayashi, I., and R. Kobaba-Wakabayashi. 2002. Effects of age on the relationship between drinking and atherosclerotic risk factors. *Gerontology* 48(3): 151–6.

Wan, Y.; J. A. Vinson; T. D. Etherton; et al. 2001; Effects of cocoa powder and dark chocolate on LDL oxidative susceptibility and prostaglandin concentrations in humans. *American Journal of Clinical Nutrition* 74(5): 596–602.

Weil, Andrew. *Eight Weeks to Optimum Health*. New York: Fawcett Columbine, 1997.

———. *Natural Health, Natural Medicine*. Boston: Houghton Mifflin, 1998.

———. *Eating Well for Optimum Health*. New York: Alfred A. Knopf, 2000.

White, I. R.; D. R. Altmann; and K. Nanchahal. 2002. Alcohol consumption and mortality: Modeling risks for men and women at different ages. *British Medical Journal* 325(7357): 191.

Whitman, Deborah B. *Genetically Modified Foods: Harmful or Helpful?* Cambridge Scientific Abstracts, April 2000.

Wolever, Thomas M. S. 1997. The Glycemic Index: Flogging a dead horse? *Diabetes Care* 20(3): 452–56.

Resources

Cooking Ingredients and Equipment

A Tea of Choice

925-551-0219

www.bodyofmine.com

This company offers an extensive online selection of green, black, and flavored teas including Gunpowder, Mugicha, and Blackcurrant. You can also create your own custom blends.

Barry Farm

419-228-4640

www.barryfarm.com

This Ohio-based organic farm and old-fashioned country store carries a number of useful ingredients, including a variety of flours, syrups, and The Spicery Shoppe Brand line of nonalcoholic extracts.

Bob's Red Mill Natural Foods

800-349-2173

www.bobsredmill.com

Stone-ground flours and unusual whole grains are Bob's specialties. Find wheat berries, flaxseed meal, and a cornucopia of flours. Most health food stores and many supermarkets carry his products.

Boyajian, Inc.

800-419-4677

www.boyajianinc.com

Manufacturers of citrus oils, flavored vinegars, and other natural flavorings, their products are available in many specialty food stores or can be ordered directly through their toll-free telephone number or Web site.

BroccoSprouts

877-747-1277

www.broccosprouts.com

Learn more about the health benefits and locate a store near you that carries these super-functional sprouts. Link to Caudill Seed Company (800-626-5357, www.caudill seed.com) to purchase home growing kits.

California Coffee Roasters

877-543-1110

www.coffee-roasters.com

Find a splendid array of flavored coffees as well as Torani brand flavored syrups.

The Chef's Resource

866-765-2433

www.chefsresource.com

A fine selection of handy gadgets and equipment including oil misters, microplane zesters, and bakeware can be found here.

Chefshop.com

877-337-2491

Visit this Seattle-based online gourmet grocer for an array of hard-to-find specialty ingredients, including many Asian products, infused vinegars, and unusual grains and beans.

Cook's Corner of Historic Smithville

800-729-9030

www.cookscorner.net

A great one-stop shopping Web site for everything from flavored coffees, tea, vanilla beans, and unusual specialty foods to an amazing array of hot sauces, including one called "Endorphin Rush"!

EthnicGrocer.com

866-438-4642

Search by country or product at this online gourmet grocer. Find orange blossom and rose waters, nut oils, and Middle Eastern spices.

faerie's finest

562-983-8397

www.faeriesfinest.com

An excellent source for the sober baking kitchen, this California-based company carries a splendid array of flavored sugars, as well as alcohol-free natural flavor powders which can be substituted for extracts, one-for-one.

Flavor Mill Gourmet Flavors

Manufacturers of excellent artificial baking flavors without alcohol, found in most candy and cake decorating stores or online through a number of distributors including www.winbeckler.com, www.countrykitchensa.com, and Sweet Celebrations, 800-328-6722.

Frontier Natural Brands

800-669-3275

www.frontiercoop.com

Makers of alcohol-free baking and cooking flavors including everything from banana to vanilla, their products are often carried in health food stores, are available on many Web sites, including www.herbalhut.com, or can be ordered directly through their toll-free telephone number or Web site.

King Arthur Flour

800-827-6836

www.kingarthurflour.com

The Bakers Catalogue Online is convenient for ordering everything from vanilla beans to fine quality chocolate and, of course, flour of every description.

The Pampered Chef

800-266-5562

www.pamperedchef.com

A variety of helpful kitchen gear including a kitchen spritzer (oil mister) can be ordered from their kitchen consultants.

Sand Mountain Herbs

256-659-2726

www.sandmountainherbs.com

Just one of many seed catalogs that sells the delicious, medicinal purslane weed. For more information on this plant, search on the Web under the word "purslane" for detailed growing instructions, history, and recipes.

Trader Joe's

A unique grocery store cropping up all over the country, their evolving product list always includes an excellent array of dried fruits, fruit juices, including blueberry juice, and a wide variety of nuts, including chocolate covered soynuts. To locate a store near you call 800-SHOP TJS, or visit www.traderjoes.com.

Recovery and Support Organizations

Adult Children of Alcoholics

310-534-1815

www.adultchildren.org

Alanon/Alateen

800-344-2666

www.al-anon.alateen.org

Alcoholics Anonymous

212-870-3400

www.alcoholics-anonymous.org

Chemically Dependent Anonymous

800-CDA-HOPE

www.cdaweb.org

Cocaine Anonymous

800-347-8998

www.ca.org

Families Anonymous

800-736-9805

www.familiesanonymous.org

LifeRing Secular Recovery

510-763-0779

www.unhooked.com

Marijuana Anonymous

800-766-6779

www.marijuana-anonymous.org

Narcotics Anonymous

818-773-9999
www.na.org

Overeaters Anonymous

505-891-2664
www.overeatersanonymous.org

Rational Recovery

530-621-2667
www.rational.org

Secular Organizations for Sobriety

323-666-4295
www.secularsobriety.org

Women for Sobriety

215-536-8026
www.womenforsobriety.org

Suggested Reading Through the Phases

Phase One

Recovery

Find out what to expect by reading about the experiences of others. *First Year Sobriety* by Guy Kettelhack is a collection of stories told by people in their first steps of recovery, with insightful and valuable commentary by the author. *Drinking: A Love Story* by Caroline Knapp, will strike a chord with every woman who battles addiction. Caroline Knapp's story of her own tumultuous love affair with alcohol is poignant and pertinent, as is her posthumously published *Appetites: Why Women Want* about learning to nourish our most basic hungers with self-respect and a healthy attitude. Pete Hamill's *A Drinking Life* provokes similar recognition for men who grew up in a hard-drinking, hard-living environment.

Basic Cooking Skills

For those who need to learn the basics or hone their technique, Betty Crocker's *Cooking Basics: Learning to Cook with Confidence* and *Learning to Cook with Marion Cunningham* will help you on your way. And don't discount the highly readable Cooking for Dummies series, which is ideal for fuzzy minds in early recovery. If looking at lots of pictures is more your style, Jacques Pepin's recently reissued *Complete Techniques* instructs on everything from chopping an onion to carving a chicken. The USDA

Table of Nutrient Retention Factors, Release 4, which includes alcohol retention percentages can be accessed at http://warp.nal.usda.gov/fnic/foodcomp/Data/retn4/. Click on retn4_doc.txt for information and retn4_tbl.pdf for the complete list (alcohol is listed at the end on page 6).

Diet and Nutrition

Nutrition for Dummies with help you sort out your macronutrients from your micronutrients, while Earl Mindell's *Vitamin Bible for the 21st Century* is a handy reference guide to vitamins and minerals. Get to know the Glycemic Index with *The Glucose Revolution: The Authoritative Guide to the Glycemic Index*, by Jennie Brand-Miller, PhD, Thomas M. S. Wolever, MD, PhD, et al. See also www.glycemicindex.com for a searchable GI database, and www.mendosa.com for a downloadable list of tested foods.

Phase Two

Recovery

Second Year Sobriety by Guy Kettelhack continues the journey, while Earnie Larsen's excellent *Stage II Recovery: Life Beyond Addiction*, and *Stage II Relationships: Love Beyond Addiction* will help in sorting through this often difficult emotional phase. Charles Whitfield's *Healing the Child Within* is a classic read for family members, as is Melody Beattie's *Codependent No More*.

Spirituality and Comfort Food

Already a classic, Jon Kabat-Zinn's *Wherever You Go, There You Are: Mindfulness Meditation in Everyday Life*, will help you learn to live in the moment. And authors such as Gary Zukav, Thomas Moore, and Deepak Chopra offer articulate insight on spiritual matters. When comfort calls and no time allows, *Comfort Food: Rachael Ray's 30-Minute Meals* can help while Graham Kerr's *Gathering Place: Comfort Food* will assist in paring down unwanted fat and calories. *Nourishing the Body, Mind, and Soul* by Deborah Kesten offers a fascinating discussion of food traditions and spirituality.

Phase Three

Recovery

Once again, Guy Kettelhack provides an insightful collection of personal stories in *Third Year Sobriety*, and Terence Gorski's many writings and workbooks on relapse prevention are invaluable additions to the recovery bookshelf.

Diet and Nutrition

Dr. Andrew Weil is the expert to consult on health, nutrition, and integrative medicine. *Natural Health, Natural Medicine,* and *Eating Well for Optimum Health* will guide you well in making smart, educated choices as you travel forward in your journey towards overall health and well-being. His monthly *Self Healing* newsletter will keep you up-to-date on current research and findings in diet, nutrition, and mind-body connections. Find a functional food guide pyramid at Southern Illinois University's Web site, www.ag.uiuc.edu/~ffh/health/ff_pyramid.html and learn more about food as preventive medicine.

Advocacy and Making a Difference

Toward a New Recovery Movement: Historical Reflections on Recovery, Treatment and Advocacy by William L. White will explain with remarkable clarity how far we have come and how much further we need to go in changing the tone of addiction and recovery in our world today. You can access this groundbreaking paper published in 2000 at www.ncaddillinois.org/whitelong.htm. Organizations such as Faces and Voices of Recovery and the online Boston-based Join Together work to remove the stigma of addiction and provide information on ways you can make a difference. September is National Recovery Month—organized through the Substance Abuse and Mental Health Services Administration—visit www.recoverymonth.gov for a participation toolkit and information on events in your area.

Index